UNDERSTANDING
THE TIMES

Also by William P. Grady:

*FINAL AUTHORITY: A Christian's
Guide to the King James Bible*

*WHAT HATH GOD WROUGHT!: A Biblical
Interpretation of American History*

*HOW SATAN TURNED AMERICA
AGAINST GOD: A Scriptural Examination
of Conspiracy History*

*GIVEN BY INSPIRATION: A Multifaceted
Study on the A.V. 1611 with
Contemporary Analysis*

*HOLY GROUND: The True History
of the State of Israel*

UNDERSTANDING THE TIMES
VOLUME THREE

PERILOUS TIMES

DEEP TRUTHS FOR SHALLOW WATERS

William P. Grady, Ph.D.

GRADY
PUBLICATIONS, INC.

DISCLAIMERS

The opinions, arguments, and conclusions contained herein are solely those of the author and do not necessarily reflect the views of the individuals who were featured, interviewed, and/or quoted.

All Scripture is taken from the King James Bible (AV 1611), with special emphasis by the author shown in bold letters.

Every effort has been made to trace all copyright holders; however, if any have been overlooked, the publisher will gladly include the necessary credits in any subsequent reprints or editions.

ISBN 978-0-9628809-5-7
Library of Congress Control Number: 2022905444
First Printing, May 2022

For information, address:
GRADY PUBLICATIONS, INC.
P.O. Box 6381
Maryville, TN 37802
Phone: (865) 216-3483
william.grady@gradypublications.com
www.gradypublications.com
Follow us on ⬛ and ⬛ @ Grady Publications

Dedication

This book is dedicated to my three Christian brothers,
Eloy Sherlock, Dameaon Dudley, and William "W. A." Jarrells,
aka *Shem*, *Ham*, and *Japheth* (along with their precious helpmeets,
Robin, Joyce, and Shiela, respectively), for being a living fulfillment
of the *beautiful* truth in this politically incorrect book!

*"How beautiful are the feet of them that preach the gospel of peace,
and bring glad tidings of good things!"* (Romans 10:15)

Acknowledgements

"For I know nothing by myself...."
(I Corinthians 4:4)

THE APOSTLE PAUL personally recognized twenty-nine co-laborers in Romans 16:1-15. I would like to thank the following people for their invaluable contributions to this third volume of *Understanding the Times for Such a Time as This:*

My devoted helpmeet of forty-seven years, Linda Shannon, who once again served as my proofreader and editor (Proverbs 31:11).

Tammy Atkins for another excellent job in text layout and design.

For the sixth straight time (beginning in 1993), Tommy and Lori Ray for their professional graphics.

Dan Erdmann for his incredible artistic skills, as evidenced by the beautiful cover for this book.

My research was aided in several particulars by Dr. Greg Nash, Gospel Light Baptist Church, Mechanicsville, MD; Pastor Mitch Serviss, Bible Baptist Church, Las Vegas, NV; Pastor Samson Ryman, Central Bible Baptist Church, Massena, NY; Assistant Pastor Brian Green, Shady Acres Baptist Church, Houston, TX (Seed for the Cities); Austin Brown; and Mrs. Paula Land.

Several individuals and churches gave generous financial assistance for this project: Pastor James and Kathy Leichty, Open Bible Independent Baptist Church, Elkhart, IN; Alvin and Debbie Edwards; Mrs. Laura Barge; Pastor Mike and Jody Watkins, Lighthouse Baptist Church, Eustis, FL; Pastor Craig Cobb, New Life Baptist Church, Dover-Foxcroft, ME; Kirk Kimley; Mrs. Teresa Dugan; and Pastor David Wagner, Branson Baptist Church, Branson, MO.

Also, considering the extensive breadth of material in this third volume, it should go without saying that the various people who graciously contributed to this book (photographs, interviews, general input, etc.) would not necessarily ascribe to every doctrinal thesis posited by "Yours Truly."

Last—and most importantly—I want to praise God for sustaining Linda and me through a myriad of Satanic attacks during the writing of *Perilous Times* (the title theme of which we personally experienced). I Thessalonians 2:18 pretty well sums up our past twelve months: *"Wherefore we would have come unto you, even I Paul, once and again; but Satan hindered us."* However, while most of the fiery darts we encountered during my five previous books were hurled at me—this time, my wife has taken the brunt. In addition to enduring several debilitating post-Covid sequelae, she also had to overcome a number of other blows (many too private to name).

By way of personal testimony, our most difficult II Corinthians 1:8 experience was having our beloved little Amica (aka "Meeky") euthanized due to an inoperable tumor. (And yes, I understand that only a fellow pet lover can empathize with the pain we felt after a decade of gladly obeying Proverbs 12:10.) And the timing could not have been more conspicuous—coming right at the critical end of this writing project! Our compassionate Christian veterinarian was dumbfounded, as only a few months earlier (after giving Meeky an exhaustive physical), she had pronounced her "one of the healthiest dogs on the planet." Of course, we discerned the greater spiritual context—that her unforeseen, *premature* death had resulted from the Devil's negotiation process with God (Job 1:12; 2:6). Were Meeky to suddenly sicken and die *after* the book was published would have been unacceptable, for Satan obviously intended to "hinder" the completion of our work.

The Heaven-sent "Balm of Gilead" that thankfully got us through this *surreal* event was twofold: the prayers of many Christian friends; and—knowing that *our pain* was for *God's gain*: *"But I would ye should understand, brethren, that the things which happened unto me have fallen out rather unto the furtherance of the gospel."* (Philippians 1:12) And so, as strange as it may sound to some—from the perspective of *this* author—to whatever degree you are edified by this book, remember that a furry little eighteen-pound "thing" was at least partially responsible, for *"God hath chosen the weak things of the world to confound the things which are mighty."* (I Corinthians 1:27).

At least *that* would be the opinion of the man who was "picked *out* to be picked *on*," enjoining us accordingly, *"But ask now the beasts, and they shall teach thee...Who knoweth not in all these that the hand of the* LORD *hath wrought this? In whose hand is the soul of every living thing, and the breath of all mankind."* (Job 12:7, 9-10)

Photo taken March 18, 2022, three hours before Meeky died in Linda's arms.

Table of Contents

Preface

IN 2019, I was preaching for a good pastor friend of mine in New England when a lady church member shared an interesting passage with me—the last two verses in the King James Bible: *"He which testifieth these things saith, Surely I come quickly. Amen. Even so, come, Lord Jesus. The grace of our Lord Jesus Christ be with you all. Amen."* The *Scofield Reference Bible* heading above these twin texts reads: "The last promise and the last prayer of the Bible." The thing that arrested the sister's attention was that the Scripture address just *happened* to be Revelation 22:20-21. I recall her saying something to the effect, "Wouldn't it be just like Jesus to *"come quickly"* —in the year 2021?"

Well, I had to admit, that prospect sure looked inviting! But then, only a nut would set any dates for the Rapture, etc. And besides, I had already received some wisdom in this area from my former pastor, Dr. Jack Hyles. As he told it, during his novice years of pastoring in Texas (circa 1950s), several of his peers *were* succumbing to the date-setting temptation. "I was too smart for that trend," he said. "However, one year I *did* get carried away and announced to my congregation that the Lord was *definitely* coming back—*this* year." He would then relate, with a chuckle, "We had a *wild* December; January was a little rough, though."

In the ensuing months, I started sharing this tantalizing Scripture address in my sermons, but *always* with the following caveat. "Of course, while this prospect looks mighty good (especially to KJV-only folks), we cannot pretend that it constitutes a dogmatic revelation. Yet, on the other hand, there's nothing wrong with *hoping* that the Lord comes back in 2021." I would then say, "In private, I plan on hanging on to this prospect till midnight, December 31, and if he *still* hasn't returned, well, I'll just get me a new text to drain for 2022." I'd then warn the brethren not to misquote me, or else, I would be forced to employ the humorous Hyles maxim— "If you repeat this, I'll deny it."

While preaching in early 2021 for a friend in Empire, Alabama, the pastor got so "shook up" when I shared the Revelation 22:20-21 nugget that he booked me on the spot to preach his Watch Night service that year— "just in case." Well, as we all know by now, the Lord didn't show in 2021. However, on that last "disappointing" night, December 31, 2021, the blessed Holy Spirit gave me that new verse to drain in 2022 (and beyond). One of the other speakers felt led to choose Acts **20:22** for his text: *"And now behold, I go bound in the spirit unto Jerusalem, **not knowing the things that shall befall me there."***

My first thought was, *"Wow,* what a Scripture to describe the utter uncertainty of where we're all headed" (though, *"bound in the spirit,"* thankfully). And, as if to dramatize the thought, the very next evening— Saturday, January 1, 2022—I literally preached under a severe tornado threat (the pastor having nearly cancelled the service). It is my sincere prayer that the "deep truths" in *Perilous Times* will enlighten you as we journey into this hidden, but hopeful, future.

"And that, knowing the time,
that now it is high time to awake out of sleep:
for now is our salvation nearer than when we believed."
(Romans 13:11)

Introduction

I N MY 2010 book, *Given By Inspiration*, I included a chapter entitled "The Old Ship of Alexandria," positing (with forty-five examples) that the Holy Spirit used a unique maritime similitude in Acts 27 to prefigure the apostate Laodicean "Bible" movement. (With twenty-seven New Testament books we might expect this chapter to deal with God's word.) Thus, in verse two Paul and Luke begin their voyage aboard an *Asian* vessel (*Textus Receptus*). However, four verses later they transfer to an *Alexandrian* ship (*Codex Sinaiticus*). The telltale destination is *Rome* (verse 6), which they eventually reach aboard a second *Alexandrian* ship (*Codex Vaticanus*). While Satan whips up Euroclydon, intending to drown the pair before they can pen their remaining books (the prison and pastoral epistles, along with Luke and Acts, a third of the New Testament canon), the *"Angel of God"* (verse 22) intervenes to ensure the divine *preservation* of this latent text (Psalm 12:7).

Fast-forward twenty centuries. Because the "more-part" (verse 12) of end-day, materialistic, English-speaking Christendom has dethroned the historic King James Bible (based on a *true* majority text), preferring any number of modern translations (traced to a corrupt, eclectic "minority text"), the closing days of *their* journey will likewise be impaired by spiritual vertigo. Notice how their *"exceedingly tossed"* conditions (verse 18) occur in the dark (verse 20), *"neither **sun** nor **stars** in many days appeared."* As both time and space are uniquely set in Greenwich, *England* (Ecclesiastes 8:4), the *Egyptian* counterfeit lacks all sense of direction, Luke recording, *"[T]hey drew near to **some** country"* (verse 27). Having *"cast out the **wheat** into the sea"* in verse 38 (wheat being an obvious type of the Bible), the very next verse states that *"they **knew not** the land."*

These technical points involving underlying text types lead to several practical applications. W. A. Jarrells (a seasoned pastor friend of mine from Alabama) has a powerful sermon on Acts 27 entitled, "How to Know When You're Nearing the End of the Church Age." Among his several points, in order to stay afloat, today's pragmatic brethren will be seen tossing "nonessential" stuff overboard like the "wheat" (verse 18). Next, *the closer you get to shore the shallower the water becomes* (initially for the ship, eventually for the men). Dr. Luke meticulously logs the depth, decreasing from twenty fathoms to fifteen fathoms (verse 28). This, in turn, will affect the fishing ("soulwinning"). The same author showed Jesus telling the disciples to *"Launch out into the **deep**, and let down your nets for a **draught**."* (Luke 5:4) When I preached this outline in Montreal, Canada, a warm-hearted Frenchman reminded me, "We must never forget the *minnows*." (See: *S. S. Minnow* from *Gilligan's Island*.)

Though Bro. W. A. took his devotional application from Luke's *historical* narrative, his spot-on accuracy is corroborated by Paul's *doctrinal* epistle of II Timothy (a book he *could* write, having been *preserved* through the storm). As a precursor to the end-time condition of *"fierce"* listed in II Timothy 3:3 (with modern-day road *"rage"* forecast in Nahum 2:4), the Alexandrian ship runs aground, *"broken with the **violence** of the waves"* (verse 41). The *good* news is that everyone survives (a beautiful type of eternal security); the *bad* news is that the last generation to "follow Paul" (verse 24; I Corinthians 4:16; 11:1) makes it in drenched! If you want a good picture of Paul's *"**perilous times**"* in II Timothy 3, read the end of his companion's account: *"[T]he centurion...commanded that **they which could swim should cast themselves first into the sea, and get to land: and the rest, some on boards, and some on broken pieces of the ship**"* (verses 43-44).

The great truth here is that the key responsibility of end-day pastors is *to help their people keep their heads above water!* This would also include helping them deal with various "jellyfish stings" sure to afflict them along the way (e.g., problems with family, finances, health, etc.). Note the same truth when our Lord's prophecy in Matthew 24:37, regarding the *"days of Noe,"* is cross-referenced back to Genesis 5:29, *"And he called his name Noah, saying This same shall **comfort** us concerning our work and toil of our hands, because of the ground which the LORD hath cursed."* The main way to *comfort* God's sheep with *hope* will always be to give them the Bible. *"For whatsoever things were written aforetime were written for our learning, that we through patience and **comfort of the scriptures** might have **hope**."* (Romans 15:4) Consequently, after Paul conveys the LORD'S words to his panicked fellow travelers (his *breaking* of the bread itself being a type of rightly *dividing* the book), *"**Then** were they all of **good cheer**"* (verse 36).

Perilous Times: Deep Truths for Shallow Water was written to *comfort* end-day Christians as they swim, float, bob, and ultimately wade their way to that glorious Heavenly shore! As I Corinthians 2:9, 11 equates *"the **deep** things of God"* with *"the things that are **freely** given to us of God,"* my exclusive source will be the Holy Bible, 1611 King James Authorized Version—the only "Bible" without a *copyright*.

"O hear us when we cry to Thee for those in **peril** on the sea!"
("Eternal Father, Strong to Save")

"...in perils in the sea..."
(II Corinthians 11:26)

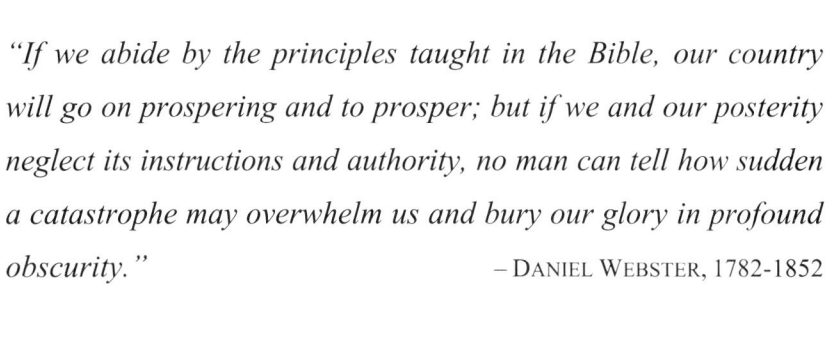

"If we abide by the principles taught in the Bible, our country will go on prospering and to prosper; but if we and our posterity neglect its instructions and authority, no man can tell how sudden a catastrophe may overwhelm us and bury our glory in profound obscurity."

– DANIEL WEBSTER, 1782-1852

1

The Last Latte

T HE CENTRAL CHARACTER in the oldest book of the Bible asked a profound question: *"Why, seeing **times** are not hidden from the Almighty, do they that know him not see his days?"* (Job 24:1) Job reasoned that if *God* knows the times, why wouldn't those who know Him discern the same? In the heart of the Old Testament, the children of Issachar are commended for being *"men that had **understanding of the times**, to know what Israel ought to do."* (I Chronicles 12:32) During the Gospel period, Jesus rebuked the Pharisees for their lack of discernment, *"O ye hypocrites, ye can discern the face of the sky; but can ye not **discern the signs of the times?**"* (Matthew 16:3). When the disciples asked Jesus to teach them to pray, He told them to insert, *"Thy kingdom come, thy will be done"* before they get to asking, *"Give us this day our daily bread."* Apparently, the Lord expects His people to know when He is doing something important, as David was told, *"[W]hen thou **hearest the sound of a going in the tops of the mulberry trees**, that then thou shalt bestir thyself."* (II Samuel 5:24)

When we examine the Church Age portion of the New Testament, Paul closes his Apostolic ministry by presenting a precise blueprint of end-day events. The critical treatise begins in II Timothy 3:1, *"This know also, that in the **last days perilous times** shall come."* (As this text refers to the last days of the Church Age, it should not be confused with the *"latter times"* of the same period in I Timothy 4:1; nor to the end of the Jewish Age or Tribulation Period in Acts 2:40, Hebrews 1:2 and I Peter 4:7.) However, by this time, Revelation 3:17-18 states that most Christians (particularly in the West) will be blinded by materialism. Dr. Jack Hyles used to say, "There are three types of people in the world. The first group *makes* things happen; the second group *watches* things happen; the third group doesn't know *what's* happening." Sadly, the average born-again believer in twenty-first century America falls into that third category regarding spiritual matters. (See April 2022 Fundamentalist fantasy, *How Christians Can Save America* by the delusional author, David Baker.)

I once attended a men's meeting in Amarillo, Texas, where a "mere" carpenter gave a ten-minute devotional showing that the first mention of the word "remnant" is in Exodus 26:12, *"And the **remnant** that remaineth of the curtains of the tent...shall hang over the **back**side of the tabernacle."* The brother concluded, "The spiritual *remnant* in any age will always have God's *back*!" Because they *really* believe "The Book" (I Thessalonians 2:13), God's current remnant of Philadelphia-minded, King James Bible believers (Revelation 3:8) will always have the decided edge when gleaning from Paul's prophetic profile. The purpose of this first chapter is to present a four-point overview of the closing days of the apostate Laodicean Church Age.

DEEP-SIX

When I began this opening chapter, the first thing I had to do was select a title. My initial choice was "The Last Days." But then I had an amazing encounter with the Holy Spirit. He impressed me that it was way too dull (LOL), and besides, He had already selected the title for me. Out of nowhere, He put "The Last Latte" on my heart. I found that quite amazing, as the only thing I hate more than lattes are skinny jeans. But then it hit me—you couldn't come up with a better catchphrase to describe America's imminent demise! (Acts 11:27-28) The Holy Spirit then directed my attention to the perfect text to illustrate this deep truth, *"They that did feed delicately are desolate in the streets: they that were brought up in scarlet embrace dunghills."* (Lamentations 4:5)

Owing to sheer curiosity, I decided to Google those three words to see what might surface. To my surprise, some attorney from Sri Lanka named Dilshan Boange, wrote a novel in 2020 with the very same title. (His only other "best-seller" is entitled *Omunkashyu*.) The storyline deals with international tension between China and India and how the resultant fallout adversely affects two Shemite dudes who run a high-end coffee house in the heart of Colombo City. (Obviously, great minds think alike.)

The theme of this insignificant appearing work of fiction—penned in Colombo, Sri Lanka—speaks to the greater reality that the entire world is currently stressed out, big time, their beaneries hanging in the balance.

The word *perilous* appears only once in Scripture. The Noah Webster 1828 *American Dictionary of the English Language* (hereinafter referred to as *Webster's 1828 Dictionary*) definition says: "Dangerous; hazardous; full of risk." One could hardly find a more fitting depiction of global conditions in the tumultuous Covid-19 era. For years I have used a simple timeline to rightly divide a major end-time truth. Now this material is alive with new relevance! While I never concern myself with the *eruption* in the Tribulation—because of the *interruption* at the Rapture—with thirteen grandchildren and one great-grandchild to pray over, I will admit to occasional fretting about the *disruption* in those perilous times (on *this* side of the interruption) caused by all the *corruption* sown into the modern "Bibles." Preachers call this the "Rapture before the Rapture." I prefer the more thought-provoking "Post-Perilous Times, Pre-Tribulation Rapture." Thus, the Rapture is called the "Blessed *Hope*" in Titus 2:13. The mid- and post-Tribulation camps misapply this text to bolster their position (right concept, wrong dispensation.) Simply put, *if* a Christian makes it to I Thessalonians 4:16, he (or she) will have to endure the perilous conditions described in I Timothy 3. Suffice it to say, the end of the Church Age will be unlike *anything* we have *ever* experienced.

While men continue to mock the Bible, they remain oblivious as to how it controls their very lives, and, in the most incredible ways. For instance, do you realize that nearly every public and commercial building in Covid-19 America has posted a sign declaring the King James Bible to be the perfect, inspired, word of God? Confused? The notice reads (in so many words), "Social Distance *Six* Feet." Why is it six and not five or seven? Do you think any of these God-haters realize that Revelation 13:18 establishes "Six" as the Bible number for *man*? Would their pro-evolution public school teachers have taught them that man was created on the *sixth* day? Would their liberal pastors (if they even attend church) have told them that the first book in the Bible named after a *man* is Joshua, the *sixth* book, *and* is spelled with *six* letters? And what about that *sixth* book of the New Testament, Ro*man*s, also with *six* letters? While having grown addicted to their "smart" phones, do you think any of them know that the *sixth* word in the *sixth* verse in the *sixth* chapter of that *sixth* book just "happens" to be—*man*?

The relationship of the number *six* to II Timothy 3:1 will surprise you. Lost men who may not attend our churches, are quite familiar with the American idiom "deep-six." Akin to placing something in "file thirteen," the expression is used as a verb meaning, "To discard, get rid of, or cancel; to completely put an end to something." An English phrase of likely nautical origin, to "deep-six" someone or something, was probably a reference to six fathoms of water being the standard depth at which to bury bodies at sea. The second, more familiar use relates to the standard six-foot depth of a grave. Thus, the looney CDC is warning *mankind* that to avoid going *six* feet under, stay *six* feet apart above ground.

In view of all this, the first point in our analysis of Paul's last-days forecast is "Deep-Six." As the definition of "perilous" has decreed, there will be plenty of *death* ahead, a *"Bad Moon Rising"* on steroids! I'm sure most of us would agree that we lost far more friends and family to Covid-19 in 2021 than we did in 2020. And if you think it's been rough lately, you ain't seen nothin' yet! A popular World War II-era cartoon in *Mad Magazine* said it all. The pilot of a B-52 bomber is struggling at the controls; his co-pilot is half-dead; his windshield is shot out; smoke is filling the cockpit. The caption has him warning his buddy, "If you think *this* is bad, *wait 'til we get out of the hanger!*" If you think Biden was bad, wait 'til you see President Kamala, President Hillary, President Nancy, or worse yet—President Oprah. Beware America—the "Last Latte" is coming to a bean boutique near you!

DEEP STATE

The exponential spread of Covid-19 sparked a debate over the true nature of the disease, i.e., Coronavirus or *"China* Virus;" pandemic, or *"plan*-demic"; coincidence or *conspiracy*? The Holy Ghost already gave us the answer some 2,000 years ago in one of Paul's twenty end-day signs. However, here, as in other eschatological texts, the Olivet Discourse in particular, Christians are understandably confused by "signs" such as wars, rumors of wars, famines, and earthquakes, as such maladies have always existed. The key to a proper exegesis is in Matthew 24:8, *"All these are the beginning of sorrows."* Cross-referencing back to the two "sorrows" in Genesis 3:16, the analogy is that the closer a woman gets to delivery, the more intense her labor pains become (ask any mother). Thus, Paul writes, *"For when they shall say, Peace and safety; then sudden destruction cometh upon them, as **travail upon a woman with child**.* " (I Thessalonians 5:3)

One must, therefore, rightly divide between "normal" wars, rumors of wars, famines, and earthquakes, and those that begin standing out for unprecedented intensity. (It remains to be seen if Vladimir Putin's 2022 invasion of Ukraine and declared rejection of Israel's sovereignty over the Golan Heights are creeping precursors to Ezekiel 38 and 39.) For instance, Paul's first sign in I Timothy 3 is *"lovers of their own selves.* " While always true of man's sin nature, the *Oxford Dictionary* named "selfie" the 2013 word of the year, adding "research suggested its frequency in the English language has increased by 17,000% in the last year." (I love to remind teenagers not to be impressed by their phones, as Moses was "downloading data" from a "cloud" onto *his* "tablets" *long* before Bill Gates had his first diaper changed.) Sign number six is *"disobedient to parents.* " In the 1800s, Mark Twain told parents, "When a boy turns thirteen, put him in a barrel and feed him through a knot hole. When he turns sixteen, plug up the hole." However, in the post-Menendez Brothers era, labor pains are off the chart, giving renewed relevance to another dictionary word, *parricide*—the killing of one's parent.

This brings us to that specific sign inserted by the Holy Ghost over 2,000 years ago that will settle the "Covid" debate. Sign number 15 is *"traitors.*" True to our "birth pangs" analogy, traitors existed in America's earliest days, Benedict Arnold being the poster child; yet they were the exception, patriots like Nathan Hale comprising the rule (Loyalists having never joined the cause to betray it). However, in our nation's final days, things are reversed. Super loyal Americans like the late Jessie Helms (aka "Senator NO") and, most recently, President Donald J. Trump (aka MAGA), are in the minority, while the Rhino Republicans, along with 99% of the "Jackass party" comprise the majority (Acts 27:12). Furthermore, after Mr. Trump's surreal win in 2016, his entire tenure was hamstrung by sign number ten, *"false accusers.* " Even Rush Limbaugh, who bashed conspiracy buffs for years with his satirical "Limbaugh Kook Test," spent the last days of his life fighting to expose the Deep State. In a subtle prophecy on the future rise of the Antichrist, the Holy Spirit tells us in Ezekiel 31:4 that *"the waters [nations] made him great, the **deep** set him up on high.*"

Of course, the proverbial "Swamp" did not begin with the "Never Trump" movement. In my 2005, 900-page tome, *How Satan Turned America Against God*, dozens of machinations were documented (only to have Sam Cohen, "Father of the Neutron Bomb," say in his afterword, "I can assure you that Bill hardly scratched the surface with regard to perfidy and corruption prevailing in our government"). Two of the more egregious cases occurred during World War II. The so-called "*Sneak* Attack" on Pearl Harbor, December 7, 1941, can be easily debunked as a *casus belli* by the November 30, 1941, *Honolulu Advertiser*. Exactly seven days *before* the infamous "sneak" attack, their front-page headline warned in bold print, "JAPANESE MAY STRIKE OVER WEEKEND." The main article, "Leaders Call Troops Back In Singapore" (also on page one), had four bullet points, the last reading, "Hawaii Troops Alerted." Wow, that was *some* sneak attack!! (Ironically, praise the Lord, the man who led the attack, Captain Mitsuo Fuchida, later trusted Christ as his Saviour after reading the testimony of Doolittle Raider, Jacob DeShazer.)

The second example of pre-Trump swamp creatures is on page 9,097 of the November 7, 1942, Federal Register. According to the *official record* of our country, one of the nation's largest banks was busted in the middle of the War for money laundering Third Reich funds! Under the authority of the Trading with the Enemy Act, the Alien Property Custodian (Leo T. Crowley) seized the Nazi assets being illegally held in the Union Banking Corporation of New York. The seven board members behind this treachery just happen to be included for your viewing pleasure. The fifth name is striking, future Connecticut Senator *Prescott S. Bush*, patriarch of the same Skull & Bones GOP clan that wouldn't spit on "The Donald" in 2016, yet had no trouble aiding "Der Führer" in 1942.

The King James Bible itself was saved from a conspiracy, the Jesuit-hatched Guy Fawkes Gunpowder Plot, November 5, 1605. In defense of genuine Bible-based conspiracy history (Luke 4:6; Acts 23:13; II Timothy 3:4, et al.), as opposed to idiotic denials of Sandy Hook, lunar landings, and a spherical earth, *How Satan Turned America Against God* exhibits the definitive "Smoking Gun" —the official death notification letter of Baptist patriot, Captain John M. Birch (John Birch Society namesake), given to me by John's brother, Robert, attributing his mysterious demise to "stray bullets" juxtaposed with the rarely-seen images of his bound, mutilated corpse lying on the ground. John had initially served as a spy for General Claire Lee Chennault's First American Volunteer Group (AVG) of the Republic of China Air Force (aka The Flying Tigers), then the 23rd Fighter Group of the 14th Air Force, before his capture and execution by Chinese Communist forces. These uncirculated photos (shown in my book), were placed in my hands by the legendary Flying Tigers triple ace, Brigadier General David Lee "Tex" Hill, during an interview I conducted with him at his San Antonio residence. (Hollywood actor John Wayne portrayed Hill's character in the 1942 film, *Flying Tigers*.) On a curious side note, when the General entered his office for the interview, he was holding his head, indicating he had a hangover. His opening words were, "Me and *Chuck* were being bad boys last night" —as in Chuck *Yeager*.

The Manhattan Project physicist, Samuel T. Cohen, wrote the afterword to my book (resulting in uncharacteristic recognition by *USA Today*). Sam was assigned to the efficiency group at Los Alamos to calculate how neutrons acted in "Fat Man" (Mark III), the plutonium bomb dropped on Nagasaki, August 9, 1945. As implied by their respective names, Sam's 10,000-lb. weapon—at 21 kilotons (21 tons of TNT), generated significantly more destruction than "Little Boy," the 16-kiloton Hiroshima warhead. In 1958, the Jewish prodigy swung to the other extreme, using a slide rule his father gave him on his fifteenth birthday to invent the controversial W70 warhead, known as the neutron bomb. While Sam's first contribution to modern-age weaponry wiped out 40% of Nagasaki, his second was a bizarre blast. A neutron bomb, officially defined as an enhanced radiation weapon (ERW), is a tactical low-yield thermonuclear device designed to maximize lethal neutron radiation in the immediate vicinity of a detonation while minimizing the physical power of the blast itself. The goal was limiting collateral damage, following medieval Just War Theory. Sam once told me that when a pacifist rabbi chided him for his creation, he replied, "What's your beef? It's a kosher bomb."

In his three-page afterword, Sam shed some timely light on the future global panic over Covid-19. "Most Americans are totally oblivious to their precarious surroundings. Several years ago, my longtime friend and colleague Joe Douglass authored a book (*America the Vulnerable: The Threat of Chemical and Biological Warfare*) whose preface contained the following statement:

While the United States debates the development of a massive defense effort against nuclear attack...the fact remains that this nation is almost entirely defenseless against chemical, biological, and toxin weapons of mass destruction. Some of these weapons may already be secreted within our borders; others could be synthesized by our enemies within a matter of hours, or days at the most. Indeed it is doubtful that most biological attacks would even be recognized for what they are. Even if it could be proven with certainty that the outbreak of a particular disease was not a natural occurrence and instead was deliberately instigated, it would be almost impossible to pinpoint the exact source.

To see how conspiracy history goes in the spirit world (Ephesians 6:12), consider the following two cases. Dean Koontz is an American author whose novels are billed as suspense thrillers, yet often incorporate elements of horror, fantasy, satire, science fiction, and mystery. Many of his titles have made the *New York Times* Best Seller list, with fourteen hardcovers and sixteen paperbacks reaching number one. In 1981, Koontz released *The Eyes of Darkness*, a thriller novel about a mother who sets out to discover if her missing son is dead or alive. Suddenly, the reader encounters a virulent infectious pandemic. Though not all elements of the fictional virus match the recent strain, the wild part is the source. While labeling it *"China's* most important and dangerous *biological* weapon in a decade," Koontz went on to say, "The Russians called the stuff '*Gorki-400*' because it was developed at their RDNA labs outside of *Gorki*, and it was the four-hundredth viable strain of man-made microorganisms created at that research center." But note the amazing change in the 2008 edition—a full twelve years *before* the "China Virus" infected America: "They call the stuff '*Wuhan-400*' because it was developed at their RDNA labs outside of the city of *Wuhan*, and it was the four-hundredth viable strain...." (In a rather eerie "coincidence," I finished writing *Perilous Times* while preaching for a pastor friend, Dustin Feaster, in Everett, Pennsylvania; Koontz, who currently lives in southern California, was born in Everett and reared in neighboring Bedford.)

For the record, the Bill Gates Institute for Disease Modeling released a video in 2018 modeling a global pandemic starting in Wuhan, China. In 2019, the World Economic Forum, in collaboration with the Bill and Melinda Gates Foundation and Johns Hopkins University, ran an exercise for an "inevitable" Corona virus pandemic (the only difference being that the virus would escape from a wet market in South America). The "Wuhan-400" reference in the 2008 edition of *The Eyes of Darkness* is even more Satanic according to the timeline submitted by my friend and "former" US Marine, Dr. Greg Nash (who has done extensive research on the Covid-19 crisis):

> Everyone has given some attention to the bio weapon SarsCovid-2. What was developed in 2005 has been weaponized as a tri-chimera virus with an HIV delivery system. It is called Covid-19, but it has never been allowed to be isolated in any laboratory because it is patented. The bio-weapon was developed in Chapel Hill, North Carolina, at Fort Detrick, which is the only DSL4 lab in the United States. Because it is illegal to fully weaponize pathogens in the United States, in 2014, Dr. Fauci sent the virus to Wuhan, China, and let our government give $150,000,000 for its manufacturing with 'gain of function' research. Dr. Fauci's mRNA research in bio weapons dates back to the 70s with HIV and the 80s with Ebola. One of the disturbing truths of these 'perilous times' is that the American government developed and paid for a virus that kills its own people.

Another dose of Satanic inspiration involves Sylvia Celeste Browne. This woman was a popular clairvoyant on the talk-show circuit in the 1980s and '90s, "gracing" *Larry King Live*, *The Montel Williams Show*, and other brain-dead venues. Typical of all witches, warlocks, and "Christian" wannabe prophets (e.g., Jean Dixon, Nostradamus, Rasputin, Edgar Casey, Aleister Crowley, Harold Camping), though some of her guesses came true, many did not. Temple University mathematician John Allen Paulos labeled this the "Jean Dixon effect." That *any* prove correct may be attributed to the deep truth in Luke 4:6 that mortals can sell their souls to the Devil (known in European folklore as a "Faustian bargain"). Thus, we observe "Sons of Arthritis" Grandpa Keith Richards and Sir Mick Jagger, a *great*-grandfather, *still* rocking it out as they near their fourscore mark (Psalms 90:10).

Just as the true God answers His children's prayers, the "god of this world" (II Corinthians 4:4) does the "same" for his. The main difference is that Satan feeds his devotees a mixture of truth and error before ultimately leaving them in the lurch. The only "perfect will" he has for their lives is that they *don't* fulfill the plan that God had for them, "*All we like sheep have gone astray; we have turned every one **to his own*** *way."* (Isaiah 53:6) While Sir Paul McCartney claims to speak with George "My Sweet Lord" Harrison—*through a tree*—John "Imagine There's No Hell" Lennon, was probably "welcomed home" with a satanic *kiss*. Dr. David Halleran, the surgeon who pronounced Lennon dead at Manhattan's Roosevelt Hospital on December 8, 1980, said that as he pulled the sheet over John's head, a Muzak version of "All My Lovin'" was eerily playing in the ER. This was the Beatles' opening song in their February 9, 1964, watershed debut at the Ed Sullivan Theater, a mere four-tenths of a mile away. It is no coincidence that *the very first lyrics* uttered on American soil by the atheist who would later say, "The Beatles are more popular than Jesus," were— "Close your eyes and I'll kiss you."

In 2008, *the same year Dean swapped "Gorki" for "Wuhan,"* Sylvia jumped onboard the "plandemic" bandwagon with her own #1 *New York Times* bestseller, *End of Days: Predictions and Prophecies About the End of the World.* As one of her last apocalyptic visions, the psycho psychic wrote on page 312, "In around *2020* a severe pneumonia-like illness will spread throughout the globe, attacking the lungs and the bronchial tubes and resisting all known treatments. Almost more baffling than the illness itself will be the fact that it will suddenly vanish as quickly as it arrived, attack again ten years later, and then disappear completely." Thus, acting apart from one another (and in the same year, no less), two of Satan's dupes picked both the *city* and *year* for the launching of Covid-19.

While other examples exist, one more will suffice. The British dystopian political action film *V for Vendetta* debuted in 2006. To give this degenerate work minimal attention, the setting is 2020, the theme is "chaos in the cosmos." The "St. Mary's virus" has crippled Europe; London is a fascist state; and America has imploded from a second Civil War. The subliminal message is that the former free world is now being *played* due to fear of an invisible bug, an eerie harbinger of how our *own* initial "two-week" quarantine continues to expand.

Make no mistake about it, *as dictated by II Timothy 3:4*, in the post-Trumpian era (discredited QAnon nuts notwithstanding), America's future is now being controlled by globalist entities (like the "Great Reset" of Davos, Switzerland). A shortlist of Satan's key players (not that you should waste any time monitoring their activities) would include Klaus Schwab, George Soros, Bill Gates, Prince Charles, Tony Blair, Bill

Clinton, Henry Kissinger, Mark Zuckerberg, Xi Jinping, Gina Gopinath, António Guterres, and Pope Francis (with plenty of bit players like Barack Obama, Anthony Fauci, John Roberts, Chuck Schumer). For the record, Joseph Robinette Biden, Jr. (aka "Sleepy Joe") has always been a pro-UN globalist puppet. Way back in 1996, I documented this in my second book, *What Hath God Wrought*. (See pages 581-82 for treasonous excerpts from the Roman Catholic Congressman's July 1992 Senate speech entitled, "The Threshold of the New World Order.") Yet, *the* most shocking deep truth concerns *who* is ultimately responsible for the Devil's extraordinary end-day power.

DEEP SLEEP

On three occasions the Apostle Paul told the Church to awaken from their spiritual sleep (Romans 13:11-14, Ephesians 5:14-18, I Thessalonians 5:6). In the powerful Philadelphia Church Age, revivals were called "Great Awakenings." However, in the Laodicean Age (the "last days" of II Timothy 3:1), a unique spiritual climate prevails. One of the least-known traits of end-time Christianity (primarily in the West), is that traditional revival will no longer occur. Though unpopular in hyper-evangelistic, "1-2-3-repeat after me" circles, the Bible is clear. Applying right division (II Timothy 2:15), the "positive" text in II Chronicles 7:14 regarding *Israel* is negated by the "negative" text in II Timothy 4:3 regarding the *Church*, *"For the time will come when **they will not endure sound doctrine**."* This Pauline text obviously concerns *saved* people, for *"the natural man receiveth not the things of the Spirit of God: for they are foolishness unto him."* (I Corinthians 2:14)

Second, note that Paul did not say they would not "believe" sound doctrine, but that they would not "endure" it. Thus, *the* prevailing characteristic of last-day Christians is an unwillingness to *endure* the politically incorrect doctrines of the "archaic" AV 1611. As Paul adds in I Thessalonians 5:2, *"the day of the Lord so cometh as a thief in the **night**,"* when Laodiceans go "nighty-night" there's no rousing them, as *their* sleep equates to rapid eye movement (REM), the fourth and deepest stage of sleep.

The connection to America's current political and cultural trajectory is astounding. Jesus said in Matthew 5:13, *"Ye are the salt of the earth: but if the salt have lost his savour, wherewith shall it be salted? **it is**"*

***thenceforth good for nothing**, but to be **cast out**, and to be trodden under foot of men."* (Like that wheat *"cast out"* in Acts 27:38 would be useless for planting, as wet seed grain causes premature germination.) While many pastors feigned outrage at their governors' declaring church services as "non-essential," the fact that these same men closed their doors so willingly proved that the initial call was right! Because the "more-part" (Acts 27:12) of Independent Baptists (not to mention the hordes of everything else) have lost their *saltiness*, the result is a *rotting* Republic! Simply put, *our* worldly state has enabled the "one-worlders" to take over. As D. L. Moody once said, "When the church affects the world you have *revival*; when the world affects the church, you have *apostasy*." On another occasion, he added, "Christians should live in the world, but not be filled with it. A ship lives in the water; but if the water gets into the ship, she goes to the bottom. So, Christians may live in the world; but if the world gets into them, they sink."

The spiritual shipwreck illustrated in Acts 27:41 was also referenced in II Timothy 3:13. After giving twenty negative end-time traits, Paul summarized, *"But evil men and seducers shall **wax worse and worse**, deceiving and being deceived."* Anyone familiar with historic revivals knows that the evidence of a genuine move of God is an improved society. Pitcairn Island was transformed from a hellhole to a moral paradise after the Bounty's survivors got saved. The same can be said concerning the primitive South Pacific island of Aneityum (New Hebrides). There, one can read the famous inscription to Missionary Dr. John Geddi:

> When he landed here in 1848
> There were no Christians.
> When he left here in 1872
> There were no Heathen.

The most graphic indictment on Laodicea is Revelation 3:15-16 where the Church is chided for being *"neither cold nor hot."* As any nurse can tell you, at one time a mixture of lukewarm water and salt was used to induce vomiting. The metaphorical application is that Covid-19 has infected Heaven itself, the Lord declaring: *"So then because thou art lukewarm, and neither cold nor hot, **I will spue thee out of my mouth**."* Aghast at reproach, a typical lukewarm Laodicean will always try to *"be a friend of the world."* (James 4:4) For instance, in 2020,

Chick-fil-A's CEO, Dan Cathy, exhorted white Christians to repent of racism and fight for their black brothers and sisters, etc. (What does this have to do with "Eat Mor Chikin?")

Another case in point is the impressive 430,000-square-foot Museum of the Bible (MOTB) in Washington, DC. While patrons will see plenty of nice scriptural exhibits, what they will not see is any definitive statement that the "Bible" (*any* version, for that matter) is the literal, inspired word of God. Steve Green, chairman of the board of the MOTB (and president of Hobby Lobby), told the *Washington Post* that the MOTB "has fence posts—limits. It doesn't overtly say the Bible is good—that the Bible is true." Instead, he says the MOTB's role is "to present the facts and let people make their own decisions."

Perhaps the classic illustration of subtle end-day, Laodicean compromise concerns an "indirect encounter" with the Ark Encounter in Williamstown, Kentucky. On a positive note—considering the Lord's words in Matthew 24:37, *"But as the days of Noah were, so shall also the coming of the Son of man be"* —such a breathtaking exhibit materializing in twenty-first-century America should provoke some serious prophetic implications. But then, Ken Ham had to try to be "cool," illuminating his life-sized Noah's Ark in orange to support the Cincinnati Bengals in their 2022 Super Bowl LVI bid on Sunday, February 13 (II Timothy 3:4).

The 70,000 fans—predominately white men who had paid roughly $6,000 per-ticket to watch a football game—were also forced to "enjoy" the so-called "Black National Anthem," plus a hedonistic halftime "spectacle" promoted as the Super Bowl's first "Hip-Hop-centric show." (Was this supposed to be Commissioner Roger Goodell's attempt to honor Black History Month?) The fifteen-minute, anti-police thug fest was led by a troupe of five "African American" rappers and one white wannabe—Dr. Dre, 50 Cent, Kendrick Lamar, the half-naked Queen of Hip-Hop Soul herself, Mary J. Blige, a doped-up Snoop Dog, and Marshal Mathers, alias Eminem (aka "The Ultimate Wigger"), who ended his "performance" by taking a symbolic knee for Colin Kaepernick). The only real perk was that SoFi patrons were spared having to endure the equally sick toilet bowl Super Bowl ads on the suspended 120-yard-long, 1,000-ton Infinity Screen. For the record, like Brother Ken's favorite "Bible," the New King James Version (changing "vials" to "bowls" in Revelation 16)—his Bengals bombed.

With many personal illustrations of REM-sleep Christianity at my disposal, I will share only two. While I was on an escalator at Detroit Metropolitan Airport in 2020, one big black dude behind me, who professed to be a Liberty University graduate, whipped a bag out of his pocket and said, "Do you want to smoke some weed, Bro?" (Should we really be surprised when the conservative icon, Dr. Jerry Falwell, Jr., had to resign from the presidency of Liberty University after posting a photo of himself—his shorts' zipper partly open, one arm around the waist of some scantily-clad ho, while holding a glass of booze in the other hand?) On another occasion, an assistant pastor of a Bible church told me that when their men had inquired about becoming a Baptist church, a state official told them the legal fees would be $1,500.00. He then remarked in a humorous tone, "And *that* wasn't gonna happen!" Our chat cooled when I asked whether they would have become Baptists if the price had been $50.00 (Genesis 18:23-33).

Closer to home, the first church of any denomination in the "Volunteer State" was the Buffalo Ridge Baptist Church of Gray, Tennessee (planted in 1779 by Tidence Lane from Sandy Creek Baptist Church in North Carolina). Typical of today's modern "Bible Belt," there are Baptists all over Tennessee, including my own city of Maryville (3,200 Baptist churches statewide). Unfortunately, most of these twenty-first century Baptists are about as spiritually discerning as a box of rocks. For instance, on March 2, 2022, the First Baptist Church of Maryville (SBC) held an "Ash Wednesday Service" where ashes were rubbed on the heads of "the faithful." (No wonder, as the Southern Baptist Holman Standard "Bible" derives from the same corrupt manuscripts as the Roman Catholic Douay-Rheims "Bible.") Also, just 1.2 miles from my house stands the largest "church" building in Blount County (no doubt, in several counties)—the colossal 80,000 sq. ft., debt-free First Apostolic Church, aka "The Maryville Miracle." This breadth of spiritual dearth is the primary contributing factor to the so-called "New South."

In 2021, *US News and World Report* did a special story on the latest bunch of contemporary apostates to infiltrate my little Smokey Mountain enclave— "HomE Church." Under the heading, "Tennessee Church Breaks with Traditional Worship Methods," the article describes the quintessential features of the area's newest example of the Satanic "Emerging Church" movement (described in another source as "fluid, hard to define, and varied.")

According to founding pastor, Jason Rogers (former pastor of Riverview Baptist Church in Rockford) and his associate, Mike Seagel (former pastor of Pilgrim Baptist Church in Maryville), their experimental work "parted ways with traditional Church in areas like dress...and music." They also "leave behind the notion that churches must hold services on Sunday morning and evening and again on Wednesday." With reference to the well-known maxim of Fundamentalist standard bearer, Dr. Lee Robertson, Rogers stated, "Some people have said you have to have three to thrive. Here is the reality of the matter. We live in a different century than when that was instituted."

Other changes include ditching the hymnals, even Sunday School. Rogers said, "The methods of reaching people for God have to keep up with the times. Sunday School has outlived its usefulness as families have become busy." (Incidentally, America's first Sunday Schools were begun by the Baptists in Rhode Island around the 1790s.) And, of course, the "archaic" AV 1611 would have to go as well: "This leadership team is not adhering to the premise that only the King James version of the Bible is the book of truth, either."

To me, the most eye-opening quote was, "HomE Church is Baptist in its theology, it just chooses to lose some of the bindings that hold no purpose or that keep people away." The bottom line is that you can simply do as you please: "At HomE Church, you can wear shorts or other comfortable clothing, bring your coffee and donuts and listen to the upbeat sounds of contemporary Christian music while also hearing the word of God."

In case you haven't figured out the meaning of that nutty name (my first impression was that a "Homie Church" must have something to do with reaching Spanish people, etc.), Pastor Rogers explains, "In the event HomE Church outgrows its current location, it will look for a more permanent home. What it won't be is a traditional church structure. It will look more like home."

The article concludes, "God is a lot nicer than we give him credit for. He is not up there waiting to strike us out of our shoes. He is a God of grace and love and mercy...If people would just loosen up and let God be the gracious God that he is, they would enjoy their salvation a lot more and more people would want what believers have." This Joel Osteen wannabe needs to read Deuteronomy 28:63, *"And it shall come to pass, that as the LORD rejoiced over you to do you good, and to multiply you; so the LORD will rejoice over you to destroy you, and bring you to nought; and ye shall be plucked from off the land whither thou goest to possess it."*

In His parable on the Kingdom of Heaven, Jesus said, *"But while men slept, his enemy came and sowed tares among the wheat, and went his way."* (Matthew 13:25) Accordingly, when the majority of genuine Christians slip into the "Land of Nod" (like Eutychus did in Acts 20:9) because they're more out than in—Heaven help us, for all Hell will soon be breaking out (Matthew 5:13)! To illustrate, on December 12, 2021, the skinny jean "fashion design seniors" at Bob Jones University (a school that has opposed the King James Bible for over half-a-century) hosted their 2nd annual, so-called "runway show featuring their capstone collections" (whatever that effeminate stupidity is supposed to mean). One of their perverted "male" models was photographed strutting his stuff—wearing an effeminate red wrap coat (with a picture of the crucifixion on it) and a crown of thorns!

The very next day, Aaron Musser, the newly "ordained" sodomite "pastor" of St. Luke's Lutheran "Church" in Chicago, hosted a special Sunday children's service—dressed in drag! The "Reverend" spoke from "its" pulpit wearing makeup, a platinum blonde wig, a long white dress and high heels (Matthew 18:6). Meanwhile, outside in Aaron's "parish," Lori Lightfoot's "Windy City" was finishing up 2021 recording more homicides than any other city in America, including New York and Los Angeles (three shy of eight hundred).

Such a potential pessimistic reality does not bode well for historic Christianity, due in part to human nature. Suicide stems from despair. Proverbs 13:12 says, *"Hope deferred maketh the heart sick"* and Proverbs 29:18 states, *"Where there is no vision, the people perish."* One of the *deepest* truths in this book is that Bible-believing soldiers in the last days face the same fatalistic temptation. *They must possess unusual grit, knowing that no amount of effort can turn things around* (i.e., like their forefathers could in the Philadelphia Church Age). Consequently, after his "Debbie Downer" forecast, Paul exhorts his soon-to-be-abandoned protégé in II Timothy 3:14, *"But **continue** thou in the things which thou hast learned and hast been assured of, knowing of whom thou hast learned them."* (Acts 13:43; 14:22; 26:22) The perfect cross-reference for *"the time will come when they will not **endure** sound doctrine"* would be, *"Thou therefore **endure** hardness, as a good soldier of Jesus Christ."*

(II Timothy 2:3) The Old Testament parallel is Haggai 2:4, *"Yet now be strong, O Zerubbabel, saith the LORD; and be strong, O Joshua, son of Josedech, the high priest; and be strong, all ye people of the land, saith the LORD, and work: for I am with you, saith the LORD of hosts."*

DEEP SPACE

A common preacher's cliché is that a good sermon outline consists of three points and a poem. The actual biblical inspiration behind this homiletical quip is based on the Trinity. As man was created in God's image, he is a tripartite being, consisting of body, soul, and spirit. Thus, most things can also be grouped into threes: time, space, and matter; past, present, and future; Moe, Larry, and Curly, etc. (Joke: Why can't Italians count to ten? Answer: Because every time they get to two, they run into a "tree.")

When I developed the first three points of this present outline, I thought I was done, but then I made the "mistake" of showing it to my wife. Because I "married up," Linda looked at the rest of II Timothy 4, specifically verses 6-8 (*"the time of my departure is at hand"*) and said, "That sounds like Paul was heading into 'Deep *Space.*'" Oh well, back to the ole drawing board…(As this subject is so important, the Holy Spirit impressed me to devote an entire chapter to our "Blessed Hope.")

2

The Trumpet's Out of the Case

L IKE THE WORD "trinity," *rapture* is not a Bible word. It stems from the Latin *raptus*, meaning "to seize a thing by force" (a related word being "rape"). Jesus's bodily resurrection involved a "seizure by force" when the *Angel of the Lord* (i.e., Jesus Himself) rolled back the stone, the attendant earthquake sending the guards into "after-shock." With the women's arrival, the greatest news the world has ever heard was uttered in a graveyard, *"He is not here: for he is risen."* (Matthew 28:6) At His earlier "forceful seizure" in Gethsemane, Jesus asked, *"Be ye come out, as against a **thief**?"* (Luke 22:52) At Calvary, we read, *"Then were there two **thieves** crucified with him."* (Matthew 27:38) Thus, when citing the Rapture in I Thessalonians 5:2, Paul likens Jesus's coming for His Church to *"a **thief** in the night,"* a good metaphor considering His return as a *body snatcher* (I Thessalonians 4:16). Interestingly, a non-theological definition for rapture is "a feeling of intense pleasure or *joy*" ("Oh, *joy*! Oh delight! Should we go without dying"), which would surely fit the mood on the way up! Fanny Crosby penned "Blessed Assurance" with these beautiful words in verse two: "Perfect submission, perfect delight, visions of *rapture* now burst on my sight."

Since the China Virus has terrorized the world, Christians have experienced a renewed focus on the Rapture. I often tell my listeners, "The trumpet's out of the case!" As previously stated, the Holy Ghost led Paul to describe the Rapture as *"that blessed hope."* (As an interesting aside to illustrate Israel's spiritual blindness, their national anthem "just happens" to be called *Hatikvah*, meaning, "The Hope," while their Star of David flag features two triangles, an ancient Christian symbol for the Trinity, one right side up, for Jehovah; the other upside down for their fallen nature.) The word "blessed" is an all-encompassing word in Scripture. As there can be no deeper truth to carry us through the perilous waters of the last days, allow me to give you eight reasons *why* the Rapture is God's "Blessed Hope."

First, and foremost, the Rapture is a *comforting* hope. Paul makes this point *twice* in I Thessalonians: *"For the Lord himself shall descend from heaven with a shout, with the voice of the archangel, and with the trump of God: and the dead in Christ shall rise first: then we which are alive and remain shall be caught up together with them in the clouds, to meet the Lord in the air: and so shall we ever be with the Lord.* **Wherefore comfort one another with these words.***"* (I Thessalonians 4:16-18) He continues in the next chapter, *"For God hath not appointed us to wrath, but to obtain salvation by our Lord Jesus Christ, who died for us, that, whether we wake or sleep, we should live together with him.* **Wherefore comfort yourselves together***, and edify one another, even as also ye do."* (I Thessalonians 5:9-11) In reference to "all things three," the Rapture is comforting because it gives a *three*-fold deliverance for those fortunate enough to experience it: from the *"perilous times;"* from *"the time of Jacob's trouble;"* and from the Grim Reaper himself! *"Behold, I shew you a mystery;* **We shall not all sleep, but we shall all be changed***, In a moment, in the twinkling of an eye, at the last trump: for the trumpet shall sound, and* **the dead shall be raised incorruptible, and we shall be changed.***"* (I Corinthians 15:51-52)

Second, the Rapture is a *sure* hope. While II Peter 3:3-4 warns of last-day scoffers saying, *"Where is the promise of his coming?"* God wants His kids to know that the Rapture is not some "too-good-to-be-true, pie-in-the-sky pipedream." Reread those words in I Thessalonians 4:16, *"***For the Lord himself*** shall descend from heaven* **with a shout.***"* The Mid-Trib crowd will cite Matthew 24:29-31 as their main proof text, confusing God's elect *nation*, Israel, with His elect *Body*, the Church. Using right division, the main difference between the two scenarios is that Matthew shows Jesus sending *angels* to gather the *Jewish* remnant *after* the Tribulation, while Paul records the *Lord Himself* coming to gather the *Christian* remnant *before* the Tribulation. Thus, we are told to wait and look for *Him* (Romans 8:25; Galatians 5:5; I Thessalonians 1:9-10; II Thessalonians 3:5), *not* for revivals, recapturing America, the WHO, Red Heifers, microchips, rebuilt Temples, or potential Antichrists, etc.

Next, the Rapture is a *purifying* hope. The apostle John states, *"Beloved, now are we the sons of God, and it doth not yet appear what we shall be: but we know that, when he shall appear, we shall be like him; for we shall see him as he is.* **And every man that hath this hope in him purifieth himself, even as he is pure.***"* (I John 3:2-3) The same author wrote in the previous chapter, *"And now, little children, abide in him; that, when he shall appear, we may have confidence,* **and not be ashamed before him at his coming.***"* (I John 2:28) The deep truth here is that the more one looks for the Lord's return, the more he or she will strive to live holy.

Fourthly, the Rapture is a *motivating* hope. Focusing on the Rapture will move us to reach our family as time is running out. Paradise was the pre-Calvary interim holding place in the center of the Earth, separating the saved from the lost in opposite locales. The rich man in Hell was motivated to see his five living brothers rescued (Luke 16:27-31). To know how terrible the Lake of Fire will be, consider that the "Great Gulf" had *two* functions. While the second purpose makes perfect sense, the first truth is almost too deep for words. When the rich man is denied water for his burning tongue, Abraham adds, *"And beside all this, between us* [himself, Lazarus, and the rest of the righteous dead] *and you* [the unsaved] *there is a great gulf fixed:* **so that they which would pass from hence to you cannot***; neither can they pass to us, that would come from thence."* You may wonder who would be crazy enough to rush into fire. When you get to Heaven, ask Susanna Wesley. As her husband's parsonage was ablaze, she tried to run in to save her five-year-old son, John. The only thing worse than seeing your loved ones burning will be the part that *you* had in sending them there! Paul wrote in I Corinthians 6:2, *"Do ye not know that* **the saints shall judge the world?***"* At the Great White Throne Judgment, *you* will have to say "Amen" when Jesus tells your lost mama, *"I never knew you: depart from me, ye that work iniquity!"* (Matthew 7:23)

Fifth, the Rapture is an *imminent* hope. When Paul wrote I Thessalonians 4, his "we" at verse 16 shows he expected to go up. However, by the time he writes, *"That thou keep this commandment without spot, unrebukeable, until the appearing of our Lord Jesus Christ"* (I Timothy 6:14), a year before his death, he passes the baton to his protégé. Note how Paul believed the Rapture would at least occur in Timothy's lifetime. The bottom line is that we should *always* be ready, as the Rapture can occur at any time. The succinct tombstone inscription for the beloved Christian physician and radio preacher, Dr. M. R. DeHaan, summarizes the doctrine of Christ's imminent return with two words, "Perhaps Today!"

Sixth, for some, the *blessed* hope is a *hateful* hope. This is the perspective of reprobate minds. The Rapture was an ancient, politically-incorrect "hate crime" that boiled down to rightly dividing between a two- and a four-letter word. Conservative Jews (the Pharisees opposed to the liberal Sadducees) had no problem with the *"resurrection of the dead"* (Acts 23:6). This was known then (and today) as the General Resurrection (of *everyone* at the end of the world).

Hence, concerning Lazarus, Mary told Jesus, *"I know that he shall rise again in **the resurrection at the last day**."* (John 11:24) However, the dude got up early! *"Much people of the Jews…came not for Jesus' sake only, but that they might see Lazarus also, whom he had raised **from** the dead."* (John 12:9) With this miracle as a type of His own resurrection, Jesus did likewise, the women being instructed, *"go quickly, and tell his disciples that he is risen **from** the dead."* (Matthew 28:7) The Jews opposed the Apostles over the same nasty nuance, *"being grieved that they…preached through Jesus the resurrection **from** the dead."* (Acts 4:2) The "problem" with the Rapture is divine discrimination— *"the dead in Christ shall rise **first**."* (I Thessalonians 4:16) When the Trumpet blows, God will separate His wheat from the Devil's tares. After the tares are gathered into bundles in the Last Days—UN, UNESCO, WHO, NATO, WTO, EU, IMF, FED, et al.—the wheat will go *up* into His loft so they don't get scorched when the bundles get burned in the Tribulation Period (Matthew 3:12; 13:30).

Seventh, the Rapture is a *profitable* hope. Returning to II Timothy 4:6-8 (our launching point for Paul's liftoff into Deep Space), the aged Apostle now *knows* he will miss the Rapture. But, no never mind, it's all good! As Paul hears the Mamertine executioner sharpening his ax, he turns his heart to Home, *"For I am now ready to be offered, and the time of my **departure** is at hand. I have fought a good fight, I have finished my course, I have kept the faith: **Henceforth there is laid up for me a crown of righteousness**, which the Lord, the righteous judge, shall give me at that day: **and not to me only, but unto all them also that love his appearing**."* Part of our reward will be for *"lov[ing] his appearing."* Thus, for nearly a half-century, I've signed Bibles with

Matthew 25:21, my life's verse: *"His Lord said unto him, Well done, thou good and faithful servant: thou hast been faithful over a few things, **I will make thee ruler over** many things*: enter thou into the joy of thy lord."* As the martyred missionary Jim Elliot said, "He is no fool, who gives what he cannot keep, to gain what he cannot lose."

Last (and perhaps strangest of all), the Rapture is a *bilocation* hope. The secular definition is, "an alleged psychic or miraculous ability wherein an individual or object is located in two distinct places at the same time." While the dark thesis is touted in the heathen realm, Bible believers realize that Satan's crowd stole it from the AV 1611. In John 3:13, Jesus stunned Nicodemus by claiming to be in Heaven and on Earth, simultaneously! Paul introduced bilocation to the church at Ephesus. Because we enter Christ's Body at conversion, we actually do live in two places at the same time: *"God, who is rich in mercy...hath raised us up together, and **made us sit together in heavenly places in Christ Jesus**."* (Ephesians 2:4-6)

He then gave the Philippians an even wilder truth, connecting bilocation to the Rapture! The first part of Philippians 3:20 reasserts this positional truth: *"For our conversation is **in heaven**."* From the *Webster's 1828 Dictionary* definition for "conversation" ("general course of manners; behavior; deportment... intimate fellowship"), we see that our *earthly* "conversation" among lost sinners (Philippians 1:27; I Peter 2:11-12) should reflect our concurrent *heavenly* "conversation" among the glorified saints. But it's that second part of our text that adds a new perspective to the Blessed Hope: *"For our conversation is in heaven; **from whence also we look for the Saviour, the Lord Jesus Christ**."* Our looking for Jesus is a bilocation phenomenon; while we do it down here, we do it up there (*"**from whence** we also look for the Saviour"*)! As Dr. B. R. Lakin would say, "Hold my mule while I shout!"

AND *AWAY* WE GO!

As we swim toward the shore of that "Unclouded Day," contemplating our *own* inevitable departure (whether by undertaker *or* "uppertaker"), the following inspirational gem will serve as a fitting end to this second chapter. During the 2020 election, a sixty-second YouTube video circulated with Joe Biden and the late Jackie Gleason sharing a split screen. Gleason appeared in his character as New York City bus driver Ralph Kramden from the 1955 hit television sitcom series, *The Honeymooners*. While Biden rambles on about his shakedown of Ukrainian president Petro Poroshenko, a frustrated, tight-lipped Ralph makes one contorted expression after another. Finally, he explodes with a classic repetitive rant, "YOU, are a BLABBER MOUTH!" He ends with a dramatic "OUT!" pointing Joe to the door.

Having grown up in that period, I laughed my head off and promptly shared it with several friends. While my peers would have loved it, being a native New Yorker, I totally related to that dismal Brooklyn apartment (especially the fire escape). However, a sorrowful spirit suddenly overtook my levity. I recalled Dr. Jack Hyles relating in a 1987 sermon how he had read a personal ad from Gleason in a newspaper asking if anyone could tell him how to go to Heaven. At seventy-one, "The Great One" was suffering from terminal colon cancer (along with phlebitis and diabetes). While most Hollywood stars take their Christ-rejecting stubbornness to the grave, Gleason was different. In a 1984 interview with Morley Safer of *60 Minutes*, Jackie openly admitted that his greatest fear in life was "not making Heaven." When his liberal Jewish host followed up with, "If you didn't make Heaven, I suspect you could *hustle* your way in, though" (an obvious reference to his Academy Award-nominated role as Minnesota Fats in *The Hustler*), Jackie became pensive, replying, "I don't think so. No, it's too much for real to con your way in."

Dr. Hyles concluded sadly that he had tried to reach Gleason but was unable to get through. The time of Jackie's "departure" was June 24, 1987, in Lauderhill, Florida. To say that the burned-out Catholic alcoholic was interested in "the great beyond" would be an understatement. His personal library (housed in the University of Miami) includes roughly 1,700 volumes of books, journals, proceedings, pamphlets, and publications in the field of parapsychology (witchcraft, folklore, ESP, UFOs, reincarnation, mysticism, spiritualism, mental telepathy, voodooism, the occult, ghosts, clairvoyance, cosmology, demons, hypnosis, life after death, mediums, psychical research, et al.), with a lesser quantity of titles relating to the entertainment industry. The bookplate on the Gleason Collection has a notable image (designed in the 1950s by Jackie himself); a stick figure preserves the iconic pose he would strike as he ended his monologue on the *Jackie Gleason Show*

(1966-1970) poised on one leg, saying, *"And Awaaay We Go!"* But *where*, exactly, *did* he go? (Job 14:10)

My melancholy was then replaced by amazement as I read a text from my good friend, Rick Proffitt, Pastor of the Bethel Independent Baptist Church of Glasgow, Kentucky (one of the men to whom I had sent the "Blabber Mouth" video).

> I like Jackie Gleason. I have a letter from his family in my possession. Years ago, a man stood up in a service where I was preaching and requested prayer for him, as he heard he was in the hospital dying. At the time I thought it rather silly. The next morning, I went to work. I was sitting drinking a cup of coffee and picked up a Louisville Courier Journal. The first thing I saw was an article about Jackie Gleason that told the hospital he was in. God began to burden me for him all day. I went home and wrote him a letter telling him of the need to be saved and included a simple gospel tract. A few days later I saw on the news that he had passed away. About a month later I went to my mail box and there was a letter from the Gleason family. When I opened it, all it said was, 'Thank you! Thank you! Thank you!' I hope that means he trusted Christ!

While no one can be sure what Jackie may have done in his heart at that eleventh hour, one thing *is* certain, Jeremiah 33:3 says, *"Call unto me and I **will** answer thee."* The Lord knows how to answer a simple ad. And while the pastor of the greatest soul-winning church of the twentieth century could not get through, a thirty-year-old "no name" pastor of a tiny "no name" church in "Podunk, Kentucky" did! The words, "AND AWAY WE GO" are inscribed on the steps of Jackie's tomb. And if he *did* make it in, I'm sure his very first words were, "How *sweet* it is!"

3

Two Ladies

T HE 2020 CHINA virus transformation of America was obviously a watershed event in the history of our nation. Yet all the unprecedented chaos can be reduced to a single profound metaphor: "Lady Justice" is an allegorical personification of the moral force in judicial systems. Her attributes are a blindfold, scales, and a sword. Far worse than "Lady Justice" depicted as peaking under her sacrosanct blindfold at the opening of the *Judge Judy* show, she has now discarded it altogether to allow her sister, "Lady Liberty," to wear it for a face covering (i.e., no *justice*, no *liberty*.) Today, people care more about "Lady Gaga" than the other Ladies. Consequently, since 2021, any freedom-loving American desiring to visit the sacrosanct Statue of "Liberty" must now provide a vaccination passport for Covid-19! Our ancestors who came through Ellis Island must be rolling over in their graves! Thus, the central question begs, *"Where did America go?"*

As usual, the answer will be found in the word of God. Unfortunately, however, as the water grows shallower, the closer we get to shore, the less appreciation the average Christian has for the *"Old* Black Book's" ability to illuminate current events. Over three millennia ago, the Holy Spirit led King David to pen those amazing twin peaks: *"Thy word is a **lamp** unto my feet, and a **light** unto my path"* and *"The entrance of thy words giveth **light**; it giveth **understanding** unto the simple"* (Psalm 119:105, 130). The purpose of this chapter is to emphasize the Bible's relevancy, especially as we will need it now more than ever. The following material will answer thirteen random contemporary questions with thirteen "ancient" answers (in their strict doctrinal context or by simple devotional application).

1. What happened to America? I once got a telephone call from a woman who said she had several of my books and wanted to know if

I would be willing to witness to her unsaved uncle. She said "He's Italian, a Roman Catholic, and a lifetime New Yorker." I immediately replied that I would and asked her for his name. She replied, "Yogi Berra" (the legendary all-star catcher for my boyhood team, the New York Yankees). Sadly, after telling me she'd get back to me with the arrangements, she never did. Yogi was famous for his many nonsensical proverbs known as "Yogi-isms," (e.g., "When you get to the fork in the road, take it" and "Baseball is 90% mental; the other half is physical"). However, his most famous saying fits today like a hand in a glove— *"It ain't over, 'til it's over!"* I'm afraid, as signaled by the 2020 stolen election, it is now "over" for America.

The weirdest thing about the Covid-19 phenomenon is how *fast* the once-great and powerful United States of America disappeared, as though she suddenly fell into a giant sinkhole. Beginning in the spring of 2020, the initial two-week trial quarantines quickly spread to several months of open-ended exponential chaos, till by the election season every patriot could smell treason in the air (II Samuel 15:12). The Bible metaphor for this abrupt transformation is found in Isaiah 59:19, *"So shall they fear the name of the LORD from the west, and his glory from the rising of the sun.* **When the enemy shall come in like a flood**, *the Spirit of the LORD shall lift up a standard against him."* Contextually, the passage applies to Israel at the Second Advent. Daniel 9:26 ends with the words, *"and the **end** thereof shall be with a **flood**."* You might say that the water cannon is the Devil's weapon of choice. Barely past her twenty-fifth anniversary, the State of Israel was nearly wiped out when elite Egyptian sapper units employed water cannons to degrade Israel's 70-ft-high sand berm along the Bar-Lev Line on the Israeli bank of the Suez Canal during the opening phase of the Yom Kippur War, October 6, 1973. Thus, a "flood" is a spot-on depiction for recent events. Like that iconic closing scene in *Planet of the Apes*, America's "torch" got extinguished by a Satanic tsunami, a modern Euroclydon.

2. But, how can we account for such accelerated evil? Revelation 12:12 says of the Tribulation, *"Therefore rejoice, ye heavens, and ye that dwell in them. Woe to the inhabiters of the earth and of the sea! for **the devil is come down unto you, having great wrath, because he knoweth that he hath but a short time**."* Running out of time to destroy Israel, Satan doubles down. The same applies at the end of the Church Age (II Timothy 3:1). Note how Satan will try to *drown* the Jewish remnant: *"And the serpent cast out of his mouth water as a flood after the woman, that he might cause her to be carried away of the flood. And the earth helped the woman, and the earth opened her mouth, and swallowed up the flood which the dragon cast out of his mouth."* (Revelation 12:15-16)

A related truth (too deep to do justice here) is the gargantuan *size* of Satan's outward form. Bible believers know that Leviathan is not some crocodile, elephant, hippopotamus, or even dinosaur (as taught in apostate IFB schools), but rather a manifestation of the Devil himself! Even Martin Luther, a sixteenth-century Jew-hating Protestant, equated Job 41:33 with Satan in *A Mighty Fortress is Our God*. The same goes for Leviathan's twin, *Behemoth*. Could Job 40:23 be the source for Satan's Super Soaker? *"Behold, **he drinketh up a river**, and hasteth not: **he trusteth that he can draw up Jordan into his mouth**."* To grasp his *"comely proportion"* (Job 41:12), just calculate how big his belly would have to be to hold the total gallonage in the Jordan. *Now* you know what Job 41:9 means, *"[S]hall not one be cast down even at **the sight of him**?"* (See the fun you miss as a "TR" man?) Though mocked by shallow fundamentalists, this notion is more relevant than their dumb "smart" phones, *"Lest **Satan** should get an advantage of us: for we are not ignorant of his **devices**."* (II Corinthians 2:11)

3. What happened to our inviolable justice system? As the Trump presidency was repeatedly waylaid by falsehoods, the bad guys kept getting away with the *real* thing, *in broad daylight, no less*. From Hillary's Steel dossier to Biden's "Blabbermouth" video, an unprecedented level of two-tier jurisprudence formed before our very eyes. While none of the criminals were jailed, President Trump was falsely impeached—*twice*. The scriptural explanation for this condition is found in Isaiah 59:14, *"And judgment is turned away backward, and justice standeth afar off: **for truth is fallen in the street, and equity cannot enter**."* Ten years after the *Revised Standard Version* ejected the Virgin birth from our churches, the NEA tossed the entire Book from our schools. As previously shown, it's a simple numbers reverse; Bible rejectors at *II Timothy 4:3* usher in the "Traitors" at *II Timothy 3:4*. Like Amasa's roadblock corpse in II Samuel 20:12, "Scriptures in the street" have done the same in America. Tired of illegal mask mandates? As revealed in our chapter introduction, "Lady Liberty's" face covering is the discarded blindfold of her sister, "Lady Justice."

4. But didn't we have a 6-3 "conservative" majority on the Supreme Court? Of the 101 men appointed to the Supreme Court from 1790-1980, Protestants filled 90 seats. Conversely, there were just six Roman Catholics. When America's CEO heard the words, "You're fired," every one of his six so-called "conservative" Justices was Catholic, nearly all of whom dumped him in the post-election turmoil, including the trio he appointed. At the time of this writing, the so-called "color blind" Joe Biden had fulfilled his pledge to do a Kamala Harris repeat by appointing far-left favorite Judge Ketanji Brown Jackson to be the first "African-American" woman on the Supreme Court, replacing the retiring liberal Jew, Stephen Breyer. When, during her Senate confirmation hearing, she was asked by Tennessee Senator Marsha Blackburn to define a woman, the "brilliant" legal mind declined to answer, saying, "I am not a biologist." (Kamala gaveled Ketanji in on April 7, 2022.)

We have the late Dr. Jerry Falwell and his Moral Majority to thank for thinking Bible-believing Baptists could lean on a bruised reed in Rome to preserve our American liberty. (See Chapter XII, "The Devil's D-Day" in my 1996 work, *What Hath God Wrought.*) But why pay attention to the Bible? With two entire chapters in Revelation (17 and 18) devoted to exposing "Holy Mother Church" as the "Mother of Harlots," Paul specifically warned that *"in the latter times some shall depart from the faith, giving heed to seducing spirits, and doctrines of devils; **speaking lies** in hypocrisy; having their conscience seared with a hot iron."* (I Timothy 4:1-2) Two of Rome's distinctives are *"forbidding to marry, and commanding to abstain from meats."* Double Duh!!

Despite the usual exceptions (Rudy Giuliani, Sean Hannity, Samuel Alito, Clarence Thomas, et al.), when you consider "fish-eaters" like Joe Biden, Nancy Pelosi, James Comey, Michael Hayden, John Kerry, John Brennan, Leon Panetta, Chris Christie, Paul Ryan, Andrew Cuomo, Susan Collins, Lisa Murkowski, Joe Manchin, Dick Durbin, Kirsten Gillibrand, Marco Rubio, Patrick Leahy, Anthony Fauci, barmaid Alexandria Ocasio-Cortez, Cardinal Timothy Dolan, Bill "Bagpipes" Barr, Opus Dei, 90% of Fox News, and "former" Catholic, Mike Pence—the Protestant Donald Trump *never* had a chance, *despite* his Scottish heritage. For the record, the Trump family "Bible," supposedly from the Hebrides revival (as promoted by Dr. Clarence Sexton), turned out to be a *Revised Standard Version*, not even published until after the revival, bringing him *and* America as much "blessing" as Peter Popoff's Miracle Spring Water.

5. Who is supposed to wear a mask? The King James Bible is very clear as to who *should* and who needs *not* wear a mask when confronting a serious disease. *"And the leper in whom the plague is, his clothes shall be rent, and his head bare, and he shall put a covering upon his upper lip, and shall cry, Unclean, unclean."* (Leviticus 13:45) Note how the next verse handles the issue of quarantines. *"All the days wherein the plague shall be in him he shall be defiled; he is unclean: he shall dwell alone; without the camp shall his habitation be."* In each case the mandated separation is limited to the *infected* person. As for social distancing, Luke 17:11-19 records the famous encounter between Jesus and the ten lepers. When the Lord shows up, the "beloved physician" notes it was the lepers who *"stood afar off."*

6. How could so many people have become so dense overnight? There was a popular song back in the day, "Blame it on the Bossa Nova." Today's version is, "Blame it on the Covid-19." Have you ever seen such goings on, like waitresses in Maine being forced to wear conehead-like inverted face shields; certain restaurants in Virginia limiting couples to one menu; swimmers wearing masks in the ocean; Catholic priests christening babies with water guns; motorcycle riders wearing masks but no helmets; people with masks and face shields on inside their cars; Walmart shoppers who look like they just landed from Mars; and let's not forget the toilet paper run, and the *craziest* one of all, *taking a Covid-19 vaccine shot* (after all, who needs three arms)? As to the cause for all the paranoia, besides basic stupidity, there are two Tribulation prophecies starting to unfold, *"men's hearts failing them for fear"* and *"for this cause God shall send them strong delusion, that they should believe a lie."* (Luke 21:26 and II Thessalonians 2:11)

7. Why has there been so little pushback by freedom-loving Americans? Isaiah 10 contains a prescient text that begins with the Assyrian King Sennacherib as he invades Israel in 713 BC, then subtly shifts to the Antichrist. The change occurs at verse 12: *"Wherefore it shall come to pass, that when the Lord hath performed his whole work upon Mount Zion and on Jerusalem, I will punish the fruit of the stout heart of the king of Assyria, and the glory of his high looks."* Obviously, God has not finished His whole work on Jerusalem yet. The Holy Ghost then reveals in verse 13 how the Beast will eliminate borders, wealth, and liberty: *"For he saith, By the strength of my hand I have done it, and by my wisdom; for I am prudent: and have removed the bounds of the* *people* (Deuteronomy 32:8; Daniel 2:43; Acts 17:26), *and have robbed their treasures* (International Monetary Fund; Federal Reserve), *"and I have put down the inhabitants like a valiant man."* ("Mask up, or else!") The deepest truth follows: *"and my hand hath found as a nest the riches of the people: and as one gathereth eggs that are left, have I gathered all the earth* (again, a feat Sennacherib never attained)*; and there was none that moved the wing, or opened the mouth, or peeped."* Sadly, pulverized by *fear*, end-day Americans will not so much as utter a "peep" as they surrender one liberty after another.

8. But why did so many Baptist pastors seemingly acquiesce as well? Plenty of sincere-minded preachers closed their doors for that initial two-week (and then some) trial quarantine, only to promptly recover and tell the government to get lost (Acts 5:29). However, to the shame of their office, others stuttered, then shuttered their churches for what seemed like an eternity, causing their sheep to go without proper feeding (Acts 20:28). One meme showed a Christian saying (concerning his online service), "I got under conviction, but when I went forward, my head hit the television screen." While John Bunyan said, "I will stay in prison till moss grows on my eyelids rather than disobey God," many a modern Baptist flinched at the mere *threat* of a fine. Yet, for that vast middle group who may have hesitated longer than necessary— realizing that many situations are unique with regard to the age and health of the membership—a timely Bible story can assuage any guilt felt.

In Judges 8, Gideon has just defeated the Midianites. When he tells his firstborn, Jether, to slay Zebah and Zalmunna, the two captured kings, Jether chokes, *"But the youth drew not his sword: for he feared, because he was yet a youth."* Twice the Holy Spirit calls him a "youth," emphasizing his lack of experience *in battle*. This is precisely why so many otherwise good preachers (like the Apostle Peter himself), performed less than expected, because of *their* inexperience in real spiritual combat. To give them the benefit of the doubt, having been spoiled so long by the protection afforded in the Bill of Rights, the men were simply *caught off guard* by their "baptism of fire" with historic Christianity (and a mere "shot over the bow" at that, compared to the "dungeon, fire, and sword" kind.) As "Jether" means *excellence*, we can only hope these genuine men of God have caught their second wind by now (like Peter did), never to repeat their misstep. And having learned these lessons, they can also help others make a comeback as well. After

John Mark (thought to be a later traveling companion to Peter) deserted Paul and Barnabas at Perga, he evidently got right, for Paul instructed Timothy, *"Take Mark, and bring him with thee: for he is profitable to me for the ministry."* (II Timothy 4:11)

9. What's up with all the woke white women? During the urban riots of 2020, young white gals became the main support base for both Antifa and Black Lives Matter, the anarchist groups behind the unrest. (Their cultural indoctrination began in their "teeny-bopper" years, when their *stupid* fathers paid their way into Michael Jackson's jungle music "concerts," so they could salivate over his crotch-grabbing antics.) YouTube videos showed white women kissing the feet of black thugs. Others had white women holding signs, "WHITE PEOPLE SUCK" and "DISOWN YOUR RACIST PARENTS." And yet, America was already in double jeopardy as the so-called "Karens," the main female target group of "angry black women," had also ditched "The Donald." In 2018, the GOP lost the House of Representatives primarily because a high percentage of suburban white Republican women bailed, due to (get this) Trump's personality.

As usual, the King James Bible can explain. After Paul finished his list of twenty signs he warned, *"from such turn away. For of this sort are they which creep into houses, and lead captive **silly women** laden with sins, led away with divers lusts."* (II Timothy 3:5-6) Thus, America's last days will be characterized by wimpy males being controlled by *"silly women."* Isaiah 3:12 adds *"children"* (like crazy Greta Thunberg) to the list of divine oppressors. The scary bottom line is found in Isaiah 13:12, *"I will make a man more precious than fine gold; even a man than the golden wedge of Ophir."* Like that *Facebook* meme where John Wayne says, "Our generation may have had its problems, but we never got offended at a label on a bottle of pancake syrup."

10. Why have I felt so emotionally drained since the 2020 election? Proverbs 29:2, states, *"When the righteous are in authority, the people rejoice: **but when the wicked beareth rule, the people mourn.**"* Daniel 7:25 says of the Antichrist, *"he shall speak great words against the most High, and shall **wear out the saints** of the most High."* John adds, *"And it was given unto him to make war with the saints, **and to overcome them**."* (Revelation 13:7) Notice that Solomon's text reads "mourn," *not* "panic." John Wesley said, "Worry is a mild form of atheism." On Inauguration Day, January 20, 2021, I preached at the

Charity Baptist Church in Amarillo, Texas. To the shock of my listeners, upon reaching the pulpit, I tore my jacket and shirt to shreds, then dumped a bag of dirt on my head! I wanted God to know that I was in mourning (Ecclesiastes 7:1-4). Furthermore, as a new, more wicked America emerges, many have also felt a growing conflict in *their* spirits over *their* native homeland, trying to walk a fine line between old-time patriotic fervor and spiritual reality. Applying God's rebuke of Samuel over *his* sustained mourning for Saul to *our* ongoing mourning for America is a tough pill to swallow. *"And the LORD said unto Samuel,* **How long wilt thou mourn for Saul, seeing I have rejected him** *from reigning over Israel?"* (I Samuel 16:1)

11. What should my response be if a civil or nuclear war breaks out? There's no telling what the future holds for this transgender, baby-killing, human-trafficking, critical race theory-promoting, God-hating, crumbling republic (Psalm 9:17). When Israel faced *her* final days, Jeremiah's "patriotic" message went over like a lead balloon:

> *Then said Jeremiah unto them, Thus shall ye say to Zedekiah: Thus saith the LORD God of Israel;* **Behold, I will turn back the weapons of war that are in your hands**, *wherewith ye fight against the king of Babylon, and against the Chaldeans...**And I myself will fight against you** with an outstretched hand and with a strong arm, even in anger, and in fury, and in great wrath...**Bring your necks under the yoke of the king of Babylon, and serve him and his people**...If thou wilt assuredly go forth unto the king of Babylon's princes, then thy soul shall live, and this city shall not be burned with fire; and thou shalt live, and thine house.* (Jeremiah 21:3-5; 27:12; 38:17)

We've come a *long* way from that "racist" statement, "Do not fire until you see the *whites* of their eyes."

12. What should my bottom line be until the Rapture? Assuming you can handle the "pessimistic" *reality* of II Timothy 4:3, the twin exhortations in Colossians 3:16 to employ Scripture and song will aid in your survival. When surrounded by the Moabites, "Jumping Jehoshaphat" ended his prayer with a pertinent petition for us: *"O our God, wilt thou not judge them? for we have no might against this great company that cometh against us;* **neither know we what to do: but our eyes are upon thee.**" (II Chronicles 20:12) Isaiah 6:1 adds, *"In the year that king Uzziah died I saw also the Lord sitting upon a throne,* **high and lifted up**, *and* *his **train** filled the temple."* King Uzziah was Israel's "President Trump," having served them well. However, just as the Jews got spoiled by their good fortune, America's Christians did the same. Isaiah does not profess to *see* the Lord until his leader is removed. Thus, though our beloved "Trump *Train*" was derailed through providence, we must continue to focus on the far greater "*Jehovah* Train" for our security (i.e., the *"train"* that *"filled the Temple"*). As for *"songs in the night,"* I recall reading an amazing article by the *British Press Association* about a British submarine that lay disabled on the ocean floor:

> After two days, hope of raising her was abandoned. The crew, on orders of the commanding officer, began singing:
>
> Abide with me!
> Fast falls the eventide,
> The darkness deepens—
> Lord, with me abide!
> When other helpers
> Fail and comforts flee,
> Help of the helpless,
> Oh, abide with me!
>
> The officer explained to the men that they did not have long to live. There was no earthly hope of outside aid, he said, because the surface searchers did not know the vessel's position.
>
> Sedative pills were distributed to the men to quiet their nerves. One sailor was affected more quickly than the others and he swooned. He fell against a piece of equipment and set in motion the submarine's jammed surfacing mechanism
>
> The submarine went to the surface and made port safely.

Finding ourselves in the perilous waters of Acts 27, we too can have *"good cheer"* (verse 36) by singing good hymns, especially, "Hold the Fort," "Keep on the Firing Line," and "'Til the Storm Passes By."

13. Finally, did Joe Biden really steal the 2020 election? While we all knew "Resident" Biden was not destined for longevity, to answer the question, Jesus said, *"Verily, verily, I say unto you, He that entereth not by the door into the sheepfold, but climbeth up some other way, the same is a **thief** and a **robber**."* (John 10:1) Though the Bible normally enjoins respect for those in authority, the author of nearly half the New

Testament was quick to show that there *are* exceptions when he blasted the local magistrates in Acts 16:37. Thus, "with all due respect," Joe was worse than a blabbermouth; he was also a *thief*; yet, one that America apparently deserved (Daniel 2:21; Romans 13:1). An old expression goes, "Once a thief, always a thief." As an odd, personal illustration, I know that Biden stole the election from my favorite *president* because he stole the wife of my favorite *customer* (in my heathen days, that is). To make a long story short, in 1972, "Bill & Jill" Stevenson opened the Stone Balloon Tavern and Concert Hall in Newark, Delaware (called by *Rolling Stone* magazine "the best-kept secret in rock and roll.") Well, it just so happens that "Yours Truly" sold the couple their highly sophisticated electronic cash register system. (At nineteen, I wasn't old enough to drink in the joint.) However, five years later, it was "Joe & Jill," as in Joe *Biden*. According to ex-husband Bill, Jill started her relationship with Joe in 1974, *while they were still married* (Proverbs 6:27-35; 9:17). Their denials have always been about as believable as their publicity photos, kissing one another through their Covid face masks. (Matching bags over their heads would have been more appropriate.) Like I said, "*Once* a thief, *always* a thief"; and, if you'll steal a man's wife, you'll steal an election, too.

4

Inventors of Evil Things

IN 2020, THE initial divide among Christians centered around pressure to wear a mask and, more significantly, whether pastors would fold under government pressure to shutter their public services. However, starting in 2021, Satan has been having a field day pitting the brethren against one another over the vaccination controversy. As of January 2022, some 204 million Americans had received at least one shot, representing sixty-two percent of the population. (Many Bible believers were included among this number.) As a "sick" sign of the times, "woke" white NFL fans were more incensed over Green Bay Packers quarterback Aaron Rodgers' Anti-Vax stand than they were about the asinine Black National Anthem ("Lift Every Voice").

This end-day phenomenon (both the outbreak and the vaccines) would fall under Paul's spot-on forecast in Romans 1:30 regarding— *"inventors of evil things."* (This same text would cover a myriad of modern-day sins such as sex change operations, test tube babies, stem cell research, and new pornographic temptations labeled "virtual vices.") While I personally oppose "the jab," several of my good friends have taken it. To give these men the benefit of the doubt, the deciding factor for most was traveling to and from the mission field. Under such conditions, their selfless willingness to jeopardize their own health would mirror Paul's words in Acts 20:24. Nonetheless, while this issue must remain an individual's private decision between God and themselves (Romans 14:4), it is also just as incumbent for spiritual leaders possessing any measure of influence to warn those who are seeking direction (Acts 20:31).

Unfortunately, as is often the case, a mixture of truth and error pervades this extremely dark subject, exacerbated by the fact that its highly technical nature is beyond the grasp of common laypeople (myself included). In an attempt to discredit the truth, Satan has infiltrated the ranks of the anti-Vaxxers with plenty of disinformation (like he did during the 2020 election crisis with the deleterious QAnon conspiracy theories). Case in point, many conservative websites state that Pfizer Chairman and CEO Albert Bourla has refused to take the shot. This is patently false, as a YouTube video clearly shows Bourla taking the booster.

Also, we are dealing with a highly fluid situation, one which appears to change weekly (I Corinthians 14:33). Therefore, I have attempted to delineate seven unassailable *facts* (along with a surprise ending), that should cause any reasonable person to think twice before getting "the jab." (As the following material may alarm those of you who have already taken the vaccination through naïveté—remember, as Matthew 6:8 says, *"your Father knoweth what things ye have need of"* and as Hosea 10:12 reveals, it is never too late to override Galatians 6:7, *"Sow to yourselves in righteousness, reap in mercy."*)

"BIO-TERRORISM BY INJECTION"

My first caution light was occasioned by the strong dissent within the medical profession itself. In standard conspiratorial debates, the so-called "crazies" are generally outed by the so-called "experts." Here, however, we have an unprecedented protest being voiced by significant numbers of the most highly credentialed individuals in the scientific community in nearly every modern nation. For instance, Robert Malone— the inventor of the Messenger RNA vaccine technology itself—has repeatedly stated that humans should avoid taking his creation because it has killed numerous test animals. "People should not be forced to take experimental COVID vaccines because risks aren't known and those under eighteen and those who've had the virus shouldn't take it." Incidentally, Dr. Malone was permanently de-platformed from his half-million Twitter followers with *no* explanation. (Duh…)

Dr. Peter A. McCullough, Vice Chair of Internal Medicine at Baylor University Medical Center, has labeled the scheme "bio-terrorism by injection." Sixty percent of doctors in private practice have not taken the jab. Former Pfizer chief scientist and vice president of the allergy and respiratory research division Dr. Michael Yeadon is a British anti-vax activist who has waged the fight on the Continent.

The most explosive revolt within the medical field is currently being led by Dr. Simone Melissa Gold, an American board-certified emergency room physician, attorney, author, and founder of America's Frontline Doctors. (As of January 2022, the AFD had nearly 1,000,000 members, including well over two thousand doctors.) Dr. Gold—the daughter of a Holocaust survivor—is passionate in her stated conviction that the whole Covid-19 "medical apartheid" myth is being employed as "a pretext to take down our great nation."

For the first time in history, doctors are being denied the right to treat their patients according to their own best judgments, particularly when prescribing Hydroxychloroquine and Ivermectin (the former being FDA approved for over sixty-five years; the latter, since 1996). The quintessential case involves Nurije Fype, a sixty-year-old Illinois woman who was admitted to Edward-Elmhurst Hospital on April 7, 2021, diagnosed with Covid-19, then placed on a ventilator on April 28. When the patient's daughter, Desareta Fype, asked the hospital to give her mother Ivermectin, they refused. She subsequently filed a lawsuit, whereupon DuPage County Judge James Orel intervened—literally telling the hospital, "Get out of the way." Nurije subsequently made a full recovery and "escaped."

Many conscientious physicians (i.e., "purveyors of conspiracies") will not even allow vaccinated people into their offices in order to protect their own staff from "shedding," a bizarre result of taking the vaccine. The shedding phenomenon explains why there were more Covid-19-related deaths in 2021 (especially in the warmer months) than in the previous year, as the injections actually help to proliferate the virus. (I lost at least a dozen preacher friends in 2021, including three former Hyles-Anderson College students in their mid-fifties who all died within a five-day period during the Thanksgiving holiday.) French virologist, Dr. Luc Montagnier—a joint recipient of the 2008 Nobel Peace Prize in Physiology of Medicine for his discovery of the human immunodeficiency virus (HIV)—has taken considerable heat for acknowledging this boomerang effect.

These medical dissenters and whistle blowers have been willing to lay it on the line, paying a hefty price to guard their patients: ridicule; slander; censorship; gag orders; black listing; litigation; termination; license revocation; forfeiture of retirement and related financial packages, et al. For example, in the first week of 2022, the sacrosanct Mayo Clinic turned seven hundred former *heroes* into *zeroes* by issuing them pink slips for refusing their chemical cocktails. By then, some twenty percent of the nation's medical personnel (nearly a half-million) had either quit or were fired from their positions.

Then—with America's understaffed hospitals already hemorrhaging—on January 13, 2022, Chief Justice John Roberts, along with fellow "conservative" Associate Justice Brett Kavanaugh, joined the Court's three liberal Justices to uphold the Biden HHS vaccine mandate for health care providers. And, as you can't make this stuff up, though all nine Justices were fully vaccinated and boosted, Sonia Sotomayor (who has diabetes) opted to attend remotely because Justice Gorsuch refused to wear a mask. Meanwhile, Justice Breyer also went dark because he wound up testing positive (though it was later ruled a false positive). The obvious bottom line is—how does Sonia justify voting to force health care workers to take an *experimental* "jab" when *she* refuses to demonstrate the faith of her own convictions? Her fleeing the chambers was a tacit confirmation that being fully vaccinated and boosted would neither stop Gorsuch, who was asymptomatic, from transmitting to her, nor protect her from getting it from him. It's no wonder that *"He that sitteth in the heavens shall laugh."* (Psalm 2:4)

"IN JUST A FEW HOURS"

The next concern I experienced involved the incredible *speed* in which these "miracle" *experimental* vaccines appeared. For most diseases, developing, testing, and regulating a safe vaccine can require ten to fifteen years. SARS-CoV-2, the virus that causes Covid-19, was first identified in December 2019. Exactly one year later, the Pfizer vaccine—though not approved or licensed by the corrupt FDA—became the first to receive "emergency use" authorization. (This end-run scam was made possible by the FDA essentially banning Hydroxychloroquine.)

According to the *Wall Street Journal,* "BioNTech co-founder, Dr. Ugur Sahin, designed the Pfizer coronavirus vaccine *in just a few hours,* on January 25, 2020." Prior to this, the fastest time for the development of a major vaccine was four years.

"JOINTS FOR JABS"

I then became troubled with the top-down, heavy-handed, Gestapo tactics employed in rolling out the vaccination. Apparently, the mRNA cure was "so good," the American people had to have it *rammed* (through their masks) *down their throats!* With the powers that be employing the old "carrot and stick" approach, "Anti-Vaxxers" have been cajoled, browbeaten, ridiculed, and threatened with workplace termination (i.e., "jabs for jobs"), while also being tempted with everything from $100 pre-paid debit cards to million-dollar lotteries (Ohio), college scholarships, even free ice cream.

Among other bribes, New Yorkers were offered: ten-trip passes on the Gotham Ferry; a courtesy ride on the Cyclone rollercoaster at Coney Island (along with free Nathan's hotdogs); and, up to $20,000 for recruiting friends and family at $100 per shot under the Big Apple's "Vaccination Referral Bonus Program." Garden State locals became eligible to win a dinner with their progressive governor, Phil Murphy (who tested positive for Covid on March 31, 2022). Nationwide, Krispy Kreme was offering two free glazed doughnuts with proof of vaccination, plus one free bonus donut daily for the rest of the year. Maine, Arkansas, and West Virginia gave away fishing and hunting licenses. Alabama's "redneck" residents sold out for much less—two fantasy laps around Talladega Superspeedway in their own cars. While Merle Haggard's kinfolk ("We don't smoke marijuana in Muskogee") were being offered free passes to the Oklahoma City Zoo, the "inmates running the asylum" in Washington State (the Liquor and Cannabis Board), inspired by the marijuana activists in the District of Columbia, were launching *their* "Purple Haze" promotion called "Joints for Jabs" —free weed for those over twenty-one. The crazy list is endless (Romans 1:28; 13:3).

The tags "vaccination racism" and "pandemic of the unvaccinated" became effective intimidation mantras. Dr. Malone said, "This is the first time in history that the ineffectiveness of a medicine is being blamed on those who haven't taken it." With the Supreme Court blocking Biden's Covid vaccine mandate for businesses, our brave men and women in uniform (along with the nation's Federal employees and frontline medical providers) remained the only viable "guinea pigs" upon whom their Commander-in-Chief could take his "kill shot." Meanwhile, in back-to-back 2022 Covid-19 vaccination rulings, Trump's Catholic chameleon "conservatives" continued to show their true colors—Brett Kavanaugh and Amy Coney Barrett joining Chief Justice Roberts and the three *open* liptards to "abandon" 35 Navy Seals on March 25, with Brett and Amy "downing" Air Force combat veteran Lt. Col. Jonathan Dunn's appeal for a religious exemption on April 16. (Given the worst-case scenarios regarding vaccine side effects, can you even imagine what kind of condition our entire military could be in were the United States to be threatened in the near future?) As a retired USMC Colonel in Kentucky told me, "The main 'incentive' remains the threat of a dishonorable discharge." (In true poetic justice, in January 2022, Biden's incompetent, mask-wearing, social-distancing "African-American" Defense Secretary, Lloyd J. Austin III, *and* the equally corrupt Chairman of the Joint Chiefs of Staff, General Mark A. Milley, *both* tested positive for Covid-19, *despite* the fact that they were fully vaccinated *and* boosted.)

"IT'S TONY. WHAT CAN I SAY?"

Then, it was the non-stop evolving theories, policy flip-flops, contradictions, disinformation, failed expectations, and outright lies told by Fauci, Gates, the CDC, FDA, and the WHO regarding any number of related issues (mask ineffectiveness; social distancing; quarantining; fraudulent death certificates; contaminated surfaces; asymptomatic transmission; herd immunity; spike proteins; faulty PCR testing; dangers to children and pregnant women; the threat of long-term immune, neurological, and reproductive diseases, et al.). Their unmitigated gall is *beyond* the pale. Like their initial bologna about those two-week, home-based quarantines—the incessant vaccines simply don't work, end of story! I mean, dude, whatever happened to, "Three 'jabs' and you're out"? (Apparently, such rationale is no longer applicable in "Woke America.")

Consequently, the highly regarded British medical journal, *The Lancet*, published an article by a University of Colorado infectious disease scientist, Carlos Franco-Paredes, concluding "Vaccine mandates should be reconsidered in light of studies finding the vaccines are not stopping transmission of the SARS-CoV-2 virus." According to the *Wall Street Journal*, Johns Hopkins professor Dr. Marty Makary said, "It's time to bring back workers who were fired for not being vaccinated." He also stated his conviction that "companies and public health officials should apologize."

While the deceitful Jen Psaki covered Biden's butt, the crooked media lied about everything else. In an explosive January 2022 interview with Laura Ingraham of *Fox News*, Dr. Malone, aka "Father of the mRNA Vaccine," spoke candidly about Dr. Anthony Fauci, Director of the National Institute for Allergy and Infectious Diseases since 1984—the nation's number one "go-to-guy" for "truth" about Covid-19: "It's Tony. What can I say? Tony has no integrity. *He lies all the time…*Me and my peers have been watching this for decades. We just shrug our shoulders and shake our heads and say, 'It's Fauci.'" (See: 2021 *New York Times* bestseller, *The Real Anthony Fauci: Bill Gates, Big Pharma, and the Global War on Democracy and Public Health* by Robert F. Kennedy, Jr.) The anti-American, arch-liberal Whoopi Goldberg (among tens of thousands of other positive-thinking progressive dupes) must have been shrugging *her* shoulders as well, having tested positive for Covid-19—despite having submitted to *three* "jabs" *and* the celebrated booster! "Its's one of those things where you think, 'I've done everything I was supposed to do.'" (Well, DUH!)

For the record, Dr. Fauci graduated from Regis High School, a private Jesuit secondary institution, located at 55 East 84th Street in Manhattan's Upper East Side. (In a creepy coincidence, I graduated from St. Stephens of Hungary Catholic School, practically around the corner at 408 East 82nd Street.) And in another sick tidbit, after graduating from Holy Cross College (another Jesuit school), Tony married Christine Grady, the current head of the Department of Bioethics at the National Institutes of Health Clinical Center. (No potential malfeasance there….)

On November 13, 2020, Johns Hopkins University's Advanced Academic Programs posted a viral YouTube lecture conducted by Dr. Genevieve Briand, entitled, "COVID-19 Deaths: A Look at US Data." Professor Briand *totally* harelipped her peers in academia (who have since maligned her credentials) by revealing that the number of Covid-19 deaths—as reported by the CDC—is grossly misleading. One of the most notable discrepancies that she highlights is the widespread reclassification of death by other diseases (such as heart disease) as Covid-19 deaths, simply because at the time of death the individuals also had Covid. Pressured by this documented exposé, the CDC's own website now acknowledges that ninety-four percent of all Covid deaths had contributing conditions. (Did ya get that, neighbor? Only *six* percent of all "Covid-19 deaths" were Covid related.) Thus, as Dr. Gold points out, "The danger is not the virus per se, but one's underlying susceptibility *to* the virus." (So, keep forcing kindergarten children to endure those scary, stifling facial diapers, etc.)

As 2022 got underway, a similar report by the highly respected Robert Koch Institute disclosed that more than ninety-five percent of reported cases of the Omicron Covid-19 variant in "The Fatherland" were in vaccinated individuals. (Roughly ninety percent of the German population has received at least two doses.) So many new Covid-19 cases have surfaced in Israel—the nation with the highest percentage of vaccinated citizens—that the Israelis are now suing their own government for having led them astray! The May 20, 2021, "Israeli People's Committee Report of Adverse Events Related to the Corona Vaccine" states, at the top of its title page, "Never has a vaccine injured so many." At best, "the Jab" was judged to be only *fourteen* percent effective; whereas, normally, a vaccine is never released unless it is at least *fifty* percent effective. Furthermore, ninety-three percent of Israel's citizens who were hospitalized with Covid were already vaccinated. Ironically, according to the post-Holocaust Nuremberg Code (Dr. Josef Mengele), forced experimental vaccinations on anyone constitutes a "Crime Against Humanity." Of course, all of this anti-Semitism is simply a precursor for the Great Tribulation: *"And the dragon was wroth with the woman, and went to make war with the remnant of her seed."* (Revelation 12:17)

Along this line of thought, one of the more "intriguing" personalities to investigate is the American naturopathic physician, Ariyana Love, an outspoken critic of mRNA technology. Her lectures are compelling, articulate, highly documented, and absolutely hair-raising to say the least. For example, in a 2021 interview on the right-wing *Stew Peters Show*, Dr. Love claimed that the Covid vaccines are effectively "bio weapons" that contain hydras and parasites that are being used to "transfect" humans into a "new species." However, the most arresting aspect of *this* particular "conspiracy theorist" is the fact that she is all over the internet, and if she is severely attacked by name (as practically all anti-Vaxxers are), I've yet to find it.

When I did a little research on Dr. Love, I discovered the secret to her unique "diplomatic immunity." According to her Bio page, "She lived in the Middle East and in the holy land of *occupied* Palestine where she studied *Apartheid*, *Zionism*, and the indigenous Falesteen (Palestinian) culture." It goes on to say, "Dr. Love is followed by international rights bodies and in 2017, she was awarded the official title of *Goodwill Ambassador* to Palestine via the Palestinian Authorities (PA)." Get the picture? With Israel boasting the highest number of vaccinated citizens, it just so happens this anti-Semitic witch doctor hosted a panel discussion of leading medical experts on April 22, 2021, entitled, "The COVID Vaxxed Must Be Quarantined!" (Warsaw Ghetto style, as in Luke 19:43.)

SCAMDEMIC

Moving right along, as the old adage goes, "Follow the money," this entire "Scamdemic" reeks of ubiquitous avarice. For instance, hospitals receive $13,000 for every Covid-19 admission and another $39,000 for every patient hooked up to a ventilator (eighty-eight percent of whom never leave the place alive). Some "death camps" receive smaller amounts for administering nasal tests. Simply put, Covid-19-doctored death certificates are "cash cows" for any hospital (i.e., regardless of how the patient *actually* died).

While the physicians with the "white hats" have been blocked from using non-traditional medications (especially Hydroxychloroquine and Ivermectin), the conflicts of interest fostered by the Gates-Fauci-CDC-Pfizer-Moderno nexus, has rendered the once-revered Hippocratic Oath—the "Hypocritic Oath." As Paul warned in I Timothy 6:10: *"For the love of money is the root of all evil: which while some coveted after...pierced themselves through with many sorrows."*

"AS THE DAYS OF NOAH WERE"

I label number six "my worst-case scenario." In March 2021, the prestigious National Institutes of Health (NIH) National Library of Medicine candidly acknowledged on its own website the results of their vaccination study: "COVID-19 vaccines designed to elicit neutralizing antibodies may sensitize vaccine recipients to more severe disease than if they were not vaccinated." Dr. Stephanie Seneff, a senior research scientist at MIT's Computer Science and Artificial Intelligence Laboratory, published an academic paper (in the peer-reviewed International Journal of Vaccine Theory, Practice, and Research), warning of long-term damage to the brain from Covid-19 mRNA vaccines, saying "it's likely there will be an 'alarming' rise in several major neurodegenerative diseases."

Several studies reveal that the mRNA "jabs" are *thirty* times deadlier than traditional vaccines. As of January 2022, the number of adverse events due to Covid-19 vaccines reported to the Centers for Disease Control and Prevention's website surpassed one million incidents (21,002 Covid vaccine deaths and 110,609 hospitalizations, along with a total of 1,000,227 Covid vaccine adverse effects). The death count alone totaled more than *all* vaccine-related fatalities over the past thirty-one years combined! By comparison, in 1976, President Gerald Ford recalled the emergency Swine Flu vaccination after the "staggering" figure of *twenty-five* unexpected deaths. And yet, many physicians and scientists believe the true numbers are much higher (by as much as a factor of twenty). This catastrophic estimate reflects the twenty side effects *formerly* listed on the CDC's own website (e.g., severe thrombosis; blood clotting; nerve damage; paralysis; heart failure; and death). This CDC "warning label" was conveniently removed by Joe Biden.

Dissenting doctors report that the first dose of Remdesivir lowers your immune system fifteen percent; the second, thirty-five percent; and the booster leaves you with practically no immune system. Dr. Sucharit Bhakdi, an award-winning Thai-German microbiologist, has lectured extensively on how and why the Covid "vaccines" trigger a breakdown of immunological defenses against infectious agents that lie dormant in our bodies. Consequently, this "cure" has a fifty percent death rate and a one hundred percent organ failure rate when given the full ten doses. As your liver and kidneys fail, your lungs fill up with fluid, and while on a ventilator, the morphine button is pushed over and over again as you are slowly killed. The process accelerates when the helpless patient is rolled over on his or her stomach, further compromising airway passages. Is it any wonder that the victim's loved ones are not permitted in these "execution chambers?" (Back in the day, consumer advocate Ralph Nader used to be ridiculed for saying that America's hospitals murdered 50,000 people annually.)

Jeremiah 1:5 remains one of the clearest Scriptures condemning abortion: *"Before I formed thee in the belly I knew thee; and before thou camest forth out of the womb I sanctified thee, and ordained thee a prophet unto the nations."* A second powerful passage is Jeremiah 20:17, *"Because he slew me not from the womb; or that my mother might have been my grave, and her womb to be always great with me."* Consequently, the main justification for a religious exception involves fetal tissue. The Pfizer, Moderna, and Johnson & Johnson vaccinations were developed with fetal cell lines (i.e., cells harvested in labs originally obtained from aborted fetuses decades earlier). The rebuttal by the "pro-Jabbers" is that these are not the *original* cells, but rather, descendants or duplicates of the originals. So, how does *that* unadulterated "rope-a-dope" sit with *your* spirit?

Now, whenever an internet search is attempted using a simple question like, "Does the mRNA vaccine alter one's DNA?" the subject is always branded a "myth," while the anti-vaccination position is rarely presented. However, a consensus among medical professionals *does* exist that such a surreal possibility is definitely in the wings. For instance, a 2017 YouTube video by Gal Zaks, chief medical officer of Moderna, Inc., confirms that the mRNA injection for Covid-19 *can* alter your genetic code (DNA). Bill Gates inferred as much in an MSN *Lifestyle* piece where he cites an article from NCBI (the National Center for Biotechnology Information) stating that "the jab" does have the *potential* of altering your DNA.

Molecular Biologist and Immunologist, Dr. Dolores Cahill (a tenured professor at the School of Medicine of University College Dublin), warns that the mRNA "jab" delivers a synthetic, inorganic molecule (medical device) that literally programs your cells to synthesize pathogens in the form of the spike proteins that your immune system will constantly have to fight off for the rest of your life. Others label it "Information Therapy" as it hacks the software of life, essentially turning the victim into a GMO (Genetically Modified Organism).

Carrie Madej is an osteopathically trained internal medicine specialist in McDonough, Georgia. (She is a 2001 graduate of Kansas City University of Medicine Medical School.) In her currently-banned video, Dr. Madej states, "COVID-19 vaccines are designed to make us into genetically modified organisms, employing the same lingo and terminology used to identify Monsanto seeds." Given the futuristic repercussions concerning the invasive vaccine patents—i.e., over our original, God-given anatomical autonomy—a creepy correlation exists with those copyrights held by the publishers of the modern "Bibles." The Jesuit agent, Dr. Fauci, is literally trying to kidnap God's children, *"What? know ye not that your body is the temple of the Holy Ghost* *which is in you, which ye have of God, **and ye are not your own?** For ye are bought with a price: therefore glorify God in your body, and in your spirit, **which are God's**."* (I Corinthians 6:19-20)

Madej further explains that the mRNA vaccination is really just the tip of the iceberg as to what is developing elsewhere in the minds of the Matrix madmen currently running this country: recombinant DNA and RNA technology; CRISPR gene editing; injecting "Luciferase" chemicals, cancer cells, metals, even animal DNA into human bodies; MRC5-bordered fetal cell lines; 5G and ultra wide-band tracking technology; nanorobotics; even hydrogels pressed into human skin, allowing AI centers to connect our brains to future smart houses. (George Orwell and Aldous Huxley would roll over in their graves if they could see these "George Jetson" blueprints.)

But this one *really* takes the cake, folks! Yuval Noah Harari is an Israeli intellectual who graduated from the Hebrew University of Jerusalem in 1998, earning his DPhil degree in 2002 from—get this—Jesus College, Oxford University. The author of several books, Professor Harari currently teaches History at HUOJ. He also claims to be happily "married" to his "husband," Itzik Yahav, whom he affectionately calls, "my internet of all things." Most significantly, however, Yuval is a leading transhumanist and top advisor to Dr. Klaus Schwab (aka "The World's Most Dangerous Man), founder and chairman of the World Economic Forum in Davos, Switzerland. (According to nutty *Wikipedia*, "Transhumanism is a philosophical and intellectual movement which advocates for the enhancement of the human condition by developing and making widely available sophisticated technologies that can greatly enhance longevity and cognition. It also predicts the inevitability of such technologies in the future.")

In January 2018, Dr. Harari was a featured speaker at the World Economic Forum. Standing on the dais before an "august" crowd of three thousand movers and shakers (which included Angela Merkel, Emmanuel Macron, Justin Trudeau, Theresa May, Benjamin Netanyahu, and Donald Trump), the Jewish sodomite went on to explain "genetic editing" in his lecture entitled, "Will the Future be Human?" A portion of his surreal remarks (as preserved on video for any skeptics), was as follows:

> Data might enable human elites to do something even more radical than just build digital dictatorships. *By hacking organisms*, elites might gain the power to *reengineer the future of life itself*, because

once you can hack something you can usually engineer it. Now in the past, many tyrants and governments wanted to do it, but nobody understood biology well enough and nobody had enough computing power and data to *hack millions of people*. Neither the Gestapo nor the KGB could do it. But soon, at least some corporations and governments will be able to systematically *hack all the people.*

And, if indeed we succeed in hacking and engineering life, this will be, not just the greatest revolution in the history of humanity, but this will be the greatest revolution in biology since the very beginning of life four billion years ago. For four billion years nothing fundamental changed. Science is now replacing evolution by natural selection with evolution by intelligent design. Not by the intelligent design *of some God above the clouds*, but by *our* intelligent design and the intelligent design of *our* clouds—the IBM Cloud, the Microsoft Cloud—these are the new driving forces of evolution.

In a follow-up taped Q & A, the mad scientist acknowledged further, "Today we have the technology to *hack human beings* on a massive scale. In this time of crisis, you have to follow science. It's often said that 'you should never let a good crisis go to waste.'" In another candid interview he explained, "People could look back in a hundred years and identify the Corona virus epidemic as the moment when a new regime of surveillance took over, especially *surveillance under the skin...*" In yet another lecture he asks, "Does the data about my brain, my body, my life belong to me, or to some corporation, or to the government, or perhaps—to the human collective?"

Finally, as his star continues to rise, in his 2020 World Economic Forum lecture, "How to Survive the 21st Century," Dr. Schwab's golden boy told his mesmerized audience, "This danger can be stated in the form of a simple equation, which I think might be the defining equation of life in the twenty-first century: B x C x D = AHH! Which means? Biological knowledge multiplied by computing power multiplied by data equals the ability to hack humans, ahh....We humans should get used to the idea that we are no longer mysterious souls—we are now hackable animals. That's what we are."

Remember, neighbor, if only *half* of these creepy reports are accurate, the Antichrist has *got* to be on the scene. Dr. Nash has also made the astute observation that Jesus actually prophesied that genetic manipulation would be a sign of His return: *"As the days of Noah were, so shall also the coming of the Son of man be."* According to a proper, rightly-divided reading of Genesis 6:1-7, fallen angels were cohabiting with women, producing a cambion race of giants. Satan wanted to corrupt the seed of the woman that he was told would ultimately crush his head (Genesis 3:15). Nash writes: "Our DNA is our code or 'software' of life that God gave us and what our Lord intends us to be as he has created us. As the DNA of mankind was corrupted, giants were born and the wickedness of man and violence filled the earth. Noah was *'perfect in his generations'* or 'genes' (Genesis 6:9), so God started over with him."

GEORGIA GUIDESTONES

Finally, for the ultimate bottom line—despite Big Tech censors and Big Pharma cash—several YouTube videos and other documented exposés have revealed Bill Gates' unabashed commitment to global population reduction (i.e., Ebenezer Scrooge's "decrease the surplus population"). Bill's father, William Gates, Sr., was a leading eugenicist and former board member of Planned Parenthood.

Well, to give you a peak into the Gates family's world view, the esoteric granite monument "Georgia Guidestones" (aka "American Stonehenge") was erected in 1980 in Elbert County, Georgia (less than three hundred miles from Jekyll Island, birthplace of the equally Satanic Federal Reserve System). As Charlie Daniels told it, "The Devil Went Down to Georgia." According to the anonymous sponsors (believed to be Jesuits), the "first" of the so-called "Ten Commandments" (i.e., of the coming Beast) prominently states, "MAINTAIN HUMANITY UNDER 500,000,000 IN PERPETUAL BALANCE WITH NATURE." Based on current figures, this equates to about a ninety-five-percent reduction from pre-Covid-19 numbers. (Hint: India has already filed suit against the Bill and Melinda Gates Foundation for inflicting sterilization and death upon their unsuspecting women via his crackpot vaccines.)

DONALD'S DEBACLE

Now—for the "bonus" material I promised. (Ya better take a *deep* breath for this one, neighbor.) When I wrote the prologue to *Holy Ground,* amidst the prevailing hype from the miraculous 2016 Trump win over

Hillary Clinton, the Holy Spirit distinctly led me to cover myself with the following prescient caveat:

> Thus, the most appropriate Scripture to define the surprising Trump victory would be Ezra 9:8, *'And now for a little space grace hath been shewed from the LORD our God, to leave us a remnant to escape, and to give us a nail in his holy place, that our God may lighten our eyes, and give us a little reviving in our bondage.'* However, if history is any guide for the future, unfortunately, like the respite under Josiah in II Kings 22 and 23, the Church will fail to profit from this window of opportunity (repeating her anemic response to [Douglas] MacArthur's request for thousands of missionaries to capitalize on Japan's post-WWII disillusionment). And just for the record—to whatever degree euphoric Laodicea '[does] *despite to the Spirit of grace'* (Hebrews 10:29)—the metaphorically deemed '[T]*rump of God'* (I Thessalonians 4:16) could just as easily become America's worst nightmare (Matthew 12:45; II Peter 2:20).

While the stolen 2020 presidential election and the subsequent disastrous Biden administration have been two of the hardest pills for the average conservative American to swallow, an even more disturbing reality has begun to dawn on some discerning patriots—particularly among Bible-believing Baptists. First, let me say that I do *not* believe that Donald J. Trump has been part of any plan to *consciously* hurt this country. However, as smart as Mr. Trump is, he is certainly no match for Satan—the arch deceiver of all mankind (Revelation 12:9; 20:7-9). As a classic illustration of a "smoke and mirrors" diversion, who could possibly miss the stark contrast between all the *good* Trump accomplished versus all the *bad* Biden has done? However, there are now several clear facts that must be considered.

First and foremost—though unrecognized by practically all of Mr. Trump's supporters—is the spiritual "coincidence" that will trace the entire Covid-19 outbreak to Donald himself! To grasp this stunning prospect, a little background review is in order. On October 30, 1991, then-President George H. W. Bush convened the historic Madrid Peace Conference by introducing his now-famous fantasy buzzphrase for securing a permanent solution to the Israeli-Palestinian conflict— "Land for Peace" (i.e., Israeli land concessions for lame Palestinian peace promises). In my 2005 book, *How Satan Turned America Against God*, I included a picture of the American president inspecting his severely damaged mansion in Kennebunkport, Maine, after the "Perfect Storm" forced him to rush home a day early.

In a second "serendipity-do," on August 23, 1992—the very day that Bush reconvened the Madrid Peace Conference in Washington, DC—Hurricane Andrew devastated southern Florida, causing $30 billion in property damage and leaving 180,000 people homeless! As David wrote in Psalm 83:4,15, *"They have said, Come, and let us cut them off from being a nation; that the name of Israel may be no more in remembrance...So persecute them with thy tempest, and make them afraid with thy storm."* I then went on to document seventeen more "coinkydinks" (as my wife likes to call them) where America suffered severe consequences for pressuring Israel to forfeit her land contrary to Amos 9:14-15. I ended my chapter with the following warning: "If you're still undecided about standing with the LORD, just start watching the Weather Channel before retiring each night...Then pull those covers snuggly against your chin. You won't have to worry about anything stirring out there in the dark—*until* the next mile marker is reached on the 'Roadmap to Peace.' Nighty night!"

Well, five months after my book was released, Hurricane Katrina wiped out New Orleans after President George W. Bush pressured Ariel Sharon to evict 10,000 Jews from the Gaza Strip and West Bank. This time, over 1.3 million Americans were abruptly made homeless, a ratio of 130-1. Then, four months after that, the complicit Israeli Prime Minister suffered a hemorrhagic stroke, remaining in a coma until his death on January 11, 2014.

This brings us to what I call the "Donald Debacle" —Trump's imperceptible role in the Covid-19 disaster. As much as I appreciate our forty-fifth President, there are at least three major areas where "The Devil" played "The Donald" like a Stradivarius (like Colonel Hogan would play Colonel Klink). First, while all of the above-cited cases of geo-political action against Israel derived from globalists like the Bush family, the Clintons, and others, what *if* a well-intentioned, anti-globalist, pro-America, pro-Israel US president—with *zero* spiritual discernment— was to make the same mistake of trying to divide Israel's land for real peace (Proverbs 14:12)? You know, a genuine patriot, like Uzzah, of whom II Samuel 6:7 says, *"and God smote him there for his **error**."*

HAPPY DR. MLK DAY!

My readers will recall a second warning that I inserted in *Holy Ground*. As a photo caption of President Trump, nine days after his inauguration on the phone with Saudi King Salman (his Jewish son-in-law and top advisor, Jared Kushner, at hand), I wrote, "Though providentially saving America from Hillary Clinton, "The Donald" will NEVER be able to make the *ultimate* "deal" —a true and lasting Middle East peace (Haggai 2:7-9) without the Prince of Peace (John 15:5). Pray that the first family gets born again."

And so—as President Trump obviously never read my book—on January 28, 2020, he and Israeli Prime Minister Benjamin Netanyahu held a joint White House press conference where they unveiled their much-touted Middle East peace plan, dubbed, "Peace to Prosperity: A Vision to Improve the Lives of the Palestinian and Israeli People." The nebulous proposal (brokered by Jared Kushner) was basically a major land concession for Israel, while mostly offering the Palestinians desert sand in the Negev. (The liberal *Times of Israel* summarized it: "Trump plan offers land without people to people who don't want the land.") However, despite the fact that the initiative was dead in the water (Mahmoud Abbas not even being invited to attend), a US-brokered olive branch for a future Palestinian State—*within Israel's Biblical borders* (not to mention a small enclave in East Jerusalem to serve as the new capital of the *pseudo* state)—would have been *more* than enough to arouse the Lord's wrath (Genesis 12:3; Daniel 11:39; Joel 3:2)!

Moving the American Embassy to West Jerusalem was a nice gesture; proposing to sever even one sliver of "Holy Dirt" is something else altogether (Exodus 3:5). Well, neighbor, take a *wild* guess what happened eight days earlier on January 20, 2020? While the nation was busy "celebrating" Dr. Martin Luther King, Jr. Day—a thirty-five-year-old "Asian-American" male patient in a hospital in Everett, *Washington* ("Joints for Jabs") was being diagnosed as the *first* confirmed case of Covid-19 in America! The anonymous prototype had just returned from visiting family members in *Wuhan*, China. Two days later, during an interview at the World Economic Forum in *Davos*, Switzerland (Ground Zero for "The Great Reset," no less), President Trump uttered his now-famous last words: "It's one person coming in from China. We have it under control. *It's going to be just fine.*"

To cite another pertinent history lesson, by October 4, 1973, the NSA knew that Egypt and Syria would launch a coordinated strike against Israel in forty-eight hours on Yom Kippur, yet President Richard Nixon refused to warn Israeli Prime Minister Golda Meir until the morning of the attack (i.e., payback for the *USS Liberty* incident). Nixon's National Security Advisor, Henry Kissinger (who is Jewish), told Defense Secretary Schlesinger, "The best result would be if Israel came out a little ahead, but got *bloodied* in the process, and if the United States stayed clean."

For the sin of allowing Jacob's bleeding on his watch, "Tricky Dicky" would become the only president in history to be *squeezed* out of office (just missing "*Jail* to the Chief")—with his second-in-command, Spiro *"Nolo Contendere"* Agnew, joining him as the only vice president forced to resign as well! Now think about this, friend—for Donald Trump's well-meaning "error" (II Samuel 6:7), he would suffer, not one, but *two* ignominious impeachments (a first for any American Chief Executive), *plus* the humiliating theft of a clear election win over "Sleepy Joe" Biden. And for the record, as with Arial Sharon, BiBi Netanyahu, Donald's likeminded, good-intentioned Jewish partner, encountered Jehovah's displeasure as well, getting bounced out of *his* office on July 10, 2021, amidst a myriad of political scandals.

The second unpalatable fact is that Donald Trump is not only recognized as the sole driving force behind the record-breaking, meteoric production of the Pfizer, Moderna, and Johnson & Johnson mRNA vaccines, but even now—after so many of the deadly side effects have become known—he *still* lauds "the jab" as the single greatest accomplishment of his presidency, etc. "I pushed the FDA like they've never been pushed before." Furthermore, in addition to Satan using Trump's ineffective vaccine to divide the Body of Christ (not to mention the potential physical harm being done to those who take it), he has also unknowingly laid the unprecedented technological framework to enable the coming Antichrist to fulfill Revelation 13:16 (e.g., vaccination mandates; vaccination passports; mask mandates; quarantines, lockdowns; internment camps; contact tracing via 5G technology).

Thus, Dr. Gold warns that the entire globe has now come under the spell of a new belief system—the "Religion of Public Health," one which scorns "facts" as irrelevant, preferring "faith" in what the new "gods" say (i.e., Pfizer and Moderna) as interpreted by their "high priests,"

Fauci and Gates. *"**And they worshiped the dragon** which gave power unto the beast: and they worshipped the beast, saying, Who is like unto the beast? who is able to make war with him?"* (Revelation 13:4) The expanding tyranny in Australia is certainly a good harbinger of where the United States is presently headed.

CONFIRMING THE COVENANT

Finally, the failed 2020 "Peace to Prosperity" initiative that triggered the Covid-19 disaster may have more prophetic significance than you think. For starters, as Proverbs 30:17 speaks to vultures picking the eye of a carcass to see if the animal is dead—who couldn't discern that all the post-Covid repressive measures constituted one big trial run to see just how far "Big Brother" could push the masses in the immediate future? So, if we *are* on the cusp of the Rapture (as *so* many of us believe), do y'all suppose that Trump's 2020 treaty proposal—bolstered by the epic normalization of diplomatic relations between Tel Aviv and the UAE (aka the "Abrahamic Accords") and, subsequently, Bahrain, Sudan, and Morocco (generating a Nobel Peace Prize nomination, no less)—just *might* have something to do with the *wording* of that prophecy in Daniel 9:27? *"And he shall **confirm the covenant** with many for one week: and in the midst of the week he shall cause the sacrifice and the oblation to cease."*

Notice that it does *not* say the Antichrist will *make* a covenant, but rather that he will *confirm* a covenant; i.e, one that is already in place. Furthermore—to play the Devil's advocate—given the traditional interpretation of Daniel 2:42-44 (that the Beast's power base will be a revived European coalition), it suddenly makes more sense that Putin, who is a strong nationalist (having banned "gays" in the 2014 Winter Olympics), would instinctively resist the true globalist aspirations of NATO and the EU, guided by their philosophical standard bearer, the previously mentioned Klaus Schwab (who published his *COVID-19: The Great Reset* less than *six* months after that initial outbreak surfaced). The odd bottom line is that *both* political theaters are evil end-day players; Russia (obvious "bad guys") versus Europe (not-so-obvious "*bad* good guys"). Thus, Russia's future clash with Israel (Ezekiel 38 and 39) will probably be over her defensive alignment with Europe (i.e., NATO ballistic missile bases on Russki borders, analogous to our own Cuban missile crisis in October 1962).

"JUS' SAYIN'…"

This would put the February 2022 Russian invasion of Ukraine in a somewhat different light. (Remember the subtitle of this book, *Deep Truths for Shallow Waters.*) First and foremost, this emotionally charged event is *way* beyond the pay grade of most Bible believers (many of whom only exacerbate matters by being incredibly opinionated, especially on *Facebook*). Trust me, it's a *vastly* disconcerting, geo-political situation. The average Christian—naive in general regarding most secular matters (see Luke 16:8 and I Corinthians 1:27)—knows practically nothing about the confusing background to the 2022 Russian-Ukrainian War, not to mention the intricate history of Ukraine itself. (My own paternal grandmother was a native-born Ukrainian who spoke six languages and lost members of her family to local terror bombings.)

For instance, don't be too quick to dismiss Putin's "denazification" paranoia till you've personally researched the facts—such as the WWII-era, pro-Nazi OUN (Organization of Ukrainian Nationalists), with their egregious genocidal acts against Jewry. Many of these atrocities (perpetrated by the Ukrainian Nazi, Stepan Andriyovych Bandera), were documented in my 2017 book *Holy Ground,* including Babi Yar—the largest Einsatzgruppen Aktion of all—33,000 defenseless Jewish civilians being gunned down in cold blood by Ukrainian Nazis in a ravine outside of Kyiv, September 29-30, 1941.

Another red flag would be the multi-*billion*-dollar funding of the "pro-Ukrainian" (anti-Russian), CIA-controlled NGO (Non-Government Organization) Renaissance Foundation, *courtesy of the Jewish globalist George Soros.* Similarly, for some strange reason, America's worst enemies—the mainstream media, "Big Tech," the corrupt Biden/Harris administration, et al., have all united behind the charismatic Jewish superhero Volodymyr Zelenskyy. After gaining notoriety by winning Ukraine's version of *Dancing with the Stars* in 2006, the former professional *actor*-turned-*politician* "endeared" himself to the LGBTQ+ community as well, with his 2014 choreographed viral video, dubbed a "queer parody" —though I prefer, "Dancing with the Sodomites" — prancing around in high heels, skintight leather pants, and a midriff-baring top. This "rising star" is *definitely* worth watching on your radar. Thus, was Donald Trump's initial foot-dragging in condemning Putin's aggression related to that ancient proverb, "The enemy of my enemy is my friend?" (Asking for a friend...) In any event, remember God's end-time bottom line: Innocent bystanders notwithstanding— *"**All** nations before him* [including Russia, Europe, Ukraine, *and* America, while excluding restored Israel, as per Numbers 23:9] *are as nothing; and they are counted to him less than nothing, and vanity* (Isaiah 40:17), and that *"the **whole world** lieth in wickedness."* (I John 5:19) Should you desire a few more, try Zephaniah 3:8 and Zechariah 12:3, 9.

So, neighbor...Ya might want to keep some of this in mind as we proceed through the 2022 midterm and 2024 presidential elections. Although I'd vote for Trump again if he ran in 2024—I'd keep both eyes open this time. Satan could be setting us up for a euphoric Fox & Friends, II Chronicles 7:14 "Republican Recoil Revival." (See blasphemous excerpt on page 155 in Helgard Muller's January 2022 book, *President Donald J. Trump, The Son of Man–The Christ*, "President Donald Trump, who is the Son of Man, must be lifted up: that whosoever believes in him should not perish, but have eternal life.") As Paul warned in I Thessalonians 5:3, *"For when they shall say, Peace and safety; then sudden destruction cometh upon them."*

Finally, as this manuscript was literally *at* the press, the germane May 2, 2022, unprecedented POLITICO-leaked Supreme Court draft majority opinion to overthrow Roe v. Wade *may* very well constitute the ultimate smoke-and-mirrors event in the history of American politics: for "Team Trump" (on the eve of the anticipated "Red Wave" mid-term elections)— "It was *my* three SCOTUS appointees who made the difference"; for the Catholic-packed Court— "See, we really *have* been the 'good guys' all along"; for the brain-dead Catholic chameleon, Joe Biden (along with Nancy Pelosi and their fellow Democratic papists intent on salvaging *something*)— "Well, at least it happened on *my* watch, by *my* religion." Only time will tell.

5

Critical Race Theory

I AM A dog lover *on steroids!* (Proverbs 12:10) However, a popular Southern expression goes, "Why keep a dog and bark yourself?" (It actually dates back to 1583, written by one Brian Melbancke in Early Modern English, "It is smal reason you should kepe a dog, and barke your selfe.") Translation: "You shouldn't do something you hired someone else to do, *as in buying, feeding, and training a guard dog, then staying up all night in case of intruders.*" (The significant application of this subject to our present chapter will be made clear later.)

Another familiar adage is, "To be forewarned is to be forearmed." This is a deep Bible truth based on Proverbs 22:3, *"A prudent man forseeth the evil, and hideth himself: but the simple pass on, and are punished."* As we are now amidst the violent waves of Acts 27:41, it behooves us to understand the clear and present danger that will incite the many defections at II Timothy 4:3. In addition to the allurements of a modern world (II Timothy 4:10; Revelation 3:17), pressure will continually grow to conform to a unique, end-time political correctness, similar to what the Tribulation saints will experience (Revelation 13:17). The pattern is now set: Yesterday, no *mask*, no service; Today, no *vaccine*, no service; Tomorrow (i.e., after the Rapture), no *mark*, no service. Think of how privileged we are to possess such timely foresight, as John (a type of the Church) had when reclining on Jesus' breast (John 13:24-26).

Satan's encroachments can be varied and subtle, though sometimes he merely inspires a "tempest in a teapot" (like using moronic "conspiracy theories" to distract from the real thing). For instance, some Christians fight over celebrating Christmas. (FYI, you can have Santa Claus, but you're *not* getting my "Baal-bush"!) Others will debate about unorthodox medical practices, such as hypnosis, acupuncture, or iridology. For others, it's the potential influence of Eastern religion on the martial arts. However, the more serious trend today, especially in corporate America, is the mandatory practice of yoga, supposedly to improve productivity, etc. Here, the Bible believer must decide—risk my job ($$$), or "laugh off" the Satanic practice as "harmless foolishness." While God may wink at a new convert doing this (II Kings 5:17-19), for the rest of us, it's "Man up!" (Luke 12:48)

COMPLIANCE OR RESISTANCE

As previously covered, when confronted with the Covid "threat," churches quickly divided into two camps: *compliance*—to avoid fines and pacify the community (like yielding to "trick or treat" shakedowns); and *resistance*—to please the Lord and pay whatever price. Families were also divided, especially by computer screens at death. The "mask shaming" and "crowd police" drove many of us crazy. San Francisco's homeless were given alcohol and cannabis during the crisis, but were still required to wear a mask while defecating in the streets. In Encinitas, California, people were being fined $1,000 just for sitting in their cars to watch the sunset at the beach. Meanwhile, a popular restaurant in Little Washington, Virginia, was seating mannequins at empty tables, to help make the dive seem livelier, while still maintaining social distancing. And who can forget that father in Brighton, Colorado, who was busted for playing catch with his six-year-old daughter on a near-empty softball field? I once had a Delta Airlines stewardess demonstrate their required inflight "chewing cycle," i.e., lift mask to bite; then replace to chew; then repeat. It was almost as bizarre as their announcement, "In the event of an emergency, remember to remove your Covid mask before placing your oxygen mask on." (Can't make this stuff up folks!) Then, the pressure over Covid vaccinations invaded our lives with dozens of technical videos to scrutinize, affording a temporary diversion from impending murder hornets, microchip implants, and alien invasions (the latter per the Pentagon's unprecedented declassification of UFO footage).

Another looming threat is *transgenderism*. According to the 2013 Diagnostic and Statistical Manual of Mental Disorders (too funny), this neurotic condition refers to "the broad spectrum of people who transiently or persistently identity with a gender different from their natal sex."

It often leads to gender dysphasia, as well. Thus, in 2016, the office of New York City's Mayor Bill de Blasio (aka Warren Wilhelm, Jr.), released a list of 31 gender identity terms that were approved by the New York City Commission on Human Rights. Should any employers or landlords refuse to honor the pronoun preference of their employees or tenants, they can be fined upwards of $250,000! No longer content with males "simply" identifying as females (and vice versa), proud New Yorkers can now legally self-identify as: agender; pangender; bi-gender; gender bender; gender-fluid; genderqueer; non-binary transgendered; trans person; transsexual; cross-dresser; drag king; drag queen; femme queen; butch; non-op; two-spirit; third sex; androgynous or Hijra (eunuchs, intersex, and transgender people in the Indian subcontinent); plus, a dozen other labels. The attached fact sheet advises: "If you don't know what pronouns to use, ask. Be polite and respectful; if you use the wrong pronoun, apologize and move on." Of course, "gender different" individuals may also use the bathroom or locker room of their choice.

Talk about casting the ultimate "Odd Couple" for America's largest city—Chirlane McCray, the Big Apple's 4' 11" Caribbean-American (heretofore lesbian) former First Lady, could not have been prouder of her 6' 5" half-Italian pothead hubby's landmark progressive policy. (Their wedding was a real hoot, featuring a pair of sodomite interracial, interdenominational "ministers" accompanied by African drummers and an Italian folk band.) As for the rest of us, with "Ladies Justice and Liberty" falling by the wayside, the pronoun perversion will be on our doorsteps in a New York minute! What began as a few Christian bakers refusing to make "gay" wedding cakes has morphed into a take-no-prisoners, multi-front war. Thus, the new normal for Bible believers everywhere is simple: "Defile your conscience by denying Genesis 5:2— or else!" Insist on addressing someone by their biological identity and you will eventually wind up in jail for a hate crime.

Yet, all of these pressure cooker trajectories *pale* in comparison to what the Bible says about "race." Two deep truths require our immediate attention concerning *any* race-related discussions. First, and foremost, while the majority of white Americans stay absolutely *pulverized with fear* regarding the sacrosanct "race card" (like they did on the eve of the O. J. Simpson verdict), most Independent Baptist pastors remain even *more* paranoid. A preacher in Alabama once advised me, "Unless one has the skills of a Philadelphia lawyer, it's better to leave it alone."

Second, the growing attack on "whiteness" (and other "Woke-ology" doctrines), is a direct assault on God's own agenda, as clearly presented in the Bible (Genesis 9:27); and as such, *should* mandate a scriptural defense by Bible-believing preachers (I Peter 3:15).

DUMB DOGS THAT WON'T BARK

While pastors have been likened to vigilant shepherds, they can also be cast in the mold of a different type, that of the Jewish prophets— alert watchdogs, ready to warn their congregations of any danger. However, by Isaiah's time, the majority of Israel's seers were depicted as *"blind...ignorant...**dumb dogs, [that] cannot bark**; sleeping, lying down, loving to slumber...greedy dogs which can never have enough...all look to their own way, every one for his gain."* (Isaiah 56:10-11) They appear to mimic the peculiar central African Basenji breed, known as the "Barkless Dog" of the Congo. During the Vietnam War, the Ruger Mark II .22 autoloader pistol, with a suppressor on the barrel, acquired the nickname "Hush Puppy," because it was used by Navy Seals to kill enemy sentry dogs. Sadly, most end-day pastors can be similarly likened to those "hushed puppies" *—silenced by Satan's rounds of race-related intimidation.* (What this means in the "Hebrew," is that Laodicean pastors are too *pragmatic* to put Biblical truth ahead of their paychecks.) This cowardice was prefigured by those Alexandrian crewmembers who got caught trying to *"flee out of the ship."* (Acts 27:30)

Such boa-constricting, lock-jaw fear has enabled Marxist groups like BLM, partnering with the liberal media, to do irreparable harm to our country. For instance, while the police are constantly berated, defunded, accosted, assaulted, and even assassinated, over unsubstantiated charges of "institutional racism" (white cops are just *dying* to shoot *innocent* young black men), the true statistics are kept from the public. (This issue hits home, as my younger son serves in law enforcement, while my son-in-law and a nephew are corrections officers.) For instance, in 2019, police officers fatally shot 1,004 people, most of whom were armed or otherwise dangerous. About a quarter of those killed were black (235). The typical blowback follows that blacks comprise only 13% of the population. However, as documented in a rare, transparent article by the *Wall Street Journal*, in 2018 that same 13% committed 53% of the nation's homicides (plus 60% of all robberies), well over *four times* their percentage of the population! That same year, there were 7,407 black homicide victims (a high percentage being black-on-black, because "Black Lives Matter," etc.). By contrast, the police fatally shot a grand total of *nine* unarmed blacks, while killing over twice that number of unarmed whites. Those nine victims represent only 0.1% of all blacks killed in 2019. Thus, a police officer is 18½ times more likely to be killed by a black male than an unarmed black male is to be killed by a police officer.

Another taboo topic concerns the quality of "life" in America's largest cities (all Democrat controlled)—the violent killing fields where the courageous men of the "Thin Blue Line" risk their lives on a daily basis (for peanut wages). Former NYC mayor Bill "Defund the Police" de Blasio's "African-American" replacement, "Smiling" Eric Adams—along with his insane, fellow "African-American," anti-prosecuting Manhattan District Attorney, Alvin Bragg, and his mysterious "African-American" political hack, Police Commissioner Keechant Sewell (the first "female" appointed to that office)—are destined to make de Blasio look like Fiorello La Guardia in comparison. (As a "great" start for the new administration, the first NYPD shooting victim in 2022 was wounded on New Year's Day, followed by four more over the next three weeks, including two fatalities.) But rather than plow through more statistics, just ask any normal income-hungry *inner-city* cabbie (or Uber driver) about his personal instincts when it comes to who he'll turn away and what neighborhoods he'll refuse to enter, especially after dark. This is the ultimate reality check, because *everyone's* money is green. And should any riders enquire about vice (i.e., hookers and/or heroin), he will tell them straight-up that the best action is usually along MLK Blvd. Would this be as good a place as any for me to ask vicariously, *"Am I therefore become your enemy, because I tell you the truth?"* (Galatians 4:16)

This censored, jungle-like behavior is not confined to the "Hood," either. I live in the serene Smoky Mountain region of East Tennessee. On April 7, 2020, just before 7 a.m., Idris Abdus-Salaam, a 33-year-old black Muslim truck driver from Durham, North Carolina, entered a Pilot Service Station in Strawberry Plains, Tennessee, *and promptly knifed three white women to death* (i.e., dead, as dead-on-the-scene dead) and seriously wounded a fourth, before the "bad ole white cops" blew him away in the parking lot. Try to find the national coverage on this sample of a real nation-wide epidemic—black-on-white crime! It doesn't exist, as such reporting would represent a major conundrum as a "hate crime" in itself. The appropriate metaphor here would be "blackout." According to the FBI, of the 776 black/white homicides in 2016, some 533 were committed by that 13% "black bloc."

And so, after long observing this pitiful and embarrassing "Don't ask, don't tell" race policy in His churches, the Lord decided to tase these "dumb dogs" by throwing the controversial issue right in their compromising faces; enter—*Critical Race Theory*.

CRITICAL RACE THEORY

Critical Race Theory (CRT) is a satanic Marxist ideology that originated in Nazi Germany in the 1930s. Its chief architect was Herbert Marcuse of the Frankfurt School at Goethe University. Rather than divide mankind along *economic* lines (bourgeoisie versus the proletariat), Marcuse did so by *race*. CRT hit America in the 1960s when Herbie partnered up with Angela Davis, the infamous black activist and avowed Communist agitator.

While few outside academia know much about CRT, it currently dominates much of American life. CRT is now being taught in every level of our already fractured education system; though, thankfully, over a dozen conservative states have blocked its implementation. The same applies to nearly all major law schools. The spineless Southern Baptist Convention has endorsed CRT, along with most dead seminaries. It pervades government, the military, even our sensitive intelligence community. In 2021, a semi-humorous "woke" recruitment ad for the CIA celebrated the intersecting identity of a black female sleuth: "I am a woman of color. I am a mom. I am a cisgender millennial who has been diagnosed with generalized anxiety disorder." (Where's 007 when we need him?) The American business community has also been infiltrated. With absolutely no regard for their faithful Polar Bear logo, in 2021 *Coca-Cola* asked its employees to fight racism by being "less white." Chick-fil-A's CEO, Dan Cathy (son of founder S. Truett Cathy), has similarly exhorted white Christians to repent of racism and fight for their black brothers and sisters. In the "religious" realm, the psychotic First United Church of Oak Park, Illinois, announced in March 2022 that it was "fasting from whiteness for Lent" (by giving up using any music or liturgy "written or composed by white folk," in favor of "the voices of African, Indigenous, and other people of color").

In 2017, the *Oxford English Dictionary* added "woke" as an adjective, defining it's updated usage as: "Originally: well-informed, up-to-date. Now chiefly: alert to racial or social discrimination and injustice; frequently in *stay woke*." How appropriate; while the Lord's children went to sleep, the Devil's crowd woke (Matthew 13:25). Thus, to guard against appearing insensitive to trannies and blacks, woke honkies must now master a modern glossary almost as mind boggling as the ex-mayor's perverted pronoun list: bigender; BIPOC (Black, Indigenous, and People of Color); BLM (Black Lives Matter); cancel culture, cisgender; cultural appropriation; dead name; DEI (Diversity, Equity, and Inclusion); diversity; emotional tax; ethnicity, gaslight; gender variant; heteronormativity; homophobe; inclusion; indigeneity; institutional racism; intersectionality, "Karens"; LGBTQ+ (lesbian, gay, bisexual, transgender, queer, and a myriad of other sexual identities); microaggression; misogyny; misgendering; neurodiversity; nonbinary; pangender; pansexual; people of color; racial profiling; queer baiting; racism; reparations; sensitivity training; systemic racism; toxic masculinity; unconscious bias; white fragility; white privilege; white supremacy; whiteness; and wokeness. The insanity of this list was seen when the "African-American" Democrat Missouri Representative and Methodist "minister," the Reverend Emanuel Cleaver, ended his "prayer" to open the 117th Congress, with the *asinine* benediction, "Amen and A-woman." (For the record, the only "woke" I care about was put to verse by Charles Wesley in 1739, "Thine eye diffused a quickening ray, *I woke*, the dungeon flamed with light; My chains fell off, my heart was free; I rose, went forth, and followed thee.")

White Americans also had to say goodbye to many friends during the "Cancel Culture Woke Revival": Aunt Jemima and Uncle Ben; Dr. Seuss; Pepe Le Pew; "Mr." Potato Head; Eskimo Pie; Mia, the Land O' Lakes' Maiden; Chiquita Banana; Big Boy (their cabbage soup will never taste the same); Peter Pan and Dumbo; Cops and Live PD; the Dixie Chicks; and my own local, politically incorrect, "Dixie" Stampede, just to name a few. The M&M characters underwent a "woke" makeover as well, "now being spotlighted for their personalities, rather than their genders." According to the communist Southern Poverty Law Center, at least 114 Confederate monuments were removed from public spaces, including my number one hero and fellow Tennessean, General Nathan "elevate them guns a little lower" Bedford Forrest (aka "Devil Forrest"). Kate Smith, the woman who made Irving Berlin's "God Bless America" a semi-national anthem, while also serving as the musical mascot of the Philadelphia Flyers hockey team, had her own bronze statue yanked from public display over a 1931 song containing an obscure reference to "darkies." (I once heard Kate belt out her signature song live in the Spectrum before the Flyers beat Boston in game six of the 1974 Stanley Cup series).

And while I would have normally expressed gratitude that the Atlanta Braves and Cleveland Indians were holding the line, I haven't watched *any* professional sports since all those ungrateful bums started kneeling during the National Anthem. At the time of this writing, negotiations were pending between Stellantis Company and the Cherokee Nation over the Jeep Cherokee and Jeep Grand Cherokee's future. Thankfully, John Wayne Airport (named after America's quintessential cowboy) is still showing "True Grit" by keeping the Duke's name alive. And finally, *Gone with the Wind* was gone, then given a reprieve with a mandatory clip of some "African-American scholar" decrying its "awful elements." (So much for that maverick "Frankly my dear, I don't give a ...." spirit.) Probably referencing Neville "Peace for our time" Chamberlain, Winston Churchill once said, "An appeaser is one who feeds a crocodile, hoping it will eat him last."

CRT FOR DUMMIES

Charles Kirk is an evangelical, conservative activist. He defines CRT in five succinct points:

1. Melanin is your master. As melanin determines skin color, humans are defined by their skin (the essence of tribal groups). Thus, *all* "people of color" are oppressed; *all* whites are their oppressors. On a 2020 preaching trip in California, I was evicted from a motel over a tepid cup of coffee, on the sole word of an Asian-American desk clerk who accused me of making ambiguous racial slurs (she probably was offended by my Trump mask). This flies in the face of M. L. King's definitive plea that his children be "judged by the content of their character," not to mention pitting unsuspecting black and white youngsters against one another from kindergarten on up.

2. Racism is ubiquitous. There is no entity, no industry, no conversation, no *anything* where racism does not exist. If you live in the West, your world was built *by* white supremacists, *for* white supremacists, and can only be "fixed" *by* black activists pulling it down (like those Rebel statues).

3. Dialogue is evil. CRT is a closed system; its tenets are non-negotiable. Thus, right-wing beliefs are suppressed as "hate" at nearly all tax-payer-funded colleges.

4. The system is totalitarian. Caucasians must accept that they were *literally* born guilty. This "wokeness" then mandates continual repentance while simultaneously laboring to destroy their own race. As it's not *what* you do, but what you *don't* do, "white silence is violence." It's not good enough to merely abstain *from* racism; one must become a pro-active CRT advocate, as well. If you don't display the "black square," the bros will come and get you.

5. Science, math, reason, and empiricism are all tools of white supremacy. After years of imbibing evolution in the name of science, America's school children are now learning that Newtonian physics, the Second Law of Thermodynamics, and other core subjects, are just excuses to keep white people in power. (No wonder they flee to online gaming addiction.) In 2021, the Smithsonian's National Museum of "African-American" History and Culture declared, "Being on time, speaking proper English, having an intact nuclear family, and staying married to one person are all attributes of whiteness." Six weeks before the disastrous 2020 election, President Trump called CRT "a cancer."

In summary, the only "whiteness" the CRT crowd will ever accept is a white flag of surrender.

"JAPHETH THE ELDER"

Paul Kennedy is the J. Richardson Dilworth Professor of History at Yale University, making him one of the leading "eggheads" in America. His 1987 tome, *The Rise and the Fall of the Great Powers: Economic Change and Military Conflict from 1500 to 2000,* contains 1,400 bibliography entries. Dr. Kennedy writes, "In the year 1800, Europeans occupied or controlled 35 percent of the land surface of the world; by 1878 this figure had risen to 67 percent, and by 1914 to over 84 percent." In 1996, fellow Ivy Leaguer, Samuel P. Huntington of Harvard, published his

own work, *The Clash of Civilizations and the Remaking of World Order.*
The author concurs with Kennedy, listing fourteen categories in which
"whitey" has no peers. Western nations:

- Own and operate the international banking system
- Control all hard currencies
- Are the world's principal customer
- Provide the majority of the world's finished goods
- Dominate international capital markets
- Exert considerable moral leadership within many societies
- Are capable of massive military intervention
- Control the sea lanes
- Conduct most advanced technical research and development
- Control leading edge technical education
- Dominate access to space
- Dominate the aerospace industry
- Dominate international communications
- Dominate the high-tech weapons industry.

That the Dilworth Professor of History was a spiritual *blank* regarding
the only infallible "history" book in the Library of Congress, was
evidenced by his concession that his colleagues and he were at a loss
to explain Europe's rise to world power. After making his case for Ming
China, the Muslim states, even Japan (as the most likely contenders), he
writes, under the heading "The European Miracle": "Why was it among
the scattered and relatively unsophisticated peoples inhabiting the western
parts of the Eurasian landmass that there occurred an unstoppable process
of economic development and technological innovation which would
steadily make it the commercial and military leader in world affairs? This
is a question which has exercised scholars and other observers for
centuries." Martin Luther once said, "The first time the Devil appears
in the Bible he was sitting under the tree of knowledge and he has yet
to leave." That these Twin Towers of *"heady...highminded[ness]"* were
mere examples of the last days, *"ever learning, and never able to come
to the knowledge of the truth"* (II Timothy 3:4,7), can be seen when
comparing them to the spiritual giants who seeded those original ivy
plants. The seventh president of Yale certainly didn't have a problem

connecting the reality of his day with Biblical prophecy. On election day, May 8, 1783, Reverend Ezra Stiles addressed the governor of Connecticut, Jonathan Trumbull, along with the General Assembly (convened in Hartford) on the subject, "The United States Elevated to Glory and Honor." In his two-hour, 30,000-word discourse, Dr. Stiles equated Genesis 9:27— *"God shall enlarge Japheth"* —to America's divine birth announcement:

> Heaven has provided this country, not indeed derelict, but only partially settled, and consequently open for the reception of a *new enlargement of Japheth. Europe was settled by Japheth; America is settling from Europe:* and perhaps this second enlargement bids fair to surpass the first...In two or three hundred years this second enlargement may cover America with [a population of three hundred million]...*Can we contemplate their present, and anticipate their future increase, and not be struck with astonishment to find ourselves in the midst of the fulfillment of the prophecy of Noah? May we not see that we are the object which the Holy Ghost had in view four thousand years ago, when he inspired the venerable patriarch with the visions respecting his posterity?*

In a speech before the American Society of Newspaper Editors in Washington, DC, on January 17, 1925, President Calvin Coolidge gave the perfect description of Japheth's God-given proclivity: "After all, the chief business of the American people is business. They are profoundly concerned with producing, buying, selling, investing, and prospering in the world." Obviously, the two secular historians wouldn't know the difference between Japheth and Jay Z. The sick thing is that end-day Independent Baptist preachers repeatedly dodge the Bible issue. Truth be told, most are so shallow they don't even understand it; they just *know* that "it's racist," etc. They remind me of the pretty girl who, when asked by an ugly suitor, "Are you doing anything Friday night?" replied, "I've *got* to be doing *something*." And to make matters worse, they always try to connect the perceived racist overtones to Dr. Peter Ruckman, second only to Donald Trump as the greatest "boogeyman" in history! (I seriously doubt that Dr. Stiles stole anything from Brother Pete.) Thus, what a combination we have: the *professors*, too dumb to realize they have the historical proof of Japheth's selection by God (I Corinthians 2:14); the *preachers*, too scared to recognize the source of this revelation

(II Timothy 4:3). In an uncanny paradox, as Japheth is the builder (USA's definitive motto being "bigger is better"), Satan will use the American pastor's spiritual DNA against him by leading him to employ *pragmatism* in denying Genesis 9:27, so he doesn't jeopardize church growth, *"supposing that gain is godliness."* (I Timothy 6:5)

This is the real legacy of Dr. Billy Graham who began using Catholic priests and liberal Protestant clergymen to get larger crowds, prompting the rebuke of Bob Jones, Sr., "It is never right to do wrong in order to get a chance to do right." Dr. Bob's prescient quote remains the greatest tie-in of Graham with Laodicea, "Billy's ministry produced a lot of fruit but his methods destroyed the orchards for future generations." Consequently, I often remind preachers that though we are *Japhethites*, our boss is a *Shemite* (like the bumper sticker says, "I work for a Jewish carpenter from Nazareth"). While we are geared for production by our genetic instincts, the "fire" at the Judgment Seat will *"try every man's work of what **sort** it is"* (I Corinthians 3:13). Note, the criterion is "sort," not "size." The God who wrote Isaiah 66:1-2 never takes so much as a baby aspirin about anything. *"Thus saith the LORD, The heaven is my throne, and the earth is my footstool: where is the house that ye build unto me? and where is the place of my rest?"* (i.e., "Yawn" in the Hebrew).

Another pre-Ruckman source is C. I. Scofield, general editor of the popular study Bible that bears his name. Over a century ago, Dr. Scofield wrote in his notes on Genesis 9:

> 5) A prophetic declaration is made that from Ham will descend an inferior and servile posterity (Genesis 9:24, 25).
>
> 6) A prophetic declaration is made that Shem will have a peculiar relation to Jehovah (Genesis 9:26, 27). All divine revelation is through Semitic men, and Christ, after the flesh, descends from Shem.
>
> 7) A prophetic declaration is made that from Japheth will descend the "enlarged" races (Genesis 9:27). Government, science, and art, speaking broadly, are and have been Japhetic, so that history is the indisputable record of the exact fulfilment of these declarations.

Incidentally, to have this critical note, God had to preserve the teenaged Cyrus through over a dozen major Civil War battles, including Antietam, the bloodiest day in US military history—a war *falsely* purported to have been fought over racial injustice.

Now in order to appreciate the historic fulfillment of these prophecies, one must study the transmigration of Noah's descendants as revealed in the ethnological table of Genesis 10. Their movement can be illustrated from a simple game of "Connect the Dots." When a map of the Middle East is viewed, three significant coordinates appear. The ancient Tigress and Euphrates Rivers join at about three o'clock. According to Genesis 2:10-14, human life began in this vicinity. After the judgment of the flood, Noah's ark rested atop Mt. Ararat at twelve o'clock and life began anew. At the western end of the "Fertile Crescent," the Nile River empties into the Mediterranean at approximately nine o'clock, not far from where man's spiritual life began. When these three dots connect, a rough triangle is formed, an ancient Christian symbol for the Trinity, i.e., God Himself. According to Genesis 15:18 (and many additional passages), the Lord promised the land within the triangle to Abraham and his descendants (through Isaac and Jacob). Everyone else (i.e., the "Gentiles") would get the leftovers.

When God broke up the "fellowship" at the Tower of Babel, He scattered the crowd into three directions. Japheth's descendants went off the *left* side of the triangle northwest into Russia and Europe. Shem goes off to the *right* and populates the East. According to Psalm 105:23, 27, Ham's people went *south* of the triangle's base onto the continent of Africa. The renowned archaeologist, Dr. Merrill F. Unger, states: "The descendants of Ham comprise the eastern and southern people who settled originally in lower Mesopotamia and subsequently in South Arabia, Ethiopia, Egypt and Canaan (Genesis 10:6-14). As the youngest son of Noah, Ham is regarded as the eponymous ancestor of the African peoples, as Japheth his brother is of the Indo-Europeans, and Shem of the Semites."

Even the lying humanist has to "fess up" occasionally, as there is only so much he can hide. The 2022 edition of *World Book Encyclopedia* states, under the heading of Noah: "Noah's sons were Shem, Ham and Japheth. Shem became father of the Semitic peoples, including the Jews and the Arabs. Ham was the father of the Hamitic peoples. Japheth was the father of Asia Minor and Europe." Under the heading "Hamites," earlier *World Book* editions add: "Hamites are certain African peoples who live mainly in eastern, northern, and northeastern Africa, including parts of Eritrea, Ethiopia, the Sahara, and the Sudan. Most Hamites are tall and have a narrow nose and brown skin. They are sometimes called Afro-Mediterranean peoples because of their physical characteristics and the region where they live. Because much of this region cannot be farmed, most Hamites tend herds of camels, goats and sheep."

Shem's descendants continued moving eastbound (note the "handfuls of purpose" buzzword in Genesis 10:30, *"a mount of the **east***") till they crossed over the Bering Strait into North America, eventually fathering the Native American Indians. Anytime you hear a man criticize the Bible's accuracy, you may rest assured that he is woefully ignorant of the historical record.

Yet, herein lies the rub! It's that bad ol' Japheth...the son God chose over the other two (like He did with Moses, Aaron, Joshua, Joseph, Abraham, Isaac, Jacob, David, Paul, and many others). According to any modern definition of the word "racism," if you believe the Bible, much less what your eyes can clearly see (i.e., *"The Emperor's New Clothes"*), YOU are a RACIST. The typical definition states, "The belief that different races possess distinctive characteristics, abilities, or qualities, especially so as to distinguish them as inferior or superior to one another." So, all races are the same, are they? Moses wrote in Exodus 11:7, *"But against any of the children of Israel shall not a dog move his tongue, against man or beast: **that ye may know how that the LORD doth put a difference between the Egyptians and Israel.***"* Sounds like God is not only divorced (Jeremiah 3:8), but a racist as well. Deuteronomy 8:18 is another "hate" passage: *"But thou shalt remember the LORD thy God: **for it is he that giveth thee power to get wealth.***"* Let me break this one down for you. Have you ever seen a pawn shop with a *black* owner negotiating with a *Jewish* customer? I didn't think so...If you believe that all races are the same—*you have a serious problem!*

GOD'S DEFINITIVE STATEMENT ON RACIAL PROFILING

It is no coincidence that the subject of race, more specifically, racial profiling, just happens to surface in our Acts 27 forecast of end-time conditions. According to verse seven and following, the shipwreck can be traced to a decision made on *Crete*. This is not insignificant given what Scripture reveals about this place. Because the Bible is a politically incorrect treatise on the *truth*, it confronts all issues of race, religion, and gender without apology. Conversely, modern translations will pacify the sinner by deleting "sensitive" passages. For instance, while the NIV removed all references to sodomites, the TNIV (*Today's New*

International Version) was "gender friendly," eliminating significant masculine or feminine usage. The presence of Crete is a veiled reference to *race*. While the average Christian may not deny the Lord *per se*, he will often deny what the Lord *says*, especially if the subject is perceived as racist in nature (II Timothy 4:3).

The book of Titus contains one of the worst statements on "hate" in the entire Bible! Having noted that God the Father is a divorced "racist," the Holy Spirit crosses the line at Titus 1:12-13 with *the* definitive statement on racial profiling. After Paul quotes one of the "slanderous" locals as stating, *"The Cretians are always liars, evil beasts, slow bellies,"* his inspired response to this intolerant characterization was, ***"This witness is true. Wherefore rebuke them sharply that they may be sound in the faith."*** Wow, so Paul must be a racist too! Three negative racial traits are ascribed to an entire culture across the board! How did 50,000,00 Christians miss this? And, then, to add insult to injury, anthropology corroborates this inspired "prejudice," acknowledging that the indigenous expression "to act the *Cretan*" was analogous to "play the *liar*." By the way, don't miss the amazing cross-reference of "sailing *slowly*" (mentioned in the same verse with "Crete") to "*slow* bellies" (in the same verse with "Cretians"). For the record, Crete is a large island off the coast of North Africa, originally populated by Ham's peeps (Genesis 10:6, 14; Deuteronomy 2:23; I Samuel 30:14; Jeremiah 47:4; Ezekiel 25:16; Amos 9:7; and Zephaniah 2:5) In the final analysis, Alexandrian "Bibles" are literally "African-American Bibles;" *produced* in *Africa* and *marketed* in *America* (Jeremiah 42:18; 44:26-30; Titus 1:11). Ya gotta give Satan credit; like "Sister" P. K. McCary said in her "scholarly" two-volume *Black Bible Chronicles* (dubbed the "Hip-Hop Bible") rendering of Genesis 3:1— "Now the serpent was one bad dude, one of the baddest of all the animals the Almighty had made."

BIG BROTHER'S BEAUTIFUL DESTINY

God clearly said that he was going to make Japheth the enlarged race, and history confirms that reality. Returning to our secular definition, this means that Japheth's kinfolk, i.e., Europeans, i.e., WHITE MEN, have *already* shown themselves to "possess distinctive characteristics, abilities, or qualities" that "distinguish them as SUPERIOR to the descendants of Shem and Ham. If this is *not* true, what did "Reverend"

Al mean in his funeral sermon for George Floyd when he said, "You [white folk] kept your knee on our neck [black folk]. We had creative skills, but we *couldn't* get your knee off our neck. It's time for us...to stand up and say, 'Get yo' knee off our necks.'" I once told a liberal woman professor at the University of Tennessee, "Y'all can't have it both ways; it's either *all* 'sub-species' of the human race are the same; or, it's natural selection, the evolutionary theory that only the strong survive." Then someone always says something like, "But I saw a black man once flying a commercial airliner." Dude, haven't you ever heard the maxim, "The exception proves the rule?" In 2021, the media sang the praises of fourteen-year-old Zaila Avant-garde for being the first "African-American" to win the Scripps National Spelling Bee—in ninety-three stinking years! (Shemites usually win the prize...)

However, the wiggle room is in the definition, as it doesn't specify *what* distinctive "characteristics, abilities or qualities." Obviously, Japheth does not excel in everything (i.e., *White Men Can't Jump*). But when it comes to "enlarging" stuff (see Dr. Kennedy's impressive list), Japheth brings his A-game. (Like that old New York joke, "How do you break up an Italian wedding? Answer: Someone yells, 'The cement's here!'") Conversely, having visited two African countries on missionary work (Kenya and Uganda), I can testify that outside of the capitals, "buildings" above two or three stories are rare. (And you *know* citing *South* Africa would be cheating). The bottom line is that Japheth's descendants have trounced Shem and Ham in the category of nation building and pioneering of modern civilizations. Call it white supremacy, white privilege, or even a white cockatoo; God calls it *fulfilled prophecy.* So, deal with it!

JAPHETH'S SPIRITUAL DESTINY

The loaded "straw man" argument follows that such a belief somehow translates to God loving Japheth more than his two brothers, etc. Nothing could be further from the truth! In fact, contrary to Cain's apathetic question in Genesis 4:9, *"Am I my brother's keeper?"* the divine purpose of Japheth's enlargement was to *get the saving Gospel of Jesus Christ to his lost siblings* (Luke 16:28). Genesis 10:21 specifically shows that Japheth is the elder brother. So—isn't that what we would expect from *our* "Big Brother" in any contemporary application?

Though my "big brother," Gregory, went to juvenile lock-up at age fourteen for burning a grocery store down (because the owner cheated him on his delivery boy paycheck); went to Sing-Sing prison for shooting a man on the front steps of a Brooklyn police precinct (for sleeping with his wife), then chasing the wounded man inside a police precinct with the smoking gun in his hand; then later dying in a shootout with the Miami police for blowing his shotgun through his neighbor's front door (because the dude refused to lower his music)—*nobody*, and I mean *nobody*, messed with me as a kid when Gregory was nearby!

Comparing Genesis 9:24 with 10:21 confirms that Japheth was Noah's first-born son. Satan hates this truth so much, the modern ESV literally changes the birth order in the text from, *"Unto Shem also, the father of all the children of Eber, the brother of Japheth the elder…"* to the corrupt, "To Shem also, the father of all the children of Eber, the elder brother of Japheth…."

And then we have this remarkable truth: The name "Japheth" (from the Hebrew root יפה) just *happens* to mean "beautiful," as in Romans 10:15, *"How **beautiful** are the feet of them that preach the gospel of peace, and bring glad tidings of good things!"* (A secondary "theory" from the Aramaic root פתה means "to extend.") Consequently, the first recorded miracle in the book of Acts (after the glossolalia at Pentecost) just happens to occur at the "Beautiful Gate," where a crippled man's feet were made "beautiful" (Acts 3:2-10).

In the providence of God, England was destined to play the key role by producing the 1611 Authorized King James Version Holy Bible. Dr. Scofield describes Gomer, the *first* of Japheth's sons, as "Progenitor of the ancient Cimerians and Cimbri, from whom are descended the *Celtic* family." (According to Jewish commentators and exegetes, Ashkenaz, *Gomer's* firstborn, settled in modern Germany, the country that would eventually produce the world's first printing press and the Protestant Reformation).

To interject a personal illustration—I left the cash register business in 1972 to work for BOAC in Manhattan. Back in the day, the acrostic stood for British Overseas Airways Corporation, Britain's state-owned international airline. (The opening words to the 1968 Beatles song, "Back in the U.S.S.R." say, "Flew in from Miami Beach, BOAC.") However, in March 1974 (five months before I was saved), the British government merged BOAC with their domestic carrier, British European

Airways (BEA). The new entity, British Airways (BA) has generally been recognized as the world's largest airline (based on fleet size and international operations.) The relevancy of this brief aviation lesson is a throwback to a familiar nineteenth-century saying, "The sun never sets on the British Empire." To illustrate the ultimate fulfillment of Japheth's "enlargement," the birthplace of the AV 1611 was once so expansive that some part of it was always experiencing daylight. (It just so happens that in 1974—eight days after my saved, Virginia-born, Baptist wife gave me a King James Bible for a wedding present—I "saw the light" at Clarence Larkin's home church, while working for British Airways at the Philadelphia International Airport, nine miles from the "Liberty Bell.") In 1922, marking the height of *Gomer's* growth, the United Kingdom comprised the largest empire the world had ever seen, ruling over 458 million people, across a quarter of the Earth's land surface, roughly 14,250,000 square miles. (Ya never can tell, neighbor, that ole King James Bible could be true!)

"To Each His Own..."

When positing the divine plan of "Japheth the Elder" evangelizing his younger siblings, the question of interracial marriage will inevitably arise. While I am personally acquainted with several born-again, mixed-couples who obviously love one another, the Holy Spirit has led me to share the following on behalf of Bible believers who do not ascribe to this heretofore unacceptable societal phenomenon.

Certainly, every parent must make their own decision as to what they teach their children, presumably Holy Spirit-led (as they've had to do with other controversial matters, like the Covid-19 vaccinations). However, should any of my more "narrow minded" Caucasian readers out there believe their daughters and sons should limit their marital choices to their own gene pool—don't let any number of "charismatic," Independent Baptist, KVJ-only, "African-American" preacher "front men" (i.e., "con men") try to lay a "guilt trip" on you for following your own conscience! I'm talking about those slick "change agents" — the ones *you're* probably thinking about right now—who only get to push their agenda because of the backslapping endorsements of those aforementioned "dumb dogs that won't bark" honky hirelings. (My good friend and former student, Pastor Dave Wagner, reminded me how they fit the profile in Jude 4 of "creeps," who *"crept in unawares."*)

Well, here's a deep news flash for ya: Like the inevitable, dead-end, population-reduction results of the "sodomy rights" perverts—if every Japhethite intermarried with either Ham or Shem, that line of Noah's descendants would plumb disappear! (Duh...) And quit getting embroiled in the debate over whether it's a "sin" or not based on Galatians 3:28. (No doubt Dr. Ruckman's critics would be shocked to learn that he has stated in his commentaries that no such scriptural prohibitions exist in the Church Age).

However, the issue is much deeper than that. Hebrews 12:1-2 states, *"[L]et us lay aside every **weight**, and the sin which doth so easily beset us, and let us run with patience the race that is set before us, Looking unto Jesus the author and finisher of our faith."* While the percentage is surely shrinking (as mankind races toward its one-world, Utopian age), there are still plenty of mixed-race youth who will testify to having felt "weighed down" by the consequences of their parents' choices. (Of course, this same idea applies to any number of old-school, black parents who feel led to heed the likeminded sentiments of Dr. Martin Luther King, Jr., who said, "The basic aim of the Negro is not to become the white man's brother-in-law, but his brother.")

And yes, I know all about the Shemite exceptions to the rule (Moses, David, Solomon, Joesph, et al.). I'm simply making a case for a remnant of Japhethites who want to preserve their God-given destiny to enlarge the greater Body of Christ. Like Polonius says in Macbeth— "To each his own, but to thine own self be true."

GOD'S "THREE R'S"

Thus, we see God's "Three R's": One *Redeemer* (to trust)—Jesus Christ; One *Revelation* (to reveal Him)—the King James Bible; and One *Race* (to spread that revelation)—Japheth, the Elder.

Now if some dummy still wants to make Genesis 9:27 a racist text, remind him that the Lord chose a Hamite to help Him carry His cross (Matthew 27:32), then chose another black man to be the first Gentile saved in the Church Age (Acts 8:26-40). And if he *still* won't listen to reason, just tell him to *blow it out his shorts* (as per the *New English*

Bible rendering of Judges 1:14, "As she sat on the ass, she broke wind, and Caleb said, 'What did you mean by that?'")

PHILLIS WHEATLEY

While I would not attempt to "white wash" any race-related atrocities associated with Japheth's expansion (Hitler's *Lebensraum* doctrine being the most egregious), the key to Genesis 9:27 will always be the Gospel-preaching missionaries and church planters who followed the materialistic pioneers (the antithesis to Hitler's *Einsatzgruppen* squads who trailed the *Wehrmacht*). To render a nominal account of British world missions would require a multi-volume set. Even the secular *Cambridge Illustrated History* conceded, "The planting of Christianity in non-Christian areas has largely been the result of efforts by British missionaries." Millions of former pagans are rejoicing in Heaven today because of courageous Brits like William Carey, J. Hudson Taylor, Charles "C. T." Studd, Robert Moffatt, David Livingston, James Chalmers, John Williams, John G. Patton, James Calvert, John Geddie, and George Grenfell (aka the "Congo Captain") who made Bogey's *African Queen* cruise look like *Scuffy the Tugboat* (circa 1946).

Take the deplorable slave trade, for instance. Do you suppose the Lord knew how to turn the thing around (Romans 8:28) for any savages who were looking for the true God while lost on the "Dark Continent" (Job 3:23)? Perhaps Phillis Wheatley can give you some light. Born in West Africa in 1753, Phillis was placed into bondage by her own people. While still a child, she was brought to Boston and sold to Mr. John Wheatley, a tailor, as a servant for his wife. Under her "cruel taskmaster," Phillis learned to read both English and Latin. More importantly, she came to know her master's Lord and Saviour after hearing George Whitefield preach. Developing a talent for poetry, she became the first published black poetess in America. The next time you visit a bookstore, ask for a copy of *Poems by Phillis Wheatley*. For one of the wildest, most politically incorrect, "Uncle-Tom" hate-literature-at-its-best examples of what *not* to read in a public gathering, try her most famous poem, entitled, "On Being Brought from Africa to America" (not to be confused with the idiotic Eddie Murphy "classic," *Coming to America*.) After all, why waste your time with kiddie-car material like *Amistad* or Maya

Angelou's "The Hope and Dream of the Slave" when you can hear something that's *really* profound?

'TWAS mercy brought me from my *Pagan* land,
Taught my benighted soul to understand
That there's a God, that there's a *Saviour* too:
Once I redemption neither sought nor knew,
Some view our sable race with scornful eye,
"Their colour is a diabolic die."
Remember, *Christians*, *Negroes* black as *Cain*,
May be refin'd and join th' angelic train.

Phillis also wrote a poem about her beloved spiritual benefactor, "On the Death of George Whitefield," calling him a "happy saint" and saying how the people would no longer be able to hear the "music of thy tongue." She then went on to extol his great preaching and life. During one of my many trips to the Old South Presbyterian Church in Newburyport, Massachusetts (where Mr. Whitefield is interred in the basement directly beneath the pulpit), the tour guide pointed up to the balcony section where Phillis read her poem during Mr. Whitefield's funeral.

And just to clear the air, while Phillis was owned by a "white guy," such was not the case for thousands of others less fortunate. Not only were the slaves initially sold by fellow Africans, but many of their new American masters turned out to be former slaves themselves! Mr. Bill Ward, a historical researcher and author of fifty-seven works of nonfiction, comments on one of the more "politically sensitive" aspects of that *peculiar* institution. "Black slave ownership is one of the most frequently overlooked parts of the slavery story. The U.S. census of 1830 showed that 3,775 free Negroes owned 12,760 Negro slaves." Furthermore, President Lincoln's iconic Emancipation Proclamation applied only to slaves being held in *Confederate* states. "Honest Abe's" reprieve did not apply to Yankee chattel in Kentucky, Maryland, Missouri, or Illinois. According to *The Gray Book* by James and Walter Kennedy, Union Commander Ulysses S. Grant's excuse for not freeing his own slaves way up in the "Land of Lincoln" was that, "Good help is so hard to come by these days."

Also, I wouldn't get too rambunctious about insane demands for reparations, until I did my homework, if I was you. According to Exodus 12:40, Ham kept his Shemite brethren in bondage for roughly four hundred and thirty years. As Dr. Peter Ruckman pointed out, "The first mention of 'Let my people go' is found in Exodus 9:1, where the oppressive race was black." And if you happen to believe in the biblical law of sowing and reaping (Galatians 6:7), that four hundred-plus-year period of Jewish bondage in Egypt just might account for the duration of the modern slave era—from the sixteenth to the nineteenth century.

And, as long as we're on the subject, those Africans got off lightly compared to the original "Million Man March" in II Chronicles 14:13, where 1,000,000 Ethiopians were *destroyed before the LORD*" in one engagement for messing with King Asa of Judah. No doubt the largest body bag count on record—some 230 times higher than the combined deaths at the 1862 Battle of Antietam, the bloodiest single day in American military history—the figure is so high that the *Scofield Reference Bible* note assumes it was a scribal mistake. (As previously noted, Scofield survived Antietam as a Confederate courier.)

"THE TENTS OF SHEM"

When our modern, politically-correct pastors are not rushing to march in solidarity with the BLM crowd, they're joining the drumbeat to fight for oppressed "native Americans" (more welfare, more slot machines, more "fire water," etc.). Dr. Kennedy's statistics about Japheth's growing global grab included the American Indians being evicted from their tepees to fulfill the second part of Genesis 9:27, *"God shall enlarge Japheth, and he shall dwell in the tents of Shem."*

Although initially subjected to many oppressive policies by the white man's government, thousands of redeemed Indians, including the celebrated Geronimo himself, eventually made it to the *real* "Happy Hunting Grounds" because a dedicated band of Gospel-preaching missionaries (like Isaac McCoy, Humphrey Posey, Evan Jones, David Brainard, John Elliot, and others) were able to break the spell of their Satanic, peyote-smoking medicine men. *"But where sin abounded, grace did much more abound."* (Romans 5:20) This was all made possible because Japheth would eventually gain the *spiritual* shelter of Shem's tents from the groundbreaking work of a Shemite *tentmaker* (Acts 18:3). Thus, many lost souls in the Philadelphia Church Age found Jesus Christ by hitting the sawdust trail under the "Canvas Cathedral."

Should anyone be interested, the very words you are now reading were originally typed into a $700 Apple iPad Air, Fourth Generation tablet, a precious gift from my West Coast Shemite "Kemo Sabe," Brother *Eloy*, a redeemed, full-blooded Navajo Indian, who plays the piano like he's on the warpath! Also, it just so happens that the first advance order I received for *Perilous Times* came from a "pale face" pastor in Georgia who forwarded his request to me through the *Facebook* page of Macedonia Independent Baptist Church—a KJV-Only Cherokee congregation, located in the town of Cherokee on the Eastern Band of the Cherokee Nation in western North Carolina—after watching a taped copy of me preaching there. (Incidentally, just before I stood to speak to a considerably larger congregation on the evening in question, the good-natured Cherokee pastor paid me one of the more unusual "backhanded" compliments of my ministry: "*Now* I know how to get more of you back on Sunday night— preach for two hours and tell Italian jokes.")

Any man of God who faithfully pushes back against this devilish, end-day incursion of Critical Race Theory will ultimately be branded a racist. (Speaking of Indians, such preachers will find themselves like the Lone Ranger did in that old joke when he says to Tonto, "Looks like we're surrounded," and Tonto replies—as he's applying his war paint— "What you mean *we*, white man?") Personally, I've heard this accusation *plenty* of times (usually from the same critics who railed against those pastors who did *not* shutter their doors during the China virus). However, owing solely to the good grace of God, every time I took a new hit in the public relations arena, my stock seemed to rise. As I well understand, 2020 was extremely tough on most hard-working evangelists and missionaries. So—for the sole purpose of emboldening young preachers who face the same temptation to wince over a potential "racist" tag (and with no intention of violating II Corinthians 10:12)—allow me to testify that at age 68-69, I was enabled by God's strength to preach in 200 churches during those first two years of Covid Chaos. In June of 2021 alone, I spoke thirty-seven times in twenty-nine days (yes, you read that right) in eighteen churches across Ohio, New York, and Pennsylvania. To state this as "tactfully" as possible (like they say down in North Carolina, "I don't want to be *ugly*"), the only practical explanation I can think of is that the crowd I *run* with—*didn't*.

THE *KEY* TO DR. GRADY'S "RACISM"

When I entered the ministry many moons ago, my pastor, Dr. Randy Carroll, gave me some wonderful advice. He said that while I could never avoid being slandered, I could always live in such a way that when the people who heard the criticism met me, they would realize that it couldn't possibly be true. Isaiah 54:17 concurs, *"No weapon that is formed against thee shall prosper."* I will therefore conclude this chapter with one of my favorite stories that I frequently tell around the country. (It's the greatest evidence that *proves* Dr. Bill Grady is a "racist"!) But first, allow me to share just a sampling of the many examples on pages 184-189 in *How Satan Turned America Against God* (along with a few bonus stories). After concluding a meeting in Mechanicsville, Maryland, I was sitting at my departure gate at Dulles Airport when Anderson Cooper suddenly appeared. While my first instinct was to give the famous CNN anchor one of my Chick tracts, the Holy Spirit immediately kiboshed that idea, reminding me of Matthew 7:6, *"neither cast ye your pearls before swine."* When I boarded the plane, the filthy animal was seated a row behind me, across the aisle. An older black lady took her seat beside me, whereupon the Holy Spirit said, "Give that Gospel tract to her." I then proceeded to witness to her throughout the entire flight. (As I recall, she was a mother of seven children and a Seventh-day Adventist.)

The "hatred" I have for black people probably began when I was in the first grade at Saint Stephen's of Hungary Catholic School in Manhattan when I was smitten with a nineteenth-century parlor song that the nuns taught us to sing— "Old Black Joe." I can still recall the sad lyrics, describing a fictional elderly black slave named Joe, who, having long missed his departed friends from the cotton fields, is now approaching his own death: "I'm comin', I'm comin', for my head is bending low; I hear those gentle voices calling, 'Old Black Joe.'" (The nuns changed the words to "I hear the angels calling....") My "racism" was probably in high gear on February 28, 1969, when I found my myself, age sixteen, one of the few white dudes surrounded by 20,000 Hamites, jiving at an SRO "Temptations" concert in Madison Square Garden.

While door-to-door soul winning when I was saved less than six months, I knelt with a black man in his living room and led his entire family to Christ as we wept and held hands together. Bro. Morris Hunt went on to pastor a black Baptist church in Media, Pennsylvania. During my five years in Hyles-Anderson College (1976-'81), I had a number of enlightening experiences. One of my black converts from Chicago came to church and walked the aisle, professing Christ as his Saviour. He must have meant business, because he handed me a bag of heroin at the altar. I then shocked my college president, Dr. Wendell Evans, by handing the white substance to him! (Not sure what he did with it...)

When I was working at Blaw Knox Foundry, I led my fellow HAC students in conducting an evangelistic preaching ministry during lunch break. Hundreds of black men were saved, including my foreman, Bill Dixon; my crane operator, Sonny Davis; and Charlie the "burner" (who once agreed to help me with a special Christmas service by dressing up as Santa Claus (though, being a tad nervous, he showed up a tad "looped"). One Sunday we had so many folks to haul to church that we filled up an entire bus!

I also had the tremendous learning opportunity of preaching in many black Baptist churches. ("Can I get a witness?") Unfortunately, however, most of these congregations were no more enlightened about the King James Bible issue, dispensational truth, and right division than are the majority of white IFB churches. However, the genuine excitement in their services (which dwarfs the nutty Charismatics) mitigates their doctrinal deficiencies somewhat. (When describing this bipolar atmosphere, Dr. Jack Hyles would say, "You don't go anywhere, but you have fun on the trip.") Black preachers are well known for their unique homiletical skills. (Translation: they normally preach circles around white boys, etc.) The late E. V. Hill's funeral sermon for his wife was a classic. "That's My King" by Dr. S. M. Lockridge was another. I recall my neighbor and good friend, Reverend Joe Hughes, who once said, upon comparing the panicked disciples on the Sea of Galilee with their snoozing in the Garden of Gethsemane, "If you can stays awake in the prayer meetin's, you can sleeps through the storms." Who could ever forget *that*? (This good man mentored me for five years while I attended Bible college, including having me preach for his congregation in Indiana Harbor.) Another brother, waxing eloquently on II Corinthians 5:17 said, "If you still *is* what you *was*—you *ain't*."

Furthermore, my "prejudice" against black people has not been limited to "African-Americans." I was with the late Dr. Wendell Runion in 1996 when he outlined his forthcoming mission board (International Baptist Outreach Missions) on a restaurant napkin in Asheville, North Carolina.

As a founding board member of IBOM, I accompanied Dr. Runion to the "Dark Continent" in September 2003, where I had the privilege of preaching in eight Baptist churches in Kenya and Uganda. We also taught in the main Bible institute and ordained six national pastors. While all the facilities were primitive, one "sanctuary" consisted of a bench and two chairs arranged under the sprawling branches of a solitary tree. In that meeting, several chickens and cows dropped by unexpectedly and caught a portion of my sermon.

Now the good news is that God also has a small, but potent, King James-Only remnant among the black churches. I've had the privilege of getting to know four such pastors (in Norfolk, Virginia; Lima, Ohio; Louisville, Kentucky; and West Memphis, Arkansas). When I preached my sermon on Israel in the Norfolk church, I related how the *USS Forrestal* suffered many disasters as a lingering judgment on the legacy of James Forrestal for his resistance to President Truman's pro-Israel policies. Was I ever shocked after the service to shake hands with one of the members, Bro. Larry Jacobs, a retired Navy man who confirmed those very events, having served on the *Forrestal* himself! A former member of my home church in Tennessee told me that he was led to God in the middle of the Mediterranean by the pastor of this same Virginia church, James Burnett, who is also a Navy veteran.

The first time I preached for the church in West Memphis, Arkansas, the pastor, Toure Carter, a former gangbanger from Omaha, Nebraska, gave me a most unusual love offering; a generous amount of cash *and* a twelve-gauge shotgun to make it out of his neighborhood! (Well, not exactly; the gun *was* a gift, but it didn't come with any shells.) This is one unique church—100% black, KJV-Only, *and* pro-Peter Ruckman! I remember a service when the entire congregation hit the altar after my sermon. (They usually hit the door.) Oh, and by the way, *please don't tell them I'm a "racist" or they might drop my monthly support!* (Just to clear the air, this generous act was totally unsolicited as I have *never* asked *any* church for support.)

However, my most treasured story involves one of their members, Bro. Dameaon Dudley. Once, after I complimented a sharp watch he was wearing, it was on my wrist in no time. (And no, I didn't lift it!) Our bond grew closer when I led one of his two daughters to the Lord. Then it was his other daughter who needed to be prayed through a heart surgery. But the wildest thing occurred when I asked the pastor if I could stay at

Bro. Dudley's home for an upcoming Bible conference, rather than the nice motel suite the church usually booked for me. He said, "Oh wow, if I ask him that, he'll be blown away!" I said, "Tell him to deal with it!" About a week later, I got a text from my "brother from another mother" asking, "Dr. Grady, what's your favorite color?" I thought to myself, "You mean, besides *white*?" (Joke!) I didn't have a clue. Personally, I didn't think "real men" have favorite colors. (I didn't know he was asking for his wife.) So, I just picked one, "Blue." Then I got another text, "Dr. Grady, what's your favorite soap?" This time I did have an honest reply, "Irish Spring" (i.e., Bro. "Grady").

About a month later, I arrived for the meeting. After the opening service I followed Bro. Dudley and his wife to their crib. When the precious couple ushered me into my room, what do you suppose I found sitting on the dresser? It was a neatly folded pile of brand-new *blue* washcloths and towels, next to several boxes of *Irish Spring*! Talk about hospitality! They even gave me my own house key so I could come and go as I pleased. Well, the week flew by with many spiritual blessings. Finally, as we were all "hugging it out" in the church parking lot, I said to my teary-eyed host, "Be sure to hold my room for next year." But when I tried to hand him his key, he shocked me by saying, "No, Dr. Grady—*you* keep it; you might be driving through the area some other time and need a place to crash." My first response was, "Well, where do you keep your valuables?"

Moral of the story: I'm probably the only white preacher in America who is anti-BLM, anti-CRT, and a "racist," who gets monthly support from a black church *and* has the house *key* of one of the *key* members on his *key* chain! (Not to mention that cool watch and shotgun!)

6

God's Cologne Bottle

THE FOLLOWING MATERIAL will constitute an abrupt devotional detour, focusing on the little-known *"endangerment of Japheth."* As mentioned in the previous chapter, the descendants of Noah's eldest son have an "Achilles Heel," one that Satan loves to exploit. Given the catastrophic conditions that are currently besetting the Church, this could be the most important study in this book. While the other sections deal with what is transpiring on the *outside*, this parenthetical chapter is about what's happening on the *inside*—i.e., inside of *you*. To survive what's coming, the Christian must be at his best spiritually.

The background for this truth is found in Luke 10:38-42. Jesus is the special dinner guest of Mary, Martha, and Lazarus of Bethany. The Scofield section heading sets the scene: "Martha and Mary in contrast." While Martha was *"cumbered about much serving,"* Mary simply *"sat at Jesus' feet, and heard his word."* With her hands full, Martha gets perturbed and asks the Lord, *"[D]ost thou not care that my sister hath left me to serve alone? bid her therefore that she help me."* Her question must have hurt Him more than her directive. While meditating on I Peter 5:7 during a personal crisis, the Methodist preacher Frank Graeff wrote the hymn, "Does Jesus Care?" He rightly concludes:

> "O yes, He cares, I know He cares,
> His heart is touched with my grief;
> When the days are weary,
> The long nights dreary,
> I know my Savior cares."

Martha must have been as startled by the Lord's reply as her sister was exhilarated: *"Martha, Martha, thou art careful and troubled about many things: but one thing is needful: and Mary hath chosen that good part, which shall not be taken away from her."* (I often remark that in "the Greek" it says, "Lighten up, Martha.")

Now, despite the fact that both women were descended from Shem, Martha's more energetic appearing profile makes her a perfect illustration of "Japheth the Elder" —the son who was destined to be the enlarged race. (While she is running around like a chicken with its head cut off, Mary, a type of Shem, "just" sits there worshipping Jesus.) Thus, the two siblings can represent a spiritual version of the classic East-West dichotomy. The deep truth here is that Martha's fixation on "gittin'er done" is what America has always been about, i.e., "Bigger is Better." Japheth instinctively equates success with how much visible evidence he has acquired— *"supposing that gain is godliness"* rather than *"godliness with contentment is great gain."* (I Timothy 6:5-6) And so the mantra goes, "My house is bigger than your house"; or, "My car is fancier than your car"; or, "My salary is bigger than your salary"; or, "My wife is prettier than your wife," etc. Someone has said that the national mentality can be summed up with the words, "If some is good, then More is Better, and TOO MUCH IS JUST RIGHT." This ethos supposedly traces back to our expansive "Go West, young man" frontier days when cattle, gold, land, and oil could be had on a first-come, first-served basis. *Whatever*—the appropriate Scripture is Proverbs 27:20, *"[T]he eyes of man are never satisfied."*

The bottom line is that Japheth is pragmatic by nature. As the "enlargement" of his immediate world is basically all that matters, he will do *anything* to accomplish his goal. Thus, his modus operandi will always be, "The ends justify the means." Consider a typical marriage where the wife mirrors Shem and the husband, Japheth. On Valentine's Day, the man is prone to buy his wife a toaster (four slicer), because he views it as a more *practical* gift (i.e., tired of waiting for his toast with the old two-slicer). Meanwhile, his better half really wanted a dozen roses, because such an *impractical*, brief shelf-life gift would prove his love, etc. Of course, this all began in the dude's childhood when he would give his sister a baseball glove for her birthday (i.e., if *she* wouldn't use it, *he* would).

Once again, Dr. Billy Graham's ministry represents the greatest example of Japhethic pragmatism in our time. America's pastors famously judge their success based on the size of their congregations. However, like the wash lady who inadvertently backs herself into a corner, this is a self-destructive curse. As previously noted, though most preachers in this country are Japhethites, their boss is a *Shemite*; a familiar bumper sticker reads, "I work for a *Jewish* carpenter from Nazareth." The greatest truth that American Christians miss is that God does not think like we do! (Isaiah 55:8) While *our* focus is on the "tangible" (enlargement), *His* focus is on the "truth." Shem relates to the *spiritual, "Blessed be the LORD God of Shem."* (Genesis 9:26) The world's three major monotheistic religions descend from Shem (Judaism, Christianity, and nutty Islam). Thus, I Corinthians 3:13 declares of the Judgment Seat: *"[T]he fire shall try every man's work of what **sort** it is."* Our rewards will be based on the *sort*—not the *size* (I Samuel 17:28-29; Luke 12:32).

And so, while Martha was busy doing the things that needed to be done (soul winning, bus calling, hospital visits, etc.), Mary was also engaged in something the Master required. Only *her* activity is rarely visible to the pragmatist's eye. Balance is the key, as God requires spiritual synergy (Proverbs 11:1). In any event, Mary learned a valuable truth as the Master spoke up in her defense. This experience emboldened her to take things to the next level.

"VERY PRECIOUS OINTMENT"

Not only do American Christians fail to realize that God does not think like they do (i.e., "Bigger is better"), they also miss the fact that Satan frequently exploits their naïveté. The main time he does this is when we fail in any number of venues. *He* knows that *we* see such down time as counter-productive to *our* instinctive, pragmatic goal of temporal success. Consequently, much of our depression results from Satan keeping our focus on this apparent, meaningless "waste." Watch how Mary destroys this Satanic illusion with her next encounter with the Lord.

The "woman" in Matthew 26:6-13 is unnamed. However, John's account identifies her as the sibling of Martha and Lazarus of Bethany. When Mary breaks her alabaster box of *"very precious ointment,"* the *"house was filled with the odour of the ointment."* (John 12:3) When she proceeds to pour the costly ingredients on Jesus's head, the disciples (led by Judas, as per John 12:4) feign outrage saying, *"To what **purpose** is this **waste**? For this ointment might have been sold for much, and given to the poor"* (verses 8-9). Does anyone really believe that Judas gave a flip about the poor? The two key buzzwords are "purpose" and "waste." Can you see their philosophical connection to Japheth's DNA? The "evangelical-Baptist" mega-apostate, Rick Warren, founder and former pastor of Saddle Brook "Church," is defined by his two *New York Times* best sellers, *Purpose Driven Church* (1995) and *Purpose Driven Life* (2002). Bible-believing pastors in Southern California will testify that Saddle Brook has some of the most extensive real estate holdings in the entire area (I Timothy 6:10).

Judas saw Mary's actions as a "waste," as there was no *visible* "purpose" for this anointing (i.e., Jesus was very much alive at the time). However, once again, the Lord came to her defense, saying, *"Why trouble ye the woman? For she hath wrought a good work upon me"* (verse 10). Note that from an earthly perspective, Mary's action was described as *"this waste,"* while from a Heavenly vantage point it was viewed as a *"**good work**."* He then says, *"For ye have the poor always with you; but me ye have not always"* (verse 11). While riding in a first-class train car, C. H. Spurgeon was similarly accosted by a Pharisaical minister with the rebuke, "I ride *second*-class and save the Lord's *money*," whereupon the "Prince of Preachers" replied, "I ride *first*-class and save the Lord's *servant*." Jesus then explains how she was forecasting His Passion. *"For in that she hath poured this ointment on my body, she did it for my burial"* (verse 12). He concludes with a remarkable prophecy that is *still* being fulfilled—this very moment in fact: *"Verily I say unto you, Wheresoever this gospel shall be preached in the whole world, there shall also this, that this woman hath done, be told for a memorial of her"* (verse 13).

FORE!

Viewing an eighteen-hole golf game as a picture of one's life span can afford a good illustration of how and where Satan regularly afflicts Christians who descend from Japheth. The front nine holes correspond to the first half of our three-score-and-ten, while the back nine relate to the second half.

The main theme of the earliest holes (2-3) can be categorized by several related words: *dreams, visions, goals, aspirations,* etc. These aims are *always* positive! For instance, little girls sitting on their "hope chests" rarely daydream about marrying a chainsaw killer, etc. Likewise, guys muse about becoming sports stars or successful businessmen, etc. Preacher boys see themselves pastoring large, growing churches. Conversely, the closing holes on the fairway (16-18) are always radically different. (At least that's where most of the cheating occurs.) Here—with the song "Sunrise, Sunset" playing in the background—the alternative theme is: *reality, truth, actuality, adjustment, acceptance,* etc. (The contrast mirrors the mood swing that exists between arriving and departing flights on any runway at Las Vegas Airport.)

The great key to this analogy is what the Lord inserts along the way of our PGA course. Remember, as Japhethites, we are consumed with "enlargement" —our onward and upward forward motion to success. However, because God is a Shemite, He has a different agenda for us; oftentimes, one that makes no sense, initially (Acts 9:16). Therefore, as the Lord's *"ways* [are] *past finding out"* (Romans 11:33), He will inevitably factor a certain percentage of unexplainable *waste* into our lives at any number of holes. For instance, my mother committed suicide right in front of me around hole three; someone reading these words was molested by a relative at number five; a young mother loses her baby at six; a teenage girl gets pregnant at seven; adultery destroys some marriage at eight; a well-meaning husband makes a disastrous financial mistake at nine; a reputation is ruined by internet slander at ten; a pastor experiences a serious church split at eleven (one that *could* have been avoided *if* he had only been more vigilant, etc.); a life ends prematurely through illness at hole twelve; a lost loved one goes to Hell at thirteen…Get the picture?

Now whenever these heartaches happen, Satan will immediately whisper in our ear, *"To what **purpose** is this **waste**?"* Sometimes, the Lord Himself causes the waste; other times, He simply *allows* it to happen (Job 1:12; 2:6). But in either case, He alone is responsible for the *apparently* senseless tragedy. This deep truth can be illustrated by a simple drawing—a circle with a dot in the middle and an arrow entering the circle, terminating at the dot. The circle represents God; the dot is any born-again believer; the arrow corresponds to the "waste" in our lives. The "waste" will always stem from one of three sources:

either *God* did it; *we* did it; or *Satan* did it. Again, in the latter two examples, the Lord obviously *permitted* it to occur. And so, for the Devil's darts to hit you (Ephesians 6:16), they must first pass through the circle! Known as the "Hedge Principle," this constitutes one of the first lessons in Scripture. When God was bragging on Job, Satan replied, *"Hast not thou made an **hedge** about him, and about his house, and about all that he hath on every side?"* (Job 1:10) Thus, whenever the Lord decides to keep the hedge *up*, there's nothing *Satan* can do to hurt you; but when He wills to take the hedge *down*, there's nothing *you* can do to keep the Devil out!

"LOWING AS THEY WENT..."

Several years ago, I arrived at a certain church in the South to preach their Sunday evening service. The pastor immediately informed me that a young married couple seated in the congregation had sustained a terrible tragedy the previous week. Their precious twelve-year-old son had ended his own life without leaving a suicide note. As they were unable to make any sense out of their tragic loss, Satan naturally had a field day. After all, how *could* they answer his question: *"To what purpose is this waste?"* All their beautiful plans for his future were wiped out for no apparent reason. And yet, though crushed, here they were, back in church. After the service, I attempted to comfort them, especially the mother, by sharing an amazing story from I Samuel 6:7-14.

After the Philistines had confiscated the *"ark of the Lord"* from the Jews, they experienced continual judgment. Therefore, they decided to return it, along with various jewels as a trespass offering. However, at the last moment the thought occurred to them that the "punishment" scenario could have been a coincidence. Thus, a plan was devised to send the cargo back to Israel in a new cart, harnessed to a pair of milch kine—with their calves separated from them in the rear. According to their reasoning, *"[I]f it goeth up by the way of his own coast to Beth-shemesh* (Israel's border), *then he hath done us this great evil: but if not, then we shall know that it is not his hand that smote us; it was a chance that happened to us."* When they released the cows, an amazing thing occurred. *"And the kine took the straight way to the way of Beth-shemesh, and went along the highway, **lowing as they went**, and turned* *not aside to the right hand or to the left; and the lords of the Philistines went after them unto the border of Beth-shemesh."*

As the calves bellowed out in one strain, their mamas answered back in a different strain. I once shared this material while preaching for my good friend, Pastor David Wagner, in Branson, Missouri, after which a veteran rancher shocked me by relating that many men in the dairy industry retire early (though they will seldom admit it), because they can no longer handle the emotional trauma of the weaning process! He further said that sometimes the calves and the cows are separated by a fence so they can at least see one another during the painful transition.

When I spoke to the mother of that twelve-year-old, I explained the application that, although her heart was broken, she was back in church, pulling *her* cart for the Lord, albeit—lowing as *she* went! Husbands, you will *never* find a text affording more insight into your wife's emotional makeup than that. And by the way men, when those milch kine completed their mission, they were sacrificed as a burnt offering to the Lord. Has God blessed you with such a helpmeet? If you married up, *treat her accordingly* (Proverbs 18:22; 19:14).

THE PURPOSE FOR YOUR WASTE

The secret to Satan's strategy is that he uses our weakness against us. He knows that our instinctive Japhethic reaction to any type of nonsensical-appearing "waste" (illustrated by Mary's spilled ointment) tends to depression, for any experience that mitigates our "enlargement" just *has* to be bad, etc. And the *last* thing the Devil wants you to discover is *why* God permitted this "waste" to occur in the first place. Believe it or not, it has to do with something the Lord wants from us! That's right; the same God who yawned in Isaiah 66:1-2 at the prospect of a trillion-dollar temple, actually has a secret desire that can only be fulfilled by you and me. And you'll *never* guess what it is.

I was saved for over forty years before the Holy Ghost showed me what an Old Testament sacrifice was basically all about. Constituting the main segue to fellowship with God, it entailed taking something of great value (as near to perfection as possible), then totally destroying it! Now ask yourself, how much sense does *that* make? And the reason for the destruction is even more astounding. Have you ever noticed that there is always an ascending aroma (like Mary's ointment) affiliated with the sacrificial system? When Noah left the ark, he *"builded an altar unto the LORD; and took of every clean beast, and of every clean fowl, and offered **burnt offerings** on the altar."* The very next verse states, *"And the LORD smelled a **sweet savour**."* (Genesis 8:20-21) Unbeknownst to most Christians, the Lord likes to smell nice! For instance, David wrote in Psalm 45:8, *"All thy garments **smell** of myrrh, and aloes, and cassia."* His son later described Jesus in Song of Solomon 3:6 as, *"**perfumed** with myrrh and frankincense."*

When these two concepts are combined, we learn that *sacrifice* provides *fragrance* for the Lord. Thus, we find that the altar of incense was located just a short distance from the brazen altar. Which brings us to the specific reason for the waste that we experience in our lives. Whenever God's will involves a *sacrifice* in your life (i.e., the total *destruction* of something very precious to you), rest assured that you are highly favored in His eyes. While Old Testament blessings were always *material* in nature (camels, sheep, oxen, gold, silver, et al.), Church Age blessings are always *spiritual* in nature, with the greatest of these being the "gift" of suffering. Paul wrote in Philippians 1:29, *"For unto you it is **given** in the behalf of Christ, not only to believe on him, but also to **suffer** for his sake."*

The great truth here is that the divine purpose for *your* apparent "waste" —once again, like Mary's spilled ointment—is to give Jesus the spiritual cologne He so greatly desires! If you want to get close to the Lord, could you get any closer than being *on* His very person? (John 13:23) *"Why trouble ye the woman? for she hath wrought a good work **upon me**"* and *"For in that she hath poured this ointment **on my body**, she did it for my burial."* (Matthew 26:10, 12) In essence, *our* waste was designed to be *His* cologne! Even the world understands the concept. As the old saying goes, "One man's trash is another man's treasure." The four cherubim in chapter four of Revelation constitute the closest created beings to God's physical manifestation. Their sole function is praising Him. Thus, David wrote, *"Whosoever offereth **praise** glorifieth me."* (Psalm 50:23) And this "praise" will always usher us into His divine presence, *"Enter into his gates with **thanksgiving**, and into his courts with **praise**: be **thankful** unto him, and bless his name."* (Psalm 100:4)

The twin New Testament cross-references for this truth are found in Ephesians 5:20, *"[G]iving thanks always for all things unto God and the Father in the name of our Lord Jesus Christ"* and I Thessalonians

5:18, *"**In everything give thanks**: for this is the will of God in Christ Jesus concerning you."* The great secret to these Scriptures reverts back to that circle illustration. As everything that ever happens to us— including the so-called "waste" —must pass through the circle, at the end of the day, it all comes from God. Thus, we are commanded to thank Him for those hard times. When our human spirit hears our lips thanking God, a tremendous peace floods our soul. Before we expressed thanks, Satan could easily convince us that it was all *our* fault, etc. However, obeying those twin texts reminds us that the Lord was personally involved in the trial with us (for He could have prevented it had He wanted to). This is precisely how we obey I Peter 5:7, *"Casting all your care upon him; for he careth for you."* As the hymn title says, "He Was There All the Time."

TEARS IN A BOTTLE

After preaching this message in a Sunday morning service in New York State (on Valentine's Day, no less), a big strapping man came up to my book table and told me that his daughter had died in her bed from a heroin overdose exactly one year ago to the day. He also said that her two young children (his grandchildren) were asleep beside her when she expired. He then shocked me by stating, "I never shed one tear all year—*until* this morning." The final lesson in our devotional detour regarding "Japheth's *endangerment*" involves a beautiful object lesson taken from Psalm 56:8. While Hank Williams, Sr. (speaking for lost men in general) popularized the country music song, "There's a Tear in My Beer," those who have *really* seen "*the* Light," know that *their* tears are preserved in a special bottle in Heaven. David wrote, *"[P]ut thou **my tears into thy bottle**: are they not in thy book?"* The question remains—*Why* are they there?

I would posit that our tears represent the Heavenly fragrance God desires to apply to His person. In my spiritual imagination, the Lord has a cologne bottle for every one of us, filled with the tears shed during our times of "waste." The great key to this analogy is that the bottles are sealed with a cap. While God *wants* to use our tears for His cologne, He can only do so under one condition. This involves the main difference between Mary's experience and that of our own. Our "very precious ointment" was *taken from* us (as in that proverbial 2:00 AM phone call). However, Mary *brought* hers *to* the Lord *voluntarily*. Because God is *not* a Calvinist, the only way He will *ever* get to enjoy *your* cologne is if *you* give Him permission to use it. He will *never* open the bottle on His own as they are *your* tears. Thus, the bottom line is that we have to advance beyond merely *adjusting* to our loss, having *learned to live with* the heartache. We have to regroup and make that painful, conscious decision to *thank the Lord* for having allowed that "waste" to devastate our life. And that is how we give Him the okay to apply *our* tears as *His* cologne! You might call it the *real* "Heaven Scent," adapted to a masculine fragrance.

"SAY ON, SISTER ANTHONY!"

When I taught at Hyles-Anderson College (1986-96), one of my night school students was a black man who pastored a Baptist church in South Chicago. Having preached in numerous black churches, I was happy to accept an invitation to speak for him on one particular occasion. During the Sunday School hour, I taught on I Thessalonians 5:18, *"In every thing give thanks: for this is the will of God in Christ Jesus concerning you."* The Holy Spirit seemed to really move through the congregation.

Just before I was to preach the main message in the worship hour, the pastor introduced one of his ladies to bring the special. She then stood up in the back left corner of the auditorium and asked the man of God if she could share a word of testimony first. Although it's been over three decades since, I can *still* remember what he said next: "Say on, Sister Anthony!" What she went on to "say" sucked all the air out of the room. (Believe me, I was there when it happened!) "I heard what Bro. Grady said during Sunday School about thanking God in all things. It's not easy to thank God when your teenage daughter is dragged down a back alley, hanging out of the car, her head literally bouncing on the pavement, then left dead in a drug deal gone bad—two weeks ago—but a few minutes ago, for the very first time, I bowed my head and thanked the Lord for taking my baby girl that way!"

She then calmly walked to the pulpit while the rest of us attempted to process what we had just heard. Standing before the microphone, "Sister Anthony" announced: "This morning I want to try and bless the church with a song entitled, "I'm Comin' *Up* the Mountain—*On the Rough Side*." I'm not sure what happened next, as the whole congregation (me included) went into a Holy Ghost fog! As they say down South, "The *big* preacher showed up!"

"LOWING AS WE GO…"

I will close this chapter with a touching illustration of the caliber of faithfulness God deserves from His servants. A year or so after I shared the story of the two milch kine with those grieving parents, I happened to drive by their church on the way to another meeting. Of course, I immediately said a prayer for them. When I got to my motel, the Holy Spirit had a special blessing waiting for me. While they had no idea that I was in the area, the father of the deceased child had sent me the following text:

> You took your time after the service at ___ Church in ___ to speak to me and my wife. Just wanted you to know that the words you spoke to me and my wife after our 12-year-old boy committed suicide has helped us more than you will know. We continue to pull forward, LOWING as we go, without our sweet boy! Thank you for taking time to help us!!

This has to be one of the most beautiful notes I have *ever* received in my nearly half-century of ministry. As with "Sister Anthony," just imagine how much Heavenly cologne the lovely Lord Jesus received from *that* precious couple. So, remember, "Japheth," while God expects you to act like you were programmed (i.e., keep "enlarging" your opportunities to advance the Gospel), just don't let Satan depress you whenever God permits him to insert some senseless appearing "waste" along *your* eighteen holes. For that is the very time Jesus is giving *you* the privileged opportunity to enhance His aroma.

> *"Be ye therefore followers of God, as dear children; and walk in love, as Christ also hath loved us, and hath given himself for us an offering and a sacrifice to God for a **sweetsmelling savour**."*
> (Ephesians 5:1-2)

7

The Battle of Guacamole

ONE OF THE great secrets to the Christian life is learning how to wait on God (Isaiah 40:31). Way back in the Wycliffe Bible era of fourteenth-century England, William Langford (sometimes Langland) coined the phrase, "Patience is a virtue." Paul reminded the believers in Nero's backyard that *"tribulation worketh patience."* (Romans 5:3) As this virtue applies in every dispensation, Tribulation saints are likewise exhorted: *"For ye have need of patience, that, after ye have done the will of God, ye might receive the promise."* (Hebrews 10:36) Tribulation is one of the Lord's greatest schoolmasters, with patience representing the evidence that the lessons were learned.

For instance, tribulation reminds us that *our* agenda and *our* happiness do not matter, as we were created for God's pleasure (Revelation 4:11). As tribulation normally produces murmuring at first, the great lesson here is that anger reveals our flawed conviction that certain self-perceived "rights" were violated, i.e., phantom rights that we never had. Tribulation often deprives us of the temporal things we falsely believed would bring us true joy, leading us to learn that God wants us to find our contentment in Him (Luke 12:15). Thankfully, the panic that follows hard on the heels of tribulation reveals a severe spiritual condition, one that we would not have known of otherwise—the onset of *atheism*. One of the most convicting statements I have heard was a quote attributed to John Wesley, "Worry is a mild form of atheism."

The most valuable lesson inevitably concerns timing. Tribulation often occurs when God has the "audacity" to interrupt *our* schedule. In our daily battle with the flesh, we often forget that *"one day is with the Lord as a thousand years, and a thousand years as one day."* (II Peter 3:8) Our negative reaction reveals our pride, as Ecclesiastes 7:8 says, *"Better is the end of a thing than the beginning thereof: and the patient in spirit is better than the proud in spirit.* " The problem with patience is that it takes *decades* to realize that God works on His own schedule, not ours. Like that old Pennsylvania Dutch expression goes, "Too soon old; too late shmart." The life of Moses illustrates this truth, dividing into three equal forty-year periods: In the first forty years, Moses learned the lesson that he was a *somebody*, second only to Pharaoh; in the second period, he learned the lesson that he was a *nobody*, second to Jethro (his father-in-law); however, in the third forty years, Moses learned the lesson of what God could do with a man who had learned the first two lessons! Joseph is another case study. When he witnessed his brothers bowing before him in Egypt, Genesis 42:9 says, *"And Joseph remembered the dreams which he dreamed of them,"* referring to the long-forgotten vision that God had given him in his youth (Genesis 37:6-9). Concerning the Lord's earthly cousin, of whom He would say, *"Among them that are born of women there has not risen a greater than John the Baptist"* (Matthew 11:11), John would spend thirty years in the wilderness preparing for a ministry lasting a grand total of three months. Surely, *"his ways* [are] *past finding out!"* (Romans 11:33)

DEBRIS IN THE SEA

This truth has great relevance with regard to Japheth's enlargement. Pharaoh's power emanated from the "Land of Ham" (Psalm 105:23, 27; 106:22). Israel's ten northern tribes were conquered and disbursed by Sennacherib, the Shemite King of Assyria (II Kings 17:5-23). Over three millennia would actually pass before Japheth's European descendants would fulfill Noah's prophecy.

Our story begins innocently enough with what appears to be another, though totally unrelated, prophecy in 590 BC recorded in Ezekiel 26 while the prophet was in Babylonian captivity. Because Israel was being subjugated by Nebuchadnezzar, her neighbors in the Phoenician city of Tyre were rejoicing. However, Israel's God was listening, declaring in verses two and three, *"Son of man, because that Tyrus hath said against Jerusalem, **Aha, she is broken** that was the gates of the people: she is turned unto me: I shall be replenished, now she is laid waste: Therefore thus saith the Lord GOD; **Behold, I am against thee, O Tyrus.**"* (Oh boy, *not* good!) In verses seven and eight, God taps King Nebuchadnezzar II to *start* the ball rolling. (My reason for this metaphor will soon be apparent.) *"For thus saith the Lord GOD; **Behold, I will bring upon Tyrus Nebuchadrezzar king of Babylon**, a king of kings, from the north, with horses, and with chariots, and with horsemen, and companies, and much people. **He shall slay with the sword.**"* And so, in 586 BC (the third and decisive time he conquers Jerusalem), Nebuchadnezzar begins the siege described in verse nine. Finally, in 573 BC, the "conqueror" triumphantly enters Tyre (verse eleven). Prophecy fulfilled—right? Well, yes *and* no. You see, there were actually *two* cities by that name, Old Tyre and New Tyre. While the former city, the one Nebuchadnezzar laid waste, was located on the coast of ancient Lebanon, the latter was situated, believe it or not, about a mile *offshore*!

According to Herodotus, the original city, now known as *Paleotyre* (Old Tyre), was founded around 2750 BC. New Tyre was a 40-acre island sitting atop two sandstone reefs. It was initially reinforced by Solomon's friend, King Hiram (969-936 BC), who also supplied material for Israel's temple, reminiscent of a far better time for Tyrian-Jewish relations. Though dependent on her land-based sister-city for food and water, New Tyre became a major religious and commercial center, known as the "Queen of the Sea." Note the subtle reference to this second, isolated island city in Ezekiel 27:32, *"And in their wailing they shall take up a lamentation for the thee, and lament over thee, saying, What city is like **Tyrus**, like the destroyed **in the midst of the sea**?"*

With the invincible Phoenician navy guarding her back, the strategic coastal base would serve as an aquatic Alamo for the inhabitants of Old Tyre whenever the mainland was threatened. Deprived of standard offensive equipment, such as siege engines and battering rams, no invader could take New Tyre, including Nebuchadnezzar. And so, after thirteen years of trying his hand in "offshore drilling," he had to settle for a humiliating negotiated truce with the Tyrian King Ethbaal III (meaning "with Baal"). The reason why this resplendent king was so slick is because he is a major type of Satan and *his* beauty, cast in the very next chapter as the *"anointed cherub that covereth."* (Ezekiel 28:13-14) Thus, an insightful cross-reference in Ezekiel 29:18 relates how Nebuchadnezzar, having messed with "the Devil," gained little for his efforts while his men literally aged, losing their hair in the protracted effort. *"Son of man, Nebuchadnezzar king of Babylon caused his army to serve a great service against Tyrus: **every head was made bald**, and* *every shoulder was peeled: **yet had he no wages, nor his army,** for Tyrus, for the service that he had served against it."*

The heathen in general, along with the religious liberals waging their own war against Biblical inspiration, made much of this evidently failed prophecy, that *Nebuchadnezzar* was supposed to have conquered Tyre, i.e., the whole enchilada, island and all! However, what they failed to notice was the specific ending of verse three. After declaring, *"I am against thee, O Tyrus,"* the Lord continued, *"and will cause **many nations** to come up against thee, as the sea causeth his waves to come up."* Thus, two-and-a-half centuries later, a young upstart Macedonian showed up, intent on *continuing* what Nebuchadnezzar had merely begun. At the time (332 BC), Alexander the Great was in a hot eastbound pursuit of Darius III and his fading Achaemenid empire. This was one tough kid, having led his father's cavalry at age sixteen. As a master tactician who never lost a battle (who would make Sun Tzu look like Private Pyle), Alexander was not about to leave his rear exposed, specifically, the crucial port city of Tyre, for the Persian fleet to exploit. Therefore, whereas the King of Babylon took thirteen years to fail, Alexander (assisted by the naval and other auxiliary forces of *"many nations"*), captured the Phoenician fortress in all of six-and-a-half months!

The key to Alexander's success literally lay in the debris of Old Tyre ("One's man's trash is another man's treasure," etc.). The royal engineers had informed him that a natural sandbar less than three yards below the surface stretched directly from the shore to the elusive stronghold. When his eleventh-hour peace emissaries were slain in full view atop the 150-foot-high walls facing the mainland, then hurled down below—such was the level of their perceived invincibility—an enraged Alexander gave the order to begin what historians view as the most complex battle in ancient warfare. Masters of the legendary phalanx, the versatile Macedonians now laid down their 20-foot-long sarissas to begin their newest tactic—constructing a mile-long, 200-foot-wide causeway out of the stone, timber, and general rubble from the old city's ruins. While the Tyrians manning the palisades initially laughed and thumbed their noses at the outrageous spectacle, their mouths soon dropped as twin, 160-foot-high, rawhide-covered siege towers began rumbling their way.

The first-century Roman historian, Quintus Curtius Rufus (who based his account on earlier Greek sources), described the fall of Tyre in his *History of Alexander the Great of Macedonia* (translated by John Yardley).

> The king himself climbed the highest siege-tower. His courage was great, but the danger was greater for, conspicuous in his royal insignia and flashing armour, he was the prime target of enemy missiles. And his actions in the engagement were certainly spectacular. He transfixed with his spear many of the defenders on the walls, and some he threw headlong after striking them in hand-to-hand combat with his sword or shield, for the tower from which he fought practically abutted the enemy walls.

To make a long story short, reinforced by a variegated armada of over 200 ships (from *"many nations,"* Sidon, Cyprus, et al.), the end was *never* in question. When the smoke finally cleared (quite literally, as Alexander burned down half the city), 6,000 enemy soldiers were dead (as opposed to 400 Macedonians). King Azemilcus and the small contingent of civilians who had sought asylum in the Temple of Melqart were duly pardoned. This was followed by the callous massacre of 8,000 civilians (mainly women and children). The "lucky" ones, some 13,000 other non-combatants, were sold into slavery. As a final testimony to Alexander's fury for having to invest so much time and blood in this protracted siege—2,000 captured Tyrians were crucified along the shore.

Another "deep truth" regards the length of Tyre's immediate punishment for having rejoiced in Israel's chastening. The explicit reason why Judah went into captivity for *seventy* years was because she had ignored her Sabbatical year obligations for 490 years (i.e., failing to let the land rest every seventh year as per Leviticus 25:1-24). Well, neighbor, guess how long *Tyre* would have to suffer for reproaching Israel? Isaiah wrote in 712 BC:

> *And it shall come to pass in that day, that Tyre shall be forgotten* **seventy** *years, according to the days of one king: after the end of* **seventy** *years shall Tyre sing as an harlot. Take an harp, go about the city, thou harlot that hast been forgotten; make sweet melody, sing many songs, that thou mayest be remembered. And it shall come to pass after the end of* **seventy** *years, that the LORD will visit Tyre, and she shall turn to her hire, and shall commit fornication with all the kingdoms of the world upon the face of the earth.* (Isaiah 23:15-17)

Note how the Holy Spirit confirms the number "seventy" three times for emphasis. History confirms that in 274 BC, roughly 58 years later, Tyre was granted independent status by Ptolemy II (one of Alexander's successors), paving the way for her eventual return to the brothel of international commerce.

However, it is when we review the rest of Tyre's history (down to the present) that we can understand the inspired metaphor employed in Ezekiel 26:3 regarding those crashing "waves." Nebuchadnezzar and Alexander's campaigns were merely the *initial* waves in what would become a continual erosion by multiplied nations. For, though temporarily restored following the completion of her seventy-year sentence, Tyre would eventually go the way of all the earth. Her ultimate fate, announced in Ezekiel 26:14, *"thou shalt be built no more,"* would not come to pass for another 2,100 years, as many more waves (nations) would have to crash in upon her: among others, the Arab hordes in 638; the "Christian" Crusaders in 1124; the Mameluke Muslims burning the *entire* city to the ground in 1291; with a devastating earthquake finishing off the old whore in 1838. Henceforth, the eyewitness testimony of modern visitors invariably shares two impressions: Still visible in the shallow water, a veritable rock quarry of granite columns and stone blocks projects an eerie double flashback to those "precious **stones**" in the breastplate of that other king of Tyre, as well as the *"**stones** of fire"* upon which he walked in that original *"garden of God"* (Ezekiel 28:13-14). As for the once-proud islet itself, it remains a desolate tract of dirt, used only for *"the spreading of nets."* (Ezekiel 26:5, 14)

As a fitting conclusion to this section, you're never going to believe what I haven't told you yet. *It's only the coolest thing in the chapter—* well, so far anyway. (You might say it's that iconic, "One more thing" line of Lieutenant Colombo.) As previously mentioned, the enemies of God's word pounced on what they viewed as a failed prophecy regarding Nebuchadnezzar's *partial* victory over Tyre. We then observed that they missed the divine caveat at verse three, that it would be Babylon *and* "many nations" that would cause Tyre's eventual and total ruination. However, the really big stuff is introduced in the next verse. *"And they shall destroy the walls of Tyrus, and break down her towers: **I will also scrape her dust from her, and make her like the top of a rock."*** (This important fact is repeated in verse fourteen for emphasis.) Of course, this is exactly what Alexander's engineers did when they stripped the ruins of Old Tyre to build their artificial esplanade. In fact, they did such a good job, modern archeologists cannot even locate the ancient site.

But how did that get into the book of Ezekiel two-and-a-half centuries before it happened? Duh—probably the same way verse twelve did— Holy Ghost inspiration! *"And they shall make a spoil of thy riches, and make a prey of thy merchandise: and they shall break down thy walls, and destroy thy pleasant houses: and **they shall lay thy stones and thy timber and thy dust in the midst of the water.**"* Wow! How's *that* for a supernatural book? After a sequence of ten singular personal pronouns following Nebuchadnezzar's debut in verse seven, indicating that all of the action in verses eight through eleven was done by *him*, the text abruptly shifts to three plural pronouns in verse twelve, introducing an unknown cast of new players (i.e., more of those *"many nations"*), the first being the king of Greece, who would own the distinction of having fulfilled this very prophecy of "laying the debris in the sea!" Y'all just jumped 258 years between verses eleven and twelve; from Nebuchadnezzar, the first "wave," to Alexander, the second "wave," with plenty of more ("waves") to follow. Get it?

ALEXANDER MEETS HIMSELF

Now when Alexander was building his causeway, he dispatched emissaries to Jerusalem "requesting" manpower and provisions for his project. Not used to being rebuffed, the Macedonian king received the shocking answer of basically, "No way, neighbor." The local authority in question is believed to have been the aged high priest, Jaddua, who ruled during the Second Temple period, mentioned in Nehemiah 12:22, *"The Levites in the days of Eliashib, Joiada, and Johanan, and **Jaddua**, were recorded chief of the fathers: also the priests, **to the reign of Darius the Persian.**"* In his "diplomatic" reply to Alexander, Jaddua tried to explain that he had signed a nonaggression pact with Darius III, and therefore could not assist one of his enemies, etc. Predictably, the message went over like a lead balloon.

After Alexander's conquest of Tyre, he set off for Gaza and Egypt with a planned "stop-over" in Jerusalem. As the king's arrival grew near, Jaddua naturally became nervous. But then—according to the pro-Roman Jewish historian, Flavius Josephus, writing in his famous twenty-volume historiographical tome, *Antiquities of the Jews* (circa AD 93)—several supernatural events suddenly occurred. For starters, Jaddua had a dream in which Jehovah basically assured him, "I've got this," and then instructed him to open the gates and go out to greet Alexander in his full priestly regalia, accompanied by his retinue (i.e., the more "pomp and circumstance," the better). Meanwhile, Alexander had apparently had his own dream three years earlier, wherein the same Jewish high priest appeared in living color, scaring the living daylights out of him! In any event, when the two finally met (after the Macedonians sacked Gaza), there was "magic" in the air. Alexander was particularly mesmerized by the high priest's mitre with its gold plate inscribed with the name of Israel's God. Josephus writes, "When Alexander saw the high priest, he reverenced God and saluted Jaddua; while the Jews with one voice greeted Alexander. When Parmenio, the general, gave expression to the army's surprise at Alexander's extraordinary act—that one who ought to be adored by all as king should adore the high priest of the Jews—Alexander replied, 'I did not adore him, but the God who hath honored him with this high-priesthood.'"

According to Josephus, Alexander then related how Jaddua had actually inspired his campaign against Darius in the first place:

> 'I saw this very person in a dream, in this very habit, when I was at Dios in Macedonia, who, when I was considering with myself how I might obtain dominion of Asia, exhorted me to make no delay, but boldly to pass over the sea, promising that he would conduct my army, and would give me the dominion over the Persians.' Alexander then gave the high priest his right hand, and went into the Temple and 'offered sacrifice to God according to the high priest's direction,' treating the whole priesthood magnificently.

Finally, with Alexander's pagan mind just about blown, Jaddua administered the *coup de grace* by whipping out a Hebrew scroll from the *Tanakh*:

> And when the book of Daniel was shown him, wherein Daniel declared that one of the Greeks should destroy the empire of the Persians, he supposed that he was the person intended, and rejoiced thereat. The following day Alexander asked the people what favors he should grant them; and, at the high priest's request, he accorded them the right to live in full enjoyment of the laws of their forefathers.

Like, *Double* Wow! Sustained for three years by a strange dream that Jaddua's God would somehow enable him to defeat the vast Persian Empire, Alexander now viewed the great truth with his own eyes, on a sacred scroll he could hold in his own hands!

Of course, while Josephus is normally accepted as a fairly reliable historian, most "scholars" dismiss his entire section chronicling Alexander's Palestine junket as mere "legend." According to one biased article that I read, the primary objection was that "Alexander is shown a book that was not yet written," reflecting the liberals' standard late-dating of Daniel. While any number of gaps and discrepancies will often hamper an accurate historiography (in this instance, one that is over four centuries old), we should also expect that Satan would pounce on such a powerful story relating to the Jews and the Holy Scriptures, not to mention the Lord Himself. Some might argue, based on Jaddua's age, that it was his son, Onias I, who actually met Alexander. (Yet, the prestigious *Jewish Virtual Library* gives Jaddua's reign as 371-320 BCE, thereby accommodating the account of Josephus.) The Talmud presents an altogether different version with Alexander meeting a different high priest, Simeon the Just. But, such variants only strengthen the general *basis* of the story—that the Macedonian King had a God-ordained historical encounter with *somebody*.

However, should you require a final "coincidence" to believe—do y'all recall how Satan tried to drown Paul and Luke on *their* way to Rome before *they* could write *their* material? Well, take a wild guess as to who else nearly had *his* writing career cut short on a similar grain run to the same destination? In his autobiographical work *Vita* (Life), Josephus writes, "But when I was in the twenty-sixth year of my age it happened that I took a voyage to Rome." After explaining the purpose, he continues:

> Accordingly I came to Rome, though it were through a great number of hazards by sea; for as our ship was drowned in the Adriatic Sea, we that were in it, being about six hundred in number, swam for our lives all the night; when, upon the first appearance of the day, and upon our site of a ship of Cyrene, I and some others, eighty in all—*by God's providence*—prevented the rest, and were taken up into the other ship.

Like Paul and Luke's deliverance in Acts 27, God obviously overruled Satan's desire to drown Josephus before he could record his account of Alexander's historic encounter with Jaddua. And, for what it's worth, with Joe born in AD 37, his wreck and subsequent arrival in Rome would have occurred in AD 63—the very same year Paul and his company left Melita and arrived in Rome! Thus, the two famous Jews were in the "Eternal City" at the same time!

Despite the fact that Alexander routinely patronized the "gods" of his conquered subjects (for obvious political capital), imagine the unprecedented convicting power of the Holy Spirit this worshiper of Zeus must have felt—*first*, upon entering the post-exilic Temple arm-in-arm with the high priest to worship the *true* God (Acts 17:23), and then, when he literally sees himself plastered across the pages of the Jews' Scriptures (Hebrews 4:12). If we assume that Jaddua gave Alexander the germane references in order, Daniel 2:39 would be the starting place, alluding to Greece as the third kingdom of brass. The next "Alexander sighting" (contrary to historic Fundamentalist positions) would be the bear in Daniel 7:5. The short explanation as to why most expositors misidentify Greece as the leopard in verse six constituting the *third* empire, would be, according to Dr. Peter Ruckman in the *Ruckman Reference Bible*, "[V]erses 17 and 24 make it perfectly clear that the Babylonian kingdom (the head of gold) is *through* before the kingdoms of these beasts arise."

However, chapter eight (cross-referenced with Daniel 11:1-4), would have made the greatest impact on the inquisitive king of Greece. While verses 19-22 clearly interpret verses 1-8, several *"handfuls of purpose"* scriptural buzz words are remarkable to behold. For instance, the uneven, two-horned ram, representing the combined forces of Media and Persia (the *"higher"* horn standing for alpha Persia), may be seen in verse four as originating in the *east* by a simple process of elimination (i.e., noting the three given directions of his "pushing"). Conversely, with the he-goat representing Alexander, verse five specifically states that he *"came from the west"* (i.e., Europe). It also says that he blew in from *"the whole earth, and touched not the ground."* The picture is reminiscent of the fast-moving Road Runner's feet spinning like wheels. In thirteen short years, Japheth's Hellenic descendant would "enlarge" *his* kingdom from Greece to India—a 3,000-mile stretch, encompassing two million square miles, representing over 90% of the then-known world!

One of the greatest fulfillments of Biblical prophecy occurs at verse seven. It constitutes the penultimate step in Japheth's "evolutionary" *enlargement* begun at Genesis 9:27. It is God Almighty's infallible answer to all asinine charges of "white supremacy" and "white privilege" — the absolute *worst* nightmare for every Critical Race theorist. (This deep truth will also explain the seemingly strange title for this chapter.) On October 1, 331 BC, Alexander the Great completed his conquest of Darius III's Persian Empire with a decisive victory at the Battle of Gaugamela (also called the Battle of Arbela), 62 miles west of Erbil, Iraq. To say that Alexander *"cast him down to the ground, and stamped upon him"* (verse seven) would be a pretty fair description of 40,000 Persian dead, against 500 Macedonians killed, and 5,000 wounded. Not too shabby for a five-foot dude outnumbered 6-1. And as verse six says that the goat *"ran unto him in the fury of his power,"* with verse seven adding, *"And I saw him come close unto the ram,"* we marvel that this is *precisely* what occurred. As Alexander was chasing Darius from the field—Ptolemy recording that he and his bodyguards literally crossed a ravine on the piled up bodies of dead Persians—he was abruptly forced to cut short the pursuit to save his left flank (only to lose his prize the next day to the sword of a traitorous Persian satrap).

As for that nutty chapter title, once when I was presenting this material, I was so tired that I accidentally said, "the Battle of *Guacamole*," and the brethren have yet to let me live it down! The bottom line in all of this is that Genesis 9:27 was finally fulfilled with Alexander the Japhethite eclipsing Darius the Shemite. And to ensure that Jaddua's "take" on Daniel 8:7 was not just a timely "Get out of jail free card" to hand to Alexander, the Holy Ghost interprets the passage at verse 21, *"And the rough goat is **the king of Grecia**: and the great horn that is between his eyes is **the first king**."* With the two iron legs of Rome replacing the remnants of Alexander's brass belly and thighs at Daniel 2:40, "Japheth the Elder" (Genesis 10:21) has never looked back—to *this* day (Daniel 2:41). Like I said, "White boys can't jump," but they *can* conquer the world!

ALEXANDER'S DEATH & LEGACY

Alexander died on June 11, 323 BC, in the palace of Nebuchadnezzar II in Babylon (where Nebuchadnezzar himself died at age 80). Until recently, the cause of his passing was shrouded in mystery, the leading guesses being malaria, typhoid, or assassination by poison. However, according to a new bombshell theory by Dr. Katherine Hall, senior lecturer at the Dunedin School of Medicine at the University of Otago, New Zealand, the young king may have succumbed to the rare, but serious autoimmune neurological disorder, Guillain-Barré Syndrome (contracted from an infection of *Campylobacter pylori*, a common bacterium at the time). As historical accounts state that his body didn't begin to show signs of decompensation for a full six days, Hall speculates that the increasing paralysis Alexander suffered, as well as the fact that his body needed less oxygen as it shut down, would have meant that his breathing was less visible, suggesting that he might not even have died when people thought he did.

A related irony, revealing Alexander's wisdom when dealing with his conquered subjects, involves Sisygambis, the mother of Darius III. After Gaugamela, Sisygambis had become devoted to Alexander while he would refer to her as "mother." Upon learning that the one who had *"cast* [her son] *down to the ground, and stamped upon him"* was dead, Sisygambis became so grief stricken that she had herself sealed into her rooms and literally starved herself to death in four days; thus, possibly expiring before him, according to Hall's startling thesis.

When asked on his deathbed who should succeed him, the heirless Alexander had purportedly replied, "The strongest." His massive empire was subsequently divided among his top *four* generals: Cassander (Macedonia), Ptolemy (Egypt), Antigonus (Asia Minor) and Seleucus (Mesopotamia), referred to as the *Diadochi* ("successors"). For a final look at Biblical prophecy, note how Daniel 8:8 prerecorded this event in 553 BC: *"Therefore the he goat waxed very great: and when he was strong, the great horn was broken; and for it came up **four** notable ones toward the four winds of heaven."* Once again, the inspired interpretation is found in verse 22, *"Now that being broken, where as four stood up for it, **four kingdoms** shall stand up out of the nation, but not in his power."*

Alexander was eventually entombed in Alexandria, Egypt. Given the fact that he was *never* defeated in battle, and that his military tactics and strategies are *still* studied at various military academies, we would expect Woke-aholics to attack his masculinity—especially since he also represents the quintessential Japhethite. Enter Oliver Stone's 2004 Warner Brothers "epic" box office *flop*, *Alexander*. David Edelstein, the chief film critic for *New York* magazine and CBS *Sunday Morning*, called the movie "a three-hour non-starter," accusing Stone of "making a mess of Mesopotamia." With absolutely no *conclusive* historical evidence, Stone cast the John Wayne of antiquity (played by Colin Farrell) as an open bisexual. He then blamed the poor showing on bad publicity (stemming from his raunchy liberties with the script).

While the LGBTQ+ perverts praised Oliver for his "boldness," the greatest outcry emanated from the male population of Greece itself. At one point a group of twenty-five Greek attorneys even threatened an international lawsuit over the perceived defamation of Alexander's manhood. Two years earlier, hundreds of Greeks stormed a conference after a speaker presented a paper on Alexander's purported homosexuality. That so many rank-and-file Greek males would be incensed by this mischaracterization speaks to the attitude his hardened combat veterans would have had in the fourth century BC. Though the Jewish Edelstein wasn't bothered by the bisexuality charge, after noting Alexander's "pouffy blond locks," he described Angelina Jolie (playing the Queen Mother) as "the only truly heroic presence in the picture," stating, "She could eat Colin Farrell for breakfast" (a more than subtle inference to Stone's effeminate character).

Incidentally, the case against Alexander's heterosexuality boils down to only two subjects: conjecture over his excessive remorse at the death of a lifelong friend, Hephaestion, and unsubstantiated allegations involving one "Bagoas the Younger," a sorry, underage, dancing Persian eunuch, and ex-favorite of Darius III, described as being "in the very flower of boyhood," thus, making Alexander a pedophile as well. The first is dismissed by a scriptural reality check revealing the picture of true friendship where David declares at the death of *his* best friend, *"The **beauty** of Israel is slain upon thy high places: how are the mighty fallen!...I am distressed for thee, my brother Jonathan: very pleasant hast thou been unto me: **thy love to me was wonderful, passing the love of women**."* (II Samuel 1:19, 26) Was "the man after God's own heart" bisexual? The other smear is too stupid to consider. To the contrary, there are numerous examples of Alexander's natural, red-blooded attraction to members of the opposite sex, not to mention his three marriages, along with 365-plus concubines who were paraded by him nightly for his selection. In the final analysis, I'll go with the *he*-goat butting Oliver's

"Alexander the Gay" fantasy back to the Jewish "Hellywood" that spawned it.

Which brings us to the end of the Macedonian's life. With an "aka" of Alexander "the Great," it was only natural that he would long to be remembered, eventually naming over *seventy* cities after himself (Psalm 49:11). Ironically, while the New Testament would cover the ancient world in Greek (a credit to his Hellenization policies), the greatest attempt to destroy its influence would emanate from the Catechetical School of *Alexandria*, Egypt (eventually producing the *Sinaiticus* and *Vaticanus* codices).

ALEXANDER IN ETERNITY

Only five barely intact accounts of Alexander's death survive to the present day (the recently discovered *Alexander Romance* being the exception). None are from eyewitnesses and all conflict to varying degrees. However, the most intriguing version, may also be the most mystifying, as it continues to enjoy a ubiquitous circulation while affording zero evidentiary corroboration. And, oddly enough, it does not even appear on *Snopes.com*, the "premier" fact-checking site that debunks fake news. Perhaps the main reason for its enduring appeal is because it rings true as the very thing a burned-out Alexander *would* have said when staring into the abyss at only thirty-two years of age. As my readers know my reputation for literary accuracy, I decided for once to relent and include this mysterious story for your scrutiny and enjoyment—for it certainly *could* be true.

The crux of "The Three Last Wishes of Alexander the Great," which were supposedly issued to his startled generals, are as follows: 1) "My physicians alone must carry my coffin because people should realize that no doctor on this earth can really cure anybody, as they are powerless and cannot save a person from the clutches of death; so let not people take life for granted." 2) "I desire that when my coffin is being carried to the grave, the path leading to the graveyard be strewn with gold, silver, and precious stones which I have collected in my treasury, to show the people that not even a fraction of gold will come with me, and that it is a waste of time to chase wealth." 3) "My third and last wish is that both my hands be kept dangling out of my coffin, as I wish people to know that I came empty-handed into this world and empty-handed I go out of this world." (That final request was a pretty good paraphrase of Paul's words in I Timothy 6:7, *"For we brought nothing into this world, and it is certain we can carry nothing out."*)

When a twenty-year-old Alexander visited the ascetic Greek philosopher Diogenes of Sinope, he asked him if there was anything he in his great riches could do for him. Diogenes replied, "Stand aside, you're blocking my sun." If Alexander did, in fact, experience remorse at life's end for having pursued temporal pleasures, the overarching factor would have to point back to that mesmerizing encounter with Jaddua a decade earlier. To review, if Josephus was accurate, Alexander was prompted to invade Persia by God Himself, his priestly emissary appearing to him in a dream; was escorted into the post-exilic Temple by the Jewish high priest (a man important enough that his name shows up in Nehemiah 12:11, 22); participated in a sacrifice to Jehovah; and fourthly, *got to see himself in the Holy Scriptures*—not to mention that by then he had also personally experienced the very fulfillment of those same prophecies!

Equally relevant would have been Alexander's acute awareness that all his "prayers" to Apollo, Hercules, Zeus, and the rest of his Pantheon pals for inner peace, real joy, and *especially*, deliverance from the *"fear of death,"* described in Hebrews 2:15 as keeping *all* men in perennial bondage—even self-perceived "demi-gods"—were about as useless as a piece of dental floss in a Willie Nelson concert! And let's not forget about those twin statements by Josephus that the Macedonian "reverenced" and "adored" the God of Jaddua. Remember, notwithstanding Alexander's lifelong religious commitment to appeasing "the gods," i.e., any and all "gods" (including those of a subjugated nation like Israel)—when push came to shove, the convicting power of the Holy Spirit would be the determining influence as to what Alexander truly felt in the *"chambers of his imagery."* (Ezekiel 8:12)

The Bible says in Job 14:10, *"But man dieth, and wasteth away: yea, man giveth up the ghost, and where is he?"* It has been said that the three greatest surprises in Heaven will be: the people who are *not* there who you expected to see; the people who *are* there who you *didn't* expect to see; and the fact that *you're* there! Do you suppose we would be shocked to meet King Nebuchadnezzar in the Glory world? Well, if the man whom God repeatedly called "my servant" wound up in "the other place," he'd be the only author of Scripture burning in the flames.

After contributing the entire fourth chapter of Daniel, the humbled Babylonian concluded, *"Now I Nebuchadnezzar praise and extol and honour the King of heaven, all whose works are truth, and his ways judgment: and those that walk in pride he is able to abase."* (Daniel 4:37)

Well, if there's a "snowball's chance in 'you-know-where'" that "Nebbie" *did* slide into Paradise, being greeted by Daniel and Ezekiel themselves, what about the possibility that his fellow Tyre team member wound up on the same side of that Great Gulf (Luke 16:26)? After all, they both expressed a reverence for the God of Israel. Ironically, they also both departed this world from the same place—that luxurious palace where Nebuchadnezzar learned that *"tribulation worketh patience."* (Daniel 4:28-33) For the record, I am no more guilty of wishful thinking regarding these polytheistic Gentile dogs than my Fundamentalist friends are for praying *their* "converts" into Heaven with a "1-2-3-repeat-after-me" sinner's prayer. And yet, having said all of this, if *my* salvation literally depended on a right guess, let's just say I'd let *you* put either one of them there. Nonetheless (and here comes my Yankee attempt at "crawdaddin'"), merely thinking positive—especially in the light of II Peter 3:9—one might posit that the best shot both kings had would lie somewhere between Acts 17:30 and Romans 2:7.

Note the beautiful cross-reference between *"And the times of this ignorance God winked at"* and Paul's witness to Alexander's descendants on Mars Hill, *"For as I passed by, and beheld your devotions, I found an altar with this inscription, TO THE UNKNOWN GOD. Whom therefore ye ignorantly worship, him I declare onto you."* (Acts 17:23) Speaking of "ignorance," most Fundamentalists *still* can't understand that *no* one was saved "looking *forward* to the cross," because *no* one had a clue as to the true reason for the incarnation of Jesus Christ—from Satan and his crowd (I Corinthians 2:8) to the first twelve "graduates" of the "Jerusalem Bible Institute" on the very eve of their Master's passion (Luke 18:34). The Holy Spirit plainly tells you in Romans 2 how pre-Calvary Gentiles were spared from Hell. Understanding that God alone remains the final judge of any man's heart, the surface formula in the Old Testament era was simple:

> *[T]he righteous judgment of God; Who will render to every man according to his deeds:* **to them who by patient continuance in well doing seek for glory and honour and immortality, eternal life:** *but unto them that are contentious, and do not obey the truth,*

*but obey unrighteousness, indignation and wrath, tribulation and anguish, upon every soul of man that doeth evil, of the Jew first, and also of the Gentile; **but glory, honour, and peace, to every man that worketh good**, to the Jew first, and also to the Gentile: for **there is no respect of persons with God**.* (Romans 2:5-11)

Y'all couldn't find Ephesians 2:8-9 in that passage if you used a SpaceX satellite. Ignorant as he was of the true God, if Alexander did *anything* "right," he certainly spent his whole life "seeking immortality" (i.e., those seventy-plus cities named "Alexandria"). Peter also chimed in on this subject, telling the Gentile household of Cornelius during the critical transition period in Acts, *"Of a truth I perceive that **God is no respecter of persons:** but in every nation **he that feareth him, and worketh righteousness, is accepted with him.**"* (Acts 10:34-35) And did you happen to notice those matching *"God is no respecter of persons"* references in Peter and Paul's inspired texts?

In any event, we'll obviously have to wait to see if Al made it in by the skin of his teeth. However, when the time arrived some 357 years later for the *"gospel of the grace of God"* (Acts 20:24) to finally reach Japheth's descendants, the Lord gave Paul His famous *"Macedonian Call,"* with the first Gentile convert on the continent trusting Christ in a city founded and named after Alexander's father, Phillip II of Macedonia (Acts 16:12-15). As my wife would say, "What a coinky-dinky!" Which leads us to the exciting theme of our next chapter…

8

The Ultimate Nugget in the AV 1611

IN 334 BC, Alexander brought an army of 48,100 soldiers, 6,100 cavalry, and a fleet of 120 ships manned by an additional 38,000 men across the Hellespont to begin his invasion of the declining Persian Empire of Darius III. As soon as Alexander landed on Asian soil, he thrust his sword into the ground and claimed the land as his own. Over three centuries later, the Apostle Paul would do the very same thing, only in reverse—thrusting his *spiritual* sword (Hebrews 4:12) into the land of Japheth, claiming it for the Lord Jesus Christ! While the previous chapter detailed the *physical enlargement* of Japheth, the present chapter will cover Japheth's *spiritual enlightenment*.

The time between Malachi, the final book of the Old Testament, and Matthew, the first book of the New Testament, is fittingly known as the intertestamental period. It has also been called the "Four Hundred Silent Years" because no new prophets were raised up by God until John the Baptist. However, should we learn in Heaven that Jaddua's indirect testimony via Alexander's dream—as preserved through the pen of Josephus—*was* true, it would constitute the stellar exception. Having left the deceased Macedonian at Daniel 8:8 with the prophecy that his "great" horn would fracture into four "notable" ones (subsequently fulfilled by the *Diadochi*), the following verse transports us 150 more years into the future for yet another "horn" to consider. *"And out of one of them came forth a **little horn**, which waxed exceeding great, toward the south, and toward the east, and toward the pleasant land."* Historically, *this* "little horn" (as opposed to the one in Daniel 7:8) was Antiochus IV (Epiphanes), king of Syria, who *"came forth"* from the Seleucid Empire in 175 BC. Seven years later, he would capture Jerusalem and fulfill Daniel 8:11 by desecrating the Temple when he offered the sacrifice of a pig on the altar to Zeus—a type of the *"abomination of desolation"* enacted in the Tribulation by the Antichrist, portrayed by that other "little horn" in Daniel 7:8 (Matthew 24:15; II Thessalonians 2:3-4).

Less than two centuries later, John the Baptist heralds the arrival of the long-awaited Jewish Messiah, Jesus of Nazareth. The despised cousins are promptly rejected and slain with our Lord's death occurring in AD 33, four years before the birth of *Yosef Ben Matityahu* (Joseph Ben Matthias aka "Flavius Josephus.") Once again, the "scholars union" has rejected the traditional account preserved by Josephus—the longest *secular* reference to Jesus in any first-century source—this time, for being a third- or fourth-century interpolation, i.e., for ringing "too Christian" to be true (as if genuine believers would resort to forgery to advance their spiritual cause). However, as modern scholarship maintains a demonstrable bias against truth, I have included the standard (and most despised) version of his extra-biblical reference to Jesus (and one to John the Baptist) as they appear in *Testimonium Flavianum* (*Testimony of Flavius Josephus*) in the extant Greek text of his *Jewish Antiquities* (circa AD 93-94).

> About this time there lived Jesus, a wise man, *if indeed one ought to call him a man.* For he was one who performed surprising deeds and was a teacher of such people as accept the truth gladly. He won over many Jews and many of the Greeks. *He was the Messiah.* And when, upon the accusation of the principal men among us, Pilate had condemned him to a cross, those who had first come to love him did not cease. He appeared to them *spending a third day restored to life,* for the prophets of God had foretold these things and a thousand other marvels about him. And the tribe of the Christians, so called after him, has still to this day not disappeared.

A second, more indirect reference to Jesus floated the belief that Rome's defeat of the Jewish rebellion in AD 70 was divine retribution for the martyrdom of James: "These things happened to the Jews to avenge James the Just who was the brother of Jesus, that is called the Christ. For the Jews slew him, although he was a most just man." He writes similarly about John:

> Now some of the Jews thought that the destruction of Herod's army came from God as a just punishment of what Herod had done against John, who was called the Baptist. For Herod had killed

this good man, who had commanded the Jews to exercise virtue, righteousness towards one another and piety towards God. For only thus, in John's opinion, would the baptism he administered be acceptable to God, namely, if they used it to obtain not pardon for some sins but rather the cleansing of their bodies, inasmuch as it was taken for granted that their souls had already been purified by justice.

To the scholars' "credit," they generally accept the last two accounts as "more" valid.

When Jesus was in the throes of agony, He prayed, *"Father, forgive them; **for they know not what they do.**"* (Luke 23:24) Because the Lord always got His prayers answered, the book of Acts opens with the Jews being given *another* chance to receive their Christ. In his second sermon, Peter shocks his Jewish audience by declaring that *they* had *"killed the Prince of life,"* after which he softens the blow, saying, *"And now, brethren, I wot that **through ignorance you did it**, as did also your rulers."* (Acts 3:15,17) He then pledges that if they would, as a *nation*, *"[r]epent and be baptized,"* after the manner of *John's* baptism (Acts 2:38; 19:3), their *national* sins would *"be blotted out, when the times of refreshing shall come from the presence of the Lord."* Such a sustained *national* repentance *would* have triggered the Tribulation and Second Advent, *"**and he shall send Jesus Christ**, which before was preached unto you: whom the heaven must receive until the times of restitution of all things, which God hath spoken by the mouth of all his holy prophets since the world began."* (Acts 3:19-21) What's that you say, preacher friend? Never heard this in your "Bible" college? (Maybe you should ask for a refund.)

Though many Jews initially responded (3,000 at Acts 2:41, with another 5,000-plus at Acts 4:4), the rulers eventually got the people under control and executed Stephen at Acts 7:59. While Stephen tries to emulate his Master's example by praying, *"Lord, lay not this sin to their charge"* (Acts 7:60), this time the Father is in no mood! With Saul of Tarsus introduced in verse 58 as a witness to Stephen's death, the end of the chapter is itself emblematic of the closing of Israel's grace period. A major shift in biblical hermeneutics follows: from Stephen's death in Acts 7, where the nation of Israel is placed on *temporary* hold, to Saul's conversion in Acts 9, where Christ's spiritual Body, comprising both Jews and Gentiles, begins to take center stage (Ephesians 3:1-12).

THE ONLY TIME JESUS REJOICED

Most so-called "Bible colleges" do a terrible disservice to their students by failing to elucidate the major *divisions* in the King James Bible (Genesis 1:4; II Timothy 2:15). Their professors are so preoccupied with "the Greek" that they can't read simple English. The Lord's contempt for "professional scholarship" is revealing. For instance, do you know the only place in Scripture where it is recorded that Jesus "rejoiced?" Shockingly, it was when He "rejoiced" because His Father made fools out of the "educated" crowd for thinking they were smarter than the common folk. *"In that hour **Jesus rejoiced in spirit**, and said, I thank thee, O Father, Lord of heaven and earth, that thou hast hid these things from the wise and prudent, and hast revealed them unto babes: even so, Father; for so it seemed good in thy sight."* (Luke 10:21) Another reference is Isaiah 28:9, *"Whom shall he teach knowledge? and whom shall he make to understand doctrine? them that are weaned from the milk, and drawn from the breasts."*

The late Dr. Ruckman, the greatest Bible teacher of the modern era, wrote accordingly: "While the Old Testament gives a history of the Father against the world, the New Testament gives a history of the Son against the Devil in the Gospels and a history of the Holy Spirit against the flesh in the Pauline Epistles." The Old Testament involves God's dealings with *nations*, while the New Testament involves God's dealings with *individuals*. Also, for every major New Testament *doctrine*, there is an Old Testament *type*: Abraham dispatching Eliezer to retrieve Rebecca for his son, Isaac, pictures God the Father sending the Holy Spirit to fetch the Church as a Bride for His Son, Jesus; while Enoch's sudden disappearance pictures the Rapture, Noah's family being subsequently preserved through the Flood pictures the Jewish remnant surviving the Tribulation, and so forth. Thus, a helpful cliché states, "The Old Testament is the New Testament *concealed*, while the New Testament is the Old Testament *revealed*."

However, the "scholars'" greatest dereliction of duty is their inability (or unwillingness) to segregate and explain the three *key* transition books of the New Testament—Matthew, Acts, and Hebrews. While *Matthew* provides the transition from the Old Testament to the New (triggered by Christ's death in Matthew 27:50), *Acts* is the dispensational bridge between Israel and the Church (triggered by Stephen's death in Acts 7:59), with *Hebrews* moving the reader from the Church Age to the Tribulation Period (triggered by the Rapture in I Thessalonians 4:16). The doctrinal heresies that arise from misinterpreting these three critical books are legion: *Catholics* break their necks on the wrong "rock" in Matthew; *Charismatics* get their generic glossolalia from Acts; while *Fundamentalists* flee to their lexicons to survive Hebrews. The great secret for successfully maneuvering through this dangerous minefield (i.e., the Holy Bible), will always be to heed Paul's admonition in II Timothy 2:7, *"Consider what **I** say; and the Lord give thee understanding in all things."* While the same author implies in II Timothy 3:16 that Christians can glean plenty of *devotional* help from *any* part of Scripture, whenever a *doctrinal* text appears to contradict a Pauline passage, *go with Paul* every time. Remember, *"God hath given thee all them that sail **with thee**."* (Acts 27:24)

For instance, the "Church of Christ" (and other soul-damning cults) victimizes many in the present Age of Grace by requiring water baptism for salvation on the basis of Peter's reasserted, exclusive charge to the *Jews* in Acts 2:41. Brother Ruckman's sermon, "Three Questions in Acts," provides a lucid outline for the "rightly divided," threefold division of *Jews*, *Gentiles*, and the *church of God* given in I Corinthians 10:32. In Acts 2:37, the men of Israel (*Jews*) ask Peter, *"Men and brethren, what shall **we** do?"* Because the "Apostle to the circumcision" is *continuing* the Old Testament message of John the Baptist to the nation of Israel, his answer contains both repentance *and* water baptism. *"Repent, **and be baptized** every one of you in the name of Jesus Christ for the remission of sins, and ye shall receive the gift of the Holy Ghost."* Then, in Acts 16:30, the Roman jailer (*Gentile*) asks Paul, *"Sirs, what must **I** do **to be saved**?"* Notice how the Jews' query does not deal with *personal* salvation, but rather appropriate restitution for having crucified their Messiah. And so, when addressing a lost Gentile in the Church Age, Paul's answer is simply faith alone with no water baptism: *"**Believe** on the Lord Jesus Christ, **and thou shalt be saved**, and thy house."* (Acts 16:31) Finally, in Acts 9—after the Lord answers the *unconverted* Saul's *"**Who** art thou, Lord?"* question with, *"I am Jesus whom thou persecutest"* —a *converted* Paul (*church of God*) asks the first "what" question for any new convert, *"Lord, **what** wilt thou have me to do?"* And note how he addresses his newfound personal Saviour as "Lord." Thus, the answer here is to get up and go into the city to await further instructions, whereupon Ananias arrives and baptizes the latest (and perhaps the greatest) Jewish convert to Christianity.

The primary reason for Paul's conversion was because God was beginning His transition away *from* Israel *to* the Church. This explains why so much doctrinal confusion can occur in the book of Acts as the "action" proceeds. The *temporary* replacement of Israel occurs in four stages: 1) In Acts 7 the process begins in Jerusalem; 2) In Acts 13 the Jews in Asia Minor are abandoned; 3) By Acts 18, God has dumped the Jews in Europe; 4) By Acts 28 they are consigned to a world-wide dispersion. Luke concludes his inspired treatise by recording Paul's departing diatribe to his lethargic brethren, *"Be it known therefore unto you, that the salvation of God is sent unto the Gentiles, and that they will hear it."* (Acts 28:28) Was Josephus listening at the door? In any event, Jerusalem was destroyed seven years later.

JAPHETH'S SPIRITUAL ENLIGHTENMENT

The study of Japheth's *spiritual enlightenment* during this period is truly amazing. Just prior to the recording of Paul's salvation experience in Acts 9, we have the conversion of the Ethiopian eunuch (a Jewish proselyte) in Acts 8. Thus, the first time Paul's *"gospel of the grace of God"* (Acts 20:24) is preached, it is delivered to a *"servant of servants,"* descended from Ham; once again, a message that was facilitated by that other Hamite "servant," helping Jesus to carry His cross. (As recently as the twentieth century, Haile Selassie I, Emperor of Ethiopia from 1930-1974, was a devout Christian who did much to evangelize his own people.) Then, while Paul temporarily disappears to Arabia, the Holy Spirit begins to wind down Peter's mostly Jewish ministry. Having opened the door of the *"kingdom of God"* to the Jews in Acts 2—by using the *"keys to the kingdom"* he received from Jesus in Matthew 16:19— Peter formally opens *"the door of faith to the Gentiles"* (Acts 14:27) with the conversion of Cornelius at Acts 10:24-48 (rehearsed in Acts 11:15). Consequently, the beautiful progression of New Testament salvation in the infant Church is complete: *Ham* in Acts 8; *Shem* in Acts 9; and *Japheth* in Acts 10.

The story of Cornelius is particularly precious to me because the Sunday morning I went forward to trust Christ (in Clarence Larkin's home church, no less), the pastor's sermon was dealing with this very subject. However, while Cornelius was not only the first full-fledged *Gentile* to be saved (the Ethiopian eunuch having been a Jewish proselyte), he also holds the second distinction of being the first *Japhethite* to trust the Gospel of the grace of God. (The centurion whose son Jesus healed, and especially the centurion at the cross, were transition believers on the cusp of the Church Age.) Yet, despite the Holy Spirit identifying Cornelius as *"a centurion of the band called the **Italian band,"*** he was not reached in his native land, rather in Asian Caesarea. But even here the Holy Spirit provides an incredible nugget. According to universal rabbinic tradition, Japheth is believed to have founded the ancient port city of Jaffa (biblical Joppa) *from which Peter was summoned to reach the first European* (Acts 10:5). One can even hear the phonetic connection between "Japheth" and "Jaffa."

When we arrive at Acts 13, the Holy Ghost calls Saul into full-time missionary work. The passage begins by mentioning two notable members of the church at Antioch—the first Gentile church and the first place where the disciples of Jesus were called "Christians" (Acts 11:26). *"Now there were in the church that was at Antioch certain prophets and teachers; as Barnabas, and **Simeon that was called Niger**, and Lucius of Cyrene, and **Manaen, which had been brought up with Herod the tetrarch**, and Saul."* Immediately following Barnabas, *"Simeon, that was called **Niger**"* is introduced. The word "niger" is Latin for "black" (no matter *what* they tell you), with two of the most important countries on the "Dark Continent" named *Niger* and *Nigeria.* Thus, while the so-called "N" word remains a major cultural conundrum (with the *same* "offended" blacks, who get apoplectic whenever a *white* person uses it, routinely shouting the *same* racial "slur" at one another), an enlightening spiritual blessing is overlooked. What the "woke" world can never grasp (I Corinthians 2:14) is that the only place in the Bible where the root word for the "N" word appears, in Acts 13:1 with good ole Bro. Niger, the Holy Spirit employs *him* as a precursor of the *beautiful* fruit that *"Japheth the Elder"* will eventually produce, i.e., Sister Wheatley and the rest of her brothers and sisters who dumped *Soul Train* for that "angelic train." Can I get a witness?

The other unusual member of the Church at Antioch is Manaen (meaning "comforter," or "counselor"), named fourth among the five main *"prophets and teachers."* As the text implies, Manaen is believed to have been a foster brother and "BFF" of Herod Antipas, the wicked

Jewish king who beheaded John and was complicit in the crucifixion of our Lord. Perhaps the soul-winning breach in Herod's household was made by Joanna, the wife of Chuza, mentioned in Luke 8:3 as being among the women followers of Jesus. A great cross-reference to further illustrate the penetrating power of the Gospel is Paul's account in Philippians 4:22, *"All the saints salute you, chiefly they that are of* **Caesar's household."**

After Saul's name shows up last on Luke's roll, verse two reads, *"As they ministered to the Lord, and fasted, the Holy Ghost said, Separate me* **Barnabas and Saul** *for the work whereunto I have called them."* It is noteworthy that Saul is called as a full-time missionary in the *thirteenth* chapter of Acts, for thirteen is the Bible number for sin and rebellion, and *this* man would spend the rest of his life going against the grain for his Lord! In Genesis chapter one, God's name appears in every verse *until* verse *thirteen*, then resumes in verse fourteen. Thus, the first time the Holy author disappears from His own Holy Book is at the first appearance of the number *thirteen*. The first mention of the word "sinner" is in Genesis 13:13, *"But the men of Sodom were wicked and* **sinners** *before the* LORD *exceedingly."* We further marvel that this text has *thirteen* words. Many other examples can be cited. The first mention of "thirteenth" is Genesis 14:4, *"Twelve years they served Chedorlaomer, and in the* **thirteenth** *year they* **rebelled."** The first mention of the word "thirteen" itself is Genesis 18:25, *"And Ishmael his son was* **thirteen** *years old, when he was circumcised in the flesh of his foreskin,"* the young man's profile and genetic posterity already given in Genesis 16:12 as being *"a* **wild** *man."*

In the New Testament, Mark 7:21-23 lists *thirteen* sins that emanate from the heart of rebellious man. In John 6:70, Jesus declares, *"Have not I chosen you twelve, and one of you is a devil?"* With thirteen people in the room, the "devil" was probably the one with *thirteen* letters in his name, Judas Iscariot (Luke 22:3). Finally, the Antichrist shows up in Revelation 13, while the same inspired author "just happens" to employ *thirteen* words for the superscription upon the Papal head of the "Great Whore" in Revelation 17:5— *"MYSTERY, BABYLON THE GREAT, THE MOTHER OF HARLOTS AND ABOMINATIONS OF THE EARTH."*

However, as previously alluded regarding Paul, while about 85% of the "thirteens" in Scripture refer to something bad, one *can* be a rebel *for* God. For instance, II Kings 18:7 says of King Hezekiah, *"And the*

LORD *was with him; and he prospered withersoever he went forth:* **and he rebelled against the king of Assyria, and served him not.***"* Thankfully for us, Britain's *thirteen* North American colonies rebelled against King George III for breaking *his* contract with *them*. One of America's earliest flags displayed *thirteen* stripes, *thirteen* stars, and *thirteen* letters, "DON'T TREAD ON ME" —a far cry from our present milquetoast, mask-wearing generation. Thus, in the closing days of Laodicean apostasy, the Lord needs some rebels *"with* a cause" to "Keep on the Firing Line" while they "Hold the Fort," *especially* regarding the AV 1611. After our departure at the Rapture, a remnant of Tribulation saints will wage their own rebellion against the Antichrist, being rallied by those *thirteen* words in the *thirteenth* verse of the *thirteenth* chapter of the book of Hebrews: *"Let us go forth therefore unto him without the camp, bearing his reproach."* I once heard of a veteran missionary to Japan having made a profound statement, "The duty of every Christian, at any time, is to discern the spirit of the age, *and then go diametrically against it.*" As Sergeant York would say, "If it's agin the *Book,* then I'm agin *it.*"

A total of *thirteen* New Testament books begin with the single word "Paul," the Lord's *thirteenth* apostle, *"born out of due time"* (I Corinthians 15:8)—and the greatest "good" *rebel* in Church history! The heart of the Pauline Epistles is I Corinthians 13:13, *"And now abideth faith, hope, charity, these three; but the greatest of these is charity."* The inspired layout in Acts 13 constitutes a revelation in itself. While the narrative begins *one* way (in two particulars), it ends in a totally *different* way. In verse two, the divine order is "Barnabas and Saul," showing that the great Apostle began his service as a "second fiddle," and, with his Hebrew name. Yet, at verse forty-three, it is "Paul and Barnabas," showing that our hero was now the "Big Enchilada," and henceforth operating under his Roman name for maximum influence with his Gentile listeners. So, where do you suppose the inspired switch occurred? Would verse *thirteen* be a good guess? *"Now when **Paul and his company** loosed from Paphos, they came to Perga in Pamphylia: and John departing from them returned to Jerusalem."*

TIME TO GO AFTER THE POLLOCKS AND WOPS

With Paul taking the reins at Acts 13:13, the Holy Spirit would now propel him toward his greatest mission—infusing the land of Japheth with the saving Gospel of the Lord Jesus Christ! While the disciples were called Christians first at Antioch in Asia Minor, Paul would now begin his westward trek by planting and/or influencing Gentile churches in Philippi, Thessalonica, Corinth, Berea, Athens, and Rome. With "Alexandrians" mentioned among Stephen's antagonists in Acts 6:9, Satan was not about to leave Paul alone while he attempted to capitalize on Alexander the Great's geopolitical conquests. While Acts 27:2 mentions *"one Aristarchus, a **Macedonian** of Thessalonica"* as accompanying Paul and Luke on their perilous voyage aboard that Roman grain ship, we note that Paul's arch nemesis was *"**Alexander** the coppersmith"* (I Timothy 1:20; II Timothy 4:14).

The great transition begins when Paul is on his second missionary journey. While engaged in his normal church-planting routine in Asia Minor, the Apostle suddenly encounters a pair of disconcerting roadblocks at Acts 16:6-7, the likes of which could only be viewed as "hate" by satanic critical race theorists. Akin to Genesis 9:27, it smacks of "white privilege," discriminating against "people of color," etc. Luke writes, *"Now when they had gone throughout Phrygia and the region of Galatia, **and were forbidden of the Holy Ghost to preach the word in Asia**, after they were come to Mysia, they assayed to go into Bithynia: **but the Spirit suffered them not.**"* The next verse has them at the coastal city of Troas, on the western shore of Turkey, adjacent to the Aegean Sea. *"And they passing by Mysia came down to Troas."* Having planted numerous churches in Shemite Asia, Paul will now learn that God wants him to go after the "Pollocks," the "Wops," and all the rest of Japheth's European descendants—with the end goal being Gomer's people in the British Isles (Genesis 10:2).

As Paul's Holy Ghost detour was destined to begin with Alexander's kin, he receives his famous "Macedonian Call" in verse nine, *"And a vision appeared to Paul in the night; There stood a man of **Macedonia**, and prayed him, saying, Come over into **Macedonia**, and help us."* The team wastes no time obeying their Captain, verse ten declaring, *"And after he had seen the vision, **immediately** we endeavoured to go into **Macedonia**, assuredly gathering that the Lord had called us for to preach the gospel unto **them**."* Finally, the next verse constitutes the climactic spiritual counterpart to Daniel 8:7 as it relates to the fulfillment of Genesis 9:27. Note the nautical terms as Paul and his company depart Asia across the Aegean Sea to Europe. *"Therefore **loosing** from*

*Troas, we came with a **straight course** to Samothracia, and the next day to Neapolis.*" After an overnight stop on the Greek island of Samothracia, Paul and Luke make their dramatic landing at *Neapolis* (meaning "New City"). When the Apostle plants his foot down, *it marks the first time the Gospel of the grace of God will have touched the Continent!* (As Horace Greeley would unknowingly concur, this insignificant appearing geography lesson illustrates the great Bible principle that the Holy Ghost generally moves East to West, while error goes in the opposite direction). As previously mentioned, the first European conversion *on European soil* will occur just three verses later in the city founded by, and named after, Alexander's father—Philip II of Macedon. *"And a certain woman named **Lydia**, a seller of purple, of the city of Thyatira, which worshipped God, heard us: whose heart the Lord opened, that she attended unto the things which were spoken of Paul."* (Those five profound words, *"whose heart the Lord opened,"* can help some of my shallower readers to see the error of their sincere but disastrous hyper-evangelistic "1-2-3, repeat after me" methodology.) After her baptism, the grateful businesswoman opens her house to become what is believed by some to be the first New Testament church in Europe (Acts 16:15, 40).

Thus, the *spiritual* "enlargement of Japheth" is off and running with Lydia being the first European Gentile to find shelter under Shem's tents (courtesy of Paul, the Gospel-preaching tentmaker). But, while you're shouting it out, allow me to ask you a question. Do y'all recall that the name Japheth means "beautiful," as in *"How **beautiful** are the feet of them that preach the gospel of peace, and bring glad tidings of good things!"* (Romans 10:15) Well, take a wild guess as to what the name *Lydia* "just happens" to mean, particularly in light of her providential role as the first born-again Japhethite on Japhethite soil. As Maxwell "Max" Smart, aka "Agent 86" (portrayed by Don Adams), might have said into his legendary shoe phone in the 1960s television sitcom, *Get Smart*— "Would you believe…BEAUTIFUL?" (Can't make this stuff up, neighbor!)

You say, "Brother Grady, is *that* the ultimate nugget in the AV 1611?" Hardly! Keep in mind that the pinnacle of Japheth's spiritual enlightenment will be the United States of America—as routed through the birthplace of the King James Bible. After all, if you want to know your exact *time* and *location* you have to go to England. The Greenwich meridian serves as the basis for the world's standard time zone system,

Greenwich Mean Time (GMT), as well as the imaginary line used to indicate 0° longitude that passes through Greenwich (a borough of London) and terminates at the North and South poles. Among other standards, in the heating and energy world, the acronym BTU does not stand for "'Beijing' or 'Botswana' Thermal Units." Consequently, if you want to know where to find the *right* Bible you might want to try Great Britain, home of the 1611 King James Authorized Version, for as King Solomon wrote, *"Where the word of a king is, there is power"* (Ecclesiastes 8:4). And so, without further ado, to discover the greatest English nugget in the AV 1611—*just look at the Scripture address where Paul's foot first touches the Land of Japheth at Neapolis!* (And like, *duh*, you want to fritter your life away on social media? Really??)

9

A Quiet and Peaceable Life

I
T IS NO coincidence that exactly *one* verse after Europe's first independent, New Testament "Baptist" church was planted at Acts 16:15, an intense Satanic attack begins, one that lands Paul and Silas in the local hoosegow, having received *"many stripes."* While some "drama queen" Christians appear to crave the spotlight of persecution, here the Holy Spirit is careful to reveal Paul's practical approach to handling the possessed damsel and her public harassment. Most Bible believers miss the first part of verse eighteen. *"**And this she did many days**. But Paul, being grieved, turned and said to the spirit, I command thee in the name of Jesus Christ to come out of her. And he came out the same hour."* Paul obviously rebuked the spirit *only as a last resort,* instinctively knowing where a confrontation would land them. I've often imagined how he would begin each day—*slowly* sticking his head out the door, looking both ways, then *tiptoeing* out, ever so quietly—only to have the crazed hellcat jump out of nowhere and renew her hysteria, *"These men are the servants of the most high God, which shew unto us the way of salvation."* (Acts 16:17)

Thankfully, the man who would pen Romans 8:28 (not to mention Romans 5:3) watched as the Lord used the ensuing fiasco—along with *their* praise-filled prayer meeting and *His* earth-shattering "Amen!" — to grow the new church by receiving the jailor and *"his house"* into the local membership as the first additions in Europe! Today's wimpy Covid-era pastors who jump *every* time the government says to— hiding behind Romans 13:1, while dancing around Acts 5:29—would do well to put their "big-boy boxers" on and note how the author of Romans 13:1 handled *his* little Napoleons. *"But Paul said unto them, They have beaten us openly uncondemned, being Romans, and have cast us into prison; and now do they thrust us out privily? nay verily;* **but let them come themselves and fetch us out.**" (Acts 16:37)

By the time Paul writes I Timothy in AD 65, he had already endured two years of house arrest in Rome (Acts 28:30). Though released for a season, he now understands that the Church would soon be facing serious civil persecution. Caesar had initially viewed the first Christians as merely a sect of cantankerous Jewry, whom the government grudgingly tolerated to avoid unnecessary confrontations over their fanatical ideologies. However, as they began to notice that the Jews themselves *"spake evil of that way"* (Acts 19:9), they promptly reassessed the followers of Jesus as a new and possibly greater threat to Rome. Even Paul's long-standing immunity afforded by his Roman citizenship would protect him no longer. Therefore, God's children would require a very special charge.

The stated purpose of Paul's first epistle to his young protégé is given in I Timothy 3:14: *"These things write I unto thee, hoping to come unto thee shortly: but if I tarry long, that thou mayest know how thou oughtest to behave thyself in the house of God, which is the church of the living God, the pillar and ground of the truth."* With chapter one comprising Paul's introduction, he gets down to business with the opening four verses in chapter two. Note the very *first* directive the Holy Spirit leads Paul to give the New Testament Church: *"I exhort therefore, that, **first of all**, supplications, **prayers**, intercessions, and giving of thanks, **be made** for all men; **for kings, and for all that are in authority; that we may lead a quiet and peaceable life in all godliness and honesty**. For this is good and acceptable in the site of God our Saviour; **who will have all men to be saved**, and to come unto the knowledge of the truth."* (I Timothy 2:1-4) It is *impossible* to overstate the importance of this watershed petition!

For our opening observation, the very one who initiated the request *lost his head the following year.* So much for that *"quiet and peaceable life."* By AD 90, *all* of the Apostles had likewise suffered martyrdom, except *"that disciple whom Jesus loved."* (John 21:7) According to the early Church leader Tertullian (AD 155-240), writing in *Prescriptions Against Heretics,* upon Emperor Domitian's order, John was "plunged, unhurt, into boiling oil," before a live audience in the Colosseum. Following his shocking, supernatural survival he was "then remitted to his island exile." Obviously, the Lord spared him so he could earn his spiritual moniker, "John the Revelator."

FORWARD TO THE PAST

God's people understand that Revelation is a *futuristic* book (Revelation 1:1; 19:10). However, given our end-day propensity to narcissism (II Timothy 3:2), we often forget that we are not the first believers to peer into the future. While the Rapture is often described as the next event on God's prophetic calendar for *us*—the *entire* Church Age was looming before the first-century Christians. Thus, the Holy Spirit uniquely structured the content in chapters two and three as a prescient panoramic view of the whole age with each "church" constituting a specific period of church history in perfect chronological order. Because God is the ultimate multitasker, John's seven letters—written to seven local first-century assemblies, addressing seven sets of particular scenarios—could also afford *any* Christian, in *any* age, general *devotional* help, while simultaneously providing specific *prophetic* coordinates in real-time for *all* believers in their respective historical periods. Thus, "lukewarm" apostates in *our* time are easier to comprehend in light of the profile contained in John's last epistle to Laodicea (Revelation 3:14-22). Finally, any passages that contradict Paul would apply *doctrinally* to Tribulation or Millennial saints. (What's that you say? You never heard any of this in your "dumb dogs that won't bark" TR school?)

And so, like those old-time Ringling Brothers Circus acts when a man was blasted out of a cannon into a large horizontal net, John became *God's* human cannonball act as the Holy Ghost fired *him* twenty centuries across the Church Age. In a surreal setting, John was literally transported into the future to write the book of Revelation. Though he awoke that morning on Patmos, he crossed over a *major* time zone at verse ten: *"I was **in the Spirit on the Lord's day."*** In a typical Bible *college*, "The Lord's *day*" means *Sunday*; in a Bible *institute*, "The LORD'S day" means, **THE DAY OF THE LORD**—as in the entire scope of apocalyptic terror culminating at the Second Advent (Isaiah 13:6-11; Malachi 4:5). Therefore, from John's heavenly perspective, he is writing with the Church Age *behind* him, the Tribulation *beneath* him, and the Millennium *before* him. To emphasize the reality that John is writing in "The day of the LORD" —*with the Church Age behind* *him*—notice how he twice states, *"And I **turned** to see the voice that spake with me, and **being turned**, I saw seven golden candlesticks."* John had to *turn around* to see the seven churches (represented by the seven golden candlesticks), because they were *behind* him—i.e., in the past—positionally. Thus, *his* present—the end of the Tribulation—is *our* future. For, although the autograph of Revelation was *officially* written roughly 2,000 years ago, the author was *actually* over 2,000 years *in the future* when he wrote it. Thus, in God's mind, *"Forward to the Past"* beats *"Back to the Future"* any day. This is why he could testify in Revelation 1:3, *"for the time **is** at hand"* —as it certainly *was*—*then*. (Still think your "smart" phone is more intriguing than the Bible?)

I was saved less than six months when I first discovered this amazing hermeneutical approach during a course on Revelation at the Calvary Bible Institute in Media, Pennsylvania. The class textbook was the popular commentary, *Revelation*, by Dr. Harry A. Ironside. Besides being pulverized by the scary-looking, retractable time-line chart in the back of the book (one that I would later discover to be mild compared to the classic work by Clarence Larkin), the main thing I recall Dr. Ironside stressing was that the very *names* of the seven churches would set the tone for the entire period. For example, to cite John's seventh letter again, *Laodicea* just happens to mean "rights of the people," a spot-on depiction of end-day, selfie-stick Christians, as forecast in II Timothy 3:2: *"For men shall be **lovers of their own selves**."* Then, some twenty years later, when I began to teach Church History at Hyles-Anderson College (1986-1996), the only "textbook" that *we* used for the sixteen-week, three-hour course was Revelation, chapters two and three. Having summarized that material in a nineteen-page thumbnail sketch in my 2010 book, *Given By Inspiration*, I will now provide a further downsizing of that synopsis as we continue our pursuit of Japheth's *enlightenment*, as the trail winds through both ancient and modern Baptist history, and *especially*, as it relates to that Pauline petition for a *"quiet and peaceable life."*

THE APOSTOLIC AGE

When John was exiled to Patmos in AD 90, the first period of church history (detailed in his opening letter to the church at Ephesus, roughly AD 33-66) was already past, the author then living in the early stages of the second (Smyrna period, AD 66-313), corresponding to his second letter. (Note that the dates in this study are not dogmatic, but flexible, and can vary depending on perspective with some overlapping of the periods also quite natural.) *Ephesus* means "desirable one" and depicts the inaugural generation of Christianity, sometimes referred to as the Apostolic Age. (This later designation would move the arbitrary ending date to AD 100 with John's death.) The Ephesus age began with a bang for being separated and hardworking, but ended in a fizzle for having *"left thy first love."*

"*FAITHFUL UNTO DEATH*"

With the Apostle's own banishment serving to illustrate the theme of his second epistle, the Smyrna period covers the scope of imperial persecution envisioned by Paul a generation earlier. The name *Smyrna* stems from the root word "myrrh," an aromatic gum resin used for embalming the dead (John 19:39-40). In Revelation 2:9, John begins, *"I know thy works, and **tribulation**, and **poverty**, (but thou art rich)."* Archeologists tell us that many of the burial inscriptions in the catacombs below Rome contain misspelled words, confirming that the early Christians were mostly from the lower echelon of society (I Corinthians 1:27). As these believers were told in verse *ten* that they would *"have tribulation **ten** days"* (the number of the Gentiles) and that they should be *"faithful unto **death**,"* *Foxe's Book of Martyrs* records *ten* lethal persecutions that occurred (eight regional and two empire-wide), beginning with Nero in AD 67 and ending with Diocletian in AD 304. The two most celebrated martyrs of this period happened to be John's personal converts.

Ignatius was the venerable Bishop at Antioch. In AD 108, he was hauled some fifteen-hundred miles along a land and sea route to die in the Roman Colosseum (the very site where his mentor was miraculously delivered). Jolting along in an oxcart while chained between Roman guards, Ignatius wrote a series of poignant letters, which he left with the grieving congregations embracing him along the route. In his epistle to the Romans, he implored them not to interfere with his sentence, stating, "Allow me to become food for the wild beasts, through whose means it will be granted me to reach God. I am the wheat of God, and am ground by the teeth of the wild beasts, that I may be found the pure bread of Christ." He then made a shocking pledge: "May I enjoy the wild beasts that are prepared for me; and I pray they may be found eager to rush upon me, which also *I will entice to devour me speedily*, and not deal with me as with some, whom, out of fear, they have not touched. But if they be unwilling to assail me, *I will compel them to do so.*" Arriving at the Flavian amphitheater just before the games were to close for the evening, Ignatius was whisked in and promptly eviscerated before the blood-thirsty patrons.

Born in AD 69, Polycarp was elevated to the Bishopric of the Smyrna church itself. Pressed by his local magistrates to recant his faith, Polycarp issued his epic reply, "Eighty and six years have I served him and He hath done me no wrong; how then can I do this great disservice against my King?" For refusing to deny Christ, he would be burned alive. Foxe transports us to the funeral scene. "When they would have nailed him to the stake with iron hoops, he said, Let me alone as I am, for he that hath given me strength to suffer and abide the fire, shall also give power, that without this, your provision of nails I shall abide, and not stir in the midst of this fire or pile of wood. Which thing when they heard, they did not nail him, but bound him." Thus, the last bishop to have personally met an apostle, perished in AD 155.

Multitudes of pagans were converted after witnessing such horrific spectacles, inspiring the maxim by Tertullian, "The blood of the martyrs is the seed of the church." Conversely, many a modern-day heathen took notice of those pastors who bowed their knees to the tyrants behind the unconstitutional 2020 China-virus *casus belli*. I mean, *really*, who could possibly miss the contrast between, "May I enjoy the wild beasts that are prepared for me" and, "But if I keep my church open, I might get a fine." However, the most important observation germane to these first two historical periods is that our ancient Baptist forefathers had *yet* to experience that *"quiet and peaceable life"* for which the Apostle Paul had exhorted them to pray! Which brings up another shocking reality check for many anemic Baptists who were taught to self-identity as just another Protestant denomination less than five-hundred years old. Charles Haddon Spurgeon, aka "The Prince of Preachers," strongly disagreed:

> We believe that the Baptists are the original Christians. We did not commence our existence at the Reformation, we were reformers before Luther or Calvin were born; we never came from the Church of Rome, for we were never in it, but we have an unbroken line up to the apostles themselves. We have always existed from the very

days of Christ, and our principles, sometimes veiled and forgotten, like a river which may travel underground for a little season, have always had honest and holy adherents. Persecuted alike by Romanists and Protestants of almost every sect, yet there has never existed a Government holding Baptist principles which persecuted others; nor I believe any body of Baptists ever held it to be right to put the consciences of others under the control of man. We have ever been ready to suffer, as our martyrologies will prove, but we are not ready to accept any help from the State, to prostitute the purity of the Bride of Christ to any alliance with the government, and we will *never* make the Church, although the Queen, the despot over the consciences of men.

God's later bestowments to His children (Ephesians 4:11)—like the great Baptist pastor and teacher, Clarence Larkin (1850-1924)—would perfect our spiritual understanding that *all* believers comprise Christ's Bride, being synonymous with the Body of Christ and *the* Church itself. My "Baptist Brider" friends who insist that any "church" (or "body") other than a *local* entity must be the "Roman Catholic Church," apparently cannot rightly divide between Satan's *universal* church (Rome) and Christ's *invisible* Church (His Body). In any event, Spurgeon's statement being primarily focused on the local church is 99% spot-on regarding our ancient Baptist heritage.

THE CHURCH MARRIES UP

The third era of ecclesiastical history ushered in a major shift in Satan's strategy. Unable to destroy the church from *without*, he would now attempt to destroy it from *within* (Acts 20:29-30). The *Pergamos* period begins in AD 313 with the coronation of Constantine I (aka "Constantine the Great"), the so-called first "Christian" emperor of Rome (at least according to most Bible colleges). Why anyone would trust some guy whose name started with "Con" is like *beyond* me (ditto Jim Bakker's homie, Jonathan "Cohn" and his *Harbinger* books). Constantine basically made the Church "an offer they couldn't refuse." As a "fellow believer" (claiming to have prayed the "sinner's prayer" after seeing a giant cross in the sky), he would now *elevate* Christianity to the official religion of the empire (*religio licita*), while subsequently banning paganism (i.e., the new *religio illicita*). Of course, the only "catch" was that the Church would now have to be married to *him*, instead of to Jesus. Thus, the name *Pergamos* just happens to be a compound word meaning "marriage and elevation." After two-and-a-half-centuries of persecution through the Smyrna era, the deal sounded sweet; so, the church "married up" — from the *catacombs* to the *cathedrals—inaugurating the first Church-State relationship in history*. The "new normal" would now entail Christ's Bride embracing a Roman Caesar—the one enthroned in *"Satan's seat."* (Revelation 2:13) Thankfully, however, a faithful remnant told their "Christian" Emperor, "Thanks, but *no* thanks," remaining underground to establish the bedrock Baptist distinctive of separation of Church and State.

The Lord added a scary warning in verse sixteen: *"Repent; or else I will come unto thee **quickly**, and will fight against them with the sword of my mouth."* (Note that qualifier, "quickly.") Connie's hirelings were so elated that the *heat* was *off* and the *honor* was *on,* that they started preaching that the Kingdom had arrived. But then, the *sword* came upon everyone "quickly." Less than twenty-five years after Constantine's death: Europe is invaded in AD 360 by Attila the Hun, aka "The Scourge of God;" the Roman Emperor Valens is killed and his army routed by the Visigoths in 378; then, Rome itself is sacked by Alaric in 410 (the first time in 800 years). However, amidst the widespread "clerical" defections, a number of *real* preachers were following the example of Christ's *"faithful martyr"* Antipas (verse thirteen); men such as, Athanasius and Chrysostom in the East, Patrick in Ireland, Columba in Scotland, and the Donatists in North Africa. About this time, Ulfilas, meaning "Little Wolf," translated the Bible into Gothic (one of the earliest translations to enter the "Land of Japheth"). Once again, however, the "deep truth" to discern here is that the persecution would *continue*—with Christ's Church *still* unable to experience that *"quiet and peaceable life."*

NONE OTHER BURDEN

John's fourth letter was to the church in *Thyatira,* Lydia's native city. The content is full of historical nuggets. The prophetic profile in the name of this "church" is a "dead" giveaway, "continual sacrifice." It references the blasphemous Roman Catholic Mass—where the wafer and wine are mysteriously *transformed* into Christ's "literal" body and blood as the Catholic priest re-sacrifices Him on the altar to be cannibalized by "the faithful" —as well as the "continual sacrifice" of the true people of God at the hand of pagan Rome itself. (The former is refuted by Hebrews 9:28; 10:2, 10-14.) The precursor to this period occurred when Constantine, seeing the handwriting on the wall (in regards to the coming barbarian incursions), fulfilled Daniel's interpretation of a second iron leg by deserting the "eternal city" in AD 330 for his new capital in Turkish Byzantium (the egomaniac promptly renaming it "Constantinople"). And so, after the last Emperor of the old Roman Empire, Flavius Romulus Augustulus, was knocked off his throne in AD 476 by the mutinous German mercenary leader, Odoacer, *a major leadership vacuum occurred among the common people.* (Crazy as it sounds, this truth can even be illustrated in the Hollywood movie, *Forrest Gump,* when—after Forrest abruptly ends his three years, two months, fourteen days, and sixteen hours of running with the words, "I'm pretty tired; I think I'll go on home" —his stunned jogging devotees exclaim, *"Now* what are we supposed to do?") Naturally, the corrupt Bishop in Rome (holding the most religious prestige among all of Europe's churches given that his parish was located in the capital itself) was only *too* happy to fill the void. (In AD 476, the child molester in question just happened to be named "Simplicius;" how appropriate.) This is precisely how the papacy would evolve from "Satan's Seat" to the "Chair of Peter," where "El Papa" would henceforth speak "ex-cathedra," i.e., "infallibly." (And should anyone be interested, the reason why all popes wear that half-a-grapefruit (*tiara*) on their head is because they are trying to emulate Jaddua's priestly mitre.)

Historically, the period covers a thousand-year span, from AD 500 to 1500. The Holy Spirit sets the tone in the opening verse, totally ignoring Mary, while having the *"Son of God,"* with His *"eyes like unto a flame of fire, and...feet of fine brass,"* address the wicked Roman hierarchy. The next verse makes a fleeting reference to an ancient practice known as "corporal works of mercy," i.e., the compassionate acts provided by local monasteries in the best of medieval traditions (hospitals, schools, orphanages, asylums, Just War theory, et al.). Surprisingly, to give credit where credit is due, God was willing to commend the biblically illiterate monks and nuns for alleviating suffering, yet have *nothing* positive to say about the professing Christians in the Laodicean Age. However, the opening word in verse twenty ("Notwithstanding"), signals that all "Purgatory" was about to break loose. The introduction of the evil Phoenician Queen, Jezebel (a flashback to Tyre), offers an insightful correlation to the Vatican's infatuation with "all things female" (Holy *Mother* Church; Mary, *Queen* of Heaven; *Mother* Theresa; Our *Lady* of Fatima; "celibate" pedophiles dressing like *mothers,* calling themselves *Fathers,* etc., not to mention the Holy Spirit's designation of Rome in Revelation 17:1 and 5 as the *"great **whore**"* and *"MYSTERY, BABYLON THE GREAT, THE **MOTHER** OF **HARLOTS** AND ABOMINATIONS OF THE EARTH").*

As Jezebel brought idolatry to Israel, Rome accomplished the same within the professing Christian church. The Vatican "wafer-god" of transubstantiation can be seen in the words, *"to eat things sacrificed unto idols."* (Revelation 2:14) The harlot's incorrigible addiction to spiritual immorality is confirmed by the words, *"and she repented not."* (Revelation 2:21) The cross-reference at Revelation 17:1-2 reveals that her fornication occurred with *"the kings of the earth."* Their offspring— *"the inhabitants of the earth"* —being *"made **drunk** with the wine of their fornication"* is an accurate depiction of the dismal conditions of medieval "life" (see William Manchester's graphic work, *A World Lit Only by Fire).* As this 1,700-year-long illicit church-state relationship began with Rome's first "Christian" Emperor, note the unmistakable likeness: "CONSTANTINE **THE GREAT**" — "MYSTERY, BABYLON **THE GREAT**."

The Lord fulfilled His threat in verse twenty-three to *"kill her children with death"* by allowing over 50% of Europe's youth to die before age thirteen. In addition to the standard "staples" of famine, drought, floods, pestilence, isolation, ignorance, fear, superstition, brigandage, warfare, depression, suicide, and genocide, other "happy times" included the Islamic and Viking invasions, the "Holy Wars" (including the insane Children's Crusade), the Hundred Years War, and the Black *Death* that wiped out one-third of the Continent (some twenty-five million people). For preferring a papal toe to a nail-scarred foot, Japheth's benighted inhabitants got to experience the "joy" of a *Satanic* Millennium.

We are now about to move into some *heavy* stuff neighbor. (Better strap on that seatbelt!) So far, the Lord Jesus has been addressing the corrupt Vatican hierarchy. However, He suddenly cracks the door open with a reference to the Pope's victims, stating, *"and all the **churches** shall know that I am he which searcheth the reins and hearts."* (Revelation 2:23) As the cross-reference in Revelation 2:11 indicates, this is an obvious reference to the *local* New Testament "churches" scattered throughout the papal-controlled Thyatira era. But *now*, note the unmistakable language as Jesus shifts His diatribe away from Rome in order to exhort our courageous Baptist forefathers: *"But unto you I say, and unto **the rest in Thyatira**, as many as have not this doctrine, and which have not known the depths of Satan, as **they** speak; I will put upon **you** none other burden. But that which **ye** have already **hold fast till I come**."* (Revelation 2:24-25)

The great epiphany here is not so much what the Lord told them *to* do— *"hold fast"* —but what He implies that they were *not* expected to do—*no city-wide crusades in the Dark Ages*. Furthermore, the phrase, *"But that which ye have already,"* indicates that this is what the churches had already *been* doing ever since Paul uttered that prayer request for a *"quiet and peaceable life."* Simply put, until God saw fit to answer that petition by providing a sympathetic government (i.e., those *"kings and...all that are in authority"*), they would have to *continue* to *"hold fast."* As with our own last-days admonition to *"continue"* in II Timothy 3:14, this is not to say that the early Christians were to ignore the Great Commission during their *"perilous times."* It meant that as their efforts would be severely hampered by Rome's overpowering intolerance, they would just have to make the best of the situation with their ecclesiastical survival being the top priority. Just as the underground congregations in Communist countries today often sing in whispered tones, believers in the Dark Ages had to fly below the radar as well. A famous nineteenth-century engraving entitled "Waldensian Peddlers" depicts two Piedmont missionaries, disguised as traveling salesmen, risking their lives by presenting the Scriptures to a well-to-do couple (whom they perceived as being open to the Gospel) during the "prospective sale."

As Paul learned within a few verses of Lydia's conversion, a less-than-favorable government will often hinder personal evangelism. He, therefore, ends his exhortation by providing the spiritual purpose behind the request, *"For this is good and acceptable in the sight of God our Saviour; **who will have all men to be saved**, and to come unto the knowledge of the truth."* (I Timothy 2:3-4) At the risk of sounding too simplistic, freedom to preach brings freedom to hear, i.e., *"the knowledge of the truth."* And so, an army of New Testament churches held on, by *whatever* moniker their particular Vatican antagonists decreed. A shortlist of these despised "sects" would include: Petrobrusians, Arnoldists, Cathari, Henricans, Paterines, Albigensians, Waldensians, and those ultimate right division advocates—the *Paulicans*. Thankfully, however, as with General Sherman's signal message to the besieged Federal forces at Altoona Pass, Georgia, "Hold the fort; I am coming," help was definitely on the way. In 1380, the first English-language Bible manuscripts were produced by John Wycliffe at Oxford. As printing was not yet discovered, the Wycliffe Bible had to be meticulously hand copied, requiring about ten months of steady work by an experienced copyist to produce just one Bible. The rental fee for a single hour with so costly a treasure was an entire load of hay.

"His Holiness" eventually threw a hissy fit! In AD 1415, the Council of Constance had Wycliffe's books and bones burned and the ashes dumped in the River Swift, which flowed through his town. A far worse fate would meet John's disciples, known as "Lollards," a derisive term meaning "babblers." (Acts 17:18) As Foxe relates, their experience was anything *but a "quiet and peaceable life."*

> The Lollards were tracked to the lonely, unfrequented places where they met, often under shadow of night, to worship God. Neighbor was made to spy upon neighbor [like the Covid-19 "mask police"]; husbands and wives, parents and children, brothers and sisters, were beguiled or forced to bear witness against each other. The Lollards' prison again echoed with the clanking of chains; the rack and the stake once more claimed their victims.

This was the movement that inspired Brian Melbancke's enduring proverb, "Patience is a virtue," for surely *"tribulation worketh patience."* (Romans 5:3) Consequently, the Lord had John conclude his fourth letter with a special "signal message" of His own for the overcomers of that age: *"And I will give him **the morning star."*** (Revelation 2:28) While the *doctrinal* interpretation of this title applies to Jesus Christ, in the *historical* application, given his epoch-making English translation of the Holy Bible, Wycliffe's "aka" just happens to be *"The Morning Star* of the Reformation."

THE PROTESTANT REFORMATION

The meaning of "Sardis," the name of John's *fifth* church, is "red ones," more specifically, *"bloodied* ones." (Five is also the Bible number for *death.*) While the *"great whore"* spent the Dark Ages *"drunken with the **blood of the saints**, and with the **blood of the martyrs of Jesus**"* (Revelation 17:6), the mother of all bloodbaths broke out when the nations of northern Europe decided to dump their "infallible" *Pontifex Maximus* and his "Holy See." The catalyst for this fourteenth-century revolt was that "Morning Star" of the previous period. The Wycliffe Bible sparked a major upheaval (both religious and political) that was quickly spread by his faithful "babblers."

John's letter to Sardis marks the end of the Middle Ages and catalogs *the* watershed event of the turbulent sixteenth and seventeenth centuries known as the mighty "Protestant Reformation," that "name" referred to in the opening verse, *"I know thy works, **that thou hast a name."*** (Revelation 3:1) Having jumped the English Channel onto the Continent, Wycliffe's message was now being propagated by the likes of Martin Luther, John Hus, Girolamo Savonarola, and one *really* sick individual, John Calvin, aided by his sycophant protégé, Ulrich Zwingli. In 1516, the Rotterdam scholar Desiderius Erasmus fanned the spiritual flames by releasing the first-ever printed copy of the Greek New Testament, basing it on the Byzantine text type. On October 31 of the following year, Luther posted his *Ninety-five Theses* on the front door of the Castle Church in Wittenberg, Germany. The fur hit the proverbial fan a full century later with the onset of the horrific Thirty Years' War in Central Europe (1618-1648). Though the concluding Peace of Westphalia gave the edge to the "harlot's daughter," it was a Pyrrhic victory at best with the slain on both sides numbering in the millions.

However, the *spiritual* losses were far more telling. While the Lord informed Sardis that *"thou **livest**,"* He was also quick to add, *"and art **dead**."* (Revelation 3:1) The next verse reveals the main problem with the Protestant movement as a whole. *"Be watchful, and strengthen the things which remain, **that are ready to die**: for I have not found thy works **perfect** before God."* (Revelation 3:2) In Scripture, the word "perfect" does not mean "sinless," but rather "mature" or "complete." Hebrews 5:8-9 says that Jesus Himself was *"made perfect,"* having *"learned...obedience by the things which he suffered."* Though the

Reformers did *some* "reforming" by way of certain individual doctrines within a corrupt, unscriptural religious behemoth, they never went far enough. For instance, by refusing to reject infant "baptism" (viewed as Christian circumcision), the Protestant denominations could never perpetuate a regenerate membership (the ritual *ordinance* replacing the born-again *experience*). As such, their "churches" were *"ready to die."*

The faithful Baptist remnant during this time can be discerned in the words, *"Thou hast a few names even in Sardis which have not defiled their garments."* Called by their enemies "Anabaptists" (*"re*-baptizers"), their key leaders would include Balthasar Hubmaier, Felix Manz, Conrad Grebel, and Menno Simons. These humble believers undoubtedly represented the bloodiest remnant of all. Whereas the *Protestants* were attempting to break away from *Rome*, the *Baptists* were constantly persecuted by *both*. An important insight to this time can be gleaned from John's later description of the *"great whore"* of Rome as *"THE MOTHER OF HARLOTS."* (Revelation 17:5) The Vatican's Protestant offspring would also become little state churches after the Pergamos tradition. This singular fact was the main reason why the professing "born-again" Protestants would come after their Baptist brothers and sisters with a vengeance, for genuine New Testament assemblies have always practiced separation of church and state. Thus, while the Protestants would emulate their mama in pursuit of the *materialistic* "Kingdom of Heaven," the Baptists would pursue the *spiritual* "Kingdom of God," and never the twain would meet!

At this juncture, nearly fifteen centuries had passed since Paul penned I Timothy 2:1-4, and the persecution had yet to cease. Thus, our faithful Baptist ancestors would continue to "hold fast." In 1529, the Protestant decree of Speyer (Germany) proclaimed: "All Anabaptists and rebaptized persons, male or female, of mature age, shall be judged and brought from natural life to death, by fire, or sword or otherwise, as may befit the persons." Under the heading "otherwise," entire Anabaptist congregations in Switzerland would pay for their anti-pedobaptism convictions by being thrown into lakes chained to their pastors. Their Protestant tormentors called it "The Third Baptism" (i.e., sprinkled as a Catholic or Protestant infant; immersed as a saved Anabaptist adult; then—immersed *permanently*). While Balthasar Hubmaier was spared this indignity, being *burned at the stake* (his beard caked with sulfur and gunpowder), his courageous wife Elizabeth was not, being *thrown*

President Donald Trump embracing Israeli Prime Minister Benjamin Netanyahu after unveiling his "Plan for a Comprehensive Peace Between Israel and the Palestinians," January 28, 2020; both leaders would find themselves turned out of office within sixteen months (Genesis 12:3; Daniel 12:39; Amos 9:15)

Bullet "Trump Train" derailed by train-wreck administration of "Amtrak Joe" and his "Caramel Caboose," forcing Bible believers to refocus their attention on the One whose *"train filled the temple."* (Isaiah 6:1) "Every nation eventually ends up with the government it deserves." (Dr. Peter S. Ruckman)

Marcus Hook Baptist Church;
Larkin baptized here in 1874

Mary Krol, my Ukrainian-born grandmother; spoke six languages

My "First Holy Communion,"
at St. Stephens of Hungary,
April 30, 1960; age seven

Cardinal Francis Spellman
signed my parochial school
diploma in 1966

Stone Balloon Tavern; I sold co-owners
"Bill and Jill" (Biden) Stevenson their
electronic cash register system in 1972

Spending my Stone Balloon sales commission in Rome

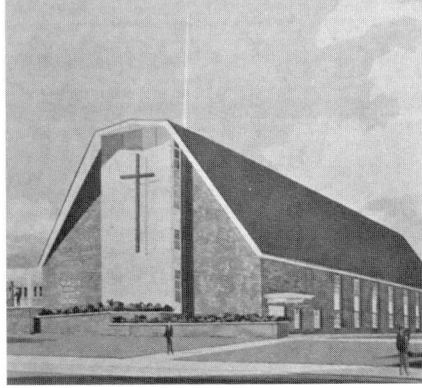

Marcus Hook Baptist Church in 1974, where
I was saved and baptized a full century after
Clarence Larkin's baptism there

Manhattan Progect physicist Samuel T. Cohen (aka "Father of the Neutron Bomb"), during my visit at his Brentwood, California home. "Most Americans are totally oblivious to their precarious surroundings" (extracted from Sam's afterword to my 2005 book *How Satan Turned America Against God*). Quoting his long-time friend and colleague, national security analyst, Dr. Joseph Douglass (from his own book, *America the Vulnerable*), "While the United States debates the development of a massive defense effort against nuclear attack…the fact remains that this nation is almost entirely defenseless against chemical, biological and toxin weapons of mass destruction."

Dr. Robert Malone, anti-Vaxxer hero, inventor of the mRNA technology

Tony and Bill, "Enemies within the gates!" (Cicero)

Ukraine President Volodymyr Zelenskyy, LGBTQ+ darling

Georgia Guidestones, Elberton, GA; "Decrease the surplus population" (Ebenezer Scrooge)

United Nations' Beast; the so-called "Guardian of International Peace and Security"; erected on Visitors Plaza, November 2021

Noah's sons were Shem, Ham, and Japheth. Shem became father of the Semitic peoples, including the Jews and the Arabs. Ham was the father of the Hamitic peoples. Japheth was the father of peoples of Asia Minor and Europe. In traditions originally unrelated to the Flood, Noah is portrayed as a gardener and credited with the discovery of wine (Genesis 9:18-27).

Dr. Ezra Stiles, "Europe was settled by Japheth; America is settling from Europe"

Seeing is believing! Page 439 in the politically incorrect 2022 edition of *World Book Encyclopedia*, Volume 4, exactly matches Genesis 9 and 10 in the King James Bible

Geronimo, famed Apache chief trusted Christ at 79; said he was "in the dark and not on the right road," wanted to "find Jesus"

Generalissimo and Mrs. Chiang Kai-shek; devoted Christians and leaders of the Republic of China during World War II

Phillis Wheatley, African slave saved under Mr. Whitefield's ministry; first published black poet, "'Twas mercy brought me from my pagan land…"

Kim Phuc, aka "the girl in the picture," the most famous photo from the Viet Nam War; today a born-again Baptist preacher's wife in Ajax, Ontario *(Associated Press)*

Left: Captain Mitsuo Fuchida, led infamous Pearl Harbor attack; *Right:* after the war converted to Christianity, then called to preach the Gospel of the grace of God *(Getty)*

Pastor Joseph Hughes; my friend and next-door neighbor; helped mentor me through Bible college, 1976-1981

Some of my other preacher pals from the greater Chicagoland area who further contributed to my "unique" homiletical development; "If you still *is* what you *was*—you *ain't*."

Me preaching during one of our third-shift lunchtime evangelistic services held at Blaw Knox foundry

James Burnett (left), pastor of Norfolk Bible Baptist Church, Norfolk, VA, and Bro. Larry Jacobs, his faithful member and fellow Navy veteran

My "brother from another mother," Dameaon Dudley; I crash at his crib whenever I preach at Morning Star Bible Baptist Church

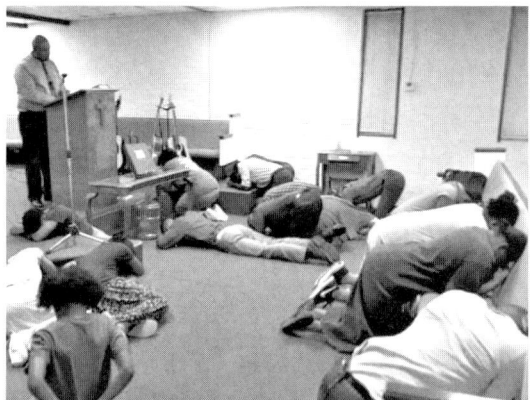

When I boarded my Dulles-JFK flight, CNN anchor Anderson Cooper suddenly appeared, taking his seat across the aisle a row behind me. The Holy Spirit distinctly prevented me from giving him a Chick tract, reminding me of Matthew 7:6. He then led me to witness to the lady beside me, a Seventh-day Adventist mother of seven.

Toure Carter, pastor of Morning Star Bible Baptist Church in West Memphis, AR, conducting the invitation after his entire congregation "hit the altar" following my sermon

Nebuchadnezzar, Babylonian king, repeatedly called "My Servant" by the God of Israel

King Nebuchadnezzar's failed 13-year siege of New Tyre, 630-561 BC (Stanley L. Wood)

Jewish historian, Flavius Josephus, who documented Alexander's visit to Jerusalem, 332 BC

Alexander the Great meets Jaddua the High Priest (Jacopo Amigoni)

Alexander in Temple of Jerusalem being shown Daniel's prophecy of his conquest of Asia (Sebastian Coca)

Battle of Gaugamela, October 1, 331 BC; Alexander defeats Darius, fulfilling Genesis 9:27 (Jacques Courtois)

Paul winning Lydia to Christ at Philippi; first Japhethite convert in Europe (Harold Copping)

Constantine the Great; instituted the Church-State relationship, beginning Pergamos Church Age

Dirk Willems, Dutch Anabaptist preacher; having just escaped from prison, turns back to rescue his pursuing Catholic guard; recaptured and burned alive in return for his selfless efforts, May 16, 1659

Waldensian missionaries posing as merchants in the Thyatiran period. *"I will put upon you none other burden. But that which ye have already hold fast till I come."* (Rev. 2:24-25)

from a bridge into the Danube with a stone around her neck three days later— *"and they shall walk with me in white for they are worthy."* (Revelation 3:4)

Many other brave Anabaptist women were martyred as well. Anne Askew was burned alive at Smithfield, London, on July 16, 1546. Carried and chained to the stake in a chair (having been racked in the Tower), the twenty-five-year-old Bible believer refused a last-minute pardon, stating, "I came not thither to deny my Lord and master." As a final indignity, Anne was then forced to endure a "sermon" (by one Bishop Nicholas Shaxton). While nodding at what she agreed with, Anne checked his errors with the incredible rebuke, "There he misseth, and speaketh without the book."

Another artistic portrayal of what life was like for our spiritual ancestors is a pen-and-ink sketch depicting a selfless act of kindness by the Dutch Anabaptist pastor, Dirk Willems. Arrested and jailed for rejecting infant baptism (and for conducting several immersions on his property), Willems was able to escape and flee across a frozen pond. When a guard gave chase, he fell through the ice and yelled for help. Though Dirk was now safely in the clear, as a precursor to the age of "Brotherly Love," he turned back to save his drowning pursuer. The famous work shows the condemned Anabaptist pulling the grateful Catholic out of the water. By this time, however, additional guards had arrived and took Willems back into custody. For saving the life of his enemy, Dirk Willems was "brought from natural life to death by fire" on May 16, 1569. According to one source, "Willems was executed in Asperen, and with a strong eastward wind blowing that day, the fire was driven away from the condemned's upper body, thus prolonging his torturous death." The wind carried his screams for miles with the words, "O Lord; my God," etc., being heard over seventy times. ("But if I keep my church open during Covid the local authorities might give me a fine...waa, waa, waa....")

Far from the *"quiet and peaceable life"* that Paul posited as the ideal conditions for spreading the Gospel, a well-known song in our Baptist hymnals describes the only "life" our forefathers knew:

> Faith of our fathers, living still,
> in spite of *dungeon, fire,* and *sword*;
> Oh, how our hearts beat high with joy
> Whene'er we hear that glorious word.

Chorus:
Faith of our fathers, holy faith,
We will be true to thee till *death*!

Our Fathers, *chained in prisons dark,*
Were still in heart and conscience free:
How sweet would be their children's fate
If they, like them, could *die* for thee!

The first part of a double irony is that "Faith of Our Fathers" was originally a *Catholic* hymn, penned in 1849 by Fredrick William Farmer to commemorate the Catholic martyrs from the time of the establishment of the Church of England by Henry VIII and Queen Elizabeth I (i.e., *Sardis*). The telling third stanza has long since been removed:

Faith of our Fathers! *Mary's* prayers
Shall win *our country* back to thee:
And through the truth that comes from God
England shall then indeed be free.

The second irony is that the modern adaptation sung in our *Baptist* churches is actually the *Protestant* version that altered the third stanza by deleting the Marian references, then adding a clear *anti*-soul-liberty, *pro*-state-church Protestant ideology:

Faith of our Fathers! We will strive
To win all nations unto thee,
And through the truth that comes from God
Mankind shall then be truly free.

THE 1611 AUTHORIZED KING JAMES BIBLE

Throughout these tumultuous times a string of printed English Bibles capitalized on the epoch translation work of William Tyndale, who sealed his life's work at the stake on October 6, 1536. His dying prayer, "Open the king of England's eyes!" was answered two years later when King Henry VIII ordered that the Miles Coverdale translation was to be used in every parish of the land. With Paul having planted the *"gospel of the grace of God"* on European soil at Acts 16:11, the 1611 Authorized King James Bible became the undisputed high-water mark of the Protestant Reformation! J. R. Green wrote in *A Short History of the English People*:

No greater moral change ever passed over a nation than passed over England during the years which parted the middle of the reign of Elizabeth from the meeting of the Long Parliament. England became the people of a book, and that book was the Bible. It was as yet the one English book which was familiar to every Englishman; it was read at churches and read at home, and everywhere its words, as they fell on ears which custom had not deadened to their force and beauty, kindled a startling enthusiasm...As a mere literary monument, the English version of the Bible remains the noblest example of the English tongue. Its perpetual use made it from the instance of its appearance the standard of our language. But for the moment its literary effect was less than its social. The power of the book over the mass of Englishmen showed itself in a thousand superficial ways, and in none more conspicuously than in the influence it exerted on ordinary speech. It formed, we must repeat, the whole literature which was practically accessible to ordinary Englishmen...But far greater than its effect on literature or social phrase was the effect of the Bible on the character of the people at large. Elizabeth might silence or tune the pulpits; but it was impossible for her to silence or tune the great preachers of justice, and mercy, and truth, who spoke from the book which she had again opened for the people. The whole moral effect which is produced nowadays by the religious newspaper, the tract, the essay, the lecture, the missionary report, the sermon, was then produced by the Bible alone. And its effect in this way, however dispassionately we examine it, was simply amazing. The whole temper of the nation was changed. A new conception of life and of man superseded the old. A new moral and religious impulse spread throughout every class...the whole nation became, in fact, a Church.

Now, while these lofty words were definitely true, the sad truth is that these same noble tenets of "justice and mercy" did *not* extend to our non-conformist Baptist ancestors trying to survive within the birthplace of the AV 1611. On April 11, 1612, the Baptist pastor, Edward Wightman, was burned alive at Lichfield. Thus, the same king who used his Ecclesiastes 8:4 power to authorize the Bible that bears his name, authorized the death warrant of a "heretic" for the "capital crime" of being a "radical Anabaptist." To whatever degree the preserved reports of what Wightman *supposedly* said are accurate (he left no written record), it would *appear* that he held various theological views, mostly orthodox, though with some possible exceptions. However, considering the fact that he was willing to *burn* for his convictions, and that none of his descendants (with the possible exception of Walt Whitman) believed any of the things for which he was burned, the odds must increase that most of his bad press was attributable to slander (Matthew 5:11; 11:19). In any event, although the freedom-loving English Baptists finally had their perfected Bible, they did *not* have the freedom to preach what it said. Thus, they would *still* need to *"hold fast"* —till the right God-ordained government could provide that ever-elusive *"quiet and peaceable life in all godliness and honesty."* (The ensuing chapters will highlight the transition from Sardis to Philadelphia, concluding with a survey of Laodicea.)

10

Sunset on Sardis

H AVING VIEWED JAPHETH'S *enlargement* at Daniel 8:7, followed by his *enlightenment* at Acts 16:11, we left him in a world of hurt after the death of Edward Wightman. For, although the Baptists finally had their perfected King James Bible, the sovereign who authorized it and the churchmen who translated it did not have the grace to allow their despised subjects to obey it. Despite the fact that Wightman's martyrdom would be the last religious execution in merry ole England, the Lord was already planning to open up a new playing field elsewhere. The power of the "Old Book" would now be transported 3,000 miles across the "Great Pond" to be unleashed in a "New World." As God makes *"everything **beautiful** in his time"* (Ecclesiastes 3:11), the Holy Ghost would fulfill Paul's long-anticipated vision for a *"quiet and peaceable life"* by connecting a string of dots through five providential colonies, attaining mankind's greatest blessing in the process—the *enablement* of Japheth.

AMOR VINCIT OMNIA

While Edward Wightman was being reduced to ashes, some fifty miles to the north a precocious three-year-old was being prepared to initiate Japheth's enablement. John Clarke was born in Suffolk, England, on October 3, 1609, then duly christened into the State church. Thankfully, he met the Lord Jesus Christ and received his "second baptism" at the first church of "Particular Baptists" in London (formed in September 1633 by Mr. John Spilsbury). Acclaimed by his contemporaries as "scholar bred," Dr. Clarke earned a master's degree in England followed by extensive medical training in Leiden, Holland.

In 1637, the twenty-eight-year-old "bi-vocational" Baptist minister landed in Boston, Massachusetts, accompanied by his wife, Elizabeth. Unlike Hubmaier's spouse, *this* Elizabeth would not be thrown off any bridge owing to the landmark religious reforms which the Lord would *enable* her husband to initiate (I Timothy 1:12). No sooner than Clarke had disembarked, he was disarmed. The Puritan-controlled Massachusetts Bay Colony was currently embroiled in a major theological and political crisis known as the Antinomian Controversy (works versus grace.) Dr. Clarke wrote, "I thought it strange that they were not able so to bear each with others in their different understandings and consciences as to live *peaceably* together." Thus, the aspiring champion of "Individual Soul Liberty" led three hundred likeminded souls out of the intolerant Protestant colony. Prior to their departure, the group drew up and signed the following compact:

> "The seventh day of the first month, 1638. We whose names are underwritten do hereby solemnly in the presence of Jehovah incorporate ourselves into a Bodie Politick and, as He shall help, submit our persons, lives and estates unto our Lord Jesus Christ, the King of Kings, and Lord of Lords, and to all those perfect and most absolute laws of His given in His Holy Word of Truth, to be guided and judged thereby."

After enduring an inhospitable winter in New Hampshire, Dr. Clarke and his flock descended on an island paradise in the Narragansett Bay, known by the Indians as *Aquidneck,* meaning, "Isle of *Peace*" (not a bad first step toward that *"quiet and **peaceable** life"*). The tranquil enclave, measuring fifteen miles long by three miles wide, was subsequently purchased from the natives for the asking price of forty fathoms of white beads (less than $100), ten coats, and twenty hoes; the deed bearing the date of 24 March 1638. Japheth the *enlarged, enlightened*, and soon-to-be *enabled*, was continuing to fulfill his part of the Noahic prophecy to *"dwell in the tents of Shem."* (Genesis 9:27) The initial settlement was established at the north end of the island in what is now the city of Portsmouth.

In April 1639, Dr. Clarke and several families organized a new community at Newport. The two towns united the following year on March 12 to form the colony of "Rhode Island." Clarke's co-laborer, William Coddington, was elected governor with suitable legislation subsequently enacted. The founding statute declared the government to be a "democracy," whose laws were in the power of the freemen by majority vote. The key tenet read, "That none should be accounted a delinquent for doctrine." The official seal was the figure of a sheaf of arrows bound together and marked with the motto *"Amor Vincit Omnia,"* meaning, "Love will conquer all things," representing a fitting memorial to Dirk Willems's selflessness and the ideal precursor to the coming age of "Brotherly Love." The historian, Dr. Conrad Glover, wrote, "As far as I am able to learn, the above document was the *first* legislative action for personal, political and religious liberty on the American continent." Despite the fact that present-day Rhode Island boasts the highest percentage of Roman Catholics of any state (42%), the city fathers of Portsmouth obviously concurred with Glover, as a prominent historical marker reads, "Welcome–Portsmouth–*Birthplace of American Democracy* Est. 1638."

Dr. Clarke then took things to the next level by sailing to London to personally lobby the Crown for twelve years on behalf of Rhode Island's fledgling religious liberties. His case was strengthened by the shameful treatment he and his assistant pastor, Obadiah Holmes, had received in neighboring Lynn, Massachusetts, in the summer of 1651. While attempting to hold Sunday services in the home of an aged church member, William Witter (no longer able to travel to Newport due to blindness), they were arrested, jailed, and fined, with Holmes receiving thirty-nine lashes at the Protestant whipping post. John Endecott, Massachusetts's longest-serving governor, said that Clarke and his company deserved death. (John would later hang four Quakers in Boston, with another fourteen women and five men being executed during the infamous Salem witch trials of 1692-1693.) Several witnesses to the Holmes whipping were saved and baptized as a result, most notably the Anglo-American Puritan clergyman, Henry Dunster, the *first* president of Harvard College! Dr. Dunster eventually got the boot from Harvard in 1654 for opposing Pedobaptism. After not so much as taking a single baby aspirin, Dunster helped found the influential First Baptist Church of Boston.

When Dr. Clarke returned to Great Britain, he published *Ill Newes from New-England*, documenting their trying ordeal. As Proverbs 21:1 says, *"The king's heart is in the hand of the LORD, as the rivers of water: he turneth it whithersoever he will,"* on July 8, 1663, Clarke obtained the signature and seal of King Charles II on a charter so democratic, both in letter and spirit, that doubts were voiced in England as to whether the king even had the right to grant it! "The charter of Rhode Island of 1663," says Thomas Bicknell, "has been universally recognized as the most liberal state paper ever issued by the English crown." An excerpt from the charter has been permanently enshrined above the main entrance of the magnificent Rhode Island State House:

TO HOLD FORTH A LIVELY EXPERIMENT
THAT A MOST FLOURISHING CIVIL STATE MAY STAND
AND BEST BE MAINTAINED WITH FULL LIBERTY
IN RELIGIOUS CONCERNMENTS

Thus, while James I, though remembered for the AV 1611, is also credited with shedding the *last* Baptist blood in *England*—it was apropos that his *grandson*, Charles II, acquiesced to the pastor of the one who shed the *first* Baptist blood in *America*! And it wasn't long before that other persecuted people discovered this haven of liberality. The first Jews arrived in Newport in 1658, with a second, larger wave landing in 1693. The Jewish community in Newport, properly, *Congregation Yeshuat Israel* ("Salvation of Israel"), constructed their synagogue in 1763, recognized today as the oldest standing synagogue in America. Based on Genesis 12:3, this one fact would have more to do with the new nation's future prosperity than can possibly be imagined. Rabbi Morris Gutstein wrote, "The blessing, which God gave Abraham, *'And in thee shall be blessed all the families of the earth,'* may be applied to America in general and to Newport of the eighteenth century in particular." When the world-famous Anglo-Irish philosopher Dean George Berkeley moved to Newport in 1729, he exclaimed, "The town of Newport is the most thriving place in all America for bigness."

Finally, though constantly busy with the affairs of state, not to mention his acclaimed medical practice, Dr. Clarke was faithful to perfect his *highest* calling. Dr. William Cathcart writes in the *Baptist Encyclopedia*: "He is spoken of by early writers as the religious teacher of the people, and as such from the beginning. A church was gathered in 1638, probably early in the year, of which Mr. Clarke became a pastor or teaching elder." For a "perfect" threefold Satanic "coincidence," nearly every "Bible" college that promotes Constantine I as the first Christian emperor and elevates "the" *Textus Receptus* over the King

James Bible for matters of final authority will also bypass John Clarke in favor of Roger Williams for having founded his so-called "first Baptist church in America." As I thoroughly document in *How Satan Turned America Against God* (pages 103-13), the Portsmouth Church began in 1638, one full year *before* Williams did his generic thing in Providence. Furthermore, as Roger's own testimony reveals, Jessie "You can't lose with the stuff I use" Jackson, William Jefferson Clinton, aka "Slick Willie," and even James Brown's former road manager, "Reverend Al" Sharpton, were probably more technically qualified to claim a Baptist tag than he was. (Immersed by one of his own baby-sprinkled followers who had never received the ordinance himself, Roger abandoned his untenable position after just six months, closing his church, never to identify with *any* denomination the rest of his life.)

Thus, we may confidently conclude that the *first church at Newport* and *not* the first church at Providence, is the *true* first Baptist church in America, and that *John Clarke, not* Roger Williams, was the founder and pastor of the *first* Baptist church in Rhode Island *and* America! For a *beautiful* postscript, as the saying goes, "A picture is worth a thousand words," a photograph in *How Satan Turned America Against God* captures the front of Congregation Yeshuat Israel (constructed in 1763)—the *oldest standing* Jewish synagogue in America—with a white steeple rising in the background affixed to the United Baptist Church, John Clarke Memorial (the current building being constructed in 1846)—the *oldest* Baptist church in America. (An American flag can also be seen flying on the synagogue property.)

AN EARLY VALENTINE

While Dr. Clarke and his vanguard Baptist enclave in Rhode Island represented the "Morning Star" of religious liberty, the whipping of Obadiah Holmes confirmed that much work remained to be done. At the tender age of thirteen, John Wightman saw his father burned alive at the stake for his religious views. In 1627, he married Katharine Frye, who bore him five sons. John emigrated to America with four of these boys, reaching Newport in 1654. (His firstborn had already resettled in the Baptist colony six years earlier.) His fifth son, George, married Elizabeth Updike in 1663. The union was blessed with four sons and one daughter. Their last child (born in 1681), was destined to seed the soil that would later produce the "Father of the American Bible Belt."

By his mid-twenties, *Valentine* Wightman—great-grandson of Edward Wightman, England's last martyr, and grandson-in-law to Obadiah Holmes, the esteemed protomartyr of American Baptists (the word *martyr* being understood by its ancient meaning of "a *witness* for Christ")—was a God-called Baptist preacher *and* a coming force to be reckoned with. Once again, as with the selfless act of Dirk Willems and the Rhode Island seal, "Love will conquer all things," the preacher's given name itself was yet *another* harbinger of a coming religious climate where Japheth's long-anticipated *enablement* would finally come to pass. In 1705, Valentine founded the first Baptist church in the colony of Connecticut at Groton with a group of twelve religious dissenters. In his "spare time," he also planted the first Baptist church in New York in 1712. Due to the local mobs, Wightman was constrained to "hold fast" in the best of Thyatiran tradition, clandestinely baptizing his five women converts at night (the others, seven men, being immersed in the morning under a protective order from the governor). He would later start many other churches throughout Connecticut and New York.

As the influence of the mother church in Groton continued, other works sprang up throughout the colony. Connecticut's second Baptist church was formed at New London with Elder Stephen Groton ordained as their pastor on November 28, 1726. The First Baptist Church in North Stonington began in 1743, with Elder Wait Palmer serving as its first pastor.

Valentine died on June 9, 1747, completing a forty-two-year ministry in Groton. Following a seven-year hiatus, the church called Valentine's son, Timothy, to be their pastor. He would lead the flock for another forty-two years before expiring on November 14, 1796. Then, in 1800, John Gano Wightman, Timothy's youngest son, became the pastor and went on to serve for an incredible forty-one more years! And, as a spiritual denouement, on June 12, 1864, Palmer G. Wightman, the grandson of John Gano Wightman was called to the Groton church and a mighty revival occurred. Truly, *"their works do follow them."* (Revelation 14:13)

In 1999, Pastor Jeff Faggart led a group of thirty-plus Baptist preachers to the Wightman Cemetery on Cold Springs Road in Groton (the site of the original church building). The top of Valentine's gravestone forms a large open Bible. After one of the pastors preached a message from behind this 250-year-old sacred desk, the Holy Ghost was pleased to blow through the hallowed site. When the dust settled, I found the late Dr. James Beller moaning and weeping beneath some bushes. He told me that the Lord impressed him then and there to write his six-hundred-page bestseller, *America in Crimson Red: The Baptist History of America*.

BIRTH OF THE BIBLE BELT

Outside of Rhode Island, the Baptist faith spread slowly throughout the colonies due to intense persecution by the Congregationalists in the North and the Anglicans down South. As the despised Baptists lacked the political wherewithal to extricate themselves from their numerically superior oppressors, the Lord got the last laugh by infiltrating Satan's lines with a Spirit-filled renegade Anglican. On a balmy spring evening in 1738, a twenty-three-year-old English missionary stepped foot on American soil at Savannah, Georgia. The gentleman's name was George Whitefield, aka "The boy preacher with a golden voice." His immediate goal was to start an orphanage in Savannah for Governor James Oglethorpe. (That work continues today as Bethesda Academy, a private boarding school for boys, where I was once privileged to speak in chapel.) However, George soon discovered that his greater purpose was to fan the flames of the first Great Awakening in America. The Lord's two-fold strategy was to increase the number of freedom-loving Baptists and to unite the colonies for their coming War of Independence.

Shuttling back and forth between the Old and New Worlds, "The Grand Itinerant" would make thirteen trans-Atlantic crossings, comprising an incredible 782 days at sea, to complete seven evangelistic tours in America. The size of his crowds in Great Britain had already made him a living legend there: 20,000 in the Moorfields; 50,000 at Kennington Common; 80,000 near Hyde Park; nearly 100,000 on a hillside in Cambuslang, Scotland. The figures he attained in the lesser-populated American colonies were not too shabby either: 6,000 in Germantown; 8,000 in New York City; 10,000 in White Clay Creek; 15,000 in Roxbury; and 20,000 in Boston. Although he didn't know it at the time, Phillis Wheatley's hero was really a *Baptist* trapped in a *Protestant's* body. When a wimpy Anglican minister in "Beantown" accosted him with the words, "I'm sorry to see you here, George," the man of God replied, "So is the devil," and proceeded to address an SRO throng of 20,000 on Boston Common!

The *main* reason Satan was sorry to see that maverick Protestant "here" was because he possessed the ministerial credentials to conduct those massive outdoor services. While the Baptists were constantly on the defensive—rarely permitted to vote or hold public office; frequently subject to fines, whippings, and/or imprisonment; and certainly, never allowed to openly proclaim their incendiary doctrines (known as "the briars of Anabaptism")—Whitefield would become God's secret weapon in the twilight of the Sardis Church Age. When his many awakened Puritan converts began reading their Bibles, it didn't take long before they discovered that infant sprinkling was nowhere to be found. The Holy Spirit was then able to move these "New Lights," as they were called, to either join existing Baptist churches or to start new ones altogether. David Benedict writes: "This work began generally among the Pedobaptists, and where they opposed it, separation ensued...They took the Bible alone for their guide, and of course, Baptist principles soon prevailed among them." Apparently, to pull off this Anglican-induced revival to benefit the Baptist cause in America, the sanctioned evangelist was not permitted to grasp what his own converts could see, encountering a "spiritual brownout" not unlike that experienced by the twelve (Luke 18:34). Thus, with some 125 new Baptist churches birthed in New England, an incredulous Whitefield could only exclaim, "All my chickens have turned into ducks."

Unfortunately, however, the South remained a spiritual wasteland. Here, the tenacious foe of religious freedom was none other than the Church of England herself, with the Baptists suffering far worse than their Yankee brethren did under the Puritans. Whitefield could not even get his fellow Protestants to listen, his crowds in Virginia and the Carolinas ranging from negligible to nonexistent. Then, the most amazing sequence of events occurred. After placing a literal curse on the town of Bath, North Carolina, on December 23, 1739, for their callous indifference to spiritual matters, an exasperated Whitefield experienced a surprising uptick just fifty miles away in New Bern during an afternoon Christmas service held in the local courthouse. His diary entry reads:

> I cried mightily to the Lord in my secret devotions, and in the afternoon when I read prayers and preached, He was pleased to

show that He had heard me, for I scarcely know when we have had more visible manifestation of the Divine Presence since our coming into America. The people were uncommonly attentive, and most were melted into tears.

Whitefield was stirred to believe that the South would be won for God, declaring further in his journal: "I looked upon it as an earnest of future and more plentiful effusions of God's Spirit in these parts. I believe, wherever the Gospel is preached in these parts with power, it will be remarkably blessed." The following day, Whitefield uttered a remarkable prayer that would alter America's spiritual destiny forever. Standing in the pine thickets of North Carolina, between Newborn Town and Trent River, he cried: "Oh, that the Lord would send forth some who, like John the Baptist, might preach and baptise in the wilderness! I believe they would flock to him from all the country round about." If anyone is interested, the extent to which this burden was honored can be gauged by the reality that there are more Baptist churches in the Tar Heel State today than in any other in the union! In "fact," there are more Baptists in North Carolina than there are people!! (Say "Amen" right there, neighbor!) What remains to be seen is the remarkable way in which the Holy Ghost brought the "baby-sprinkling" Whitefield's "immersing" preacher into the wilderness of North Carolina.

Returning to the fertile soil in Valentine's "parish," six years after that anointed prayer meeting in Carolina, George was privileged to become the means to achieving the answer to his prayer, albeit unknowingly. Shubal Stearns, an unsaved church member of the Congregational Church in Tolland, Connecticut, was converted under a powerful Whitefield sermon in Boston. He immediately became a stalwart preacher among the "New Lights" (also called the "Separates" from II Corinthians 6:17), the revived faction of dead Congregationalism (i.e., the "Old Lights"). After a six-year pastorate in Tolland, Stearns also repudiated infant "baptism," morphing into one of Whitefield's ducks at the hands of Wait Palmer at the First Baptist Church in Stonington. He was immediately ordained into the Baptist ministry on March 20, 1751, by Palmer and Elder Joshua Morse. With his own flock following the shepherd's lead, the First Baptist Church in Tolland was duly formed.

Three years later, the dramatic jumping-off point had finally arrived. In July 1754, Stearns baptized Noah Alden of Stanford. The following month, Shubal and his wife Sarah, accompanied by seven devoted couples (including his brother-in-law, Reverend Daniel Marshall and his spouse), headed south for Whitefield's designated target (leaving the Tolland work with Elder Alden). In a letter to Alden during a brief sojourn in Hampshire County, Virginia (the northeast corner of present-day West Virginia), Shubal stated that an advance party in North Carolina had written back that "there was no established meeting within a hundred miles of them, and that the people were so eager to hear, that they often came from *forty miles each way* when they could have an opportunity to hear a sermon." Consequently, on November 22, 1755, Whitefield's "John the Baptist" planted the Sandy Creek Baptist Church in the barren wilderness of Orange County, North Carolina (modern-day Randolph County).

At the time, the so-called "Bible Belt" was actually in New England, with forty of the forty-seven Baptist churches in colonial America existing north of the coming Mason-Dixon Line. However, a supernatural paradigm shift was about to occur! Do y'all recall Mr. Whitefield's prayer vision regarding his yet unknown missionary to the South that "the multitudes would flock to him from roundabout?" Shubal's vanguard work of sixteen souls experienced a veritable infusion of Holy Ghost power—*enlarging* to over 600 members in the first two years alone! Thomas Armitage cited a Dr. Howell as writing, "Everywhere the ministry of these men was attended with the most extraordinary success. Very large numbers were baptized. Churches sprang up by scores. Among the converts were many able men, who at once entered the ministry, and swelled continually the ranks of the messengers of salvation."

Henry Vedder gives the number of local assemblies directly started by Sandy Creek at forty-two and adds that one hundred and twenty-five ministers were sent out over a five-hundred-mile area. This statistic would appear to represent about 99 percent of the male membership. A nearby historical marker further affirms that by the year 1829 over 1,000 churches traced their origin to the Sandy Creek Baptist Church! Another monument credits Sandy Creek with being the "Mother of all Separate Baptist churches of the South." And for what it's worth, the main reason why students in our modern Baptist colleges are more familiar with Protestantism (John Wesley, D. L. Moody, Billy Sunday, et al.) is because historic Baptist methodology is anathema to "purpose-driven kingdom building." *Our Baptist forefathers believed in multiplication through division, not addition.* And the converts who got dunked didn't dry *up* after they dried *off* (Acts 2:41-42).

"VIRGINIA IS FOR LOVERS" —REALLY?

Having followed the Holy Ghost from England to Rhode Island, over to Connecticut, then down to North Carolina, Virginia would constitute the next-to-the-last stop in the long-anticipated enablement of Japheth. The most strategic new churches to branch out from Sandy Creek were gathered in the back woods of neighboring Old Dominion (Deep River, Abbot's Creek, Little River, Neus River, Black River, Dan River, and Lunenburg City, et al.). An army of leather-lunged, gun barrel-straight Baptist pastors became household names overnight. A short list would include: the "Murphy Boys," Joseph and William; Colonel Samuel Harris; James Ireland; Lewis, Elijah, and Joseph Craig; Dutton Lane; Thomas Jefferson's neighbor, Andrew Trimble; John Weatherford; David Tinsley; Elijah Baker, aka "The Apostle of the Eastern Shore;" Jeremiah Moore; John Corbley; Lewis Lunsford; John "Swearing Jack" Waller; and Elder John Leland.

The inevitable backlash from Satan was swift and severe (I Thessalonians 2:18). Since 1969, "Virginia is for Lovers" has been the highly successful tourism and travel slogan of the US Commonwealth of Virginia. Yet, *whatever* that cutesy phrase supposedly means today (i.e., given the state's expanding political liberalism), the mid-eighteenth-century Anglican-ruled Virginia that our Baptist forefathers had to confront represented anything *but* a "Love Fest" atmosphere. True to the adage that "an Episcopalian is a Catholic who flunked Latin," for the "crime" of preaching the Gospel of Jesus Christ without a state license, Baptist ministers suffered a myriad of afflictions: doors bashed in and services interrupted by cursing mobs; communion tables smashed to bits; ministers hauled down from their pulpits by the hair and publicly horse-whipped; pelted with projectiles; stabbed with knives; wounded by gunfire; baptismal services scattered by drunken rowdies on horseback; dunked in creeks themselves and nearly drowned; sued and run out of the country. ("But if I don't close my church for Covid, I might get a fine…")

And that was just *some* of what happened to these men *before* their arrests and kangaroo-court trials. Most pastors received outrageous sentences to Virginia's "Gulag of Gaols" (the loathsome, rat-infested jails meant to confine legitimate criminals). To add insult to injury, the "convicts" were compelled to pay for their "room and board" as well. Several years ago, during a Baptist history tour in Virginia, the attendees and I traversed a tranquil pasture in search of a particular grave marker. It was my honor to discover it—a small brass plaque, lying flat on the earth beneath the cow patties: "James Ireland buried in this vicinity." The ordeal of this Baptist pastor from Culpepper County, as recorded in Lewis Peyton Little's work, *Imprisoned Preachers and Religious Liberty in Virginia*, speaks for itself: "Jailed for preaching. Five months; Tried to suffocate him with smoke; Tried to blow him up with gunpowder; Tried to poison him. Injured for life (a daughter died from the poisoning); Drunken rowdies put in the same cell with him (he led them to the Lord); Threatened with a public whipping; Horses ridden over his hearers at jail; *Men made their water in his face*; Opposition everywhere."

That entry about "horses ridden over his hearers at jail" refers to a rarely known phenomenon whereby the busted parsons would deliver their Sunday sermons to their separated flocks through the grates of their "gaols!" The dramatic practice even had a name— "Denying the prison bounds." The embarrassed magistrates would do everything they could to disrupt the abnormal proceedings. While some beat on drums, others would hurl snakes and hornets nests at the crowd. Still others tried to disperse the faithful by sending blaspheming drunks on horseback into their midst. I was once privileged to speak for a former student of mine who pastors in Chesterfield, Virginia. In my sermon I told the congregation about a major historical marker displayed at the Chesterfield County Courthouse a mere seven miles away that dealt with the subject at hand.

On May 15, 1773, Pastor John Weatherford, a father of fifteen, was arrested in Chesterfield County for "preaching and assembling the people together without having any license for so doing." He and five other pastors were subsequently jailed for five months. As John was wont to extend his arms through the grates while preaching, the guards would keep the *Sardis* theme relevant by slashing the flesh off his hands with their swords. While he preached on, undeterred, so many locals were getting saved outside the windows that the incensed officials had a twelve-foot stone wall constructed directly in front of Weatherford's iron cell grate. They even lined the top with broken glass set in mortar to prevent John's more daring disciples from utilizing the strategic perch. However, as II Timothy 2:9 states that *"the word of God is not bound,"* when the pastor's unseen congregation were all in their place, a handkerchief on a pole would be raised as the signal that they were ready for "church." The man of God then proceeded to throw his voice *through* the grates, *up* and *over* the twelve-foot impediment, and *out* to the waiting crowd. The attendant drama only ensured that the jailhouse revival continued, baptisms being performed by twilight. Pastor Weatherford was eventually released after an "obscure" lawyer by the name of *Patrick Henry* paid his fine—personally. The names of those six pastors are inscribed on a brass plaque affixed to a *stone wall* less than twenty feet from the present Chesterfield County Courthouse and roughly fifty feet from the site of the incarceration itself. To my surprise, when I asked my listeners for a show of hands as to how many knew about this story, less than a half-dozen were raised.

BAPTIST CONTRIBUTIONS TO THE REVOLUTION

The American Revolution put a temporary hold on what James Madison described in a letter to a friend as, "That diabolical, hell-conceived principle of persecution that rages among some." One of the more practical reasons for the "time out" was because the despised Baptists constituted the most active patriots of the war. The evidence is so voluminous that only a brief synopsis can be attempted here. In fact, many of the iconic events of the war were actually trumped by unknown acts of Baptist valor.

For instance, the revolution *supposedly* began with "The Shot Heard Round the World," adapted from Ralph Waldo Emerson's "Concord Hymn," erroneously related to the skirmish at Concord Bridge, April 19, 1775. (The opening shot on *that* first day was actually fired on a Congregational Church yard in Lexington.) However, the *bigger* mistake regarding the so-called "first shot" involved a time discrepancy "slightly" longer than four hours—as in, one of four *years*. Alamance Battleground is a North Carolina State historic site south of Burlington, commemorating the Battle of Alamance on May 16, 1771. Unbeknown to most brain-dead social media addicts in America, a giant obelisk erected on the Alamance Battleground in 1880 reads: "FIRST BATTLE OF THE REVOLUTION." The Battle of Alamance was the final engagement in the brief "War of the Regulation" fought between the triumphant forces of Royal Governor William Tryon and a band of Western North Carolina settlers dissatisfied with Tryon's tyrannical policies. The "Regulator" moniker essentially reflected the historic Baptist distinctive of individual soul liberty, as in the inalienable right of a man to "regulate" his own affairs.

The breeding ground for the revolt contained the heaviest concentration of Baptists in the state. Thus, while the majority of the Regulators may not have been Baptists (or even saved for that matter), they were certainly inspired by their freedom-loving neighbors. Though Shubal Stearns actually attempted to assuage a shooting rebellion, most of the Sandy Creek Association membership opted to protect their property. Consequently, after Tryon's decisive victory, his forces bivouacked on the Sandy Creek Baptist Church grounds. Six of the Regulators were hung in Hillsborough, chief among them being Benjamin Merrill, a Baptist deacon and captain in the Rowan County militia. Standing on a barrel with a noose around his neck, James Pugh's last words were, "Our blood will be as good seed in good grounds that will soon produce one hundred fold." Rather than sign a loyalty oath to the king, the Sandy Creek membership, already greatly diminished by church planting, plummeted to just fourteen, the majority following Elder Tidence Lane to what is now Gray, Tennessee. The Buffalo Ridge Baptist Church became the first church of *any* denomination in the Volunteer State.

Moving right along, while a handful of Protestant Freemasons disguised as Indians became famous for merely throwing some tea overboard during the much-touted "Boston Tea Party" on May 10, 1773, eleven months earlier, the Baptist merchant, John Brown (brother of Nicholas Brown, founder of Brown University), rallied a contingent of his neighbors to capture and *blow up* the HMS Gaspee off Warwick, Rhode Island, on June 9, 1772, wounding the British commander, Lieutenant William Dudingston. Dr. William Cathcart called it "the first British blood shed in the War of Independence." Within weeks of Lexington and Concord, the predominantly Baptist Rhode Island legislature voted to send 1,500 volunteers to the conflict and was also the *first* colony to sever ties with England, doing so on May 4, 1776 (two months *before* the signing of the Declaration of Independence).

In the village of Hopewell, New Jersey, stands an unpretentious little church building, which was erected in 1747. An internet article from Mercer County Genealogy Trails (Mercer, New Jersey) reads in part, "…the building has acquired much fame by reason of the fact that within its shadows repose the remains of Hon. John Hart, one of the signers of the Declaration of Independence." Though raised a Presbyterian, Hart identified with the Baptist cause enough that he donated the needed land for the Hopewell Baptist Church and Cemetery. (John Gano, founding pastor of the First Baptist Church in New York City was saved, baptized, and ordained at the Hopewell church.) Thirteen orphans, a deceased wife, and the destruction of all his property, not to mention his own premature death on May, 11 1779, was the legendary price Honest John paid for that sacred signature in the final hours of the Sardis Church Age. (On a personal note, one of my most prized possessions, received from a friend, is a fifteen shilling New Jersey colonial note, classified as "About Uncirculated," displaying John Hart's signature, dated March 25, 1776—*less than four months* before he signed his own death warrant.)

One could even argue that a Baptist pastor had a profound influence on the Declaration of Independence itself. In a small, insignificant burial plot off the northbound lane of I-75 in Kentucky (roughly mile marker 91.5) lies the body of Reverend Andrew Tribble, founding pastor of the Albemarle Baptist Church (Chester Grove Baptist Church today), near Charlottesville, Virginia. In the providence of God, Elder Tribble, a veteran of the notorious gaols himself, was also a neighbor and confidant of Thomas Jefferson. The following quote is from the Andrew Tribble Memorial at the Tates Creek Baptist Church near Richmond, Kentucky (the site of Tribble's last pastorate):

MR. JEFFERSON ATTENDED THE MEETING OF THE CHURCH SEVERAL MONTHS IN SUCCESSION AND AFTER ONE OF THEM ASKED ELDER TRIBBLE TO GO HOME AND DINE WITH HIM, WITH WHICH HE COMPLIED. MR. TRIBBLE ASKED MR. JEFFERSON HOW HE WAS PLEASED WITH THEIR CHURCH GOVERNMENT? MR. JEFFERSON REPLIED, THAT IT HAD STRUCK HIM WITH GREAT FORCE, AND HAD INTERESTED HIM MUCH; THAT HE CONSIDERED IT THE ONLY FORM OF PURE DEMOCRACY THAT THEN EXISTED IN THE WORLD AND HAD CONCLUDED THAT IT

WOULD BE THE BEST PLAN OF GOVERNMENT FOR THE
AMERICAN COLONIES. THIS WAS SEVERAL YEARS BEFORE
THE DECLARATION OF AMERICAN INDEPENDENCE.

Though nearly twenty different religious denominations existed in
eighteenth-century colonial America, Baptist preachers filled one-third of
the 102 chaplain positions in the Continental Army. General Washington
declared, "Baptist chaplains were among the most prominent and useful
in the army." Even the British General Howe was forced to concede,
"The Baptists were among the more strenuous supporters of liberty."
Many of these courageous men (like Washington's favorite, John Gano)
were frequently found in harm's way, enshrining their motto of "toxic"
masculinity: "Pray, read your Bible, *and keep your power dry*."

Three weeks after the Declaration was signed, General "Mad
Anthony" Wayne found himself cut off from Philadelphia. On July 29,
he dispatched an important letter to Benjamin Franklin via his most
reliable courier, the Reverend Dr. David Jones, pastor of the Great Valley
Baptist Church in Devon, Pennsylvania. I once had the privilege of
reading the original in a museum. Wayne's defining line would send
most of today's wimpy, Covid-conscious pastors into shock: "Through
the medium of my chaplain (David Jones), I hope this will reach you as
*he has promised to blow out any man's brains who will attempt to take
it from him*." After Jones single-handedly captured a British spy,
General Howe put a bounty out for his capture! When the Continental
Congress called for a day of prayer and fasting on July 20, 1775, the
gun-toting parson preached his classic sermon, "Defensive War in a
Just Cause Sinless." Drawing on the text of Nehemiah 4:14, which
enjoins the Jews to defend their homes and families, Jones articulated
the prevailing Baptist sentiment that to fight for their liberty was
honest in the sight of God. Over 3,000 listeners sat spellbound.

Another "lightweight" story surpassed by its long-suppressed Baptist
counterpart would be the "Midnight Ride of Paul Revere" (William
Wadsworth Longfellow's slightly embellished version). Most students
of the Revolution agree that the American victory at King's Mountain,
South Carolina, on October 7, 1780, was the turning point of the war.
What they *don't* know is how a Virginia-born Baptist patriot and
Regulator veteran was more than partially responsible. Far eclipsing
Paul's brief route (both in miles and time), Martin Gamble, a faithful
member of Roaring River Baptist Church (Hollow Baptist Church then),

traveled over one hundred miles in twenty-four hours, *wearing out three horses in the process*, to warn the militia in western North Carolina and Virginia that Major Patrick Ferguson (aka "The Bulldog") was marching to reinforce General Cornwallis. This timely heads-up enabled some 1,800 backcountry "Overmountain Men" (including many of the original Sandy Creek exiles) to reach King's Mountain just in time (Martin being credited with having led 350 men himself).

And *so*, for having boasted, "I am king of this mountain, and *God Almighty Himself* could not drive me from it," not only was the major's entire force of Loyalist militia wiped out by their more freedom-loving brethren (225 killed, 163 wounded, and 716 captured, as opposed to twenty-eight Patriots killed, with another sixty-two wounded, one being Gamble himself), but "Patty Boy" also got *riddled with lead* as he attempted to flee on horseback (*eight* musket holes to be exact). The added irony that some one-hundred-and-fifty "supposedly" superior *Ferguson* rifles were used (the first breechloaders employed in the war)—*designed by the dead dude himself*—meant little when matched against the deadly Kentucky Long Rifle. Even one of Ferguson's dual accompanying mistresses, the red-headed "*Virginia* Sal" (the other sharing the same nickname, "*Virginia* Paul"), was also blown away.

On a "positive" note, the Lord *did* honor the highly detested Brit's conviction that he "would not be driven off *his* mountain." After Major Ferguson's mutilated body was stripped naked, unceremoniously urinated on, and wrapped in an ox hide, he and his "ho" were buried together, on site. On a more serious note, the main takeaway is that this pivotal victory—gained by a rabble of Alleghany mountaineers and Baptist jingoists (without the aid of a single Continental regular)—was facilitated by the untold "Twenty-four-hour Ride of Martin Gamble."

Finally, after "Lord" Cornwallis's ignominious surrender at Yorktown on October 19, 1781, George Washington repudiated his Anglican pedobaptism (a symbol of the unscriptural alliance of church and state begun in Pergamos), having his personal chaplain, John Gano, immerse him in the Hudson River (some accounts cite the Potomac). The early twentieth-century painting depicting his baptism (as well as the battle sword Washington presented to Gano), are displayed at William Jewell College in Liberty, Missouri. (While the "heathen rage" over this event, claiming a lack of "credible" corroboration, two of Gano's descendants, a medical doctor grandson and a ninety-year-old great-niece and widow, swore out notarized affidavits in Lexington, Kentucky, on August 16, 1899, affirming that their ancestor's testimony of baptizing Washington was well known within the family, photocopies appearing on pages 902-903 of *How Satan Turned America Against God.*) Furthermore, when the official proclamation by Congress of a formal cessation of hostilities was made, it was Washington's personal request that "prayer be offered to the Almighty ruler of the world by Reverend John Gano." Baptist historian John T. Christian pretty well sums things up, writing:

> They (American leadership) were surrounded with enemies from without; and Tories and traitors within. The most careful watchfulness was demanded. Only patriots could be trusted; and true men with the American spirit and liberty were imperatively demanded. *The Baptists were such men.* They were accustomed to a hardy life; and had long been trained in the rugged school of experience; were loyal and trusted citizens; and above all were endued with the spirit of wisdom and liberty. *Not a man of them proved a traitor. They cast their united strength into the American cause.*

Yet, despite their many noble contributions to the cause of American independence, the Baptists remained aware of their reproachful tag as "dissenters." Baptist chaplains were compelled to seek written permission that they "might be allowed to preach to the troops during the campaign with the same freedom as chaplains of the established Church." A full two years after the signing of the Declaration of Independence, Baptist ministers were *still* being confined to the gaols for crimes of conscience. My precious helpmeet (and the proofreader for these very lines) was saved and immersed as a child in a Baptist church in Accomac County, Virginia. The first Baptist works on the Eastern Shore were established by Elder Elijah Baker. Linda's spiritual progenitor was shamefully incarcerated in the Accomac County jail from July 1 to August 25, 1778. Thankfully, however, the sun was just about to set on Sardis...

11

The Long-Awaited Answer

GEORGE WHITEFIELD CALLED Pennsylvania the garden of America. Song of Solomon 4:16 says, *"Awake, O north wind; and come, thou south; **blow upon my garden, that the spices thereof may flow out**. Let my beloved come into his garden, and eat his pleasant fruits."* In time, the Holy Ghost would blow upon the Keystone State (particularly her capital) and the resultant aroma would be "beautiful." After the colonists broke with their mother country, the Second Continental Congress approved the woefully inadequate Articles of Confederation; the states ratified the same on March 1, 1781 (seven months before the British surrender at Yorktown). However, the Lord was not about to bless the governing apparatus of an aspiring country that would still deny religious liberty to all.

In May 1782, a mob in Hingham, Massachusetts, broke into a house where a certain Reverend Lee was preaching. The Baptist minister was cussed and beaten with a "long club," then had soft cow dung cast in his face, whereupon he was physically dragged out of town and threatened with worse if he ever returned. Lee replied, "That is not so much as they whipped Paul." Having occurred just twenty miles from the so-called "Liberty Tree," another Baptist sarcastically remarked, "These Sons of Liberty ought rather to be called Sons of Violence."

VIRGINIA STATUTE OF RELIGIOUS LIBERTY

Several of the Founding Fathers had witnessed the persecution of the Virginia Baptists firsthand. As a teenage lad, James Madison had stood alongside his father outside the Orange County jail and listened in astonishment as several Baptists preached from their cell windows. Some had even defended these pastors in court. Lewis Little wrote, "The Baptists found in Patrick Henry, an unwavering friend." Thus, Andrew Tribble's ally, Thomas Jefferson (another litigator for the Baptists), teamed up with James Madison to begin work on what would become the prototype legislative reform in this arena. In 1785, Madison prepared the way with his prescient treatise entitled, *Memorial and Remonstrance*, arguing from history that Christianity would flourish best *without* the support of the government. On January 16, 1786, the Virginia General Assembly passed Jefferson's seminal masterpiece, the *Virginia Statute of Religious Liberty*, disestablishing Emperor Constantine's Episcopalian harlot in the process:

> Be it enacted by the General Assembly, That no man shall be compelled to frequent or support any religious worship, place or ministry whatsoever; nor shall be enforced, restrained, molested or burthened in his body or goods, nor shall otherwise suffer on account of his religious opinions or belief; but, that all men shall be free to profess and by argument to maintain, their opinions in matters of religion, and that the same shall in no wise diminish, enlarge or affect their civil capacities.

Jefferson thought so highly of this achievement that he directed his tombstone to read:

HERE WAS BURIED
THOMAS JEFFERSON
AUTHOR OF THE
DECLARATION
OF
AMERICAN INDEPENDENCE
OF THE
STATUTE OF VIRGINIA
FOR
RELIGIOUS FREEDOM
AND FATHER OF THE
UNIVERSITY OF VIRGINIA

Japheth's *enablement* to proclaim his *enlightenment* in the land of his *enlargement* was drawing close, as was the long-awaited actualization of II Timothy 2:1-4. Consequently, as James 4:8 says, *"Draw nigh to God, and he will draw nigh to you,"* it wouldn't take long for the Lord to show His approval. Within a few months, Madison was moved to pen a second significant document. On May 25, 1787, the historic Constitutional Convention assembled in *Philadelphia's* Independence Hall. Apparently, some new and improved ideas were *blowing* through the air. Yet, only God Almighty could blend them perfectly. On September 17, 1787, following several months of dramatic debate, forty distinguished Americans affixed their signatures to *another* parchment of providence. Mr. Madison would henceforth be known as the "Father of the Constitution." However, the critical document still required verification by a minimum of nine state conventions. In a truly remarkable occurrence, the Lord decreed that a single Baptist pastor would be in the right place at the right time to literally decide the fate of Madison's venerable achievement. Japheth the Elder was standing on the very cusp of his long-awaited destiny.

ELDER JOHN LELAND

As previously stated, when Shubal Stearns left Connecticut in 1754 he turned the Tolland work over to Noah Alden (a Massachusetts native and direct descendant of John Alden, one of the Plymouth Pilgrims). In May of that same year, a male child was born into a Congregational family in Grafton, Massachusetts. Foreordained to determine the very future of America, John Leland would have to first experience the *second* birth. In the providence of God, the Lord led Noah to leave Groton in 1766 to pastor the Baptist church in Bellingham, Massachusetts. After a sustained period of Holy Ghost conviction in his late teen years, John trusted Christ and was baptized by Alden on June 1, 1774. He preached his first sermon on the twentieth day of the same month (there being no preacher at the meeting in Grafton to which he had gone). Surrendering to the call of God on the spot, he would deliver another eight thousand messages over the next sixty-seven years.

Two months after the Declaration of Independence, John married Sally Devine of Hopkinton, Massachusetts on September 30, 1776. They spent their "honeymoon" traveling to Virginia to begin a lifetime of service to God. John initially labored as an itinerant evangelist, baptizing hundreds of converts during the turbulent war years. Eventually settling in Orange County, he came to pastor two thriving churches simultaneously, one in Black Walnut, Orange County, and the other in Goldvine, Louisa

County. In the critical year of 1788, the Lord sent a mighty revival and John baptized three hundred additional souls. The combined membership in the two churches swelled to over five hundred. The timing of this awakening, with its commensurate *political* influence, would help tweak Mr. Madison's remarkable creation. The Constitution required ratification by nine state conventions. Of the thirteen voting states, Leland's Virginia was by far the noblest, wealthiest, and most influential. As her boundaries took in the Ohio territory, it was also the most populated, claiming one in every four Americans. Thus, Old Dominion's approval would be absolutely essential.

Patrick Henry, George Mason, and Richard Henry Lee led the opposition party (the Anti-federalists), objecting that a bill of rights had not been included. Henry was particularly troubled by the absence of any statutes regarding religious liberty. Agreeing that various amendments were indeed justified, Federalists Madison and Washington recommended ratifying the Constitution first, then adding a string of amendments afterward. It was their conviction that a failure to approve the Constitution as initially put forward would doom the entire project.

As each county had to elect delegates to the state convention, the "Father of the Constitution" naturally *assumed* that he would be a "shoe in" candidate in his own county of Orange. This proved to be anything *but* the case. While tarrying in Philadelphia to complete *The Federalist Papers*, Madison was unaware that opposition was fomenting back in Orange County. After enduring decades of persecution, Baptists in all states were appalled at the lack of specific religious guarantees in the proposed Constitution. As "fate" would have it, a significant number of voters in Madison's home county "quacked." And the same ratio prevailed state-wide, Thomas Jefferson recording in his *Notes on Virginia* that two-thirds of the population had become religious dissenters (Baptists, Presbyterians, Methodists, or Quakers) by the eve of the Constitution's ratification. While missionary outreach from Sandy Creek had established eighteen Baptist works in Virginia by 1770, the resultant persecution quadrupled that figure within four years! Francis Hill Hawk, an Episcopalian historian, acknowledged the obvious ramifications:

> The Baptists were not slow in discovering the advantageous position in which the political troubles of the country had placed them. Their numerical strength was such as to make it important to both sides to secure their influence...Persecution had taught them not

to love the establishment, and now they saw before them a reasonable prospect of overturning it entirely.

The Virginia Baptist General Committee met and agreed unanimously that the Constitution, as proposed, did not "make sufficient provision for the secure enjoyment of religious liberty." And, as they would ultimately decide who went to Richmond—you might call them the *original* "Mighty Ducks." A letter was subsequently dispatched to Madison (from his own father) warning him of the precarious situation. The paranoid candidate subsequently battled his way back to Orange through a severe snowstorm, arriving only days before the March 25 county election. Other notable personages such as Samuel Adams and John Jay had failed to be appointed delegates from their states. Would Madison be the most embarrassing casualty of the Convention? If he of all statesmen was not present, who could possibly oppose the eloquent Patrick Henry, of whom Jefferson once remarked, "He appeared to me to speak as Homer wrote"?

The man destined to be the nation's fourth chief executive had only one option. While traveling on the road from Fredericksburg to Montpelier, Madison went out of his way to call on the influential Pastor, John Leland. In his acclaimed *History of Virginia* (as cited by Armitage), Robert Semple recognized the former Massachusetts native as probably "the most popular preacher who ever resided in Virginia." Historian L. H. Butterfield pointed to Leland's "simple but graphic language, his avoidance of doctrinal refinements, his humor and his sincerity" as character traits that endeared him to his listeners. His homespun antidotes were legendary. The former governor of Massachusetts, the Honorable G. N. Briggs, related that the popular preacher was himself one of the two declared anti-Constitution candidates to be nominated; Colonel Thomas Barbour being the other. *The Dictionary of American Biography* states of Leland, "He was nominated by the Baptists of Orange County as a delegate to the Virginia convention of 1788, to oppose the Constitution." Furthermore, an extant copy of *Elder John Leland's Objections to the Federal Constitution* (as found in the Madison Papers housed in the Library of Congress) documents Leland's *initial* public commitment to the anti-Federalist platform.

Despite the profitable Leland-Madison political alliances of the past, not to mention their warm personal friendship, Mr. Madison would have his lobbying work cut out for him. The specifics of what was said during that rendezvous with destiny will never be known this side of eternity. Obviously, Madison would have given his pledge to do all within his power to secure a bill of rights *after* the Constitution was safely in place. But the man of God would have to pray down the Spirit's leading to trust his neighbor's commitment enough to reverse his own well-known and widely followed conviction.

Within a few days of their timely conference, a throng of liberty-loving "good ol' boys" assembled near the Orange County courthouse to literally decide the future of America. James Madison was introduced as the first speaker. Upon ascending a hogshead of tobacco, the 5'6" statesman promoted the Constitution for nearly two hours in a voice barely above a whisper. When he concluded his remarks, Pastor Leland took the stump and spoke for less than ten minutes. *He promptly shocked the crowd by reversing his position to endorse Mr. Madison's candidacy.* The preacher explained that his decision was predicated on Madison's pledge to provide a Bill of Rights once the Constitution was secure. The "brethren" took it from there! The actual tallies gave Madison 202 votes, and his Federalist running mate, James Gordon, 187, while Thomas Barbour and Charles Porter received 56 and 34 votes, respectively.

With his eleventh-hour reprieve, Madison was cleared to advance to Richmond while Tom unpacked his suitcase in a stupor (i.e., "What was the license number of that truck?"). The ensuing debate between Madison and Henry raged on for two-and-a-half months. During this time, news of Leland's defection had spread like wildfire. Consequently, a number of Henry's supporters grew more tolerant of Madison's proposal. When the final count was taken, eighty-nine delegates voted for ratification while seventy-nine opposed. (This was five days after tiny New Hampshire's endorsement had "technically" secured the nine-state minimum.) The significance of Leland's Spirit-led paramount endorsement is evidenced by the slim margin of victory *despite Mr. Madison's weighty presence.* A mere *ten* votes had enabled Madison to prevail over Patrick "Give Me Liberty or Give Me Death" Henry, a living legend who would be reelected to five terms as Virginia's governor. What do you suppose the final outcome would have been if the *very author* of the Constitution himself would have been barred from the proceedings?

"CUNNINGLY DEVISED FABLES"...NOT!

The Bible says in II Peter 1:16, *"For we have not followed **cunningly devised fables**, when we made known unto you the power and coming of our Lord Jesus Christ, but were eyewitnesses of his majesty."* As with the account of Washington's baptism, the standard naysayers and "Debbie Downers" would try to discredit the historicity of the Leland-Madison confab as just another "Baptist legend." Unfortunately for them, the high-profile corroboration is overwhelming. To cite just a sample of the voluminous documentation provided in *How Satan Turned America Against God*, in his definitive three-volume set, *James Madison: A Biography* (available at Montpelier), Dr. Ralph Ketcham of Syracuse University stated:

> On his way from Fredericksburg to Orange, with the election but a few days away, Madison stopped to see the influential Baptist preacher John Leland, who had drawn a vigorous memorial protesting, among other things, the failure of the new Constitution to guarantee religious freedom....In return for Leland's promise to withdraw his objections, Madison reaffirmed what he and other federalists had increasingly agreed to: they would support a bill of rights, including a firm article on religious freedom, as amendments to the Constitution *after* it's ratification....At the traditional court day election, the fourth Tuesday of the month (March 25), planters and tradesmen, despite a "very cold wind," gathered early, and "Colonel" Madison, Francis Taylor noted, "...addressed himself in a speech to the people in defense of the new Constitution, and there appeared much satisfaction."

William Lee Miller was an American journalist, academic, and historian who taught in the University of Virginia's religious studies department for seventeen years. In his acclaimed *The Business of May Next* (also available at Montpelier), Dr. Miller wrote:

> Then on the way on to Orange he had a meeting with the noted Baptist preacher John Leland. Leland and many Baptists had objected to the Constitution's failure to include a protection for religious liberty, but Madison, an old comrade-in-arms from the great Virginia struggle on that issue, was able to persuade him that the failure to ratify the Constitution would not serve religious liberty or any other

good purpose. Madison made a speech defending the Constitution, and was an easy winner over his anti-federalist neighbor…

From the prestigious American Antiquarian Society, we have the following comments given by Dr. L. H. Butterfield in *Elder John Leland, Jeffersonian Itinerant*:

> Elder John Leland is not often mentioned in histories of the United States, even the comprehensive ones. When he is, it is invariably in connection with the gift of an enormous cheese to President Jefferson on New Year's Day in 1800…But if John Leland is best known for an exploit typical of our engaging and probably harmless desire to break records, he deserves to be remembered for a better reason. *He played a substantial part in molding another American tradition that is full of meaning to all of us today—the separation of church and state in the United States.* The success of the Baptist revivalist was phenomenal in the years before the Revolution…On 30 January, James Madison, Sr., wrote his son that sentiment against ratification was decidedly rising in Orange County. "The Baptists are now generally opposed to it…." There followed a meeting between Madison and Leland that has been celebrated in local history and in Baptist annals.

Dr. Samuel Chiles Mitchell (1864-1948) was a former president of the University of South Carolina, as well as the first president of the Medical College of Virginia. In 1914, he also became president of what is now the University of Delaware. On September 26, 1934, Dr. Mitchell delivered an address at the Bicentennial of Orange County. The august gathering convened in the grove at Gum Spring at the Leland-Madison Memorial Park, located on Highway 20 (Route of the Constitution), four miles east of Orange. In his remarks, Dr. Mitchell cited two historical references to the summit that occurred in the grove itself (the site of Leland's parsonage at the time). The first of these was a eulogy for James Madison that was delivered at Culpepper Courthouse on July 18, 1836, by John S. Barbour, a long-time friend and associate of Mr. Madison. (Mitchell also affirms that the address was published in the *National Intelligencer* of Washington, DC, on August 2, 1836.) Concerning Madison's role in securing religious liberty for all, he stated:

In the accomplishment of this great object, the sect denominated Baptists took the foremost part...But for James Madison, we should have no Constitution: I call history to be witness. He above all others, created it. He above all others gave to it the ratification of Virginia. Without Virginia, the Union was disjointed, and was no Union, had every other state accepted, adopted and ratified the Constitution. His election to the Convention itself, in Virginia, was brought about by his sudden return to his county on the eve of the election. His soft and assuasive and lucid elocution changed two ministers of the Gospel of the Baptist church on the day preceding the election and that conversation carried him into Virginia. The celebrated John Leland was one of them. (It is thought by some that Reverend Aaron Bledsoe of Pamunkey was the other.) His mind was thrown open to the lights of reason and the power of argument...*and I speak but the voice of faithful tradition in saying that these changes were decisive in the election.*

Finally, Miller's other point of evidence was a letter by the Honorable George N. Briggs, Governor of Massachusetts (1844-1851), dated, Pittsfield, Massachusetts, April 15, 1857 (as found in William Sprague's nine-volume tome *Annals of the American Pulpit*). The letter's content relates to a special visit Governor and Mrs. Briggs made to the Lelands three or four years before the preacher's death when "Elder" Leland was in his early eighties. Briggs states how he informed Leland of Mr. Barbour's eulogy, then asked him for his personal recollection of that providential meeting with his now-departed friend. Briggs' version of Leland's account follows:

On his way home from Philadelphia, Mr. Madison went some distance out of his direct road to call upon him. After the ordinary salutations, Mr. Madison began to apologize for troubling with a call at that time; but he assured Mr. M. that no apology was necessary—'I know your errand here,' said he, 'it is to talk to me about the Constitution. I am glad to see you, and to have an opportunity of learning your views on the subject.' Mr. Madison spent half a day with him, and fully and unreservedly communicated to him his opinions upon the great matters which were then agitating the people of the State and the Confederacy.

They then separated to meet again very soon, as opposing candidates before the electors, on the stump. The day came, and they met, and with them nearly all the voters in the County of

Orange, to hear their candidates respectively discuss the important questions upon which the people of Virginia were so soon to act. 'Mr. Madison,' said the venerable man, 'first took the stump,' which was a hogshead of tobacco, standing on one end. For two hours, he addressed his fellow-citizens in a calm, candid and statesman-like manner, arguing his side of the case, and fairly meeting and replying to the arguments, which had been put forth by his opponents, in the general canvass of the State. Though Mr. Madison was not particularly a pleasing or eloquent speaker, the people listened with respectful attention. He left the hogshead, and my friends called for me. I took it—and went in for Mr. Madison; and he was elected without difficulty. 'This,' said he, 'is, I suppose, what Mr. Barbour alluded to.'

The Governor's remarks conclude:

A noble Christian Patriot! That single act, with the motives which prompted it, and the consequences which followed it, entitle him to the respect of mankind.

AMERICA THE BEAUTIFUL

The rest is history! Mr. Madison remained true to his word. Within months of becoming the nation's first chief executive, George Washington, accompanied by his secretary of state, Thomas Jefferson, embarked upon a colonial tour to promote the ratification of the Bill of Rights. Although the new president was expected to call upon the principal cities of the fledgling republic, receiving their delegations and letters of adulation, Newport would enjoy a special unspoken relationship (akin to his sacred baptism at the hands of John Gano). Not only was Newport the site of the first Baptist church in America, but also the home of what had formerly been the largest and most prosperous Jewish community in the nation.

Washington and his entourage arrived in Newport in August 1790. The Baptist-inspired conviction for religious liberty was so strong in Rhode Island that two months before the Declaration of Independence was proclaimed by the General Congress in Philadelphia, the General Assembly of the Colony of Rhode Island and Providence Plantations had gathered in the Old State House in Providence on May 4, 1776, and passed their *own* Declaration of Independence from the British

Crown! Washington understood what the modern educated fool does not—in the words of Charles Carroll, as quoted in the first volume of his work *Three Centuries of Democracy*— "Rhode Island, from that moment, became, and is at this day, *the oldest sovereign and independent state in the western world.*"

Furthermore, President Washington was well aware of what the Baptists had meant to his eight-year struggle. In a letter to the General Committee of the United Baptist Churches of Virginia following his April 30, 1789, inauguration, Washington wrote:

> While I recollect with satisfaction that the religious society of which you are members have been throughout America, uniformly and almost unanimously, the firm friends to civil liberty, and the persevering promoters of our glorious revolution, I cannot hesitate to believe that they will be faithful supporters of a free yet efficient General Government. Under this pleasing expectation I rejoice to assure them that they may rely upon my best wishes and endeavors to advance their prosperity.

His added blessing was an exchange of letters with the previously mentioned Hebrew congregation in Newport, *Yeshuat Israel*. Like the Baptists, the few Jewish Americans had made a substantial contribution to the war effort disproportionate to their number. For example, the Polish-born Philadelphia businessman, Haym Solomon (aka "Washington's Banker") had advanced to Congress, for the Revolutionary War, the incredible sum of $658,007.13, practically bankrolling the entire conflict singlehandedly. Appropriately enough, a Jewish woman, Emma Lazarus, would later pen those noble words found on the future Statue of Liberty ("Give us your tired..."). An excerpt from Touro Synagogue's formal letter of greeting to their distinguished visitor, dated August 16, 1790, reads as follows:

> Permit the children of the stock of Abraham to approach you with the most cordial affection and esteem for your person and merits, and to join with our fellow Citizens in welcoming you to New Port....Deprived as we heretofore have been of the invaluable rights of free Citizens, we now (with a deep sense of gratitude to the Almighty disposer of all events) behold a Government, erected by the Majesty of the People—a Government which to bigotry gives no sanctions, to persecution no assistance—but generously affording to

All liberty of conscience, and immunities of Citizenship:—deeming everyone, of whatever Nation, tongue, or language, equal parts of the great governmental Machine:—*This so ample and extensive Federal Union whose basis is Philanthropy, Mutual Confidence and Publick Virtue, we cannot but acknowledge to be the work of the Great God, who ruleth in the Armies of Heaven and among the Inhabitants of the Earth, doing whatever seemeth him good.*

The "Father of Our Country" dictated and signed his warm reply dated the following day. His concluding paragraph reads:

It would be inconsistent with the frankness of my character not to avow that I am pleased with your favorable opinion of my Administration, and fervent wishes for my felicity. *May the Children of the Stock of Abraham, who dwell in this land, continue to merit and enjoy the good will of the other Inhabitants, while everyone shall sit in safety under his own vine and fig tree, and there shall be none to make him afraid.* May the father of all mercies scatter light and not darkness in our paths, and make us all in our several vocations useful here, and in his own due time and way everlastingly happy.

And so, with Elder Leland's main task completed, he allowed the Spirit to "catch *him* away" i.e., from the local spotlight (like Philip's dramatic departure in Acts 8:39), taking Sally back to their native Massachusetts in March of 1791. Nine months later, the Bill of Rights was born! Collectively ratified by Congress on December 15, 1791, the First Amendment to the United States Constitution was an early Christmas present to the American people:

Congress shall make no law respecting an establishment of religion, or prohibiting the free exercise thereof; or abridging the freedom of speech, or of the press; or the right of the people peaceably to assemble, and to petition the government for a redress of grievances.

The renowned Baptist historian, Thomas Armitage, commented accordingly:

Thus, the contemned, spurned and hated old Baptist doctrine of soul-liberty, for which blood had been shed for centuries, was not only engrafted into the organic law of the United States, but for the first time in the formation of a great nation it was made its chief corner-stone. For the first time on that subject the *quiet*, pungent old truth asserted its right to immortality as expressed by Scripture: 'The stone which the builders rejected is become the head-stone of the corner.'

Dr. Armitage's use of that word "quiet" constitutes the perfect correlation between the Bill of Rights and the threaded theme of the last three chapters. Some 1,757 years after the Lord's first preachers were confronted by local authorities—at the "***Beautiful** Gate*" (Acts 3:2, 10)—who *"laid hands on them, and put them in hold unto the next day"* (Acts 4:3), the dawn of a new era had definitely arrived! Seventeen centuries after Paul exhorted the brethren to pray for a sympathetic government to provide a *"**quiet** and **peaceable** life in all godliness and honesty,"* in order to inaugurate the Lord's agenda for *"all men to be saved,"* a significant portion of the Body of Christ would *finally* get to experience I Timothy 2:1-4! Not only would the descendants of "Japheth the Elder" be *enlarged* and *enlightened*, but now, *thanks to the First Amendment*, they would also be *enabled*; as in, legally protected to use their "***beautiful** feet"* to bring the *"gospel of **peace**"* to the *rest* of the human family (i.e., their *Hamite* and *Shemite* nephews and nieces). With the "coinky-dinky" that the names *Japheth* and *Lydia* just *happen* to mean "beautiful," the Baptists' new home base for world evangelism would come to be known as *"America the BEAUTIFUL."*

Along with the "Star Spangled Banner" and "America the Beautiful," "America" ("My Country 'Tis of Thee") rounds out the nation's three most popular patriotic tunes. This selection is unique for one reason. Because the Lord used His "despised sect" to perform the geo-political miracle, a Baptist preacher was tapped to pen the classic number. Samuel Francis Smith was a Boston native and a contemporary of John Leland. (Leland was then spending the last thirty years of his life and ministry traveling as an itinerant evangelist out of Cheshire, Massachusetts.) Reverend Smith, a graduate of Harvard, produced his hymn in 1831 while attending Andover Theological Seminary. The lyrics resound with the theme of Japheth's enablement. The opening line sets the tone: "My country, 'tis of thee, Sweet land of *liberty*." He then continues with phrases such as "Let *freedom* ring"; "Land of the noble *free*"; "Sweet *freedom's* song"; "Author of *liberty*"; and "*freedom's* holy light."

And as long as we're on the subject, *another* Baptist preacher, Francis Bellamy of Rome, New York, authored The Pledge of Allegiance.

Once again, as Jesus said in John 8:36, *"If the Son therefore shall make you free, ye shall be free indeed,"* the American flag itself is one gigantic Gospel tract! In 1896, John Philip Sousa wrote *his* famous song, *Stars and Stripes Forever.* Does that *blue* field adorned with *stars* make you think of a direction you want to go when you die? Of course, the problem is that sinners are barred from Heaven because of sin. Therefore, the other part of Sousa's title reflects the divine remedy. "Old Glory" features *thirteen* stripes, the Biblical number for rebellion. These stripes further divide into *seven* red and *six* white. In the Bible, *seven* is God's number of perfection (seven notes on a scale, seven colors in a rainbow, etc.), while *six* represents man (Revelation 13:18). Thus, we see that the combination of both numbers pictures a "God-man" (I Timothy 2:5) who would embody the fulfillment of Isaiah 53:5— *"...with His **stripes** we are healed."* And the added fact that it is *six white* and *seven red* (rather than the other way around) reveals that you cannot get into the *white* (imputed righteousness) without passing through the *red* (Christ's blood); as the hymn *Grace Greater Than All Our Sins* puts it, "Look there is flowing a *crimson* tide; *whiter* than snow you may be today." Consequently, one could say—no *stripes*, no *stars*. And for the record, there just happens to be *fifty* stars, *that* particular number being the Bible number for *liberty* (Leviticus 25:10).

Perhaps the most succinct statement defining what the Baptists bequeathed to mankind occurred during a stately dinner party in Madrid, Spain, in the late 1800s. Two men were conversing, the famous British philosopher, John Bright, and Jabez Lamar Monroe Curry, President Grover Cleveland's Minister Plenipotentiary to Spain. A graduate of Harvard University in 1825, Dr. Curry's lifetime achievements required three columns of print in the renowned *Dictionary of American Biography.* Most importantly, however, J. L. M. Curry was a faithful Baptist minister. His fame was so pronounced in his native Alabama that his bust remained one of the two representing that state in the Capital's Statuary Hall in Washington, DC (until replaced in 2009 by the agnostic, Helen Keller). In the course of their discussion, Bright was expounding on the many contributions England had made to the world. He then asked Curry, "What distinct contribution has *America* made to the science of government?" After a brief pause, the Baptist ambassador replied, *"The doctrine of Soul Freedom."* Following a moment of reflection, the befuddled philosopher conceded, "A tremendous contribution indeed."

THE DOOR OPENS IN PHILADELPHIA

Upon completing his first missionary journey Paul rehearsed to his sending church at Antioch *"all that God had done with them, and how he had **opened the door of faith to the Gentiles**."* (Acts 14:27) This vanguard Gentile harvest was in Asia. However, by the time Paul writes to his European converts in I Corinthians 16:9, the Lord's focus has turned to the land of Japheth: *"For **a great door and effectual is opened unto me**, and there are many adversaries."* Representing one of the most amazing correlations of sacred prophecy with secular history, the Bill of Rights which opened the door to the Philadelphia Church Age at Revelation 3:8 "just happened" to be signed *in the city of Philadelphia* itself! Once again, first we had Dirk Willems' selfless act of *love* (i.e., the one that got him *killed*); then it was *Valentine* Wightman preparing the soil for Shubal Stearns; then the precursor Rhode Island Coat of Arms, "*Love* Conquers All"; and last of all—with our Baptist ancestors having persevered through that original *"battleground state,"* the future "Virginia is for *Lovers*" —it finally came together in the "City of Brotherly *Love*."

The city of Philadelphia also has an amazing Jewish connection. Philadelphia and Pennsylvania both contain *twelve* letters, the Bible number for Israel. Haym Solomon, the previously mentioned banker who financed the American Revolution, is buried in a Hebrew cemetery in Philadelphia. One might call him *the* "key" that opened the door to the Philadelphia Church Age, being situated in the "*Key*stone State" (especially since Revelation 3:7 mentions a *Jewish* "key," i.e., as in *"the key of David"*). The first native-born and longest serving prime minister in Israel's history, Benjamin "Bibi" Netanyahu, graduated from Cheltenham High School, located in the Philadelphia suburb of Wyncote. It has been said that he speaks perfect English with a Philadelphia accent and that a miniature "Liberty Bell" often sat on his desk. (For the record, Bibi was ousted by the same end-day, globalist cabal that eliminated Donald Trump, as per II Timothy 3:4.) Finally, even the "Italian Stallion" got into the act. Michael "Mickey" Goldmill was the fictional Jewish character created by Sylvester Stallone and portrayed by Burgess Meredith in the *Rocky* film series. Based on the fellow

Hebrew bantamweight, Charley Goldman, Mickey plays the ex-pug-turned-trainer who winds up guiding the Catholic Balboa to fame and fortune.

No doubt, Brother Whitefield smiled up in Glory. (Through God's mercy, the British evangelist was called Home on September 30, 1770, seven years before he would have had to choose sides in the war.) Having labeled Pennsylvania as the "Garden of America," Whitefield chose Philadelphia as his Capernaum. Whereas Clarke and Williams had described Rhode Island as an *"Efficacious* Experiment," William Penn labeled *his* colony as a *"Holy* Experiment." Whitefield's outdoor crowds often surpassed the city's entire population of 12,000 (the largest American city at that time). On Sunday, May 11, 1740, the "Grand Itinerant" addressed 15,000 souls in the morning and 20,000 more in the evening! After measuring the area reached by his voice in one particular service, Benjamin Franklin confirmed, "I computed that he might well be heard by more than thirty thousand." Others testified that they could hear him on the Jersey shore—a *mile* away!

Whitefield also knew that the Baptists had something his dry Protestant brethren lacked. "I went and heard Mr. Jones, the Baptist minister, who preached the truth as it is in Jesus. He is the only preacher that I know in *Philadelphia,* who speaks feelingly and with authority. The poor people are much refreshed by him, and I trust the Lord will bless him more and more." However, *most* of all, George saw the spiritual electricity in Mr. Franklin's city as a powerful harbinger of the approaching transition *from* Sardis *to* Philadelphia. His amazing follow-up diary entry for November 28, 1739, reads:

> Blessed be God, for the great work begun in these parts. Oh, that what God says of the Church of Philadelphia in the *Revelation,* may be now fulfilled in the city called after her name! *"I know thy works.* **Behold I have set before thee an open door, and no man can shut it.** *Behold I will make them of the synagogue of Satan to come and worship before thy feet, and to know that I have loved thee."*

So there you have it—the éclat of Western civilization! With the "Bloody Whore" three thousand miles away and her harlot Protestant offspring checked by the powerful First Amendment, the Baptists were liberated at long last to bring about the vindication of their holy and jealous Creator (Isaiah 42:8). Thanks to the words "freedom of speech," no American minister would be burned at the stake for street preaching. And, owing to the "free press" clause, no one would be burned for printing the Holy Bible, either. With these two safeguards in place, an army of Baptist soul winners rushed through their Philadelphia door to obey the scriptural charge atop the Liberty Bell, *"Proclaim **liberty** throughout all the land unto all the inhabitants thereof"* (Leviticus 25:10). Should we be surprised to learn that the modern city of *Liberty*, North Carolina, "just happened" to spring up around the still-functioning Sandy Creek Baptist Church?

Over the next two hundred years, the United States of America would rise to a level of prominence and prosperity unparalleled in the annals of mankind. As the Roman Empire had limited the *"Holy One of Israel"* (Psalm 78:41), the Baptists in America had inspired a form of government that would unleash the mighty power of God. Promises such as, *"Blessed is the nation whose God is the Lord"* (Psalm 33:12) and *"Righteousness exalteth a nation"* (Proverbs 14:34), could now be appropriated. Whitefield's "ducks" had come a *long* way. And, to ensure that the public never forgets, the words inscribed on Leland's impressive memorial in the Leland-Madison Park cement the historical reality of this glorious event once and for all!

1754-1841
ELDER JOHN LELAND
COURAGEOUS LEADER OF
THE BAPTIST DOCTRINE
ARDENT ADVOCATE OF THE PRINCIPLES
OF DEMOCRACY
VINDICATOR OF SEPARATION
OF CHURCH AND STATE

NEAR THIS SPOT IN 1788 JOHN LELAND AND
JAMES MADISON, THE FATHER OF THE AMERICAN
CONSTITUTION, HELD A SIGNIFICANT INTERVIEW
WHICH RESULTED IN THE ADOPTION OF THE
CONSTITUTION BY VIRGINIA. THEN MADISON
A MEMBER OF CONGRESS FROM ORANGE PRESENTED
THE FIRST AMENDMENT TO THE CONSTITUTION
GUARANTEEING RELIGIOUS LIBERTY, FREE SPEECH AND
A FREE PRESS. THIS SATISFIED LELAND AND HIS
BAPTIST FOLLOWERS.

PRESENTED BY EUGENE BUCKLIN BOWEN PRESIDENT
BERKSHIRE COUNTY MASSACHUSETTS CHAPTER
SONS OF THE AMERICAN REVOLUTION.

In closing, *the* single most important observation to make about the birth of the Philadelphia Church Age was the statement in Revelation 3:8, *"[T]hou hast kept my word."* For, although the Baptists had received their King James Bible in 1611, they were compelled to *"hold fast"* for another 180 years until the freedom to spread it was granted in 1791. Enlarged and enlightened, Japheth would finally be enabled to fulfill his pre-ordained purpose as given in I Timothy 2:1-4.

12

Paradise Lost

I
T TOOK SEVENTEEN centuries for a privileged portion of Christ's Body to experience I Timothy 2:1-4. However, it would take only 230 years for "America the Beautiful" to become "Paradise Lost." (*Paradise Lost* is an epic poem about the fall of Adam and Eve, written in 1667 by English poet John Milton.) This chapter will reveal the primary cause for her loss, the terminus occurring at the low-water mark of the 2020 presidential election. It is no coincidence that the door to America's freedom would *close* in the very locale where it *opened*—the worst voter fraud taking place in the "City of Brotherly Love." (In April 2022, Philadelphia became the first major US city to reinstate indoor mask mandates.)

The Philadelphia Church Age (1791-1901) was the most fruitful period in Church history (to be followed by the worst era). This epoch produced the greatest church planters, pastors, evangelists, missionaries, and soul winners of all time. And, according to the loony anti-KJV crowd, it was somehow built upon a "flawed" *translation* of "inferior" *copies*. Nonetheless, working in tandem with the Bill of Rights, Japheth's AV 1611 would experience an unprecedented proliferation of one billion copies, translated into some three hundred languages. As Peter (Simeon) told the Jerusalem church how *"God at the first did visit the Gentiles, to take out of them a people for his name"* (Acts 15:14), Japheth "the Elder" would now be *enabled* to reach significant numbers of his younger Shemite and Hamite siblings around the globe.

Even the Protestant translators discerned that a special door was opening before them. Dr. Miles Smith (aka "A very walking library"), wrote the new Bible's preface, stating:

And in what sort did these assemble? In the trust of their own knowledge, or of their sharpness of wit, or deepness of judgment, as it were in an arm of flesh? At no hand. *They trusted in him that hath the key of David, opening, and no man shutting*; they prayed to the Lord, the Father of our Lord....

While the Baptists opened the door, all evangelical denominations would benefit as well.

"GIMME THAT OLD-TIME RELIGION"

Although the Baptists differed from their Methodist and Presbyterian brethren in many doctrinal issues, there was a surprising amount of commonality, especially in the area of soul winning. For one thing, everyone used the same Bible, the 1611 Authorized Version. This was the age where folks were still "simpleminded" enough to grasp the concept of a singular, or final, authority. While the preacher was known as the *parson*, meaning *person*, thus, "*the* person" —the Bible, meaning *book*, was likewise understood to be "*the* Book" (i.e., "Mamma's sick; call *the* person with *the* Book.") The modern perversions would not show up for another century.

Not only did these frontier parsons have the right Bibles on their pulpits (often alongside a gun), they also knew how to use them, especially when preaching on Hell. While modern sinners in post-Billy Graham America hide in Hell-denying "worship centers," this was not always so. Back in the day, when a lost person would visit the First Baptist Church in any town, he was sure to hear, *"If you don't git borned ag'in, you'll split Hell wide open!"* Petrified, he would run out and try the First Presbyterian Church next door. Because the robe-wearing "Rev" there seemed more reserved, the sinner would lower his guard. This time, however, the shocking message was, *"If you're not one of the elect,* you will split Hell wide open, and there's *nothing* you can do about it either!!"* Having staggered out the back door and across the street into the last church in town, the poor wretch is last seen jumping out the window with the Methodist preacher screaming, "Even if you *are* borned ag'in, you can *still* lose it and split Hell *wide* open anyhow!!!" Preaching like this kept a nation on the edge of its pew.

As a Tennessee resident, I was thrilled to learn of an incident involving the "Volunteer State" that epitomizes the power of the Philadelphia

Age. Our story begins in 1852 with a one-room schoolhouse graduation in neighboring Alabama. The students of Oak Bowery School chose a precocious five-year-old to serve as a novelty commencement mascot. Standing on a table, the closing line of the lad's memorized speech was a showstopper: "In coming years and thundering tones, the world shall hear of Sam P. Jones!" (In a personal aside, when I was nine years old, the New York Mets ended their 1962 inaugural season with a disastrous 40-120 record, prompting the *New York Times* to dispatch a roving reporter to Manhattan's Central Park to interview disgruntled fans. When he stopped to chat with my father, who was playing ball with my sister and me, he made the mistake of asking what I thought, whereupon I replied, "I got two words for the Mets— 'They're lousy!'")

After his family moved to Georgia, Sam went on to become a successful lawyer. However, he later yielded to alcoholism. Sobered up by the death of his Christian father, Sam accepted Christ in a revival meeting conducted in his grandfather's Methodist church. He preached his first sermon a week later from Romans 1:16. Sam's ministry was transformed when he heard a Methodist circuit rider, Simon Peter Richardson, say, "The preacher is not a vassal, not a slave, but a king and his throne is his pulpit." His love for the plain text of the AV 1611 was exceeded only by his contempt for dead scholarship. He'd often say, "I'd rather study my ABCs in Heaven then my Greek and Hebrew in Hell." With most of his meetings in the Bible Belt, the fire-breathing, "Hellfire-and-Damnation" Jones rarely preached on Heaven. When a certain committee complained that they had invited him to preach *to* sinners but that he ended up preaching *at* them, Sam replied, "Never mind, I will get to the sinners. I never scald hogs until the water is hot." When asked why he didn't attack the Catholics, he answered, "When I get through with the Methodists, it's bedtime."

If "Reverend" Jones were alive today, do you think he would get many invitations? In *The Life and Sayings of Sam P. Jones* (written by his wife), Mrs. Jones tells how her hubby once stirred the town of West Point, Georgia, to revival by having his door-to-door visitation teams (consisting only of Sam, the host pastor, and two elderly ladies) greet the unsuspecting folk with the blunt announcement, *"You are going to Hell!"* On another occasion, the mayor of Palestine, Texas, was so mad when Sam exposed the corruption in his administration that he literally

attacked the evangelist at the local train depot. In a telegraph message
to his wife, Sam related:

> The one-horse mayor of Palestine, Texas, tried to cane me at the
> train this morning. He hit me three times. *I wrenched the cane from
> him, and wore him out.* I am well. Not hurt. Will lecture tonight at
> LaGrange.

"CAPTAIN TOM"

In 1885, the ministers in Nashville, Tennessee, erected a tent (at
Broadway and 8th Avenue) seating 6,000 and watched Sam pack it out
four times a day for over thirty consecutive days! The "early" meeting
was at 6:00 AM Nearly 10,000 decisions for Christ resulted from that
month-long revival! (The city's entire population was only 50,000.) On
the evening of May 10, the popular riverboat magnate, Captain Thomas
"Tom" Green Ryman, slipped into the tent (with a few "associates") to
"confront" the controversial preacher who was affecting his livelihood.
At the time, the forty-four-year-old Nashville native owned and operated
thirty-five steamboats—the largest fleet of passenger and cargo ships
on the Cumberland—many providing gambling and liquor. The happily
married father of eight also owned several bars, including the largest
waterfront saloon in town. With Sam's hard preaching against "John
Barleycorn," a head-on collision with one of the original "Tennessee
Titans" was inevitable.

Thankfully, Captain Tom would be no match for Sam's Captain
(Hebrews 2:10). The evangelist preached and the entrepreneur listened.
To everybody's shock, Ryman fell under conviction and left the tent a
born-again Christian! As per II Corinthians 5:17, when his contracts
with the riverboat liquor concessionaires expired, Tom chose not to
renew them, costing him plenty. His greatest burden now became the
souls in Nashville who were still unsaved, especially his family and
friends. Thus, he informed his spiritual mentor that God had led him to
build a state-of-the-art venue worthy of the message he preached. The
construction would take seven years at a cost of $3,000,000 in today's
money. On May 25, 1890, Sam held his first revival at the site with
only the foundation and six-foot walls standing. Meanwhile, Ryman
built a Gospel Wagon, complete with pulpit, organ, and choir platform
to take God's salvation into the local areas.

Finally, the new, cutting-edge, acoustically designed 2,362-seat auditorium opened in 1892 as the Union Gospel Tabernacle (the humble patron refusing to have the place named after himself). Thomas Ryman died on December 23, 1904. At his funeral on Christmas Day, Sam eulogized his convert, saying, "A purer, stronger, nobler man, truer to God than he, I have never met." He also recommended to the thousands of mourners that the Tabernacle be re-named in Captain Tom's honor. From that day till now, the edifice at 116 Fifth Avenue North has been known as the "Ryman Auditorium." (Sam joined his pal on October 15, 1906, his own memorial being conducted at "The Ryman" as well.)

"WINE IS A MOCKER, STRONG DRINK IS RAGING"

On June 28, 1907, the Women's Christian Temperance Union gathered for its national convention in the Ryman. However, it wouldn't take long for Sam and Tom's old beer guzzling crowd (aligned with the martini sippers) to capture the sanctified structure. As a sad harbinger, on July 31, 1915, Captain Tom Ryman, Jr., was shot six times and killed on his own ship (the Jo Horton Fall) by a disgruntled former employee. By now, a brash promoter, Lula Clay Naff, had leased the Ryman to steer it into the "Roaring Twenties." The former Union Gospel Tabernacle soon became the haven of Nashville's cultural elite. Ever since that first 1885 Crusade, the high society crowd had been gunning for Sam, a *Nashville Union* editorial stating:

> If Mr. Jones's style and language suit the good people of our city, then we can no longer rightfully maintain our boast that Nashville is the "Athens of the South"…We have as much culture, refinement and esthetic taste in Nashville as any city of its size in the Union, and that this so-called reverend gentleman should be permitted to say such things in our leading pulpits, and then be invited to come again, amazes us beyond expression.

Thus, whereas John Philip Sousa performed his famed "Stars and Stripes Forever" on October 25, 1894, some of the "new" headliners would include: Charlie Chaplin (1918); Vatican Choirs of the Sistine Chapel (1919); Jazz Hounds (1921); Harry Houdini (1924); W. C. Fields (1928); Ziegfeld Follies (1935); and Katherine Hepburn in *The Philadelphia Story* (1941). During World War II the Ryman began its legendary three-decade run as "Home to the Grand Ole Opry." The Bible Belt would now make its sad transition from *Sam* Jones to *Spike* Jones and *George* Jones.

Among Garth "Beer Run" Brooks' many "Friends in Low Places," the latest wave of future "stars" would include: Hank Williams, Sr. ("There's a Tear in My Beer"); Hank Williams, Jr. ("Whiskey Bent and Hell Bound" and "Family Tradition"); Hank Williams III ("Smoke and Wine"); Willie Nelson ("Whiskey River" and "I Gotta Get Drunk"); Roy Acuff ("Wreck on the Highway"); George Jones ("White Lightning"); Loretta Lynn ("Bartender" and "Wine, Women, and Song"); Merle Haggard ("I Think I'll Just Stay Here and Drink"); Conway Twitty ("Wine Me Up"); Bob Wills ("Bubbles in my Beer"); Tex Ritter ("Rye Whiskey"); Johnny Cash ("I Hardly Ever Sing Beer Drinking Songs" and "He Turned the Water Into Wine"); Jerry Lee Lewis ("Who Will Buy the Wine?"); Kenny Chesney ("Drink it Up"); Greg and Duane Allman ("Drunken Hearted Boy"); Carrie Underwood ("Drinking Alone" and "My Savior"); Brad Paisley ("Whiskey Lullaby"); and Toby Keith's great advice ("Get Drunk and Be Somebody").

On October 23, 1994, the first *Sam's Place* showcased a plethora of contemporary Christian, Country, and Gospel "artists." The series was obviously named after the original inspiration for their iconic, red-bricked, Victorian-Gothic styled palace—Reverend Samuel Porter Jones! ("In coming years and thundering tones....") Truth be told, he'd hardly recognize the joint! Imagine Mae West strutting around on the very stage where Sam had preached the Gospel! Captain Tom's legacy has devolved to "The Carnegie Hall of the South," then "The Birthplace of Bluegrass," and finally, worst of all, "The Mother *Church* of Country Music." On June 25, 2001, the Ryman was designated a National Historic Landmark. Then, smack dab in the Covid era, on June 10, 2021, Madonna wannabe Miley Cyrus hosted a free Pride Month-themed concert at the pride of "Music City," *but*, only for vaccinated patrons (sure wouldn't want any potential AIDS victims being infected by the China Virus). So, *what* in the world happened, you say? Believe it or not, it all had to do with an unheeded warning…from beyond the grave.

SERPENTS IN PARADISE

As a bedridden James Madison approached his earthly departure, his burden for America was heavy. Having no children of his own, the "Father of the Constitution" determined to bequeath his national progeny a last word of paternal consolation. In the Fall of 1834, the ailing statesman penned, for posthumous disclosure, his poignant final "Advice to My Country."

> As this advice, if it ever see the light will not do it till I am no more, it may be considered as issuing it from the tomb, where truth alone can be respected, and the happiness of man alone consulted. It will be entitled therefore to whatever weight can be derived from good intentions, and from the experience of one who has served his country in various stations through a period of forty years, who espoused in his youth and adhered through his life to the cause of its liberty, and who has borne a part in most of the great transactions which will constitute epochs of its destiny. The advice nearest to my heart and deepest in my convictions is that the Union of the States be cherished and perpetuated. Let the open enemy to it be regarded as Pandora with her box opened; *and the disguised one, as the Serpent creeping with his deadly wiles into Paradise."*

This amazing testament speaks to the truth that *"the god of this world"* was not *about* to relinquish any turf without a fight. Mr. Madison warned his posterity that their freedom would be threatened by enemies, seen and unseen. In *How Satan Turned America Against God,* I posited three main "serpents" that the Devil would employ to eventually destroy our liberties: *slavery, secret societies,* and *Roman Catholic immigration.* One does not have to be a rocket scientist to see how this Satanic trilogy has spit its venom since the 2016 election.

The "Peculiar Institution" is *still* encumbering Japheth's descendants (despite 750,000 Civil War deaths) vis-à-vis Critical Race Theory, Black Lives Matter, urban riots, reparations demands, Al Sharpton's ugly puss, et al. Then, who could miss the secret societies' (aka the "Deep State") orchestration of the China Virus "Plandemic" *and* their successful coup d'état of President Trump's re-election? Did these modern *"traitors"* fulfill II Timothy 3:4? As for Rome's part in our present chaos, how did "the Donald's" Catholic Supreme Court appointees do when push came to shove? Did those nice right-wing ideologues throw him under the bus via I Timothy 4:1-6? Has anyone noticed that the escalating "Border Crisis" just *happens* to mirror the *exact* blueprint I gave in *What Hath God Wrought!* ... in 1996? Did all those warnings by Samuel Morse about the Vatican's clandestine plan to invade America with illegal immigration come to pass (i.e., *The Saint Leopold Foundation for the Furtherance of Catholic Missions in America*)? Did the 2002 Hollywood film *Gangs of New York* illustrate the identical material in my chapter, "The Devil's D-Day?" And, did the floodgates open under a pro-abortion, Roman Catholic president named Joe Biden, supported by his Catholic House Speaker, Nancy Pelosi? Did the specific transfer of these Covid-infected illegals to the leading Red states (Texas and Florida) spark a resurgence of the Covid-19 panic? Was the Jesuit-trained Dr. Anthony Fauci involved?

However, the Whore's deadliest attack occurred when she sank her fangs into the King James Bible. As President Andrew Jackson lay dying, he pointed to an AV 1611 and said, "That book, Sir, is the Rock upon which our Republic rests." Every Pope has known this from the night the Jesuit-led Guy Fawkes Plot to kill James I was foiled on November 5, 1605. Heretofore, the growth of English Protestantism has been linked to her possession of a vernacular Bible. So, in 1582, Rome endorsed the adage, "If you can't beat 'em, join 'em," producing her own English New Testament, rendered by Jesuits at Rheims (the Old Testament in 1610 at Douay). A marginal reference in the first Catholic English "Bible" predicted that the king's revisers would "be abhorred in the depths of Hell." (Yawn...) The anti-KJV poison began to work as soon as the "Monarch of the Books" appeared. The liberal Protestant, Dr. Hugh Broughton, said he "had rather be rent in pieces by wild horses than any such translation by my consent should be urged upon poor churches."

The main difference between the two competing Bibles was in their underlying texts. The KJV New Testament (along with its six precursors) was translated primarily from the *Textus Receptus* ("received text"), the predominant Greek tradition of the manuscript era (also known as the *Majority, Traditional, Byzantine* and *Antiochian* text). The Douay-Rheims issued from the same flawed manuscripts that Jerome used for his *Latin Vulgate,* the "Bible" that ushered in the Dark Ages. The manuscript authority for Rome's 1610 counterfeit were those two infamous fourth-century Alexandrian codices, *Vaticanus* ("B") and *Sinaiticus* ("Aleph"), prefigured by those two Alexandrian vessels in Acts 27 and 28.

Satan's strategy was simple. While American Christians could never be duped into dumping their beloved AV 1611 for a Catholic "Bible," the trick was to get them to swap *up* to a "better" Protestant version— yet based on the same corrupt Greek text *below*. The plan called for revising the KJV in England, then exporting it to the United States for some good ole Yankee tweaking. The main culprits were Anglican Bishop Brooke Foss Westcott and Cambridge professor Fenton John Anthony Hort. Though technically Protestants, their extant letters reek with pro-Catholic sympathies (Mariolatry, Purgatory, Popery, Oxford Movement). Unbeknown to many, both men *hated* the United States of America. In one of his letters, Dr. Hort wrote:

> I...cannot say that I see much as yet to soften my deep hatred of democracy in all its forms. I care more for England and for Europe than for America, how much more than for all the niggers in the world! And I contend that the highest morality requires me to do so...Whatever people may say to the contrary, the American empire is a standing menace to the whole civilization of Europe, and sooner or later one or the other must perish...Surely, if ever Babylon or Rome were rightly cursed, it cannot be wrong to desire and pray from the bottom of one's heart that *the American union may be shivered to pieces.*

Having covered this history in *Final Authority,* only a brief review is necessary. From 1853-71, the two academics secretly made a new Greek text from *Vaticanus* and *Sinaiticus*. It was then smuggled into the Church of England Revision Committee, then unleashed on the gullible, mostly conservative participants (after being duped into agreeing to an "iron rule of silence").

After ten years of combative "revision," the *English Revised Version* (New Testament) slithered out on May 17, 1881. The Old Testament completed the project in 1885—the same year 20% of Nashville's populace got saved listening to Sam Jones preach out of a King James Bible! With the "Dynamic Duo's" release of *The New Testament in the Original Greek,* having replaced the *Textus Receptus* readings in over 5,000 places, the *Revised Version* ultimately altered the KJV in some 36,000 particulars! The key observation is that the so-called "revised AV 1611" caused *great* rejoicing within the ranks of Roman Catholicism.

The "Very Reverend" Thomas S. Preston of Saint Ann's Roman Catholic Church in New York was quick to report:

> The brief examination which I have been able to make of the Revised Version of the New Testament has convinced me that the Committee have labored with great sincerity and diligence, and that they have produced a translation much more correct than that generally received among Protestants. It is to us a gratification to find that in very many instances they have adopted the reading of the Catholic Version, and have thus by their scholarship confirmed the correctness of our Bible.

The *Dublin Review* for July 1881 predicted, "The New Version will be the death knell of Protestantism." Literally *hundreds* of modern perversions have come and gone over the past century, showcasing such "spirituality" as: *The Black Bible Chronicles'* Ebonics translation of Genesis 3:1 (mentioned in chapter five), "Now the serpent was one bad dude;" a "sodomite friendly" version, *The Queen James Bible*, released in 2011 (the 400th anniversary of the AV 1611), pitched as a King James Bible "edited to prevent homophobic misinterpretation;" and the exclusive (just for Trekkies) *Klingon Language Version's* rendering of Psalm 23:1—"joH'a' 'oH wIj DevwI' jIH DIchDaq Hutlh pagh." (All I can say is, "Beam me up, Scotty, there's no intelligent life down here.")

"PILGRIM'S APOSTASY"

The all-time greatest selling book (apart from the King James Bible) is the 1678 classic by John Bunyan, *The Pilgrim's Progress* (a spiritual commentary on the AV 1611). Bunyan's allegory has been translated into more than two hundred languages and has never been out of print. Even the secular world regards it as "one of the most significant works of religious, theological fiction in English literature." Bunyan was a non-conformist Baptist preacher in England who spent twelve years in the Bedford Prison for refusing to take a license. It was here that he wrote *The Pilgrim's Progress*, mostly using charcoal for ink and crumpled milk churn lids for paper.

Nearly all Christians are familiar with the story line of his book. It revolves around the spiritual "progress" of the main character, "Christian," from his conversion to his arrival in the Land of Beulah and victorious crossing over the "River of Death." Of course, the "shining light" of the AV 1611 forms the centrality of Pilgrim's journey. One of God's greatest luminaries during the "Sunset of Sardis," Bunyan would go on to author sixty books before his death at age fifty-nine. The following "dispute with a scholar" is taken from *The Struggler*, and will serve as an apropos illustration of Bunyan's devotion to the King James Bible:

> As Mr. Bunyan was upon the road near Cambridge, there overtakes him a scholar that had observed him a preacher, and said to him, How dare you preach, seeing you have not the original, being not a scholar?
>
> Then said Mr. Bunyan, Have you the original?
>
> Yes, said the scholar.
>
> Nay, but, said Mr. Bunyan, have you the very self-same original copies that were written by the penmen of the scriptures, prophets and apostles?
>
> No, said the scholar, but we have the true copies of those originals.
>
> How do you know that? said Mr. Bunyan.
>
> How? said the scholar. Why, we believe what we have is a true copy of the original.
>
> Then, said Mr. Bunyan, so do I believe our English Bible is a true copy of the original.
>
> Then away rid [sic] the scholar.

Unfortunately, however, as we shall now see, "Pilgrim's *Apostasy*" would begin with a small cabal of fellow *Baptist* "scholars" intent on overthrowing the AV 1611.

AMERICAN BIBLE UNION VERSION (ABUV)

While most Bible believers know of the pro-Vatican Westcott and Hort scam behind the modern-day tsunami of "improved" Protestant Bibles, few realize who fired the first shot. According to Dr. Larry Vance, there were thirty-eight attempts to dethrone the KJV from 1653 to 1867. Though most were not worth the dynamite to blow them up, two would prove more troublesome than all the rest combined. Five years after Andy Jackson's death (and three before Westcott and Hort began their furtive work), a self-deluded *Baptist* mission board in *America* attempted a major hammer blow to Old Hickory's "Rock." The ill-fated groundwork for *this* abomination was laid by another group of misguided gnat-strainers eight years previous.

If you can believe it, neighbor, in 1842—just *fifty* years after the Philadelphia door was opened by the liberating First Amendment to the Constitution—a new edition of the King James Version "carefully revised and amended by several Biblical scholars" was published in *Philadelphia.* However, more shocking than its publication site was the title that later appeared on its binding—*Baptist Bible.* To make a long story short, a cabal of Baptist "scholars" led by David Bernard and A. C. Kendrick, got the bright idea to produce an "Immersionist" version (i.e., John the "Immerser"). Basically, the Baptist intelligentsia, *"ever learning, and never able to come to the knowledge of the truth"* (II Timothy 3:7), disliked the *transliteration* of the Greek verb *baptizo* into the English "baptize," preferring the stricter *translation* into "immerse." Supposedly, this was a prejudicial conspiracy by the Church of England to mask their Pedobaptism error (despite the *Oxford English Dictionary* confirming that "baptize" was in use as early as the eleventh century). Another "doctrinal" hang-up was for "congregation" or "assembly" over "church."

A sample of the multiplied earth-shattering "improvements" they made to the AV 1611 would include (beginning in Genesis): "food" instead of "meat" (Genesis 1:29); "Cherubim" instead of "Cherubims" (Genesis 3:24); "bore" instead of "bare" (Genesis 6:4); "spoke" instead of "spake" (Genesis 8:15), "begot" instead of "begat" (Genesis 10:24). (*Please*—tell me I don't have to go on....) And of course, "Day-star" was substituted for "Lucifer" in Isaiah 14:12; and, most appropriately, Mr. Madison's "vipers" replaced "cockatrice" in Isaiah 59:5. Perhaps their most essential "upgrades" in the New Testament (apart from "immerse" and "congregation"), were inserting "John the Baptist" for "John Baptist" in Luke 7:20, along with dumping "Jesus" for "Joshua"— *twice,* in Acts 7:45 *and* Hebrews 4:8. (Like I said, "Beam me up, Scotty!")

Well now, the Holy Spirit was *so* "impressed" with the *Baptist Bible* that He let it crash and burn on the runway! Had *you* ever heard of it before? (The Baptist History Preservation Society has a copy of the 1847 version.) Unfortunately, it would jumpstart the second, far more influential Baptist effort to replace the KJV. On June 23, 1850, several prominent Baptists in the American Bible Society left to form the American Bible Union at the Baptist Tabernacle on Manhattan's famed Mulberry Street. Still irked by the "baptizo" fiasco, *this* time the goal was to take the defunct *Baptist Bible* to the next level. The only problem was that the higher *up* you take a bad idea, the further *down* you will fall. The site itself represented quite an "omen," as Mulberry Street would soon become the heart of "Little Italy" and eventual ground zero for the American Mafia (i.e., the Ravenite Social Club, 247 Mulberry Street, aka "John Gotti's Bunker").

The leading force behind *this* proposed revision was the celebrated intellectual, Spencer H. Cone, DD. Now before "Brother Spence" became a Baptist in 1814, he spent seven years honing his future "homiletical" skills as a *professional actor*. Too early for the Ryman Auditorium, Spence made his debut in July 1805 at the Chestnut Street Theater in— *Philadelphia*. (Here we go again, folks.) His breakthrough role was playing the minor character Achmet in the tragedy, *Mahomet* (a play by the atheist Voltaire about Mohammed). So, now we have a former actor on Mulberry Street about to perform his grand denouement, i.e., trying to convince the Baptists to dump their King James Bibles! Cone also felt there were plenty of other problems besides the "baptism thing," stating, "Yet, this is but one of numerous errors, which, in our estimation, demand correction."

The fateful *American Bible Union Version* (ABUV) project began in 1852 with over two dozen "reputable" scholars. The New Testament was published in sections: Gospels in 1862; Acts through II Corinthians, 1863; Galatians through Revelation, 1864, with a final revision in 1865. The Old Testament was not completed until 1912 (Thomas Armitage citing embarrassing debt as the cause). Cone boasted that his Baptist opus had corrected 24,000 errors in the "Protestant" KJV. However, to see how pleased "The Book's" Author was, you might want to take a second look at that data—from *His* view: Gospels, 1862 (The Seven Days Battles, 36,000 total casualties; Shiloh, 24,000; Antietam, 22,700); Acts through II Corinthians, 1863 (Gettysburg, 51,000; Chickamauga, 35,000; Chancellorsville, 30,000); Galatians through Revelation, 1864 (Spotsylvania, 30,000; Wilderness, 21,000; Cold Harbor, 18,000); final revision, 1865 (Abraham Lincoln assassinated).

At the end of the day, "Achmet" never had one curtain call. While the Baptist intelligentsia got swept up in the moment, the common folk (Mark 12:37) dumped the ABUV like a bad habit. Thomas Armitage (a translation member himself) said, "While many men of learning and nerve espoused the movement, a storm of opposition was raised against it from one land to the other." Referring to that "storm," the otherwise conservative Dr. Armitage humbly admitted, "Every consideration was presented on the subject but the main thought: that the Author of the inspired originals had the infinite right to a hearing, and that man was in duty bound to listen to his utterances, all human preference or expediency to the contrary notwithstanding." (What that means in the "Greek" is— "It is what it is!") Writing in 1907, even the notoriously liberal Baptist historian, Henry C. Vedder, was forced to concede:

> *The project of circulating a denominational version of the Scriptures in English has been tested once for all and proved to be a disastrous failure.* The version was successfully made and possesses many merits, but it could not be circulated; Baptists could neither be forced nor coaxed to use it. They were greatly the losers and are still by reason of this apathy, but we must take the facts of human nature as we find them; and one fact now unquestioned is that the attachment of English-speaking Christians to the version of the Scriptures endeared to them by long use and tender association has proved to be too strong for the successful substitution of any other.

Although the ABUV flopped like its precursor, *this* time Satan would use Cone's junk to inspire a *serious* revision across the Atlantic. News of the American attempt to replace their sacrosanct "baptize" with "immerse" created panic within the Church of England. Armitage wrote that the ABUV "so completely revolutionized public opinion on the subject of revision that a new literature was created on the subject, both in England and America, and a general demand for revision culminated in action on that subject by the Convocation of Canterbury in 1870." A year later, the 1871-1885 Revision Committee (totally dominated by Westcott and Hort with their secret Greek New Testament) was up and running thanks to Spence and his Baptist Coneheads! According to Armitage (*A History of the Baptists*, Volume 2, p. 911), one of the key translators on this sinister committee stated, *"We never make an important change without consulting the Union's version."* You just read one of the *most* important statements in this entire book!!

No sooner had our early nineteenth-century Baptist leaders grown spoiled with the political cover afforded by the Bill of Rights than they allowed Satan to deceive them into attacking the very translation that God had already sanctioned for over two centuries. Truer words were never spoken than, *"Great men are not always wise."* (Job 32:9) Even the spiritual giant Clarence Larkin was taken in for a time. Thankfully, the rank-and-file Baptists had enough sense to follow the Holy Ghost instead; which speaks to one of the key observations of our time. The average Independent Baptist preacher today appears to be "stuck on stupid" when it comes to striking a proper balance between their Baptist heritage and their King James Bible (Proverbs 11:1).

Many of my "Ruckmanite" friends will defend the KJV to the death while displaying a mediocre attitude regarding their Baptist identity. The "Baptist Briders" (or "Landmarkers") exhibit a double hang-up. Not only is their lauded "Baptist with a 'Big B' position" over the top (as it denies the invisible Body of Christ, relegating this New Testament mystery to *local* Baptist assemblies), but like Cone and his cronies, they will normally disavow the AV 1611 by elevating "the" underlying *Textus Receptus* as their final authority. My fellow HAC alumni can no longer know what to believe as Jack Hyles is gone (i.e., old joke about question-and-answer luncheons when pastors would ask, "Dr. Hyles, can you tell us what we believe about such and such?") And the camp-meeting crowd is too busy "shouting it out" (when they're not blasting "double-married preachers," etc.) to even grasp the issue. Thus, the Lord's sheep are running out of time for some of you knucklehead shepherds to get your act together (Luke 12:32)!

AMERICAN STANDARD "COMMODE" VERSION (ASCV)

The disastrous Reconstruction-induced Fourteenth Amendment ending states' rights was ratified only four years after the ABUV's release. But there would be more dots to connect. On January 22, 1881, a sixty-nine-foot tall, two-hundred-ton granite obelisk arrived in New York City from *Alexandria*, Egypt. Known as "Cleopatra's Needle," the 3,500-year-old monolith was erected in Manhattan's Central Park before 10,000 awed spectators. (Conversely, the Latin phrase "Laus Deo," meaning "Praise be to God," adorns the east face of the aluminum cap atop the American-made Washington Monument, completed in 1884.) Two months later, on March 4th, the cream of Washington society assembled in the Smithsonian's Arts and Industries Building for the inaugural ball of

President James Garfield. Once inside its rotunda, the refined guests were transfixed by a giant allegorical female statue of America holding a lamp in her right hand. The inauguration "treat" was a display of the first electric lighting in Washington, DC. With Jesus stating in Luke 10:18, *"I beheld Satan as **lightning** fall from heaven,"* and Paul describing him in Ephesians 2:2 as *"the prince of the **power of the air**,"* one might think that 1881 was a major turning point for America and the world. At least the spooks did, occultist researcher David Ovason writing, "This idea, that electricity would promote a new life for mankind, was endorsed in a thousand books and works of art."

As previously mentioned, only seventy-four days after that electric lamp lit the Arts and Industries Building, the Church of England released its *Revised Edition* of the New Testament. With the Old Testament finalized in 1885, the new "Bible" exhibited 36,000 departures from the KJV. A final "highlight" of the year was Garfield's own murder on September 19. Felled by two bullets fired by a deranged Chicago lawyer, Charles J. Guiteau, the crime occurring just a short distance from where the president had thrown that electrifying switch. As Ovason notes, "It was clear to everyone that *electricity* had opened vast vistas on a new age." (See freaky lyrics of the Johnny Cash song, "Mr. Garfield.")

At this point the question begs—Was there a nexus between the United States and the *Revised Version*? (Hint: An identical "Cleopatra's Needle" was previously gifted to the British government, arriving in London in 1877.) When the Revision Committee began its fifteen-year project, two American teams were selected (one for each Testament) to critique the work. Although the Yanks had no vote on revision points, they were expected to pass their editorial advice to the mother committee for consideration. The notorious "scholar," Philip Schaff of Union Theological Seminary in New York City, was the unanimous choice to chair both panels. A liberal Protestant, Schaff had earlier served on the final editing board of Cone's ABUV debacle.

"Dr. Phil" chose thirty American scholars for the project. A hodgepodge of denominations was represented, including Baptist, Congregationalist, Dutch Reformed, Methodist, Episcopal, Friends, and "anti-Jesus" Unitarians. As the motive in any modern Bible project is filthy lucre (I Timothy 6:10), the Americans were willing to wait *fifteen* years before they could cash in on *their* efforts. And so, on August 26, 1901, the "illustrious" *American Standard Version* (ASV; officially, the *Revised Version, Standard American Edition*) was published by the *copyright* holder, Thomas Nelson & Sons (Acts 27:11). Oh, and by the way, *this* time it was President William McKinley who got whacked, *eleven* days later in Buffalo, *New York*. (If anyone's keeping score, that's *three* chief executives out, with one on deck, after as many attempts to assassinate the King James Bible.)

As previously stated, the dates for the seven church ages of Revelation chapters two and three are arbitrary. Having assigned the opening of the Philadelphia Age to 1791—corresponding to the liberating Bill of Rights signed in Philadelphia—I would date the Laodicean Age from 1901, corresponding to the first major assault on the AV 1611 upon American soil. This watershed event marks the moment America crossed a critical line. Henceforth, every English translation would be a bastard "Bible" birthed by their RV and ASV parents. The National Council of Churches' *Revised Standard Version* (RSV), changing "virgin" to "young woman" in Isaiah 7:14, would be delivered in 1952. (Their double-minded idiocy was exhibited by retaining "virgin" in Matthew 1:23.)

The *New American Standard Bible* (NASB) would replace the bankrupt ASV in 1971. Dr. S. Franklin Logsdon (pastor of the Moody Church, 1951-53) was the project manager and co-founder (with Dewey Lockman) for the NASB. He wrote the format, interviewed several of the translators, and wrote the Preface. However, when he was eventually made aware of the many corruptions in the finished text, he formally repudiated his involvement. His famous, oft-repeated testimony was, "I'm afraid I'm in trouble with the Lord."

The good ole Southern Baptist Convention released their *Holman Christian Standard Bible* in 2004 following the "standard" aberrations, like deleting Christ's deity in I Timothy 3:16. And on it would go. Perhaps the consummate example of the "scholarship" behind the new "Bibles" is Jeremiah 10:5. The NASB (and the others) replaced the KJV reading, *"They are upright as the **palm tree**"* with "They are like a scarecrow in a cucumber field" (despite the fact that they all get it right at Judges 4:5 when dealing with the exact same Hebrew word).

By now you are probably wondering why the current paragraph heading is "American Standard Commode Version." I chose that title for two reasons: First, over half of the toilets in the United States display the words "American Standard" —*and that's exactly where these new Bibles belong!* (In 2013, the Japanese potty producer, Lixil Corporation, spent $342 million to purchase American Standard Brands, the 138-year-old US maker of toilets and bathroom/kitchen fixtures.) My second reason is a real stretch. You will recall that Paul's Alexandrian grain ship wrecked because the "more part" (i.e., the lukewarm majority in Laodicea) insisted on leaving the fair havens for Phenice, a mere forty miles away. In Acts 27:9-12, the Holy Spirit tells us exactly *why* the fateful decision was made, despite the fact that *"sailing was now dangerous."* (Now, here comes the "stretch," neighbor.) How's *this* for Laodicean logic? *"And because the haven was not **commodious** to winter in, the more part advised to depart thence."* According to *Webster's 1828 Dictionary*, "commodious" means something "convenient" or "suitable," as in the difference between an *outhouse* and an *indoor commode.* (*Somebody* say "Amen!!")

And just in case any of my "high-minded" critics care, an internet article at *vocabulary.com* states, "Yes, you see the word, *commode*—i.e., toilet—in *commodious.* Both words once had the meaning of *convenience* attached to them from their Latin roots. Indoor plumbing is in fact convenient when you compare it with the alternative." Laodiceans view the KJV as a major *inconvenience.* "I can't understand the archaic words," or "Certain passages offend my sensibilities," etc. And they surely don't want the strain of any strife with family and friends. No sir, that "KJV-Only" fanaticism is not *commodious* one bit. While the AV 1611 rendered Paul's words in Philippians 3:8 as, *"I count all things but loss for the excellency of the knowledge of Christ Jesus my Lord: for whom I have suffered the loss of all things, and do count them but **dung**,"* the more delicate ASV says, "for whom I suffered the loss of all things and do count them but *refuse*." Mark it down, friend—America took her first major step toward "Paradise Lost" when she dumped the AV 1611 for the *dung* in the "ASCV" 1901.

"CIVIL RIGHTS"

The word *Laodicea* means "rights of the people," or "civil rights." The end-day Pauline cross-reference is II Timothy 3:2, *"For men shall be lovers of their own selves."* Whereas the "Church of the '*Open* Door'" is easily discerned against the historical backdrop of the Bill of Rights, the "Church of the '*Closed* Door'" is equally conspicuous, being defined by the modern age of unprecedented materialism. The Lord's specific indictment against Laodicea, *"[T]hou sayest,* **I am rich, and increased with goods,***"* mandates an exclusive application to the twentieth and twentieth-first centuries (i.e., no shopping malls in the Dark Ages). Thus, our present-day entitlement culture was forecast two thousand years ago through the very name, Laodicea— *"rights* of the people" (i.e., 1964 Civil Rights Act).

The current Laodicean apostasy is the main cause for the loss of American freedom. In the Philadelphia Age, Jesus sent the Christians out through an *open* door, an obvious symbol of liberty. God's formula has always been simple: to whatever degree local New Testament churches would "keep the *word*," He would "keep the *door*" (Revelation 3:8). In order to fully understand the "door" metaphor, remember that there are actually *two* concepts that blend. While an "open door" symbolizes the unique freedom that American Christians have to come and *go* at will (i.e., with the *Go*spel), it also pictures Jesus in control of the Church itself (Ephesians 5:23).

With this in mind, Laodicea has an obvious problem. In Revelation 3:20, Jesus is standing on the *wrong* side of a *closed* door. In Philadelphia, *He* sends the *Christians* out; in Laodicea, *they* keep *Him* out! Shocking as it sounds, this is the Age where the Lord is thrown out of His own church! Note how John's salutation to Laodicea is the only greeting that reads, *"And unto the angel of the church **of** the Laodiceans"* (i.e., as opposed to *"the church **in** Laodicea,"* as all previous letters read, beginning with Smyrna). The main reason that Jesus—*along with His Philadelphia remnant*—is now on the outside looking in, is because the Church *belongs to* the Laodiceans! (Is that plain enough, neighbor?)

Yet, to be more precise, the Laodiceans did not actually show Jesus (and us) the door per se. It's more sinister than that. In Revelation 3:7-8, the Lord is shown being able to open and shut the Philadelphia door at will. This is because He has a *key. "These things saith he that is holy, he that is true, he that hath the **key** of David."* Simply put, *keys* open doors. (The added fact that it is a *Jewish* key, cross-referenced to Isaiah 22:22, speaks to the previous material regarding the Jews' role in America's founding.) However, in the Laodicean epistle, the text implies that a change has occurred. Apparently, He must now be *let* in— *"if **any** man hear my voice, and **open the door***, I will come in to him."*

Consequently, the prevailing enigma of a "closed door" is reduced to a single, thought-provoking question— *"Who changed the lock?"*

Apparently, the key that opened the Philadelphia door does not fit the Laodicean lock. When an estranged wife is determined to keep her husband out of the house, the first thing she does is change the locks. According to II Corinthians 11:2 and Ephesians 5:20-32, the Church is the Bride of Jesus Christ. Thus, in Laodicea—in a figurative sense—the Lord Jesus has been *locked out* of His own Church by His own apostate Bride. (It is no coincidence that the ancient city of Laodicea just happened to be named after a woman—the third-century BC Seleucid queen, Laodice I, a *real* piece of work, morally.)

THE END OF JAPHETH

When "America the Beautiful" crossed that fateful line in 1901, the ultimate "Doomsday Clock" began ticking. With Japheth the Elder's *enlargement, enlightenment,* and *enablement* now in his rearview mirror, his ignominious *end* would soon be here. The "ten toes" of Daniel 2:34 and 42 reveal that the "Times of the Gentiles" will terminate at the Battle of Armageddon (Revelation 16:16). Thus, the events of the final two centuries would simply pave the way, then pass away as a bad dream (Job 20:8). From the notorious anti-Semite, Henry Ford (one of Hitler's greatest supporters), to the familiar tagline, "Love. It's What Makes a Subaru, a Subaru," employed by the first automaker to target the LGBTQ+ market with specific ad campaigns ("It's Not a Choice. It's the Way We're Built")—they would all make "Mr. Toad's Wild Ride" look like a walk in the park.

To begin, on April 18, 1906, a massive 7.9 earthquake levels San Francisco, killing 3,000. Hollywood's first movie studio appears on Sunset Boulevard in 1911. The 1913 Federal Reserve Act establishes the Federal Reserve Board two days before Christmas. In June 1917, the first 14,000 American "Doughboys" land in France; 116,708 will never return alive. While they're dying "Over There," 675,000 additional Americans die "over here" in the 1918 influenza epidemic. The "Roaring 20s" roar in with liquor, prostitution, and organized crime. The Stock Market crash on October 24, 1929 (aka "Black Thursday"), cripples the economy for years. The 21st Amendment, ending Prohibition by repealing the 18th Amendment, is ratified on December 5, 1933 ("Happy Days Are Here Again," etc.).

The so-called "sneak attack" on Pearl Harbor occurs on December 7, 1941, dragging America into WWII; 405,400 American casualties will follow. On November 6, 1943, Prescott S. Bush and his fellow Union Banking Corporation of New York board members are busted by the Alien Property Custodian for money laundering German Marks for the Third Reich. On August 25, 1945, Baptist missionary and intelligence officer, Captain John M. Birch is secretly executed by Red Chinese troops; the deed is covered up by our State Department, prompting the formation of the conservative, anti-Communist John Birch Society. (The thirty-four-year-long Cold War begins in the aftermath.) The United Nations is launched in San Francisco on October 24, 1945. Of far greater "significance," Benjamin "Bugsy" Siegel's Flamingo Hotel opens in Las Vegas a year later on December 26, 1946.

At the century's midpoint, the surest sign that man's days are numbered occurs at midnight, May 14, 1948, when the tiny State of Israel becomes *"a nation...born at once."* (Isaiah 66:8); America's Baptist president, Harry Truman, shocks even his own Cabinet by issuing a surprise, de-facto recognition eleven minutes later. On January 6, 1957, Elvis Presley's hips are censored from the waist down while gyrating at the Ed Sullivan Theater. (A sixteen-foot bronze statue of Elvis, the world's largest, currently stands in an Arab village a mile outside Jerusalem.) Four months later, Billy Graham (aka "The Pride of Laodicea") makes his pragmatic foray into ecumenical evangelism beginning his sixteen-week New York City Crusade, supported by dozens of liberal Protestant and Catholic clerics. The first fruits of this "revival" occur in 1962 with twin bans on Bible reading and prayer in the public schools. (After all, if the *Church* ditched "The Book," why shouldn't *Caesar*?) For the record, on December 22, 1963, John F. Kennedy becomes the *fourth* president to be assassinated after a major attack on the KJV.

The Beatles begin the "British Invasion," debuting on "The Ed Sullivan Show" on February 9, 1964. The Age-defining Civil Rights Act follows on July 2. The first US combat troops hit Vietnam on March 8, 1965; some 58,000 names will appear on the Vietnam Veterans Memorial Wall, honoring the first Americans to die in a war they *couldn't* win. On March 4, 1966, John Lennon says the Beatles are more popular than Jesus. From April 4 to May 27, 1968, the greatest social unrest the United States had felt since the Civil War occurs as black mobs torch their own "hoods" after MLK's murder. On October 10, 1973, and August 9,

1974, respectively, the dynamic-duo of Spiro "Nolo Contendere" Agnew and Richard "Tricky Dicky" Nixon resign amidst the legendary Watergate Conspiracy (the spiritual cause traced to Dick's betrayal of Israel in the Yom Kippur War).

Meanwhile, on January 22, 1973, a shocking 7-2 Supreme Court decision grants "a woman's right to choose," with over sixty-two million legalized murders perpetrated right on through Covid-19. On August 16, 1977, Elvis Presley—the so-called "King of Rock and Roll" —is found dead on his bathroom floor at Graceland, being "knocked off his throne" (American Standard?) while "taking care of business." On December 8, 1980, John Lennon tries to "Imagine there's no Hell." The first AIDS patient is logged in San Francisco on April 24, 1981. John Birch Society president, Senator Lawrence McDonald, is murdered on September 1, 1983, in the mysterious disappearance of KAL flight 007. The trial run attack on the World Trade Center occurred on February 26, 1993, followed by the bombing of the Alfred P. Murrah Federal Building in Oklahoma City on April 19, 1995. President Bill "It depends on what the meaning of the word 'is' is" Clinton (aka "Slick Willy") is impeached on December 19, 1998.

The century ends in panic over an impending "Y2K" threat that never materializes. A year later, the United States barely escapes a Constitutional crisis when a 5-4 Supreme Court decision gives G. W. Bush the presidency. The horrors of September 11 occur eight months later, followed by successive (and never-ending) military deployments to Iraq and Afghanistan. After Bush coerces Israel to evict 10,000 of its own citizens from Gaza and the West Bank in a giant "Land for Peace" gift to Yasser Arafat, 1.3 million Americans find *themselves* homeless, August 29, 2005, in the wake of Hurricane Katrina. In the middle of our so-called "War on Terrorism," with two hot wars being fought simultaneously in two Islamic countries, an anti-Semitic, Indonesian-bred (some would add, Kenyan-born) closet Muslim with three Middle Eastern Islamic names, is somehow elected to the highest office in the land on November 4, 2008.

In June 2013, Lionsgate Films releases a supernaturalist comedy, *Rapture-Palooza*, about a young couple left behind after the Rapture. The Antichrist, who is black, is after the white chick, so her "skinny-jeans" millennial boyfriend tries to save her. The "highlight" occurs when the wimp takes a giant laser and accidentally smokes Jesus *and*

His winged horse, nixing the Second Advent. On June 26, 2015, a 5-4 Supreme Court decision replaces "Adam and Eve" with "Adam and Steve," ruling that the Fourteenth Amendment requires all states to grant same-sex marriages. America's first "Christian Witches Convention" convenes in Salem, Massachusetts, in April 2019. Four months later, "Dr. Phil's" old Union Theological Seminary has a chapel service in which they confess their sins against plants *to* a collection of plants on stage. In December 2020, Sir Paul McCartney relates that he talks to deceased ex-Beatle George Harrison—*through a tree.*

By 2020, the most unusual phenomenon occurs. With the "more part" of *enlightened* Japheth reduced to Divine vomit (Revelation 3:16), his *unenlightened* globalist kinfolk (based at the World Economic Forum in Davos, Switzerland) have aligned with *Shem* ("China Virus") and *Ham* (Critical Race Theory) in a Satanic death wish to destroy the United States of America, effectively *ending* Japheth's spiritual destiny. And so, after the "Deep State" exploits the Covid-19 "Plandemic" to orchestrate the greatest in-your-face presidential election theft in American history, Joseph R. Biden (aka "Sleepy Joe") is inaugurated as the forty-sixth president of the United States on January 20, 2021. Donald Trump's earlier White House exit is emblematic of the last act in Japheth the Elder's "Paradise Lost" saga. With the ruinous end traced to that filthy "ASCV," the Constitution would henceforth be as worthless as a pay-toilet in a diarrhea ward.

And we haven't even touched on a myriad of other societal maladies, such as: human trafficking; legal and illegal drug addiction; open borders (leading to burgeoning Democratic voter rolls); permanent election rigging; vaccine passports; internet censorship; shadow banning; social media tracking; drone surveillance; bitcoin mysteries; artificial intelligence sprawl; nuclear, chemical, biological, and electromagnetic pulse threats; a national "Debt Clock" that struck $30 trillion on February 1, 2022 (currently growing at $45,486 dollars per second); and a shortlist of future Democratic presidential hopefuls that include: Kamala Harris, Jill Biden, Caitlyn Jenner, Gavin Newsome, Pete Buttigieg, Stacey Abrams, Elizabeth Warren, Cory Booker, Amy Klobuchar, Gretchen Whitmer, Michelle Obama, Oprah Winfrey, Lori Lightfoot, Alexandria Ocasio-Cortez, Kanye West, and Snoop Dogg. (And some of the brethren *still* want to debate about a flat earth.)

Finally, on August 12, 2021—right in the middle of the Covid-19 crisis—multitudes of the earth's "finest" participated in a free online event entitled, "Global Middle Finger to End Christianity." Under "What to Expect," the unintelligible *Facebook* post read, "At 2PM on August 12th, everybody give a big middle finger to the sky to end Christianity and create more Atheists, while fighting the Global Prayer so their sky daddy won't snatch us up." (A photo of three smiling young white couples flipping the bird accompanied the post.)

THE LAST CHARGE TO PHILADELPHIA

We have now arrived at the most critical juncture of this book. As previously seen, it took roughly 1,725 years for a select portion of the Body of Christ to experience the blessings of I Timothy 2:1-4, courtesy of the First Amendment to the US Constitution. But it required only 230 years for the Church to lose its unprecedented freedom, with a cabal of mostly misguided Baptist academics literally inaugurating the entire modern "Bible" revision movement by commissioning the American Bible Union Version in 1850 (a mere sixty years after the Bill of Rights).

Those initial Baptists who transitioned from the Sardis Church Age to the Philadelphia Age were commended accordingly: *"I know thy works: behold, I have set before thee an open door, and no man can shut it: for thou hast a little strength, **and has kept my word**, and has not denied my name.* (Revelation 3:8) That first generation of "bloodied" Sardis refugees entered the Philadelphia era having kept His word (the AV 1611), refusing to recant (as their martyrologies testify). Throughout Philadelphia the *majority* of born-again believers (both Baptist and Protestant alike) exhibited the scriptural distinctives of their age—going out through an "open door," to spread the "word of God," with hearts of "brotherly love." Meanwhile, a *minority* of Laodicean-minded Christians maintained their own definitive traits of civil rights, lukewarmness, and materialism (Revelation 3:15-17).

However, when the Laodicean Age begins with the "ASCV" 1901, the numbers start to reverse themselves; the Philadelphia remnant grows smaller and smaller while the new Laodicean majority grows larger and larger; which brings us to that fateful voyage in Acts 27. With the "more part" of Laodicea at the helm, the "Old Ship of Zion" will eventually wreck on the rocks, forcing the last generation of Pauline, rightly-dividing, post-perilous times, pre-Tribulation, KJV-Only, Independent Baptists overboard (II Timothy 3:1).

Now, at such a pivotal moment the Holy Spirit was not *about* to leave His Philadelphia remnant without a final charge and exhortation. Whereas verse eight clearly applies to the *start* of the Philadelphia Age, the rest of John's sixth letter speaks to the faithful Philadelphia Bible believers at the *end* of the Laodicea Age. Continuing the historical approach, verse nine could easily point to such flash-in-the-pan, anti-Semitic "nutjobs" as Steven Anderson who spread the Catholic-Protestant heresy that the Church replaced *Israel* (i.e., fellow doctrinally-deficient Baptists "discovering" that they were "actually" Jews).

The significance of verse ten cannot be overstated. It constitutes the all-important final charge to the Philadelphia remnant! Note how the Holy Spirit is now addressing those believers who are *still* keeping His word—on the very cusp of the Rapture itself. *"Because thou **hast kept the word** of my patience, **I also will keep thee from the hour of temptation, which shall come upon all the world, to try them that dwell upon the earth.***" (If that's not a pre-Trib Rapture proof text, I don't know what is.)

With the 2020 presidential election having rendered the once-powerful US Constitution a feckless document, the Church will obviously have to revisit the defensive holding pattern depicted in Revelation 2:25. However, the surviving Philadelphia remnant at the end of Laodicea have a unique possession that their Thyatira forefathers could only dream about. (Hint: We received it in 1611.) Therefore, while the ancient charge to *"hold fast"* is obviously implied, the Lord also enjoins us in Revelation 3:11 to *continue* "holding" that priceless King James Bible—while we are *"hold[ing] fast"* ourselves! *"Behold, I come quickly: hold **that** fast **which thou hast**, that no man take thy crown."*

On January 26, 1986 (in the NFL's pre-kneeling era), I watched my Chicago Bears perfect their famous "Super Bowl Shuffle" by defeating the New England Patriots 46-10 in Super Bowl XX in New Orleans. The most memorable play of the game occurred in the third quarter when "da Bears" were first and goal on New England's one-yard line. While everyone *assumed* that Chicago's punky QB, Jim McMahon, would give the ball to his all-star running back, Walter Payton (aka "Sweetness"), he instead handed off to his 6-foot-3-inch, 335-pound (overweight) rookie defensive tackle, William "Refrigerator" Perry—who promptly steamrolled Pat's linebacker Larry McGrew, rumbling into the end zone for a stadium-shattering touchdown! (Alan Ameche's winning one-yard run in the 1958 "Greatest Game Ever" and Bart Starr's quarterback sneak in the 1967 "Ice Bowl" were promptly relegated to second and third place for iconic NFL drama.)

This is *exactly* what the Philadelphia remnant has to do in the closing minutes of *our* Super Bowl contest against the "god of this world!" We, too, must put *our* heads down—*protecting our precious King James Bibles just as tightly as the "Fridge" protected that football*—then steamroll *Satan's* linebackers as we rumble into Heaven's end zone at the Rapture. (Then the *real* "Super Bowls" will begin, as in those seven Bowl Judgments in Revelation 16.) For, soon after that Philadelphia door closes, another door opens up above (Revelation 4:1). And remember, that impressive ten-karat-gold, forty-diamond encrusted Super Bowl ring (including Perry's record size 25) will seem as nothing more than a worthless fugazi when compared to *our* eternal rewards; so don't let the Devil's defense strip that Book from your hands— *"that no man take thy crown."*

ESCAPE FROM "MUSIC CITY"

We will now close this negative-appearing chapter with two positive stories. The following testimonies from the closing days of Laodicea will clearly demonstrate that God is *still* in the saving business—even *after* "Paradise Lost."

Jerry Monday was born on June 13, 1945, in Mt. Ayr, Iowa. As a youth he developed a love for music and began honing his exceptional skills. He once described his early honky-tonk apprentice years as "playing in bars and sleeping in cars." After a two-year stint in Colorado, Jerry moved to "Music City," Tennessee, in 1963, where he would finally break into the "Big Time." Between 1965-69, he appeared three times on the Grand Ole Opry in the historic Ryman Auditorium. He debuted playing the dobro for Johnny Cash. (The "Man in Black" was so high on amphetamines that night he gave Jerry a considerable "nudge," thinking he was not standing close enough to the microphone.) In the other two shows he played dobro for the Stonemans, singing "Looking Out My Back Door" on the second (naively unaware that the lyrics were about taking dope).

By now Jerry was in strong demand as a musician, singer, and songwriter, playing various instruments for such major headliners as Mac Wiseman, Jimmy Martin, and "Pop" Stoneman. On April 18, 1967, Jerry appeared with the Stoneman Family on the iconic *Tonight Show*. Naturally, he interacted with many country music "legends" of the day. He co-wrote "We Had All the Good Things Going," one of Dolly Parton's greatest hits. I once saw a video of Jerry—with a full head of bushy hair—accompanying Tammy Wynette on the dobro as she brought the house down singing "Don't Come Home A-Drinkin' (With Lovin' on Your Mind)." He was good friends with Jeannie Seely, known for "Don't Touch Me." In his "spare time," Jerry also played bit parts in various movies: *The Road to Nashville* (1967), starring Johnny Cash, Marty Robbins, and Waylon Jennings; *Hell on Wheels* (1967), with Marty Robbins and Connie Smith; and *Dear Dead Delilah* (1972), featuring Will Geer, Michael Ansara, and Agnes Moorehead.

However, as Hebrews 11:25 warns that *"the pleasures of sin"* last only *"for a season,"* Jerry was getting weary of singing for the Devil. Thus, on Sunday morning, April 5, 1970, he visited the Belmont Baptist Church in Nashville. Seated in the balcony, he came under strong conviction and went forward at the invitation, trusting Jesus Christ as his personal Saviour. The rest is history. To match his three Ryman gigs, Jerry would go on to pastor three Baptist churches (Fayetteville, Tennessee; Fairmont, West Virginia; and Grafton, West Virginia). In 1977, he married his better half, Betty Marie, who resigned her job as a Circuit Court clerk to travel with him. Over the past four decades Jerry and Betty have sung in countless revivals, camp meetings, and Bible conferences. As former heavyweight boxing champion George Forman would always stand in his corner between rounds, Jerry would likewise famously play the piano standing up. Writing over 150 songs for the Lord, his two most popular remain "In, Amen," and "So That You Can Catch Up with Me" (about the passing of Dr. J. Harold Smith's wife, Myrtice).

Following Paul's exhortation in II Timothy 3:14 for end-time Bible believers to *"continue,"* Jerry has remained a fervent soul winner. One of his poignant memories involves his long-time friendship with the late Faron Young. Known as the "Hillbilly Heartthrob" and "The Singing Sheriff," Young was a successful producer, singer, and songwriter from 1951-1994. His top chart single was "Hello Walls" (selling over one million copies). Sadly, his life was plagued with depression, alcoholism, and health issues. Early on, Faron befriended Jerry, paying his way into the Musicians' Union. The two spent much time together. In fall 1996, Faron promised Jerry that he would call him soon to discuss his need of salvation. Unfortunately, that call never came. True to the words of his other 1957 chart topper, "Live Fast, Love Hard, Die Young," on December 10, 1996, Faron Young shot himself at age sixty-four in his Nashville home. His ashes were sprinkled over the lake on Johnny Cash's estate. In 2000, Young was inducted into the Country Music Hall of Fame. Reflecting on his secular career—to paraphrase the words of Job's servants, *"I only am escaped alone to tell thee"* —Jerry once told me, "I'm sure thankful God delivered me from that mess!" Brother Monday's life story was dramatized on the *Unshackled* program in December 2004 under the pseudonym "Clayton Miles." (Refusing to retire in their senior years, Jerry and Betty have a live *Facebook* hymn-sing every Friday morning at 7:30.)

"GIVE..."

By age fourteen, Alan was already headed in the wrong direction. Born the youngest of four children into a *severely* dysfunctional home outside Washington, DC, in 1956, Alan would be remanded to several county jails (*jails*, not youth facilities) at least *ten* times before his eighteenth birthday. (During that milestone year he would "graduate" to the Baltimore Penitentiary.) His rap sheet would make James Dean look like Fred Rogers. In the seventh grade he was commuting to school in a '67 GTO, having forged his own license. After taking out at least five telephone poles (while driving intoxicated), accumulating sixty-eight points in the process (fifty-six over the normal limit), Alan finally had his bogus license revoked. At fifteen he was expelled from the eighth grade, never to return again. His most egregious offense was packing a loaded gun to class. (Throughout his adolescent years he would have at least five guns put to his head.) The last straw occurred when an eleventh-hour counseling session went south. The incorrigible profligate simply stole a Colt 45 Malt Liquor truck and promptly shared some of the contents with his so-called "advisor," whereupon the pair got thoroughly wasted.

His elder brother, Norman, a Vietnam vet, was no Japheth, but rather a federal prisoner serving a life sentence for a crime spree too horrible for words (let's just say, short of a Leonard Lawrence profile in *Full*

Metal Jacket). While most siblings occasionally "fight" with each other (like the Flynn brothers from the "City of Brotherly Love" in the John Wayne classic, *Sands of Iwo Jima*), Alan was a bit "over the top" — shooting his other brother, Homer, on two occasions, stabbing him on a third. Thankfully, Homer survived all three encounters, got saved, and started witnessing to Alan, but was always rebuffed. Whenever they would wrestle, Alan, being the smaller of the two, would refuse to yield. Thus, Homer would say, "Alan, you need to *give!*" (He would frequently use the same metaphor regarding Alan's need for Christ.) In 1972, Homer died in a freak incident involving a garbage truck owned by the family business. Alan would often reflect on that word— "Give...."

The following year (when Alan was seventeen), he and two friends *stole a police S.W.A.T. team armored carrier* while they were all high on PCP. Alan was riding shotgun, a Mexican named Robert was seated in the middle, while Jet, a dude with long red hair, was *attempting* to drive. Going eighty-miles-an-hour they passed a police car parked in front of a 7-11 store. As Jet now had his head hanging out of the window, the officers could hardly miss his long red locks waving in the breeze. During the ensuing high-speed pursuit (on the Baltimore-Washington Parkway), Alan and Robert suddenly discovered that their chauffeur was no longer with them. Hardly a candidate for the Rapture, "Red" had simply baled in motion. Hemmed in by approaching roadblocks, the pair quickly went airborne, careening off the expressway onto an adjacent building, then sliding off the roof, before landing on the street— upside down! (Obviously, "Roberto" was no Latino version of Steve McQueen, etc.)

When the smoke cleared, Alan, dazed but unhurt, was staring at his partner in crime, who, having survived as well—presently had his buttocks ignominiously stuck in the shattered windshield. As the sirens and lights were closing in, the two juvenile delinquents were attempting to con each another. "Tell them *you* picked *me* up hitchhiking," Alan implored, whereupon his "amigo" replied, "No way, Jose; tell 'em *you* were the hombre driving, etc." Minutes later, with the police having recaptured their own Humvee, and drawing down on the perpetrators, the two "yutes" peacefully surrendered. (It was probably hard to figure which side felt more humiliated, though the tripping teens weren't "feeling" much at the time). Reunited at the jail, Alan discovered that

Robert had thrown him under the bus for a ham sandwich, *so*—he proceeded to beat the snot out of him.

The paradigm shift in Alan's life came a few months later while he was out on bail. During a meeting with his parole officer, Alan grew indignant over a stern lecture he was having to endure. (Being half drunk didn't help matters any.) Suddenly, Alan sucker-slapped the official across the face—hard enough that he fell to the floor. (*Not* good…) He then proceeded to flee the County building (i.e., exit stage right). Waiting in the parking lot was the guy who'd driven Alan to his appointment. John was a young man who had grown up idolizing Alan's criminal lifestyle. However, he too had recently gotten saved and now had a *big* "surprise" planned for his mentor.

When Alan came flying out of the building, he literally dove into John's green pinstriped '69 Camaro Z28 (what else?) and said (in so many words), "Lets' get the 'blankety-blank' out of here," to which John immediately replied, *"Wanna go to a revival?"* Alan asked, "What the 'blank' is that?" whereupon John "innocently" answered, "It's where they have singing and preaching and stuff." With the alarm blaring and one very perturbed parole officer leading the pursuit, Alan said, "I don't care *where* the 'blank' we go, as long as it's away from here." And so, "Hoke Colburn" burned rubber, fishtailing out of the parking lot with "Miss Daisy" hunched down out of sight. However, unbeknown to Alan, his protégé had set him up by giving the guest evangelist a heads-up about the "special" visitor he was planning to bring to the meeting that night.

Due to the parole session lasting longer than expected, by the time the fugitives pulled up at the giant tent (hosted by the First Baptist Church in Riverdale, Maryland) the service was already over. (Alan would later relate how his paranoia led him to believe that John had lied to him, thus, one of them was probably going to die). However, they soon found the faithful man of God sitting on a folding chair, patiently awaiting their arrival. As the Lord knew that His future soldier was not your "typical prospect," He had an equally unique "Reverend" picked out to lead him to salvation.

Dr. James W. Delashmit was a former dopehead who had sold drugs to support his own $75-a-day habit. He was also the founder and president of a rogue chapter of the Hell's Angels motorcycle club in St. Louis. Sixty-five "One-Percenters" rode with him, including nine bodyguards. Meanwhile, pestered by his godly mother to visit her church, "Sonny

Boy" finally relented. On the big morning, he swallowed three "red devils" and showed up wearing his colors. Fortunately for him, as with "Captain Tom" Ryman, he also fell under old-time, Holy Ghost conviction and hit the mourners' bench.

His fellow "biker brothers" nearly killed him for quitting the gang (sending him to the hospital after literally riding their choppers over his body). As a new creature in Christ, Jim simply shrugged it off and surrendered to preach. While Lester Roloff took his cow to Baylor University to milk his way through school, Jim sold his prized lavender-purple Harley to offset *his* tuition at Baptist Bible College in Springfield, Missouri. After graduating, he pastored several churches in the 1970s and '80s, while also conducting powerful revival meetings. Hundreds were saved upon hearing his signature sermon, "From Dope to Hope."

This was the caliber of "man" (John 1:6) that extended his hand to Alan in that deserted tent. The only problem was his opening greeting: "I've heard about *you*, that you're dying without Christ and are on your way to Hell and need to get saved." Clenching his fists, while debating in his mind whether to slug the professed ex-"Fallen Angel" or not (no one would speak to *him* that way and get away with it), Alan was suddenly disarmed when the preacher got the jump on *him* instead. Holding Alan's right hand in a death grip, Brother Delashmit quickly closed the distance, got right in his prospect's face, then *pulverized* him by saying, *"One time in your life, why don't you just—give?"* The Holy Spirit used this to trigger an immediate flashback to the very expression Homer would tell him.

For the first time in years, tears streamed down Alan's cheeks. When the soul winner asked Alan if he wanted to be saved, he said "Yes." However, when Jim began taking him down the "Roman's Road," Alan blurted out, rather sheepishly, "I can't read; can you read them to me?" Praise the Lord, in short order Alan finally "gave" and was gloriously saved! The date was Monday, September 30, 1974 (six weeks after my own conversion, roughly two hours away).

Like the Apostle Paul, Alan immediately took off, "terrorizing" his old crowd (with that old "black-backed, 66-caliber" AV 1611). His longtime sweetheart, Linda Thierauf, trusted Christ two months later. Because Alan has always been the "romantic" type (LOL), they tied the knot on Valentine's Day 1976 (the former hooligan having "married up" *big time*). The Lord would bless the couple with three daughters and two sons. As Alan laughingly told me once, "I met Linda when I was fourteen and *tried* to pick her up on my bicycle. Then I got my 'license.' I was fourteen and came by in a '67 GTO. She got in. Now we have eighteen grandkids."

In 1979, Alan relocated his young family to the Florida Panhandle so he could attend Pensacola Bible Institute (where he learned to read and write), finishing up four years later. Dr. Ruckman would often recognize Alan as one of his favorite graduates. (During this time, he also completed a short-term stint with the Army National Guard Reserves.) In 1987, Alan became Pastor of Faith Baptist Church in Smyrna, Delaware. The firm KJV-Only work (allied with Heritage Bible Baptist, another strong church in nearby Greenwood, pastored by Garry Manaraze), has since become a shining lighthouse in that benighted area of liberal Delaware.

While attending his son's high school commencement in 1995, Alan witnessed to the keynote speaker—*Senator* Joe Biden. When the politician insisted that he was "saved" in 1988 when God healed him from a brain aneurysm, Alan informed him that he would split Hell wide open if he didn't dump his Catholic religion and trust Jesus Christ! Though Delaware's "greatest" contribution to America "promised" to visit Faith Baptist, the adulterer—who stole Bill Stevenson's wife— has *yet* to show.

In conclusion, the main reason I shared this beautiful testimony is because of that prayer burden of Thomas Ryman from over a century ago, that his extended family and friends would come to Christ (the vision that led him to build the massive structure that bears his name today). For you see, as Revelation 14:13 says, *"Blessed are the dead which die in the Lord...and their works do follow them,"* Pastor Alan's last name just happens to be—*Ryman*. According to oral family tradition, Alan's third great-grandfather in Germany was a distant cousin of Thomas Ryman. (In fact, Alan's facial profile bears such a striking resemblance to his famous ancestor that the first time he visited the Ryman Auditorium, they honored him by refusing to charge him the admission fee.) As an added bonus, not only are all of Alan and Linda's children saved (four of whom faithfully serve at Faith Baptist Church), but their firstborn, Samson, continues to carry the Ryman torch, pastoring the Central Bible Baptist Church in Massena, New York.

13

Trapped in a Terrified City

LESS THAN ONE year after my salvation experience in 1974, my wife and I were peering down into the main archeological tell of ancient Jericho, considered the world's oldest continually inhabited city, containing the remains of twenty successive settlements. (The second-most important dig is New Testament Jericho.) It was quite an exhilarating experience for a new convert. I can still recall our guide pointing out the visible evidence confirming that the city walls did indeed fall flat according to the Biblical narrative (Joshua 6:20).

The story of "Rahab the Harlot" offers an insightful application for Christians living in America in the "last days" of the Church Age. Rahab was *trapped in a terrified city*. So are we! Present-day USA, like Jericho of old, is under a curse and is *definitely* going down; the only question is— *"When?"* (Someone has said that enduring the Biden administration is like being strapped in a chair and watching a two-year-old playing with a loaded gun.) According to Genesis 10:6, Canaan's occupants would have been black, being descended from Ham. There are seven powerful lessons from the fall of Jericho that will help you to survive the "perilous times" ahead.

JERICHO WAS IN PANIC MODE

As an old Italian joke goes, two Mafia hitmen are walking through the forest at night when one of them says, "I have to admit, it's pretty scary out here." The other replies, "You think *this* is bad? I have to walk back alone!" Having afforded the two spies a surreptitious refuge, Rahab was quick to inform them that her fellow citizens were likewise paralyzed by fear because of Israel's widely-known exploits.

*"[A]nd she said onto the men, I know that the LORD hath given you the land, and that **your terror is fallen upon us,** and that **all the inhabitants of the land faint because of you.** For we have heard how the LORD dried up the water of the Red sea for you, when ye came out of Egypt; and what you did unto the two kings of the Amorites, that were on the other side Jordan, Sihon and Og, whom you utterly destroyed. **And as soon as we had heard these things, our hearts did melt, neither did there remain any more courage in any man, because of you:** for the LORD your God, he is God in heaven above, and in earth beneath."* (Joshua 2:9-11)

The rub in Rahab's report is that the Israelites would never have stalled at Kadesh Barnea had they been privy to this intel then. Thus, an entire generation perished in the wilderness for refusing to trust the same God who delivered them from Egypt (Numbers 10:11-14:45). Who could miss the twenty-first-century application to the Covid-19 "*Quarantined* States of America," Joshua 6:1 stating, *"Now Jericho was **straitly shut up** because of the children of Israel: **none went out, and none came in**"*?

Their main cause for panic can be found in the words, *"For we have heard...**what ye did** unto the two kings of the Amorites, that were on the other side Jordan, Sihon and Og, whom ye **utterly destroyed.**"* (Joshua 2:10) The definition of *"utterly destroyed"* —the imminent reality for Jericho (Joshua 6:21), as well as the rest of Canaan (Joshua 10:40)—may be found in the precise instructions given by Moses: *"But of the cities of these people, which the LORD thy God doth give thee for an inheritance, **thou shalt save alive nothing that breatheth.**"* (Deuteronomy 20:16) This may come as a shock to many of you—but that directive would include little two-year old girls as well. So, who do y'all suppose got the nod to cut their throats—Joshua's troops, or perhaps a special hit squad comprising the soldiers' wives (like modern-day female members of the IDF, toting their M16s)? Dr. Ruckman used to ask, "Did any babies drown in the flood?" The bottom line is that *none* of us have a clue about the words in Proverbs 1:7, *"The **fear of the LORD** is the beginning of knowledge."*

As Jericho's peeps started shaking in *their* boots about forty years *before* Joshua arrived (1491-1451 BC), the same is true with our nation. On February 26, 1993, the LORD dispatched a special "truck" to the basement of the North Tower of the World Trade Center to deliver a "late notice" (via the Middle East) that America's "rent" was overdue. Eight years later, a *more* intense "warning" arrived on September 11— "Pay up or have your furniture moved to the curb!"

You say, Dr. Grady, what "rent" are you talking about? The answer is contained in the first five verses of Isaiah 26, forecasting the long-awaited security conditions that Israel will experience in the Millennium. The passage begins: *"In that day shall this song be sung in the land of Judah; We have a **strong city**; salvation will God appoint for **walls** and **bulwarks**."* While technically a Kingdom Age text, the truth of God's willingness to protect any nation that honors His word was appropriated by Great Britain and the United States on numerous occasions. From the defeat of the Spanish Armada, through the evacuation at Dunkirk, to the victorious Battle of Midway, the Lord has manifested His ability to deliver whomsoever He will.

Throughout the centuries, people desiring to move within the "walls and bulwarks" of *this* "strong city" had only to agree to the one condition given in verse two: *"Open ye the gates, that the **righteous nation which keepeth the truth** may enter in."* You could say that "righteousness" is the sole "rent" that God requires countries to pay. If a tenant would fulfill his part of the lease, the "landLORD" would gladly reciprocate. Thus, verses three and four state, *"Thou wilt keep him in perfect peace, whose mind is stayed on thee: because he trusteth in thee. Trust ye in the LORD for ever: for in the LORD JEHOVAH is everlasting strength."*

Consequently, the only question that pertains to 9/11 is whether or not our nation's "rent" was current. The answer should be painfully and *frightfully* obvious. America's sins are too many and too vile to rehearse here. Suffice it to say that abortion, human trafficking, witchcraft, sodomy, and transgenderism were hardly the cultural staples that inspired hymns like "America the Beautiful," "My Country 'Tis of Thee," and "God Bless America." Verse five reveals how JEHOVAH deals with deadbeats. As your King James Bible is as current as tomorrow's headlines, the passage contains a four-part similitude related to the implosion of the Twin Towers: *"[F]or he bringeth **down** them that dwell on **high**"* [*high*-rise buildings brought *down*]; *"the **lofty city**"* ["The Big Apple," or, more specifically, Manhattan— "The City"], *"he layeth it low; he layeth it low, even to the **ground**"* [as in "Ground Zero"]; *"he bringeth it even to the **dust**"* [as in 10,000 plaintiffs awarded $657 million in damages for their exposure to toxic *dust* during rescue-related efforts].

Applying the hermeneutical "Law of First Mention" to a lethal implosion orchestrated by Satan, we find an exact type in the oldest chapter in the Bible: *"[A]nd, behold, there came a great wind from the wilderness, and smote the four corners of the house, **and it fell upon the young men, and they are dead.**"* (Job 1:19) Why mess around with "Hebrew Codes" when the *real* action is in the English? (You might take a second look at that unassuming Scripture address—*backwards*.)

And so, after twenty *more* years of trembling, the citizens of this once-proud nation got to witness Afghanistan's new Taliban "government" (caliphate) installed on the twentieth anniversary of 9/11—literally celebrating from the abandoned US embassy! The "late fees" alone were roughly $2.3 trillion, plus 23,150 American servicemen killed and wounded (not to mention another $10 billion in abandoned military hardware along with hundreds of crucifixions and decapitations following Joe Biden's catastrophic "drawdown"). The bottom line is that America is now literally *teetering* on the *eve of eviction* for refusing to pay her rent! Meanwhile, the global Covid-19 paranoia is serving as a precursor to the Tribulation conditions described in the third Gospel, the *"great earthquakes...famines, and **pestilences**"* resulting in *"[M]en's hearts failing them for **fear**."* (Luke 21:11, 26)

BE SURE YOU HAVE A SCARLET THREAD

The name *Rahab* means "broad" (now used as a slang term for females). She represents all of us before we met the Lord Jesus Christ, for ***"broad** is the way that leadeth to destruction, and many there be which go in thereat"* ("Broadway Joe" Namath, "Funky Broadway," etc.). Rahab was no common hooker either, but rather a high-end call girl, for even Jericho's king knew her by name (Joshua 2:3). But, hallelujah, because of God's amazing grace, she went from being a street *walker* to being a street *worker*. Herbert Lockyer described her as "the woman God took from the dunghill."

Now, from Rahab's perspective, she let the two spies escape out of her window by a common *"cord"* (verse 15). However, looking back up to her, they emphasized that their means of escape—as well the same for her future hope—was a *"**scarlet** thread"* (verse 18). Thus the expression, "hanging by a thread." The 1909 *Scofield Study Bible* note states, "The scarlet line of Rahab speaks, by its color, of safety through *sacrifice* (Hebrews 9:19, 22)." Rahab's "token" (verse 12) was a type of the precious blood of Jesus Christ (I Peter 1:18-19). You could say that it prefigured our "spiritual umbilical cord" for the new birth (John 3:3, 5). Lockyer posits that the flax she spread on her roof and the scarlet cord she used as a sign indicated that Rahab probably manufactured colored linen, a *beautiful* forerunner of another converted female entrepreneur specializing in dyes (Acts 16:14). Both women are in Heaven today because of that related pledge in Isaiah 1:18, *"Come now, and let us reason together, saith the LORD: though your sins be as **scarlet**, they shall be as white as snow; though they be **red like crimson**, they shall be as wool."*

Although Rahab could not have understood it at the time (Luke 18:34), the Church Age Gospel that would eventually save her soul (I Peter 4:6), was hidden in the very instructions she gave the spies. *"Get you to the **mountain**, lest the **pursuers** meet you; and hide yourselves there **three days**, until the **pursuers** be returned: and afterward may ye go your **way**."* (Joshua 2:16, 22) When Satan's pursuers were after *us*, i.e., "Death and Hell" (Revelation 6:8)—Hallelujah—the one who died on *"the mountain,"* i.e., Mount Calvary, and then rose *"three days"* later, enabled *us* to find *our "way,"* i.e., *"**I am the way**, the truth, and the life: no man cometh unto the Father, but by me."* (John 14:6)

Furthermore, notice how Rahab did not waste any time getting started. Whereas the spies had instructed her, *"Behold, **when we are come into the land**, thou shalt bind this line of scarlet thread in the window which thou did let us down by,"* verse 21 states, *"And she sent them away, and they departed: **and she bound the scarlet line in the window**,"* emphasizing the urgency of salvation (I Samuel 21:8; II Corinthians 6:2.) My friend, eternal damnation in the Lake of Fire will be a *lot* worse than dying of the Coronavirus (Revelation 20:15). Make sure *you* have a *"scarlet line"* hanging *down* from *your* window—as it's the only way to go *up* at death or the Rapture! When Satan tries to unsettle you about America's imminent destruction, just remind yourself who is outside the walls directing that assault:

> *"And it came to pass, when Joshua was by Jericho, that he lifted up his eyes and looked, and, behold, there stood a man over against him with a sword drawn in his hand: and Joshua went unto him,*

*and said unto him, Art thou for us, or for our adversaries? And he
said, **Nay; but as captain of the host of the LORD am I now come.**
And Joshua fell on his face to the earth, and did worship, and said
unto him, What saith my lord unto his servant? **And the captain of
the LORD'S host** said unto Joshua, Loose thy shoe from off thy foot;
for the place whereon thou standest is holy. And Joshua did so."*

This truth is so profound that modern Bible correctors teach that the
King James translators made an error when they called Joshua "Jesus"
in Acts 7:45, *"Which also our fathers that came after brought in with
Jesus into the possession of the Gentiles, whom God drave out before
the face of our fathers, unto the days of David."* They throw the same
conniption fit at Hebrews 4:8, *"For if **Jesus** had given them rest, then
would he not afterward have spoken of another day."* So quick to criticize
our precious AV 1611, they apparently miss the simple reality that Jesus's
name in Hebrew was *Yeshua*, which translates into English as *Joshua*.
(Duh!) The central truth to remember is that the "Captain's" attitude
toward *you*—as opposed to everyone else He's fixin' to *vaporize* in
America—was conveyed to Rahab with the words: *"And it shall be,
when the LORD hath given us the land, that we will deal **kindly** and
truly with thee."* (Joshua 2:14)

OBEY *YOUR* INSTRUCTIONS

In our story, Rahab's "salvation" technically relates to her escaping
physical death, i.e., at the hands of the Israelites, *"[A]nd that ye will
save alive my father, and my mother, and my brethren, and my sisters,
and all that they have, and **deliver our lives from death."** (Joshua 2:13)
However, it also pictures the unique, dispensational combination of
"faith and works" regarding spiritual salvation in the Old Testament
economy. Her "faith" was clearly present, having testified, *"[F]or the
LORD your God, **he is God** in Heaven above, and in earth beneath."*
(Joshua 2:11) However, James 2:24-25 adds, *"Ye see then how that by
works a man is justified, and not by faith only. Likewise also **was not
Rahab the harlot justified by works,** when she had received the
messengers, and had sent them out another way?"*

The Scripture further implies that Rahab's "work" was the main reason
she survived the destruction: *"By **faith** the harlot Rahab perished not with
them that believed not, **when she had received the spies with peace."***

(Hebrews 11:31) The point is that "faith" *alone* would not have saved her life, *if* she had not *acted* on that faith by: 1) receiving and hiding the spies; 2) streaming the scarlet thread from her window; and, 3) being in the house when the walls came down (as conditioned in Exodus 12:22 on Passover, indicating *no* eternal security *before* the Church Age *sealing* ministry of the Holy Spirit was revealed in Ephesians 1:13).

And so—*with the world just about to end*—it might be nice if some of the more "shallow brethren" (i.e., those "closet Ruckmanites" who read the Doc's material under their blankets by flashlight) might *finally* get this sticky-wicket right before it's too late. For the umpteenth time: *Nobody* in the Old Testament had a *clear* understanding of the saving, *Church Age* Gospel of the death, burial, and resurrection of Jesus Christ (Mark 9:9-10; 9:30-32; 16:11; Luke 18:31-34; 24:21; John 20:9; I Corinthians 2:8; Ephesians 3:5; and Colossians 1:26); *Nobody* in the Old Testament period entered Heaven *when* they died; *Nobody* from the Old Testament period entered Heaven *after* Calvary because of their "works." As shown in Luke 16:19-31, when folks kicked the bucket *before* the cross, they all descended into the "heart of the earth." (Airhead "TR Fundies" deride this important Bible doctrine as a "Baptist Purgatory.") Most, like the rich man, went to Hell; the rest landed in Paradise, like Lazarus. The key passage that unravels this ongoing bone of contention is Exodus 34:6-7 (cross-referenced with Exodus 20:6, Numbers 14:18, and Deuteronomy 5:10).

> *"And the* LORD *passed by before him, and proclaimed, The* LORD, *The* LORD *God,* **merciful** *and* **gracious**, **longsuffering**, *and abundant in goodness and truth, keeping* **mercy** *for thousands,* **forgiving** *iniquity and transgression and sin, and that will* **by no means clear the guilty.***"* (Exodus 34:6-7)

The Holy Spirit has Moses repeat the same thought in Numbers 14:18, *"The* LORD *is longsuffering, and of great* **mercy**, **forgiving** *iniquity and transgression, and* **by no means clearing the guilty.***"* The "deep truth" here is threefold. First, God extended *mercy* to whosoever He judged "deserved" it—based on the all-important criteria laid out in Romans 2:6-10. Moses then adds, *"And showing* **mercy** *unto thousands of them that* **love me and keep my commandments.***"* (Deuteronomy 5:10) This arrangement simply allowed the "qualifying" transgressor (i.e., those who love Him and obey His commandments—precisely as Jesus told the rich young ruler in Matthew 19:17) to *bypass* Hell. Thus, Jeremiah wrote, *"It is of the LORD'S* **mercies** *that we are not consumed, because his compassions fail not."* (Lamentations 3:22)

However, while God was willing to *"forgive transgressions and sin"* (especially in anticipation of His Son's prayer in Luke 23:34 and Peter's interpretation in Acts 3:17-21), He would not "clear" the recipient of His mercy, *"For it is not possible that the blood of bulls and of goats should **take away** [clear] sins."* (Hebrews 10:4) The Old Testament usage of the Hebrew word for "clear" is the equivalent of the New Testament word "justify" (Titus 3:7). The ninth definition for "clear" (when used as a transitive verb) in the *Webster's 1828 Dictionary* says, "To purge from the imputation of guilt; to *justify* or vindicate." (In addition to Exodus 34:7, *Webster's* cites Genesis 44:16, *"[H]ow shall we* **clear** *ourselves?"*)

This brings us to phase two. The Lord's graciousness consigned Old Testament saints to "Abraham's bosom" (i.e., where Lazarus went). Now did you get that? God's *mercy* ensured that they avoided Hell, while His *grace* allowed them to slip into a temporary, spiritual "layaway," if you will. Finally (and most importantly), His *longsuffering* enabled Him to await that liberating day when His Son would descend into *Paradise* (Luke 23:43) to preach the imminent Church Age Gospel to the "righteous dead" (Hebrews 12:22-23; I Peter 3:19; 4:6). Isaiah points to the Father's *foreknowledge* as the key to His patience: *"Yet it pleased the LORD to bruise him...**He shall see of the travail of his soul**, and shall be satisfied: **by his knowledge** shall my righteous servant **justify** [clear] many; for he shall bear their iniquities."* (Isaiah 53:10-11)

> *"[B]eing **justified** freely by his grace through the redemption that is in Christ Jesus: whom God hath sent forth to be a propitiation through faith in his blood, to declare his righteousness for the **remission of sins that are past, through the forbearance of God**; to declare, I say, at this time his righteousness: that he might be **just, and the justifier** of him which believeth in Jesus."* (Romans 3:24-26)

The Apostle employed the word "remission" as the Church Age equivalent for the Old Testament concept of a *"temporary* covering." The problem with remission was that it was never permanent. While one's cancer may go into "remission," the patient is never totally out of the woods as the disease can always return. Thus, the Jews required an *annual* "Day of Atonement" (Hebrews 10:1-3, 11). Though the Old Testament saints "deserved" to go to Hell (according to the law of sowing and reaping in Galatians 6:7), a little-known safety net in Hosea 10:12 would enable them to raise a different harvest: *"Sow to yourselves in righteousness, **reap in mercy.**"*

To summarize, until the sins of Old Testament saints could be fully "taken away" (John 1:29), they could only be "pardoned" (like President Richard Nixon): *"And he said, If now I have found **grace** in thy sight, O Lord, let my Lord, I pray thee, go among us; for it is a stiffnecked people; and **pardon our iniquity and our sin**, and take us for thine inheritance."* (Exodus 34:9) Consequently, after Jesus finally "cleared" them in Paradise, He *"ascended up on high* [leading] *captivity captive."* (Ephesians 4:8-10) The bottom line is simple. Having watched the tormented souls across the "great gulf" *burning in Hell* for multiplied centuries, *every* Old Testament saint (from Adam to the dying thief) "hit the altar" after Jesus finished preaching the *first* evangelistic sermon in history!

Returning to a Church Age application, the *only* "instruction" you need to heed for your *spiritual* salvation is to have that "*scarlet* thread" hanging from *your* window (II Corinthians 13:5; I Peter 1:18-19). However, as a black preacher friend of mine used to say, "You may be *saved* down here, but you ain't necessarily *safe* down here." Given the strong potential of America's imminent destruction, the best way to improve *your* "chances" for a *physical* deliverance as well would be to obey as many Biblical mandates as possible; for, *"When a man's ways please the LORD, he maketh even his enemies to be at peace with him.* (Proverbs 16:7) Therefore, make sure *you're* inside the house when "the walls come a-tumblin' down." Then, as Rahab declared in Joshua 2:21, simply hold God to *His* token: *"And she said, **According unto your words, so be it**."* (The most practical "instruction" to follow will be given in chapter nineteen, "The Christian's 9-1-1 Number.")

GET *YOUR* FAMILY AND FRIENDS INSIDE

Rahab exhibited an immediate burden for her family. *"Now therefore, I pray you, swear unto me by the LORD, since I have shewed you kindness, that ye will also shew kindness unto my father's house, and give me a true token: and that ye will save alive my father, and my mother, and my brethren, and my sisters, and all that they have, and deliver our lives from death."* (Joshua 2:12-13) She well understood the gravity of Isaiah 26:20, *"Come, my people, enter thou into thy chambers, and shut the doors about thee: hide thyself as it were for a little moment, until the indignation be overpast."*

This was the identical pattern at the start of the Church Age. Acts 10:24 states, *"And Cornelius waited for them, and had called together his **kinsmen and near friends**."* The first two converts in the land of Japheth were burdened for their lost loved ones as well. Regarding Lydia, Acts 16:15 says, *"And when **she** was baptized, **and her household**."* After Paul exhorted the Philippian jailor, *"Believe on the Lord Jesus Christ, and **thou** shalt be saved, **and thy house**,"* he preached to *"all that were in his **house**,"* baptizing *"[him] and **all his**, straightway,"* the new convert, *"believing in God **with all his house**."* (Acts 16:31-34)

I was saved in the Sunday morning service of the Marcus Hook Baptist Church on August 25, 1974. The very first thing I did when I pulled out of the parking lot was to make a beeline for my father's house. My initial attempt at soul winning *totally* bombed! I didn't exactly use a lot of wisdom. My opening line was, "Dad—guess what? I just changed religions!" Believe me, my hot-blooded Irish Roman Catholic father was *not* impressed. Within moments, he had his finger pointed in my Southern Baptist wife's shocked face as he snarled at her, "You stole my Billy!" Man, was it *ever* on from there (knock-down, drag-out shouting, cussing, and total chaos)! Thankfully, he eventually *did* trust Christ. I was even privileged to baptize him in front of 6,000 witnesses at an evening service at the First Baptist Church of Hammond, Indiana. But those intervening twenty-plus years were fraught with burden and despair. (By the grace of God, I was also able to lead my sister to the Lord, as well as my wife's older brother, both of whom are now in Heaven.)

Peter Ruckman made an astute observation regarding what transpired in the harlot's case. As Rahab was undoubtedly the "black sheep" of the family—given her chosen "profession" —in order for her kinfolk to get "saved," they would have to go down to the seedy part of town and *stay* in one of Jericho's better-known "houses of ill repute." They had to be *"numbered with the transgressors"* (Mark 15:28) and ostracized by "respectable" society. And *anyone* who ever gets saved will have to do the same (Luke 5:32; Romans 5:6; I Corinthians 4:13). Of course, the modern translations remove Mark 15:28 to appease Laodicean minds.

(Dr. Ruckman also noted that the *scarlet* thread was hung out of the window of a prostitute, so to this day, the area of town frequented by the same is called a "*red*-light district.")

Standing on the very cusp of the Rapture, we would all do well to follow Rahab's example. One of the scariest verses I have ever read is I Corinthians 6:2, ***"Do ye not know that the saints shall judge the world?*** *and if the world shall be judged by you, are ye unworthy to judge the smallest matters?"* Combined with the cross-reference in Daniel 7:9-10, the central truth is that we will be assisting at the Great White Throne judgement. So, when Jesus says to your unsaved mama, *"I never knew you: depart from me, ye that work iniquity"* (Matthew 7:23), the last word she will ever hear—as she is cast into the Lake of Fire to burn forever— will be a resounding "Amen" from the lips of the very one she brought into the world (see Matthew 10:36). Thus, we read in Revelation 21:4, *"And God shall wipe away all tears from their eyes,"* not to mention Isaiah 65:17, *"For, behold, I create new heavens and a new earth: **and the former shall not be remembered, nor come into mind"*** (see also Job 24:20). Unfortunately, your mama's memory will forever remember you! (See Luke 16:25.)

To illustrate this point, early one morning while I was pastoring in Post Falls, Idaho, a man in a pickup truck collided with a pregnant woman driving a small automobile, literally knocking it onto our church property. The expectant mother was rushed to the local hospital unconscious (the man was uninjured). Within an hour, the head nurse called me to ask if I could help minister to the husband. Upon arriving at the emergency room, I was told that their near full-term, red-headed baby boy had been taken by Caesarean section, but lived only twenty minutes. The grieving husband was seated in a folding chair alongside his wife's body, which was hooked up to several machines. I was standing directly behind him with my hands on his shoulders. The nurse informed him that she could not survive and that he should therefore tell her he loved her and such, as she could probably still hear him. It was a very sober scene.

After what seemed like an eternity (probably only twenty minutes), that ominous beeping on the screen went **Beep, Beep, Beep, Beep, Beep, Beeeeeeeeeeep.........** *"Or ever the silver cord be **loosed**, or the golden bowl be **broken**, or the pitcher be **broken** at the fountain, or the wheel **broken** at the cistern. **Then** shall the **dust return to the earth** as it was: **and the spirit shall return unto God who gave it**."* (Ecclesiastes 12: 6-7)

The couple had only recently moved into the area. Their parents asked me if I could conduct the funeral in our church. The odd thing is that they were Mormons. The service was one of the strangest I have ever had in nearly fifty years of ministry. *The mother and son were laid out in the same casket!* I preached on II Samuel 1:23, *"Saul and Jonathan were lovely and pleasant in their lives, and in their death they were not divided."* Someone has rightly said that truth is stranger than fiction. According to the Bible, when that innocent baby took his last breath, the angels carried him straight to Heaven (Deuteronomy 1:39; II Samuel 12:23; Luke 16:22; and II Corinthians 5:8). Conversely, when his Mormon mother took *her* last breath—assuming that she was trusting in Joseph Smith's "gospel" —sadly, she dropped into the fires of Hell where Joe already was (Luke 16:22-23; John 3:3; 14:6; Acts 4:12).

In 1972, Paul Simon released a song entitled "Mother and Child Reunion," inspired by a pet dog run over by a car. The stupid world doesn't have a clue. The *real* "reunions" will take place at the Great White Throne Judgment (Revelation 20:11-15). On that "Great and Terrible Day," that mother will finally be released from the pangs of Hell to stand before Jesus Christ. When the Lord says, *"Depart from me ye cursed into everlasting fire,"* the horrible reality will be that the little son, whom she carried for eight months but never saw, will now be standing next to Jesus in a thirty-three-year-old glorified body, and will say "Amen" to his own mother's sentencing! Moral of the story: Better reach *your* loved ones before the walls come down!

YOUR DELIVERANCE WILL ALSO BE MIRACULOUS

When General Joshua and his army closed in for the kill the Israelites marched around Jericho seven times and then let 'er rip! *"So the people shouted when the priests blew with the trumpets: and it came to pass, when the people heard the sound of the trumpet, and the people shouted with a great shout, **that the wall fell down flat**, so that the people went up into the city, every man straight before him, and took the city."* (Joshua 6:20)

While that was certainly a spectacular event, Rahab's deliverance was equally miraculous. Do you happen to recall just *where* the harlot lived? *"Then she let them down by a cord through the window: **for her house was upon the town wall**, and **she dwelt up on the wall**."* (Joshua 2:15)

Y'all see a "problem" yet? (Hint: Sure looks like Rahab was sitting on a powder keg, as her house was situated on Ground Zero for Joshua's incursion.) When the wall came down, Joshua commanded the spies in verse twenty-two, *"**Go into the harlot's house**, and bring out thence the woman, and all that she hath, as you sware unto her."* (Joshua 6:22) So, tell me again, *Where* was that popular bordello located?" The next verse confirms, *"And the young men that were spies **went in, and brought out Rahab**, and her father, and her mother, and her brethren, and all that she had; and **they brought out** all her kindred, and left them without the camp of Israel."*

Well, I'm a-tellin' ya, neighbor, there are only three possible solutions to this here conundrum. 1) The section of wall attached to Rahab's house was the *only* section that *didn't* fall; 2) Her house came down *with* the wall, though she and her family survived like Dorothy in *The Wizard of Oz*; or, 3) Should we take the more extreme, literal interpretation (i.e., regarding "*the* wall," as in *every* wall enclosing Jericho falling down flat) that that scarlet thread was a-danglin' down from a "*hovering* house?" (*Somebody* say "Amen!") Did the Lord have to supply another ladder as he did for those angels in Genesis 28:12? Well, one thing's for sure—in either case, that "scarlet thread" was never even needed to *identify* the sanctified whore house. I mean, who could have missed *that* joint amidst all the dust and rubble?

The Church Age application to *our* future deliverance from *our* "terrified city" will be no less miraculous. The best-case scenario would obviously be the Rapture. Next best would be our supernatural preservation *through* whatever God throws at America *before* the trumpet blows. Just prior to the fall of Jerusalem, Jeremiah was left for dead in a muddy cistern, having offended King Zedekiah's princes. However, in God's providence, a faithful Hamite named Ebed-Melech (meaning "Servant of the King") spoke to Zedekiah on Jeremiah's behalf, securing his release. Note the beautiful reappearance of a "cord" employed in the prophet's rescue: *"So they drew up Jeremiah with **cords**, and took him up out of the dungeon: and Jeremiah remained in the court of the prison."* (Jeremiah 38:13) When the horrific end came a year later, not only did the Lord spare Jeremiah, but Ebed-Melech as well:

> *Now the word of the LORD came unto Jeremiah, while he was shut up in the court of the prison, saying, **Go and speak to Ebed-melech the Ethiopian**, saying, Thus saith the LORD of hosts, the God of*

*Israel; Behold, I will bring my words upon this city for evil, and not for good; and they shall be accomplished in that day before thee. **But I will deliver thee in that day**, saith the LORD: and thou shalt **not** be given into the hand of the men of whom thou art afraid. For **I will surely deliver thee**, and thou shalt **not** fall by the sword, but thy life shall be for a prey unto thee: **because thou hast put thy trust in me, saith the LORD**.* (Jeremiah 39:15-18)

The final option for our supernatural deliverance would be the grace of God to endure the worst! Moses assured the Jews, *"[A]s thy days, so shall thy strength be."* (Deuteronomy 33:25) Like that beloved hymn, "Old Time Religion" says, "It will do when you're a-dyin'." Thus, no matter *what* we will have to face in the "perilous times" ahead, our Lord's promise is all that we will ever need: *"My grace is sufficient for thee."* (II Corinthians 12:9)

UNDER THE RUBBLE

True to Rahab's name relating to *"**broad** is the way, that leadeth to destruction,"* the eventual body bag count in Jericho confirmed the second half of Matthew 7:14, as well— *"and **few** there be that find it."* The city's entire population was wiped out *except* for Rahab and her houseguests. However, when the text is scrutinized, a disturbing nuance surfaces regarding specific family members. In her petition for their lives, the list is quite exact: *"[A]nd that ye will save alive my father, and my mother, and my brethren, **and my sisters**, and all that they have, and deliver our lives from death."* (Joshua 2:13) The spies readily agree, stating in verse eighteen, *"and thou shalt bring thy father, and thy mother, and thy brethren **and all thy father's household**, home unto thee."*

With no reason for the spies to have excluded Rahab's request for her sisters' deliverance as well, commentators generally feel that the women were included under the umbrella phrase, *"all thy father's household."* However, the survivors list in Joshua 6:23 reveals a marked distinction: *"And the young men that were spies went in, and brought out Rahab, and her father, and her mother, and her brethren, and **all that she had**; and they brought out **all her kindred**, and left them without the camp of Israel."* The obvious flag is that Rahab's sisters were conspicuous by their absence. Rather than employing that initial term, *"all of thy father's household"* (which is thought to have included the sisters), the text now reads, *"all that she had,"* her original phrase used in addition to her sisters, ostensibly a synonym for her family *and* the wording she used in Joshua 2:13 referring to her family's family (i.e., any nephews and nieces). The new expression, *"all her kindred,"* is believed to represent a larger unit than *"thy father's household,"* functioning here as a summary statement.

Therefore, the question begs—*Were Rahab's sisters in the house when the walls came down?* Sadly, while the linguistic evidence is inconclusive, the very real possibility exists that these siblings perished in the subsequent sacking of Jericho. Such a scenario is not without precedent. In the destruction of Sodom, Lot lost both his wife and his two sons-in-law (Genesis 19:14, 26). The potential application to our own loved ones is sobering. When the dust settles on the other side of the Rapture, some of *them* may be under the rubble. Thus, as the lyrics to "Brethren, We Have Met to Worship," state, the time for action is now!

> Brethren, see poor sinners round you
> Slumbering on the brink of woe;
> Death is coming, Hell is moving,
> Can you bear to let them go?
> *See our fathers and our mothers,*
> *And our children sinking down;*
> Brethren, pray and holy manna
> Will be showered all around.

Mazel Tov!

When the book of Joshua was written, the author confirmed that Rahab *"dwelleth in Israel even unto this day; because she hid the messengers, which Joshua sent to spy out Jericho."* (Joshua 6:25) Now, although Rahab may have lost her sisters, the Bible confirms that she did gain a husband, an Israelite named Salmon (believed by many adherents of Judaism to be one of the two spies). And this wasn't just *any* ole "catch" either. According to Numbers 10:14, her new father-in-law, Nahshon, son of Amminadab, was so important that Moses appointed him Supreme Military Commander of the Tribe of Judah, the lead eastward camp. Not bad for an "ex-hooker." However, there is much more than that.

Rahab made such a new life for herself that the Holy Spirit mentions her three times in the New Testament alone. Her first appearance is in

Matthew 1:5, *"[A]nd Salmon begat Booz of Rachab; and Booz begat Obed of Ruth; and Obed begat Jesse."* (Here, the King James committee transliterated her name as *Rachab* after its literal spelling in the Greek.) The following verse confirms that this former Canaanite courtesan became the great-great-grandmother of King David, Israel's greatest monarch. Finally, verse sixteen enshrines Rahab as one of four female Gentiles in the royal line from which Jesus Christ descends as the Saviour of all mankind. Matthew would also record an apropos rebuke that Jesus leveled at the chief priests and elders: *"Verily I say unto you, That the publicans and **harlots** go into the kingdom of God before you. For John came unto you in the way of righteousness, and ye believed him not: but the publicans and **harlots** believed him: and ye, when ye had seen it, repented not afterward, that ye might believe him."* (Matthew 21:31-32)

Thus, at the end of the day it would appear that *Salmon* was the one who "married up." As the proverbial "cherry on top," Rahab was also the only woman besides Sara to be inducted into the exclusive "Hall of Faith" in Hebrews, chapter eleven. Verse thirty-one reads: *"By faith the harlot Rahab perished not with them that believed not, when she had received the spies with **peace**."* The word "peace" constitutes an amazing picture of the II Corinthians 5:17-style transformation Rahab would later experience when compared to her initial, vicarious identification with her fellow citizens, *"your terror is fallen upon **us**,"* and *"as soon as **we** had heard these things, **our** hearts did melt."* (Joshua 2:9, 11) As Paul would later write, *"Therefore being **justified by faith**, we have **peace** with God through our Lord Jesus Christ."* (Romans 5:1)

And so, my fellow King James Bible believers— "trapped in our *own* terrified city" —let us honker down with *our* blessed "scarlet thread" dangling as we await that trumpet blast outside the walls, followed by that glorious shout (Joshua 6:16, 20).

> *"For the Lord himself shall descend from heaven with a **shout**,*
> *with the voice of the archangel, and with the **trump** of God: and*
> *the dead in Christ shall rise first: then we which are alive and*
> *remain shall be caught up together with them in the clouds, to*
> *meet the Lord in the air: and so shall we ever be with the Lord.*
> ***Wherefore comfort one another with these words.***"
> (I Thessalonians 4:16-18)

14

Fear Not, Little Flock

THE PURPOSE OF this chapter is to revisit Jericho's "fear factor" as it applies to the faithful Philadelphia remnant in the closing days of the Laodicean Church Age. In Luke 12:32, Jesus told His listeners, *"Fear not, little flock; for it is your Father's good pleasure to give you the kingdom."* We will now examine this important text in its *historical, doctrinal,* and *devotional* context.

The extended passage from Luke 12:22-34 is an excerpt from the familiar "Sermon on the Mount" in Matthew 5:1-7:29 (specifically, 6:25-34). The basic subject matter deals with trusting God for one's temporal needs. The historical setting is found in verse thirty: *"For all these things do the **nations of the world** seek after: and **your Father** knoweth that ye have need of these things."* (Matthew says *"Gentiles"* instead of *"nations of the world."*) In Amos 3:2, the Lord declared to Israel, *"**You only** have I known of all the families of the earth."* Consequently, Moses was instructed, *"And thou shalt say unto Pharaoh, Thus saith the LORD, **Israel is my son, even my firstborn.**"* (Exodus 4:22) Thus, in contrast to the pagan deities enshrined in the Roman Pantheon, Jesus portrayed Jehovah as the exclusive Father of the *Jewish* nation (*"[Y]our Father knoweth that ye have need of these things"*).

Having opened His discourse to Israel as a whole, the Lord then downshifts doctrinally with the phrase, *"little flock."* Here He begins to address the embryonic remnant that will embrace Him on the other side of Calvary. (These future messianic Jews were forecast in Eliab's derisive question to David in I Samuel 17:28, *"[W]ith whom hast thou left those **few sheep** in the wilderness?"*) Upon Stephen's murder in Acts 7:59, God dumps the *physical* seed of Abraham for their rejection of Him (I Samuel 8:7). He then blends His *"little flock"* with that Gentile remnant prophesied in John 10:16 to form a new *spiritual* nation:

> *But ye are a chosen generation, a royal priesthood, **an holy nation,** a peculiar people; that ye should shew forth the praises of him who hath called you out of darkness into his marvellous light; **which in time past were not a people, but are now the people of God**: which had not obtained mercy, but now have obtained mercy.* (I Peter 2:9-10)

The Apostle to the Gentiles explained this glorious merger to the Church at Rome by quoting the prophets Hosea and Isaiah accordingly:

> *As he saith also in Osee, **I will call them my people, which were not my people**; and her beloved, which was not beloved. And it shall come to pass, that in the place where it was said unto them, Ye are not my people; there shall they be called the children of the living God. Esaias also crieth concerning Israel, **Though the number of the children of Israel be as the sand of the sea, a remnant shall be saved**.* (Romans 9:25-27)

In contrast with *"Israel after the flesh"* (I Corinthians 10:18), Paul labeled this new *"little flock"* within the greater (predominantly Gentile) Body of Christ as *"the Israel of God"* (Galatians 6:16), for *"they are not all Israel, which are of Israel."* (Romans 9:6) Thankfully, at the Second Advent, *both* Hebrew factions shall be reunited— "National Israel" *and* "Remnant Israel" —for, to the eternal consternation of Steven Anderson and his NIFB freak show, *"[A]ll Israel shall be saved: as it is written, There shall come out of Sion the Deliverer, and shall turn away ungodliness from Jacob: For this is my covenant unto them, when I shall take away their sins."* (Romans 11:26-27)

FEAR, FLOCK, FATHER

The all-important devotional application in Luke 12:32 unfolds in its natural three-word alliteration: *"**Fear** not, little **flock**; for it is your **Father's** good pleasure to give you the kingdom."* To begin in the middle, *"[W]e are his people, and **the sheep of his pasture**."* (Psalm 100:3) As noted above, we are the ones Jesus referenced in John 10:16, *"**And other sheep I have, which are not of this fold**: them also must I bring, and they shall hear my voice; and there shall be one fold, and one* *shepherd."* We were also the ones Jesus had in mind when He told Peter, *"Feed my **lambs"*** and *"my **sheep."*** (John 21:15-17). The same applies to Paul's exhortation to the Ephesian elders, *"Take heed therefore unto yourselves, and to **all the flock**, over the which the Holy Ghost hath made you overseers, to **feed the church of God**, which he hath purchased with his own blood."* (Acts 20:28) Ditto, Peter's command to *"**Feed the flock of God** which is among you."* (I Peter 5:2)

Then, in addition to being *God's* flock, we are also a *little* flock (like those *"few sheep"* in I Samuel 17:28). At the end of the day, the Church of Jesus Christ would constitute the *"**few** there be that* **[found]** *it."* (Matthew 7:14) Consequently, as noted throughout this book, at the Judgment Seat of Christ, our Shemite Shepherd will try our work, *"of what **sort** it is."* (I Corinthians 3:13)

And, as a *"little flock"* —in nutty twenty-first-century America— we are also a *threatened* flock. Satan's predators are everywhere! Paul warned the shepherds in Ephesus, *"For I know this, that after my departing shall **grievous wolves** enter in among you, **not sparing the flock**."* (Acts 20:29) Peter adds, *"Be sober, be vigilant; because your adversary **the devil, as a roaring lion**, walketh about, **seeking whom he may devour**."* (I Peter 5:8)

Being a *threatened* flock leads to our first word in Luke 12:32—*fear*. Because Christians can be tempted to experience the same anxiety as the unsaved, the Holy Spirit's message to us is simple, *"**Fear not**, little flock."* The main reason we can heed this simple charge is because of the last word in our outline—*Father*. Though we are *little,* our Shepherd is *big!* (If you'd like to see just *how* big, read Daniel 2:35.) In the 1960s, "What, Me Worry?" was the enduring mantra used by the freckle-faced Alfred E. Neuman for *Mad Magazine*. So, why should any Bible believer "worry" about anything, considering the Shepherd we have? (See John 10:11.)

PSALM 23

The beloved 23rd Psalm ranks alongside John 3:16 and the Lord's Prayer as a trilogy of the most well-known Scriptures by both saved and lost folks alike. Untold funerals have begun with the words, *"The Lord is my shepherd; I shall not want."* (Or, like the little girl famously said, "The Lord is my shepherd; *that's all I want.*) The all-important cross-reference to our chapter title, *"Fear Not, Little Flock,"* is that beautiful fourth verse— *"I will fear no evil."* Because the Lord is "our" Shepherd, we never "want" for anything, especially in dire-appearing circumstances (i.e., Biden/Harris, CRT, BLM, Covid-19, Vaccine Passports...yada, yada, yada). For while we may not know *why* it is that *"He maketh [us] to lie down"* in certain pastures, some we would not choose for ourselves (verse 2), because of Romans 8:28, we can *always* be assured that they are *"green pastures"* (i.e., *green*, as in life-giving).

The Jews did not understand why *they* were being made to "lie down" under the boot of Roman oppression (Luke 1:71; 24:21). Unfortunately, they missed *"the time of their visitation"* (Luke 19:44), despite the fact that the long-awaited anti-type of their great shepherd/king David was standing in their very presence—fulfilling Psalm 23:2 by commanding them to *"sit down by companies upon the green grass."* (Mark 6:39) But thankfully (as noted above), a better day is coming for Jehovah's covenant nation: *"Thus saith the LORD of hosts; Again in this place, which is desolate without man and without beast, and in all the cities thereof, shall be an habitation of shepherds causing their flocks to lie down."* (Jeremiah 33:12)

And of course, *Israel's* loss was *our* gain (Romans 11:19, 28), the Shulamite woman declaring, *"Behold, thou art fair, my beloved, yea, pleasant: also our bed is green."* (Song of Solomon 1:16) Paul completes the analogy by relating that the divine purpose of a *"green* bed" is for the predominantly Gentile Bride— *"dead to the law"* and newly *"married to another, even to him raised from the dead"* —to *"bring forth fruit unto God."* (Romans 7:4) I recall my good friend, Daniel Buchanan (pastor of New Beginning Missionary Baptist Church, Lenoir, North Carolina), sharing some "Southern theology" on this holy text: "Ole-time worship during church occurs whenever the Bride is romancing her Husband, which frequently results in *babies* getting born (again) at the altar."

As indicated by the opening verse, *"The Lord is my shepherd,"* the entire Psalm revolves around our personal relationship with Jesus Christ. Thus, to obey His command, *"Fear not, little flock,"* it will behoove us to remember the following seven truths regarding *our* Shepherd.

First of all, He *receives* us. Do *you* remember the day the Good Shepherd received *you* into His fold? (See John 10:3.) One of the most beautiful things I have ever read is a widely circulated internet piece:

The Bummer Lamb

Every once in a while, a ewe will give birth to a lamb and reject it. There are many reasons she may do this. If the lamb is returned to the ewe, the mother may even kick the poor animal away. Once a ewe rejects one of her lambs, she will never change her mind. These little lambs will hang their head so low that it looks like something is wrong with its neck. Their spirit is broken. These lambs are called "bummer lambs." Unless the shepherd intervenes, that lamb will die, rejected and alone.

So, do you know what the shepherd does? He takes that rejected little one into his home, hand-feeds it and keeps it warm by the fire. He will wrap it up with blankets and hold it to his chest so the bummer can hear his heartbeat. Once the lamb is strong enough, the shepherd will place it back in the field with the rest of the flock. But that sheep never forgets how the shepherd cared for him when his mother rejected him. When the shepherd calls for the flock, guess who runs to him first? That is right—the bummer sheep. He knows his voice intimately. It is not that the bummer lamb is loved more, it just knows intimately the one who loves it. It's not that it is loved more, it just believes it because it has experienced that love one-on-one.

Many of *us* are bummer lambs, rejected and broken. But He is the good Shepherd. He cares for our every need and holds us close to His heart so we can hear His heartbeat. We may be broken, but we are deeply loved by the Shepherd.

After He receives us, our Shepherd *nourishes* us: *"I shall not want"* (verse one). This lifelong process begins at birth: *"[A]s **newborn babes, desire the sincere milk of the word**, that ye may grow thereby."* (I Peter 2:2) Jeremiah adds, *"**Thy words were found, and I did eat them**; and **thy word** was unto me the joy and rejoicing of mine heart."* (Jeremiah 15:16) Having begun with *"sincere milk,"* the end goal is *"strong meat,"* for that is the diet that *"belongeth to them that are of **full age**."* (Hebrews 5:14)

Thirdly, the Shepherd *leads* us: *"[H]e **leadeth** me beside the still waters"* and *"in the paths of righteousness for his name's sake"* (verses two and three). Now, without wanting to seem "insensitive," a sheep is one of the *dumbest* animals God ever created! Among other self-injurious practices, sheep will often wander off and get lost (Luke 15:4). Therefore, the Chief Shepherd said, *"I will give you **pastors** according to mine* *heart, which shall feed you with knowledge and understanding."* (Jeremiah 3:15)

Pastors are listed among the special gifts God gave to the Church, *"for the perfecting of the saints, for the work of the ministry,* [and] *for the edifying of the body."* (Ephesians 4:11-12) The twin admonitions in Hebrews 13:7,17 are excellent cross-references for *remembering, following, obeying,* and *submitting* to *your* God-given undershepherd. (If some spooky-looking, anti-pastoral authority, hyper-dispensationalist tells you that Hebrews is not a Church Age book, tell him to read I Timothy 3:5.) Remember, the main reason Christians need pastors to lead them is because *"God hath chosen the **weak** things of the world to confound the things which are mighty."* (I Corinthians 1:27)

After receiving, feeding, and leading us, the Shepherd also *comforts* us: *"[T]hy rod and thy staff they **comfort** me"* (verse four). Oddly enough, this "comfort" derives partially from *chastening,* as the "rod" is always a reminder that God loves us, *"for whom the Lord **loveth** he **chasteneth**, and **scourgeth** every son whom he receiveth."* (Hebrews 12:6) The flip side of the "comfort coin" is that this same "staff" (sometimes referred to as the two ends of a shepherd's crook) is also used to keep the predators at bay.

This, in turn, leads to benefit number five, the Shepherd *protects* us: *"Thou preparest a table before me **in the presence of mine enemies**"* (verse five). Saved by the precious blood of the perfect Lamb of God, born-again Christians were spiritually circumcised in the process (Colossians 2:11), being cut away from their sinful flesh and reattached to the *"members of his body, of his flesh, and of his bones."* (Ephesians 5:30) As such, we have a supernatural antibody coursing through our veins. (Is it any wonder that Bill Gates and his globalist minions want to pump their poisonous vaccines into our bodies?) For many years scientists have studied ways to produce antidotes for poisonous snakebites. While horses were used in the old days, modern research now confirms that the best anti-venoms actually come from sheep. The process starts with a lamb being injected with a specified quantity of venom. The sheep's blood would then immediately begin producing antibodies to neutralize the poison. When enough antibodies were generated, they would be extracted from the lamb's blood and presto—an antidote for snakebite to neutralize the venom within the victim. Thus, the *blood of the Lamb* destroys the *venom of the serpent*! (John 3:14)

Sixth, the Shepherd *cleanses* us: *"[T]hou anointest my head with oil"* (verse five). Paul further declared in Ephesians 5:26-27, *"Husbands, love your wives, even as Christ also loved the church, and gave himself for it; that he might sanctify and **cleanse it with the washing of water by the word.**"* (Ephesians 5:25-26) Another enlightening internet post addresses this subject:

Anoint My Head with Oil

Sheep can get their head caught in briers and die trying to get untangled. There are horrid little flies that like to torment sheep by laying eggs in their nostrils which turn into worms and drive the sheep to beat their head against a rock, sometimes to death. Their ears and eyes are also susceptible to tormenting insects. So the shepherd anoints their whole head with oil. Then there is peace. That oil forms a barrier of protection against the evil that tries to destroy the sheep.

Do you have times of mental torment? Do worrisome thoughts invade your mind over and over? Do you beat your head against the wall trying to stop them? Have you ever asked God to anoint your head with oil? He has an endless supply! His oil protects and makes it possible for you to fix your heart, mind, and eyes on him today and always! There is peace in the valley! May our good Father anoint your head with oil today so that your cup overflows with blessings! God is good and He is faithful.

Finally, number seven, the Shepherd *escorts* us—particularly, at the end of our journey: It was my privilege to write the foreword for the 1994 edition of *Gathered Fragments* by Pastor Willard Thomas. Though ever reticent to discuss the disputed subject, Bro. Willard is believed by many to be the true, unsung hero who penned the earliest version of the famous poem, *Footprints in the Sand* (appearing in his earliest work.) He obviously believed in "working for a cause, not for applause." As Harry S. Truman once said, "It is amazing what you can accomplish if you do not care who gets the credit." (With no pun intended, Ronald Reagan is also identified with a slightly different version of this quote.)

Though I never broke the "Debbie Downer" news to my good friend while he was still alive, the crux of Bro. Willard's inspirational verse was, shall we say, slightly—unscriptural? In his dream, the author asks the Lord why the two sets of footprints dissolved to just one during difficult times: "I don't understand why, when I needed You the most,

You would leave me" (presumably at the very lowest and saddest times.) The well-known response is, "My precious child, I love you and will never leave you...When you saw only one set of footprints, it was then that I carried you."

Can there be any doubt that the greatest temptation to fear would be at the hour of one's death? (Hebrews 2:15) Tell me then—how many sets of footprints does Psalm 23:4 indicate there will be at the end of your life: *"Yea, **though I walk** through the valley of the shadow of death, I will fear no evil: **for thou art with me.**"* The truth is, the Shepherd walks *before* you through *life* (verse three) and *beside* you through *death* (verse four). His *presence* is all you need to stay on your own two feet! (See Psalm 18:33 and 94:18.) When it was Moses' time to go, the Lord, who would ultimately bury him in secret, told him directly, *"**Get thee up** into this mountain...and behold the land of Canaan, which I give unto the children of Israel for a possession: **and die in the mount whither thou goest up,** and be gathered unto thy people."* (Deuteronomy 32:49-50)

And—as if all of the above was not enough—while the Shepherd has been out in front *throughout* your life, and by your side at the *end* of your life, He has also *had your back* the entire time! To ensure that no beasts of prey sneak up on any stragglers in the rear of the flock, two faithful sheepdogs have been guarding the way: *"Surely **goodness and mercy shall follow me** all the days of my life and I will dwell in the house of the LORD for ever"* (verse six). Dr. Harry Ironside once had a delusional church lady tell him that she believed she was being followed by two strangers. He wisely shared the above passage with her and her fears dissipated.

THE MAIN CAUSE FOR FEAR

In his 1933 inaugural address, Franklin D. Roosevelt famously said, "The only thing we have to fear is *fear* itself." The deepest truth for Bible believers to grasp, as the water continues to grow shallower, is that the central cause for our fears is the subconscious belief—planted by Satan— that current events are *totally* off the rails. A shortlist of such panic-button, doomsday scenarios would include: Joe and Kamala are just about to destroy America; the FED is on the verge of sinking our economy; the Chicoms are about to unleash an even *worse* virus than Covid-19; China is preparing to invade Taiwan in response to Russia's invasion of

Ukraine; those *Red Dawn* Soviet paratroopers will probably land in my yard tomorrow; pretty soon we'll *all* be in one of Bill Gates' "Anti-vaxxer camps"; and, did I take the Mark of the Beast when I received the jab?

Now, while every one of those examples (except the last) is certainly possible (and, *more* likely than not), the difference is that these debacles are *not* happening by "chance" (I Samuel 6:9). As Paul would put it (from I Timothy 1:17; 6:15), *every single bit of it* is under the *complete* control of the **"King eternal, immortal, invisible, the only wise God...the blessed and only Potentate, the King of kings, and Lord of lords"** (I Chronicles 29:11; Job 23:13; Psalm 115:3; Proverbs 19:21; Isaiah 46:10; Lamentations 3:37; Daniel 4:35; Matthew 19:26; Acts 4:28; Romans 8:28; Ephesians 1:11; Revelation 4:11). Simply put, Christians become *fearful* when they lose sight of the *Lord's* involvement in deteriorating events. Consequently, **"I will fear no evil: for thou art with me."** Thus, the great secret to the Shepherd leading you *"beside the still waters"* is to constantly remind yourself that He is there to *do* that very thing!

THE BEST REMEDY

The quickest route to those *"still waters"* of Psalm 23:2 is to obey the Pauline charge, **"In everything give thanks**: *for this is the will of God in Christ Jesus concerning you."* (I Thessalonians 5:18) As discussed in chapter six, this liberating truth is related to that threefold analogy of the circle, dot, and intrusive arrow. To review, the circle is God, the dot is any saved person, and the arrow represents all of our experiences, especially the so-called negative ones engineered by Satan. Thus, the reason we are to thank God for *everything* is because *everything* occurs within the scope of His permissive will. (Nothing can touch the dot without passing through the circle.)

Applying this principle to our emotional survival through America's last days (not to mention of the Church Age itself) is the great key to gaining victory over the Devil's attempt to steal our peace of mind. The trick is to use the negative news as the Lord's antibodies to destroy the venom of Satan's fear. Your whole perspective will change when you remind yourself that God Himself is orchestrating (*allowing*) the present chaos. Before you employ this mental discipline, your subconscious can keep you depressed by convincing you that current events are literally spinning out of control ("chaos in the cosmos," etc.). Your only perceived solution is to thrust your head in the sand, believing that "out of sight is out of mind" (Job 39:17). However, if you will slap yourself and confront those nonstop "negative waves" ("Odd Ball," *Kelly's Heroes*)—but with the all-important caveat of acknowledging God's providence at work— then *"the **peace of God**, which passeth all understanding, shall keep your hearts and minds through Christ Jesus."* (Philippians 4:7)

Unfortunately, the difficult part of this guaranteed therapy is coming to grips with the two-fold reality that this is *no longer* the "America of John Wayne" ("Toto, I've a feeling we're not in Kansas anymore"), and it's just a matter of time before Joshua blows the walls down! This should give us some empathy for Jeremiah (aka the *"Weeping* Prophet") as he penned the book of Lamentations. *"Mine eye runneth down with **rivers of water** for the destruction of the daughter of my people. Mine eye trickleth down, and ceaseth not, without any intermission."* (Lamentations 3:48-49)

No matter how many psychotic, II Chronicles 7:14-quoting Fundies get apoplectic at the novel idea of interpreting Scripture in its rightly-divided, dispensational context (see II Timothy 2:15; 3:1-4:13)—the United States of America is presently on a ventilator, with the God who originally elevated her about to pull the plug! The miracle is that our nation lasted as long as it did, for *her* destiny—along with the rest of the so-called "Community of Nations"—was sealed long ago: *"**Behold, the nations are as a drop of a bucket**, and are counted as the small dust of the balance: behold, he taketh up the isles as a very little thing...**All nations before him are as nothing**; and they are counted to him **less than nothing**, and vanity."* (Isaiah 40:15, 17)

Only *one* nation has an unequivocal exemption from that broad stroke (and it *sure* ain't us, neighbor). *"Therefore fear thou not, **O my servant Jacob**, saith the LORD...**For I am with thee, saith the LORD, to save thee: though I make a full end of all nations whither I have scattered thee.**"* (Jeremiah 30:10-11) After a Moabite king solicited Baalam to place a curse on Israel, the hireling hit-man prudently declined the contract as his knees began smiting one another at the very prospect, stating:

> *How shall I curse, whom God hath not cursed? or how shall I defy, whom the LORD hath not defied? For from the top of the rocks I see him, and from the hills I behold him: lo, **the people shall dwell alone, and shall not be reckoned among the nations**.* (Numbers 23:8-9)

Connecting the dots will reveal that our so called "American Exceptionalism" was related to our befriending that despised Jew. For while "all nations" have been *before* the Lord (i.e., in His direct line of fire), the *"apple of his eye"* (Zechariah 2:8) has obviously been *behind* his back (Exodus 14:19; 33:23). And any nation wise enough to befriend her would find itself behind Jehovah's back as well (Genesis 12:3). You might describe the Lord's attitude as, "Any friend of Jacob is a friend of mine, etc." But of course, all that changed with the criminal eviction of President Trump on January 20, 2021 (not to mention BiBi's ouster six months later by the same globalist cabal). While "The Donald" moved our Embassy to JerUSAlem, when the new Israeli Prime Minister, Naftali Bennett, conferred with Biden in the Oval Office on August 27, 2021, a masked "Sleepy Joe" was observed nodding in and out of consciousness. (On September 22, 2021—while I was literally typing these words—the news broke that the Democratic House, hijacked by AOC and her Muslim "Squad," had shot down funding for Israel's Iron Dome missile defense system.) Oh well....

FROM HOSPICE TO HELL

America has not always been on life support; far from it. "Lady Liberty" once proudly shined as the envy of all the world. And no matter what the Marxist NEA spews forth, Bible-believing Christianity was *the* historical impetus for her unique status. After touring the prison systems of this country, Alexis de Tocqueville wrote his classic work, *Democracy in America.* Less than a decade after Thomas Jefferson's death, the famous French aristocrat, scientist, political philosopher, diplomat, and historian codified *this* about *our* nation:

> *Upon my arrival in the United States the religious aspect of the country was the first thing that struck my attention;* and the longer I stayed there, the more I perceived the great political consequences resulting from this new state of things. In France I had almost always seen the spirit of religion and the spirit of freedom marching in opposite directions. But in America I found they were intimately united and that they reigned in common over the same country.
> *Religion in America...must be regarded as the foremost of the political institutions of that country;* for it does not impart a taste for freedom, it facilitates the use of it. Indeed, it is in this same point

of view that the inhabitants of the United States themselves look upon religious belief.... *In the United States the sovereign authority is religious...there is no country in the world where the Christian religion retains a greater influence over the souls of men than in America,* and there can be no greater proof of its utility and if its conformity to human nature than that its influence is powerfully felt over the most enlightened and free nation of the earth.

The following de Tocqueville quote, though relegated to oral tradition, is totally consistent with his published sentiments in *Democracy in America*:

> I sought for the key to the greatness and genius of America in her harbors...in her fertile fields and boundless forests; in her rich mines and vast world commerce; in her public school system and institutions of learning. I sought for it in her democratic Congress and in her matchless Constitution.
> *Not until I went into the churches of America and heard her pulpits flame with righteousness did I understand the secret of her genius and power.*
> America is *great* because America is *good*, and if America ever ceases to be *good*, America will cease to be *great*.

But, alas, that was yesterday. Today, the United States is taking her final, stuttering steps from Hospice—to Hell (I Samuel 20:3). In preparation of an appropriate eulogy, a brief history of "America the Beautiful" can be summarized in three salient Old Testament Scriptures:

• America's Past: *"**Blessed** is the nation whose God is the LORD."* (Psalm 33:12)

• America's Present: *"Righteousness exalteth a nation: but sin is a **reproach** to any people."* (Proverbs 14:34)

• America's Future: *"The wicked shall be cast into **hell**, and all the nations that forget God."* (Psalm 9:17)

Though hard to believe, the United States, along with her historically King James Bible-believing Japhethite cousins (Great Britain, Canada, Australia, and New Zealand) will be the *first* to go down the tubes in the Tribulation (Revelation 9:15-18), for they are the lead nations capable of *forgetting* the true God; Red China, Communist Russia, North Korea, Muslim Iran, and most of Catholic Europe never *knew* Him to *forget* him!

In the hymn, "Come, We that Love the Lord," Isaac Watts concurred, "Let those refuse to sing *who never knew our God.*" Accordingly, I Peter 4:17 reads, *"For the time is come that **judgment must begin at the house of God**: and if it first begin at us, what shall the end be of them that obey not the gospel of God?"* (Ezekiel 9:6)

AN EFFECTIVE THERAPEUTIC EXERCISE

I will end this chapter with an effective therapeutic exercise that I employ to avoid being depressed by the current catastrophic cacophony. Whenever I hear the latest lunatic development—in order to trigger the escape hatch of I Thessalonians 5:18—I simply repeat to myself something like this: "Man, oh man! God must *really* be mad at America!!" (to have permitted this latest disaster). No matter how silly it may sound—I'm a-tellin' ya, neighbor—it works! The equivalent of obeying the Pauline charge, *"In everything give thanks,"* it's the very means to experience the emotional relief promised in I Peter 5:7, *"Casting all your care upon him; for he careth for you."* If you doubt my "sage" advice, try the following exercise:

- Biden Cancels Pipeline, Then Begs OPEC for Oil as Gas Prices Soar
  You: Man, oh man! God must *really* be mad at America!!!

- Family Members Forced by Draconian Hospital Policy to Die in Isolation
  You: Man, oh man! God must *really* be mad at America!!!

- CJCS Mark Milley Promises to Warn China if US Plans Attack
  You: Man, oh man! God must *really* be mad at America!!!

- Male Perverts Allowed to Shower Alongside Girls in Public Schools
  You: Man, oh man! God must *really* be mad at America!!!

- Virginia Middle School Removes Urinals from Boys' Bathrooms
  You: Man, oh man! God must *really* be mad at America!!!

- Realtors Can No Longer Refer to "Master" Bedrooms or Bathrooms
  You: Man, oh man! God must *really* be mad at America!!!

- Thousands of Covid-Infected Illegals Entering USA Daily from Mexico
  You: Man, oh man! God must *really* be mad at America!!!

- USA Borrowing from China to Give It Back in Foreign Aid
  You: Man, oh man! God must *really* be mad at America!!!

- Evangelical Lutheran Church Installs First Transgender Bishop
  You: Man, oh man! God must *really* be mad at America!!!

- Florida Elementary School Kids Taken on Field Trip to LGBTQ+ Bar
  You: Man, oh man! God must really be mad at America!!!

- Mothers Must Now Be Called "Birthing Persons"
  You: Man, oh man! God must really be mad at America!!!

- Experts Now Advise Asking Babies if it's Okay to Change Their Diapers
  You: Man, oh man! God must *really* be mad at America!!!

- NFL Schedules Black National Anthem for Every Game
  You: Man, oh man! God must *really* be mad at America!!!

- Robert E. Lee Statue in Richmond Removed After 130 Years
  You: Man, oh man! God must *really* be mad at America!!!

- New York University Offers Class on Taylor Swift
  You: Man, oh man! God must *really* be mad at America

- Professor Wants "Pedophile" Changed to "Minor-Attracted Person"
  You: Man, oh man! God must *really* be mad at America!!!

- Joe Biden's pick for Deputy Assistant Secretary of Spent Fuel and Waste Disposition in the Office of Nuclear Energy for the Department of Energy was Sam Britton, a drag queen and proponent of "pup play," which involves grown men (i.e., "sick puppies") putting on dog masks and behaving like animals for sexual kicks. No relation to Paul Anka's "Puppy Love," this Satanic garbage started in 1977 with Rodney Howard Brown, and his so called "Toronto Laughter Revival" where "Christians," barking like dogs, would be led around the services by a leash.
  You: Man, oh man! God must *really* be mad at America!!!

- On the very cusp of Vladimir Putin's threatened February 2022 invasion of the Ukraine—the same day Joe Biden warned US citizens there that their military would not be coming to their rescue—another Vladimir was running interference for his boss, distracting America's brain-dead sports addicts (II Timothy 3:4) with an "epic" inter-gender, two-on-one, bare-knuckle Russian MMA "spectacle" (reminiscent of the Roman Colosseum); a seventy-five-year-old, tattooed pensioner with a red Mohawk hairdo named Vladimir Spartak and his eighteen-year-old equally-tattooed grandson, "Big Igibob," duking it out for six three-minute rounds with a 268-pound, twenty-eight-year-old Russian female, Yuilia Mishko, aka "The Tomboy."
  You: Man, oh man! God must *really* be mad at America!!!

- Finally (as this book was just about to go to press), after half the "Christians" on *Facebook* went apoplectic over the publicity stunt Jap-slapping of Chris Rock by Will Smith—while the national media was predictably ignoring the hate-crime carjacking of Mrs. Linda Frickey, a white, 73-year-old grandmother, by four "African-American" teenagers who left her to bleed out in the street due to a severed arm—Fox News hired Caitlyn Jenner as a contributor (calling the pervert "an inspiration to us all"), then, 24 hours later, slammed Disney for going "woke" by removing "gender greetings" from its parks.
  You: Man, oh Man! God must really, *really* be mad at America!!!

In summary, the process is quite elementary. Fear always results from losing sight of the Lord's personal involvement (Psalm 23:4). Thus, without a conscious reminder that He is solidly in charge, you're bound to get stressed. *"Fear not, little flock"* is not a suggestion; it's a command! Let this convicting exhortation by John Wesley keep you on your knees: "Worry is a mild form of atheism." When an atheist chided him saying, "Your followers are a bit too emotional," the Methodist founder replied, "You're probably right—*but they die well.*" Reposing on his own deathbed at eighty-seven years of age, Wesley's famous last words mirrored Psalm 23:4 perfectly: "Farewell, farewell…The best of all is, God is with us!"

"For God hath not given us the spirit of fear;
but of power, and of love, and of a sound mind."
(II Timothy 1:7)

15

The Terminal Generation

THIS CHAPTER WAS especially written for the young people in our King James-Only Independent Baptist Churches (along with their parents and youth directors). To whatever degree the *"perilous times"* of I Timothy 3:1 are upon us, this demographic will constitute "The Terminal Generation." As such, our kids deserve particular attention for they have obviously been chosen to fulfill a unique role in the divine denouement of the New Testament Age.

In AD 1212, tens of thousands of Catholic boys were butchered (literally) in the so-called "Children's Crusade" (a bizarre harbinger of Rome's modern pedophilia epidemic). While these striplings are to be commended for their bravery, their handlers deserve the condemnation of history for sending them—unprepared, unarmed, and underaged— into harm's way (not to mention Hell itself). It is my prayer that the following material will mitigate the number of casualties our own youths will suffer as they square off against a far deadlier foe than their thirteenth-century predecessors.

KING JOSIAH

King Josiah was one of the most extraordinary personalities in Scripture. As God often employs Old Testament types to shed light on New Testament truth, Josiah was no exception. His life affords several critical lessons for Christian youth to assimilate as they find themselves, alongside their moms and dads, floating to Heaven's shore in those perilous waters of Acts 27.

Josiah was the sixteenth monarch of the southern kingdom of Judah (encompassing the tribes of Judah and Benjamin). According to

II Chronicles 34:1, his reign lasted thirty-one years (640-609 BC). His succinct legacy follows in verse two: *"**And he did that which was right in the sight of the LORD**, and walked in the ways of David his father, and declined neither to the right hand, nor to the left."*

His name means, "Who Jehovah heals." As no mention is made of any physical maladies, the implication is that his "healing" involved *emotional* issues (probably sadness). Josiah was crowned at the tender age of eight following the untimely death of his father Amon. His "glorious role model" (Proverbs 17:6) was so wicked that, after reigning only two years, the twenty-four-year-old neophyte was "bumped off" by one of his own servants. (Though Amon got what he deserved, the double use of the word *"conspired"* in verses 24 and 25 represents an insightful cross-reference to those end-day *"traitors"* listed in II Timothy 3:4.)

PAPAW MANASSEH

Now to give ole Amon the benefit of the doubt, he probably didn't have much of a childhood either, for Josiah's grandfather made his daddy look like a saint. Manasseh lorded over Judah fifty-five years, the longest reign in Jewish history. So, exactly how bad was Josiah's papaw? A synopsis of Josiah's inherited kingdom can be seen in II Chronicles 33:1-10. The litany of Manasseh's sins would include: idolatry (verse 3); pagan altars *in* the Temple (verses 4 and 5); witchcraft (verse 6); and child sacrifice (verse 6); II Kings 23:7 adds that he also sanctioned *"houses of the sodomites...**by the house of the LORD.**"*

The ultimate slam-dunk indictment on his half-century-plus reign was, *"So Manasseh made Judah and the inhabitants of Jerusalem to err, **and to do worse than the heathen, whom the LORD had destroyed before the children of Israel"*** (verse 9). Whereas even wicked King Ahab was willing to humble himself and repent in sackcloth (I Kings 21:27), Manasseh's profile concludes: *"And the LORD spake to Manasseh, and to his people: **but they would not hearken"*** (verse 10). And did I mention that Manasseh was also guilty of "shooting the messengers" who delivered those warnings? According to strong rabbinical tradition, Isaiah's martyrdom, being sawed in half (Hebrews 11:37), was ordered by his *own* grandson, good ole King Manasseh himself. (What a guy!)

His political career can be defined by the meaning of *his* name: "One who causes to forget." More than any other monarch, Manasseh caused Israel to *forget* God— *"The wicked shall be turned into hell, and **all the nations that forget God.**"* (Psalm 9:17) Ultimately, Manasseh was the main reason that Jehovah dispatched Nebuchadnezzar and his Babylonian hordes in the first place. *"And I will appoint over them four kinds, saith the LORD: the sword to slay, and the dogs to tear, and the fowls of the heaven, and the beasts of the earth, to devour and destroy. And I will cause them to be removed into all kingdoms of the earth, **because of Manasseh** the son of Hezekiah king of Judah, for that which he did in Jerusalem."* (Jeremiah 15:3-4)

BE CAREFUL WHAT YOU WISH FOR

In Jeremiah 15:4, the Holy Ghost was careful to delineate that our villain was *"Manasseh the **son of Hezekiah**."* Do y'all happen to remember what happened when Isaiah informed Hezekiah, *"Thus saith the LORD, Set thine house in order; **for thou shalt die**, and not live"*? (II Kings 20:1) The startled king turned his face to the wall, wept, and prayed down fifteen more years. The great Baptist prayer warrior George Mueller revealed that the secret to his devotional life was losing his will in a matter. As he would naturally have several reasons why he thought it would be *good* for him to secure the particular thing he was praying for, he would then cancel out *his* will by listing a matching number of reasons why it might be *bad* to have it. The key was to always pray, *"nevertheless not my will, but thine, be done."* (Luke 22:42)

Well, it would *appear* that in Hezekiah's case, he should have stuck with the Lord's original schedule, as three years into the "bonus round," Queen Hephzibah gave birth to Manasseh. Twelve years later, the "little devil" took over the kingdom when "daddy's dial" ran out (II Kings 21:1). Thus, not only did the apathetic king leave Judah's security jeopardized from *without* (II Kings 20:12-19), but he also bequeathed them a ticking time bomb *within*. (Oddly enough, the latter would precipitate the former; the sins of Hezekiah's son sparking God's judgment vis-à-vis Nebuchadnezzar, the invasion itself facilitated by his earlier indiscretions with those Babylonian "emissaries.")

Yet the Lord always knows what He's doing, for if Manasseh had never been born, neither would Josiah have arrived. (See: George Bailey's epiphany in the Christmas classic, *It's A Wonderful Life.*) Josiah *had* to be born—at least according to a remarkable prophecy recorded in the book of I Kings. Following Solomon's death, *his* dingbat son, Rehoboam, sparks a civil war that results in Jeroboam reigning over the ten northern tribes (leaving Benjamin aligned with Judah). To combat the centralized worship in Jerusalem, Jeroboam erected two secondary altars, one in Beth-el and the other in Dan. When He decided to offer a sacrifice at the southern location, the Lord sent a prophet to rebuke him. What happened next was so astounding, it would only occur one other time in the entire Bible (not including our Lord's case in Isaiah 7:14). In 712 BC, the Holy Spirit announced that a Persian potentate by the name of *Cyrus* would free the Jews from their seventy-year captivity (Isaiah 44:28); according to Ezra 1:1-8, this came to pass 176 years later. Notice how this same miracle occurred in the earlier prophecy regarding Jeroboam's generic sacrifice. This time, Jehovah's celebrated "poster-*child*" is pre-named some three centuries ahead of time!

> *And, behold, there came a man of God out of Judah by the word of the LORD unto Beth-el: and Jeroboam stood by the altar to burn incense. And he cried against the altar in the word of the LORD, and said, O altar, altar, thus saith the LORD; Behold, a child shall be born unto the house of David,* **Josiah by name***; and upon thee shall he offer the priests of the high places that burn incense upon thee, and men's bones shall be burnt upon thee. And he gave a sign the same day, saying, This is the sign which the LORD hath spoken; Behold, the altar shall be rent, and the ashes that are upon it shall be poured out.* (I Kings 13:1-3)

JOSIAH'S UNIQUE INNER MOTIVATION

This would probably be a good place to "pull over and park" to remind my young readers that *you* were also created for a divine purpose. Dr. Bob Jones, Sr., used to say, "Success in life is finding the will of God and doing it!" And so, let us return to II Chronicles 34 and take a closer look at this amazing eight-year-old sovereign and see what *you* can apply to *your* life.

When Josiah turned sixteen, *"in the eighth year of his reign, while he was yet young,* **he began to seek after the God of David his father"** (verse 3). Notice that he did this while he was *totally* on his own! (Though Jeremiah was a contemporary, the Holy Spirit does not reveal any interaction between the two men.) Four years later, he begins to *"purge Judah and Jerusalem from the high places, and the groves, and the carved images"* (verse 3). My man then goes *wild*, busting up more stuff than Eliot Ness and the Untouchables would ever dream of (even burning the bones of the pagan priests upon their own altars); and not only in Judah, but in the Northern Kingdom as well (verses 4-7). At age twenty-six, he begins repairing the Temple (verses 8-13).

Now, here comes the unbelievable part. How many of you teens have your Bible with you as you are following this narrative? So...look what comes next: *"And when they brought out the money that was brought into the house of the LORD,* **Hilkiah the priest found a book of the law of the LORD given by Moses**. *And Hilkiah answered and said to Shaphan the scribe,* **I have found the book of the law in the house of the LORD"** (verses 14-15). The critical takeaway here is that *everything* Josiah accomplished—beginning as an eight-year-old in the wickedest time of Israel's history—he did *without* a Bible (much less a godly father, spiritual advisors, and/or an indwelling Holy Spirit). *How are we to account for this?*

Next, note his personal reaction to the holy discovery: *"And Shaphan read it before the king....And it came to pass,* **when the king had heard the words** *of the law, that* **he rent his clothes"** (verses 18-19). He then issues an all-points bulletin for any spiritual advisors that might be *"left in Israel and in Judah* [who could basically tell him what to do next], *concerning the words of the book that is found: for great is the wrath of the LORD that is poured out upon us"* (verse 21). Things were so bad, the best they could come up with was a "lady preacher" named Huldah. (Again, the Holy Spirit makes no mention of Jeremiah's whereabouts.) Talk about the original "Debbie Downer," Huldah's forecast was no Joyce Meyer hug-it-out pep talk (verse 22-28)! The almost-humorous, subliminal (Isaiah 3:12) feminism in play can be seen in the opening directive by the *"college"* professor (KJV word employed in verse 22 for Jerusalem's Second Quarter) to the *royal* emissaries of *King* Josiah— *"Tell ye* **the man** *that sent you to me...*yada, yada, yada..." (verse 23).

Anywho, the crux of her message was that God was going to clean Judah's clock—period! *"Thus saith the LORD, Behold* **I will bring evil upon this place**, *and upon the inhabitants thereof, even all the* **curses** *that are written in the book which they have read before the king of Judah"* (verse 24). These "curses" are listed in Deuteronomy 27:15-26; 28:15-68. However, because Josiah's *"heart was tender"* (verse 27),

Jehovah would grant him a pass (well, sort of…). Like that old saying goes, "Everybody wants to go to Heaven, but nobody wants to go today," the "good news" was, *"Behold, I will gather thee to thy fathers, and thou shalt be gathered to thy grave in peace, **neither shall thine eyes see all the evil that I will bring upon this place, and upon the inhabitants of the same"** (verse 28). This deep truth was captured in Isaiah 57:1, *"The righteous perisheth, and no man layeth it to heart: and merciful men are taken away, none considering that **the righteous is taken away from the evil to come."** (One of the greatest illustrations of this truth was the death of super patriot, Senator Jessie Helms of North Carolina on the 4th of July, 2008—six months before the inauguration of Barack Hussein Obama II, aka Barry Soetoro).

Josiah responds by personally taking the newfound Law of Moses to his subjects posthaste: *"And the king went up into the house of the LORD, and all the men of Judah, and the inhabitants of Jerusalem, and the priests, and the Levites, and all the people, great and small: **and he read in their ears** all the words of the book of the covenant that was found in the house of the LORD"* (verse 30). He then *"**stood in his place, and made a covenant before the LORD"*** to renew the Mosaic mandates and *"caused all that were present in Jerusalem and Benjamin to **stand to it**. And the inhabitants of Jerusalem did according to the covenant of God"* (verses 31-32).

Afterwards, the fired-up king inaugurated a sweeping reformation, detailed in II Kings 23:4-14. Among other acts, Josiah removed and burned all the Baalite paraphernalia polluting the Temple (verse 4); fired the idolatrous priests (verse 5); dismantled the sodomite houses adjacent to the Lord's house (verse 7); closed the Molech infanticide clinics (verse 10); and destroyed numerous altars, images, and groves (verses 12-13 and 19). And then, the dramatic moment finally arrived for Josiah to fulfill that three-hundred-year-old prophecy:

> *Moreover **the altar that was at Beth-el**, and the high place which Jeroboam the son of Nebat, who made Israel to sin, had made, both that altar and the high place he brake down, and burned the high place, and stamped it small to powder, and burned the grove. And as Josiah turned himself, he spied the sepulchres that were there in the mount, and sent, and took the bones out of the sepulchres, and burned them upon the altar, and polluted it, **according to the word***

of the LORD which the man of God proclaimed, who proclaimed these words (verses 15-16).

As a parting gesture (to leave the right impression, etc.), Josiah *"slew all the priests of the high places that were there upon the altars, and burned men's bones upon them, and returned to Jerusalem"* (verse 20). Back at home he restored the Passover, but not in just *any* old fashion: *"Surely there was not holden such a passover from the days of the judges that judged Israel, nor in all the days of the kings of Israel, nor of the kings of Judah"* (verse 22). He then *"put away"* all the Harry Potter freaks (verse 24), with II Chronicles 35:3 adding that he also had the Ark of the Covenant returned to the Temple.

Now *that's* what you call reform! The Holy Spirit summarized Josiah's reign accordingly: *"And like unto him was there **no king before him**, that turned to the LORD with all his heart, and with all his soul, and with all his might, according to all the law of Moses; neither after him arose there any like him"* (verse 25). Do y'all realize that King David—the man after God's own heart (I Samuel 13:14)—would have to be included in that superlative, *"**no king before him**"*? Let *that* sink in, neighbor. While *Manasseh* was Israel's *worst* king, his grandson *Josiah* was Israel's *greatest* king. (Sadly, Manasseh was too busy *burning in Hell* to rejoice at Proverbs 17:6.)

THE CHARIOT HEARSE

True to "Sister Huldah's" prophecy, being the spiritual VIP that he was, Josiah received a true RIP sendoff; i.e., *before* he could *see* God's judgment on his kingdom:

> *Now the rest of the acts of Josiah, and all that he did, are they not written in the book of the chronicles of the kings of Judah? In his days Pharaoh-nechoh king of Egypt went up against the king of Assyria to the river Euphrates: and king Josiah went against him; and he slew him at Megiddo, when he had seen him. And his servants **carried him in a chariot dead** from Megiddo, and brought him to Jerusalem, and buried him in his own sepulchre. And the people of the land took Jehoahaz the son of Josiah, and anointed him, and made him king in his father's stead.* (II Kings 23:28-30)

I recall hearing an old black preacher say once, "You never sees a U-Haul behind a hearse," while another said, "You can'ts takes it wit' you, but you can sho' sends it on ahead!" Josiah lived his "whole" life for the Lord, and now, at the young age of thirty-nine—it was suddenly over (Hebrews 9:27).

HERE'S WHERE *YOU* COME IN

There are at least *four* powerful truths from the "Life and Times of King Josiah" that can apply to the young people in our Bible-believing churches. First of all, Josiah was living in the "last days" of Israel's independence. He died in 609 BC; a mere twenty-three years later, the Temple he cleaned up was razed to the ground by Nebuchadnezzar. You Christian teens are likewise living in the "last days" of the Church Age (II Timothy 3:1).

Second, Josiah inherited a kingdom contaminated by unprecedented wickedness—i.e., sodomy, witchcraft, child-sacrifice—all of it occasioned by Israel's *worst* king who *"caused [them] to forget"* the God of Abraham, Isaac, and Jacob. Similarly, *your* nation has taken a turn for the worse after eight years of *America's* worst president, Barack (aka "Lightning," i.e., Luke 10:18) "Barry" Hussein Obama II—followed by four additional years of an Obama-led shadow government to hamstring Donald J. Trump, the most *productive* president in US history—followed by the stolen 2020 election and the continuation of Barry's underground proxy presidency through the *dumbest* president in US history (aka "El Cid," as he, like the dead Castilian knight, must be constantly propped up, only by drug cocktails instead). And, whereas Israel's main sin was *idolatry*, America's main sin (in both sacred and secular arenas alike) is *materialism* (Matthew 6:24; II Timothy 3:2; 4:3; Revelation 3:17), pre-addressed by the Holy Ghost with *"and **covetousness** which is **idolatry**."* (Colossians 3:5)

Third, and one of the most painful truths of all, just as Josiah—through no fault of *your* own—*you* folks are suffering for the sins of *your* parents' generation as well. Josiah understood this reality as soon as he heard the Law read for the first time: *"[G]reat is the wrath of the LORD that is poured out upon us, **because our fathers have not kept the word of the LORD**, to do after all that is written in this book."* (II Chronicles 34:21) A pastor friend of mine once said that he "felt bad for animals because they got a bum rap, being punished for the sins of humans" (Romans 8:22). In similar fashion, the "Terminal Generation" will have to pay for the sins of *my* peer group. The proverbial "can" of the US National Debt ($30 trillion as of 2/22) that's been "kicked down the road" for decades cannot *begin* to compare with what's coming (II Timothy 3:1).

Fourth, and no doubt the toughest part of this message, as King Josiah discovered, no matter *what* you do—you represent the first generation since 1791 that *cannot* alter the coming judgment of God Almighty! Immediately after the Holy Spirit said of Josiah, *"And like unto him was there no king before him, that turned to the LORD with all his heart...neither after him arose there any like him,"* the next two verses state,

> **Notwithstanding the LORD turned not from the fierceness of his great wrath**, wherewith his anger was kindled against Judah, **because of all the provocations that Manasseh had provoked him withal**...I will remove Judah also out of my sight, as I have removed Israel, and will cast off this city Jerusalem which I have chosen, and the house of which I said, My name shall be there. (II Kings 23:25-26)

Josiah had inherited a 100%, bona fide, no-win situation. So has the "Terminal Generation." Sadly, as discussed in chapter one under the heading "Deep Sleep," whereas multiplied "Great *Awakenings*" defined the Philadelphia Church Age, in the closing days of Laodicea, when the lukewarm Christians enter the "Land of Nod," they nod out *permanently*, for theirs is a REM sleep (II Timothy 4:3). Is it any wonder, therefore, that the *bum* who followed Donald Trump was nicknamed "Sleepy Joe?"

THE REST OF THE STORY

There is an inscrutable contrast between the death of Josiah and the righteous life he lived (Hebrews 6:10). Why would Israel's godliest king meet such an ignominious end; slain in his own land by a heathen pharaoh? Given how much work remained to be done, Josiah's untimely death would surely evoke the question, "What purpose was *this* waste?" Of course, as we have already seen in chapter six, there is always a divine purpose for everything that happens in our lives, whether we can see it or not at the time (Romans 8:28). Thus, to grasp "The Rest of the Story" (as Paul Harvey used to say), one must examine the lengthier account of his demise as preserved in II Chronicles 35:20-23:

> *After all this, when Josiah had prepared the temple, Necho king of Egypt came up to **fight against Carchemish by Euphrates**: and Josiah went out against him. But he sent ambassadors to him, saying, What have I to do with thee, thou king of Judah? I come not against thee this day, but against the house wherewith I have war: **for God commanded me** to make haste: forbear thee from meddling with **God, who is with me**, that he destroy thee not. Nevertheless Josiah would not turn his face from him, but disguised himself, that he might fight with him, and hearkened not unto the words of Necho **from the mouth of God**, and came to fight in the valley of Megiddo. And the archers shot at king Josiah; and the king said to his servants, Have me away; for I am sore wounded.*

The historical context, set in April 609 BC, is that Egypt's Pharaoh Necho II *"came **against** Carchemish by Euphrates"* (an important ancient capital in the northern part of the region of Syria) to help the Assyrians beat back a challenge from the emerging Neo-Babylonian empire. (The word "against" is sometimes misunderstood; the fifth definition in *Webster's 1828 Dictionary* states, "opposite in place, abreast." Thus, Necho was intending to be "opposite" Carchemish geographically, i.e., as an ally, rather than opposing it.) When the Hamite force was approaching Megiddo, King Josiah led his army to engage them. Militarily, Assyria was perceived to be the greater threat than fledgling Babylon, especially with Judah's traditional buffer zone of the ten northern tribes now gone.

The real mystery that has puzzled Bible teachers for years was Pharaoh Necho's message to Josiah, *"**God** commanded me to make haste"*; in essence, "Don't *even* interfere with *me*, or you'll be messing with '*God, who is with me.*'" However, even more baffling than Necho's *recorded* statement is that *inspired* pronouncement by the unnamed chronicler, *"and hearkened not unto the words of Necho **from the mouth of God**, and came to fight in the valley of Megiddo"* (verse 22). This would appear to rule out the possibility that Necho was lying in order to dissuade Josiah. In any event, Judah's king wasn't buying it and abruptly sealed that decision with his royal blood.

The Bible contains several illustrations of God speaking directly to heathen rulers (Genesis 12:17-20; 20:3-7; Daniel 4:1-3) Other unorthodox mouthpieces include a jackass and a profane priest (Numbers 22:28-31; John 11:51; II Peter 2:16). In this instance, Necho seemed convinced that the "true" God (at least the one he was willing to momentarily recognize and even share with Josiah) had indeed communicated with *him*. But why would Israel's God have done so?

JEHOVAH FOOLS NECHO

The supernatural message evidently emboldened Necho to make his incursion (like the dream Alexander would later profess to have had where Jaddua coaxed him to invade Asia.) So, the question begs, did God actually *want* Necho's message to dissuade Josiah from attacking him? Of course, owing to divine foreknowledge, God knew that Josiah would ignore Necho's "rope-a-dope." And, if necessary, He could have easily moved him to distrust the Egyptian.

The answer lies in several Old Testament prophecies that reveal Jehovah's evolving role in the geo-political arena: in the *long* run—to smash Egypt; in the *short* run—to have Josiah hinder Necho's efforts to prevent the rise of Babylon (the *"head of gold"* in Daniel 2:38):

> *Therefore thus saith the Lord GOD; Behold,* ***I am against Pharaoh king of Egypt, and will break his arms****…and I will cause the sword to fall out of his hand.* ***….And I will strengthen the arms of the king of Babylon****, and put my sword in his hand: but I will break Pharaoh's arms, and he shall groan before him with the groanings of a deadly wounded man.….And I will scatter the Egyptians among the nations, and disperse them among the countries; and they shall know that I am the LORD.* (Ezekiel 30:22, 24, 26)
>
> *Thus saith the LORD of hosts, the God of Israel;* ***Behold, I will send and take Nebuchadrezzar the king of Babylon, my servant…And when he cometh, he shall smite the land of Egypt****, and deliver such as are for death to death; and such as are for captivity to captivity; and such as are for the sword to the sword.* (Jeremiah 43:10-11)

After Josiah's death, Necho's army fought the Babylonians at the Battle of Carchemish but were unable to prevail, most likely due to their winnowing at Megiddo. Having penned a lamentation for Josiah (II Chronicles 35:25), the prophet mentions this specific battle in

Jeremiah 46 (and with the phrase in verse 10, *"For this is **the day of the LORD** GOD of hosts,"* we perceive there are prophetic overtones as well.)

> The word of the LORD which came to Jeremiah the prophet against the Gentiles; against Egypt, against the army of **Pharaoh-necho** king of Egypt, which was by the river Euphrates in **Carchemish**...Order ye the buckler and shield, and draw near to battle....Wherefore have I seen them dismayed and turned away back? **and their mighty ones are beaten down**. (Jeremiah 46:1-3, 5)

Thus, in retrospect, we may safely conclude that the Lord pulled a fast one on Necho. You might even say He "sucker-punched" ole Pharaoh (a ruse previously employed on the original biblical Pharaoh in Exodus 14:2-4 and on Ahab in I Kings 22:20-23). Funnier still, Jehovah could not even be technically charged with "dishonesty." Yes, he may have told Necho to invade the Babylonians, passing *through* Josiah's turf on the way; He just let the idiot misinterpret *why*—i.e., so Judah's king could weaken him enough to determine Necho's subsequent defeat at the hands of Nebuchadnezzar at Carchemish.

JOSIAH AND TRUMP

Following his Mesopotamian flop, Pharaoh Necho stopped in Jerusalem on his way back to Egypt. Learning that Josiah had been succeeded by his youngest son, Shallum (under the name "Jehoahaz"), Necho promptly deposed him and installed his equally inept sibling, Eliakim (under the name "Jehoiakim"). Henceforth, the *"Kingdom* of Judah" would be subject to the Twenty-sixth Dynasty of Egypt. Thus, at the end of the day, Josiah sacrificed his life to facilitate the fulfillment of prophecy—the imminent destruction of his nation and the burning of Jerusalem and her Temple, followed by the deportation of his beloved subjects, events he was at least shielded from witnessing. (For the record, as an Assyrian vassal herself since 671 BC, Egypt would soon be transferring her own monthly reparation payments from Nineveh to Babylon.)

An insightful parallel exists between King Josiah and President Trump. Josiah's big "mistake" was that he *almost* pulled off a political miracle. At the pace he was going, he might have reunited the two Jewish kingdoms. And so—as strange as it sounds—the Lord had "no other choice" than to take him out (again, through no fault of his own).

A similar example was when Jonathan had to die to make room for King David (I Samuel 18:1-3; 31:2-6). Another case was when the Lord called Moses home, apparently for just *one* tiny infraction (Deuteronomy 32:51-52). Yet, hadn't Moses himself reminded the Jews, *"[T]hou shalt worship no other god: for the LORD, whose name is **Jealous**, is a jealous God."* (Exodus 34:14) Well, one of the *real* problems Moses had was that he was getting *way* too popular with the people. Despite the fact that the Lord had to personally bury His servant in a secret location to prevent his tomb from becoming a shrine (Deuteronomy 34:6), the people settled for worshiping the brazen serpent instead (II Kings 18:4).

This is probably why Paul got so rattled in Lystra when those Gentiles started goo-goo-eyeing Barnabas and him (Acts 14:14). Ditto for the "first Pope" before Cornelius at Acts 10:26 and that angel in Revelation 19:10 before John. (I even had a nutty Southern preacher tell me that the reason God allowed General Thomas "Stonewall" Jackson to die by friendly fire was because he couldn't stand refusing to answer his prayers for a Confederate victory in the "War of Northern Aggression.")

The main truth is that God was *dead* serious about judging Judah for the sins of King Manasseh—*despite* Josiah's greatness in the opposite direction. It would all revert back to II Kings 23:26: *"**Notwithstanding** the LORD turned not from the fierceness of his great wrath, wherewith his anger was kindled against Judah, because of all the provocations that Manasseh had provoked him withal."* Two incredible verses bear further witness to Jehovah's recalcitrant attitude. As the "weeping prophet" revealed, by the time God's patience wore out, there was *nothing* that *anyone* could do: *"Then said the LORD unto me, Though **Moses** and **Samuel** stood before me, yet my mind could not be toward this people: cast them out of my sight, and let them go forth."* (Jeremiah 15:1) Ezekiel added three more heavy-hitters to the list: *"[T]hough these three men, **Noah**, **Daniel**, and **Job**, were in it, they should deliver but their own souls by their righteousness, saith the Lord GOD."* (Ezekiel 14:4)

So, can you see the obvious similarity to the presidency of Donald J. Trump? The day I was born (November 27, 1952), Harry S. Truman was celebrating Thanksgiving in the White House. That makes fourteen different chief executives (including "El Cid"), through which I have lived—and I'm a-tellin' ya, neighbor—there hasn't been a close second to Donald J. Trump for integrity, patriotism, efficiency, and overall accomplishment. Unfortunately, however, "The Trumpster" experienced the same irreversible problem with America that Josiah did with Israel. His herculean feats clashed with God's determination to punish this nation! Just like King Josiah's "Make Judah Great Again" agenda could not stay Jehovah's hand, neither could President Trump's valiant efforts prevail. The poor man just had no idea *how* deep that "swamp" actually was.

"AMTRAK JOE" AND HIS "CARAMEL CABOOSE"

Dr. Peter S. Ruckman once said, "Every nation eventually ends up with the government it deserves." As far back as 1974, the year I was saved, preachers were already saying that if God spared America He'd have to apologize to Sodom and Gomorrah. And so, like those disillusioned Jews who had to endure the inept "leadership" of *their* last "empty suits" (Jehoahaz, Jehoiakim, Jehoiachin, and Zedekiah), the citizens of this once-great nation, including you teens, are now experiencing the identical nightmare in the catastrophic, post- "Trump Train" era, which is now being "led" by the "train wreck" administration of "Amtrak Joe" and his "Caramel Caboose," Kamala Harris.

The bottom line is that the USA will have to pay for those *65 million* murdered babies—and a *whole* lot more. Second only to the abortion holocaust is the woefully under-reported (suppressed) $150 billion-per-year global human trafficking epidemic (Matthew 18:6; Luke 17:2), involving countless American and foreign political elites (Bill and Hillary Clinton, Prince Andrew, et al.). Representing the proverbial tip of the iceberg, millions and even *billions* of tax-payer dollars flow through a special legislative "hush-hush" slush fund for settling "sexual allegations" —and worse. For example, in 2015, Detroit Democratic Rep. John Conyers (the most senior member of Congress and foremost advocate of reparations for "African-Americans") got nailed paying a former female staffer twenty-seven "large."

And let's not forget about Joe and Jill's "church." According to the *Associated Press,* the estimated total legal settlements from sex abuse cases perpetrated by Roman Catholic "clerics" in America from 1950-2007 exceeded $2 billion. (Updated figures put the figure at $3 billion by 2012.) This is why Paul wrote *"it is better to marry than to burn."* (I Corinthians 7:9)

Many believe that Jeffery Epstein's "missing" Rolodex would make J. Edgar Hoover look like a piker by comparison. Those clandestine "Lolita Express" junkets to his infamous "Virgin" Islands resort (aka "Pedophile Island") eventually resulted in his untimely "suicide" on August 10, 2019, while sequestered in Manhattan's Metropolitan Correctional Center (like your loved ones in their Covid-19 "cells"). For the record, the onetime British socialite, Ghislaine Maxwell—currently imprisoned for recruiting and grooming Jeff's underage girls—just happens to be the daughter of Robert Maxwell, the late publishing tycoon and former British Parliament member who literally saved Israel by securing their weapons in the 1948 War of Independence. (See pages 461-65 in my 2017 book, *Holy Ground: The True History of the State of Israel.*)

As with my prior statement in chapter four that if just a fraction of the "vaccination conspiracies" were true, it would be bad enough—the same rationale applies to the most outlandish sex-trafficking allegations— i.e., ranging from "Pizza Gate" to CIA-funded DUMB (deep underground military bunkers). While there will always be plenty of QAnon-style nonsense to distract genuine patriots from the real conspirators, with over 10,000 "reported" cases of child exploitation annually in America, I'm more than willing to keep an open mind as to any reputed scenarios, no matter how dark they may be.

Someone has to warn the *"silly* [teen] *women"* (II Timothy 3:6) in our churches how they can be wearing their silly masks while hanging out in the local mall one moment, then wearing a bag over their head while strapped to a chair in a distant land the next—waiting to be slowly tortured to death. On July 7, 2020, CNN broke the story that Dutch authorities had discovered a torture site (south of Rotterdam) hidden inside seven shipping containers, lined with sound-proofing material. Among other medieval-styled devices, police found pruning shears, loppers, a branch saw, scalpels, pliers, finger cuffs, tape, balaclavas, black cotton bags, handcuffs (attached to the floors and ceilings), and a dental chair complete with straps for the feet and arms. The torture chambers were also fitted with cameras for remote monitoring—so that perverts watching over the dark-web could bid against one another (facilitated by EuroChat, an encrypted chat network providing "worry-free communications") to determine who got the privilege of deciding *how* someone's daughter would die. (The "lucky" ones were processed into global prostitution as portrayed in the 2008 film, *Taken*.) So, laugh about "Pizza Gate" all you want, but over eight hundred arrests were eventually made across Europe in this rare bust.

THE *REAL* "RED DAWN"

And so, my young friends, the obvious bottom-line to all of this is that *you* are "The Terminal Generation." While *your* parents and grandparents got to live out *their* natural lives in the comfort and freedoms afforded by the greatest nation in history, *you* will probably spend *your* "best" years shackled in Babylonian bondage (not only as America expires, but through the death throes of the apostate Laodicean Church Age as well).

However, the *good* news—and I can't *possibly* emphasize this enough—is that *you* represent God's *spiritual* Josiahs! Like Israel's sixteenth king (and further illustrated by Queen Esther later), the LORD personally handpicked *your* arrival into this world *"for such a time as this."* (Esther 4:14) As God knew Jeremiah *before* He formed him in the womb (Jeremiah 1:5), He knew *you* in a similar way. Based on Psalm 139:14, *your* Creator must have equipped *you* with all the specialized gifts that *you* will need to glorify Him in the troublesome times ahead (Job 1:8; 2:3). Someone has said, "The Lord always gives His *toughest* battles to His *best* soldiers" (Acts 9:16; Philippians 1:29). It was no "coinky-dinky" that God chose a ruddy "teenybopper" to take out a giant named Goliath (I Samuel 17:42).

When Jesus rebuked the Pharisees in Matthew 16:2-3, he referenced the prevailing meteorological belief, *"When it is evening, ye say, It will be fair weather: for the sky is red.* **And in the morning, it will be foul weather to day: for the sky is red and lowring.***"* The contemporary equivalent is the adage, "Red sky at night, sailor's delight. *Red sky in morning, sailor take warning."* Consequently, with the *"Sun of righteousness* [about to] *arise with healing in* **his** *wings"* (Malachi 4:2), as *"unto a* **light** *that shineth in a dark place, until the* **day dawn,** *and the* **day star** *arise in your hearts"* (II Peter 1:19), don't be surprised if the weather around you gets a tad rough. As Satan's paratroopers are currently landing all across our land, *your* role is the spiritual equivalent to the 1984 film, *Red Dawn*; *you* are the Lord's chosen Wolverines for this final Church Age conflict! So, *"lift up your heads"* (Luke 21:28) and keep your eye on that eastern sky (Matthew 24:27), for the *"morning star"* of Revelation 2:28 is just about to come up!

THE SECOND BATTLE OF MEGIDDO

I'm told there's a military policy known as "Obey the last command." This is meant to provide a soldier with direction amidst the fog of battle. Nearly 2,000 years ago, the *"Captain of* [our] *Salvation"* said, *"Occupy till I come."* (Luke 19:13) As we are now standing on the cusp of I Thessalonians 4:16, *our* "last command" to obey as Christ's spiritual soldiers (II Timothy 2:3) is the same, whether as youths or adults. We must all *keep on the firing line* and *hold the fort!*

On our previously mentioned trip to Israel (when we visited Tell Jericho), my wife and I motored across the tiny country in a rental car. One of the most breathtaking sites we took in was a massive open area overlooking the fertile Jezreel Valley—the very place where the final battle of the Tribulation will take place: *"And he gathered them together into a place called in the Hebrew tongue **Armageddon**."* (Revelation 16:16) What I didn't know at the time was that we were also gazing at the site where Josiah was defeated by Pharaoh Necho. We would later discover that the word "Armageddon" derives from a Greek transliteration of the Hebrew "Har Megiddo"; "Har" meaning "a mountain or range of hills;" hence, Armageddon means, "Hill of Megiddo."

Thus, the greatest news (in this otherwise "heavy" chapter) is that seven years after we are "beamed up" out of this nuthouse, we get to return for the *"Second* Battle of Megiddo!" And, for this rematch, we will be led by the *great, great, great, great, great, great, great, great, great, great, great, great, great,* "grandson" of King Josiah (through Joseph)— King Jesus Himself! (Matthew 1:10-16) And the last time I checked, the final chapter in the Bible "strongly indicates" that we win—Glory! (Revelation 19:11-21) It sure can't get much better than that, neighbor!!

"STAND TO IT"

Whenever I preach this message to young folks, I generally end by inviting them to join me at the altar to reaffirm the covenant Josiah led *his* people to make with the Lord. As I prayed over this chapter, the Holy Spirit impressed me to challenge any young man or woman reading these words to do the same:

> And the king stood in his place, and made a covenant before the
> LORD, to walk after the LORD, and to keep his commandments, and his

testimonies, and his statutes, with all his heart, and with all his soul, to perform the words of the covenant which are written in this book. ***And he caused all that were present in Jerusalem and Benjamin to stand to it.*** *And the inhabitants of Jerusalem did according to the covenant of God, the God of their fathers.* (II Chronicles 34:31-32)

Remember, you *must* be very special to God, for He's the one who positioned *you* in this critical time frame in history. So don't let Him down! Stand to it!!

16

God's Preeminent Stone

WARNING: THE NEXT three chapters involve a *heavy* Bible study. As we continue to delve further into the *"perilous times"* of II Timothy 3:1, our focus must remain on the lovely Lord Jesus Christ, particularly our soon *"gathering unto him,"* and *not* on the ubiquitous preparations being made by the *"god of this world"* for the equally imminent, though short-lived, kingdom of Antichrist (Daniel 11:21; II Corinthians 4:4; II Thessalonians 2:1; Revelation 13:1-18).

The previous chapter referenced Israel's shepherd/king smiting Goliath with a *stone* (I Samuel 17:50). This is a preview of *"what shall come to pass hereafter"* (Daniel 2:45)—specifically, how Jesus will crush the Beast and his end-day global government at the end of the Great Tribulation. *"Thou sawest till that **a stone was cut out without hands**, which smote the image upon his feet that were of iron and clay, and brake them to pieces...and the **stone** that smote the image became a **great mountain**, and filled the whole earth."* (Daniel 2:34-35)

Our Lord also prophesied of this event saying, *"The **stone** which the builders rejected, the same is become the head of the corner...And whosoever shall fall on this **stone** shall be broken: **but on whomsoever it shall fall, it will grind him to powder**."* (Matthew 21:42-44) When five Muslim nations attacked the fledgling State of Israel on May 15, 1948, the embryonic IDF prevailed, primarily due to the leadership of a clandestine Jewish-American Army advisor, Colonel David "Mickey" Marcus—aka "Michael *Stone*." This chapter will examine "God's Preeminent Stone" in Holy Ghost detail! (It will make those granite Georgia Guidestones look like low-grade gravel in comparison.)

"STAY AVAY FROM MY VINDOWS!"

My late father grew up in the 1930s on the West Side of Midtown Manhattan in New York City amid the infamous Irish neighborhood known as "Hell's Kitchen." One of the funniest stories I recall him telling me was when he and his fellow "dead-end kids" would hang in front of the local jewelry store. The Jewish owner would inevitably come out, broom in hand, and chase them away, screaming with a heavy Yiddish accent (and plenty of drama), "Stay 'avay' from my 'vindows' and let the sun shine in on my diamonds!"

Anyone the least bit familiar with the real world knows that Jews have no competition when it comes to fiduciary matters. From America's pawn shops to the Federal Reserve Board, the truth of Deuteronomy 8:18 remains on permanent display: *"But thou shalt remember the LORD thy God: **for it is he that giveth thee power to get wealth**, that he may establish his covenant which he sware unto thy fathers, as it is this day."* Thus, Dr. Ruckman would say, "The main reason Gentiles hate Jews is because Gentiles love money and Jews know how to make it." Consequently, most Jewish jokes revolve around mammon. For instance, Sam Cohen once told me that a real Jewish dilemma was a free ham sandwich. This God-given acumen is particularly true in the precious stones industry. (Why, the first three letters in the word "jewelry" should be a dead giveaway.) The practical reason for this "racist reality" is because the Jewish people, perennially on the run throughout the Diaspora, needed to scoot with their loot; handheld assets being preferable to real estate holdings.

The book of Exodus records the Jews' inaugural Sinai exile inspiring that other familiar Gentile quip that the reason why the Israelites wandered forty years in the wilderness was because somebody lost a quarter. In any event, Jehovah God utilized all manner of jewels when He designed the garments for the high priest, a major type of *our* Heavenly intercessor, the Lord Jesus Christ (Hebrews 4:15; 7:22-28).

HOLY EPAULETTES

In Exodus 28:2 the Lord instructed Moses: *"And thou shalt make holy garments for Aaron thy brother for glory and for beauty."* These items included: the mitre, golden plate and blue lace; curious and linen girdles; linen breeches; linen and upper robes; shoulder pieces and golden clasps;

ephod and breastplate of judgment; Urim and Thummim; along with the golden bells and pomegranates. (Rarely noticed, the high priest wore no footwear as he ministered on holy ground.) Each of these sanctified accoutrements (detailed in Exodus 28 and 39), like everything in the tabernacle itself, represented a special type of Jesus Christ. For this present study our attention will focus on the shoulder pieces and the breastplate.

The two shoulder pieces may be likened to the epaulettes on a traditional army uniform (used to affix ornamental shoulder straps or decorations). The breastplate of judgment would rest upon the ephod, suspended by two gold chains attached to the golden clasps on the shoulder pieces. (Numerous visual study aids abound on the internet.) The directions regarding Aaron's epaulettes state: *"And thou shalt take two onyx stones, **and grave on them the names of the children of Israel**: six of their names on one stone, and the other six names of the rest on the other stone, **according to their birth**."* (Exodus 28:9-10) The same pattern is replicated on the table of shewbread, twelve loaves broken into two rows of six. This is not without significance, as the loaves picture Jesus as the "bread of life," i.e., the *"living* Word of God" (Matthew 4:4; John 6:22-51). While the Apostle John, a type of the New Testament Church (John 13:23, 20:2; Ephesians 5:23), identifies Jesus as the *"living* Word of God" seven times in the *"written* word of God" (John 1:1-3; 14: I John 1:1; 5:7; Revelation 19:13), the Holy Spirit led the King James translators to employ exactly sixty-six words when rendering the Apostle's introduction of Jesus in John 1:1-5.

The important point here is that the names of Jacob's twelve sons were to be engraved on the two onyx stones—*in their birth order*. Thus, according to Genesis 29:32-35, Leah supplies the first four names on onyx stone number one: Reuben, Simeon, *Levi* and Judah. (As the *third* son, Levi represents an unseen English nugget, as the *third* book in your King "Jacob" Bible—*James* being the New Testament equivalent of *Jacob* when translating from Hebrew into Greek, then to English— just happens to be *Levi*ticus.) With Rachel temporarily barren, she gets the "bright" idea of loaning out her handmaid Bilhah to Jacob, to fill in the remaining two names on the first stone, Dan and Naphtali (Genesis 30:6-8). Deciding that two can play at the proxy game, Leah employs her own handmaid Zilpah to produce Gad and Asher, the opening two names on Aaron's other epaulet (verses 11-13). Having secured her second wind, Leah then births Issachar and Zebulun for the ninth and tenth slots (verses 18-20).

By now Rachel has apparently repented of her initial bad attitude toward Leah. *"And God remembered Rachel, and God hearkened to her, and opened her womb. And she conceived, and bare a son; and said, God hath taken away my reproach: And she called his name Joseph; and said, The LORD shall add to me another son."* Thus, Joseph becomes the eleventh name (verses 22-24). Finally, the birth of Joseph's brother, Benjamin, not only brings an end to the list, but to their mother's life as well (Genesis 35:16-18).

The two engraved onyx stones *"set in **ouches** of gold"* (a bezel or pocket in which a precious stone or seal is set) were subsequently placed *"upon the shoulders of the ephod for stones of memorial unto the children of Israel:* **and Aaron shall bear their names before the LORD upon his two shoulders for a memorial.***"* (Exodus 28:11-12) With the brother of Moses being an important type of Christ, the multiple cross-references are beautiful. As the "Good Shepherd" of John 10:11, Jesus began His earthly ministry by attempting to seek, find, and rescue the lost flock of Israel, if by any means *"**laying it on his shoulders**, rejoicing."* (Luke 15:5) However, though rejected at His first coming (Luke 19:44; John 1:11), Jesus will reign as King of kings and Lord of lords throughout the Millennium: *"For unto us a child is born, unto us a son is given: **and the government shall be upon his shoulder.**"* (Isaiah 9:6) Undoubtedly, the restored Jews of Romans 11:26 will play a major role in that global governance, Luke 22:29-30 further revealing that the twelve Apostles will supply the key leadership positions within Israel itself. (You might want to keep this in mind the next time some jackleg Steven Andersonite tries to "enlighten" you that God is done with the physical seed of Jacob.)

THE BREASTPLATE OF JUDGEMENT

The all-important breastplate of judgment was likewise to be made *"with cunning work; after the work of the ephod...of gold, of blue, and of purple, and scarlet, and of fine twined linen"* (verse 15). It measured approximately nine inches square, being doubled to form an interior pocket to hold the mysterious Urim and Thummim (verse 16). Twelve settings of precious stones, arranged in four rows of three each, adorned the forepart of the breastplate. When the high priest would gingerly enter *"the most holy place"* (Numbers 18:10)—the tinkling bells on his bare feet signaling to the people that he was still alive—the following view is what Jehovah demanded:

> *[T]he first row shall be a sardius, a topaz, and a carbuncle: this shall be the first row. And the second row shall be an emerald, a sapphire, and a diamond. And the third row a ligure, an agate, and an amethyst. And the fourth row a beryl, and an onyx, and a jasper: they shall be set in gold in their inclosings (verses17-20).* [Once again, the names of Israel's twelve sons were to appear.] *And the stones shall be with the names of the children of Israel, twelve, according to their names, like the engravings of a signet; every one with his name shall they be according to the twelve tribes* (verse 21).

Now if something was incongruent, if the high priest messed up somewhere, the bells would suddenly go silent. (*Not* good!) Rabbinic tradition has always posited that Aaron had a rope attached to his ankle so he could be dragged out if he met the same fate as Nadab and Abihu (Leviticus 10:1-2). And by the way, like the missing footwear, there were no chairs among the designated furniture in that scary place, the message being clear—do your business and *get out* (hopefully, with your life). Therefore, not only did Aaron, as a type of Christ, bear the names of Jacob's sons on his *shoulders* for a memorial, but on his *heart* as well: *"And Aaron shall bear the names of the children of Israel in the breastplate of judgment **upon his heart**, when he goeth in unto the holy place, for a memorial before the LORD continually"* (verse 29). Once again—so much for the perverted heresy of replacement theology espoused by Catholics, Protestants, and the dwindling NIFB disciples of Stevie Anderson.

Along this line, the Holy Ghost inserted another nuance to emphasize Israel's eternal preeminence, *"With the work of an engraver in stone, **like the engravings of a signet**, shalt thou engrave the two stones with the names of the children of Israel: thou shalt make them to be set in ouches of gold."* (Exodus 28:11; see also, 28:21; 39:6, 14) These stones were to be graven as signets—so they could be used as a seal! The names were not just scratched *into* the stone, they were carved *out* to form a raised signet. A spiritual lady geologist who helped me with this material said in a text, "How awesome is it that God uses the names of the twelve tribes as His signet?" As Esther 8:8 confirms, *"[T]he writing which is* *written in the king's name, and **sealed** with the king's ring, **may no man reverse.** "* This ancient practice is also referenced regarding the decree of Darius: *"[A]nd the king **sealed** it with his own **signet**...that **the purpose might not be changed** concerning Daniel. "* (Daniel 6:17) Thus, the nation of Israel is Jehovah's personal signet as illustrated in Haggai 2:23: *"In that day, saith the LORD of hosts, **will I take thee, O Zerubbabel, my servant,** the son of Shealtiel, saith the LORD, **and will make thee as a signet: for I have chosen thee, saith the LORD of hosts.** "* (The same beautiful principle applies in the Church Age as per II Timothy 2:19.)

And furthermore, neighbor, iffen ye don't think "Dem Bones" in Ezekiel 37:1-14 are a-gonna jiggle back together one day—you'd best take *another* look at them thar' shoulder pieces. Whereas the raised Hebrew letters spelling out the names on eleven of those corresponding breastplate gems would have appeared in whatever color band was beneath their individual surfaces, the two onyx stones upon Aaron's "epaulettes" would have exhibited a *uniform* look. The alternating layers in a typical onyx run black, white, black, white, black. Conforming to common engraving practices of the time, the black surface would be completely removed exposing the first underlying white layer. When the appropriate Hebrew letters were carved out of this limestone, they would be sitting atop the second underlying black band. Well, what about that—*white* letters raised up out of a *black* base; not a bad picture of Israel's future resurrection in answer to Jehovah's question, *"Son of man, **can these bones live?** "* (Ezekiel 37:3)

THE STONE WHICH IS ABOVE EVERY STONE

We have now arrived at the central truth of this chapter. Take another look at those twelve stones. One of them exhibits a notable distinction. Can you discern God's preeminent stone? I'll give you a hint; the gem in question filled *two* functions in Aaron's attire. Give up? As this jewel was a cut *above* the other eleven—look *up* (i.e., to Aaron's shoulders).

The great Creator, Who *"searcherth out...**all the stones of darkness**"* (Job 28:3), decreed that the *onyx* should not only bear the names of Israel's twelve sons upon Aaron's epaulettes but also serve as one of the twelve stones in his breastplate. Do you suppose this was mere *"chance"* (I Samuel 6:9), as if such a crazy thing was even possible? A brief Bible study will yield some amazing discoveries regarding *this* particular

John Wycliffe's bones burned to ashes

William Tyndale burned to ashes

"But, if I don't close my church for Covid…

…I might get fined by the Health Dept.!"

Ann Askew racked and burned to ashes

Edward Wightman, burned to ashes

Laodicean Baptists *receiving* ashes

Shubal Stearns, founder of Sandy Creek Baptist Church in Orange County, NC, November 22, 1755; this vanguard work of 16 souls grew to over 600 members the first two years; regarded as the "Mother of All Separate Baptist Churches in the South," with roughly 1,000 churches birthed by 1800. (Don Adair/Baptist History Preservation Society)

Lawyer Patrick Henry defending Baptist minister John "Swearing Jack" Waller in Fredericksburg, VA (the "colorful" appellation reflecting his pre-conversion life); indicted for "preaching the gospel contrary to the law." The liberty-loving Henry represented many imprisoned Baptists, frequently paying their fines anonymously, such as John Weatherford below. (Sydney King/Virginia Baptist Historical Society)

Left: Pastor John W. Weatherford, "denying the prison bounds," in Chesterfield Co., VA (Sydney King/Virginia Baptist Historical Society)

Right: Grave of Pastor Andrew Tribble, in Terrill, KY; a neighbor to Thomas Jefferson, his monthly church business meetings influenced the future president's views on democracy

Left: Regulator monument observing Battle of Alamance, NC, May 16, 1771; first battle of the American Revolution; strong Baptist participation

Right: Burning of the HMS Gaspee by Baptist patriots off Warwick, RI on June 9, 1772; first British blood shed in the War of Independence

Baptist Martin Gambill rides to alert militia (Ron Adair/Baptist History Preservation Society)

Chaplain Gano's prayer of thanksgiving, April 19, 1783 (Ron Adair/Baptist History Preservation Society)

Elder John Leland atop a hog's head of tobacco, March 25, 1788, endorsing James Madison for Orange County delegate to Virginia's State Constitutional Convention in Richmond; the most important Baptist contribution to America, as it ultimately secured the Bill of Rights in 1791. This marvelous watershed achievement, often ignored and/or challenged by revisionist historians, is conspicuously validated by the Leland-Madison Memorial Park on Highway 20 (Route of the Constitution), four miles to the east of Orange. (Sydney King/Virginia Baptist Historical Society)

Ryman and Jones families on steps of Ryman home in Nashville (Ryman on back row, second from left; Jones seated before French horn player)

Union Gospel Tabernacle under construction in 1891; renamed the Ryman Auditorium in 1904; former home of Grand Ole Opry, 1943-1974; aka "The Mother Church of Country Music"

Thomas Green Ryman aka "Captain Tom"

Mystery look-alike distant cousin

Jerry Monday (left) playing the dobro with the Stonemans on the iconic *Tonight Show*, April 18, 1967; trusted Jesus Christ as his Saviour three years later

Jerry and Betty Monday, composing and singing music for the Lord over the last four decades; "In, Amen!"

Clockwise: Ira D. Sankey, Phillip Paul "P. P." Bliss, Dwight L. Moody, and Lucy Jane Bliss

Ashtabula, Ohio, train disaster, December 29, 1876, killing prolific Baptist hymnist P. P. Bliss and his wife, Lucy

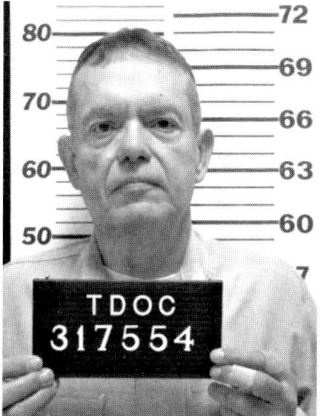

Bible corrector/pedophile Joe Combs

"What you do with the Bible will determine what God does with you."

My KJV and charger cord, minus stolen cell phone, after I slept through a burglary of a church RV in San Antonio, Texas; *"...for so he giveth his beloved sleep"* (Psalm 127:2)

Collapsed seats of Aeroflot plane after near-crash landing during my 2002 research trip to Solovetsky Island, Russia ("The Gulag Archipelago")

Pastor Anthony Ekakol of the Malaba Outreach Baptist Church, West Nigeria, Africa, along with Dr. Runion and me during our 2003 mission trip

Preaching under primitive conditions; *"For where two or three are gathered together in my name, there am I in the midst of them."* (Matthew 18:20)

Suffer little children to come unto me, and forbid them not...."
(Luke 18:16)

"Red and yellow, black and white, they are precious in His sight."

Training faithful Nigerian nationals in their local Bible Institute as per the Pauline model in II Timothy 2:2

Ordaining six new pastors; since this photo was taken, Pastor Ekakol has started 200 churches

"Japheth the Elder" winning his Hammite siblings to Jesus

Bill and Janet Eubanks

"Some wish to live within the
sound of church, or chapel bell;
I want to run a rescue shop,
within a yard of Hell!"
(C. T. Studd)

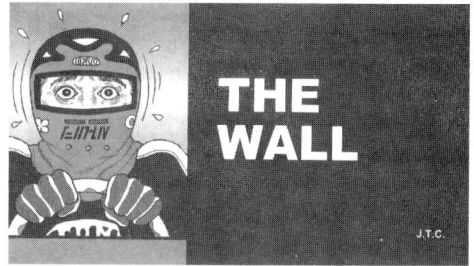

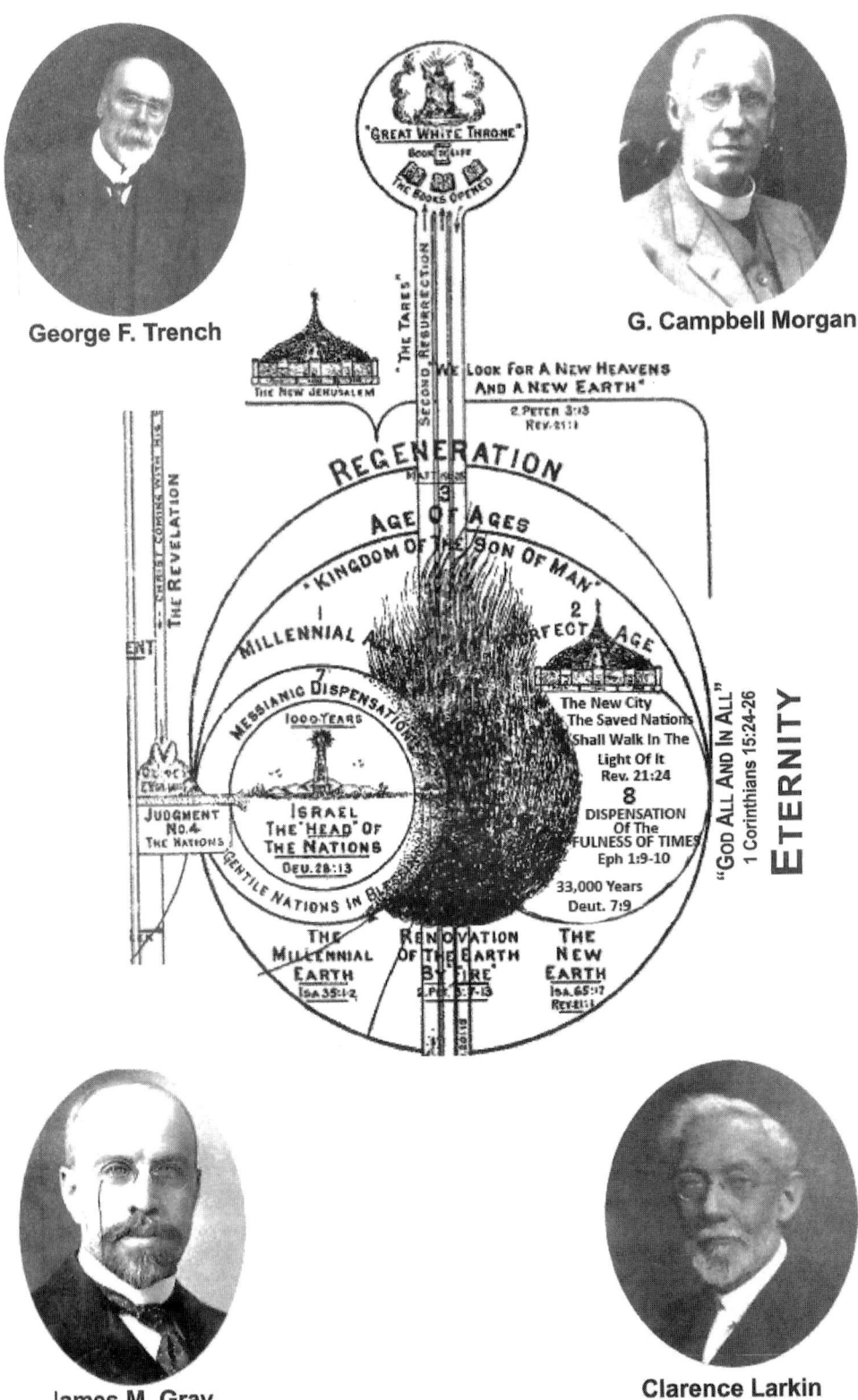

George F. Trench

G. Campbell Morgan

James M. Gray

Clarence Larkin

Dispensational Truth, Clarence Larkin (page 17)

*"stone of **darkness**."* For instance, consider the list of materials Moses solicited for the Tabernacle:

> *Take ye from among you an offering unto the LORD: whosoever is of a willing heart, let him bring it, an offering of the LORD; gold, and silver, and brass, And blue, and purple, and scarlet, and fine linen, and goats' hair, And rams' skins dyed red, and badgers' skins, and shittim wood, And oil for the light, and spices for anointing oil, and for the sweet incense, And **onyx stones, and stones** to be set for the ephod, and for the breastplate.* (Exodus 35:5-9)

Notice that the only stone specifically mentioned by name was the *onyx*, the other eleven simply falling under the generic heading, *"and stones"* (plural). Far from mere happenstance, some 475 years later, David repeats this noticeable snub when gathering items for the Temple:

> *Now I have prepared with all my might for the house of my God the gold for things to be made of gold, and the silver for things of silver, and the brass for things of brass, the iron for things of iron, and wood for things of wood; **onyx stones, and stones** to be set, glistering stones, and of divers colours, and all manner of precious stones, and marble stones in abundance.* (I Chronicles 29:2)

The importance of the onyx can also be determined by the hermeneutical principle of "First Mention." This preeminent stone was so important, its debut predated Adam and Eve!

> ***And a river went out of Eden** to water the garden; and from thence it was parted, and became into four heads. The name of the first is Pison: that is it which compasseth the whole land of Havilah, where there is gold; And the gold of that land is good: there is bdellium **and the onyx stone.*** (Genesis 2:10-12)

Furthermore, from a chronological standpoint, the onyx shows up even earlier than this. Do you recall our study of Tyre's overthrow in chapter seven? King Ethbaal III was *so* wicked that the Holy Spirit cast him as a major type of the Devil (the Lord addressing Satan through him exactly as He addressed him through Peter in Matthew 16:23). When describing the resplendent glory which this *fifth* cherub (the one missing in Ezekiel 1:5) possessed in the *original* Garden—before his *own* fall—look what shows up in *his* breastplate, and in the *fifth* slot (Bible numeric for death).

> *Son of man, take up a lamentation upon the king of Tyrus, and say unto him, Thus saith the Lord GOD; Thou sealest up the sum, full of wisdom, and perfect in beauty. Thou hast been in Eden the garden of God; every precious stone was thy covering, the sardius, topaz, and the diamond, the beryl, the **onyx**, and the jasper, the sapphire, the emerald, and the carbuncle, and gold: the workmanship of thy tabrets and of thy pipes was prepared in thee in the day that thou wast created. Thou art the anointed cherub that covereth; and I have set thee so: thou wast upon the holy mountain of God; thou hast walked up and down in the midst of the **stones of fire**. Thou wast perfect in thy ways from the day that thou wast created, till iniquity was found in thee.* (Ezekiel 28:12-15)

"THE STONE OF ISRAEL"

At this point the obvious question is—*why?* Why did Jehovah choose the onyx as His preeminent stone? The solution to this mystery can be solved by reviewing the birth order. (Although Exodus 28:21 does not specify that the twelve names on the breastplate were likewise listed according to their birth, the insinuation is reasonable, especially given the following material.)

As the eleventh *stone*, the onyx would correlate with Jacob's eleventh *son*—Joseph. (It is also noteworthy that *eleven* is the Bible numeric for crisis, as in 9/11, Matthew 20:6-7, et al.) The dual usage of the onyx on the shoulder pieces *and* on the breastplate is also consistent with the honor Joseph experienced having his land allotment doubled for his two sons, Manasseh and Ephraim. Though Reuben should have received the "double portion" afforded the firstborn, I Chronicles 5:1 confirms, *"[F]orasmuch as he defiled his father's bed* [with Bilhah, Genesis 35:22], **his birthright was given unto the sons of Joseph the son of Israel."** (While some may speculate whether Levi and Joseph's names were replaced on their respective stones by Manasseh and Ephraim due to the phrase in Exodus 28:21, *"everyone with his name shall they be **according to the twelve tribes"*** —beside the fact that the breastplate was produced *before* Joseph's land was allotted to his sons, and *after* Canaan's conquest, at least three Scriptures affirm Joseph and Levi's status as tribal patriarchs: Genesis 49:5, 22, 28; Deuteronomy 33:8,13; and Ezekiel 48:31-32, cross-referenced with Revelation 21:12.)

That the Father would bypass the *emerald,* corresponding to the messianic tribe through which His beloved Son would descend, may surprise some (the "subliminal significance" of which was not lost on the Jewish moguls in Hollywood, as per their naming of the Emerald City in the timeless blockbuster, *The Wizard of Oz*). However, Judah appears to have been hamstrung by the same proclivity as Reuben, the Holy Ghost devoting an entire chapter to his "indiscretion" with his daughter-in-law, Tamar (Genesis 38). Judah was also the one who recommended selling Joseph to the Ishmeelites, that Jewish ethos seen in the words, ***"What profit is it*** *if we slay our brother, and conceal his blood?"* (Genesis 37:26)

Any question related to Joseph's legitimate claim to being God's preeminent stone was settled by the deathbed prophecy of Jacob in Genesis 49:22-24:

> *Joseph is a fruitful bough, even a fruitful bough by a well; whose branches run over the wall: The archers have sorely grieved him, and shot at him, and hated him: But his bough abode in strength, and the arms of his hands were made strong by the hands of the mighty God of Jacob;* ***(from thence is the shepherd, the stone of Israel:)***.

As some 160 examples bear witness to Joseph being *the* central type of Jesus in Scripture, that last part of verse twenty-four would have its later and greater fulfillment in Israel's foremost shepherd/king, the undisputed *Rock* of Ages! (See Exodus 33:22; I Corinthians 10:4)

Whereas the high priest bore the names of Jacob's sons upon his *shoulders,* he also carried them on his *heart*: *"And Aaron shall bear the names of the children of Israel in the breastplate of judgment **upon his heart.**"* There is a beautiful nugget here that reveals yet another illustration of Joseph's prominence. Of the twelve stones that sat upon Aaron's heart, which one do you suppose was literally the closest? Do y'all recall that the breastplate was doubled to provide a pocket for the Urim and Thummim? While Scripture does not explain *how* the "U and T" were utilized to ascertain the divine will (Numbers 27:21; Deuteronomy 33:8; I Samuel 28:6; Ezra 2:63), these arcane Hebrew "thing-a-ma-jigs" must have been crucial because of what the next verse says: *"And thou shalt put **in** the breastplate of judgment the Urim* *and the Thummim;* **and they shall be upon Aaron's heart,** *when he goeth in before the* LORD: *and Aaron shall bear the judgment of the children of Israel* **upon his heart** *before the* LORD *continually."* (Exodus 28:30) If the "U and T" were sitting *in* that breastplate pocket, they would obviously be resting at the *bottom* of that pouch. And that, my dear friend, would position them directly behind the *eleventh* stone (the one in the middle of the fourth row)!

"BLACK IS BEAUTIFUL?"

When that eleventh stone adorning Aaron (a major type of *our* intercessor) is matched with Jacob's eleventh son (the Bible's premier type of Christ), several beautiful lessons result: First, as Joseph was "refused" by *his* brethren (Genesis 37:4), David prophesied of Jesus in Psalm 118:22, *"The* **stone** *which the builders* **refused** *is become the head stone of the corner."* (The Lord applied this verse to Himself in Matthew 21:42.) Second, as Joseph was unfairly viewed as the proverbial "black sheep" of the family, the definitive onyx is the "black onyx" (while containing bands of white within). Next, as Joseph was hated for his *"coat of many colors"* (Genesis 37:3-4), the onyx can also display any number of additional shades. (Onyx is a banded variety of the oxide mineral chalcedony with the colors of its bands ranging from white to almost every color, except some shades such as blue and purple). Fourth, as Joseph would not only save his immediate family from the famine, but also provide salvation for the entire world (Genesis 18:18; 22:18), the main color of "black" is striking in its tripartite typology.

To begin, the word "black" appears eighteen times in your King James Bible, along with one reference to "blacker," one to "blackish," and six to "blackness." Now, as the Holy Ghost ordained matters, of these twenty-six references, a full 86% display a *negative* context (the only three "positive" exceptions describing the color of marble, hair, and horses). Roughly the same conspicuous percentage applies to "Black's" twin brothers, "Dark" and "Darkness." You say— "Dr. Grady, that's a *racist* observation!" Well, neighbor, would your problem be with basic *arithmetic* (a definite CRT trait), or with the *author* who put those "politically insensitive" verses into His Book without even checking with you (II Timothy 3:16)?

A small, scientific sample for both of these colors would include: Genesis 1:2—the second verse in the Bible—where the first post-Gap description of the world says *"**darkness** was upon the face of the deep;"* Jeremiah 14:1-2; Lamentations 5:10; and that ominous *"**black** horse"* in Revelation 6:5, describing famine; Job 30:28, 30, depicting mourning and sorrow; Jeremiah 8:21 and 14:2, for a period of time void of "spiritual light" (i.e., from God); Job 3:5 and 10:21-22, as the location of the dead; and Jude 13, where both words appear as the terminus where evil spirits spend eternity— *"the **blackness** of **darkness** for ever."* Numerous other references represent affliction, calamity, or adversity as the penalty for sin: Lamentations 4:8; Psalm 107:10; Isaiah 5:30; Joel 2:6; Zephaniah 1:15; Zechariah 6:2; and Revelation 16:10.

The main usage here (especially for "darkness") signifies eternal damnation: Matthew 8:12; 22:13 and 25:30. Paul sums it up accordingly: *"Because that, when they knew God, they glorified him not as God, neither were thankful; but became vain in their imaginations, and their foolish heart was **darkened**."* (Romans 1:21) Consequently, until contemporary times, all Bibles were bound in a black cover. People traditionally hung black crepe on their doors when a loved one passed, the corpse being transported in a hearse called a "Black Mariah."

Next, with the AV 1611 setting the pace, the hymnals followed suit. Hundreds of spiritual songs portray these same colors in an equally negative context. "*Dark* the stain that spoiled man's nature; Long the distance that he fell" ("Deeper Than the Stain Has Gone"); "One day when sin was as *black* as could be" ("One Day"); "For the dear Lamb of God, left His Glory above to bear it to *dark* Calvary" ("Old Rugged Cross"); "*Dark* the night of sin has settled" ("Let the Lower Lights Be Burning"); "In this *dark* world of sin" ("Peace, Perfect Peace"); "When surrounded by the *blackness* of the *darkest* night" ("Finally Home"); "*Dark, dark* hath been the midnight" ("The Sands of Time Are Sinking"); "It may be, perchance, that the *blackness* of midnight will burst into light in the blaze of His glory" ("Christ Returneth"); "When *darkness* veils his lovely face" ("The Solid Rock"); "He arose a Victor from the *dark* domain" ("Christ Arose"); "Though all around me is *darkness*" ("Never Alone"); "The prince of *darkness* grim, we tremble not for him" ("A Mighty Fortress is Our God"); "The sky is o'ershadowed with *blackness*" ("Master, The Tempest Is Raging"); "The whole world was lost in the *darkness* of sin" ("The Light of the World is Jesus");

"*Darkness* be over me" ("Nearer My God to Thee"); "*Dark* is the stain that we cannot hide; What can avail to wash it away? Look! There is flowing a crimson tide; *Whiter* than snow you may be today" ("Grace Greater Than All Our Sins").

So many examples abound, we can barely scratch the surface, other *"hymns and spiritual songs"* (Ephesians 5:19) incorporating these "dark lyrics" include: "There'll Be No Dark Valley"; "The Ninety and Nine"; "Holy, Holy, Holy"; "O Worship the King"; "Some Golden Daybreak"; "Surely Goodness and Mercy"; "Zion's Hill"; "Face to Face"; "Bring Them In"; "When We See Christ"; "Oh, How I Love Jesus"; "Follow On"; "Oh, I Want to See Him"; "I've A Home Beyond the River"; "We've a Story to Tell to the Nations"; "Heaven Came Down"; "Make Me a Blessing"; "I'll Go Where You Want Me to Go"; "We'll Understand It Better By and By"; "No, Not One"; "Jesus Never Fails"; "Yield Not to Temptation"; "Faith of Our Fathers"; "If Jesus Goes With Me"; "Be Calm My Soul"; "I Heard the Voice of Jesus Say"; "Joyful, Joyful, We Adore Thee"; "May Jesus Christ Be Praised"; "Jesus, I Am Resting, Resting"; "Holy Ghost, with Light Divine"; "Jesus, Thou Joy of Loving Hearts"; "I Will Sing the Wondrous Story"; "In Heavenly Love Abiding"; "Jesus Bids Us Shine"; "Christ Is King"; "The Touch of His Hand"; "Lead Me Gently Home, Father"; "When Love Shines In"; "Who at My Door Is Standing?"; "Come Unto Me"; "God Leads Us Along"; et al.

With Ezekiel 28:13 showing that Lucifer was created as a musical instrument (all modern versions hiding this revelation by deleting the words "tablets" and "pipes"), the world's hymnists discerned this spiritual reality instinctively. In his "gospel" classic, "I Saw the Light," Hank Williams, Sr. ("Tear in My Beer"), wrote, "No more *darkness*, no more night. Now I'm so happy, no sorrow in sight. Praise the Lord, I saw the light." Truth be told, in a well-known story, Minnie Pearl related that while she was driving to a show with Hank, she started singing his signature number, whereupon he interrupted her saying, "Quit! Hush! I don't want to hear that. I don't want to hear it, 'cause there ain't no light."

Representing the antithesis of God's *preeminent* stone, the Hell-bound *Rolling* Stones released their smash raga rock hit, "Paint It Black," in 1966, written by Mick Jagger and Keith Richards. When "Sir Mick" was asked why he wrote a song about death, the fornicating, dopehead knight replied, "[Duh...], I don't know." (The depressing lyrics appear to revolve around a lover who has died.)

I see a **red door**
And I want it painted **black**
No colors anymore
I want them to turn **black**

I see the girls walk by
Dressed in their summer clothes
I have to turn my head
Until my **darkness** goes

I see a line of cars
And they're all painted **black**
With flowers and my love
Both never to come back

I've seen people turn their heads
And quickly look away
Like a newborn baby
It just happens everyday

I look inside myself
And see my heart is **black**
I see my **red door**
I must have it painted **black**

Maybe then, I'll fade away
And not have to face the facts
It's not easy facing up
When your whole world is **black**

No more will my green sea
Go turn a deeper blue
I could not foresee this thing
Happening to you

If I look hard enough
Into the setting sun
My love will laugh with me
Before the morning comes

I see a **red door**
And I want it painted **black**
No colors anymore
I want them to turn **black**

I see the girls walk by
Dressed in their summer clothes
I have to turn my head
Until my **darkness** goes

I wanna see it painted
Painted **black**
Black as night
Black as coal

I wanna see the sun
Blotted out from the sky
I wanna see it painted, painted, painted
Painted **black**, yeah....

Of course, *Rolling Stone* magazine rated "Paint It Black" as "one of the greatest songs of all time." One reviewer said, "The Rolling Stones wrote this as a much slower, conventional soul song. But then Charlie Watts improvised a double-time drum pattern, echoing the rhythm heard in some Middle Eastern dances. This new more *upbeat* rhythm was then used in the recording as a counterpoint to the *morbid* lyrics." Apparently, the truth about plunging into *"the **blackness** and **darkness** forever"* was too much for even these hardcore rockers. Sadly—unless "reached" in time by that "professing" born-again preacher's kid, Alice Cooper— eighty-year-old Charlie, having apparently painted over *his* potential "**red** door" exit (Isaiah 1:18), "rolled" into that very **blackness** on August 24, 2021, joining John "Imagine There's No Hell" Lennon and George "My Sweet Lord" Harrison! Like that other Stones hit, "You Can't Always Get What You Want," Charles discovered, "You can't have your cake and eat it too," for eternity will either be wonderfully "upbeat" —or frightfully "downcast" (John 3:36). As for that "line of cars all painted **black**," like their other eternal cellmate, the *former* anti-Semite, Henry Ford, used to say about *his* Model T, "You can have any color— as long as it is painted **black**." (Currently on deck is the bat head-eating, former lead vocalist, Ozzy Osborne, aka "The Prince of **Darkness**.")

Finally, added to "The Book" and the "Hymn Book" is the English dictionary itself. Reflecting the inspired KJV pattern, about ninety percent of all words with "black" are negative also. A politically incorrect shortlist would include: blacklist; blackball; blackmail; blackbird; blackface; blackjack; blackjacked; blackheads; black magic; black book; blackout; blacken; blackish; black water; black widow; black hole;

black eye; blackboard jungle; blackout; black market; black ice; black box, Black Friday (1929); Black Death; black humor; black and blue; black helicopters; Black Mariah; black swan; black cat; black lung; black hat; Black Bart; Black Sabbath; Black Panthers; black power; and Black Lives Matter. (A similar log would apply to *dark*, i.e., dark horse; dark secret; dark web; etc.)

In a timely "coincidence," during the writing of this very chapter (October 12, 2021), Hollywood's "Captain James Kirk," ninety-year-old William "Beam Me Up, Scotty" Shatner, blasted into the Lord's domain (Psalm 115:16) aboard a rocket owned by Jeff Bezos. An *Associated Press* reporter covering the "iconic" sci-fi actor's ten-minute adrenaline rush into the second Heaven stated, "He said that going from the blue sky to the utter *blackness* of space was a moving experience: 'In an instant you go, "Whoa—that's *death*." That's what I saw.'"

"X" MARKS THE SPOT

Another uncanny stat is that an inordinate percentage of words ending in "X" are also bad news. Some of the more recognizable examples would include: anthrax; boombox; Botox; box (coffin); crucifix; crux; detox; ex ("All My Exes Live in Texas"); faux; fix (rigged bet); flummox; flux; fox (the Lord's sarcastic nickname for Herod); *Fox News* (literally worse than *CNN*, as per Revelation 3:15-16); hex; hoax (China virus vaccines); jinx; jukebox; lax (also, Los Angeles airport code, i.e., "Land of fruits and nuts"); lummox; Lux (Satan's Latin name, "Light bearer"); Malcom-X; Marx (i.e., Karl Marx, aka "Father of Communism"); nix; perplex; phoenix; pontifex (i.e., papal title, Pontifex Maximus); pox and smallpox; sphinx; surtax; sweatbox; tax (IRS); sex (outside of marriage); six (i.e., six feet under, not to mention 666); unisex (transgender insanity); vex; X-Mas and X-rated. (The following fifteen "bonus round" words— all guaranteed to be negative—were included for scrabble veterans everywhere: auspex; banjax; bollix; brux; cicatrix; culex; desex; haruspex; kex; minx; noyaux; pemphix; prolix; scolex; and varix.)

Thus, we see that God's preeminent stone—the black onyx—appears to have two strikes against it: the color *black,* and the fact that it ends in "X." And so, with all this Scripture, hymnology, and vocabulary considered, we are now prepared to discover the ultimate type of Christ embedded in Aaron's breastplate of judgment.

BLACK LIVES MATTER

In Exodus 26:7, we learn that part of the Tabernacle's layered covering consisted of *eleven* curtains of goat hair (not goat skin). In Psalm 120:5, we are further informed of an area in Arabia known as Kedar, the regional export center for this ancient commodity. The significance of these two seemingly insignificant tidbits has to do with a most astounding revelation in the Song of Solomon. This particular "deep truth for shallow waters" will reveal *why* mankind needed a "Black Onyx" —specifically, the Lord Jesus Christ—and *how* He was uniquely qualified to fill that need.

The book begins with the Shulamite woman (a picture of the Church) speaking of her beloved (a picture of Jesus). She then makes a key statement about herself: *"I am black, but comely, O ye daughters of Jerusalem, as the tents of Kedar, as the curtains of Solomon. Look not upon me, because I am black, because the sun hath looked upon me"* (verses 5-6).

Twice the Holy Spirit states that the main Old Testament type foreshadowing the *espoused* Bride of Christ (i.e., *you* and *me*) was— *black*. Historically, Solomon's favorite wife was an Egyptian princess, the Hamite daughter of Pharaoh (I Kings 3:1). And it just so happens that this was the identical case with Joseph. Not only did the exiled Hebrew marry a *Gentile* bride, but a *black* one as well (Genesis 41:45).

The key take-away here is that this "blackness" represents a major type of man's *sinfulness*, i.e., the lost condition of *all* humanity, whether Shem, Ham, or Japheth, with absolutely *no* distinction (Romans 3:10, 23). Therefore, what the world desperately needed was a Saviour who was *not* black (spiritually speaking), one who was not "darkened" with sin as they were (*"Dark* the stain that spoiled man's nature"). And so, enter Jesus Christ (*eleven* letters) in chapter *five* (death number) as Joseph's great antitype. Now, just how do you suppose the Holy Spirit will prompt this love-struck bride to describe her *olive*-skinned, *Jewish* lover from the *Middle East*? *"My beloved is white and ruddy, the chiefest among ten thousand."* (Song of Solomon 5:10)

That, my friend, is the *ultimate* WHITE SUPREMACIST! And the main reason He came in the first place is because—**BLACK LIVES MATTER!** ("Hold my mule while I shout, *again!"*) For God *so* loved us (John 3:16) that He was not only willing to change *places* with us, but *color* as well! Though he was *"white* as snow" (typifying sinlessness), he became *"black* as" —not the proverbial "Ace of Spades" —but as

"His Father's preeminent Onyx Stone!" Like those other two hijacked Bible words, *"[rain]bow"* (Genesis 9:13) and *"gay"* (James 2:3), this is the one and only *true* BLM agenda!

> *Now then we are ambassadors for Christ, as though God did beseech you by us: we pray you in Christ's stead, be ye reconciled to God.* **For he hath made him to be sin for us, who knew no sin; that we might be made the righteousness of God in him.** (II Corinthians 5:20-21)

Once again—as with the scriptural explanation for "white superiority" and "white privilege," viewed through the prism of Japheth the Elder's destiny to evangelize his two younger siblings—accepting the clear "black-and-white" color types in Scripture will result in discerning *God's* version of Black Lives Matter. According to Romans 5:12, we were *all* spiritually "black" because of our parents' fall in the Garden. (And, as Adam means "red," like the clay he was taken from, you could say that we morphed from red to black, and finally, to white.) But praise God, Jesus Christ descended from Heaven's *"ivory* palaces" to *"dark* Calvary" to become *our* "Black Onyx" stone (Psalm 45:8). And by the way, neighbor, as previously mentioned, that's why the Father ordained that a *black* man would enable Jesus to complete that very odyssey (Luke 23:26).

The pagan New Age devotees have an instinctive attraction to the onyx stone (like their instinctive aversion to the number thirteen). One lapidarist put it this way: "The onyx is believed to be a powerful protection stone, *absorbing* and transforming negative energy. It is also believed to bring happiness and good fortune." What an insightful depiction of the Gospel by an unsaved person (I Corinthians 2:14). The heathen Pharaoh was certainly drawn to Jacob's *eleventh* son.

And so, because of the truth of Romans 8:28, Joseph could assure his guilt-ridden, paranoid brethren, *"But as for you, ye thought evil against me; but God meant it unto good, to bring to pass, as it is this day, to save much people alive."* (Genesis 50:20) Thus, the book of Genesis ends **six** verses later, with an **"onyx"** in a **box** in the shadow of a **sphinx**. *"So Joseph died, being an hundred and ten years old: and they embalmed him,* **and he was put in a coffin in Egypt.**" (Genesis 50:26)

"BLACK *IS* BEAUTIFUL!"

Evangelist Sammy Allen used to say a person can't "get saved" until they first "get lost." Thus the *greatest* day in a sinner's life is when they come to realize they *are* lost; the *second* greatest day is when they follow through and get saved! As the second stanza of "Amazing Grace" says, "'Twas grace that taught my heart to fear, and grace my fears relieved." Applying this truth to our present study, the greatest day in *our* life was when the Holy Spirit showed us that our spiritual condition was "black" (Acts 16:14). Therefore— "Black *Is* Beautiful."

I will close with one of the most beautiful experiences of my entire ministry that perfectly illustrates this thought. I was preaching a revival when an Italian lady, recently saved out of Catholicism and faithfully attending the church, walked in Sunday morning with a visitor, who happened to be as black as Rahab. At the invitation, both women came forward. I'll never forget what happened next. When the visitor got to the altar, she slowly bowed—as if curtsying before a literal king—then knelt, her head bent so low that her forehead nearly touched the ground, her arms spread out, extending upward behind her back.

The pastor's wife knelt alongside her and learned that she had trusted Christ only a week ago. It was a great start to the meeting. But the real blessing would come the next evening. Both gals were back and as excited as they could be. The new lady, who was sharp as a tack, said she was a real estate appraiser. She was so outgoing that the Pastor and I felt led to ask her a personal question. On Sunday morning, she had dressed all in black. It stood out so much that we asked her about it. Her answer blew us both away. Now, remember, she had not even been saved a week and this was her first time to visit a Bible-believing Baptist church. She said, "The reason I dressed in black was because I had just died five days earlier." (I doubt if she had read Romans 6, 7, and 8 as yet.) Neither she nor her Italian friend missed a single service that week.

Five months later, I texted the Pastor to see how she was doing and received the following reply: "She's a firecracker, Preacher. Keeps me on my toes. Asks good questions. Bible all marked up. She started writing Gospel tracts, too." Like I said— "Black *is* Beautiful" because "Black Lives Matter!"

"He hath made everything beautiful in his time...."
(Ecclesiastes 3:11)

17

The Greatest Blackout in History

I HAVE AN Israeli-born Jewish friend who lives in Nashville, Tennessee, with whom I have been sharing the Gospel for many years. When the Music City experienced a serious power outage in 2019, I "exploited" the situation by texting him an intriguing question. After enquiring as to how he and his wife were coping with the down time (making good use of candles, etc.), I asked him if he was aware that the greatest "blackout" in history had emanated from *his* native country, and in the city of Jerusalem, no less. *"And it was about the sixth hour, and there was **a darkness** over **all the earth** until the ninth hour. And the sun was **darkened**, and the veil of the temple was rent in the midst."* (Luke 23:44-45)

Now, notice that it wasn't just *any* ole *local* darkness—but a *specific* darkness covering the *entire* planet! The reason for this eerie global phenomenon was to hide the horrific fulfillment of II Corinthians 5:21. Even Mick Jagger conceded in "Paint It Black" that "I wanna see the sun blotted out from the sky." Thus, the great British hymnist, Isaac Watts, wrote in his beloved 1707 classic, "At the Cross":

> *Well might the sun in darkness hide*
> And shut his glories in,
> When Christ, the mighty Maker died,
> For man the creature's sin.

Not only did God the Father pull the curtain down on Earth, but He also lowered Heaven's shades to shield the inquiring angels from the terrible spectacle (Matthew 26:53; Ephesians 3:10; I Timothy 3:16; I Peter 1:12). Yet, the gates of Hell may have opened to permit the devils to join *their* "captain" in heaping their own abuse on Jesus. Psalm 22:12-13 says,

*"Many **bulls** have compassed me: strong **bulls** of Bashan have beset me round. **They gaped upon me with their mouths, as a ravening and a roaring lion"** ("bulls," as in that fifth cleft-footed cherub, aka "Ole Slewfoot," Ezekiel 1:7).* Notice how John reveals the method Satan will use in the Tribulation to cause the sun to go dark: *"And he [Apollyon] **opened the bottomless pit**; and there arose a smoke out of the pit, as the smoke of a great furnace; **and the sun and the air were darkened by reason of the smoke of the pit**. And there came out of the smoke locusts upon the earth."* (Revelation 9:2-3)

"TREASURES OF DARKNESS"

But, praise the Lord, because *this* curtain descended at Calvary, that *other* curtain could open in the Temple (Luke 23:45). However, what transpired during those three hours is not specified in Scripture. Whatever it was, it undoubtedly had something to do with God's promise in Isaiah 45:3, *"And I will give thee the **treasures of darkness"*** (i.e., something *valuable* hidden in the shadows). To connect the dots, this mystery should relate to a *perfect* "stone," for the Bible further declares, *"He setteth an **end to darkness**, and searcheth out all perfection: the **stones of darkness**, and shadow of death."* (Job 28:3)

This "information blackout" itself has occasioned much spiritual speculation. Being good Baptists, we are blessed with the historic Baptist distinctive of "individual soul liberty." This means that we are free to follow the dictates of our conscience regarding any non-heretical matters (Romans 14:4; Acts 17:11). For instance, some Christians debate whether Jesus spent those three hours burning in literal Hell fire as our genuine substitute, etc. Now, to be honest, I have never been able to wrap my head around this question to form an opinion one way or another. However, a different conjectural topic has increasingly engaged my attention over the years. Do y'all remember *where* that black onyx appeared on Lucifer's breastplate? The Holy Ghost listed it as the *fifth* stone—the number of *death* (e.g., five letters in death, grave, devil, Satan, and—*snake*). Some Bible believers posit that in the Lord's death *on* "the tree" (Galatians 3:13), our onyx stone may have shared some sort of a veiled, metamorphic connection with the *serpent* who beguiled our first parents *under* "a tree" (Genesis 3:13).

To explain, most Christians spend their entire spiritual lives oblivious to any number of weightier doctrines (Hebrews 5:11-14). For example, Jesus said, *"For what shall it profit a man, if he shall gain the whole world, and **lose his own soul**?"* (Mark 8:36) Tell me, neighbor, how would a human being *lose his soul*, presumably throughout eternity? Your average Peter Ruckman-bashing "TR Funnymentalist" could not even begin to handle this question as he would draw a similar blank regarding David's related enquiry in Psalm 8:4, *"**What** is man?"* Paul answered the second query when writing to his Japhethite converts in Thessalonica: *"And the very God of peace sanctify you wholly; and I pray God your whole **spirit** and **soul** and **body** be preserved blameless unto the coming of our Lord Jesus Christ."* (I Thessalonians 5:23) Man is a tripartite being, consistent with the statement in Genesis 1:27, *"God created man in his own image"* (i.e., the Holy Spirit is the spirit within the Godhead; the Father is the soul; and the Son is the body).

While John 1:18 says, *"No man hath **seen God** at any time,"* Scripture does *not* say that God is shapeless. To the contrary, Jesus admonished the Pharisees by stating, *"And the Father himself, which hath sent me, hath borne witness of me. Ye have neither heard his voice at any time, **nor seen his shape**."* (John 5:37) The precise trinitarian doctrine would teach that although no man has ever seen the "soul" of the Godhead (God the Father), numbers of Old Testament saints *were* privileged to see Jehovah's "bodily shape," as the "Angel of the Lord," specifically— Jesus Christ in His pre-incarnate state (Genesis 32:30; Exodus 24:10; Deuteronomy 34:10; Hosea 12:4-5; Isaiah 6:5). Thus, Paul wrote of the second member of the Trinity, *"Who, **being in the form of God**, thought it not robbery to be equal with God."* (Philippians 2:6)

The key takeaway truth is that the *human* "soul" is likewise defined by *its* "shape" (II Corinthians 12:3). Several germane passages reveal that a human soul literally fills out the shape of its physical house (II Corinthians 5:1-4). For instance, in Luke 16:24, the rich man's soul has a "tongue," while the soul of Lazarus sports a "finger." Revelation 6:11 shows that the souls of martyred Tribulation saints will don robes, etc. Paul, therefore, explains in I Corinthians 15:44, *"There is a natural body, **and there is a spiritual body**."*

Consequently—regarding the actual meaning of the Lord's words, *"lose his own soul"* —as the never-dying soul of an unsaved person can never be annihilated (like the nutty Jehovah's Witnesses teach), the "loss" must relate to its basic composition, i.e., the loss of its shape. This would also explain the meaning of *"perish"* in John 3:16, for that which perishes is not the sinner's conscious existence, but merely the *shape* of his or her soul from conception. The same would apply in Matthew 10:28, *"but rather fear him which is able to **destroy** both **soul** and body in hell."* And so, after an indeterminate sentence in God's holding cell of Hell, "lost" souls wind up in the eternal Lake of Fire (called the second death in Revelation 21:8). Here, they are destined to surrender their bodily shape, as their non-glorified bodies would already have disintegrated in the grave (Job 19:26; 24:20).

In John 8:44, Jesus told his Jewish detractors, *"**Ye are of your father the devil**, and the lusts of **your father** ye will do."* The Lord made other references to their "family tree" as well: *"but the tares are the **children of the wicked one**"* (Matthew 13:38); *"ye make him twofold more the **child of hell**than yourselves"* (Matthew 23:15); *"**Ye serpents, ye generation of vipers**, how can ye escape the damnation of hell?"* (Matthew 23:33) When Paul confronted Elymas the sorcerer, he addressed him as *"thou **child of the devil**."* (Acts 13:10) Similarly, when the second-century Bible-correcting gnostic, Marcion "The Heretic," accosted Polycarp, demanding, "Acknowledge us," the convert of "John the Beloved" fired back, "I acknowledge the *firstborn of Satan*!"

Thus, Dr. Ruckman believed that the souls of unsaved people would forfeit their original, divinely designed *shape* (Psalm 139:14-16), eventually morphing into the form of *their* father (i.e., "Like father, like son"). And, as Satan initially appeared to Adam and Eve in the "shape" of a *serpent*, "the Doc" further reasoned that in the Lake of Fire, these souls—the majority having espoused Darwinian *evolution*—would eventually *devolve* into *red* maggots (Revelation 12:3), i.e., "little serpents," no longer destined to inhabit a glorified body like Jesus received (I John 3:2).

As usual, the greatest (and most hated) Bible teacher in the twentieth century had Scripture validation for his so-called "peculiar doctrines." When the Lord issued His solemn warning of Hell in Mark 9:42-50, He repeated a terrifying statement thrice: *"[I]t is better for thee to enter into life maimed, than having two hands **to go into hell**, into the fire that never shall be quenched: Where their **worm** dieth not."* (Of course, the NIV deletes all three references.) Notice how *this* "worm" is singular, against the plural "worms" in Job 19:26. Would you agree that a "worm" is essentially a "little serpent?" The cross-reference is Isaiah 66:24, where future "Holy Land Tours" will include a "scenic stop" at the Lake of Fire (located near the Dead Sea, as per Isaiah 34:5-10): *"And they shall go forth, and look upon the carcases of the men that have transgressed against me: **for their worm shall not die**, neither shall their fire be quenched; and they shall be an abhorring unto all flesh."*

"I *SCARCE* CAN TAKE IT IN"

Now, here comes the *really* heavy stuff. (Remember, as a good Baptist, you can take it or leave it.) So, the question remains, what exactly *did* transpire in that darkness? The traditional ("safe") explanation is that, given the totality of the world's sin being placed *upon* Jesus, He must have *appeared* like the Devil himself to His Father (Revelation 12:9). But, could there be something *worse* than this?

The Bible plainly teaches that Jesus did more than merely "bear our sins *on* his body" and "take away our sins." Paul wrote in Galatians 3:13, *"Christ hath redeemed us from the curse of the law, **being made a curse for us**: for it is written, **Cursed** is every one that hangeth on a tree:"* As previously noted, II Corinthians 5:21 specifically states that God *"**made him to be sin** for us, who knew no sin."* Therefore, the Holy Spirit led Peter to add, *"Who his own self bare our sins **in** his own body on the tree."* (I Peter 2:24)

Ironically, the great key to where I am going was provided by the Lord Himself. If you think you're brave enough to venture a sneak peek behind that curtain at "Dark Calvary," consider what Jesus told Nicodemus when citing Numbers 21:8: *"And as Moses **lifted up the serpent** in the wilderness, **even so must the Son of man be lifted up**: That whosoever believeth in him should not perish, but have eternal life."* (John 3:14-15)

To illustrate the power of that view, C. H. Spurgeon was converted at age fifteen as the result of a ten-minute sermon on Isaiah 45:22, *"Look unto me, and be ye saved."* Smack dab in between John 3:3 and John 3:16 you have Jesus revealing a more in-depth "exposition" of Isaiah 52:14, *"As many were astonied at thee; **his visage was so marred more than any man, and his form more than the sons of men.**"* The *Scofield Bible* note states, "The literal rendering is terrible: 'So marred from the *form* of man was His aspect that His appearance was not that of a son of man' —i.e., not human—the effect of the brutalities described in Matthew 26:67, 68;

27:27-30." However, while the cat-o-nine tails changed the visage of what one could see in the *light*, that Holy *form* was "marred" far worse in the *dark*.

What Jesus basically said was, "If you want to have some advanced perspective on my Passion—look at a serpent on a pole." (See counterfeit "Rod of Asclepius" logo for the increasingly morally bankrupt medical profession). Consequently, not only did the "Son of Man" exchange his spiritual *color* with His creation (i.e., from white to black), but quite possibly his spiritual *shape* as well. If lost men have Satan for their father (and they do, as per John 8:44), then Job's seemingly nebulous words make perfect sense. Having previously stated in Job 17:14, *"I have said...to the **worm**, Thou art my **mother**,"* he later declares, *"How then can man be justified with God? or how can he be clean that is born of a woman? Behold even to the moon, and it shineth not; yea, the stars are not pure in his sight. **How much less man, that is a worm? and the son of man, which is a worm?**"* (Job 25:4-6)

Here, the Holy Ghost not only tells us that a lost man is somehow related to a *worm*, but that the God-man, *who would vicariously represent him in judgment*, would also have to "form" a similar relationship. Thus, after Jesus' dying words from the cross, *"My God, my God, why has thou forsaken me?"* were pre-recorded through David a millennium earlier, the inspired text has Jesus add, *"**But I am a worm, and no man; a reproach of men, and despised of the people.**"* (Psalm 22:6) A pastor friend once asked me if I thought the Lord's declaration in verse 14— *"I am **poured out** like water and **all my bones are out of joint**"* — might have something to do with a temporary alteration of his bodily composition? Isaac Watts certainly understood *his* vermiform roots:

> Alas, and did my Saviour bleed?
> And did my Sovereign die?
> Would He devote that sacred head
> For such a *worm* as I?

While the modern milquetoast rendition changes that fourth line to: "For *sinners* such as I," that old beloved standby, "How Great Thou Art," contains *the* enduring line defining our ineffable recoil:

> And when I think that God, His Son not sparing;
> Sent Him to die—*I scarce can take it in*;

That on the cross, my burden gladly bearing,
He bled and died to take away my sin.

The *first* Adam partook of fruit *from* a tree; the *last* Adam replaced it by putting Himself *on* a tree. *"But now is Christ risen from the dead and become the **first fruits** of them that slept."* (I Corinthians 15:20, 45) And yet, there is more; the serpent was cursed *"under* the tree" (Genesis 3:13), the Saviour was cursed *"on* the tree." (Galatians 3:13) While Micah 7:17 says, *"They shall **lick the dust like a serpent**,"* Jesus cried out from His cross, *"My strength is dried up like a potsherd; and my tongue cleaveth to my jaws; **and thou hath brought me into the dust of death**."* (Psalm 22:15) To whatever degree our II Corinthians 5:17 transformation from "Earth Worms" to "Heavenly Saints" may have mandated the "Son of Man" to take our place on that "pole," *literally*, one species would appear to represent the most appropriate type for that *"brazen serpent...lifted up"* at Calvary. With the *"black* onyx" constituting God's preeminent stone, *Pantherophis Obsoletus* (a non-venomous species of Colubridae found in central North America) fits the bill, being also known as the western rat snake, *black* rat snake, pilot *black* snake, or simply—*black* snake. (Should you desire something more blood curdling, the African *black* mamba, the late Kobe Bryant's moniker, is considered one of the deadliest snakes on the planet.)

And *this*, my dear friend, is what Jesus was burdened about in the Garden. *"Then saith he unto them, **My soul** is exceeding sorrowful, **even unto death**."* (Matthew 26:38) Did you TR people get that? (Don't be so shocked, the subtitle of this book is *"Deep Truths for Shallow Waters."*) The Lord was *not* apprehensive about the approaching death of His *body*, but rather of His *soul*! Whereas the *"second death"* of Revelation 21:8 will be the destruction of the *soul*, Jesus was about to get a foretaste of that very unfathomable experience by "drinking the cup" for you and me! The very *thought* of this ordeal caused His blood to literally spew forth from His pores (Luke 22:44). Dr. Peter Ruckman wrote:

> When Christ was 'made a curse for us' (Gal. 3:13), He, in some mysterious and horrible way, became so much the epitome of SIN that for all practical purposes He took the Devil's place. He took upon Him the responsibility of someone who had been guilty of letting SIN into the world. *This* is the heart of the crucifixion, and

this is the 'cup' that He was praying about in Gethsemane. Some day YOU will take the Devil's place if you do not take the Lamb that took YOUR place.

ISAIAH 53

Now the standard Fundie exposition of Genesis 3:14 has Jesus bruising Satan's head at Calvary. However, Paul would disagree, having written in Romans 16:20 some thirty years *after* the crucifixion, *"And the God of peace **shall bruise Satan under your feet shortly"*** —at the Second Advent (Psalm 68:21; Habakkuk 3:13; Ephesians 1:22; 5:30). However, while the serpent at Genesis 3 was not bruised at Golgotha, the serpent of John 3 most certainly was! (And it happened in that *darkness*.)

Isaiah 53:5 affirms, *"But he was wounded for our transgressions, **he was bruised for our iniquities**."* The really scary part is—bruised by *whom*? Manasseh's grandfather began his messianic treatise with an arresting statement. After *"grow*[ing] *up before **him"*** (God the Father), Jesus is described as having *"**no form** nor comeliness"* (verse 2). While the rest of the verse clearly relates to His physical appearance (*"and when we shall see him, there is no beauty that we should desire him"*), that first part about His being without "form" (i.e., any *human* form?), sure sounds like what we've been positing thus far (a subtle prophetic reference to His "soul death"). The confirmation as to *who* bruised our Lord begins in verse four: *"Surely he hath borne our griefs, and carried our sorrows: yet we did esteem him stricken, **smitten of God**, and afflicted."* Further validation as to whether this "bruising" was particularly directed at His *soul* was then repeated thrice (in as many verses) for emphasis:

> **Yet it pleased the LORD to bruise him**; *he hath put him to grief:* **when thou shalt make his soul an offering for sin**, *he shall see his seed, he shall prolong his days, and the pleasure of the LORD shall prosper in his hand.* **He shall see of the travail of his soul, and shall be satisfied**: *by his knowledge shall my righteous servant justify many; for he shall bear their iniquities. Therefore will I divide him a portion with the great, and he shall divide the spoil with the strong;* **because he hath poured out his soul unto death**: *and he was numbered with the transgressors; and he bare the sin of many, and made intercession for the transgressors."* (Isaiah 53:10-12)

Consequently, as Hebrews 9:28 declares, *"So Christ was once **offered** to bear the sins of many,"* the *pouring out* of His soul—i.e., rendering it "formless" (as a *human*)—became the ultimate "sin offering" for all of mankind.

"A SERPENT UPON A ROCK"

There is something more unspeakable than even this conjectural metamorphosis regarding God's preeminent stone. The consummate picture of what our Black Onyx endured for us may be found in Exodus 17:1-7. It constitutes one of the holiest texts in Scripture, and, strangely enough, one of the least understood. (If I was you, neighbor, I'd take my shoes off before turning to the passage.)

Like I said, long before the *serpent's* head is bruised at *Armageddon*, the *Saviour's* head was bruised at *Calvary*. The prescient scene in Rephidim is one of those rare occasions in Scripture where all three members of the Trinity are represented. Here, God is shown conversing with Moses; the rock depicts Jesus Christ (I Corinthians 10:4), while the water pictures the Holy Spirit (John 7:37-39). Though your average Christian knows that the Crucifixion was prefigured by Moses smiting the rock, the part that is too surreal for our finite comprehension concerns *where* the Father was *standing* when the rock was smitten!

> *And the* LORD *said unto Moses, Go on before the people, and take with thee of the elders of Israel; and thy rod, wherewith thou smotest the river, take in thine hand, and go. Behold, **I will stand before thee there upon the rock** in Horeb; **and thou shalt smite the rock**, and there shall come water out of it, that the people may drink. And Moses did so in the sight of the elders of Israel.* (Exodus 17:5-6)

The Holy Spirit made a veiled reference to that ghastly, yet "wonderful" scene through the words of Solomon in Proverbs 30:18-19: *"There be three things which are too **wonderful** for me, yea, four which I know not...the way of **a serpent upon a rock**."* Thus, according to the solemn typology suggested here, the "Light of the World" went *out* at high noon—because the Father *stomped* it out! While Moses had warned Israel in Deuteronomy 28:63, *"the* LORD *will **rejoice** over you to **destroy** you,"* Isaiah 53:10 affirmed that their Messiah could be treated no differently— *"Yet it **pleased** the* LORD *to **bruise** him."* For having been apprised, *"**Thy bruise** is incurable,"* how *else* could the Jewish nation be *"set at **liberty**?"* (Jeremiah 30:12; Luke 4:18) And the same holds true for us, for *"If the Son therefore shall make you **free**, ye shall be **free** indeed."* (John 8:36)

"O SACRED HEAD, NOW WOUNDED"

Regardless of how you may view these theoretical "worst-case scenarios" involving what happened behind the veil, we can *all* agree that God must really love us! (John 3:16; Romans 5:8) The ancient hymn, "O Sacred Head, Now Wounded" (some 300 years older than "A Mighty Fortress Is Our God")—traditionally ascribed to Bernard of Clairvaux—is now believed to be the work of an obscure poet-abbot, Arnulf of Leuven (c.1200-1250). If the author was not one of those rare, born-again, rogue Romanists (in the tradition of Thomas à Kempis and Desiderius Erasmus), the Lord sure has blessed his musical adaption of John 19:2 for nearly a millennium. These poignant words never fail to bring tears to my eyes. Four of the eleven better-known stanzas follow:

O sacred head, now *wounded*,
With grief and shame weighed down;
Now scornfully surrounded
With thorns, Thine only crown;
O sacred head, what glory,
What bliss, till now was Thine!
Yet, though despised and gory,
I joy to call Thee mine.

What Thou, my Lord, hast suffered,
Was all for sinners' gain:
Mine, mine was the transgression,
But Thine the deadly pain.
Lo, here I fall, my Saviour!
'Tis I deserve Thy place;
Look on me with Thy favor,
Vouchsafe to me Thy grace.

What language shall I borrow
To thank Thee, dearest Friend,
For this my dying sorrow,
Thy pity without end?
O make me Thine forever;
And should I fainting be,
Lord, let me never, *never*
Outlive my love to thee.

Be Thou my consolation,
My shield when I must die;
Remind me of Thy passion
When my last hour draws nigh.
Mine eyes shall then behold Thee,
Upon Thy cross shall dwell,
My heart by faith enfolds Thee.
Who dieth thus dies well.

"ENJOY—BUT *PLEASE* DON'T FORGET ABOUT ME"

The word "onyx" is found *thirteen* times in the KJV. (How appropriate, given that thirteen is the Bible numeric for sin and rebellion.) However, there is a fourteenth usage, but in a mutated sense. I once heard a black pastor friend say, "I'm gonna preach from *Genocide* to *Revolution*." The *first* mention of onyx is in the second chapter of *Genesis*; the *final* reference is in the second-to-the-last chapter of *Revelation*.

In the twenty-first chapter of Revelation, the Holy Spirit provides a preview of the Heavenly New Jerusalem. According to verse sixteen, the massive city (suspended between Heaven and Earth) is foursquare, measuring 1,500 miles long, by 1,500 miles wide (62,726,400,000,000 square feet), by another 1,500 miles high. (So much for Denver's celebrated status as the "Mile High City.") And by the way, neighbor, praise God for the KJV's reading at John 14:2, *"In my Father's house are many **mansions**,"* for the asinine ESV says, "In my Father's house are many *rooms*." (Only a moron would prefer a room to a "crib.")

The four walled sections are entered through twelve gates of pearl (permanently open) attended by twelve angels (verses 12 and 21). And what do you suppose you will find engraved on each pearl? *"And had a wall great and high, and had twelve gates, and at the gates twelve angels, **and names written thereon, which are the names of the twelve*** *tribes of the children of Israel"* (verse 12). As previously mentioned, the great cross-reference confirming that Levi, and especially Joseph, were not replaced on the breastplate by Manasseh and Ephraim is given in the last chapter of Ezekiel: *"And the gates of the city shall be after* **the names of the tribes of Israel***: three gates northward; one gate of Reuben, one gate of Judah, one gate of* **Levi***. And at the east side…three gates; and one gate of* **Joseph***, one gate of Benjamin, one gate of Dan."* (Ezekiel 48:31-32)

As Joseph was honored by a double exposure on Aaron's garment, the greatest type of Jesus Christ will own a similar status in the New Jerusalem (howbeit the *real* attention will be on his antitype, the Lord Himself). That final use of the word onyx—in its mutated sense—will be found *underneath* the city's massive walls:

> And the **foundations of the wall of the city** were garnished with all manner of precious stones. The first foundation was jasper; the second, sapphire; the third, a chalcedony; the fourth, an emerald; **The fifth, sardonyx***; the sixth, sardius; the seventh, chrysolyte; the eighth, beryl; the ninth, a topaz; the tenth, a chrysoprasus; the eleventh, a jacinth; the twelfth, an amethyst.* (Revelation 21:19-20)

Interestingly, while the names of Jacob's sons appear on the twelve gates, the names of the twelve Apostles are etched on the twelve bejeweled foundations (verse 14). According to Matthew 10:2, Philip was the fifth apostle, yet for some unknown reason the Holy Ghost is silent as to why he was the one honored to be matched with the sardonyx through eternity. We'll obviously have to wait till we get Home to discover the answer (John 13:7).

Regarding a spiritual connection between the sardonyx and level five, an article I read stated, "A sardonyx is a type of an onyx, but with a brownish-red rather than a black base." The term, "brownish-red" is basically a description of dried blood. Over time, spilled blood that starts out bright red turns darker and darker as it dries, eventually exhibiting a shade of light brown. This reflects the ruse Joseph's brethren employed to deceive their father: *"And they took Joseph's coat, and killed a kid of the goats, and* **dipped the coat in the blood***."* (Genesis 37:31)

Now, in my opinion, what you are about to read is the most precious truth in this chapter (maybe even in the entire book). Would you agree that we'll all be having the *time* of our lives spending *eternity* in that

"Pearly *White* City?" The lyrics to that blessed hymn by Arthur F. Ingler constitute the antithesis to "Paint It Black."

There's a holy and beautiful city
Whose builder and ruler is God;
John saw it descending from Heaven,
When Patmos, in exile, he trod;
It's high, massive wall is of jasper,
The city itself is pure gold;
And when my frail tent here is folded,
Mine eyes shall its glory behold.

Refrain:
In that bright city, pearly *white* city,
I have a mansion, a harp, and a crown;
Now I am watching, waiting, and longing
For the *white* city that's soon coming down.

No sin is allowed in that city
And nothing defiling or mean;
No pain and no sickness can enter,
No *crepe* on the doorknob is seen;
Earth's sorrows and cares are forgotten,
No tempter is there to annoy;
No parting words ever are spoken,
There's nothing to hurt or destroy. [Refrain]

No heartaches are known in that city,
No tears ever moisten the eyes;
There's no disappointment in Heaven,
No envy and strife in the sky;
The saints are all sanctified wholly,
They live in sweet harmony there;
My heart is now set on that city,
And some day its blessing I'll share. [Refrain]

My loved ones are gathering yonder,
My friends too are passing away,
And soon I shall join their bright number,
And dwell in eternity's day;
They're safe now in glory with Jesus,
Their trials and battles are past.
They overcame sin and the tempter,
They've reached that fair city at last. [Refrain]

My friend, did you have a precious loved one taken by the China Virus? (My own ninety-year-old mother-in-law went home to Glory two days before Christmas in 2020.) What a blessing to meditate on how they are now playing tag with the angels in that Heavenly City. But there is something else. As beautiful as those lyrics are, did you notice that there is no mention of the *foundations*, especially that *fifth* level garnished by the sardonyx stone? The great truth of this section is a throwback to what Jesus had previously asked His Bride do throughout the Church Age. Paul instructed his Japheth converts in Corinth:

*For I have received of the Lord that which also I delivered unto you, That the Lord Jesus the same night he was betrayed took bread: And when he had given thanks, he brake it, and said, Take, eat: this is my body, which is broken for you: **this do in remembrance of me**. After the same manner also he took the cup, when he had supped, saying, This cup is the new testament in my blood: **this do ye, as oft as ye drink it, in remembrance of me**. For as often as ye eat this bread, and drink this cup, ye do shew the Lord's death till he come.* (I Corinthians 11:23-26)

The holy bottom line of this is that—believe it or not—the mighty Creator of the Universe did not want to be forgotten by His puny creation (Psalm 8:3-4). And the same will hold true throughout eternity! While we'll all be thrilling to our glorious living conditions *upstairs*—the way our Groom intended it to be—the only thing He'll ask is that we occasionally remember that "brownish-red" foundation *down* on level five. Prefigured by that kid's coagulating blood permeating Joseph's coat of many colors, Jesus—as His Father's preeminent sardonyx stone—had to shed *His* blood as well so that we could enjoy that beautiful Pearly White City forever! (Revelation 1:5-6)

"IN SIGHT"

I will now *appear* to contradict the last statement I made about our memorializing that "brownish-red" foundation. The reason for this borderline retraction is because Jesus has a beautiful surprise prepared for His Bride regarding her "little" *500 quintillion* cubic-foot "Honeymoon Cottage" (a quintillion being a one with *eighteen* zeros behind it). While it's true that sardonyx stones do sport a brownish-red tint—on Earth—

the ones you and I will see in that fifth foundation will undoubtedly take our celestial breath away. (The same will apply to those other eleven gems adorning the remaining levels.)

Upon receiving his first glimpse of the Lord in His throne room, John began his depiction accordingly: *"And he that sat was to look upon like a jasper and a sardine stone: and there was a **rainbow** round about the throne, **in sight** like unto an **emerald**."* (Revelation 4:3) Now, neighbor, what you have just read constitutes a major conundrum. All emeralds have a distinctive, common denominator—their green color. Yet "in" John's "sight," that same gemstone radiated like a multi-colored rainbow. How is this possible? The explanation will astound you. The key to this "optical illusion" is that little, two-word phrase, "in sight" (i.e., not previously visible). Thus, "The Revelator" was describing something that could only be seen in Heaven. While the emerald looked one way on earth, it looked totally different in the presence of God.

Optical mineralogy is the study of minerals and rocks by their optical properties. Thinly sliced rock and mineral samples are studied in laboratories with a cutting-edge piece of equipment known as a petrographic microscope. Only within the past fifty years have petrologists made a watershed discovery involving certain light rays and their relationship to precious stones. To explain this highly complex procedure in laymen's terms—when a particular sliver is penetrated by an innovative luminescence known as cross-polarized light (i.e., direct light verses bent light; nicknamed "pure light"), the gems divide into two categories— isotropic or anisotropic (ISO meaning "not colorful in polarized light"; ANISO meaning "is colorful in polarized light").

If a stone is isotropic, the polarization effect will render it colorless; the once-beautiful jewel simply goes black. Conversely, if the stone is anisotropic, the effect is literally mind-blowing; this beautiful jewel gets a serious makeover, resulting in a kaleidoscope of dazzling colors in unique patterns. Anisotropic minerals (also referred to as birefringent or birefractive) contain an optical property that causes them to appear differently in various kinds of light. In Revelation 21:23, John described "the light" he had "in sight" —from his Heavenly vantage point: *"And the city had no need of the sun, neither of the moon, to shine in it: **for the glory of God did lighten it, and the Lamb is the light thereof**."* The very light of God's presence is what separates the precious stones into their isotropic or anisotropic categories.

The accompanying salient truth is equally bedazzling. Would you believe that all twelve foundation stones just happen to be anisotropic? Conversely, many gems that were popular down here are never mentioned as making it up there, being isotropic all along (e.g., rubies, opals, garnets, ambers, fluorites, halites). While diamonds may have been "a girl's best friend" during the materialistic Laodicean Age, most (if not all) being isotropic as well, would be about as "stunning" as coal dust in eternity. (Regarding Lucifer's breastplate, which contains a diamond, one theory I've heard is that he manufactured it himself on earth.) Therefore, the hymnist A. S. Bridgewater could write, "Rare jewels of splendor are glowing; How beautiful Heaven must be" (Malachi 3:17). Now, neighbor—if the Bible is just an ordinary book, how was a first-century exiled fisherman able to handicap a perfect twelve-out-of-twelve anisotropic stones some 2,000 years before the process of cross-polarization microscopy was even developed? (Now *that* would be a coinky-dinky-and-a-half!)

By the way, should we be surprised that the words "in sight" are conspicuously "out of sight" in all modern translations—from the New American Standard Commode Version to the New International and English Standard Versions? With their historic aversion to the Blood, these perverse imposters also change sardonyx back to onyx. And if that's not bad enough, the NASCV and the NIV also replace the anisotropic sardius with the isotropic ruby at level six, making a liar out of God!

In closing, while Jesus certainly wants us to remember the pensive symbolism involving death level five, He apparently was willing to enhance that original drab brownish-red hue with any number of bright and beautiful colors (red being the dominant shade)—primarily for His lovely Bride's sake. After all, "giving honor unto the wife" would involve honoring her innate scriptural propensities as the consummate (and sole) "Heavenly homemaker" throughout eternity (Proverbs 31:27; I Timothy 5:14; Titus 2:5). In fact, the two are so closely intertwined that the Holy Spirit has the angel tell John, *"Come hither, **I will shew thee the bride, the Lamb's wife**. And he carried me away in the spirit to a great and high mountain, **and shewed me that great city, the holy Jerusalem**, descending out of heaven from God."* (Revelation 21:9-10)

But then—why *wouldn't* the stone representing the very blood of God (Acts 20:28) be the most beautiful of all? Suffice it to say, having altered His preeminent onyx from black to brownish-red, the "Master Mineralogist" will surely arrange the most resplendent finale imaginable, for as Paul assured the Church in Corinth:

> *But as it is written,* **Eye hath not seen***, nor ear heard,*
> *neither have entered into the heart of man,* **the things**
> **which God hath prepared for them that love him***.*
> (I Corinthians 2:9)

18

Strength for the Journey

W HEN I PREACH in Amarillo, Texas, the host pastor (my good friend, Ben Hickam) inevitably takes his guests to the "The Big Texan Steak Ranch." This historic Route 66 landmark is world-famous for offering a free 72-oz steak to anyone who can devour it in one hour. To illustrate the adage that "truth is stranger than fiction," according to the restaurant's website, the current record holder is a rather petite lady named Molly Schuyler (weighing in at 124 pounds), who reportedly finished off *three* 72-oz slabs in an incredible twenty minutes!

In the book of Hebrews, we learn that certain portions of the Bible are likened to meat (in contrast to other portions likened to milk). In his comments on Melchizedek, the writer chastised his Jewish readers for their unwarranted inability to digest deep doctrine:

> *Of whom we have many things to say, and **hard to be uttered**, seeing ye are dull of hearing. For when for the time ye ought to be teachers, ye have need that one teach you again which be the first principles of the oracles of God; and are become such as have need of **milk**, and not of **strong meat**. For every one that useth **milk** is unskilful in the word of righteousness: for he is a babe. But **strong meat** belongeth to them there are of full age, even those who by reason of use have their senses exercised to discern both good and evil.* (Hebrews 5:11-14)

The previous two chapters were "prime" (rib) examples of strong meat. Whereas that material focused primarily on the Lord Jesus Christ, the current section will focus "primarily" on you. The main reason God the Father wants His "kids" to include meat in their spiritual diet is because meat is protein and protein builds muscle. Say what you will, but having observed this thing for nearly half-a-century, I can tell you that one of the leading causes for burnout among "hyper"-Fundamentalists (no doubt a redundant expression) is a lack of serious doctrinal teaching. Neighbor—you can't run 24/7 on pablum; you need protein.

When the mighty prophet Elijah got so depressed that he wanted to die, the Angel of the Lord (Jesus Christ) revived him with a Heavenly "Whataburger." Note the result: *"And he arose, and did eat and drink, **and went in the strength of that meat forty days and forty nights** unto Horeb the mount of God."* (I Kings 19:8) Therefore, this chapter was specifically written to provide a similar meal, so that *you* may have "strength for the journey" that *you'll* soon be having to endure. (Consider it *your* third "72-oz steak" in as many chapters.) And because we are discussing "meat," the main similitude will involve an ox.

ROMANS 6, 7, AND 8

It is generally agreed that the most perplexing portion of Scripture for the "digestive tract" of the *"Body* of Christ" are chapters six, seven, and eight of the book of Romans. This has no doubt remained an elusive text throughout Church history, for even Peter (the so-called "first Pope") acknowledged that his *"beloved brother Paul"* had left *him* befuddled from the get-go, stating that *"in **all** his epistles…*[were] *some things **hard to be understood**."* (II Peter 3:16) This forms a double dilemma, for this Roman trilogy is also regarded as holding the secret to attaining the sacrosanct "victorious Christian life." Talk about a spiritual conundrum—as with Laodicea being the epoch that received the most blessing, but produced the least fruit—the most important Scripture in the Bible (apart from the Gospel) is now the least understood by the Body (including the majority within the Philadelphia remnant). This unmitigated disaster represents the perfect illustration of an ignorant "Puke Pot 'Church' Age" stemming from a polluted "Chamber Pot 'Bible' Version."

I have often heard preachers announce that they were going to explain these chapters, only to find myself even more confused when they finished. For instance, consider the following sample of enigmatic texts from Romans, chapter six—the ones you have been scratching your head about your entire Christian life: *"Knowing this, that **our old man is crucified with him**, that **the body of sin might be destroyed**,* *that henceforth we should not serve sin"* (verse six). With absolutely *no* disrespect directed to the Holy Ghost—What in the *world* is *that* supposed to mean? Ditto for the next verse, *"For he that is **dead** is freed from sin."* Did you know that you were "dead" and consequently "free" from sin? Then we have, *"dead with Christ"* in verse eight. Cool—but, again, *what does it mean*? (No problem with verses nine and ten.) The real kicker is verse eleven, *"Likewise **reckon ye also yourselves to be dead indeed unto sin**, but alive unto God through Jesus Christ our Lord."* Really? Like the catchphrase associated with the TV show "I Love Lucy" that had Ricky Ricardo say, "Lucy, you got some 'splainin' to do" —can't *anyone* "splain" these abstract passages?

When trying to exegete the key word "reckon," one Greek "expert" on the internet said, "This is a term of faith where we count something as true. *It is not enough to understand verses one to ten; we need to believe them as true.* The word 'reckon' means to calculate or compute something as true. As an accounting term it carries the idea of put to an account." Do you really think this bum *understands* the ten verses in question? Which reminds me of that old joke about the Christian Science boy and his Roman Catholic friend. When the Catholic asked his pal to pray for his mother because she was sick, the Christian Scientist replied, "She's not really sick, she just *thinks* she's sick." When they ran into each other a few days later the positive thinker asked his friend, "How's your mother doing lately? Whereupon he replied, "Well—now she thinks she's *dead*."

What Paul essentially said is that all you have to do is to "reckon" yourself to be *dead* to sin and it will be so! Isn't that a "comforting" reality? But wouldn't it be even *more* comforting—if you understood what in the world he was talking about? To be honest, I was saved for over forty years before the Holy Spirit gave me enough light to finally get a handle on this difficult doctrine (Psalm 119:18). The secret to understanding what this "reckon" business means (with chapter six being the catalyst that opens seven and eight) is to grasp *how* this occurs. And the key to understanding *how* this occurs is found in a simple Old Testament similitude concerning an ox. (And don't *even* miss that conspicuous last letter "x".)

A MOSAIC LEASH LAW

One of the great principles for learning Scripture is that the Holy Spirit has permeated the Old Testament with numerous types, pictures, and illustrations of various New Testament doctrines. For instance, Enoch is a type of the Rapture, while Noah's family surviving the deluge pictures the Jewish remnant being preserved through the Tribulation. Abraham dispatching his servant, Eleazar, to find a bride for Isaac previews God the Father sending the Holy Spirit to procure a Bride for His Son, Jesus Christ. Hence, the Bible institute cliché: "The Old Testament is the New Testament *concealed*, while the New Testament is the Old Testament *revealed*."

Consequently, it would only be natural for the Lord to employ something in the Old Testament to unseal the great mystery of Romans 6, 7, and 8 in the New Testament, and in this we are not disappointed. Because the King James Bible is such an amazing "Book," the solution to understanding *how* to "reckon oneself dead indeed unto sin" is found— believe it or not—in an insignificant-appearing *leash law* tucked away in the inspired legalese of the ancient Mosaic Code! Just one chapter after the Ten Commandments are revealed in Exodus 20:6-17, Moses warns the Jews not to let their oxen run wild through the neighborhood. He also lays out the various penalties if someone dies from such negligence:

> *If an ox gore a man or a woman, that they die: then the ox shall be surely stoned, and his flesh shall not be eaten; but the owner of the ox shall be quit. But if the ox were wont to push with his horn in time past, and it hath been testified to his owner, and he hath not kept him in, but that he hath killed a man or a woman; the ox shall be stoned, and his owner also shall be put to death.* (Exodus 21:28-29)

The next verses deal with the appropriate judgments commensurate with the status of the victim. If the ox killed a family member of a neighbor (as opposed to a servant), the householder could set whatever fine he desired, and if the defendant could not afford to pay, he would be executed. As verse twenty-nine implies, the man could just as well waive any fine in favor of capital punishment.

> *If there be laid on him a sum of money, then he shall give for the ransom of his life whatsoever is laid upon him. Whether he have*

gored a son, or have gored a daughter, according to this judgment shall it be done unto him. (Exodus 21:30)

Now, remember what we're looking for, neighbor—something hiding in an Old Testament text that will unravel a New Testament doctrine— in this case, a connection to the death of Jesus Christ. With that in mind, go back and reread verse thirty and see if something doesn't jump off the page. (I purposely didn't put *this* buzzword in bold.)

Surely you have spotted it by now. If not, here's a couple of cross-references: *"And whosoever will be chief among you, let him be your servant: Even as the Son of man came not to be ministered unto, but to minister, and to give his life a* **ransom** *for many."* (Matthew 20:27-28) *"For there is one God, and one mediator between God and men, the man Christ Jesus; Who gave himself a* **ransom** *for all, to be testified in due time."* (I Timothy 2:5-6) P. P. Bliss put this great truth to music with his beautiful hymn, "I Will Sing of My **Redeemer**." (See the providential origin of this hymn in the following chapter.) The word "ransom" is found in Scripture *thirteen* times (the Bible numeric for sin and rebellion). Furthermore, the *first* mention just *happens* to be our text prescribing the "ransom" to be paid for a death inflicted by a man's ox.

The second buzzword phrase is even more exhilarating. While the fatal goring of a freeman could mandate any size ransom (i.e., *"whatsoever is laid upon him"*), a servant had a set figure assigned to his death. *"If the ox shall push a manservant or a maidservant; he shall give unto their master thirty shekels of silver, and the ox shall be stoned"* (verse 32). So, tell me, neighbor, do y'all see anything in particular there that might be pointing to something *way* out in the future (i.e., relative to the scene in 1491 BC)? Would *"thirty shekels of* **silver***"* ring any bells, as in "Silver Bells" (silver being a type of redemption)? Can you think of anyone's *servant* being "gored" that was connected to a precise monetary figure of *thirty pieces of silver*? Did you happen to catch that "random" reference to the word *"servant"* in Matthew 20:27? Do you know what Philippians 2:7 says? (Just think how many "ho-hum" times you have speed-read through this Exodus 21 minutia in the past...*yawning* as you went.)

Now, turn to the great Psalm 22 (second only to Isaiah 53 concerning Calvary). Did you notice how this messianic Psalm begins? *"My God, my God, why hast thou forsaken me?"* (spoken by Jesus from the cross in Matthew 27:46). The Holy Spirit then gives a graphic depiction of the crucifixion in verses fourteen through eighteen. The prophetic pinnacle in verse sixteen is hard to miss— *"they **pierced** my hands and my feet."* However, while our Saviour's members were *technically* "pierced" by Roman *nails*, the bigger spiritual picture has to do with Jesus Christ— as a *servant*—being "gored" by someone's *ox*. As noted in the previous chapter, that surreal scene was captured in verse twelve: *"Many **bulls** have compassed me: strong **bulls** of Bashan have beset me round."*

Those bulls represent the sinners for whom Christ died. With Isaiah 51:20 calling Israel *"a wild **bull** in a net,"* Acts 3:13-15 and I Thessalonians 2:14-15 clearly state that the crucifixion *began* with the Jews. (The background to this "anti-Semitic" premise can be traced to that "golden *calf*" in Exodus 32:4.) However, when the *Jewish* Apostle Paul addressed his *Gentile* flock in the "Eternal City," his text read, *"But God commendeth his love toward **us**, in that, while **we** were yet sinners, Christ died for **us**."* (Romans 5:8) If those "bulls" represent the Jews, those "dogs" in verses sixteen and twenty represent us, pictured by those Roman executioners (Matthew 15:26). Thus, the "Heebs" *started* it and the "Goys" *finished* it. Like the songwriter said, *"I Should Have Been Crucified."* Not only were our *sins* nailed to His cross, but our sins nailed *Him* to the cross (Colossians 2:14).

Did you ever wonder *why* those thirty pieces of silver got too hot to handle (like the Ark of the Covenant did with the Philistines)? First, Judas decided *he* didn't want them as bad as he thought. But when he tried to return them to the chief priests, they didn't want them, either. The reason for this relates directly to our text. Legally, those thirty shekels of silver belonged to the *"master"* of the slain servant (Exodus 21:32). As Jehovah called Jesus *"**my** servant"* in Isaiah 52:13, obviously, neither Judas nor the Jewish leaders had any rightful claim to the "blood money." Do you suppose the priests were thinking of Exodus 21:32 when they told Judas in Matthew 27:6, *"It is not lawful for to put them in the treasury, because **it** is **the price of blood**"?* (The Scriptures appear to be silent on the exact meaning of this phrase.) Therefore, in fulfillment of the *spoken* words of Jeremiah (preserved in the *written* text of Zechariah 11:12), the funds went to purchase the *"**potter's** field."* (Matthew 27:6-10) And so, at the end of the day, those thirty pieces of silver wound up going to the *rightful* claimant, for we all know who "The Potter" is (Jeremiah 18:6).

TIME FOR REVIEW

In summary, the progression of our Lord's Passion unfolded as follows: Jehovah's Servant was "girded" in the upper room (John 13:4); "gored" on the cross (John 19:34); "guarded" at the tomb (Matthew 27:66); and "glorified" by the resurrection (John 17:5). The capstone of this sequence facilitated the "deepest truth" in human history! Remember that our working premise posits that the key to understanding Romans 6, 7, and 8 is an Old Testament type (in this case, that arcane leash law).

To recalibrate your spiritual faculties, a quick check of I Corinthians 10:6-11 will show how Paul reminded his Gentile readers that all those disastrous choices the Jews made in the wilderness were recorded for the Church's benefit: *"Now all these things happened unto them for ensamples:* **and they are written for our admonition,** *upon whom the ends of the world are come"* (verse eleven). He then shared the same principle with the church at Rome: *"***For whatsoever things were written aforetime were written for our learning,** *that we through patience and comfort of the scriptures might have hope."* (Romans 15:4) This is essentially what Paul was saying in II Timothy 3:16 when you consider that the main "Scriptures" *then* constituted the Old Testament: *"***All scripture** *is given by inspiration of God, and is* **profitable.***"*

More precisely, notice how the Holy Spirit uses an ox in Old Testament Israel to teach another truth; this time, regarding proper compensation for a New Testament pastor. Quoting from Deuteronomy 25:4, Paul instructs the carnal (i.e., "tightwad") Corinthians accordingly:

> **For it is written in the law of Moses, thou shall not muzzle the mouth of the ox that treadeth out the corn. Doth God take care for oxen? Or saith he it altogether for our sakes? For our sakes, no doubt, this is written***: that he that ploweth should plow in hope; and that he that thresheth in hope should be partaker of his hope. If we have sown unto you spiritual things, is it a great thing if we shall reap your carnal things?* (I Corinthians 9:9-11)

He gave his youthful protégé similar instruction: *"Let the elders that rule well be counted worthy of* **double honour,** *especially they who labour in the word and doctrine.* **For the scripture saith, Thou shall not muzzle the ox that treadeth out the corn.** *And, The labourer is* *worthy of his reward."* (I Timothy 5:17-18) That root word "honour" is where we get "honorarium" (i.e., "love offerings").

With all this considered, a final review of the seven obvious facts of our story will help to prepare you for the critical doctrinal application: 1) A man owns an ox. 2) Such beasts of burden were profitable assets in an agrarian economy (Proverbs 14:4), likened to modern tractors. 3) However, one's ox could also be a deadly asset. 4) Here, the hypothetical case has a man's ox killing a human (or another man's animal in verse thirty-five). 5) Now—here's where the door to our great truth is cracked open for the first time. While God *definitely* holds the owner of the ox responsible, note that he is *not* indicted for *committing* the act—but rather, for not *preventing* the tragedy. You might call it an Old Testament form of "negligent homicide." 6) The final judgment costs the guilty party severely, his liability ranging from *"thirty shekels of silver"* to *"whatsoever is laid upon him"* to even his own life. 7) The ox is destroyed at the end of the story.

DOCTRINAL APPLICATIONS

We are now ready to throw the door *wide* open regarding how all of this applies to you (specifically, Romans 6, 7, and 8). So, get ready for a blessing! First of all, *we* have *our* own "ox" to contain. It goes by various New Testament names (and/or theological terms), i.e., our "Old Man," our "flesh," our "sin nature," or, more specifically, our "Adamic nature." And again, did you catch that amazing "coinkydink" that the word "ox" just *happens* to end with the letter "x"?

Second, like the animal in Exodus 21, our "spiritual ox" can be a profitable asset—as well as a deadly one. In his comments on the tongue, James writes, *"But the tongue can no man tame...**Therewith bless we God...and therewith curse we men**, which are made after the similitude of God. **Out of the same mouth proceedeth blessing and cursing."*** (James 3:8-10) Those same "beautiful 'feet'" that can carry the Gospel to some unsaved person can just as easily walk you to a liquor store (or worse). The same finger that rings the prospect's doorbell can tap the internet keys on some unholy site. Get the picture, neighbor?

Now, here comes the *really* big one. In fact, it's *so* big, I have to prepare you for the attendant shock. The main benefit of finally understanding Romans 6, 7, and 8 has to do with eliminating those proverbial "skeletons in your closet." While I have never been troubled by the sins I committed *before* my salvation (Paul's "pattern" of going from "the guttermost to the uttermost," as discussed in I Timothy 1:12-16, having cared for that), I *have* frequently struggled with the guilt stemming from the sins I committed *after* I trusted Christ. Am I alone in this experience? *"I trow not."* (Luke 17:9) So, here goes, neighbor…Thirdly, from God's perspective—*we* don't "gore" anybody; our *ox* does the goring! Translation: The Lord *never* sees *us* as sinning; He *always* sees the "sinning" being done by our ox (i.e., by our "Old Man"). So, say bye-bye to all those skeletons in your closet! They don't belong there because you never committed *any* of those sins in the first place; your *ox* did—but *you* did *not*! Now *that's* a 72-oz steak, folks!

PAUL'S AFFIRMATION

According to the old adage, "If it seems too good to be true—it probably is!" Fortunately, in this case, what you have just read about that clean slate is *absolutely* true and forms the heart of the "victorious Christian life." The secret to comprehending the Pauline doctrine in Romans 6, 7, and 8 is correlating that Old Testament similitude of an ox with Paul's blanket statement in Romans 7:17-20, then studying his expanded explanation in Colossians 2:9-13.

Paul begins in Romans 7:15 by describing the frustration every child of God feels when their holy desires are constantly upended by their unholy realities. *"For that which I do I allow not: for **what I would, that do I not;** but **what I hate, that do I.**"* He then makes one of the most illuminating statements in all of the Bible: *"**Now** then it is **no more** I that do it, but sin that dwelleth in me"* (verse 17). The opening conjunction *"Now"* alerts you that a paradigm shift has occurred; the words *"no more"* implying that there *was* a time when Paul *was* guilty, but that was yesterday—i.e., when "Paul the Apostle" was "Saul of Tarsus." In his pre-conversion years, Saul had only *one* nature and you can rest assured he seldom (if ever) hated *anything* he did (as there was no indwelling Holy Spirit to convict him). However, *"Now"* Paul's "New Man" is no longer even *capable* of sinning. As he testifies in his own words, *"Now"* the only culprit is the *"sin that dwelleth in me."* Resulting from his Damascus Road encounter, Paul is now spiritually *bipolar*! (As we learned in chapter two, he will later inform the Philippians that they are "bilocative," as well.)

This Pauline truth is *so "hard to be understood"* that even this writer could barely handle it. After I preached a sermon on the AV 1611 for a church in Ada, Ohio, the pastor got so excited, he jumped up on the platform and exclaimed, "I believe the King James Bible is the inspired, infallible, inerrant, perfect, word of God; and *if* there are any errors in it—they'd have to be *inspired* errors!" Paul was *so* blown away by his own revelation, he actually penned an "inspired error" in his autograph— then, quickly corrected himself with a parenthesis (it probably being too hard to erase it on the original parchment, LOL). If you think I'm crazy, just read the next verse for yourself. *"For I know that **in me (that is, in my flesh,)** dwelleth no good thing: for to will is present with me; but how to perform that which is good I find not."* (Romans 7:18)

Paul had to catch himself after writing the word "me," clarifying that what he *really* meant was that no good thing dwelt—in his "flesh." Remember, as a saved man the *real* Paul was no longer *in* his "flesh"; he was now *in* someone *else's* "flesh" (Ephesians 5:30). The Holy Spirit then led Paul to repeat himself for emphasis: *"For the good that I would I do not: but the evil which I would not, that I do. **Now if I do that I would not, it is no more I that do it, but sin that dwelleth in me"*** (verses 19-20).

PAUL'S EXPLANATION

Most Christians never do get a grip on Romans 6, 7, and 8 because they unknowingly skirt Colossians 2. Paul uses the latter to elucidate the former. With reference to the Lord's pedagogical method of employing Old Testament types as precursors to New Testament doctrines, here the object in view is circumcision. When God introduced this practice to Israel, through Abraham, He instructed him to remove a tiny sliver of flesh from the male foreskin. In the Church Age, the anti-type of *spiritual* circumcision calls for the *entire body of flesh* to be cut away from the born-again believer. *"For **in** him dwelleth all the fullness of the Godhead bodily. And ye are complete **in** him, which is the head of all principality and power: **In** whom also ye are **circumcised** with the **circumcision** made without hands, **in putting off the body of the sins of the flesh** by the **circumcision** of Christ."* (Colossians 2:9-11)

Do you see those two *positional* references to the new convert being "***in*** him" (as well as that third reference, "***in*** whom")? When the real you—

your *soul*—is cut away from your *sinful* flesh, it is reattached to Christ's *sinless* flesh (Romans 7:1-6). Thus, Paul could write in Ephesians 5:30, *"For we are members of his **body**, of his **flesh**, and of his **bones**."* Once again, the "real you" is taken "out" of *your* physical body and placed "in" *Christ's* spiritual body! Talk about the doctrine of eternal security—for a Christian to lose his salvation in the Church Age, Jesus would have to have a "reverse skin and bone graft." (And we know that the only Baptists who can orchestrate *that* rupture are "Free Will" Baptists.)

Notice how precise the AV 1611 text reads at verse twelve, *"Buried with him in baptism, wherein also ye are risen with him through the **faith of the operation of God**, who hath raised him from the dead."* Would you not label "circumcision" a *surgical* procedure? If you're still hangin' in there with me, Paul then explains that the key to getting everything to come together is that tiny word "faith." All you have to do is repeat the process that *got* you saved in the first place. *"For by grace are ye saved through **faith**."* (Ephesians 8:9) After you heard the *facts* of the death, burial, and resurrection of Jesus Christ, you chose to exercise "faith" in God's promise to save all who would believe (Acts 16:31). It's the same way with Romans 6, 7, and 8. The way you *"**reckon** ye also yourselves to be dead indeed unto sin, but alive unto God,"* is to simply *believe* what God said about His "operation." That procedure is what separates *you* from your *ox*.

To summarize, in the Old Testament, a person's soul and body were attached to one another. Consequently, if a Jew touched a dead body, *he* became defiled, as his body and soul were stuck to one another (Numbers 19:13). Thus, the oft-repeated phrase, *"The **soul** that sinneth, **it** shall die."* (Ezekiel 18:4) However, in the Church Age, the moment a sinner yields his/her will to the convicting power of the Holy Spirit and believes the Gospel of the grace of God (Acts 20:24), the most amazing process occurs. As the Father initially withdrew His presence from Adam the moment his "primary residence" became contaminated, He must now separate the soul of a saved man from *his* corrupt flesh, so that God the Holy Spirit can re-enter his spirit (I Corinthians 6:17). While most Christians are familiar with the *fact* of that glorious reunion— *"The Spirit itself beareth witness with our spirit, that we are the children of God"* (Romans 8:16)—few ever discover *how* this encounter was facilitated; namely, through spiritual circumcision.

And so, we have a surgical "operation," and we certainly know the identity of the "Great Physician" (Mark 2:17). All we need is an allusion to the right "scalpel." Enter Hebrews 4:12: *"For **the word of God** is quick, and powerful, and **sharper than any twoedged sword, piercing** even to the **dividing asunder** of soul and spirit, and of the joints and marrow, and is a discerner of the thoughts and intents of the heart."* The Bible is obviously the "instrument" that performs our spiritual circumcision. Once again, note the precision of the AV 1611 text. As I Thessalonians 5:23 shows man to be a tripartite being (body, soul, and spirit), the question arises: How would one "divide" *three* entities "asunder" (i.e., in half)? Look how the Holy Spirit does this. On one side, He has the soul and spirit, and on the other, the equation is balanced by using two synonyms to represent the flesh—joints and marrow! How "cool" is that? The main observation is that the soul and spirit together are detached from the body—period! And that's what happened to you at your salvation. The "real you" (i.e., your soul) was cut away from your flesh and reattached to Christ's body. Unlike "souls" in the Old Testament dispensation, we are *in* our bodies but no longer *attached* to them. So, *now* do you understand why you can no longer *technically* sin, even if you wanted to?

Speaking of "cool," the coolest illustration I ever heard to "splain" this holy concept is a common ice tray. The tray, representing our physical body, holds frozen cubes of ice, representing our soul and spirit. The cubes start out stuck to the tray. But, when warm water is applied (representing Holy Ghost conviction through that scalpel as per John 6:44 and Ephesians 5:26), then the tray is twisted slightly—that *crack* represents the split second we say yes to the Gospel; the cubes break loose but remain *in* the tray. However, while you and I are still *in* the tray, we're no longer stuck *to* the tray. Praise God, one day we're going to leave these old ice trays behind, preferring *"rather to be absent from the body, and to be present with the Lord."* (II Corinthians 5:8) As the beautiful lyrics of "Until Then" say, "The soul of man is like a waiting falcon; when it's released, it's destined for the skies." And it won't be long before we get *new* "trays" to boot! *"It is sown a natural body; it is raised a spiritual body...**as we have borne the image of the earthy, we shall also bear the image of the heavenly.**"* (I Corinthians 15:44, 49)

JOHN'S DISAGREEMENT

However, as if to represent the ultimate "Debbie Downer" moment, about the time you were just about to shout it out—regarding all those skeletons being evicted from your spiritual closet—the Holy Ghost has to bust up the party, informing you that Dr. Bill Grady is nothing but a big heretic for saying such crazy things. (And of course, all his critics could not be happier.)

Well, all you have to do is read what the Apostle John had to say about this "sinlessness stuff." After all (if you *really* want to push the "right division" envelope), if there's ever a disagreement between Paul and John, you'd have to go with the "disciple whom Jesus loved," for he received truths from God over thirty years after Paul's martyrdom (not to mention the book of Revelation). So, why not ask him what he thinks about Grady's false teachings?

The Bible says in I John 1:8, *"If we say that we have no sin, we deceive ourselves, and the truth is not in us."* There, wha'd I tell ya, neighbor? The man is not only racist, long-winded, and a conspiracy nut, but he's also a self-deceived apostate who would make Steven Anderson look like Charles Spurgeon! And, just so you don't think that verse was a random fluke, John gave Grady a *second* shot for good measure two verses later: *"If we say that we have not sinned, we make him a liar, and his word is not in us."* Now the "Book" is calling him out for trying to make God out to be a liar! All I can say is, you pastors better get your calendars out and start canceling this deceiver or else you will enter into his sins.

JOHN'S AGREEMENT

Now, hold the phone, neighbor; if I were you, I wouldn't let those skeletons creep back into my closet quite yet—at least not till you ask John to clarify his position. You see, having penned the book of Revelation while he was in two different places at the same time (the Island of Patmos and the Day of the Lord), you might say that he also wrote the book on "bilocation theology."

You say, "Dr. Grady, now *you* sound like *you're* talking out of both sides of *your* mouth." Well, for one thing, I *could* whip out some of that right division, "hyper-dispensational" double-talk about sticking with Paul if any text from Hebrews through Revelation appears to clash doctrinally with what he wrote for the Church Age. I even have a verse for this "crazy" idea—that Paul is the chief spokesman for the New Testament Church: *"Consider what I say; and the Lord give thee understanding in all things."* (II Timothy 2:7) Yet, "on the other hand" (as Tevye the dairyman would say), maybe that won't be necessary. Perhaps we should ask John if he has anything else to say about that *"hard to be understood"* Pauline view that spiritually circumcised Church Age saints can no longer sin because they're now in Christ's body. (After all, the pair *did* have time for a "sit down" with the Lord when John "dropped *up*" at Revelation 4:1.)

Alright already; *enough* of all the funny business! Let's hear it. Ok, how's this, neighbor? *"He that committeth sin is of the devil...**Whosoever is born of God doth not commit sin***; for his seed remaineth in him: ***and he cannot sin**, because he is born of God."* (I John 3:8-9) And just because John left the door open for Dr. Grady's critics to attack him twice in chapter one, he evened the record with a second offsetting text in I John 5:18, *"**We know that whosoever is born of God sinneth not**; but he that is begotten of God keepeth himself, and that wicked one toucheth him not."* (And don't *even* get me started with how many times Fundamentalist "scholars" butcher I John 3:9 with "the Greek," i.e., substituting "practice sin" for *"commit sin."*)

While much of the doctrine in I John *does* apply to Tribulation saints (get over it, you shallow Fundies), I John 1:8, 10 do *not* contradict I John 3:8 and 5:18 for Church Age believers. It's just another example of that "bilocation" phenomenon. Whereas the first two verses deal with the *practical* aspect of a Christian's "sin" (simply what the believer *allows* his or her "ox" to do), the latter pair deal with the *positional* aspect (that a circumcised soul can no longer sin because he or she is *in* Christ). We know that the positional truth holds the *doctrinal* authority, for Jude 24 says, *"Now unto him that is able to keep you from falling, **and to present you faultless** before the presence of his glory with exceeding joy."* Thus, Paul would write to the Church at Corinth, *"For I am jealous over you with godly jealousy: for I have espoused you to one husband, **that I may present you as a chaste virgin to Christ**."* (II Corinthians 11:2) And don't forget about that beautiful promise in II Corinthians 5:21, *"that we might be made the righteous of God **in him**."*

SINLESS, BUT STILL LIABLE

At the outset of this chapter, I informed you that the main way to unlock Romans 6:11 will be found in an Old Testament type involving an arcane leash law. So, let us return to that impenetrable text and see if it reads more clearly now. *"Likewise **reckon ye also yourselves to be dead indeed unto sin**, but alive unto God through Jesus Christ our Lord."* The enhanced illumination that you should now sense results from "bipolarizing" yourself into two distinct entities: the *real* "you" (your soul) and your "ox" (your sinful flesh). Building upon this anti-type, the reason you can now *"**reckon** your*[self] *to be dead indeed unto sin"* stems from your exercising simple *faith* in the Holy Ghost-revealed *facts* about that "operation" of God (your spiritual circumcision). Thus, you *live* the Christian life the same way you *began* the Christian life— *believing* what God says (Ephesians 2:8-9).

And, as already stated, the great liberating reality of this doctrine is that you never really committed that sin that has *"so easily"* haunted your conscience for so long (your *ox* did it). Wouldn't it be amazing if we discover in Heaven that the so-called "besetting sin" of Hebrews 12:1 was somehow connected to those very skeletons? Don't you think Satan has used *guilt* to hamper many Christians *"who are taken captive by him at his will"* from running their race? (II Timothy 2:26)

However, as good as this news is, don't get *so* carried away that you lose sight of the offsetting caution light. In Deuteronomy 16:19, Moses warned the magistrates, *"Thou shalt not wrest judgment; thou shalt not respect persons, neither take a gift: **for a gift doth blind the eyes of the wise**, and pervert the words of the righteous."* The devotional application here is that even the goodness of God can blind a Christian (Ecclesiastes 7:10, 14). For instance, while it's true that the Lord no longer sees us as sinners, he *does* hold us accountable for the actions of our ox—exactly like the Mosaic Law did with the Jews. Notice how Paul's unfolding context stresses this very responsibility:

> **Let not sin therefore reign in your mortal body**, *that ye should obey it in the lusts thereof.* **Neither yield ye your members as instruments of unrighteousness unto sin**: *but yield yourselves unto God, as those that are alive from the dead, and your members as instruments of righteousness unto God. For sin shall not have dominion over you: for ye are not under the law, but under grace.* (Romans 6:12-14)

This means that the closest a Christian ever comes to "sinning" — as a circumcised believer detached from his defiled body and reattached to Christ's glorious Body—is to *allow* his or her sinful flesh do what it wants; i.e., *letting* your ox participate in the "Running of the Bulls" (goring anything that moves, etc.). This would constitute the doctrinal explanation for the "sinning" in I John 1:8, 10. So remember this on the next trip you make to the altar at your church. If you want to be more scripturally precise, don't say, "Lord, please forgive *me* for doing such and such" but rather, "Lord please forgive me for letting my sorry *ox* do such and such." (Glory!)

"BIBLE BUCKS" AT THE JUDGMENT SEAT

Paul wrote in II Corinthians 5:10, *"**For we must all appear before the judgment seat of Christ**; that every one may receive the things done in his body, according to that he had done, whether it be good or bad."* In his first epistle to the same local assembly, he stated, *"If any man's work abide which he hath built thereupon, **he shall receive a reward**. If any man's work shall be burned, he shall suffer loss: but he himself shall be saved; yet so as by fire."* (I Corinthians 3:14-15) I will now present you with the most "imaginative" preview of that approaching event that you have ever heard.

The hallmark of my allegorical depiction of our Heavenly "rewards," or lack thereof, is what I call "Bible Bucks." And yes, I know *all* about those five specific *crowns*. (Duh, whoever said this was supposed to be scriptural anyway?) When I give this closing illustration in my ox sermon, I dazzle my listeners with all the "stuff," i.e., rewards, they stand to redeem with the Bible Bucks they'll receive at the Judgment Seat. After all, I'm just trying to obey Colossians 3:2, *"Set your affection on **things above**, not on things on the earth."* For instance, there's got to be furniture up there that we'll need for our mansions. What about intergalactic spaceships to check out that new heaven? (Dude, *humor* me…use your imagination!)

And so, as my fancy goes, *every* believer will hear about the same opening commendation from Jesus. "Welcome home, my child. I have *good* news and *bad* news for you. The good news is that you never sinned one single time since you trusted me as your Saviour! You compiled a perfect record. The best we can compute, you earned roughly ten million Bible Bucks for your service on earth. *'Well done, thou good and faithful servant.'"*

As only God can ordain such matters, when I preached this sermon for my good friend, Mitch Serves, pastor of Bible Baptist Church in Las Vegas, Nevada, a youth worker literally gave me a handful of green bills, each sporting the words "Bible Buck, Redeemable at the Bible Baptist Church store!" (The teenagers would earn these as promotions at their activities.)

Now, when I act out this illustration with a random church member, I hand a number of Bible Bucks to the unsuspecting chump, with a warm pat on the back. However, just before he bolts away for the nearest celestial mall to blow his wad, I remind him—in the most compassionate tone—that I do have some *bad* news for him as well. "My child, while it's true that *you* never committed any sins since the day you got saved, unfortunately, your ox caused quite a bit of havoc down there." I will then hand the stupefied brother an invoice itemizing all the damages he is liable for—even though *he* never did any of it *himself* (Exodus 21:30).

My fantasy skit usually concludes something like this: "My child, I'm *so* impressed that *you* never messed up one time, but, like I said, that animal of yours, well, to tell you the truth, he was like a "wild bull in a china shop." So, on the way out, would you mind stopping by the desk over there and settling up with our treasurer, Brother Matthew? Your damages come to only eight million Bible Bucks. I'm sure you can get some neat stuff with the remaining two million. See you at the Marriage Supper. *Next….*" And just like those starry-eyed game-show winners who exit the spotlighted stage with *their* winnings only to sit down with the IRS agent behind the curtain (so the "gubmint" can take *its* cut), *we* will surely see a portion of *our* rewards go up in smoke as well (I Corinthians 3:15); primarily for not obeying Romans 6:12.

About this time, some dipwad will be heard complaining, "Well that's just not fair, I personally never tore anything up; it was my ox, *he's* the guilty party, not me!" (Yada, yada, yada…) Of course, carnal believers like this have no clue how the whole thing shakes out anyway (Proverbs 24:7). Returning to spiritual reality, the reason why we ultimately throw "our" crowns at the Lord's feet is because *He* was the one who earned them *for* us in the first place! While Philippians 2:13 says, *"**For it is God which worketh in you** both to will and to do of his good pleasure,"* Galatians 2:20 adds, *"I am crucified with Christ:*

nevertheless I live; yet not I, but Christ liveth in me: **and the life which I now live in the flesh I live by the faith of the Son of God**, *who loved me, and gave himself for me."* (Galatians 2:20) Thus, it's no big deal if an ox causes you to lose rewards you never really earned. (Duh…)

THE *REAL* TITLE OF THIS CHAPTER

I will now let my readers in on a little secret. "Strength for the Journey," though perfectly apropos, is *not* the real name for this chapter. Whenever I preach this sermon, I always wait till the very end to announce the title. Though all of *three* words and consisting of only *nine* letters, it perfectly summarizes the great theme of the message. It explains the practical reason as to *why* an Old Testament Jew could get into serious trouble because of his ox. And the same truth will apply for you and me today.

According to Exodus 21:29, the negligent party would ultimately be indicted for one reason: *"But if the ox were wont to push with his horn in time past, and it has been testified to his owner,* **and he hath not kept him in**, *but that he hath killed a man or a woman; the ox shall be stoned, and the owner also shall be put to death."* (This statement is repeated in verse thirty-six.) Therefore, to maximize the number of "Bible Bucks" that you could clear at the Judgment Seat of Christ, you only have to do one thing between now and the Rapture…*Box Your Ox!*

In closing, I will share a rather "cute," but insightful, anecdote. The incident occurred in a North Georgia church where I had preached my Exodus 21 message in the morning service. During the evening preliminaries, the pastor was taking testimonies when an older married woman rose to her feet to "share" how my message had already helped her. To paraphrase her account, she said, "My husband and I went to Walmart this afternoon to get a prescription filled. The place was busy, so we were having a long wait. Well, ole Harold (fictitious name) started getting "ugly" with the pharmacist. Finally, I turned to him and said, "Harold—*box your ox*!!"

19

The Christian's 9-1-1 Number

W E HAVE OFTEN heard preachers say that Jeremiah 33:3 is God's personal phone number. *"**Call unto me, and I will answer thee**, and shew thee great and mighty things, which thou knowest not."* While we won't have to worry about the Beast's number of 666 in Revelation 13:18 because of that *prior* "call" we'll be getting in Revelation 4:1, *"Come up hither,"* we definitely will need to acquaint ourselves with God's emergency 9-1-1 number to help us survive the *"perilous times"* that will usher in that very event (II Timothy 3:1; Titus 2:13). Thus, what you are about to read may prove to be the most practical material of this entire book, as it was written to help you weather that impending shipwreck in Acts 27.

THE LIGHTS WERE ON IN GOSHEN

The Bible says in Job 22:21, *"Acquaint now thyself with him, and be at peace."* In Philippians 2:5, Paul adds, *"Let this mind be in you, which was also in Christ Jesus."* The thought here is that the more you become "acquainted" with the Lord—particularly as to how He has always delivered His own—the less you will be tempted to panic when Satan shows up. And so, before we get to God's 9-1-1 number, a brief review of His consistent track record is in order.

When Pharaoh refused to "let God's people go," the Lord brought a series of ten plagues on his nation. The judgments were cataclysmic, beginning with the Nile River turning to blood and ending with the death of the firstborn. However, throughout this ordeal, the Jews were afforded a special sanctuary status. Moses informed Pharaoh that the frogs would be specifically *"upon **thy** people."* (Exodus 8:4) When God was preparing the flies, Moses was instructed to tell Pharaoh, *"And I will sever in that day the land of Goshen, in which my people dwell, **that no swarms of flies shall be there**; to the end thou mayest know that I am the* LORD *in the midst of the earth"* (verse 22). He then smoked all the cattle in Egypt, with one exception, of course: *"[B]ut of the cattle of the children of Israel **died not one**."* (Exodus 9:6) Likewise, when the grievous hail, mingled with fire, started wiping out man, beast, and trees alike, *"Only in the land of Goshen, **where the children of Israel were, was there no hail**"* (verse 26).

Are y'all beginning to notice a pattern here? After the locust *"covered the face of the whole earth, so that the land was **darkened**,"* the little critters devoured every green thing in Egypt (Exodus 10:15). Then, with God continuing to harden Pharaoh's heart, the ninth judgment descended over the pyramids. *"And the* LORD *said unto Moses, Stretch out thine hand toward heaven, that there may be **darkness** over the land of Egypt, even **darkness** which may be felt. And Moses stretched forth his hand toward heaven; and there was a thick **darkness** in all the land of Egypt three days. They saw not one another, neither rose any from his place for three days"* (verses 21-23).

By the way, if anyone's counting, that's *three* negative uses for the word "darkness" in two Scriptures (not to mention that earlier reference at verse fifteen). However, notice how things end at the Hebrew haven: ***"[B]ut all the children of Israel had light in their dwellings"*** (verse 23). Praise God—the lights were on in Goshen! When it comes to "keepin' a light on for ya"—I'm a-tellin' ya, neighbor—Tom Bodett ain't got *nothin'* on Jesus! And He'll also do the same for *you* in the dark days ahead!

JEHOVAH'S RACIST RANT

The politically incorrect bottom line in all of this is that, contrary to popular opinion, God does *not* look at all people the same way. You see, He's a tad *prejudiced* when it comes to His own young'uns. For instance, folks are often shocked when they eavesdrop on the Lord's upper room prayer to His Father: *"I pray for them* [the apostles]*: **I pray not for the world**, but for them which thou hast given me; for they are thine."* (John 17:9) The following "insensitive" remark that Jehovah made on the eve of the exodus speaks for itself:

> *And Moses said, Thus saith the* LORD*, About midnight will I go out into the midst of Egypt: And all the firstborn in the land of Egypt*

shall die, from the firstborn of pharaoh that sitteth upon his throne, even unto the firstborn of the maidservant that is behind the mill; and all the firstborn of beasts. And there shall be a great cry throughout all the land of Egypt, such as there was none like it, nor shall be like it anymore. ***But against any of the children of Israel shall not a dog move his tongue, against man or beast: that ye may know how that the LORD doth put a difference between the Egyptians and Israel.*** (Exodus 11:4-7)

Dude—can you believe how *racist* God is? He talks like He thinks He's the Creator of the universe or something! (See Job 42:2; Ecclesiastes 3:14; Isaiah 14:27; 45:5-12) And (as noted above), His Son doesn't seem any better either: *"But he answered and said, It is not meet to take the children's bread, and to cast it to **dogs**."* (Matthew 15:26)

A FEW CLOSE CALLS

Soon to reach my three-score-and-ten on November 27, 2022, I can testify that the Lord has protected me from many a premature run-in with the "Grim Reaper" (Ecclesiastes 7:17; Hebrews 2:14), both before and after my conversion to Jesus Christ. Thus, in the hope of encouraging some faint-hearted soul, I felt led to share a few of my own memorable "escapes" (Job 1:15-19; Acts 9:23-25; 12:5-11; 27:24; II Timothy 4:17). Remember what they say, "Truth is stranger than fiction."

To begin with, as I would later learn, my mother was not able to have any more children after my half-brother, Gregory, was born (from her first marriage). However, after several years of trying to start a new family with my dad, her doctor informed her that her womb had somehow miraculously "turned" (Psalm 71:6). I was therefore able to enter the world, on November 27, 1952—Thanksgiving Day, no less—the perfect birthday gift for a "thankful" father who was also born on 11/27 in 1919, falling on Thanksgiving as well. My first brush with reality occurred seven years later when I was in the first grade. My best friend, a happy-go-lucky Hungarian boy named Zoltan, was beaten to death in broad daylight at a deserted construction site while walking home from school. A few years later, while headed to the convent at my parish "church" to shake down a few nuns for some Halloween candy, I was mugged by a gang of juvenile delinquents.

Returning from a Boy Scout weekend campout, I met my father on a Sunday afternoon in Ned's (one of three Irish taverns where I was practically reared). For some unknown reason, as I laid my backpack down near the doorway, a man at the other end of the joint hurled a beer glass at me, missing my face by inches. My father flew off his barstool in a flash. Fortunately for the fool who threw that glass, the bartender, along with two other patrons, were able to restrain my dad. Over sixty years later I can *still* remember what one of those men said to that startled rummy as he pointed at me— "Don't you know who *that* is? That's John Grady's son!"

At age ten I woke up in the middle of the night to find my inebriated mother trying to suffocate me with my own pillow. Upon extricating myself I ran out of my tiny bedroom into the kitchen to discover that all the gas jets were turned on. Thankfully, I was able to turn them off in time, get our apartment door open, and run to my father who was working the night shift at his doorman job nearby. My mother, who was normally the greatest, had a variety of physical and chemical maladies and was also suffering severe depression over the recent loss of her own mother. (My alcoholic grandfather had beaten her with a shoe; a resultant brain bleed contributed to her death.) Trying to communicate with her through a Ouija board certainly didn't help matters. She ended her own life on March 17, 1964.

My wife often reminds me that "God looks after his dingbats." In my case, He continued doing so long before I formally belonged to Him (I Corinthians 6:20; Hebrews 1:14). During the summer of 1967, I was innocently lured to the apartment of a pedophile in Queens (no pun intended) but was shielded from harm by the unexpected (and providential) arrival of the homo's homie. Another near-miss occurred while hitchhiking in Pennsylvania. I climbed into a pink caddy with a French poodle cuddled up next to the driver (short ride...*real* short). In 2008, several lawsuits (going back to the 1960s) were launched against Joe Biden's Roman Catholic Archdiocese of Wilmington, Delaware, for—you guessed it—dudes, dressing like mothers, calling themselves "Fathers," raping the children in their charge. Three of the twenty-plus "celibate sodomites" happened to teach at Salesianum, the all-male Catholic High School that I attended between 1966-1970 (moving intermittently between Delaware and New York). On this occasion, the thing that saved my neck was the fact that none of these sickos were my own instructors. (As I recall, in the "providence of God," most of my priests hailed from the womanizing minority.)

While working for my dad at a local Manhattan candy store, an "African-American" would-be robber fired a pistol at him at point-blank range. Thankfully, it jammed. Not sure if this one qualifies, but about this same time (summer 1966), the Lord definitely spared this future preacher some serious grief in a dingy nightclub one night in Yonkers (just a few blocks from where the future serial killer, David Berkowitz, aka "The Son of Sam," was living his teenage years at the time). Having just graduated from St. Stephens *grade* school, "Yours Truly," age *fourteen*, slipped into the Ninety-Two Club to rendezvous with my eighteen-year-old Italian paisan, Vinny. The only "problem" was that the legal drinking age in New York was eighteen. (The silver sharkskin suit I wore in those days was so impressive, I rarely got carded at the door.) So, while busting some moves on the dance floor, I got "busted" —by an undercover detective. When he asked me to show him my draft card (the law at that time), I was so dumb (not to mention wasted), I replied, "Where I go to school, they don't issue our draft cards until senior year." As he started laughing (along with the crowd that had encircled us by now), I broke down and "confessed" that I was really only "seventeen," but would turn "eighteen" in two months. While I could have gotten formally arrested and detained, "thankfully," the woman who owned the dive passed her "envelope" to the officer and we walked—believe it or not, to *another* club nearby (Proverbs 23:35).

On December 31, 1968, I welcomed in the New Year by passing out stone-cold drunk in Times Square, just as the historic ball was descending from the Allied Chemical Building. Later that morning I woke up in some good Samaritan's apartment (probably a *real* NY Guardian Angel), lying on his living room floor—stuffed in a vomit-soiled plastic trash can. The Lord must have also been "keeping the light on for me" during my single year at the University of Delaware (1970-'71) when I divided my riotous living between drinking 100-proof Southern Comfort and doing various drugs, including the strong psychedelic hallucinogen, mescaline (responsible for at least one bad all-night "trip" on campus).

On March 8, 1971, I arrived at Manhattan's Penn Station to attend the epic heavyweight title fight between Joe Frazier and Muhammad Ali. I was "greeted" by a delegation of "African-Americans" intent on "relieving" me of my $75 ticket. However, four of New York's finest showed up just in the nick of time. When Madison Square Garden opened its doors several hours later, the only way I was able to make it in alive was due to my taxicab driver (a recent good ole boy transplant from down South) personally escorting me through the rampaging mobs outside, his snarling Doberman, "Satan," clearing a path like God did at the Red Sea. Glory!

Way back in the scary Cold War year of 1972, my boss and I were in Germany, sitting on a bus at Check Point Charlie, waiting to pass through the Berlin Wall into East Berlin. That cash register sale to Jill "Biden" Stevenson and her soon-to-be cheated on husband helped me win a sales contest, generating enough commission to spend a month in Europe with my employer. (Oddly enough, my second biggest deal during the promotion was for twenty electric typewriters to the Elkton Christian School of Bible Baptist Church, in Elkton, Maryland, just missing Tom Wallace's pastorate by a few months. When I assumed that the staff member negotiating the transaction was trying to "save my soul," i.e., with a faithful Gospel witness, I attempted to "save my sale" by praying a "sinner's prayer.") Well, anyway, back on the bus, an apoplectic, goose-stepping Communist guard sprang in and hauled us off the bus; my boss had been spotted holding a West Berlin newspaper. Later that week, while traveling from Vienna to Warsaw, our train made an unexpected stop in Prague. Realizing that we didn't have visas for Czechoslovakia, I tried to hide in the "water closet," but was promptly corralled by another gun-toting Commie who forced us to pay the equivalent of a full day's stay. (For what it's worth, being duly counseled by the locals, we spent much of our hotel time in Poland sweeping the rooms for "bugs," i.e., the electronic kind.)

Not long after I was saved in 1974, Satan totaled my car on a Philadelphia expressway. He must have really *hated* that vehicle, as the Holy Ghost had used it to get the Gospel to me through a fifteen-minute daily radio broadcast that literally mesmerized me as I commuted to work each morning (John 6:44). Years later, I would be blessed to discover an old hymn entitled, "I Heard it First on the Radio." (When I pastored in the Flint, Michigan, area, "General Motors country," my fanatical male church members had a difficult time "accepting" my testimony, as they couldn't imagine how God would use a *Toyota* speaker.)

My wife and I moved to Northern Indiana in August 1976 so I could attend Bible college in preparation for the ministry. At the beginning of my second year, I cut my leg while working at a local foundry (building the M60 tank) and developed swelling at the wound site, which eventually went away. But, having nearly collapsed at the guard shack on my way in to work shortly thereafter, I was taken by ambulance to an area hospital where the diagnosis was *two* pulmonary emboli—one in each lung. With her nurse's training, Linda was acutely aware of how dangerous this was. But God…!

Later that same year, after dining out at a Red Lobster restaurant in Dolton, Illinois, during the Christmas season, we were robbed at gunpoint in the parking lot by two doped-up "African-Americans." (Linda was seven months pregnant with our daughter.) So, get this—*after* the brutha with the *Mod Squad* afro *had* our wallet and pocketbook, he *continued* pointing his .357 Magnum in my face, saying, *"I don't know if I ought to do this, or not, man."* Suddenly, he saw "some*thing*" or "some*one*" (that *we* sure didn't see), and blew out of there in a New York minute, taking his "dawg" with him. (Having lost our $90 Christmas shopping money, we received an unexpected windfall of nearly $300 from concerned family and friends.) Once again, "I escaped" (along with my wife and unborn child).

Fast-forward to 1988 when I experienced another bad car wreck, while teaching at Hyles-Anderson College. This time, some drunken Iranian blew through a red light at a South Chicago intersection, plowing into a taxi that then plowed into me. The result was a risky herniated disc surgery on two of my cervical vertebrae. Supposedly one of the more painful operations as well (my surgeon practically scaring me to death during our pre-op conference the day before), I experienced *zero* discomfort and never took a single pain pill. My only post-op "problem" was a severe chest pain scare (prompting several costly middle-of-the-night emergency tests), which turned out to be nothing more than acid reflux from a pizza I had "browbeaten" Linda into smuggling into my room. (Not sure how long it took for the hospital staff to discover the discarded pizza box under my mattress after I left.)

However, two miracles resulted from this *providential* "accident" with that tanked-up Muslim (Romans 8:28). During my recovery, God opened my eyes to the KJV issue through a set of cassette tapes by Peter Ruckman (originally owned by a PBI student who just happened to be the former road manager for the Allman Brothers Band). After developing a course on the subject, I began writing *Final Authority* in January 1992.

To put it mildly—*all Hell broke loose,* sending my guardian angels into round-the-clock shifts, with plenty of overtime! With no exaggeration whatsoever, Linda and I encountered Satanic persecution for fifty-two straight weeks! (See I Thessalonians 2:18)

Though *we* both survived, my unsaved brother, Gregory, did not. While writing the book's closing chapter in December, I received an unexpected phone call from him and wound up giving him a solid Gospel witness, my first time ever in eighteen years. Two weeks later he was dead. According to the Miami Police, when he told his Cuban neighbor to lower his Salsa music the guy cussed him out, whereupon my 6' 4", 230-lb., former Sing-Sing inmate brother decided to turn it down himself—*with a shotgun blast through the hombre's front door.* A police pursuit and shootout ensued. The "official" report states that he shot himself (Matthew 26:52).

As for the second miracle, my Heavenly Father enabled me to finance the first 5,000 copies of *Final Authority* with residual funds from the cash settlement I eventually received from the insurance claim. (They sold out within sixty days, followed by the Lord's blessing of two more printings of 5,000 each within a few months; fifteen printings to date.)

Several years later, while conducting a revival meeting in San Antonio, Texas, I was sleeping in an RV on the church property when two "African-American" Hurricane Katrina refugees broke in and cleaned the place out, including my cellphone from off the night stand—*eighteen inches from my head.* Thankfully, I slept through the whole affair (Psalm 127:2). Like that line from the song, "He's in the Midst," says: "And every night as you lay down, Angels are camping all around" (Psalm 34:7). Not long after this, while riding through Johnson City, Tennessee, on an exciting Baptist history tour, things got even *more* exciting when our bus (packed with preachers) slid off the road and careened down an embankment. This time, I got away with only a partially dislocated clavicle. (On a "positive" note, they tell me we made the CBS *Evening News* with Dan Rather.)

While doing research for my third book, *How Satan Turned America Against God,* a pastor friend, Randy Gibson, and I visited the Solovetsky Islands on the White Sea in northern Russia. Encountering dense fog, our pilot hit the runway *so* hard that half of the twenty seats in the Aeroflot "puddle jumper" collapsed flat. The three holding Bro. Gibson, our Moscow University guide, and me held in place. The greater danger

I survived was when the rather "hefty" Russian stewardess ("Olga Somebody") tried to confiscate my camera after I had documented the chaotic cabin. Later that same week, we were detained at the Ukraine-Russia border by scowling Ukrainian guards with AK-74 Kalashnikov rifles. (To my "surprise," they weren't at all impressed that my paternal grandmother was born in Ukraine. Imagine that!) After our interrogator told us that our papers were "incomplete" (lacking "paper" US dollars), we paid the "surcharge" and slipped back into "Mother Russia."

More recently, in 2014, after contracting food poisoning in Jerusalem, I was diagnosed with type-two diabetes. In 2016, I was rushed to my local emergency room with an extreme blood pressure spike (over 200). Within minutes the alarm bells started clanging and the nurses started running when blood began *flowing out of my left eye.* After I was stabilized, they sent me home that same day. (Not the best decision…) The next morning, I suffered a life-threatening heart attack while eating breakfast with my grandchildren. This time my son-in-law drove me to the emergency room. Known as the "widow-maker," my left anterior descending artery (LAD) was 95% blocked. However, after receiving a single stent from a great lady cardiologist from India, I was as good as new. (During my recovery, a black, Scripture-quoting, Christian doctor from Africa appeared to come out of nowhere to play a major role in stabilizing my condition.)

In November 2019, while driving across Pennsylvania in the middle of the night, I hit a gargantuan deer with my Chrysler Town & Country minivan. (Probably had it coming for not driving a more "toxic" masculine vehicle. Laugh, folks, that's a joke!) With over 240,000 miles on the odometer, I sold it to a scrap yard that evening for a whopping $100.00. For the record, the good Lord sent in $35,000 within two weeks allowing me to purchase a new Honda Pilot. (Like Hudson Taylor used to say, "God's work, done in God's way, will never lack God's support.")

While preaching in Texas in January 2020—just *before* "the Covid" became a household expression—I got terribly sick, exhibiting *every* China Virus symptom except one. A San Antonio emergency room physician told me it was "probably" walking pneumonia. Somehow, I never had to cancel one meeting, naively preaching fifteen times, in fifteen days, in twelve churches! Then, having spoken in a total of ninety-two churches in the dreaded Covid-19 year of 2020 (including a week-long camp meeting in Dresden, Germany), I received what must have been a false positive (having shown zero symptoms) in January 2021, after which Jesus "kept the light on," allowing me to continue running the "Corona gauntlet," ministering in *another* 108 churches through 2021.

On November 18, 2021, Linda and I were guests of Pastor David Wagner and his wife Jeanine at Silver Dollar City in Branson, Missouri. We arrived early to wait in line for the opening of the play "A Christmas Carol." Suddenly, plumes of ominous black smoke rose in the sky directly in front of us. Unknown to us at the time, a grease fire had started near the theater where we were headed. The immediate danger was fourfold: most of the park's structures were made of wood; there were plenty of dry leaves swirling around in a moderate breeze; and the entire park was packed. As ashes began raining down, "the natives started getting restless." Thankfully, directions were given for an orderly evacuation and a stampede was avoided. Three buildings were consumed before local fire fighters saved the day.

Finally, on Friday evening, December 10, 2021, I closed out a three-day Christmas Jubilee for my friend, Gary Eaton, pastor of Solid Rock Baptist Church in Franklin, Kentucky. As I drove home to Maryville, Tennessee, that night, I noticed the weather acting extremely erratic. My smart phone began issuing one storm warning after another. Various sirens could be heard in the distance. Unbeknown to me at the time, twenty-two deadly tornadoes were ripping a path of devastation across six Midwest states. The next morning, I was shocked to learn that an F-5 tornado had killed nearly eighty people in Mayfield, Kentucky—just over two hours to the west of our meeting in Franklin.

THE GUARDIAN OF OUR WAY

Three of the men that God greatly used during the Philadelphia Church Age were evangelist Dwight "D. L." Moody, his famous song leader (and former IRS employee) Ira Sankey, and the bass-baritone Gospel singer who wrote much of the music Ira sang, Philip Paul "P. P." Bliss. (Mr. Sankey also penned many beautiful hymns, his most memorable being, "The Ninety and Nine.")

On Christmas Eve 1876, Moody and Sankey were traveling up the Delaware River by steamboat. With the passengers being in a festive mood, they approached the well-known Sankey for a song or two. Agreeing to do so, he prayed for the Lord's leading as to what he should do. He later said that *he* wanted to sing a Christmas hymn, but the Holy Spirit led him to choose a *shepherd's* tune instead (i.e., *"Fear not, little flock."*):

> Saviour, like a shepherd lead us,
> Much we need thy tender care.
> In thy pleasant pastures feed us,
> For our use thy folds prepare."
>
> Chorus:
> "Blessed Jesus, blessed Jesus,
> Thou hast bought us, Thine we are;
> Blessed Jesus, blessed Jesus,
> Thou hast bought us, Thine we are.

His audience was deeply moved. Suddenly, a rather rugged looking fellow stepped forward and asked Sankey if he had served in the Union Army in the recent War Between the States. When the Hoosier replied, "Yes," the stranger recoiled, then asked a second question, "Can you recall if you were doing picket duty on a particularly bright moonlit evening in 1862?" Well, now it was Ira's turn to take a breath. When he answered that he did, in fact, remember such an unnerving night, he got the shock of his life.

The man related that he had also served in the conflict, but with the Confederacy. On the night in question, he was lurking in the woods along the perimeter of the Federal camp when he saw Sankey standing guard, illuminated by the moon. "I can't possibly miss at this range," he thought to himself. So, he raised his musket and took aim, fully shrouded by the darkness. However, as he informed his now-enthralled listener, "Just as I was about to squeeze the trigger—*you* began to sing." But the Spirit-filled crooner didn't pick just any ole ditty ("She Was Bred in Old Kentucky, but She's Just a Crumb Up Here," et al.). The Lord led him to sing the *same* hymn he had just performed for his Christmas Eve audience— "Saviour Like a Shepherd Lead Us" (Romans 8:14). Given his Bible Belt roots, the semi-startled Johnny Reb decided to wait till Ira finished his hymn, *then* he'd blow his brains out. But as the future song leader for the great D. L. Moody crusades continued, obeying Ephesians 5:19, he got to that second line in the second stanza:

> We are Thine, do Thou befriend us;
> *Be the guardian of our way…*"
> Keep Thy flock, from sin defend us,
> Seek us when we go astray

As the story goes, the would-be sniper related that precious memories from his childhood began to flood his soul. His Christian mother had sung that very hymn to him on numerous occasions. Sadly, she died young, leaving her unsaved boy to face the world alone. By the time Ira finished singing, the man, having already lowered his musket, retreated back into the shadows, wiping the tears from his eyes.

Both Americans could sense the reality of the divine appointment. Deeply stirred, Mr. Sankey embraced his former enemy, the man who could have taken his life. Praise God, for as Jesus promised in Matthew 18:20, *"For where two or three are gathered together in my name, there am I in the midst of them,"* it didn't take long for the man who wrote "The Ninety and Nine" to lead that lost sheep to the Shepherd.

IT'S ALL GOOD!

Now, of course, as Romans 8:28 is still in the Book, not all believers will experience the same supernatural deliverance in their trials and tribulations. Some, like Job, are "picked out to be picked on" for the greater glory of God. As Paul told his Japhethite believers in Philippi, *"For unto you it is **given** in the behalf of Christ, not only to believe on him, but also to suffer for his sake."* (Philippians 1:29) Just *five* days after that glorious Christmas Eve riverboat reunion, another holiday drama played out; only this time, it occurred on a train. The ending would be quite different as well.

On the snowy evening of December 29, 1876, a lovely Christian couple was traveling to Chicago after visiting family in their home area of Rome, Pennsylvania. One hundred-and-sixty fellow passengers filled the eleven cars. At around 8 PM, as the Pacific Express train was puffing its way across a ravine near Ashtabula, Ohio, an eerie cracking sound was heard. Suddenly, and without warning, the 160-foot iron trestle gave way and the train plunged into the stormy abyss. Before the wooden cars hit the bottom of the watery gorge—some seventy feet below—many were already ablaze due to the jostled lamps and kerosene stoves (Daniel 6:24). By midnight, the horrible cremation was complete. One survivor, a Mr. J. E. Burchell, testified:

> Those who came from the wreck said they could see into the cars and could see the charred trunks of those who had been literally burned to death. They described them as wholly unrecognizable beyond

identification, and presenting the most ghastly scene they had ever looked on. Some of the unfortunates were burned literally to ashes, and in some cases only calcined bones were left to tell that human beings had ever been there.

Railroad officials acknowledged that nearly one hundred had perished. The man in our story miraculously survived the plunge and was able to extricate himself through a window. However, when he attempted to pull his wife through, alas, he could not, as she was caught in the twisted ironworks of the seats. Burchell wrote, "Finding that he could not save her, he stayed there with her—and died." The couple in question was Philip and Lucy Bliss; Philip, as in—Philip Paul Bliss, the prolific Baptist hymn writer.

Known as P. P. Bliss, Philip had penned the words and/or music to over three hundred sacred songs, many that we still sing today: "Let the Lower Lights Be Burning"; "The Light of the World is Jesus"; "Whosoever Will"; "Dare to Be a Daniel"; "Wonderful Words of Life"; "It is Well With My Soul"; "I Gave My Life For Thee"; "Hallelujah, What a Saviour"; "My Redeemer"; "Once For All"; "Jesus Loves Even Me"; and his two most famous, "Almost Persuaded" and "Hold The Fort." (Survivors of the *RMS Titanic* disaster reported that even passengers rowing in lifeboats sang the Bliss hymn, "Pull for the Shore.")

In His divine wisdom, the Lord had allowed His *"three-fold cord"* of Moody, Sankey, and Bliss to be *"quickly broken"* (Ecclesiastes 4:12). Given that this gifted servant of God was taken at just thirty-eight years of age, Satan must have really tried to tempt the Body of Christ with his disconcerting question, *"What purpose was this waste?"* Of course, on the other side, just imagine how much cologne the Lord gained in the exchange! Several years ago, I was privileged to join a host of Baptist preachers (led by Pastor Jeff Faggart) in singing "Hold The Fort" at the mass gravesite of the Ashtabula River Railroad Disaster.

Ironically, the very night before his death, Bliss had sung, "We're Going Home Tomorrow" (a hymn by Sophia T. Griswold, for which he had composed the music). While the Blisses' bodies were never identified, Philip's trunk was miraculously discovered intact. Inside, a treasure was preserved—the words to a song he had just completed. James McGranaham set the lyrics to music, bequeathing God's Church a fitting memorial to P. P. Bliss:

I will sing of my redeemer,
And His wondrous love to me;
On the cruel cross He suffered,
From the curse to set me free.

Chorus:
Sing, oh sing, of my Redeemer.
With His blood, He purchased me.
On the cross, He sealed my pardon,
Paid the debt, and made me free.

However, there was another hymn found in that suitcase, "He Knows," written by Mary Brainard; Bliss had just set it to music. Because of the song's obvious relevance to the tragedy, it was sung at the close of the couple's funeral, January 7, 1877. As this beautiful number is rarely heard today, it's as if the Holy Ghost retired it in honor of Philip and Lucy. In our contemporary vernacular, the lyrics would be captured by the phrase— "It's all good."

I know not what awaits me,
God kindly veils my eyes,
And o'er each step of my onward way
He makes new scenes to rise;
And every joy He sends me
Comes a sweet and glad surprise.

Chorus:
Where He may lead I'll follow,
My trust in Him repose;
And every hour in perfect peace,
I'll sing, "He knows, He knows";
And every hour in perfect peace,
I'll sing, "He knows, He knows.

EZEKIEL 9:1-11

Thus, though God is certainly able to *"save [us] to the uttermost"* (from our temporal dangers), He can just as easily will that we become *"pressed out of measure,"* even to the point of death (John 16:2; II Corinthians 1:8; Hebrews 7:25). Thinking "positive" therefore, to improve the *possibility* of securing divine deliverance from circumstantial threats (the *"perilous times"* unfolding around you), the great secret is to simply do what Rahab and *her* family did—heed your instructions!

While the Bible presents clear *commands* to be *obeyed*, it also contains spiritual *principles* to be *applied*. Some of these practical truths may even be lifted from a different dispensation, for *"**All scripture** is given by inspiration of God, and **is profitable** for doctrine, for reproof, for correction, **for instruction in righteousness**."* (II Timothy 3:16) In my opinion, one of the best-kept survival secrets in the AV 1611 is tucked away in Ezekiel 9:1-11. You might call it God's 9-1-1 number.

This semi-nebulous prophecy will probably unfold in the Great Tribulation (though it may have happened during the Babylonian invasion). According to the opening two verses of Ezekiel 9, Jehovah summons six *"men"*—some really bad dudes who are obviously angels—*"even every man with his **destroying** weapon in his hand."* After making a second reference to their *"**slaughter** weapons"* (the deadly Uzi machine gun being a major Israeli export), one of the Heavenly hitmen is singled out as *"clothed with linen with a **writer's inkhorn** by his side"* (verse 2), i.e., "The pen is mightier than the sword." The Lord orders him to, *"Go through the midst of the city, through the midst of Jerusalem, and **set a mark upon the foreheads of the men that sigh and that cry for all the abominations that be done in the midst thereof**"* (verse 4).

He then continues with the all-important qualifier: *"And to the others he said in mine hearing, Go ye after him through the city, and smite: let not your eye spare, neither have you pity: Slay utterly old and young, both maids, and little children, and women: **but come not near any man upon whom is the mark**; and begin at my sanctuary"* (verses 5-6). Do y'all recall that "signet" business from chapter sixteen, "God's Preeminent Stone"? Could the "seal" in Ezekiel 9 be the same as in Exodus 28:36? *"And thou shalt make a plate of pure gold, and grave upon it, like the engravings of a signet, HOLINESS TO THE LORD."* (See also: II Timothy 2:19)

There is a similar situation in Revelation 7:3 and 9:4. Whereas the random number of Jews in Ezekiel 9:4 is distinguished by *"a **mark upon** their foreheads,"* the 144,000 male virgins are protected by *"the **seal** of God **in** their foreheads."* Both are in "marked" contrast to the infamous "Mark of the Beast" in Revelation 13:16-18. (So now you know where the *Antichrist* got the inspiration for *his* generic stamp.)

Also, notice how that phrase *"and **begin at my sanctuary**"* parallels the great cross-reference in I Peter 4:17, *"For the time is come that **judgment must begin at the house of God**: and if it first begin at us, what shall the end be of them that obey not the gospel of God?"* This truth is also contained in Psalm 9:17, *"The wicked shall be turned into hell, **and all the nations that forget God**."* As previously noted, Isaac Watts put this theme to music in the second stanza of "We're Marching to Zion" — "Let those refuse to sing *who never knew our God*." Mark it down, neighbor—as y'all can't return from a place where you've never been—the first billion body bags in the Tribulation period will *not* be coming from China, India, Russia, Iran, or North Korea; they'll be coming from the United States, Great Britain, Canada, Australia, and New Zealand—nations that, once upon a time, *knew* the true God of the AV 1611—then *dumped* Him.

As Jehovah's massacre begins (reminiscent of Joshua's horrific genocide in Canaan), Ezekiel is literally blown away: *"And it came to pass, while they were slaying them, and I was left, **that I fell upon my face**, and **cried** and said, **Ah Lord GOD!** wilt thou destroy all the residue of Israel in thy pouring out of thy fury upon Jerusalem?"* Whereupon God answers His prophet: *"The iniquity of the house of Israel and Judah* [and the United States of America] *is exceeding great* [human trafficking], *and the land is full of blood* [65,000,000 abortions], *and the city full of perverseness* [LGBTQ+]*: for they say, The LORD hath forsaken the earth, and the LORD seeth not. And as for me also, mine eye shall not spare, neither will I have pity, but I will recompense their way upon their head"* (verses 8-10). Ezekiel then completes his coverage at the conspicuous Scripture address of—9:11, *"And, behold, the man clothed with linen, which had the inkhorn by his side, reported the matter, saying, I have done as thou hast commanded me."*

Thus ends one of the strangest chapters in the Holy Bible. But don't miss the all-important bottom line. The Holy Spirit has carefully delineated the main criteria for survival in the Tribulation period— *sighing* and *crying* for the abominations in Jerusalem. Notice in verse eight how even Ezekiel was quick to heed the divine mandate (only in reverse order; crying, *then* sighing).

Now, while Jehovah is under no *obligation* to extend this Tribulation arrangement to Church Age saints, He *might* be so inclined should we exhibit a *similar* burden for the abominations of our *own* country. To cite

Zephaniah 2:3, *"[I]t may be ye shall be hid in the day of the LORD's anger."* We, therefore, observe that two different types of tears can serve two different ends: *cologne* for *God* and *deliverance* for *us*. Again, though clearly not a *doctrinal* promise for the Body of Christ, the *devotional* principle *could* save *your* life (as well as the lives of your loved ones) amidst the approaching *"perilous times"* predicted in II Timothy 3:1. As Ezekiel 9:6 clearly reveals that God *will* spare folks *after* the Rapture for sighing and crying over sin—considering His assurance in Malachi 3:6, *"For I am the LORD, I change not"* —why *couldn't* He replicate this way of escape *before* the Rapture as well. (As "The Donald" was famous for saying, "What do you have to lose?")

This theme of broken-heartedness over sin is a constant throughout Scripture. For instance, the "man after God's own heart" declared, ***"Horror hath taken hold upon me** because of the wicked that forsake thy law"* and ***"Rivers of waters run down mine eyes**, because they keep not thy law."* (Psalm 119:53; 136) With reference to the interracial marriages between the Jews and the heathen, Ezra wrote, *"And when I heard this thing, I rent my garment and my mantle, and **plucked off the hair of my head and of my beard**, and sat down astonied."* (Ezra 9:3) (Conversely, according to Nehemiah 13:25, Ezra's co-laborer got so "tore up," he plucked the hair off the *perpetrators* instead.) Wicked ole King Ahab himself found mercy, I Kings 21:27 recording that *"he rent his clothes, and put sackcloth upon his flesh, and fasted, and lay in sackcloth, and **went softly**."* In fact, during the mighty revival at Nineveh, even the *beasts* got a reprieve when their humans covered them in obedience to Jonah's ultimatum to *"be **covered with sackcloth**, and **cry mightily** unto the Lord."* (Jonah 3:8)

With Isaiah 53:3 describing the Lord as *"a man of **sorrows**, and acquainted with **grief**,"* Luke 19:41 recorded His reaction before Jerusalem, *"And when he was come near, **he beheld the city, and wept over it**."* In the Sermon on the Mount, Jesus taught, *"Blessed are they that **mourn**: for they shall be comforted."* (Matthew 5:4) During Paul's labors in the land of Japheth, Acts 17:16 states, *"Now while Paul waited for them at Athens, **his spirit was stirred in him**, when he saw the city wholly given to idolatry."* The Apostle would later write to the Church at nearby Corinth that *"**godly sorrow** worketh repentance to salvation."* (II Corinthians 7:10)

Of course, Jeremiah—aka the "Weeping Prophet" and author of the book of *Lamentations*—represents the quintessential model for human tears working in tandem with divine deliverance. Having written, *"Oh that my head were waters, and mine eyes a fountain of tears, **that I might weep day and night** for the slain of the daughter of my people"* (Jeremiah 9:1), when Jerusalem fell to the Babylonians in 586 BC, Jeremiah was released from his dungeon and shown great kindness, the king himself issuing an edict allowing him to choose the place of his residence.

*Now Nebuchadrezzar king of Babylon gave charge concerning Jeremiah to Nebuzar-adan the captain of the guard, saying, **Take him, and look well to him, and do him no harm**; but do unto him even as he shall say unto thee. So Nebuzar-adan...sent...and took Jeremiah out of the court of the prison, and committed him unto Gedaliah...that he should carry him home: so he dwelt among the people.* (Jeremiah 39:11-14)

King Solomon wrote in Ecclesiastes 7:3, *"**Sorrow is better than laughter**: for by the sadness of the countenance the heart is made better."* However—if you plan on dialing God's 9-1-1 number in the coming crisis, allow me to clarify one critical caveat: We're not talking about shedding crocodile tears over a drop in your property value or your looted 401K; it's more like weeping over those poor defenseless infants being eviscerated in their mothers' wombs (Jeremiah 20:17). The ongoing Communist coup d'état of our original God-ordained government—designed (according to I Timothy 2:1-4) for the propagation of the Gospel, both home and abroad—would also qualify for a display of godly sorrow. Thus, Solomon also wrote, *"When the righteous are in authority, the people rejoice: **but when the wicked beareth rule, the people mourn**."* (Proverbs 29:2)

On the Wednesday evening when "El Cid" was illegally inaugurated (January 20, 2021), I was preaching at the Charity Baptist Church in Amarillo, Texas. Mere moments into my opening remarks, I tore my suit jacket to shreds. Then my shirt and tie suffered the same fate. As the congregation looked on in disbelief (a solid church where I have preached for over twenty years), I took a bag of dirt (previously hidden in the pulpit) and poured it on my head. You say, "Dr. Grady—why in the *world* would you do such a bizarre thing, especially behind the sacred desk?" My answer is simple: I was mourning, as per Proverbs 29:2.

(For the record, I did this on one other occasion, in my own pulpit in Swartz Creek, Michigan, on the Sunday morning following the Supreme Court decision legalizing same-sex marriage on June 26, 2015.)

And so, my dear friend, *if* an angel was passing out those same marks in the closing chaos of the Laodicean Church Age—would *you* receive one? How many tears have you been shedding lately over America's sins? Have you been able to influence your loved ones to do the same? Would *they* get a mark? You'd better think long and hard about these questions. Should you require a little "inspiration," I will close this chapter with a pair of stories that are almost too hard to believe.

"YOU'RE KILLIN' ME, SMALLS!"

As the coming of the Lord draws nigh, the intensifying insanity within the *professing* Body of Christ is growing beyond the pale. At the time of this writing, a gun-barrel-straight, KJV-Only pastor, with a wife and five children, for whom I preached in 2021—is shacked up with a 22-year-old sodomite! With each new over-the-top revelation, I am reminded of that iconic pop culture one-liner from the 1993 baseball movie, *The Sandlot*, when an exasperated Ham Porter exclaims to the naive Scotty Smalls, "You're killin' me, Smalls!"

For instance, while holding a meeting in 2021 for my pastor friend, Mark Velder in Independence, Missouri, I heard one of the *craziest* stories in my entire forty-eight years in the ministry. The pastor of another KJV-Only, soul-winning, independent Baptist Church began a sordid, decade-long affair with one of his own church members, who also happened to be the wife of his best friend and confidant. The 51-year-old preacher's name was—David *Love*. (Can't make this stuff up folks!) Having dreamed up an insane life insurance scam, the wife, Teresa Stone, slipped her former Marine hubby's gun to her hitman pastor/lover who promptly murdered "Brother Randy" in his own office on March 31, 2010.

But you've not heard anything yet, neighbor. The cold-blooded killer then delivered the touching eulogy at the funeral ten days later! Standing before the "grieving widow," hundreds of visitors, and his own sorrowful flock, the "man of God" waxed eloquent: "We weep, not just because of the separation of our loved one, but because of the questions that death brings. Questions like, '*Why*? *Why* him? *Why* now?'" Of course, "Brother Love's Traveling Salvation Show" came to a screeching halt with the pair being caught in their lies, convicted, and jailed. I was grateful to my host for introducing me to the replacement pastor who had stabilized Dave's disoriented congregation (having met him while he was out preaching on the street). He even graciously assured me that he had enjoyed reading several of my books.

For what it's worth, the same day I learned about this twisted travesty, I visited the tiny Hill Park Cemetery in Independence and gazed upon the grave of the famous outlaw, Alexander Franklyn James, better known as Frank James (the older brother of fellow outlaw Jesse James, founder of the legendary James-Younger Gang). Between the years 1868 and 1876, Frank participated in at least four robberies that resulted in the deaths of bank employees or citizens (including the disastrous Northfield, Minnesota, raid on September 7, 1876). Somehow, I cannot conceive of either Frank or Jesse, Billy the Kid—or even Captain Jack Sparrow— sinking to the level of that former IFB pastor. But wait till you hear the next story (particularly, it's bizarre relevance to God's 9-1-1 number).

"THE SINISTER MINISTER"

During my five years as a student at Hyles-Anderson College (1976-81), one faculty member remained in a class by himself. Joe Combs was, without a doubt, the most popular teacher in the school. (What we didn't know at the time was that much of his lecture material was plagiarized.) *He was also the most outspoken critic of the King James Bible on campus.* For instance, I distinctly recall him challenging the italicized words in Psalm 14:1, telling us that the correct reading—after deleting *"there is"* —should be, "The fool has said in his heart, 'NO, God.'"

As the Lord ordered things, I eventually became his main student assistant, doing a myriad of things, such as grading test papers; washing his car; charging his airline tickets on my American Express card; even grocery shopping for his wife, Evangeline. (I can still remember two of their favorite items, Bugles and Mr. Pibb.) When I later became a HAC faculty member myself (1986), Combs was just leaving. In our parting conversation, he asked me what I planned to do about "Hyles' nutty new view on the King James Bible issue." (Dr. Hyles took his KJV-Only stand in April 1984.) After leaving the college, Joe eventually ended up in Bristol, Tennessee, pastoring a small church. By then their family had grown to five children, four biological and one adopted.

On March 24, 2000, the Fundamentalist world was rocked as "Brother" Combs and his wife were sentenced to 179 years behind bars for the unconscionable crime of torturing—for nearly two decades—their adopted daughter Esther (today living under a different name). My favorite "Bible" teacher received a one hundred-fourteen-year sentence for a litany of offenses, including aggravated kidnapping; aggravated assault; and *seven* counts of aggravated rape. His "helpmeet" and co-conspirator got off lightly, receiving "only" sixty-five years for aggravated kidnapping and aggravated child abuse. The medical record confirmed that *layers* of scar tissue (scars upon scars) appeared over most of the victim's body, revealing over *four hundred* from burns and cuts! (A germane example of another negative word ending in the letter "x" would be the noun "cicatrix," defined as "the scar of a healed wound.")

According to official court transcripts, every imaginable thing was done to this poor girl, short of death (mirroring that Draconian torture trailer in the Netherlands): her skin was ripped open with pliers and sewn back together with darning needles; she was burned with scalding water; hung by her neck until unconscious; thrown down stairs while strapped in a high chair; beaten with ball bats and hoses; her teeth were knocked out and her bones were broken. While told by her "mother" that her scars were the "Mark of the Beast," her pastor-father allegedly told her, "David had concubines, too." (How ironic, having named her after a queen in the Bible.)

The jury was out for all of three hours. Needless to say, this surreal blockbuster created a media circus for several years with Combs billed as the "Sinister Minister" on such programs as ABC's *Prime Time* and *20/20*. For the record, I immediately visited the pair (in adjacent sections of the Sullivan County Jail), where they both "assured" me of their complete innocence, etc. I didn't know what to believe. After all, in addition to having served as the closet pedophile's main college assistant, when the Combses brought five-month-old Esther home from the adoption agency, my wife and I purchased a beautiful baby dress for her. Good night, his creepy signature even defiles my ordination certificate! And now *this* shocking turn of events? Like I said— "You're killin' me, Smalls!"

Joe Combs died behind bars in 2015 at the age of 67. Given his animus for the AV 1611, his ignominious end was at least consistent with his favorite classroom saying (accompanying his picture in any HAC yearbook during his tenure)— "What *you* do with the Bible will determine what *God* does with you!" (In his case, it was more like, "...what God does *to* you.") By now, many of my readers must be wondering what this grotesque story has to do with "God's 9-1-1 Number." The "Sinister Minister" certainly could not have cared less about sighing and crying over America's sins as he was obviously obsessed with his own, torturing his adopted daughter over eighteen years, for one.

Well, be that as it may, way back in 1979 I took a Bible class at HAC on the book of Ezekiel. Take a wild guess *who* my professor was. It was then and there that I learned the great truth of Ezekiel 9:1-11. And to this day—over forty years later—I have *yet* to hear (or read) anyone else repeat this valuable, life-saving principle. So, if you were helped by this material, you have a monster to thank. How ironic! I'm sure when "Brother Love" and the "Sinister Minister" started out in the Lord's work, prison jumpsuits never entered their minds. Which brings me back to my original question: *If* an angel was passing out those same marks today—would he give one to *you*?

"Till the Storm Passes By"

In the dark of the midnight have I oft hid my face,
While the storm howls above me, and there's no hiding place
'Mid the crash of the thunder, Precious Lord, hear my cry
Keep me safe till the storm passes by

Chorus:
Till the storm passes over, till the thunder sounds no more
Till the clouds roll forever from the sky
Hold me fast, let me stand, in the hollow of Thy hand
Keep me safe, till the storm passes by

Many times Satan whispered, "There is no need to try
For there's no end of sorrow, there's no hope by and by"
But I know Thou art with me, and tomorrow I'll rise
Where the storms never *darken* the skies

When the long night has ended and the storms come no more
Let me stand in Thy presence on the bright peaceful shore
In that land where the tempest, never comes, Lord, may I
Dwell with Thee when the storm passes by

20

The Closing Illustration

THE "DEEP TRUTH" that you are about to discover in this chapter constitutes the ultimate spiritual reality for the Philadelphia remnant maneuvering through the "shallow waters" of Acts 27:28. The main reason this truth is *so* deep, is because it is totally unique to the Laodicean Church Age. As we are readying to abandon ship at II Timothy 3:1, we'll not even be able to encourage ourselves with that Bliss hymn, "Pull for the Shore" —for we won't have a life boat to pull from (Acts 27:44).

This content is also distinct for another reason. Like the little-known salvation concept in Ezekiel 9:1-11, it has fallen through the cracks in our Independent Baptist churches as well. Saved for nearly half-a-century, I've *yet* to hear a single sermon explaining this concept. Whereas the last chapter dealt with how to *survive* what's coming, the present one will explain *why* it's coming.

"BECAUSE...HE GOD!"

As previously mentioned, I received a providential "leg-up" in my ministry preparation by visiting (and preaching in) numerous black churches in the Gary, Indiana-Chicagoland area (1976-81). I rarely heard a sermon that did not stimulate my soul. (And the tradition continues forty-plus years later as the "racist" Dr. Bill Grady preached for three different black congregations during the one-year writing of this "racist" book.)

One of the earliest black Baptist pastors I recall hearing was a Chicago minister who left a lasting impression on me to this day. Not only was his preaching style unique, but his appearance was as well. An older gentleman with white hair, he stood all of 4' 11" tall; throw in a long purple robe and you're starting to get the picture. As he stepped out onto the dais, my first impression was of the eighth-century Frankish king, "Pepin the Short." (Thought to have been about the same size, Pepin was rumored to drag a clanking, seven-foot sword from his belt.)

I recall this man of God bringing two outstanding sermons in the Bible conference that I attended. The first was titled, "Watch Dem Woims," a message about the coming grave (based on Job 19:26 and Hebrews 9:27). However, it was his second one that really blew this young "preacher-boy" away! The key to his approach on that occasion was two-fold: first, the sermon was very short; second, the introduction took up about ninety-nine percent of the elapsed time. (Can I get a witness?)

He began by saying, with the utmost drama, "This evening…I'm going to answer the paramount question— 'Why?'" He then proceeded to recite a *long* list of related, rhetorical queries dealing with the Lord: i.e., "*Why* He deserves your utmost devotion"; "*Why* He is worthy"; "*Why* you should love Him supremely"; "*Why* He will never desert you"; "*Why* you may always depend on Him," etc., etc. The laundry list went *on* and *on* and *on*. (*Believe* me, neighbor, you *had* to be there!) And all the time he continued rattling off these reasons, he was prancing back and forth across the length of the platform, his long purple robe flowing behind him. And, most importantly, at every "Why" he would stop on a dime, pivot, and then just *stare* at the riveted congregation. Dr. R. G. Lee he was not, but brother—I ain't *never* forgotten that night!

However, it was his one-percent, *coup de grâce* finale that really brought the house down. After roughly fifteen minutes, with everyone (and I mean *everyone*) sitting on the edge of their seats, the "Rev" reached his last "Why." Immediately after that, he leaned slightly forward to give the long-awaited climactic answer to those twenty-plus questions: He finally said, and I quote— "Because…He *God!*" Before we knew what had happened, the preacher closed his Bible (though come to think of it, I'm not even sure that he ever opened it), tucked it under his arm, did a 180° half-spin, and then promptly "left the building" (like it was an Elvis concert).

The direction of this chapter will follow the same format as that preacher's "sermon." The introduction will comprise the great majority of the material. Then, with the necessary foundation laid, the Holy Ghost will supply the knockout punch. Enjoy!

HEAVENLY HOMILETICS

Included in any standard Bible college curriculum will be a course titled *homiletics*, defined as "the art of preaching or writing sermons." One of the key features of any effective sermon (or book) is the "closing illustration." For instance, with reference to R. G. Lee, his signature message, "Pay Day Someday," ends with Toni Jo (one of his former church members) *frying in the electric chair*. (In fact, the details were so gruesome, the entire account has been deleted in most modern copies of the sermon.) This is why that black pastor's sermon was so effective; the main emphasis came at the conclusion.

However, what might surprise you is that this homiletical principle stems from God Himself. Remember, Matthew 4:17 says, *"From that time Jesus began to **preach**, and to say, Repent: for the kingdom of heaven is at hand."* The main way to discern the Lord employing this technique is through another related discipline, *hermeneutics*, defined as "the branch of knowledge that deals with interpretation, especially of the Bible or literary texts." From a Bible believer's perspective, the key hermeneutical approach itself is further known as *dispensationalism.*

Shortly after getting saved in 1974 at the historic Marcus Hook Baptist Church in Lynwood, Pennsylvania (Clarence Larkin's home church), I enrolled in Philadelphia College of the Bible (co-founded by C. I. Scofield as Philadelphia Bible College). In 1976, the Dean of PCB, Dr. Clarence Mason, published a book titled *Dispensationalism Made Simple.* A portion of his cogent definition for "dispensation" follows:

> The word dispensation means literally a stewardship or administration or economy. Therefore, in its biblical usage, a dispensation is a divinely established stewardship of a particular Revelation of God's mind and will which is instituted in the first instance with a new age, and which brings added responsibility to the whole race of men or that portion of the race to whom the revelation is particularly given by God.

After finishing my Sunday morning sermon while conducting a KJV seminar in a Michigan church, I was accosted in the doorway by a fifteen-year-old, snot-nose visitor who wanted to debate me over the "evils" of dispensationalism, etc. (Isaiah 3:5, 12). As his pro-Steven Anderson parents looked on with pride, I finally asked the persistent (pain-in-thederriere) stripling, "What part of 'get lost' don't you understand?" The reason why these airheads are taught to hate dispensationalism (the same way the majority of "normal" Independent Fundamental Baptists do) is because the central tenet of this theological discipline is maintaining a strong distinction between Israel and the Church. Both "IFBs" (Old and New) blindly follow the Catholic-Protestant position of Covenant Theology, which in turn generates the heresy of *Supersessionism*, more commonly known as Replacement Theology (the Church replaced Israel).

Now, if "dispensationalism" *is* a heresy, someone should have given the Holy Ghost a "heads-up," for He "ignorantly" inserted the "blasphemous" word into the New Testament—four separate times (I Corinthians 9:17; Ephesians 1:10; 3:1-3 and Colossians 1:24-29). The *Webster's 1828 English Dictionary* defines "dispensation" as: "A period of time during which God deals with the human race in a particular way…a general state or ordering of things: a system of revealed commands and promises regulating human affairs…Something dispensed or distributed."

Essentially, dispensationalism is the Bible method of outlining God's expanding interaction with His creation—from the Garden of Eden to the River of Life. If there were no significant speed bumps along the way, Jehovah would *still* be executing us for "gathering sticks" (cooking) or for traveling over 2,000 cubits from 6:00 PM Friday to 6:00 PM Saturday (Numbers 15:32-36; Exodus 16:29; Acts 1:12). Dispensationalism is the engine that drives the Pauline injunction of *"rightly dividing the word of truth"* into its three-fold "division" of *"Jews…Gentiles…* [and] *the church of God."* (II Timothy 2:15; I Corinthians 10:32)

Most Bible teachers have traditionally divided the seven thousand years of human history (including the Millennial Kingdom) into seven dispensations. (Some, like my friend, Pastor Corey McCaw, count the Tribulation as a separate dispensation.) It is when we view how each period *ends* that the Lord's homiletical use of a "closing illustration" is manifested. (And let me give ya a heads-up, neighbor, *every* dispensation ends in a colossal failure.)

MYSTERY SOLVED

Once, while preaching for a friend of mine in South Carolina, the pastor told me the following story. His church men conducted regular meetings at the local jail. The facility would occasionally bring in various sports celebrities as a promotion. One evening, as the pastor and some of his workers were entering the place, out walked heavyweight boxer Marvis Frazier (son of the legendary former champion, Joe Frazier). My friend told me that he was dumbfounded by how unusually flat Frazier's nose appeared. (During his bitter public relations war with "Smokin' Joe," Muhammad Ali was often quoted as ridiculing his opponent for having a "flat nose and big ears, like a gorilla.") While any boxer can get a flat nose from his particular career choice (I mean, who hasn't heard the expression, "I'm gonna flatten your nose" or, "I'm gonna beat the snot out of you," etc.?), yet in Marvin's case, there was an added explanation for this mystery, and, believe it or not (as I went on to enlighten the pastor)—one that perfectly illustrates the greatest truth as to *why* all dispensations end in failure.

On November 25, 1983—with "all" of ten professional fights under his belt—Marvis entered the ring at the Caesars Palace Sports Pavilion with the undefeated, World Boxing Council heavy-weight champion, Larry Holmes, aka "The Easton Assassin" (*Big* mistake…). The massacre lasted less than three minutes. The insightful part of the mismatch occurred after Marvis was sent sprawling to the canvas at the two-minute, twenty-second mark. Holmes can then be seen repeatedly hand gesturing to Frazier's corner to throw in the towel. While Marvis' father-manager refused to concede, referee Mills Lane finally stopped the bout—after Holmes landed *nineteen* consecutive punches, the last sending his opponent's mouthpiece flying out of the ring. So, guess where most of those punches landed? (Three years later, "Iron Mike" Tyson would further reconfigure Marv's nasal cartilages by knocking him out in thirty seconds *flat*.)

The spiritual application from this pugilist illustration is that Marvis, and especially his stubborn father, represent the human race, with Holmes a picture of God. While getting *their* noses flattened—*dispensation* after *dispensation*—unsaved men have adamantly refused to throw *their* towel in, thus forcing the Lord to *continue* pummeling the snot out of them! Therefore, the main reason why *every* dispensation ends in failure is because man simply will *not* acknowledge God's appraisal of him: *"[M]an at his best state is altogether vanity."* (Psalm 39:5) Paul adds in Romans 3:10-12, *"As it is written, There is **none** righteous, no, not one: There is **none** that understandeth, there is **none** that seeketh after God.*

*They are all gone out of the way, they are together become unprofitable; there is **none** that doeth good, no, not one."* As a relevant, personal aside to illustrate the depravity of man, after that good-natured cabbie helped me get into the Garden to witness Marvis's Pop whoop Ali, he was so distracted—keeping Satan from biting someone's buttocks—he forgot to collect the fare and started to leave. Having initially let him go, thinking, "What a dope, etc.," my conscience (even as a lost man) smote me, and I called him back, paid the money, and even gave him a tip, bless God!

SEVEN CLOSING ILLUSTRATIONS

To begin, the first dispensation—known as *Innocence*—opens with "innocent" man in a perfect environment, with only one command to keep. The period ends with Adam and Eve's fall, followed by their expulsion from the defiled Garden of Eden (Genesis 2:17; 3:23-24).

The second dispensation, *Conscience*, begins with God providing our first parents with a *temporary* restoration through a blood sacrifice, capped by His promise of a coming Redeemer with *permanent* potency (Genesis 3:15, 21; Hebrews 10:4). With their newly acquired *"knowledge of good and evil,"* the fledging human race "evolves" to the world's first *murder*, followed by women copulating with angels (Genesis 3:7; 4:8; 6:1-4). The overall assessment came to be, *"every imagination of the thoughts of his heart was only evil continually."* (Genesis 6:5) The Lord's closing illustration on this frightening occasion was a worldwide deluge (Genesis 7:21-23)!

The third dispensation, *Government,* starts with God giving man the desire of his heart; i.e., the ability to govern his own affairs. The Biblical sanction for capital punishment follows in Genesis 9:6, *"Whoso sheddeth man's blood, by man shall his blood be shed."* (By now you should be able to envision the Lord—*fist in glove*—signaling recalcitrant humanity's corner to throw in the towel.) The period ends with the colossal Tower of Babel fiasco (Genesis 11:8-9).

The fourth dispensation, *Promise,* begins with Jehovah's double pledge to call out from among the nations a chosen people for Himself, *and* to give them their own land (Genesis 15:18-21). The descendants of Abraham (through Isaac and Jacob) had but to abide on their own turf to inherit every blessing. The period ends with them "slaving away" in a brick factory in Egypt. (No towel…)

The fifth dispensation, *Law*, begins with Moses delivering the Jews from bondage, then forging them into a nation atop Mount Sinai. After receiving and reviewing God's proposed covenant (in writing), they hastily affirm, *"**All** that the LORD hath spoken **we will do**."* (Exodus 19:5-8) This time, the dispensation would end with a double disaster: the destruction of Jerusalem, including Solomon's Temple in 586 BC, followed by the seventy-year Babylonian captivity, then the Holy City's renewed devastation and razing of the Herodian Temple in 70 AD, followed by the worldwide Diaspora of Jewry. (*Still* no towels…)

The sixth dispensation, *Grace,* is clearly seen by the doctrinal waymark at John 1:17, *"For the **law** was given by **Moses**, but **grace** and truth came by **Jesus Christ**."* Luke 16:16 is another: *"The law and the prophets were **until John**: since that time the kingdom of God is preached, and every man presseth into it."* Better known as the Church Age, this epoch begins with the arrival of Jesus Christ and his subsequent rejection by Israel, *twice*, followed by Paul's specialized ministry to the Gentiles (John 1:12; Acts 11:18; 14:27; 28:28). The wild and wooly closing illustration of *this* dispensation (the one you and I belong to) is just around the corner; and let me tell ya—there ain't a *towel* in sight (Matthew 24:37; Luke 18:8; II Thessalonians 2:3; II Timothy 3:1-13; 4:1-4)!

The seventh dispensation, *Kingdom*, will follow the abbreviated dispensation of the seven-year Tribulation period known as *"the time of Jacob's trouble."* (Jeremiah 30:7) This era opens with the glorious Second Advent, the Battle of Armageddon, the rescue of the Jewish remnant, the Judgment of the Nations, the binding of Satan, *and* the dawn of the Millennial Age (Matthew 24:27; Revelation 16:16; Zechariah 12:10; Matthew 25:31-46; Revelation 20:2-3). However, by the close of this unprecedented time of blessing, man is *still* not willing to "fess up" as to what he is, the evidence being his march on Jerusalem with the insane goal of *killing* God Almighty! And so, the "referee" is *finally* forced to step in and stop the 7,000-year beatdown with the mother of all closing illustrations! *"And they went up on the breadth of the earth, and compassed the camp of the saints about, and the beloved city: **and fire came down from God out of heaven, and devoured them**."* (Revelation 20:9)

THE SEVEN CHURCH AGES

The closing illustration for the *sixth* dispensation, *Grace*, is unique in that it also serves as the closing illustration for the seven Church Ages (as laid out in Revelation chapters two and three). As these periods have already been addressed in this book, I will just review them briefly here. They constitute the "Seven Golden Candlesticks" of Revelation 1:12-13. (Remember, the dates and definitions are not dogmatic but flexible and can vary depending on perspective with some overlapping of the periods being quite natural, as well.)

- **Ephesus** (AD 33-100), meaning "desirable one," portrays the Church of the Apostolic Age, ending with the death of John near the close of the first century (Revelation 2:1-7). The Church at Ephesus was a hard-working, highly separated body that *hated* the things that Jesus *hates*, namely, *"the deeds of the Nicolaitanes"* (clergy-laity distinction; Greek-teaching professors and pastors lording over beholden ministerial students and church members). However, by the time Revelation was completed, a spirit of complacency had settled into the Church, resulting in the Lord's rebuke, *"thou hast left thy first love,"* and subsequent command to *"repent and do the first works."*

- **Smyrna** (65-313), meaning "myrrh" (an aromatic gum resin used for embalming the dead), is the primarily negative age, characterized by imperial Roman persecution (Revelation 2:8-11). It begins with the martyrdoms of Paul and Peter (II Timothy 4:6; II Peter 1:14) and ends with the Edict of Milan establishing toleration for Christianity within the Empire. As John forecast that the Church would *"have tribulation ten days," Foxe's Book of Martyrs* highlights ten imperial persecutions (eight regional and two empire-wide).

- **Pergamos** (313-500), meaning "marriage and elevation," features the birth of the so-called "Church-State" relationship (Revelation 2:12-17). The Satanic catalyst for this unholy aberration (sidestepped by nearly all TR and pseudo-KJV-Only "Bible" colleges), was the coronation of Constantine "The Great," Rome's first *professed* "Christian" Emperor (Acts 20:29-30). As with the stereotypical villain, Snidely Whiplash, the price for this vaunted "elevation" of Christ's Bride—up and out of the Catacombs to a new and glorious persecution-free status— would be her "marriage" to good ole Emperor Constantine himself

("Nice knowing you, Jesus…"). Meanwhile, the godly ancient Baptist remnant that spurned Satan's *"Con*-man," choosing rather to remain the true, underground Church, was prefigured by Antipas, the Lord's *"faithful martyr."*

• **Thyatira** (500-1500), meaning "continual sacrifice," represents a dual reference to the blasphemous Roman Mass, with its doctrine of transubstantiation (cannibalism and clinical vampirism), along with the perpetual suffering of God's people for opposing these heresies (Revelation 2:18-29). This letter (the longest of the seven), covers the rise of Roman Catholic power in Western Europe, jumpstarted by her exploiting the empire's leadership vacuum following the fall of Rome in 476. Thyatira's popes continued the Church-State union (begun in Pergamos) by their ongoing *"fornication"* with the *"kings of the earth."* (Revelation 17:2) Having preferred to kiss a "papal toe" over a "nail-scarred foot," earth's inhabitants would be "blessed" with a Satanic Millennium (aka the "Dark Ages"). Two of the more salient texts comprise the Holy Spirit exhorting our Baptist ancestors to *"hold fast"* (verse 25), as the *"morning star"* (verse 28) was on the horizon (the first translation of the Bible in English, rendered by John Wycliffe, aka "Morning Star of the Reformation").

• **Sardis** (1517-1791), meaning "bloodied ones," covers the period of the Protestant Reformation, the "blood" being equally shed by the opposing Catholic and Protestant forces in the Thirty Years War, as well as by the Anabaptists subsequently martyred by their Protestant and Catholic tormentors alike (Revelation 3:1-6). A veiled reference to our courageous Baptist forefathers can be seen in the words, *"Thou hast **a few names even in Sardis** which have not defiled their garments."* The Sardis period is dated from Martin Luther's Ninety-five Theses to James Madison's Bill of Rights. The crowning event was the publication of the Authorized King James Bible of 1611.

• **Philadelphia** (1791-1901), meaning "brotherly love," previews the "Church of the Open Door" in America, *opened* and *kept* open by the providential First Amendment to the United States Constitution, signed in the "City of Brotherly Love" (Revelation 3:7-13). The outstanding characteristic of this age is *spiritual fruitfulness* ("Japheth's enablement"). No longer enjoined just to "hold fast," as in the "Old World" because of the "Bloody Whore," an army of pastors, missionaries, evangelists, church planters, and soul winners—armed with their King James Bibles—would now pass *through* that "open door" to accomplish the greatest exploits in Church history! The beginning of the end of this period dates from 1901 with the arrival of the American Standard "Commode" Version (ASCV).

- **Laodicea** (1901-?), meaning "rights of the people" (or "civil rights"), is the last of the seven ages and constitutes the "Church of the *Closed* Door" (Revelation 3:14-21). Representing the perfect metaphor, Laodicea literally closes the door to the entire Church Age itself. Whereas the Philadelphia epistle depicts Jesus standing *inside* His own church—holding the door open to send the Christians out (to spread the Gospel)—by the time Laodicea rolls around, the situation has flipped. Now *they* are back inside, behind a closed door (with the lock newly changed, making the *"key of David"* in verse seven of no effect) and *He* is outside trying to get back in (verse 20) with the most pitiful cry, *"Behold, I stand at the door, and **knock**: if any man hear my voice, and **open the door**, I will come in to him, and will sup with him, and he with me."* (For what it's worth, if Jesus was a Calvinist, He would have broken the door down.) Thus, in just one hundred years, the Body of Christ falls from its highest peak to its lowest abyss.

LABORING IN LAODICEA

Now, this is where *you* come in. We are all laboring in the closing days of the Laodicean Church Age. Above everything else, your spiritual survival depends upon discerning the unique character of this time. To begin with, consider the current era in light of the following two passages: *"For unto whomsoever much is given, **of him shall be much required"*** and *"[D]espisest thou the riches of his goodness and forbearance and longsuffering; not knowing that the **goodness of God leadeth thee to repentance?**"* (Luke 12:48; Romans 2:4)

Christians who grew up in post-WWII America, i.e., amidst the unparalleled culture initiated by "Rosie, Elvis, and Billy" (as explained in chapter nineteen in *What Hath God Wrought!*), share three common denominators (unlike any other believers in any of the other six ages). First of all, as illustrated by the opening chapter title, "The Last Latte," we have all enjoyed the *most* physical comforts: Big Macs, appetizers, timeshares, gym memberships, virtual reality, Alexa and Siri, AI Chat box companions, smart beds, car wash upgrades, flat screen TVs, high-speed internet, Black Fridays, tailgate parties, Bit Coins, IPods, app stores, video games, drive-up windows, smart watches, Xboxes, et al.

Secondly, we have all enjoyed the *most* access to Scripture, in a variety of venues: printed page; audio; smart phones; etc., and, at ridiculous prices. In 2011, Walmart "recognized" ("cashed in on") the epic 400th anniversary of the AV 1611 by selling miniature hardback reproductions of the King James Bible for—$3.00. Conversely, to *rent* a Wycliffe Bible in fourteenth-century England for just *one* hour, our ancestors had to fork over an entire load of hay (no pun intended). Oh, so you love listening to Alexander Scourby, do you? Yeah, tell me *all* about it; Baptist martyrs were burned at the stake with portions of Scripture chained around their necks! (And if you *really* want to have your end-day "comfort zone" rattled, check out the foremost narrator of the King James Bible "moonlighting" as ranch foreman "Old Polo" in the Hollywood blockbuster, *Giant,* starring Rock Hudson, Elizabeth Taylor, and James Dean, Al's main scene being where he serves up booze for everyone at the closing bash in the film.)

Third, and most importantly, from the perspective of self-preservation, we have all enjoyed the *most* physical protection (from religious persecution). I mean, really, what is the worst thing you ever suffered when trying to share the Gospel in America? What's that you say, someone cussed you out and told you to "get the blank" off their porch? Wow! What's that? *Another* person ripped up your Chick tract? Dude—Waldensian mothers in sixteenth-century Europe had their *wombs* "ripped up" so psychopathic Roman Catholics could extract, cook, and *eat* their unborn babies! (See: *Wylie's Illustrated History of the Waldenses.*) And, as the old adage goes, "Everyone wants to go to Heaven, but no one wants to go today," the last generation of Christians will not even have to experience death (I Corinthians 15:51-52; Hebrews 9:27)!

Now, when you compare these sober realities with Luke 12:48 and Romans 2:4, you get an equation that looks something like this: The Church Age that received the *most* blessings *from* God—produced the *least* fruit *for* God. How do you suppose *that's* going to fly at the Judgment Seat of Christ? (Hint: I wouldn't want to be caught standing anywhere *near* those Waldensian mothers.)

A HUMBLING ILLUSTRATION

When the post-Exile Jews were constructing the second Temple, Ezra 3:12 relates, *"But many of the priests and Levites and chief of the fathers, who were ancient man, that had seen the first house, when the foundation of this house was laid before their eyes, wept with a loud voice."* The humbling application here is that the best of the Philadelphia remnant, laboring in Laodicea, could not begin to compare with our spiritual forefathers.

To render a telling personal illustration, one of my morning routines (when I am home between meetings) is to watch back-to-back episodes of *Hogan's Heroes* with my wife while we eat breakfast together. (For the benefit of my younger readers, *Hogan's Heroes* was a television sitcom set in a Nazi Germany prisoner-of-war camp during World War II; it ran for six seasons from 1965 to 1971, totaling 168 hilarious episodes).

One morning (during the writing this manuscript, no less), the Holy Spirit reminded me that many, if not most of us—*despite* our devotion for the King James Bible and our commitment to preserving the "Old Time Religion" —represent the textbook illustration for the adage, "The best of men are men at best." (Like former Israeli Prime Minister Golda Meir would say, "Don't act so humble; you're not that important.") While laughing my head off at a particular episode, a *"still, small voice"* reminded me that the late Werner Klemperer (Colonel Wilhelm Klink), John Banner (Sergeant Hans Schultz), Leon Askin (General Albert Burkhalter), and Howard Caine (Gestapo Major Wolfgang Hochstetter— all four being unsaved Jews—were undoubtedly *burning in Hell* while they were entertaining me during breakfast. (Robert Clary, who played Corporal Louis LeBeau, a fifth Jewish cast member who actually spent time in the Buchenwald concentration camp, was still alive as of 2022, age ninety-five.) The same goes for most of the deceased Gentile actors, especially the star of the show, Bob Crane (Colonel Robert Hogan), a Roman Catholic and closet sex-addict who died on June 29, 1978, in a mysterious unsolved murder. (His net worth at the time of his death was $150,000.)

So, how's all of *that* for a mega "Debbie Downer" reality check? But it gets even more bizarre. In Season 1, actor Gavin MacLeod (of *The Mary Tyler Moore Show* and *The Love Boat* fame) appeared as Major Zolle in "Hello, Zolle." He did such a good job that he was cast as two different characters only three episodes apart. In Season 3, Episode 27,

"The Collector General," he played General Metzger; then in Season 4, Episode 1, "Clearance Sale at the Black Market," he appeared as Gestapo Major Kiegel, a corrupt entrepreneur. Later in Season 4, he also played General von Rauschenberg in "The Witness," his final *Hogan's Heroes* appearance.

MacLeod died on May 29, 2021, the very month I began writing this book, at the age of ninety in Palm Desert, California. However, while practically everyone involved with *Hogan's Heroes* was burning in fire, Gavin went the other direction. According to his personal testimony, he accepted Jesus Christ as his Saviour on September 15, 1974 (less than three weeks after my own conversion). He went on to make several Christian films (primarily appealing to the evangelical, "Pat Boone" genre). Thus, we have the incongruent scenario (similar to my story of the mother and baby who died from that car accident at my church) that at the Great White Throne Judgment, Klink, Shultz, Burkhalter, Hochstetter, LeBeau, along with Colonel Hogan and all the rest of his "Heroes," will stand before Jesus Christ and be sent into the Lake of Fire—while Gavin MacLeod says, "Amen!" (Oddly enough, Crane's last role was a single episode on *The Love Boat* in 1978, just months before his head was bashed in, and four years into Gavin's new life in Christ.)

THE "ORIGINAL" ORIGINAL SIN

One of the more "indelicate" texts in Scripture is the Lord's rebuke to *"the church of the Laodiceans"* as given in Revelation 3:16, *"So then because thou art lukewarm, and neither cold nor hot, I will spue thee out of my mouth."* After putting up with His espoused Bride— "warts and all" —for nineteen hundred years, what could have possibly induced Jesus to regurgitate her overnight? To comprehend the uniqueness of this age, you'll have to discover the source of the "holy vomit," i.e., the actual *origin* of *the* "Original Sin."

In our Lord's rebuke to Satan (as spoken through the King of Tyrus), He says, *"Thou wast perfect in thy ways from the day that thou wast created, till iniquity was found in thee."* (Ezekiel 28:15) Have you ever wondered what this particular "iniquity" was? Well, a Spirit-filled deacon's wife in Kentucky gave me the answer (during the writing of this book). Notice what the Holy Spirit points out earlier in this same chapter: *"With thy wisdom and with thine understanding thou has gotten* *thee riches, and hast gotten gold and silver into the treasures: By thy great wisdom and by thy traffick hast **thou increased thy riches**, and **thine heart is lifted up because of thy riches**.*" (Ezekiel 28:4-5)

By verse sixteen, the context constricts solely to Lucifer, "***By the multitude of thy merchandise** they have filled the midst of thee with violence, **and thou hast sinned**: therefore I will cast thee as profane out of the mountain of God: and I will destroy thee, **O covering cherub**, from the midst of the stones of fire.*" The Devil's problem seems to have begun at Ezekiel 27:22, "*The merchants of Sheba and Raamah, they were thy merchants: they occupied in thy fairs with chief of all spices, **and with all precious stones, and gold**.*" (Remember that the first mention of "gold" is in Genesis 2:12.)

And so, whereas Satan himself apparently fell to the allurement of riches, he has subsequently spent his entire "career" tempting mankind with the same "bling." As documented by Avro Manhattan in *The Vatican Billions,* material gain has been *the* driving force of every Pope in history. Describing the Roman Catholic "Church" in Revelation 17:5 as *"MYSTERY, BABYLON THE GREAT, THE MOTHER OF HARLOTS AND ABOMINATIONS OF THE EARTH,"* John went on to itemize her many wares throughout the centuries:

> *And the merchants of the earth shall weep and mourn over her; for no man buyeth their merchandise any more: The merchandise of gold, and silver, and precious stones, and of pearls, and fine linen, and purple, and silk, and scarlet, and all thyine wood, and all manner vessels of ivory, and all manner vessels of most precious wood, and of brass, and iron, and marble, And cinnamon, and odours, and ointments, and frankincense, and wine, and oil, and fine flour, and wheat, and beasts, and sheep, and horses, and chariots, and slaves, **and souls of men**. (Revelation 18:11-13)*

Thus, while the AV 1611 translators rendered I Timothy 6:10, "*For the love of money is **the** root of all evil,*" every major modern perversion— all traced to *Codex Vaticanus*—exchanged the definite article "the" for the indefinite article "a," downgrading the text to "For the love of money is ***a*** root of all sorts of evil." In his 1981 tome, *The English Bible from KJV to NIV: A History and Evaluation,* the evangelical Harvard academic, Jack P. Lewis, was candid enough to concede:

If one should ask if there are too many translations, the reply must be that the question is really irrelevant. The translations are here; they are not going away; and they must be dealt with. To hide one's head in the sand will not make the translations disappear; it will not bring back the so-called 'good old days' when everyone read one translation. *As long as there is financial gain in it, publishers will push translations, old or new.*

"RICH AND INCREASED WITH GOODS"

Continuing along this line, the reason why the majority of born-again folks in twenty-first-century Laodicean America are described as being "lukewarm" spiritually, is due to the following divine assessment: *"Because thou sayest, **I am rich, and increased with goods, and have need of nothing**; and knowest not that thou art wretched, and miserable, and poor, and blind, and naked."* (Revelation 3:17) I've often said that the best inscription to put on America's tombstone would be "BELLS AND WHISTLES." As much as I *love* Christmas, I'll have to admit that the Devil's indoctrination period must have begun with all those presents crowding out that dinky manger scene under the tree. By the time my generation was old enough to be further controlled by the power of music, Satan used the Beatles to decimate our culture. Is it any wonder that one of their most popular tunes ("Can't Buy Me Love," notwithstanding) was titled "Money (That's What I Want)"?

When Revelation 3:17 is cross-referenced with Matthew 6:24, the whole picture comes into focus. *"No man can serve two masters: for either he will hate the one, and love the other; or else he will hold to the one, and despise the other. **Ye cannot serve God and mammon**."* Here, our Saviour categorically declares that no human can submit to God *and* money simultaneously. All men, saved or lost, must choose between the two. Because *"no man can serve two masters,"* Christians who choose to sell out for material gain become incapable of submission to God. He who willfully succumbs to the cares of this world and the deceitfulness of riches could not submit to God if he wanted to—for (duh…) *"no man can serve two masters."* Once the Laodicean apostate "goes for the gold," his singular face-saving profile becomes unmistakable: *"Having a form of godliness, but denying the power thereof."* (II Timothy 3:5) Is there any doubt that the Bible is the power of godliness? Therefore, we perceive that the source of John's "puke" in Revelation 3:16 is *"the deceitfulness of riches"* in Mark 4:19.

Conversely, the opposite profile is true as well. With *"covetousness"* identified as *"idolatry"* in Ephesians 5:5 and Colossians 3:5, one of the sure signs of a spiritual man (or woman) is a total disregard for "things." Whereas your typical Japhethite in Laodicea moves and breathes by the materialistic mantra, *"gain is godliness,"* Philadelphia believers understand that *"godliness with **contentment** is great gain."* (I Timothy 6:5-6) In the Old Testament, Joseph apprised his worldly-wise brethren, *"Also **regard not your stuff**; for the good of all the land of Egypt is your's"* (Genesis 45:20); in the New Testament, Paul told the Church, *"Therefore let no man glory in men. **For all things are your's.**"* (I Corinthians 3:21) The colorful evangelist, Lester Roloff, once told a judge, "I'm really a millionaire, your Honor; just temporarily separated from my assets."

Someone has rightly said, "When the church became a nightclub, and the pulpit became a stage, the church became a carnal show to entertain the masses who are bored with spiritual things." As America grows more and more carnal, every hardworking Philadelphia-minded pastor, along with his devoted church members, should understand how this applies to their shrinking attendance. When this concept of "materialistic paralysis" is comprehended, several other theological maladies are found to be related. For instance, there are three central reasons why most of the saved Laodiceans in your area will avoid your "house of worship" like the plague. (The same applies as to why those first-time visitors rarely come back.) The first reason is because of *pastoral authority*. When these lucre-driven bums discern that your shepherd is faithful to his charge in I Peter 5:2 of *"taking the oversight thereof,"* they'll not hang around to flaunt their secular credentials, i.e., hoping to acquire "political power" within the congregation. (Like Jack Hyles used to say, "A camel is a horse put together by a Baptist committee.) Their core problem with "pastoral authority" is the "authority" part.

The second hang-up that materialistic Christians have with *your* "kind of church" is the pastor's *preaching*. Teaching is rarely the problem; it's the preaching they can't handle, once again, because of its authoritative nature. (News flash for my anti-pastoral authority Ruckmanite friends: I personally heard "the Doc" say, "The best churches I've ever seen were pastored by dictators, as somebody has to keep the little dictators from taking over.") And by the way, when milquetoast "prophets" (like Charles

Stanley) sit on stools behind their "sacred desks" and "talk" to their Sunday morning congregations—that's *not* preaching! Authentic Bible "preaching" normally resembles that which God commanded Isaiah to do: ***"Cry aloud, spare not, lift up thy voice like a trumpet, and shew my people their transgression, and...their sins."*** (Isaiah 58:1)

As one who both taught *and* preached, Jesus left us the pattern: *"In the last day, that great day of the feast, **Jesus stood and cried**, saying, If any man thirst, let him come unto me, and drink."* (John 7:37) Dr. Hyles likened the difference between teaching and preaching to a public cafeteria and a military chow line; in the former, you simply select what you want (without spitting on what you don't like), while in the latter you "gladly" take what's "flung" at you (by that snarling cook with the "Mom" tattoo on his arm)! Paul thusly warned that in the last days, those who would not *"endure sound doctrine"* would be controlled by *"their own **lusts**"* (for the "stuff" of this world), and would thus *"heap to themselves **teachers**, having itching ears."* (II Timothy 4:3)

Of course, problem number three will arise as soon as they discover that your pastor is one of those narrow-minded, King James-Only "dictators." Because the "rich young rulers" of our day have become spiritually incapacitated, they will not accept a Bible that lays exclusive claim to the English-speaking world. Instead, they will take cover behind the assurances of Christian "scholarship" that one conscientious "toilet translation" (ASCV) is as good as the next, etc. They'll embrace *anything* but a dreaded submission to *one* book. (Translation: There are no such things as "NIV-Only" or "ESV-Only" folks; just "anti-KJV-Only.")

Therefore, the central observation to make is that our present unrivaled variety of "Bibles" just happens to coincide with an unrivaled age of materialism. To put it another way, America's "scripture" selections increase commensurate with her living standard. Appreciating the reason for this will explain the growing animosity toward the King James Bible. In conclusion, your precious AV 1611 is under attack by today's money-worshiping, lukewarm Laodiceans simply because it commands the same unconditional surrender that its author *did* (and *does*). *"For he taught them as one having **authority**, and not as the scribes."* (Matthew 7:29) As I stated in the opening chapter of my first book thirty years ago—the problem with the King James Bible is a problem with *final authority.*

THE CLOSING ILLUSTRATION FOR LAODICEA

We have now arrived at the dramatic "closing illustration" of this chapter (i.e., equating to that last one percent of the black preacher's sermon). In theater parlance, the word "denouement" is defined as "The final part of a play, movie, or narrative in which the strands of the plot are drawn together and matters are explained or resolved." What you are about to read is the "spiritual denouement" of not only the Laodicean Church Age, but of the entire sixth dispensation, *Grace*. It applies to our appearance before the Judgment Seat of Christ (I Corinthians 3:12-15; II Corinthians 5:10).

In the opening monologue of the 1970 Hollywood movie, *Patton* (winner of seven Academy Awards), George C. Scott is shown standing with an enormous American flag displayed behind him, addressing an unseen audience of American soldiers. This iconic image led the Library of Congress to select *Patton* for preservation in the United States National Film Registry as being "culturally, historically or aesthetically significant." Believe it or not, a cut from that same opening scene contains a principle that can be *"spiritually* significant" for you and me. To further motivate his men to kill Nazis on the front line, "Old Blood and Guts" says, in a sustained snarl,

> You may be thankful that twenty years from now when you are sitting by the fireplace with your grandson on your knee and he asks you what you did in the great World War II, you *won't* have to cough, shift him to the other knee and say, 'Well, your granddaddy shoveled ['manure'] in Louisiana.' No, Sir, you can look him straight in the eye and say, 'Son, your Granddaddy rode with the Great Third Army and a [blankety-blank-blank] named George Patton!

This secular theme of "no regrets" was previously captured in the title of the 1966 film, *What Did You Do in the War, Daddy?* Another application from the sports world would be the stereotypical third-string, would-be high school football star who is trying to impress his girlfriend in the stands but comes off the field with a clean uniform as his coach never sent him in. (Had she only disappeared for a brief trip to the ladies' room he would have immediately soiled his jersey with dirt.)

Now, as many of you are undoubtedly scratching your heads by now, allow me to send *you* sprawling to the canvas (like Larry did to

Marvis). With reference to that bilocation phenomenon discussed in chapter two, project *yourself* momentarily to the Judgment Seat of Christ (assuming of course, that you're saved). Imagine that all of the Church Age saints are lined up in chronological order (according to their appropriate historical sequence in Revelation). After witnessing all those brave martyrs receive their crowns (James 1:12; Revelation 2:10), especially the women and children—what are *you* going to say when it's *your* turn to give an account? "Ah...duh...well, I ah, *left a tract at a KFC once.*" Get the picture, Ace?

And so, for the sole purpose of illustrating a critical truth, I'll tell you what I "plan" on saying to Jesus. (In reality, I'll be shaking in my boots just like you). My fantasy spiel goes something like this, "Lord, first of all, thank you for the cream puff, persecution-free lifestyle you ordained for me in twenty-first-century America. While I never asked for it, I certainly appreciated it. However, what I *really* want to thank you for (drum roll, please) is for—*having given me the necessary grace to withstand the greatest weapon you ever permitted Satan to unleash on the Church.*" Did you grasp the significance of what you just read? Do you realize that the "Church Triumphant" was able to battle through nearly eighteen centuries of *dungeons*, *fire*, and *sword* in Europe and Great Britain, then labor through another two hundred years of hassle-free, fruit-bearing evangelistic endeavors in America—only to be stopped *dead in her tracks* by the unprecedented age of Laodicean materialism? (See Revelation 3:17) What the rack and stake couldn't do, Visa, Master Card, and "Wally World" did!

The bottom-line for the Philadelphia remnant attempting to labor in Laodicea, is that *you* are the *first* generation of born-again Baptists—in the history of the New Testament Age—that is being assailed by *the* weapon that finally takes the Church out! *"For the time will come when they will not endure sound doctrine."* (II Timothy 4:3) That time is here, folks! The shrinking attendances in your Sunday and Wednesday services bear witness to this "negative" anti-II Chronicles 7:14 reality.

While most "TR Fundamentalists" ignorantly reject the prophetic character of chapters two and three of Revelation, they are too shallow to recognize that the main projected character trait of Laodicea— *"rich and increased with **much goods"** —historically, could *not* have fit in any of the previous six periods, especially in the Dark Ages (500-1500), when "stick men" were eating the bark off of trees. (See *A World Lit*

Only by Fire, by William Manchester.) This concept of requiring a precise order for things similarly unhinges the evolution crowd when their "fossil fantasy" charts are upended by the actual geological record aligning with the Genesis flood.

The ramifications of this truth are mind-boggling. For instance (as sick as this may sound) those same godly Waldensian mothers who permitted their wombs to be sliced open rather than deny their Lord—*if given the opportunity*—might very well have succumbed to the modern temptations of too many "mani-pedis"! What this means is that *none* of those same martyrs we shall witness receiving their crowns (Ignatius, Polycarp, et al.) could have possibly imagined the extent of what that final generation of Christian soldiers were destined to face (II Timothy 2:3).

Now, in my day (when the best Italian jokes were told by Wops, and Pollocks had the best Polish jokes—i.e., when nobody could even spell "disparaging"), an amusing story from the genre of black comedy perfectly illustrated this vital truth (though in our present whacked-out "woke world" it would probably be deemed "hate speech;" oh well, yawn...remind me to take a baby aspirin, etc., *especially* if it offends all those "dawgs" who throw the "N" word around 24/7). As the tale goes, these two senior black gents, Rufus and Amos, were walking down a dusty country road when the one suddenly says to the other, "Rufus, as good a friend as you and I is, if'n you had a million dollars, would you gives me half? Rufus answers without any hesitation, "Amos, as good a friend as you and I is, you *knows* I'd give you half." A few moments later, Amos asks his buddy a second question, "Rufus, as good a friend as you and I is, if'n you had a *half*-a-million dollars, would you give me half?" Again, Rufus replies, "Amos, as good a friend as you and I is, you *knows* I'd give you half. As they arrive at the fork in the road, Amos, says, "Rufus, let me aks you one last question. If'n you had two *hogs*, would you gives me one?" Rufus immediately turns to the brother and says, "Shoooot man, dat's no fair—you *knows* I gots two hogs!"

Just as it was *so* easy for Rufus to *think* he would be willing to "give away the store" —when it wasn't his to give—*no* Church Age saint, from Ephesus through Philadelphia, could say what he or she *would* have done *if* faced with the end-time temptation of unparalleled materialism. Yet, it gets worse than that. As covetousness continues to immobilize the carnal Christians, who form the majority in Laodicea, the fact that *their* defection has rendered national revival impossible, is neutralizing many within the Philadelphia remnant through despair (II Timothy 3:13; Daniel 7:25).

This added dilemma poses a serious threat, as hopelessness is the main cause for suicide among saved *and* lost people (Proverbs 13:12; 29:18). And so, not only must the Lord's end-day night fighters overcome the *greatest* weapon Satan has ever unleashed, materialism (*the* weapon that finally knocks out the Church), but they must *also* face that other related psychological danger—being the first generation of Baptists that could *not* turn things around, no matter *how* much they tried (exactly like King Josiah's frustrating experience). Thus, already battling "spiritual PTSD" from engaging Satan's "super weapon," God's men must also ward off the depression caused by the reality that things *must* inevitably crash— on *their* watch (II Timothy 3:13-14; 4:3).

CHAMBER POT "BIBLES" AND PUKE POT "CHURCHES"

You say, "Dr. Grady, I'm afraid to ask; could there *possibly* be anything *else*?" Well, as Lieutenant Columbo used to say, "Just one more thing...." King David wrote in Psalm 11:3, *"If the **foundations** be destroyed, what can the righteous do?"* Added to this is that heavy prophecy in Amos 8:11, *"Behold, the days come, saith the Lord GOD, that **I will send a famine in the land**, not a famine of bread, nor a thirst for water, **but of hearing the words of the LORD**."* Yet at the end of the day, should we really be shocked that Satan will have used a "Chamber Pot 'Bible' Version" to produce a "Puke Pot 'Church' Age"?

The third part of God's correlated "Closing Illustration" for the Age of Grace will be the *near*-destruction of *our* "foundation" —the Authorized King James Bible, 1611 Version. (Notice, I said "near" destruction.) The Holy Spirit led the Apostle John to describe Jesus as the "Word of God" seven times: John 1:1,14; I John 1:1; 5:7; and Revelation 19:13. He also moved the King James translators to employ exactly *sixty-six* words when introducing Jesus in John 1:1-5. (Jesus is called the "Word" because, as John 1:18 explains, He came *out* of the Godhead to make the invisible Father known—just as a word comes *out* of the mind to reveal the invisible thought.) Thus, we see a parallel between Jesus Christ as the *"living* Word of God" and the King James Bible as the *"written* word of God."

The key truth to discern from this similitude involves the *physical* abuse our Lord absorbed in His human body. For instance, with His first blood shed at His circumcision eight days after arriving in Bethlehem, Jesus surely skinned His knees on several occasions while playing as a normal Jewish child in Nazareth. Contrary to the stereotypical "effeminate" portrayal of Jesus by organized religion, how's *this* for being far out— what about the possibility that He *might* have even bruised His knuckles defending His sisters or any of His four younger brothers (Mark 6:3; Psalm 69:8) from some bullies, like Moses intervened for Jethro's daughters in Exodus 2:17? (I'd hate to think where *that* poor slob wound up; i.e., "Fly Me to the Moon.") Then, there were those unavoidable splinters at Joseph's carpenter shop. But, of course, the greatest affliction that the "*living* Word of God" endured was inflicted by the Roman cat-o'-nine tails and the cross—at the *end* of His life.

The same is true concerning the "*written* word of God." Even the pagan editors at *Wikipedia* understand this amazing fact:

> The *Authorized Version* maintained its effective dominance throughout the first half of the 20th century. New translations in the second half of the 20th century displaced its 250 years of dominance (roughly 1700 to 1950), but groups do exist – sometimes termed the King James only movement – that distrust anything not in agreement with ("that changes") the *Authorized Version*.

The main idea to discern here involves a second correlation. In AD 33, God the Father *allowed* the "*living* Word of God" to be arrested and mercilessly ravaged at the whipping post—*with no warning, explanation, or intervention.* Having falsely assumed that they were about to be led in a successful revolt against Rome, the eleven disillusioned disciples fled Gethsemane, fulfilling Matthew 26:31 by taking personal "offense" at their apparent abandonment.

In the twenty-first century, God is likewise allowing His "*written word*" to be ravaged, only this time by the World Wide Web. Allow me to explain. Back in the day, a sincere KJV pastor could easily wean a novice believer away from the modern perversions. The standard approach *used* to involve showing him the seventeen whole verses deleted in the NIV (Matthew 17:21; 18:11; 23:14; Mark 7:16; 9:44, 46; 11:26; 15:28; Luke 17:36; 23:17; John 5:4; Acts 8:37; 15:34; 24:7; 28:29; Romans 16:24; and I John 5:7) However, that same naive prospect will have his momentary euphoria ended by a dozen "friends" who immediately bombard him with some serious information overload, emailing him dozens of anti-KJV websites (KJV-Only cult; Ruckman's Heresies; 100,000 errors in the AV 1611, etc.). The sheer magnitude of today's highly technical, language-related textual argumentation is slowly but surely "destroying the foundation" —and just like at Calvary, God is *allowing* it to happen! For the record, after studying this issue for a third of a century, I am convinced—based on Isaiah 7:9; Romans 1:29; I Thessalonians 2:13; and Hebrews 11:6—that the King James Bible, *as a supernatural book*, must ultimately be accepted by *faith*, and *not* by the preponderance of intellectual evidence.

However, as I said, we're only witnessing the "near" destruction of the King James Bible. The Father is presently permitting the internet to accomplish the same thing that the thirty-nine lashes were designed to do—bring the victim as *close* to death as possible. Thankfully, we know that no human can ultimately "destroy" the "*written* word of God," for as the "*living* Word of God" testified of His own life in John 10:18, *"No man taketh it from me, **but I lay it down of** myself,"* He fulfilled that pledge on the cross, Matthew 27:50 confirming, *"**Jesus,** when he had cried again with a loud voice, **yielded up the ghost**."* And so, while we will surely experience a *"famine...of hearing the words of the LORD"* in the last days, *we* are privy to something that the disciples were not; as previewed by that empty tomb three days later—the "written word" will also be gloriously resurrected, in *"a little while!"* (John 16:16-19)

GOD'S "REPO MAN"

In his three-page afterword to *How Satan Turned America Against God*, the late Manhattan Project physicist, Sam Cohen, wrote, "Bill Grady is one of the most unusual friends I have known in my eighty-four years." (Following our seven-year relationship, I would have to say that the feeling was mutual.) In 1984, Universal Pictures released a science fiction "dark" comedy entitled *Repo Man* (starring Emilio Estevez, Dean Stanton, Tracy Walter, and Olivia Barash). The bizarre plot centers on a repo man and a lobotomized nuclear scientist (loosely based on Cohen) driving a "hot" 1964 Chevrolet Malibu around Los Angeles—with an extraterrestrial hidden in the trunk, clutching a neutron bomb. On the DVD of *Repo Man* (which has since gained a cult following), Sam is interviewed in his Brentwood, California, home by the film's director, Alex Cox. (Ironically, Mr. Cohen told me that Stanley Kubrick's *Dr. Strange Love* was *his* favorite movie, the main character, played by Peter Sellers, being patterned after the preeminent nuclear strategist and Hudson Institute founder, Dr. Herman Kahn, one of Sam's good friends, whom he personally recruited to the RAND Corporation in 1947.)

Two decades later, America's "foremost" closet-Muslim President, Barry Soetoro Barack Hussein Obama II, made his "long-awaited" delayed as long as possible) diplomatic visit to Israel on March 20, 2013. The "highlight" of his trip was captured by a *Washington Times* headline: "President Obama's limo breaks down at Israeli airport." Apparently, one of Barry's security personnel put the wrong fuel in his armor-plated "Caddie" (appropriately named "The Beast"). One of my favorite photos in *Holy Ground* shows the broken-down vehicle being hauled away on an Israeli tow truck (a long line of Hebrew characters prominently displayed along the side panel).

Obama's embarrassment has a subtle connection to the opening chapter of this book, particularly that fourth point, "Deep Space." While we are all awaiting the "Blessed Hope" to take us out of this insane asylum, few believers realize that it is also a *"Misunderstood* Hope." For instance, neighbor, did it ever dawn on you—*why* the Lord yanks His Church out in the first place? Well, why was Barry's presidential "pimp mobile" hauled away? If you still haven't caught on, allow me to give you the text that explains the practical purpose *for* the Rapture. Jesus told his followers, ***"Ye are the salt of the earth****: but if the salt have lost his savour, wherewith shall it be salted? **it is thenceforth good for nothing**, but to be **cast out**, and to be trodden underfoot of men."* (Matthew 5:13)

The Christian can be likened to salt, devotionally speaking. He is to make people "thirsty" for Christ and his witnessing should have a "savor" in it (Colossians 4:6). As a preservative, we are told in Mark 9:50 to have *"**salt** in ourselves"* and to *"have peace one with another."* However, as the first part of the verse reads, *"if the **salt** have lost its **saltiness**,"* the longer text in Matthew 5:13 says what's to be done when this occurs— *"it is...to be **cast out**."* In Israel's case (the historical-doctrinal application), the phrase "cast out" occurs thirteen times in the book of Jeremiah, which precedes the Babylonian captivity, typifying Israel's future persecution under the Antichrist (Revelation 12:1-4;13-16).

When the Church of Jesus Christ loses *its* "saltiness," it is likewise, *"good for **nothing**,"* requiring the same treatment that Barack's limo received. And if you *still* haven't figured it out, try this old saying on for size: "If it ain't broke, don't fix it" (i.e., if the Church wasn't broken, it wouldn't need to be removed). The Rapture is basically Heaven's tow truck and the Lord Jesus is the Father's "Repo Man!" As the Bride is currently broken down on the tarmac, it's time to haul her on up to that big "*body* shop" in the sky, so she can *"[make] herself ready"* for the Wedding (Revelation 19:7). How's that for a "Debbie Downer" similitude for that Laodicean majority—entering Heaven at the back of a tow truck! (Before you get too critical, you'd better read I John 2:28.)

Imagine how many cigarettes and beer cans will fall from those sanctified hands at who knows *how* many worldly venues? (If I was God, I'd have the trumpet blow during a scheduled church service for added effect.) And yet, that gracious reality regarding spiritual circumcision will even hold true for these "worst-of-the-worst," lukewarm Laodiceans; the majority of whom will be "under water" at the Judgment Seat regarding their "Bible Bucks."

Finally, if you need any more evidence that the Church has "run out of *gas*," just consider the press headlines from Veterans Day 2020 that reveal the caliber of president we have reaped as a nation: "Biden Giving Veteran's Day Remarks After His 'Fart' in Front of the Royals;" and, "Parker Bowles Caught in the Line of Fire When Biden Passes Gas;" then, "Duchess of Cornwall 'Can't Stop Talking' About Joe Biden's 'Long, Loud' Fart at COP26"; and—sure couldn't leave *this* one out— "Camilla *Blown Away* After Hearing Joe Biden Fart 'Loud.'" (And remember, neighbor, "El-Cid's" flatulence problems "came out" less than two weeks after a similar number of headlines highlighted his "Presidential Poopy Pamper Papal Audience" with Pope Francis.)

GOD'S SPECIAL REWARD

When the Pilgrims were attempting to secure investors for their proposed journey to the New World, they composed a letter listing the reasons they would constitute a worthy investment. The fifth one read in part, "Lastly, *it is not with us as with other men*, whom small things can discourage, or small discontentment cause to wish themselves at home again." They were comparing themselves with the rank and file of humanity in their day. The faithful Philadelphia remnant of today are unlike other men of *any* age for they are facing that which no other Christian had to face.

Therefore, to end this chapter on a spiritual note, the most edifying truth related to the concept of God's "Closing Illustration" is the special reward He will give to those who overcome these unprecedented conditions (Revelation 22:12). In the late 1920s, a dirt-poor farmer in Dawson, Texas, brought his wife and three sons to a large city church to attend Sunday morning worship. As the place was packed out, the slightly out-of-place appearing folk seated themselves near the rear of the auditorium. However, the youngest boy, apparently not content to remain in the nosebleed section, scampered away and claimed the sole empty seat on the front row pew for his own.

This did not go over well with the head usher. As the service was about to begin, the man told the twelve-year-old he would have to move elsewhere (the lad was apparently sitting in the dude's seat). Well, having come to hear preaching, the young Texan in his dusty bib overalls was not about to surrender his turf without a fight ("Come and Take It!") With the confrontation escalating, the platform door suddenly opened and the pastor walked out. He immediately inquired as to the problem (that by now was causing quite a distraction). When the man of God discovered the reason, he addressed the boy accordingly, "Son, if you want to hear me preach that much, then come up and *sit with me* on the platform." And *that's* where a young Lester Roloff (future pastor of Peoples Baptist Church, Corpus Christi, Texas, and founder of Roloff Evangelistic Enterprises) sat that Sunday morning—directly alongside the legendary Dr. J. Frank Norris (dual pastor of the First Baptist Church of Fort Worth, Texas, and Temple Baptist Church in Detroit, Michigan).

In like fashion, the Apostle John closed his epistle to Laodicea with the exhortation, *"To him that overcometh will I grant **to sit with me in my throne**, even as I overcame, and am set down with my Father in his throne."* (Revelation 3:21) You see, the Lord knows *exactly* what the Philadelphia remnant has had to endure, resisting that all-powerful end-day allurement of riches. We discern this from His words, *"**even as I also overcame**, and am set down with my Father in his throne."* The cross-reference that elucidates this empathetic spirit is Matthew 4:8-9,

"Again, the devil taketh him up into an exceeding high mountain, **and sheweth him all the kingdoms of the world, and the glory of them;** *And saith unto him,* **All these things will I give thee,** *if thou wilt fall down and worship me."*

Whereas the *"god of this world"* succumbed to covetousness (Ezekiel 27-28), our faithful High Priest faced down *and* overcame that same temptation *for* us (Hebrews 4:15-16). And as the Father rewarded His Son by inviting Him to sit with Him on *His* throne, Jesus has promised to do the same for those of us who similarly overcome. While I'm not exactly sure how that will play out doctrinally, it *sure* sounds like the perfect "Closing Illustration" to me!!

21

There's a Better Day A-Comin'

DURING MY NINE-year pastorate in Michigan, whenever current events seemed darker than usual, I would announce to my Sunday congregation that it was time to take another one of our periodic "excursions into Cloudland" (a positive spin on the phrase coined by Dean Burgon, who ridiculed Westcott and Hort's textual fantasies as "excursions into Cloudland"). My members would immediately perk up for they knew that meant I had prepared a special message designed to transport us all into the "Heavenlies" for a momentary respite.

That is my purpose here. With conditions in America darker than ever, I guarantee we are about to ascend further then Rod Serling, Captain Kirk, or Luke Skywalker ever dreamed of going. So, buckle up; lift off is in ten seconds. Next stop—only the Lord knows….

"THY KINGDOM COME, THY WILL BE DONE"

In June 2019, Pope Francis, the first Jesuit Pontiff, shocked the "Christian" world by approving changes to the wording of the so-called "Lord's Prayer" (also known to "The Faithful" as the "Our Father"). Instead of *"lead us not into temptation,"* Catholics would now be chanting "do not let us fall into temptation." Fran piously pontificated that the English rendering was incorrect.

> It is not a good translation because it speaks of a God who induces temptation. I am the one who falls. It's not him pushing me into temptation to then see how I have fallen. A father doesn't do that; a father helps you to get up immediately. It's Satan who leads us into temptation, that's his department.

Protestants conclude their version with the doxology, *"For thine is the kingdom and the power, and the glory, forever. Amen."* (Matthew 6:13) While Bible-believing Baptists generally reject formal prayers, they do endorse the longer account as the full text. Yet, there is something more shocking than "El Papa's" animus for Scripture in general (his rejection of Matthew 6:13 in particular). As the following "devotional" will show, about ninety-nine-percent of the true Church is just as ignorant regarding the real meaning of Jesus' words.

A LOST DOCTRINE?

Within seven decades of John Nelson Darby's epic disclosure of a seven-year Tribulation (based on Daniel's seventieth week), fellow Irishman and Plymouth Brethren revivalist, George F. Trench (1841-1915), published a book in 1895 attempting to give God's children further light. (Trench was an associate of Sir Robert Anderson and E. W. Bullinger.) His book was titled *After the Thousand Years*. Unfortunately, as the release date shows, by the time this Philadelphia believer released his years of private study, the dawn of Laodicea had arrived. Therefore, while his work *was* endorsed by several prominent contemporary leaders (G. Campbell Morgan, James M. Gray, Clarence Larkin, George Soltau, et al.), it eventually disappeared behind the "somber shadows" which Burgon predicted would engulf the Church by codices Aleph and B. (The spiritual deception of the 1885 *Revised Version* was so pronounced that otherwise spiritual giants, like R. A. Torrey and Larkin, were initially beguiled themselves.)

The last time Trench's work saw the fading light of day was in 1920, appearing in Larkin's enlarged and revised edition of *Dispensational Truth*. And so—like that 1876 Ashtabula train wreck—what we have is a *deep* theological thesis, developed at the height of the Philadelphia Church Age, vanishing while its patron was attempting to transport it across the bridge into Laodicea. Unlike the Bliss manuscript that was found, the Trench treatise has now remained dormant for a century. In 2018, a dispensational (non-KJV-Only) Bible church pastor named Bob Bolender delivered an eyebrow-raising lecture on this topic before his peers at the Chafer Theological Seminary Pastor's Conference in Houston, Texas. About this same time, I also discovered Trench's book and read it. I was smitten! Learning that Larkin was the last advocate of this view (before it dissipated), my spirit was arrested by the "coincidence" that I was saved, baptized, and called to preach at the historic Marcus Hook Baptist Church in Lynnwood, Pennsylvania—Larkin's home church! Soon the inevitable thought struck me—was I supposed to revive this prophetic baton for the Bible believers of the last generation?

"SHOW ME THY GLORY"

Before we tackle our heavy subject, I have an important "Service Announcement." While this position is one you've probably never heard, it would *not* be a breach of orthodoxy if you felt Spirit-led to embrace it (Romans 8:14). The main reason is because it doesn't adversely affect any crucial doctrine as much as it *augments* "a" doctrine—i.e., Christ's preeminence. Translation: Backed by your historic Baptist distinctive of "individual soul liberty," you can relax, while prayerfully contemplating the presentation; for, as I Corinthians 7:28 says (wrenched from its context), *"thou hast not sinned."* (Smiley Face…)

The opening line in *After the Thousand Years* reads: "The vision of God, as it is the beginning of life in the soul of man, is, ever after, the longing desire of every true believer." The author then comments on Exodus 33:18. "*'Show me Thy glory'* was not a prayer suitable only to Moses' hour of great perplexity: it is the prayer of every quickened soul of men, for every day, in every circumstance of life, and then the hour of death itself." It would take fifteen centuries for God to grant a partial answer: *"And **the Word** was made flesh, and dwelt among us, **(and we beheld his glory, the glory as of the only begotten of the Father,)** full of grace and truth."* (John 1:14) While *more* glory will surely come, the question remains, how much, where, and *especially*—when?

Therefore, if what you are about to read (regarding Christ and any future glory) turns out to be true, the "*worst*-case scenario" would be that Jesus will simply have *more* splendor for His Bride to behold (Ephesians 2:7; Revelation 21:23). As Trench wrote, "[I]f any ask what are the moral or spiritual benefits of such investigations as the following, we answer, all that exalts the Son of God helps us to discern His glory" (John 17:5).

RUBS REQUIRING RESOLUTION

The *Oxford Language* dictionary defines "rub" as: "A difficulty, especially one of central importance in a situation." Mr. Trench's initial following resulted from his ability to uncover, expose, and resolve certain disconcerting "rubs" within the existing eschatological construct. The two main rubs involve the *moral* character of the "glorious" Millennial Kingdom (the "highlight" occurring in Revelation 20:7-9) and "The Great Abdication" in I Corinthians 15:24-28.

According to the best eschatological timelines—tweaked by the best Philadelphia-minded expositors (though laboring in the shadows of Laodicea)—the course of events will be: 1) After the seven-year Tribulation Period and Second Advent, the thousand-year "Golden Age" begins, constituting the *peak* of Christ's earthly glory. 2) When *this* period ends, Jesus gets off His throne and gives the Kingdom to His Father. I don't know what *your* experience was, neighbor, but I ain't *never* heard one sermon on I Corinthians 15:24. 3) The Great White Throne Judgment comes next, followed by the new heaven, new earth, and new city. 4) Then, finally, "Eternity Future" begins (contrasted with pre-Genesis 1:1 "Eternity Past").

But then, everything suddenly *blurs*, beginning with those foggy *details* in Revelation 21 and 22. As we're all feeling our way through the final Church Age—the one requiring "eye salve" to see (Revelation 3:18)—when was the last time you heard *any* preacher make *any* sense out of these two chapters? Though most Christians will say (while sipping their lattes), "Oh well, at least we're going to Heaven," etc., *some* of us would like some clarity, if possible (the more glory for Jesus, the better.)

RULING WITH A ROD OF IRON; BUT WHY?

We have always heard that the Millennium would be the apex of Christ's glorious reign on planet earth (a near-perfect state of sinlessness, harmony, and prosperity). However, Scripture itself would strongly disagree. The problem is that we've never noticed certain "negative" passages. Teddy Roosevelt said, "Walk softly, but carry a big stick." Have you ever wondered why King Jesus will have to control His "glorious" realm with a "big stick" (Revelation 2:27)—when everything is *supposed* to be

"Kumbaya" time? For instance, have you ever pondered all the darkness in Psalm 2?

> *Why do the heathen rage, and the people imagine a vain thing?* *The kings of the earth set themselves, and the rulers take counsel together, against the LORD, and against his anointed, saying, Let us break their bands asunder, and cast away their cords from us.* *He that sitteth in the heavens shall laugh; the LORD shall have them in derision. Then shall he speak unto them in his **wrath**, and vex them in his sore displeasure.* ***Yet have I set my king upon my holy hill of Zion.*** *I will declare the decree: the LORD hath said unto me, Thou art my Son; this day have I begotten thee.* ***Ask of me, and I shall give thee the heathen for thine inheritance, and the uttermost parts of the earth for thy possession. Thou shalt break them with a rod of iron; thou shalt dash them in pieces like a potter's vessel.*** *Be wise now therefore, O ye kings: be instructed, ye judges of the earth. Serve the LORD with fear, and rejoice with trembling.* ***Kiss the Son, lest he be angry, and ye perish from the way, when his wrath is kindled but a little.*** *Blessed are all they that put their trust in him.*

Obviously, *this* opposition—by the *"kings of the earth"* —cannot be referring to Rome, but rather to Christ's *rebellious* Millennial subjects, the ones He'll keep *constrained* with "bands and cords." The context is that of a conquered people who feign surface submission, though retaining an entrenched hostility (like the pupil told to "sit down" by his teacher, muttering to himself, "I may be sitting down, but I'm *standing up* inside"). This future resistance was captured by the citizens' rancor in the parable of the ten pounds: *"We will **not** have this man to **reign over us**."* (Luke 19:14)

The Lord's iron-fisted rule will include a threat to turn the spigots off (and worse) of any nation that boycotts the Feast of Tabernacles:

> *And it shall come to pass, that every one that is left of all the nations which came against Jerusalem shall even go up from year to year to worship the King, the LORD of hosts, and they keep the feast of tabernacles. And it shall be, that whoso will not come up of all the families of the earth unto Jerusalem to worship the King, the LORD of hosts, **even upon them shall be no rain**. And if the family of **Egypt** go not up, and come not, that have no rain; **there shall be***

the plague, wherewith the LORD will smite the heathen that come *not up to keep the feast of tabernacles.* (Zechariah 14:16-18)

Dozens of references in the Psalms also speak to this seething "Golden Age" rebellion. Space constraints allow but a sample:

Make a joyful noise unto God, all ye lands…Say unto God, How **terrible** *art thou in thy works!* **through the greatness of thy power shall thine enemies submit themselves unto thee***…He ruleth by his power for ever; his eyes behold the nations:* **let not the rebellious exalt themselves***. Selah.* (Psalm 66:1, 3, 7)

The Lord reigneth; let the earth rejoice…Clouds and darkness are round about him: righteousness and **judgment** *are the habitation of his throne.* **A fire goeth before him, and burneth up his enemies round about***. His lightnings enlightened the world: the earth saw, and trembled.* (Psalm 97:1-4)

The LORD said unto my Lord, Sit thou at my right hand, **until I make thine enemies thy footstool***. The LORD shall send the* **rod** *of thy strength out of Zion:* **rule thou in the midst of thine enemies***.* (Psalm 110:1-2)

Perhaps the wildest precursor alludes to the swift, possibly daily, *executions* (as per Zephaniah 3:5) fulfilling Ecclesiastes 8:11. *"I will* **early** *destroy all the wicked of the land; that I may cut off all wicked doers from the city of the LORD."* (Psalm 101:8)

To explain, while the *first* generation of "Millennials" will begin as grateful residents (inspired by "precious memories" of their recent past), the *successive* waves will soon "rise to the occasion," allowing their non-circumcised human natures to revert to that age-old anti-Semitism. However, now their "ox" must not only submit to a "Jew" enthroned in Jerusalem, but to an entire regime of elevated Hebrews—telling *them* what to do, etc. And to exacerbate matters, Israel will also exact a hefty annual tribute from their Gentile vassals (Psalm 72:9-10; Isaiah 60:5, 7, 11, 16), compelling subjection: *"The sons also of them that afflicted thee shall come* **bending unto thee***; and all they that* **despised** *thee shall* **bow themselves down at the soles of thy feet."** (Isaiah 60:14) Woe be to any Gentile state that slights the Jews: *"For the nation and kingdom that* **will not serve thee shall perish***; yea,* **those nations shall be utterly wasted."** (Isaiah 60:12)

Consequently, far from the lofty notion that God's Millennial blessings will be showered upon *all* of earth's "happy" inhabitants *equally*, it appears that Jewry will receive the lion's share of the "good times," *and*, at the expense of the Goyim: *"And the sons of **strangers** shall build up **thy** walls, and **their kings shall minister unto thee.**"* (Isaiah 60:10) Again, *"And **strangers** shall stand and feed **your** flocks, and **the sons of the alien** shall be **your** plowmen and **your** vinedressers."* (Isaiah 61:5) David summarized this reality in Psalm 67:7 *"God shall bless **us;** and **all the ends of the earth** shall fear him."* So, can you "guess" what inspires this "racist revival" amidst so much Kingdom Age "glory"? In reality, as pre-figured by the Jews' spoiling of the Egyptians in Exodus 12:36, this preferential Millennial treatment is simply a long-overdue payback on a mammoth scale. (And did you catch Jehovah's lingering animosity for the "Land of Ham" in Zechariah 14:18-21?)

"AS THE SAND OF THE SEA"

The greatest indicator of the true character of dispensation seven is the instantaneous global uprising that occurs when the Devil is released from his own "millennium" in the bottomless pit.

> *And when the thousand years are expired, Satan shall be loosed out of his prison, And shall go out to deceive the nations which are in the four quarters of the earth, Gog, and Magog, to gather them together to battle: **the number of whom is as the sand of the sea**. And they went up on the breadth of the earth, and compassed the camp of the saints about, and the beloved city.* (Revelation 20:7-9)

Nearly a century ago, the opening line from the dramatized radio adaption of the fictional detective series, *The Shadow*, would rhetorically ask, "Who knows what evil lurks in the hearts of men? The Shadow knows." That the "King of kings," reigning as the recognized Son of God, will experience *so* much prolonged resistance from the human race—*in* the Devil's absence*, and,* after enjoying ten centuries of supernaturally enhanced living conditions—speaks volumes to the power of the Adamic nature. When you cross-reference Matthew 24:37, *"But as the days of Noe were, so shall also the coming of the Son of man be,"* with Genesis 6:3 and 15:16, the application for now and in the Millennium is that man's sin nature devolves. This reveals the scope of "evil lurking within the hearts" of the very people to whom we witness (Acts 7:54-59; 14:19; 21:31; 22:22-23).

The magnitude of this siege is seen by the fact that Satan's unholy coalition derives from the four corners of the earth, its number likened to the *"sand of the sea"* —a most poignant metaphor, given its original positive depiction of Abraham's seed (Genesis 22:17; 32:12). This gargantuan force is also in stark contrast to the remnant *"camp of the saints"* it encircles (the ultimate confirmation of Matthew 7:13-14). And then, history's *ultimate* denouement abruptly completes verse nine (comprising all of twelve words): ***"And fire came down from God out of heaven, and devoured them."*** (Note: For those who desire the *ultimate* glory for Jesus, the more we hear about the *real* "Golden Age," the more we identify as "Millennial minimalists," *in search of something better* (hence, the current chapter title *and* the following heading).

THE PAULINE MODEL

If we stick with the standard schematic regarding I Corinthians 15:24, it is here that Jesus will give up His throne and deliver what's left of His "glorious" Kingdom to the Father, the remnants of their just-completed "scorched earth" finale notwithstanding. While I anticipate plenty of blowback by "the brethren" for this chapter (Job 21:3), the hilarious thing is that most of these doctrinal lightweights are not even familiar with the basic scriptural position that Trench labored to elucidate ("The Great Abdication"). But a far *bigger* "rub" requires resolution. After Paul expired in Lystra (Acts 14:14-19) he was *"caught up into paradise,* [where he] *heard unspeakable words, which it is not **lawful** for a man to utter."* (II Corinthians 12:4) While unlawful to utter—*for a time*—the Jewish "Apostle to the Gentiles" apparently got the Holy Ghost's okay to "dump the truck" in Rome, where the last colony of Diaspora Jews had rejected their Messiah (Acts 28:25-29). Thus, in three of Paul's prison epistles, Jesus is depicted reigning over a glorious Kingdom *vastly* different from the chaos we've examined. The two are mutually exclusive in both their character and domain. Paul's version is absolutely *perfect* in *every* aspect, therefore anything *but* what the Millennium will be. Tell me if you see any iron scepters in the following passage:

Wherefore God also hath highly exalted him, and given him a name
*which is above every name: that at the name of Jesus **every knee***
*should bow, of **things in heaven, and things in earth, and things***
***under the earth**; and that **every tongue** should confess that Jesus*
Christ is Lord, to the glory of God the Father. (Philippians 2:9-10)

While this passage will have its first fulfillment on Judgment Day
(those *"things under the earth"* being conspicuously absent in Ephesians
1:10), it will also apply to that "better day a-comin," when *everyone*
will praise Him instinctively. For instance, do you really anticipate that
during the Millennium, anti-Semitic Egyptians, concealed in Cairo's
back alleys, will react *that* way at the dropping of Jesus' name? Why,
they'll spit in the gutter! Furthermore, did you notice the greater sphere
of rule in *this* realm, compared to Psalm 2:8? Whereas the Pauline
perspective encompasses things *terrestrial, celestial,* and even *infernal,*
the "slightly downgraded" dimensions in the Davidic model state: *"Ask*
of me, and I shall give thee the heathen for the thine inheritance, and
the uttermost parts of the earth for thine possession."

This same contrast between the Pauline and the Millennial models
can be seen in the Apostle's letter to the Church at Ephesus:

*[H]e...set him at his own right hand **in the heavenly places**, far*
above all principality, and power, and might, and dominion, and
*every name that is named, **not only in this world, but also in that***
***which is to come**: and hath put all things under his feet, and gave*
*him to be head over all things to **the church, which is his body**, the*
*fullness of him that filleth **all in all**.* (Ephesians 1:20-23)

Furthermore, during the Millennium, Jesus governs in Jerusalem,
but in the Kingdom that *Paul* describes, He's ruling from a throne, *way*
up there in *"heavenly places."* While this relates to our Lord's *present,*
exalted position over His Church, the "Fullness of His Body" —the
phrase *"not only in this world, **but also in that which is to come,"*** speaks
to something future; something *beyond* even the Millennium (a vista
that I Corinthians 13:12 and Hebrews 2:8 say is not visible to us as yet.)
Thus, the designation *"this world"* matches the *old* earth, while the world
"which is to come" matches the *new* earth. Then, Ephesians 2:7 states,
***"[T]hat in the ages to come** he might show the exceeding riches of his*
grace in his kindness toward us through Christ Jesus.") Here, the
plural "ages" will uniquely accommodate both the seventh and eighth

dispensations. Paul reiterates this "colossal" post-Millennial domain in Colossians 1:13, 18, 20-21, calling it *"the kingdom of his dear Son."* Again, *this* realm cannot be Millennial, for verse twenty shows that the blood of His cross had enabled Him *"to reconcile all things unto himself; by him, I say, whether they be things in earth, or things in heaven"* (a condition that *never* occurred while Jesus was "cracking heads"). But, neither does it fit in eternity, as I Corinthians 15:24 reveals that *"the end,"* i.e., of *time* (among other things) follows "The Great Abdication."

THE GREAT ABDICATION

Paul's revelation in I Corinthians 15:24-25 is one of the most profound truths in Scripture! *"**Then cometh the end**, when he shall have **delivered up the kingdom to God, even the Father**; when he shall have put down all rule and all authority and power. **For he must reign, till** he hath put all enemies under his feet."*

On December 10, 1936, Britain's King Edward VIII shocked the world by abdicating his throne to marry Wallis "Wally" Simpson, an American divorcée. (On a personal note, my dad once got "inebriated" with the Duke of Windsor after a Christmas Eve party in the late 1950s.) At some unknown future time, Jesus will abdicate *His* throne, transferring all *mediatorial* power to His Father. One of the Bible's least-known and most arresting doctrines is that Jesus Christ will *not* rule *forever* as a perfect "Man," particularly, as the "Son of Man." That's what those four startling words mean— *"then cometh **the end**."* This is not to say that His royal glory and majesty will ever cease; it will surely continue, but, from within the self-imposed "confines" of the Godhead itself, so *"that God may be **all in all**."* (I Corinthians 15:28) You see, according to John 17, Jesus has a dual title to glory: The first, *"**the glory** which thou gavest me I have given them"* (verse 22), refers to His earthly, visible, temporal glory, scheduled to "end" at His abdication; the second, *"**the glory** which I had with thee before the world was"* (verse 5), remains His essential, inherent, invisible glory that will *never* "end."

Regardless of *when* "The Great Abdication" occurs (after the Millennium or following yet another, indeterminate length of time more conducive to the pristine Pauline construct), the general consensus among the "old-timers" was that *"the end"* meant Jesus will have completed

His *temporal* role as the "Son of *Man*," vindicating His vicarious role as the "Redeemer of Man." Consequently, our precious Saviour will step down to *reenter* the Trinity, resuming His *eternal* role as "The Word," the position He held *before* He was begotten as the "Son" (John 1:1-3, 14-18).

No longer to be *"manifested* in the flesh" (before *"our* eyes," according to Larkin), the second Person of the Godhead will then return to a singular essence and substance with the Father, henceforth reigning as God—*period.* Paul thusly relates in I Corinthians 15:28, *"then shall the Son also, himself be subject unto him that put all things under him that God may be all in all."* Notice the cross-reference in Ephesians 1:23, *"Which is his body, the fulness of him that filleth all in all."* The bottom line is that "The Great Abdication" constitutes *the* watershed catalyst that precipitates eternity *future,* replicating the conditions of eternity *past* (prior to Genesis 1:1).

MIC DROP!

We have now arrived at the central thesis of this chapter. In the 1800s, Independence, Missouri, was called the "Queen City of the Trails," the jumping-off point for "Wagons Ho!" westward on the Oregon Trail. Applying this to my readers, for the faint-hearted, this marks your *last* chance to turn back. So, climb up at your own risk and don't say you weren't warned. (Smiley face!)

You will recall that dispensationalists typically divide "time" into seven eras (the last being the Millennium). However, in his Introduction, Trench posits an *eighth* dispensation (to reconcile the "rubs"):

> [I]f the reign of Christ in its perfection cannot be *millennial,* and shall not be *eternal,* it follows that between the end of the one, the millennial, and the beginning of the other, the eternal state, must of necessity intervene that *'dispensation of the fulness of times'* (Ephesians 1:10), that KINGDOM of the Son of God's love, that KINGDOM that cannot be shaken, which it is Christ's to enjoy as Heir of all things, and Head of the new creation.

Wow! While Paul describes the present dispensation of Grace in Ephesians 3:1-3, he also references another future dispensation. This would make "The Great Abdication" God's "Closing Illustration" for the eighth and final period! Larkin identified this second, "post-Millennial" reign of Christ as, "The Restoration of All Things," conforming to the *"mystery of his will"* (Ephesians 1:9). Thus, the inherent typology in the Davidic era of "War" will precede the Solomonic era of "Peace." Larkin summarizes:

> The *'Millennial Age'* and the *'Perfect Age,'* between which the Earth is renovated by Fire, make up the *'Age of Ages,'* which period is called the *KINGDOM OF THE SON OF MAN*. At the close of the 'Age of Ages' when Christ *'shall have put down all rule and all authority and power. For he must reign till he hath put all enemies under his feet,'* then Christ as the Son of Man, shall surrender the Kingdom to God, that God may be *ALL IN ALL*. I Corinthians 15:24-28 This is known as *The Great Abdication*...He will abdicate because He has *Finished the Work That Was Given Him to Do as the Son of Man*. He will not surrender His *Human Nature*, but his title *'Son of Man'* will merge back into that of *'Son of God'* so that the Divine *Godhead* shall thereafter act in its *Unity*, and God shall be *'ALL IN ALL.'* This will end what we understand by *Time*. Then *Eternity* will begin, which will be divided up into the *Ages of the Ages*. Of its end there is no hint.

The renowned nineteenth-century Bible teacher, G. Campbell Morgan, concurred. In his 1898 work, *God's Methods with Man*, Morgan called Trench's book "a scholarly and lucid exposition of this subject." Commenting on mankind's universal submission to Jesus in Philippians 2:5-11, he states, "That will never be until the Millennium is past *and the great Kingdom comes* which lies in the fullness of time beyond." Regarding Revelation 21-22, "Remember that these are only passing glimpses of the glory of *a kingdom on earth, beyond the Millennium,* the Great White Throne, and the final casting out of evil. This is a picture of the fulness of the times, when all things shall be subdued to the sway of Jesus."

James M. Gray was a protégé of D. L. Moody and the third president of Moody Bible Institute. In his 1903 lecture, "The Millennial Age," he lauds *After the Thousand Years* as a "notable book." Citing Trench repeatedly, Dr. Gray comments on Philippians 2:5-11 (in contrast to the Millennial disarray): "And yet, although this is something beyond, something greater than the Millennial Age, *it is at the same time not the final Eternal Age,* as the closing words of verse eleven indicate.

God, i.e., God the Father, or God distinguished from Christ the Mediator, is not yet seen as the All in All of I Corinthians 15." Speaking of *"the end,"* he wrote, "This 'end' will not follow immediately on the Second Coming, but be preceded by the Millennial Age. *And, we may now add, will be preceded also by the Dispensation of the Fullness of Times."*

Now before anyone faints, take a *deep* breath, then venture *another* look at Revelation 21 and 22, for here John reveals the opening scenes of this parenthetical "post-Millennial Kingdom," (*prior* to Eternity Future). You say, "But Brother Grady, according to all my prophecy charts, this is where eternity begins." Really? (Lol, so do mine!) During my seven-year "phone-pal" rapport with Mr. Cohen, I would often ask, "Sam, how ya doin' today?" The retired octogenarian *physicist* would reply with a quip that speaks to this very conundrum. "Bill, I'm killing *time* till time kills *me*." Laura Barge wrote one of my book cover endorsements for *Holy Ground*. This former research astrophysicist earned her Master's degree and PhD in Physics from Baylor University. I'd be willing to "go out on a limb" and say that both of these scientists would agree with *my* pea-brained layman's assessment that the fundamental difference between *time* and *eternity* is that (duh), "In eternity—there *is* no time" (thus the expression, "Time without end").

So, if these final two chapters in our Bible are *supposed* to be set in eternity—*where time is no longer being marked by a sequence of moments*—how do we reconcile Revelation 22:2? *"In the midst of the street of it, and on either side of the river, was there the tree of life, which bare twelve manner of fruits, **and yielded her fruit every month: and the leaves of the tree were for the healing of the nations."*** Isaiah 66:22-23 presents a similar "rub" regarding another purported scene in the eternal state. *"For as the **new heavens and new earth**, which I will make, shall remain before me, saith the LORD, so shall your seed and your name remain. And it shall come to pass, that **from one new moon to another, and from one sabbath to another**, shall all flesh come to worship before me, saith the LORD."* Feeling a little stumped, neighbor? (The Neutron Bomb inventor once exhibited a similar "deer in the headlights" reaction after I related that a redneck preacher friend of mine from North Carolina said he "done rejected" the "Big Bang Theory" because, and I quote, "Ain't no round things come out of explosions!")

Also, if Jesus abdicated at the *"end"* of the Millennium—what's He doing *back* on a throne at Revelation 21:5-6? *"**And he that sat***

upon the throne said, *Behold, I make all things new. And he said unto me, Write: for these words are true and faithful. And he said unto me, It is done.* **I am Alpha and Omega, the beginning and the end."** (We know who the "Alpha and Omega" is from Revelation 1:8.) Jesus is also shown enthroned in Revelation 22:1.

Then there's that little "rub" concerning the abolishment of death. I Corinthians 15:25-26 says Jesus *"must reign,* **till** *he hath put all enemies under his feet.* **The last enemy that shall be destroyed is death."** Funny, I didn't see any "death of death" in the Millennium—did you? (Sure seemed like they would've needed plenty of body bags at Revelation 20:9.) However, with Jesus *still* on "a" throne in Revelation 21:4, John writes, *"And God shall wipe away all tears from their eyes;* **there shall be no more death,** *neither sorrow, nor crying, neither shall there be any more pain: for the former things are passed away."*

Therefore, it appears that Jesus will enjoy *several* levels of authority: the first stage as the glorified "Headship of the Body" (His Church) during the sixth dispensation (to be perfected at the Second Advent); the second as the "Son of David," the homage of all Israel during the Millennium; the third would be as His concurrent exaltation over the Angelic Hosts; the fourth, His co-regency as "The Lamb," alongside His Father (Revelation 22:1) during the "Dispensation of the Fullness of Times"; and finally, His reign as "The Word" throughout eternity. An ancillary outline would be: Millennial Kingdom, with Jesus reigning *alone* on the old earth; Perfect Kingdom, with Jesus reigning *with* the Father on the new earth; Eternal Kingdom, with the Triune God reigning *"all in all"* from within the Godhead. (As an interesting aside, Evangelist Kevin Mann has noted that the word "Godhead" is specifically found *three* times in the King James Bible: Acts 17:29; Romans 1:20; and Colossians 2:9.)

You say, "Brother Grady, I can hardly wrap my mind around what you're suggesting!" Well, join the club. Even Dr. Ruckman—the single greatest Bible expositor in our time—conceded in his commentary on I Corinthians, "While all the material in verses 20 to 23 is well laid out in the Scriptures, I must admit, verses 24 to 29 are not quite as clear...I don't understand everything about these verses." In fact, after writing in his *Reference Bible* note at I Corinthians 15:28, "If we are 'in Christ,' that would imply that we would go with Him into the Godhead and merge with the Trinity," he concluded by reverting to his ethnic heritage, signing off with the German equivalent of *duh*— "Now, when I get this far out into infinity and eternity, trying to explain a matter as heavy as this one, my standard response is *Ich weiss nicht*." (Translation: "I do not know.")

"TO A THOUSAND GENERATIONS"

For my faithful readers who have not trashed this book (not yet, anyway), I have a special blessing for you. The one remaining factor is *duration*; the obvious buzzword in *"fulness of times"* being *"fulness."* Whereas all prior dispensations were curtailed due to "human error" (including the Tribulation as per Amos 8:9, Matthew 24:22, and Revelation 8:12), *this* dispensation will have *plenty* of time to run its course—especially since the centerpiece is Christ's glory.

However, the main contribution of the following revelation (beyond its establishing the length of this era) is the fact that it cements the orthodoxy of Trench's thesis itself—unless, of course, one is hesitant (too intimidated by "the brethren") to take what the Holy Ghost declared at face value. How's *this* for a hot potato? Moses wrote in Deuteronomy 7:9, *"Know therefore that the LORD thy God, he is God, the faithful God, which keepeth covenant and mercy with them that love him and keep his commandments* **to a thousand generations.** *"*

One could say that the decision to resurrect this long-lost doctrine (perhaps *"for such a time as this"*) boils down to a simple willingness to acknowledge the second principle of logic, the "Law of Contradiction," i.e., "Things that are different are not the same." For instance, would we agree that a "year" and a "generation" are clearly dissimilar? Well, whereas John established Israel's Millennial Kingdom as lasting a thousand *years*, Moses spoke of another, "slightly" longer period, lasting a thousand *generations.* What's that you say— "Moses wasn't referring to a *literal* 'thousand generations,' just engaging in hyperbole by employing *figurative* language? And besides, who needs *secular* logic for a *spiritual* issue?"

Okay, so let's drop reason and revert to traditional hermeneutics. The primary law to follow when interpreting any Biblical text is to accept it *literally*, unless the context mandates a *figurative* (allegorical) approach ("innocent until proven guilty"). Thus, Graves, Larkin, Morgan, Gray, Soltau, and their allies actually took the *orthodox* position, while their detractors unknowingly embraced the *unorthodox* view. But now you counter, "So who needs theology either? Besides, Deuteronomy 7:9 was just a *random* passage anyway." Okay, okay, we'll drop the logic *and* the hermeneutics. May we use the Bible?

Citing Deuteronomy 19:15, Paul wrote, *"In the mouth of two or three witnesses shall every word be established."* (II Corinthians 13:1) Guess what Psalm 105:8 says? *"He hath remembered his covenant for ever, the word which he commanded to a thousand generations."* And, as the old saying goes, "Third time's the charm," I Chronicles 16:15 completes the trilogy: *"Be ye mindful always of his covenant; the word which he commanded to a thousand generations."* Note that in Psalm 105, Jehovah says that *"He hath remembered His covenant"* (was deliberately mindful), while I Chronicles enjoins *us* to *"be mindful."* Imagine how God feels about this century-long blackout of His pledge. Other verses imply multiple generations (Exodus 20:5-6; 34:7; Deuteronomy 5:9-10; 32:7). Also, the shorter-numbered generations are always taken literally, prompting George Soltau to state in his 1912 book, *Past—Present—Future,* "It is therefore consistent to allow the higher number, 'a thousand,' to signify a definite number rather than an indefinite one."

TIME TO GET OFF THE FENCE AND VOTE!

Like I said up front, nobody *has* to accept *any* of this spiritual "speculation" —but you *do* have to get off the fence now and vote! (See I Kings 18:21) Either you will pick the *literal* or the *allegorical* mode. And don't forget, if you choose the latter, the onus is on *you* to enlighten the rest of us "literalist heretics" as to what the allegory was designed to teach. Thus, as "Santino Corleone" famously asked his father, "So, what's your answer gonna be, Pop?" the Holy Ghost requires the same answer from you.

For the record, my late friend and doctrinal mentor, the peerless Dr. Peter Sturges Ruckman, "appears" to have opted for the *figurative.* However, as he esteemed Larkin so highly, he states in his Corinthians commentary: "Now, Clarence Larkin has a different view…And since Clarence Larkin is the source for all prophetic exposition among pre-Millennial Fundamentalists and conservatives in the twentieth (and twenty-first) century, I would be doing you a disservice if I did not try to describe his system to you." (The foremost KJV defender was even willing to overlook Larkin's occasional misguided use of the *Revised*

Revision.) After summarizing Larkin's position, Ruckman humbly concludes, "Now, brethren, if there is any explanation *beyond these two*, I do not know what it is, and it will take someone who has put more prayer and study into it then I have to figure the thing out."

And so, the "mother of all rubs" remains—if any would be so "reckless" as to take this *thrice*-made Holy Ghost pronouncement *literally*...well, let's just say they'll need an updated prophecy chart. Thus, the question begs, where would you insert a period lasting a thousand *generations*? Which brings up the concomitant issue of a generation's length. Larkin picked thirty-three years, matching the lifespan of Jesus. (My good preacher friend, Jamie Twardzik, reminded me that II Samuel 5:5 reveals that David reigned thirty-three years over all Israel and Judah.) Bob Bolender prefers a century, based on Isaiah 65:20. Most Bible teachers use forty-seven years.

Perhaps the most precise formula would stem from Matthew 1:17, *"So all the generations from Abraham to David are **fourteen** generations; and from David until the carrying away into Babylon are **fourteen** generations; and from the carrying away into Babylon unto Christ are **fourteen** generations."* This makes forty-two generations comprising a period of approximately 1,990 years, equating to about forty-seven years each. This would make Christ's "Perfect Kingdom" last roughly 47,000 years! The stark contrast to a "mere" ten-century Millennium illuminates Moses' words (possibly a prophetic utterance to the rebels besieging Jerusalem), *"Thou turnest man to destruction; and sayest, Return, ye children of men. For **a thousand years** in thy sight are but as yesterday when it is past, **and as a watch in the night**."* (Psalm 90:3-4) Dr. Bolender summarizes accordingly:

> This paper makes the case for the Dispensation of the Fullness of Times. It is a stewardship distinct from the Millennial Kingdom of Jesus Christ. It is a finite temporal stewardship with a beginning and an end. It follows the Great White Throne judgment and associated Lake of Fire expulsions. It commences with the creation of new heavens and a new earth. It concludes when Jesus Christ παραδίδωμι paradidōmi delivers the kingdom to God the Father. (I Corinthians 15:24,28) It is a dispensation without sin or death. It is a dispensation populated by a thousand generations of those who love Jesus Christ and keep his commandments.

"OF THE INCREASE OF HIS GOVERNMENT...THERE SHALL BE NO END"

Larkin relates that the Jews will, once again, play a significant role in this dispensation. In addition to Deuteronomy 7:9 noting that the object to be extended for a *"thousand generations"* will be none other than God's covenant with Israel, Manasseh's papaw wrote, *"For as the new heavens and new earth, which I will make, shall remain before me, saith the LORD, **so shall your seed and your name remain.**"* (Isaiah 66:22)

However, the most surprising aspect of this schematic is that of ongoing *procreation* throughout. Unknown to typical Fundamentalists, who attribute every "heresy" in history to "Ruckman," the doctrine of "post-Millennial procreation" included a wide breadth of adherents in the Philadelphia Church Age, spanning several denominations, including accomplished academics from various theological institutions (John Darby to Lewis Sperry Chafer, et al.). Obviously, one cannot have "generation" without "procreation." Pastor Bolender articulates this period as "a finite temporal [i.e., within the bounds of time] humanly-procreative dispensation in the New Heavens and on the New Earth prior to The End (the Omega moment) beyond which will transpire Eternity Future."

Of course, the main objection has to do with an inability to read simple English. You say, "Dr. Grady, haven't you seen what Jesus said in Matthew 22:30. *"For **in the resurrection** they neither marry, nor are given in marriage, but are as the angels of God **in Heaven.**"* Dude— where do you find a single verse in Revelation 20-22 showing that Millennial *survivors* get raptured and/or translated into glorified bodies like Church Age believers? Remember, as "things that are different are not the same," *glorified saints* do not equate to *purified humans*; neither do *celestial* beings equal *terrestrial* beings. (The same error is applied concerning Genesis 6:1-4, where Bible deniers delete *"in heaven"* from *"the angels of God"* in Matthew.) As Tribulation survivors enter the Millennium, Millennial survivors will enter the new earth. The question arises, *how* will these people be preserved through earth's fiery renovation to land unscathed on their purged planet? (Isaiah 65:17; 66:22; II Peter 3:7-12) Well, duh—maybe by the same supernatural means God used to preserve Noah and *his* family through the Flood. And if the Lord could remove Elijah, only to retrieve him later to herald the Second Advent (II Kings 2:11), why...I'm sure He'll "think" of *something*.

The problem is that the average Christian has forgotten God's original charge to Adam and Eve, *"Be **fruitful**, and **multiply**, and **replenish** the earth."* (Genesis 1:28) After 7,000 years, the Lord will finally get what He always wanted *and* for nearly 50,000 years! Glory!! Tell me, neighbor— what's so hard to understand about that? Is this really so terrible? Then another asks, "Dr. Grady, how will this new earth hold all those people that will form those thousand generations, especially with no death?" Excellent question; for one thing, we don't know how large the new sphere will be. God could even design it to be constantly enlarging. But I believe He has a much more spectacular blueprint in store. (Hint: It might have something to do with Psalm 19:1, *"The **heavens** declare the glory of God; and the **firmament** sheweth his handywork."*)

The unraveling of this beautiful plan revolves around Revelation 21:1-2, *"And I saw a **new heaven** and a **new earth**: for the first heaven and the first earth were passed away; and there was no more sea. And I John saw the holy city, **new Jerusalem**, coming down from God out of heaven, prepared as a bride adorned for her husband."* While you probably never learned this in "Bible" college—conforming to the Pauline outline in I Corinthians 10:32, the new Earth will be "rightly divided" to the *Jews*; the new Heaven to the *Gentiles*; and the new City to the *Church*. To give my Fundamentalist readers a further leg up, that "sea" is not talking about any "sea" *you* ever "saw," but rather that great body of water between the second and third Heavens, referenced in Psalm 148:4, and blasted away at II Peter 3:10. (Note: As no two theologians agree on everything—the Ruckman-Larkin divide over the thousand generations being a perfect example—Trench erroneously believed that the new Jerusalem will be for Israel.)

You say, "Dr. Grady, what do y'all mean the new Heaven is for the Gentiles?" Well, didn't God tell Abraham, *"Look now toward heaven, and tell* [count] *the stars, if thou be able to number them: and he said unto him, **so shall thy seed be**"*? (Genesis 15:5) With Abraham's *physical* seed (through Isaac and Jacob) destined to inhabit the new earth (Ezekiel 37:24-28), and his *spiritual* seed (through Jesus Christ) destined to inhabit the new Jerusalem (Revelation 21:9-10), we perceive that those renovated worlds above our heads (Deuteronomy 4:19) are destined for Abe's *physical* seed—through *Ishmael* and *Esau*—constituting the Gentiles that will transit through the Millennium.

Have you ever read Isaiah 45:18? *"For thus saith the LORD that created the heavens; God himself that formed the earth and made it; he hath established it, **he created it not in vain, he formed it to be inhabited**: I am the LORD and there is none else."* While the "it" here is *technically* referring to earth, our precious home is just *one* planet in the vast solar system. Thus, God calls His visible, physical realm the "Kingdom of Heaven" (as opposed to His invisible, spiritual "Kingdom of God"), as the earth sits *in* "the heavens." So, what do you suppose would have happened *if* Adam and Eve hadn't sinned, and the human race obeyed that original command to repopulate the earth—with painless childbirth, no death, endless age, no wars, no sickness, no disease, and no poverty? Would God have called things off when the human race ran out of room to keep multiplying?

The greatest proof text confirming that Jesus will colonize the new Heaven with perfected Gentiles—beginning with the thousand generations of His ever-expanding "Perfect Kingdom," right on through eternity— is Isaiah 9:7. While most Christians love verse six, the mega-heavy implication hidden in the opening line of verse seven has virtually fallen through the cracks for a century: *"**Of the increase of his government and peace there shall be no end**, upon the throne of David, and upon his kingdom, to order it, and to establish it with judgment and with justice **from henceforth even for ever**. The zeal of the LORD of hosts will perform this."* Note, the text is not talking about *time*, but rather, *size*; it does not say, "Of the *existence* of...," or, "Of the *presence* of his government," but rather, *"Of the **increase** of his government...there shall be no end."* Christ's glorious domain will *continually* grow throughout the universe for some 47,000 years! This will constitute the "main harvest," as James 1:18 says *we* are merely the *"firstfruits of his creatures."* (Sadly, the average Baptist pastor is probably more familiar with the seventeenth-century Puritan minister, *Increase* Mather.)

And, one more thing, while the Bride's heavenly address will remain the new Jerusalem forever, her main responsibility throughout the "Dispensation of the Fullness of Times" will be managing her Husband's ever-growing realm (Proverbs 31:23, 27). In Revelation 19:16, Jesus is called a "King *of* kings" and a "Lord *of* lords." Well, neighbor, *we* are those very "kings" and "lords" who will oversee everything, especially after Jesus re-enters the Godhead. Being *"born* again," we'll be *"formed* again," i.e., in God's image (Genesis 1:27), only *this* time, in the image of God the Son (I Corinthians 11:7; Colossians 3:10). As Charles Wesley wrote, "*Adam's* likeness now efface. Stamp *thine* image in its place" (Genesis 5:1-3; I Corinthians 15:45).

So, don't pass out when you arrive in the new Jerusalem and discover there are no "family circles" there, *broken* or *unbroken* (Sorry about that, "Man in Black"), for we will probably all appear as thirty-three-year-old, sinless, male replicas of Christ's resurrected body—able to eat food, become visible or invisible at will, and travel through outer space at about 1,000,000,000 miles per second! Believe it or not, even Billy Graham believed much of this and actually said so on Johnny Carson's *The Tonight Show* in 1967 (the same year Jerry Monday appeared), "I think that we are going to be able to go from planet to planet, and from one part of the universe to the other…as fast as thought…and have tremendous enterprises to do on other planets; and I think there are many indications in the Bible about this." ("Come on, man!" as "El-Cid" would say. Read the verses before you go apoplectic on me: Psalm 17:15; Matthew 22:30; Luke 24:38-43; Romans 8:29; II Corinthians 5:16; I John 3:1-3.)

HOLD ONTO YOUR HAT, NEIGHBOR!

As we previously established, the *worst*-case scenario of this holy conjecture is that Jesus would get *more* glory—ruling over, and eventually *turning* over to His Father, a *real* Kingdom of Perfected Righteousness (rather than having had little time to "enjoy" His long-awaited "inheritance," having to suppress perennial insurgencies, not to mention leaving His Father a fried globe littered with a few billion corpses). As Bolender notes, "Whereas the amount of New Testament space attributed to the 'thousand *year* Kingdom' is relegated to the 'white space' between Revelation 20:6-7, the '1,000 generation Kingdom' is allotted two entire chapters!"

However, for any of my readers who are still acting like Saul's people, who "*followed him trembling*" (I Samuel 13:7), let me offer you a final spiritual sedative. If y'all just don't have the stomach to exercise your "individual soul liberty" by telling the "heresy police" to get lost, all you have to do is visualize Revelation 21 and 22 as *the first forty-seven thousand years of eternity*. "But," you say, "Dr. Grady, that sounds like a contradiction of physics." Oh, hush—*you* started this!

Besides, we also agreed that the Trench-Larkin schematic does *not* alter anything in the Church Age; does *not* affect the pre-Trib Rapture; does *not* shorten the traditional length of the *seven*-year Tribulation (Hello!); and does *not* change the Millennium (apart from noting the nonstop "negative waves"). In fact, if it wasn't for the God-given courage I received to commit this material to print—ninety-five percent of my critics would have never even *known* about "The Great Abdication." (Can't make this stuff up, folks!)

Now, while Dr. Ruckman interpreted the "thousand generations" *figuratively* (in his commentaries on Psalms and Corinthians, along with his reference Bible), his exposition of Revelation 21-22 is the most profound I've ever read! (But, to let you in on a "little" secret, in an "all's well that ends well" scenario, Clarence Larkin's influence on "Brother Pete" was *so* pronounced that when "the Doc" penned his Revelation commentary, he actually "flinched" —siding with Clarence, *twice*; but wait till I get there, neighbor.)

As Revelation 21:4 declares, *"there shall be no more death"* in the *eighth* dispensation (much less throughout eternity), it appears that the source of this supernatural constitution for perfected humans will be the "Tree of Life." Revelation 22:2 says, *"In the midst of the street of it, and on either side of the river, was there **the tree of life**, which bare twelve manner of fruits, and yielded her fruit every month: and **the leaves of the tree were for the healing of the nations.**"* We therefore discern the circular fashion of God's eternal word, for having started with the "Tree of Life" in Genesis 2:9, the Bible will end beneath the same branches. (Joyce Kilmer would appropriately write, "I think that I shall never see a poem lovely as a tree…Poems are made by fools like me, but only God can make a tree.") This is precisely why the last two chapters of Scripture pick up where the first two chapters left off—perfect humans preparing to perform their divine mandate to *"[b]e fruitful, and multiply, and replenish the earth."* (Genesis 1:28)

These "healed nations," along with their sovereigns, appear in Revelation 21:24, in conjunction with the new Jerusalem: *"And the **nations of them which are saved** shall walk in the light of it: **and the kings of the earth do bring their glory and honor into it.**"* And so, before proceeding, if you *still* think you might crash and burn over what you are about to read—just ask yourself: When was the last time *anyone* made *any* sense out of these two chapters for *your* benefit?

What's that you say, *"Never?"* (I thought so...) We both know that most of "the brethren" are more familiar with "flat earth" theories than "new earth" realities. So, hold onto your hat, neighbor!

The reason these kings enter the Holy City through *twelve* gates is because they hail from *twelve* nations on the new earth (one nation per gate). God fixed that number back in the "Table of Nations," right after Moses pre-recorded the future migrations of Japheth and his two siblings: *"And unto Eber were born two sons: **the name of one was Peleg; for in his days was the earth divided.**"* (Genesis 10:25) Take a *wild* guess what "Peleg" means; would you believe, "division"? As the next dot to connect will show, this division refers to the Lord separating the earth's population at Genesis 11:8...

> *Remember the days of old, **consider the years of many generations:** ask thy father, and he will shew thee; thy elders, and they will tell thee. When the Most High **divided to the nations their inheritance,** when he separated the sons of Adam, **he set the bounds of the people according to the number of the children of Israel.** For the Lord's portion is his people: **Jacob is the lot of his inheritance.** He found him in a desert land, and in the waste howling wilderness; he led him about, he instructed him, **he kept him as the apple of his eye.*** (Deuteronomy 32:7-10)

Reinforced by Luke's reference in Acts 17:26 to the *"times before appointed, and **the bounds of their habitation,"*** the LORD has apparently divided this planet into *twelve* regions, *vis-à-vis* the *"**number** of the children of Israel."* While there's no way to be sure, a sample would include: the Arctic Circle; North, Central, and South America; Antarctica; Greenland; Europe; Asia; India; Africa; Australia; and New Zealand. According to Isaiah 10:13, these divine borders will be removed by the globalist polices of Antichrist. No matter, however, with perfected Jewry still the preeminent race, God will employ these same regions (or possibly an updated dozen) on the new earth for twelve Gentile fiefdoms as a veritable launching pad to "regions beyond" (for some *real* excursions into cloud land).

You say, *"Good night,* Dr. Grady, what in the *world* are you talking about now? Enter dot number three: *"And lest thou lift up thine eyes unto heaven, and when thou seest the sun, and the moon, and the stars, **even all the host of heaven,** shouldest be driven to worship them, and serve them,* *which the Lord thy God hath divided unto all nations under the whole heaven.* " (Deuteronomy 4:19) As any pagan astrologer will tell you, our solar system is "divided" into twelve constellations, which constitute the twelve sectors that the twelve Gentile nations will inhabit (arriving via angelic airlifts (Luke 16:22). *I'm* crazy, you say? Maybe you should take another "look" at II Peter 3:12-13: "*Looking for and hastening unto the coming of the day of God, wherein the heavens being on fire shall be dissolved, and the elements shall melt with fervent heat? Nevertheless we, according to his promise, look for **new heavens** and a new earth, **wherein dwelleth righteousness**.* " Trench writes:

> Again, let us ask ourselves whether it would be consistent with the revelation and history of God's dealings with the world, that He should permit it to be flooded with sin and rent with rebellion for nearly six thousand years, and then when His rule, temporarily and imperfectly reestablished, has been once more impiously disputed in the great revolt, to receive back from His Son that Kingdom stained with blood, and charred with fires of judgment, and that He should have no further opportunity of rule as Son of Man? Should we not rather expect that His reign in the '*new heavens and a new earth, wherein dwelleth righteousness*' (II Peter 3:13), would at least equal, if not greatly exceed in its length, the reign of Satan in the world of sin?

Then there's that hidden nugget David left us:

> *When I consider thy heavens, the work of thy fingers, the moon and the stars, which thou hast ordained; What is man, that thou art mindful of him? and the son of man, that thou visited him? For thou hast made him a little lower than the angels, and hast crowned him with glory and honour. **Thou madest him to have dominion over the works of thy hands**; thou hast put all things under his feet.* (Psalm 8:3-6)

The last time I checked, neighbor, my *fingers* were part of my *hands.* (Hallelujah!) Perhaps this ever-increasing, intergalactic, "Isaiah 9:7" Kingdom will now come into sharper focus through the Pauline lens of Ephesians 1:10, "*That in **the dispensation of the fullness of times** he might gather together in one all things in Christ, **both which are in heaven, and which are on earth; even in him**.* "

Lastly, one of the more amazing benefits of this schematic is that it finally explains the role of Jesus as *"the everlasting Father"* in Isaiah 9:6. Notice what God the Son promises relative to His still-temporal rule alongside His own Father in Revelation 21:6-7 (what will occur after *"the end,"* in eternity): *"And he said unto me, **it is done**. I am Alpha and **Omega**, the beginning and **the end**...He that overcometh shall inherit all things; and I will be his God, **and he shall be my son**."* (By the way, neighbor, do y'all think half those "yahoos," who love debating about modalism, have ever connected *these* dots?) But first, back to the "Tree of Life," for that is where all Millennial survivors must make their initial stop.

"THE TREE OF LIFE"

Unanimously declared the undisputed winner by default (no IFB critic rendering any sane alternative exposition), Dr. Ruckman posits that the humans who pass through these twelve gates—to partake of the *"tree of life"* —will likely do so on their birth month. He then clarifies, "This does not mean that each nation has a separate month, but everybody born in September, for instance, goes in through the gate assigned to their particular nation."

As Revelation 22:14 proclaims, *"Blessed are they that **do his commandments, that they may have right to the tree of life**, and may enter in through the gates into the city,"* a combination of "faith and works" (Revelation 12:17; 14:12; 16:15) will enable surviving Millennial saints to gain their eternal life by eating the fruit of that tree. (Owing to a combination of pseudo-King James Onlyism and anti-dispensational bias, Fundamentalists, including the late John R. Rice and Jack Hyles, have traditionally broken their spiritual necks here, substituting "wash their robes" for *"do his commandments."*) According to Revelation 22:3, the "curse" in Genesis 3:17 will then be lifted. Most Christians are unaware that the main reason humans (and animals) die is because everything they eat comes from contaminated soil (Romans 3:13). However, as foreshadowed by Psalm 65:9, the soil on the new earth will be irrigated by that *"pure river of **water of life**, clear as crystal, proceeding out of the throne of God and of the Lamb."* (Revelation 22:1)

Now, watch as my late mentor, Dr. Ruckman—the man who taught me more Bible than any ten other preachers combined—displays his first shift toward *his* own mentor:

> So in eternity, we might assume that if the people who are born do not partake of the 'tree of life,' *they die.* But in Revelation 20, we read that *'death and hell were cast into the lake of fire,'* so this conclusion may not be the truth. *Therefore, we will alter it just a little and say this*: for 33,000 years (*This is the period that Larkin calls the 'Age of Ages' before eternity begins. See Deut. 7:9 and I Chron. 16:15-19*), or a period of time that only God knows, people will have to take of the 'tree of life.' There is a possibility that once a man partakes of the 'tree of life,' and reproduces seed, his seed receives eternal life and the offspring does not have to take of the 'tree of life.' This means that people in the Tribulation and Millennium who 'keep His commandments,' will be able to partake of the 'tree of life' in their month—the month of their birth—and from then on their offsprings (sic) are *born with eternal life.*

Dr. Ruckman then explains:

> This is impossible to figure for certain because nobody knows what would have happened if Adam had taken of the 'tree of life' *before* he fell (see Gen. 2:9,16). But the indication is that if he had taken of the 'tree of life' before he fell, he would have lived forever, and the seed that he would have produced would live forever too.

By the time "God's junkyard dog" got to page 780, Brother Larkin must have *really* been smiling in the Glory World! (Are any of you Ruckmanites still with me?)

> This 'dispensation of the fullness of times' is supposedly based on a passage in Deuteronomy 7:9, the idea being that God made promises to Israel which will endure for 1,000 generations. (*Clarence Larkin has figured thirty-three years to a generation; the figure being based on the life of Christ. This would make a period of 33,000 years for this expansion before eternity begins.*) If a generation is one hundred years, *as it is in Genesis 15*, then the passage of time would be 100,000 years. If a generation is forty-seven years, *as it is in Matthew 1:17*, the figure would be 47,000 years. *So, varying between 33,000, 47,000, and 100,000 years, there seems to be a period of*

time, marked off by days, weeks, and months, before eternity begins. In this time, outer space will be populated. Think of outer space being populated for 33,000 years! What a small slice of time was cut out for those of us who lived seventy or eighty years, and then died, worrying all our life about 'making a living!' God is in no hurry. 'One day is with the Lord as a thousand years, and a thousand years as one day.' (2 Pet. 3:8) The fact that the Devil has detained God for 6,000 years is of no concern to Him. *His plans are going to take 33,000 years to carry out anyway, at a minimum.*

He then concludes:

> The gist of Revelation 22:2 is that on the new earth, in eternity, there are twelve nations divided off by twelve boundaries, and these nations are composed of nations who were saved during the tribulation (Matt. 25) and during the Millennium (Rev. 19). These 'saved nations' go into the city, partake of the 'tree of life' to get their eternal life, and then they spend eternity reproducing and multiplying infinitely and going out into outer space, and popularizing first the twelve constellations that make up the zodiac, and then from there they move on out into outer space.

Thus, James 1:18 (matching I Corinthians 15:23) states: *"Of his own will begat he **us** with the word of truth, that **we should be a kind of firstfruits of his creatures."*** The "main harvest" is reaped throughout those "thousand generations" and beyond. (Don't ask me about the "gleanings" 'cause I ain't got nary a clue.) Of course, by now there's *got* to be some unhinged Fundies who would reject all this unbelievable sirloin because the equally whacked-out Mormons have hijacked a sizable portion. During a Hyles-Anderson chapel service, I recall hearing a popular evangelist (who was always boasting about reading his Greek New Testament every morning) defame Dr. Ruckman (without mentioning his name): "I know of a preacher who is so sex-crazed, he thinks we'll be having sexual relations for eternity." Well, that sure won't apply to the Body of Christ (nor to the third category of inhabitants, glorified Old Testament, Tribulation, and Millennial saints). For one thing, *we* won't need the "Tree of Life" to get eternal life, for we already have it (I John 5:11-12). I received *my* "eternal life" from a "tree of *death"* (Galatians 3:13). And secondly, even if we *could* engage in physical relations (which we will absolutely *not* be doing), we'll be too busy superintending that eternally expanding empire (*especially* after Jesus reenters the Trinity).

Finally, the surreal concept that drove Dr. Ruckman to glossolalia (*"Ich weiss nicht"*) was that our bilocative position of being *"in* Christ" implies that we will accompany Jesus back into the Godhead (where He will "rejoin" the Triune God—in *whatever* sense is implied by the phrase *"all in all"*). While this has also befuddled "Yours Truly," one day the Holy Spirit *seemed* to direct me to Ephesians 1:13-14: *"In whom ye also trusted, after that ye heard the word of truth, the gospel of your salvation:* **in whom also after that ye believed, ye were sealed with that holy Spirit of promise,** *Which is the earnest of our inheritance **until** the redemption of the purchased possession, unto the praise of his glory."* My initial reaction was euphoric, believing that "I" had discovered a great scriptural nugget, i.e., *on my own* (the downfall of many Peter Ruckman wannabes).

Based on that little word *"until,"* I reasoned that *our* being sealed by the Holy Ghost into Christ's spiritual Body would end when we entered Heaven. There, "the seal" would be broken, like when our wives and mothers open their canning jars, etc. (Might we then be like Paul, musing in II Corinthians 12:3, *"whether in the body, or out of the body, I cannot tell: God knoweth"?*) However (to quote our old friend Tevya again), "But on the other hand...," I Thessalonians 4:17 *still* says, *"and so shall we **ever be with the Lord**."* So, maybe we *do* retain our "positional presence" *in* Him as we disappear inside the Godhead—while simultaneously retaining our "practical presence" out in that "wild black yonder" as Christ's viceroys, governing His eternally expanding realm. Yet, in any event, I too feel left with no other response but, *"Ni' thuigim"* (Gaelic for, "I don't understand"). And because so many folks have the strange idea that William *Patrick Grady* is an *Italian* name (perhaps because of all my "Wop" jokes), well, here ya go, neighbor— *"Non capisco."*

"THE MORROW AFTER THE SABBATH"

One final "teenie-weenie" Bible study will form a fitting conclusion to our chapter, "There's A Better Day A-Comin'." (The significance of the word "day" will soon be apparent.) In II Peter 3:8, God reveals His prophetic model of Millennial "days" based on the "seven" system of

Leviticus 23 and 25. *"But, beloved, be not ignorant of this one thing, that **one day** is with the Lord as a thousand years, and a thousand years as **one day**."* (Hosea 6:2 exhibits a similar example.)

According to the traditional schematic, following *six* "prophetic" days (comprising a thousand years each—*four* thousand in the Old Testament and *two* thousand in the Church Age), a glorious Millennial Sabbath day's rest will occur. Yet, as we have discovered, it will be a *turbulent* "rest." But for His divinity, King Jesus would have worn Himself out "wearing out" Millennial rebels with that iron scepter. However, while the Millennium is definitely typified by the Sabbath (or seventh day), the same chapter also makes a subtle reference to an *eighth* day.

> *And you shall count unto you from **the morrow after the sabbath**, from the day that ye brought the sheaf of the wave offering; seven sabbaths shall be complete: Even unto **the morrow after the seventh sabbath** shall ye number fifty days; and ye shall offer a new meat offering unto the Lord.* (Leviticus 23:15-16)

Jehovah also had Moses instruct the people regarding special "*eighth* day" celebrations:

> *Seven days ye shall offer an offering made by fire unto the LORD: **on the eighth day shall be an holy convocation unto you**; and ye shall offer an offering made by fire unto the LORD: it is a solemn assembly; and ye shall do no servile work therein....Also in the fifteenth day of the seventh month, when you have gathered in the fruit of the land, ye shall keep a feast unto the LORD seven days: on the first day shall be a sabbath, **and on the eighth day shall be a sabbath**.* (Leviticus 23:36, 39)

The seventh day applied to the "*old* creation," for that is when God rested, then passed it to Man for his own day of rest (Exodus 20:9-11; 34:21). But as the human race (later, Israel, more specifically) began to disrespect the seventh day (Isaiah 58:13-14), the future Millennium was doomed to be a flawed "rest" at best; i.e., just one more *imperfect* "day." However, the *eighth* day, as the *first* day of a new week—the day of our Saviour's resurrection—points to a "*new* creation" rest. (In Bible numerology, eight relates to new beginnings: e.g., *eight* souls left the ark to re-establish life; Jewish males, including Jesus, were circumcised on the *eighth* day; Jesus showed Himself alive *eight* times; the New Testament was penned by *eight* men.) Following the *imperfect* "rest of nature" on the *seventh* day, comes the supernatural and *perfect* "rest of resurrection" on the *eighth* day. Thus, the perfect glory of the risen Christ, in conjunction with a resurrected Kingdom, will come on the "morrow" *after* the Sabbatical Millennium. Conforming to the "Dispensation of the *Fullness of Times*," you could call it *The Longest Day* (film title commemorating June 6, 1944, Allied landing on Normandy Beach). Trench concludes:

> Note, therefore, that this eighth day cannot point to the Millennium, which is represented by the seventh; and it cannot be Eternity, for it is a day or definite period, like each of the preceding days...The first division of time for man is called the first day, the last is called the eighth day. Eternity lies behind the first and beyond the last. The eighth day must therefore be a dispensation lying between the Millennium and the subsequent Eternity.

THE FATHER'S DEBUT

One of the most overlooked truths in Scripture has been staring at us for years in Revelation 21:3, *"And I heard a great voice out of heaven saying, Behold, the tabernacle of God is with men, **and he will dwell with them**, and they shall be his people, **and God himself shall be with them**, and be their God."* With John 1:18 stating, *"No **man** hath **seen God** at any time,"* and the Lord reiterating in John 5:37, *"Ye have neither **heard his voice** at any time, nor **seen his shape**,"* the greatest blessing Jesus will undoubtedly enjoy at the start of this final, 47,000-year-long "day," is when He gets to introduce His Father (and co-Regent) to the real "New World Order" of perfected humanity! (See Revelation 21:22; 22:1, 5) This would appear consistent with the intimate relationship that Adam and Eve enjoyed with God before the Fall (Genesis 3:8).

The remedial explanation for man's restored ability to "see" the Father (alongside "the Lamb") will probably fall somewhere between the ingredients in that miraculous "fruit" (the *real* "Balance of Nature") and those supernatural "swabs" God will use to *"wipe away all tears from their eyes."* The typical language for this grand event has likewise been sitting undetected in our Bibles all along: *"And it came to pass on **the eighth day** that Moses called Aaron...and he said...**to day the LORD will appear unto you**."* (Leviticus 9:1, 2, 4)

To employ a popular metaphor— "at the end of *this* day," *the* ultimate "closing illustration" in history will literally *end* history, forever! Thus, the great Philadelphia Age missionary, George Soltau, wrote over a century ago, "This is the closing act in the history of the human race as recorded in Scripture—the limit of prediction, not of existence." And so, all I can say is—What an ineffable finale!! According to *"our beloved brother Paul"* (II Peter 3:15), *if* we retain our positional presence *"in* Christ," God the Father, accompanied by "the Word" and the Holy Spirit (Revelation 22:17), will be taking you and me into *their* eternal abode (I Corinthians 2:9; 15:28).

RETURNING FROM CLOUDLAND

So, kiddies, did y'all have a refreshing diversion on our round-trip excursion to "Cloudland" today? Did you especially enjoy the inflight "meal" service? As the runway lights are now approaching, we might as well end where we took off.

Remember when that Satanic Jesuit imposter altered the text of the so-called "Lord's Prayer"? And do y'all recall how I said the average Baptist was just about as ignorant as "Franny" concerning this "prayer"? Well, how's your present understanding? Did the Holy Ghost *"[make] known unto* [you] *the mystery of his will"* concerning the future *"gather*[ing] *together in one **all things in Christ?***" (Ephesians 1:9) Can you now see to which "Kingdom" Jesus was referring? ***"Our Father*** *which art in heaven, Hallowed be thy name.* ***Thy kingdom come, Thy will be done*** *in earth, as it is in heaven...**For thine is the kingdom**, and the power, and the glory, **for ever**. Amen."* (Matthew 6:9, 10, 13)

Obviously, the "kingdom" referred to *there* was *not* Christ's Millennial reign, nor the thousand generations, but rather the *Father's* kingdom. Therefore, the true "Lord's Prayer" for the perfect "will" of "God the Father" —concerning *"His* Kingdom" —will never "be done" *until* "the end" comes at "The Great Abdication!"

POSTSCRIPT

In closing, I sincerely hope this study has been a blessing to your soul. When I wrote my conspiracy tome, *How Satan Turned America Against God*, I devoted an entire chapter ("Attitude Check") on behalf of my many pastor friends, warning my readers not to become self-appointed missionaries intent on spreading their "eye-opening discoveries" within their local churches (becoming unhinged pains in the derrière.) I would strongly issue a similar caution here. If your pastor ultimately does not embrace a literal interpretation of the thousand generations (or any other part of this chapter)—while you do—*keep these blessings to yourself!*

Let me also state that I do *not* claim to be the final authority on this subject. Only a fool would be so pretentious. And by the way, neighbor, don't let all my bravado fool ya; truth be told, I barely have a handle on the heavier particulars myself. (But, as Jack Hyles used to joke, "If you repeat that, I'll deny it.")

I recall eating breakfast with Dr. Ruckman at a Perkins Pancake House near Monroe, Ohio, in 1992. While chomping on some crispy bacon, he began diagramming the twelve constellations on a napkin and said, "Somebody needs to do some further study on this." Perhaps someone will do the same regarding *this* holy subject—pursuing the very real possibility of a "finite, temporal, humanly-procreative dispensation" that will last for one thousand literal generations, situated between the Millennium and Eternity. (And if you don't wind up buying any of this, at *least* admit that it was cool while it lasted.)

Remember, none of us will ever totally "arrive" down here (Proverbs 3:7; Galatians 6:3; Philippians 3:12), for that "Book" is pretty deep! Thus, George Trench concludes *After the Thousand Years* with a profound statement that should humble us all: "To man it is given but to dabble in the broken waters on the shore. The ocean of Truth lies beyond."

While the Ages Roll
(Mosie Lister)

Someday this stammering tongue
will falter no more
And a grander, sweeter song I shall sing
Then I'll join the ransomed choir
On Heaven's bright shore
Forever to praise the King

Chorus:
And while the ages roll
I'll keep on praising Him
and my voice will never tire or grow old.

And my song shall ever be
Praise the Lamb, who died for me
And I'll sing it while ages shall roll.

When a million years have passed
in that wonderful place,
My song of praise will just have begun;
For my song will never end
While I look on His face,
And my song will never be done.

(Repeat Chorus)

O the depth of the riches both of the wisdom and knowledge of God! how unsearchable are his judgments, and his ways past finding out! For who hath known the mind of the Lord? or who hath been his counselor? Or who hath first given to him, and it shall be recompensed unto him again? For of him, and through him, and to him, are all things: to whom be glory for ever. Amen. (Romans 11:33-36)

22

I Want to Die on the Battlefield

MY EARLIEST MEMORY of Brother "U-B" was in the late 1980s, appropriately, at one of Dr. Peter Ruckman's "Bad Attitude Baptist Blowouts." He was running up and down the aisles waving a bright red handkerchief. I distinctly remember that his colorful suspenders stood out as well. Although he definitely had a wild-eyed look, there was also something very transparent, almost childlike about him.

William (Bill) Eubanks was born in Portland, Oregon, on June 16, 1941. Before reaching his tenth birthday, he was already experiencing the *"trouble"* mentioned in Job 14:1 (the product of a broken home). However, about that same time (July 1951), Bill's father sent him to a week of summer camp in the Sierra Mountains of California, east of Modesto. On the final night, a male Christian worker witnessed to Bill and led him in a "sinner's prayer."

He then spent his formative years working in sawmills and logging camps in Oregon and Northern California. By 1967, he was already serving an eighteen-month sentence in the Oregon State Penitentiary for drug possession. It was at this particularly dark time in Bill's life that he "happened" upon (and read) a little, inconspicuous appearing, black-and-white illustrated pamphlet titled, "This Was Your Life" (Jack Chick's signature Gospel tract). God was reaching out to "U-B."

CIRCUS CIRCUS

No sooner had Bill reached the *age* of twenty-one than he was dealing the *game* of "Twenty-one" (among other card games). He would pass the next seventeen years in the highly toxic gaming industry, eventually graduating to the coveted position of "pit boss," overseeing a dozen poker dealers in Las Vegas (*Casino*) and Lake Tahoe (*Godfather II*). For my privileged readers who grew up in church, a pit boss (known today as the "pit manager") is the top enchilada (originally the casino manager, or one of the other floor managers) who directs the employees that work in the casino pit. This "Hell-hole" arena typically contains several tables for Blackjack, Poker, Craps, Roulette, and other games.

Apart from illicit activities, it doesn't get much worse than earning a "living" as a pit boss in Sin City (legalized gambling and prostitution with plenty of liquor, all under the watchful eye of Bugsy Siegel's "descendants"). Certain worldly Christians insist they can't see what's so wrong with an occasional lottery ticket, etc. Apparently, they're so carnal they can't discern that the bedrock philosophy of all "gambling" is abject *atheism*; why do you think they're called "games of *chance*" (I Samuel 6:9)? You'd think they'd catch on from the soldiers *"casting lots"* for our Lord's garments at Calvary (Psalm 22:18; Matthew 27:35).

One of the more bizarre dens of iniquity where Bro. Bill did his thing was the famous Circus Circus on the Las Vegas strip (eventually morphing into one of the most "successful" casinos in Nevada). Monkeys were trained to pay out jackpot winnings. An elephant named Tonya roamed the joint in a pink outfit, pulling slot machine handles and tossing dice with her trunk. In one short-lived publicity stunt, baby elephants were transported around the casino via an overhead tram, giving the illusion that they were flying.

Dr. Bob Jones, Sr., used to say, "You can't win at the game of sin." Before my father got saved late in life, he spent much of his adulthood plying his dual trade as a *bookie* ("bookkeeper") and a *shylock* ("loan officer") throughout the five boroughs of New York City. I can still remember his paternal advice (regarding horse racing), "Billy, the only way to beat those ponies is with a whip." Over half-a-century later, I am blessed to *preach* in Las Vegas (for my good friend, Pastor Mitch Serviss, and the wonderful people of Bible Baptist Church).

ASSURANCE OF SALVATION

In January 1979, Bill was working as a pit boss over a dozen poker dealers on the day shift at the Sahara Tahoe Hotel and Casino in Stateline, Nevada. Bored with life in general, he began to watch various televangelists on the Christian television channel in his plush apartment overlooking Lake Tahoe. "Strangely" (as he would later testify), the more *preaching* he viewed, the less *weed* he smoked. The Lord was tracking His future "tract star" (John 8:44).

Thankfully, after several providential events—including a broken ankle, a powerful earthquake, a six-part Christian television mini-series (*Jesus of Nazareth*), a brief experimental stint in a Bible college (three whole days), and one *really* unusual visitor (Hebrews 13:2)—Bill finally got it nailed down. As he would later testify,

> It was about 10 P.M., April the 8th 1979. I dropped off that couch, fell on my knees and cried out to *God* for mercy. I prayed, '*Lord Jesus*, please forgive me of my sins, come into my heart and save me.' I am sure I prayed and said some other things I can't remember, but *light* came into that room, *salvation* flooded my soul, and the captive was *set free! It was over...it was done!* The great transaction was made, and for *sure* I knew I was *born again*...John 3:7. Thank *God* for His wonderful *Son, Jesus Christ; God* in the flesh.

"A PECULIAR PEOPLE"

In I Peter 2:9, God's children are called *"a **peculiar** people."* The accuracy of this inspired assessment is confirmed by three unexplainable truths: 1) we believe a message we cannot explain; 2) we love a person we've never met; and 3) we're homesick for a place we've never been! (Glory!!) However, as that famous last line in George Orwell's *Animal Farm* says, "All animals are equal, but *some* animals are *more* equal than others" —some of *God's* children are more "peculiar" than others. If you turn to the word "peculiar" in any dictionary, Bill Eubanks' picture will be there. After all, he *was* born in pre-"Autonomous Zone," Portland, Oregon. (His future bride would represent the stellar exception.)

For instance, take the matter of how Bill's youthful nickname appears in his book. While most people would abbreviate Eubanks as "Eubie," he invented the *peculiar* hyphenated spelling of "U-B." (Therefore, to appease my proofreader/editor wife, hereafter, Bill Eubanks will be referred to as "Eubie.")

And so, as I was saying, Brother Eubie was *definitely* a mold-breaking designer's model, which, by the way, is the definitive trait of a true

King James Bible believer. (Conversely, the "TR" crowd produces mostly clones.) That Bill was greatly influenced by "Ruckmanism" would also factor into the equation, as the "Doc" was always quick to acknowledge, "The brighter the bulb, the more bugs it attracts." Of the scores of "KJV-Only" preachers who loved Eubie, I'm sure they would all agree that he was one of the *most* "peculiar" of all. The stereotypical image would be of him parading down any number of inner city streets wearing an old-fashioned, double-sided Scripture sandwich board! As Lester Roloff used to say, "I'm a fool for Christ; whose fool are you?" Bill's attitude was, "If I'm a nut, I'm screwed onto the right bolt!" His friends knew he was likely to do *anything* under the right circumstances. For instance, on one particular mission trip:

> We're tractin' in Vera Cruz, Mexico, we split up, and I come upon a Catholic Church that's packed out. There are three doors open, and the joint is so full the people can't get in because of the press. As I walk onto the property, I give out some tracts, and I feel some opposition, so I don't know why I do it, but the next person I give a tract to, *I cross myself.* That person smiles and lights up like a Christmas tree. It's going good now. I get to the doors of the "church," crossing myself, bowing, and saying 'Maria, Maria.' They love it! Eager hands reach for my Chick Tracts. People in the 'church' are smiling and asking for my Chick tracts with their eyes and outstretched hands. I pass them out like a hotdog vendor at Yankee Stadium. I don't know what's going on in the 'church,' but I'm getting 'The Death Cookie', 'Why is Mary Crying?', 'Are Roman Catholics Christians?', and many other titles to these precious Mexican people. In fifteen minutes, I had gone to the three doors that were open and passed out four hundred tracts to a packed house, kneeling, crossing myself, and repeating, 'Maria, Maria.' I've found that works every time around a crossback church.

We also knew that Bill had absolutely *no* use for the Baalite Nicolaitanes, who kept their Catholic parishioners in bondage. The former Augustinian monk, Martin Luther, was known to say, "I used to think the Pope was the Vicar of Christ; now I think he's the Vicar of Hell!" Brian Green informed me:

> Bill was in the Verizon store in Houston trying to get a cell phone and an old Catholic priest and a young priest walked in, wearing

their clerical garb. Bill got up from the counter where the Verizon employee was helping him and went straight for the older priest. He pointed his finger in his face and told him, 'I can't wait for the day that God chucks you into the Lake of Fire for preaching your d*#m damnable doctrine.' They kicked him out of the Verizon store and on his way out he 'tracted' everyone in there.

One reason that Bill exhibited more "eccentricities" than the rest of us "less peculiar" folks, had to do with God's unique call on his life (Romans 14:4). The Lord led His servant to spearhead a ministry called "Seed for the Cities," through which he would eventually distribute well over a million Chick tracts via "hand-to-hand" contact ("combat"), mostly on the "mean streets" of this world—locales where few of us "normal" Christians would venture. His life's verse defined his world-view: *"O give thanks unto the LORD; call upon his name: **make known his deeds among the people.**"* (Psalm 105:1)

However, a more subtle reason for Bro. Bill's "unconventional" personality was not as easily discerned. Eubie was the Bible believer's version of the late Fundamentalist evangelist, Carl Hatch (1929-2002). Both men had similar sub-missions—to motivate average preachers to become more aggressive; i.e., to come out of their shells. The principle was simple. To draw their more reserved prospects *five* steps to the right, *they* would have to go *ten* steps.

For instance, it was nothing "unusual" for Dr. Hatch to climb up onto a table in a McDonald's restaurant to "pray over his food" —like, *really* loud (sometimes with a few added "comments" thrown in as well). Once, while preaching a revival in Georgia in 1977, he surprised his host pastor by taking him to the nearby movie set where "Smokey and the Bandit" was being filmed. "Brother Carl" promptly conned his way through the main gate by flashing some kind of a "badge" and muttering "FBI." He then boldly banged on Burt Reynolds' trailer, introduced himself and the pastor, then invited "The Bandit" to the meeting. The world's top box office star at that time was so taken aback, he invited the two Baptist preachers in and endured a twenty-minute Gospel witness. Take it from me, neighbor, Carl Hatch and Bill Eubanks were not *half* as crazy as they may have acted (they were "crazy like a fox!")

"*A WOMAN SHALL COMPASS A MAN*"

Because Bill's Creator knew him better than anyone else (Jeremiah 1:5), He provided him with the perfect helpmeet to balance him out. In 1982, Bill met a sweet, spiritual widow named Janet. The two Oregonians were married the following year on February 11. Bill would often describe his bride as "the glue that holds our ministry together." Having known the couple for over thirty years, I once told sister Janet that the Holy Spirit had impressed me to share Jeremiah 31:22 with her as the perfect text to describe *her* particular role in *their* lifetime of service together. *"[F]or the LORD hath created a new thing in the earth, A woman shall compass a man."* (For the record, Dr. Ruckman saw a double application for this "woman;" a reference to the virgin Mary bypassing Joseph to bear Jesus Christ, along with prophetic overtones associated with Isaiah 66:7-9 and Revelation 12:4-5.)

Jack Hyles had a sermon entitled "Woman, The Holy Spirit of the Family." The idea was that a Christian wife was designed to be the unseen influence in a home, just as John prophesied that the third member of the Godhead *"shall not speak of himself."* (John 16:13) True to this characterization, Janet Eubanks has never coveted attention for herself. Suffice it to say that her hubby could never laud her enough, especially when it came to surpassing him in "tracting." Whether facing an intimidating gang of bikers, an arrogant Rabbi, or a restaurant full of Roman Catholic priests, Janet's courage is legendary. As Bill tells it:

> We're on a subway train in New York City, and one of the *meanest* guys I'd ever seen got on the car. He's about twenty-five and has black engineer boots on, a black t-shirt, and a black leather jacket. His hair is long and greasy, combed straight back. He has a big silver earring in each ear and sunglasses on. He's growling and snorting, and looking real mean. I bury my face in the newspaper, you know, looking to see how the Knicks are doing, and Janet gets up, and goes and tries to give him a tract. He snorts and growls something that I took to be a 'NO,' and just then, the train stopped and he got off...*Thank God!*"

On another occasion in Bangor, Maine, Bill and Janet came across the very scary-looking Victorian mansion owned by the American horror author, Stephen King. (I saw this overrated dump in 2021 when preaching for my good friend, Pastor Craig Cobb.) Too intimidated to go himself,

Bill says to Janet, "Honey, go up and tract that house." He continues, "She immediately heads for the side gate that's open. I get in the car, *lock the doors,* and ask *God* to protect her. I mean, that's the way you do, ain't it? Janet said there were video cameras all over the place and a sign saying, *'Don't ring the doorbell for autographs.'* Anyway, because of the team, Stephen King got the *Gospel.*"

Bill's timidity was no different than Paul's experience (Acts 27:24; I Corinthians 2:3). Because the great Apostle labored without a helpmeet, the Lord would have to occasionally fill that cheerleader role Himself (Acts 18:9-10). However, for the rest of us married preachers (especially those of us who "married up"), our Heaven-sent "better halves" are the ones who quicken our resolve (Proverbs 19:14). Once, when George Whitefield was field-preaching, an incensed mob approached and began hurling stones at him. Naturally, his courage began to fail. His wife, Elizabeth (also a former widow), who was standing behind him, pulled his gown, and said, 'Now, George, play the man for God!' His moral strength renewed, he preached on and the enemy soon retreated. This was Janet's *modus operandi* with *her* evangelist hubby.

BIRTH OF A VISION

Like I said, Bill Eubanks despised everything about the Roman Catholic hierarchy. That righteous indignation came to a head in May of 1983 (when Bill and Janet had only been married three years). To further illustrate Janet's role in Bill's life, the Holy Ghost led her to give Bill a book titled *Missiles Over Cuba: The Tom White Story,* the true account of missionary-pilot Tom White, who, for seven years, dropped more than 400,000 Gospel tracts behind the "Sugar Cane Curtain" (eventually spending seventeen months in Castro's prison for his efforts).

Bill read the 222-page book in one sitting; he was mesmerized. Then the thought struck him, "[I]f Brother White could drop tracts on Havana, Cuba, why couldn't I learn how to fly and drop tracts on the Vatican in Rome, Italy?" He then began feeding his vision by reading several other books regarding leaflet dumps in both spiritual *and* shooting wars. To make a long story short (long, as in eight years long), Brother Eubie set his face like a flint to accomplish this holy mission for his Saviour.

Fast-forward to 1991; not only had the former Vegas pit boss learned how to fly and earned his pilot's license, but he had also won his wings from the *Repubblica d'Italiana*. Furthermore, having taken several survey trips, Bill had made the needed local contacts to achieve his coming assault on the "Holy See." By then, he had also shipped thousands of Gospel tracts to a clandestine safe house. On the negative side, two aborted missions occurred in this nearly decade-long preparation. His main problem was securing the all-important bombardier. Apparently, no one wanted to risk rotting away in Castel Sant'Angelo. Anyone can act macho in America, but messing around over *there* is something else.

By way of a personal illustration, I made my first visit to Rome in the summer of 1972 (courtesy of "Bill and Jill" Stevenson). I still have a photo of myself posing as a proud Roman Catholic with the Vatican dome in the background. However, returning as a Christian three years later, I can *still* recall the anxiety I felt when trying to leave a few of Alex Dunlap's anti-Catholic tracts around the Vatican ("I Was a Nun" and "I Was a Priest"). I'm a-tellin' ya, neighbor, those Italian *Guardia Svizzera* (Swiss Guards)—the world's smallest and oldest continuously serving military unit, brandishing their ancient swords, pikes, and halberds—look *mighty* intimidating up close!

Well, true to Jeremiah's prophecy that *"a woman shall compass a man,"* after all of Bill's male bombardier prospects washed out (or went AWOL), guess who volunteered for duty? Even before the last *dude* "bombed," the Holy Spirit laid it on Janet's heart to fill the number two position on the mission. Though paranoid at the prospect of Vatican retaliation, Janet stepped up in the spirit of those legendary World War II female Soviet pilots known as "The Night Witches." Bill would later write, "[M]y brave wife loves *God* and will obey *God! She won't obey me 100% of the time, but she will God!"*

THIRTEEN MINUTES OVER THE VATICAN

In 1944, Metro-Goldwyn-Mayer released its wartime blockbuster, *Thirty Seconds Over Tokyo,* chronicling the historic April 18, 1942, "Doolittle Raid," America's reprisal bombing of Tokyo following the Japanese attack on Pearl Harbor four months earlier. (Ironically, when Bill was one year old, his home state was attacked by the Japanese on September 9, 1942, when a solitary floatplane, catapulted from a submarine, dropped incendiary bombs on Brookings, Oregon, in a "tit-for-tat" retaliatory raid for the Doolittle strike; fortunately, the payload fizzled in the damp woods, failing to do any long-term damage.) Capitalizing on the MGM title, Eubie would document his own historic bombing run over Vatican City in a book titled, *Thirteen Minutes Over the Vatican.* (On a personal note, Janet's role as "tract bombardier" reminded me of how my own mother, barely twenty years of age, worked as a wartime finals supervisor at the Norden Laboratories plant in lower Manhattan, producing the top-secret Norden bombsight, carried onboard all sixteen of Doolittle's B-25 Mitchell bombers.)

The pair rented a tepee cabin, nine miles north of Rome, at a place called Seven Hills Camping. (How appropriate, given Rome's moniker as "The City of Seven Hills" lining up with the "Great Whore's" location, as per Revelation 17:9.) The date chosen for the "Eubanks Raid" was March 30, 1991, the Saturday before Easter, guaranteeing a packed SRO crowd in Vatican Square down below. Given Bill's early nickname of "Eubie," it was only appropriate that his epic quest would begin at a small airport in Rome named "Urbe." That morning, Bill took off alone in a rented Cessna 172 Skyhawk (a four-seat, single-engine, fixed-wing aircraft). Diverting from his official flight plan, he then made an "unscheduled" landing at the equally tiny airport in nearby Reitta to rendezvous with Janet and the "bombs." There they quickly loaded their powerful payload—250 lbs. of leaf tracts and 200 lbs. of Chick tracts (in English and Italian), roughly 85,000 Gospel leaflets! (Mama Mia!!)

With their Hertz rental car discretely left behind a hanger, "Bonnie and Clyde" waited nervously onboard. (The tension must have mirrored that felt by those Mossad agents on board *their* EL AL airliner at the Buenos Aires Airport awaiting takeoff clearance, holding a sedated Adolf Eichmann, dressed in an EL AL uniform.) Finally—the announcement came over the radio: *"Cessna Tango-Alpha-X-ray, cleared for take-off."* Moments later, they were roaring down the 4,000-foot grass runway at 50 mph. Satan must have been watching.

"IF WE EVER GET OUT OF THIS THING ALIVE..."

It was now about twelve noon and the drama was off the charts (from *Twelve O'clock High* to *High Noon*). Bill writes, "Janet had moved to the back of the airplane and was adjusting the bags of tracts. She told me she was taking her contacts out and for me 'to tell her what to do and she'll do it.' You know, that's a beautiful thing for a husband to hear from his wife." But then it happened—a typical Eubie moment! As Bill relates on the opening page of his book:

> I can't believe we're lost. A man said once, a good pilot is *never lost;* he just doesn't know where he's at. Well, I *never* was a very good pilot, and I'm afraid I am lost. This morning, I took off from Urbe Airport in Rome, and flew north thirty-eight minutes to the mountain airport, Reitta, and picked up Janet, and the tracts. When we took off, and headed south towards Rome, I had the Tiber River right under me, and it looked like a lead pipe cinch to find the Vatican, I mean, the Tiber runs *right by* the Vatican. I mean, *Ray Charles could find it!* But now, after flying almost an hour south, all I see down there is rolling hills and a few cows.
>
> How did this all get started? What am I doing in an airplane, with my wife, and 450 pounds of Gospel tracts, flying over a bunch of cows in Italy? *Help me, Lord Jesus!*

When I asked Janet for one of her more memorable recollections, Bill's devoted helpmeet answered:

> I just remember wanting to get it over with. Just before we were over the Vatican, Bill was lost and I remember saying to him, *'If we ever get out of this alive, I will never fly with you again.'* Then he remembered he had something on the plane (a direction finder or something) and he zeroed right in to the directions to the Vatican. It was quite a trip to remember!

BOMBS AWAY!

As Janet said, the Lord answered Bill's desperate Nehemiah prayer, and just in the nick of time. Thanks to his trusty ADF (automatic direction finder), *"Mystery Babylon"* was finally in sight. Descending from 5,000 to 1,500 feet, Bill flew *straight* to Vatican Square at 90 mph. Suddenly, they spotted their first sign of trouble. A red government helicopter was already hovering suspiciously above the Sistine Chapel at about 2,000 feet. Having purposely kept his radio off, Bill could only imagine how many security alerts he had already triggered.

I opened my side window and locked it in the open position, and over the roar of the motor, and wind noise, I yelled back to Janet, *'Dump the first bag!'* Right then was a critical part of the tract bomb run. I wanted the helicopter and the Vatican to see our intentions…*to drop literature, not bombs!* As we crossed the Tiber, Janet was dumping the first bag out, the prop wash threw the tracts back at her, and she got hit in the eye right off. From then on she would take handfuls, and dump them out, as opposed to trying to empty the bag out the window…As the Obelisk was looming before me, I banked right, then pulled hard on the left rudder and set myself up for the drop. The plane fell into place like I'd trained for this all my life.

With 90% power, and one notch of flaps, we started around the obelisk in a left-hand turn at 900 feet. The left wing was pointed down, and we were in about a 40-degree bank. Now it was up to me to fly the airplane, (*and not stall it*), and it was up to Janet to get the tracts out! The noise was deafening, and the tracts were flying around the inside of the plane like a man in a money machine on a quiz show, when you can keep all the money you can grab in three minutes. The red air search-and-rescue helicopter was still hovering over the Sistine Chapel, and some people in the square were pointing up to us. Janet was having a hard time getting the tracts out, and she yelled up to me, *'I can't do anymore it's too hard!'* Over my shoulder, I yelled, *'Get them out! It's been five years, and we're here now, and I'm not landing this thing 'till they are all out!'*

A Shot Over the Bow

About this time, I'm wondering how many of my readers are discerning enough to grasp the spiritual depth of this incredible true story. If I had to guess, I'd say that about 99 percent of "professing" Laodicean Christians would be "aghast" at such a "preposterous act." That's probably how most of the backslidden Jews reacted when they saw that other religious "fanatic," Phinehas, shish-kabob Zimri and Cozbi (Numbers 25:6-15). And they were probably *more* shocked at how the Lord rewarded Phinehas for *"being zealous for his God"* (verses 12-14). When I wrote the foreword for *Ruckmanism Ruckus*, Dr. Geneha Kim's 2010 book defending the ministry of Dr. Peter Ruckman, I went on record, stating, "I've often said that should the Rapture occur today and we discover that the Judgment Seat of Christ will not take place for a week, you'll find me hanging with the "Doc" in Hallelujah Square (I Timothy 5:17; II Timothy 1:16)!"

That is *exactly* how I feel about Bill and Janet Eubanks. What they accomplished on March 30, 1991, was one of the most spectacular events in all of Church history! Paul wrote in I Corinthians 1:27, *"But God hath chosen the **foolish** things of the world to confound the wise."* Could you possibly think of anything more "foolish" *appearing* than 85,000 Gospel tracts being dumped on a Pollock Pope named John Paul II—by a former "Sin City" pit boss-turned-Baptist evangelist, named Bill Eubanks?

If anyone is interested, the true, subliminal purpose for Bill's mission was the same as the "Doolittle Raid." While those sixteen bombers did minimal damage, their main accomplishment was sending Tojo a psychological message— "You'll be getting *your* comeuppance soon" ("Little Boy" and Sam Cohen's "Fat Man"). Likewise, Bill's foolish *appearing* paper "bombs" represented a figurative "shot over the bow," a forecast of the surreal destruction prophesied by the Apostle John: *"Therefore shall her plagues come in one day, death, and mourning, and famine; and she shall be utterly burned with fire: **for strong is the Lord God who judgeth her.**"* (Revelation 18:8)

MISSION ACCOMPLISHED

"Meanwhile, back at the ranch" (about 800 feet above Vatican City):

> [Janet] went back to the *not so easy task* of grabbing great handfuls of tracts out of bags and throwing them out the side window beside me. The plane was running good. There was no opposition, and around, and around we went...the tracts were dropping on the square and in Vatican City itself, with surprising accuracy...It was sure great to see the *Word of God* floating down over the Great Whore. I estimated we had around 85,000 tracts, and it looked like 90% of them were hitting the target. After about thirteen minutes, Janet yelled, *'They're all out, all of them!'* I pulled the plane out of the left hand turn we'd been in, climbed to 2,500 feet, and turned the plane north to land back at *Urbe* Airport.

Having requested and received permission to land, Bill set the Cessna down for a near-perfect landing—then *slowly* taxied to "Judgment Day." Within seconds, the ominous message crackled over the radio: *"Cessna,*

Tango-Alpha-X-ray, please continue to taxi up to the end of the runway, **someone wants to talk to you.** *"*

YOU'LL NEVER EAT LUNCH IN THIS TOWN AGAIN

At that very moment, a book destined to be one of the fastest-selling volumes in history was just starting to hit the bookstores. Published March 6, 1991, by the first week of April, *You'll Never Eat Lunch in This Town Again,* by Academy Award-winning producer and author, Julia Phillips, had already moved to the top of the *New York Times* non-fiction bestseller list, staying there for thirteen weeks. One Hollywood source called the 573-page, career-ending, tell-all autobiography, "the longest suicide note in history." While blood-washed, Bible-believing Baptists could not care less about such tripe, the irony of this book title was that it represented the perfect preview of the *persona non grata* status the Eubankses would receive for their little "stunt."

But first—while we're on this subject about *New York Times* best-selling authors—allow me to testify about something to which I have first-hand knowledge. About ten years ago (while I was pastoring in Michigan), I received a phone call from a Vice President of *Newsweek* magazine in Manhattan. The man said that he had tried contacting Jack Chick at his office in Rancho Cucamonga, California, but his calls were not returned. (Duh…) He said that when he saw *Final Authority* on the Chick Publications website, he decided to ask me if I would "reach out to Mr. Chick" on his behalf. (Man, do I *hate* that "skinny-jeans" expression.) Of course, when I talked to Brother Jack, he gave me the response I already anticipated, "Bill, I *never* talk to the press; you can't trust them." Oh, by the way, in case you'd like to know *why* such a high-profile magazine desired that interview, their own VP told me they wanted to do a feature article on Jack—*recognizing him as the most prolific author alive!!* Though he never wrote a single "book," his animated Gospel "booklets" (measuring 3"x5"), have now been translated into over one hundred languages with total sales closing in on *one billion*!

Well, returning to Bill and Janet…As soon as they climbed out of their plane they were met by a livid, six-man "reception committee" (as in *Italian* livid, the color of their faces matching that security helicopter parked less than a hundred feet away). After a thorough search of both their persons and plane, the couple was led away to a security office for some intense interrogation. The first order of business was surrendering their passports and airline tickets. As Eubie tells it:

> [F]or the next six and a half hours, we were among the wildest crew you could ever imagine. I mean, telephones were ringing off the wall, fax machines were faxing, police and airline pilots (*they said they had to divert two airliners that day, and it cost them 10,000 gallons of jet fuel*) were staring at us like they wanted to kill us. Others thought we were crazy, and others looked at us in amazement. There was one man who offered Janet his hand, and shaking it said, 'Good business!' That guy must've been *saved!*

One sure thing about the Lord is that—if you go out on a limb for *Him*, He'll always have *your* back (Exodus 14:4). Thus, in the providence of God, one big "coinky-dink" saved Bill and Janet. The Italian government is famous for being in constant flux. Since WWII, the nutty nation has endured *sixty-six* "governments," averaging one every 1.14 years! Well, it just so "happened" that the particular weekend Bill felt "led" to bomb the Vatican State—*there was no one running the main country next door!* And *that* was the reason he related, "It was a madhouse in there!" The one "stable" leader, John Paul II, aka "Sovereign of the State of the Vatican City" (Revelation 17:18), had already made a damage-control television appearance, playing down the embarrassing incident, "Summa our Americano friends-a gotta little-a excited." (As Bill would later discover, this papal broadcast even aired briefly on an American network.) In the meantime, while all the little "Berlusconi's" were arguing amongst themselves as to how the Baptist invaders should be punished (e.g., Thumbscrews, Wheel, Strappado, Rack, etc.), the chief "head knocker" (Bill's expression) decided on giving Bill an ultimatum—one he would gladly accept, like a blind dog in a meat factory.

> [T]he head man brought me a sheet of paper and a pen, and said to me, *'I want you to confess!'* I said, *'Excuse me?'* About to blow his gasket and raising his voice, he said, *'I want you to confess your crime!* I want you to write on this paper what you did, and why you did it, and sign the paper.' *'Oh, yes, confess,'* I said. *'Yes, I'd be happy to confess.'* I took the pen and paper, and sat at a table, and started writing, *'There's one mediator between God and men, the man Christ Jesus. There's no hope in the Pope. Jesus alone saves.'*

I wrote that we dropped Gospel tracts on precious Italian people to warn them that a church cannot save them, Mary cannot save them, but only the finished work of the *Lord Jesus Christ* can save *anybody!* I quoted Romans *10:9-10, John 3:7, John 1:11-12*, and every verse I could think of, and explained in *'the confession'* that we weren't trying to hurt anybody, but show how the Catholic people had been deceived; that Mary, although a great woman, couldn't possibly hear the prayers of millions, or she would be a member of the *Godhead*. She didn't ascend from the grave, as the *Lord Jesus* did, and the Catholic Church was the biggest fake this side of the Mormon church (*golden plates, yeah, right*). I filled up both sides of the paper, signed it, and took it to the big boss and waited another hour.

And so, as Bill had obeyed the first part of Proverbs 3:6, *"In all thy ways **acknowledge him**,"* His God was only too glad to fulfill the second part, *"and he shall **direct thy paths**."* To everyone's shock, the chief interrogator was about to be *"moved by the Holy Ghost"* to direct Bill and Janet's steps—out the door! But first, he would acquaint them with the theme of Julia Phillips' book:

Standing before us he said, looking right at me, *'You've done a very bad thing, and you can no longer fly an airplane in Italy!'* As I bowed my head to the floor in subjection, it was all I could do to keep from bursting out laughing. Then, he continued, *'And, Mr. Big Shot, you are through flying. I get your license yanked in the States!'* I tried to put a sad look on my face, (*as though I really cared if I ever flew a plane again*), and his voice was rising to a shrill. He lost all his composure and handed me our passports and airline tickets. Pointing to the door, he screamed, *'Now, you take'a your wife, and you get outta my country, and never come back!!!'* Taking Janet by the hand, I said, *'Let's go, Honey,'* and we *ran for the door.*

"SOME HAVE ENTERTAINED ANGELS UNAWARES"

A final incident remains to be told. It was dark when they hit the street outside Urbe Airport. Running as fast as they could, they were able to catch a bus to downtown Rome. Then, owing to the grace of God, they were able to connect with the last bus of the evening going to the mountain city of Reitta where they could retrieve their rental car. During the two-and-a-half-hour ride, they chatted with a young Italian soldier who spoke English. Anticipating the dismal conditions at their small destination so late at night, they asked the "man" if he could help them secure transportation to the *"aeroporto."* He readily agreed. Bill writes:

> I sat back in my seat and tried to control my nervousness. Downtown Reitta looked like it was closed up for the night as the bus unloaded, but the soldier, true to his word, went and talked to a couple of men warming their hands on a fire burning in a barrel. What happened next about blew my mind. Out of an alley crept a *brand new, black, Mercedes Benz, 450 SL sedan.* The car pulled right up to where we were standing at the bus stop. Two men in suits and neckties were in the front seat. The driver said in broken English, *"You want aeroporto? Avanti, get in, we take!'* I opened the door for Janet, as we got in the backseat of the car. As the car pulled away towards the airport, I tried to offer the men money. *'No, put your money away,'* the driver said. *'No problem, we take you to aeroporto.'*
>
> Am I dreaming? Are these men *angels*? Are they *Mafia*? [What's a four-letter Italian word for 'Goodbye?' — 'Bang!'] I don't know to this day who they were, or where they came from. They dropped us at our rental car and waited as I reached under the seat and found the key was where I'd left it that afternoon and started the car. The note that Janet had left on the dashboard was still there, and it read, 'Please return this car to Hertz, any location, thank you.' I thanked the two men before they drove off into the night. It was close to 2 A.M. as we sped down the mountain highway to the *Leonardo da Vinci Airport*, parking the car in the Hertz Car Rental lot.

The Lord even fixed things so they could change the departure date on their tickets from April 3 to March 31. Thus, on that beautiful *Resurrection Sunday* morning 1991, Bill and Janet made their "Great Escape" from *"that **great city**, which reigneth over the kings of the earth."* (Revelation 17:18) As their 9:00 AM TWA departure lifted off the runway, headed for Los Angeles, the "land of fruits and nuts" never looked better! Bill could finally breathe easy, especially since *he* wasn't doing the flying. All through check-in he had been a total wreck, recalling, "I was so nervous *I don't know which was loudest, my teeth chattering, or my knees knocking!"* For the record, Bill had plenty of cause for alarm "in the flesh." As he relates, *"We found out later, that on Monday, a warrant was issued for my arrest, and if we had still been at Seven*

Hills Camping, or been caught while trying to leave the country, I'd still be in jail."

AFTERGLOW

Two hours into the flight, they were served lunch. Janet chose chicken salad, and would you believe it—Bill chose the pasta! Then it dawned on them what they had just been through. "I can see God's mighty hand in all of this…God wouldn't let us do the mission until Italy was without a government for Easter weekend, 1991." While the majority of their fellow passengers seated around them were tourists and business people, *they* had just gone *To Hell and Back* (1955 WWII Audi Murphy film).

> Halfway through the meal the stewardess started to pour me a glass of red wine. Janet put her hand over my glass and told the stewardess, *'No wine for him, he's a Christian.'* I looked at her, and she at me, and we burst out laughing. I mean…I couldn't stop! I spit food out all over my shirt, and we just *roared!* You see, it really got a hold of us, and we were laughing the laughter of *deliverance! God* let us do a daring and probably foolish thing, and *He delivered us!*

Brother Bill ends his story with a final reflection:

> Was the mission crazy? Maybe. Was anything accomplished? Well, over 300,000 gospel tracks were distributed [counting the many thousands given out during their survey trips]. But the most important thing that happened while preparing and doing the mission was that it was *exciting*, and God gave me something to work on and I got through those critical years after being saved. If not for this I might've gone back into the world. Eternity will show the results of the mission, but I believe *God* allowed it to happen for the good of the author.

Two years after their adventure, Bill and Janet Eubanks stepped out into full-time missionary work. As to Bill's question, "Was the mission crazy?" allow me to reiterate what I have already stated. Being a converted, hard-core, Latin-rite Roman Catholic; a serious student of history; a six-time visitor to Italy; and, a friend of the Eubankses for over three decades, I repeat—while Eubie may have been a tad "unhinged" himself (LOL)—what he and Sister Janet *did* during those "thirteen minutes over the Vatican," will eventually be recognized as one of the most spectacular events in Church history! I double-dog guarantee it, neighbor, the surreal contempt they single-handedly cast against *"MYSTERY, BABYLON THE GREAT, THE MOTHER OF HARLOTS AND ABOMINATION OF THE EARTH"* will garner *plenty* of attention at the Judgment Seat of Christ! (The whole mission, praise God, will probably be replayed on a giant jumbo screen.) *"For God is not unrighteous to forget your work and labour of love, which ye have shewed toward his name, in that you have ministered to the saints, and do minister."* (Hebrews 6:10)

BILL'S DEATH WISH

Committed to Gospel tracting, Bill had written his own Gospel tract early-on, a tri-color illustrated one, tailor-made for his old gambling crowd, titled, "Beat the Odds." (Pictures of cards and dice were featured on the cover.) The onetime pool hustler would don a suit and tie and "greet" arriving tourists as they stepped off their buses in front of the various casinos. "I would stand right at the door and every passenger that would get off I would pretend I was a casino host, I'd give them the tract and with a big smile say, 'Welcome to Reno.' I never had a turndown."

Now, from the world's perspective, Bro. Bill certainly "beat the odds" regarding his and Janet's successful Vatican City sortie. However, when the adrenaline rush subsided, Eubie started getting antsy for new worlds to conquer. Unfortunately, unlike tract-bombing Rome during Easter, this time, he set his bombsights on a no-win situation—Mecca during Ramadan! I'm a-tellin' ya, neighbor, buzzing 300,000 Catholics crammed into Vatican Square is one thing. Dropping a payload of anti-Islamic Chick tracts (*Allah Had No Son; Who is Allah?; Is Allah Like You?; The Little Bride; Camel's In The Tent; Men of Peace?;* a 9-11 reminder, *Who Cares?;* a special Muslim version of *This Was Your Life*, titled *Your Best Life;* and especially, *The Pilgrimage*) on the heads of 2.5 million Muslim "pilgrims" doing their Hajj thing around the Kaaba is something else entirely!

Israel's "Islamophobic" God already prophesied of Ishmael's seed, *"And he will be a **wild man**; his hand will be against every man, and every man's hand against him; and he shall dwell in the presence of all his brethren."* (Genesis 16:12) As a certain Taliban father is entertaining another, the two Mohammedans are gazing at photos of the kiddos atop the mantle when the host suddenly exclaims with a sigh, "Ah—they blow up so quickly." (See: Chick tract, *The Sky Lighter*.)

For anyone else to make such a boast, it could easily be laughed off as hot air; but not by some wild child who had already bombed St. Peter's Square. For instance, when Bill gave me an autographed copy of his book, he wrote on the back inside cover, "Please pray for Mecca 2009, survey trip 3/5/09. We need a safe printer and a co-pilot." As he was fully committed to his "death wish" vision (Acts 21:13), he literally made terminal cancer the main qualification for prospective bombardiers. (Janet was not a candidate this time.)

Thankfully, and hallelujah, during a camp meeting at Landmark Baptist Church in Stamford, Connecticut, my friend, Pastor Vince Massa, and I were able to "reason" with Bill, eventually "coaxing him down from his ledge," etc. And so, apart from visiting a few Indian reservations in Arizona, this was as close as Bill ever got to getting the Gospel to *full-blooded* Shemites. (He did venture south of the border frequently, once leading a church group in Mexico City to distribute 85,000 Chick tracts along a parade route of three million cheering Mexicans during a "1917 Revolution Day" fiesta.)

THE QUINTESSENTIAL JAPHETHITE

The main reason I felt led to conclude *Perilous Times* with Bill's testimony is because it represents the classic closing illustration for my thesis regarding the spiritual purpose for "Japheth thc Elder's" enlargement—to get the Gospel to his fellow Japhethites *and* to his two younger siblings as well! Ironically, Janet once told me that when she and her husband were working at the Long Beach Rescue Mission, Bill asked an Oriental volunteer, "Why don't you go back to your homeland and reach your own people?" Whereupon the Shemite replied with a grin, "That's what we have *you* for!"

As the Holy Spirit obviously felt that downtown Tokyo (and other such Asian fields) were not quite ready for Bro. Eubie and his sandwich board, the born-again card shark would find his ultimate niche in the "Land of Ham" (Psalm 78:51). Therefore, constituting the quintessential Japhethite, Bill would spend the last of his "golden years" on the Dark Continent, reaching his "brothers from other mothers" with the saving

Gospel of Jesus Christ. (As the lyrics from "Oh Holy Night" state, "Chains shall He break, for the slave is our brother.")

You see, Bill actually had a double life's verse. While Psalm 105:1 related to his *mission*, Luke 23:33 related to his *Master*—the consummate focus of his life: *"And when they were come to the place, which is called Calvary, there they crucified him, and the malefactors, one on the right hand, and the other on the left."* Having wasted his early years as a pit *boss* for Satan, Bill would now devote the rest of his life as a pit bull for Jesus! (Ecclesiastes 9:10)

Saved at the age of twenty-seven, Janet felt just as disenchanted with this world's goods as her hubby. Her life's verse (as she signed it in my book) was II Peter 3:11, *"Seeing then that **all these things shall be dissolved**, what manner of persons ought ye to be in all holy conversation and godliness?"* She exhibited the same "long-view" mindset as Priscilla Stewart, who, on her wedding day to the famous cricketeer-turned-missionary, Charles "C. T." Studd, wore a sash across her plain dress, sporting the terribly "romantic" message— "United to fight for Jesus." Whereas Priscilla was needed back in England to run her husband's mission office, leaving him to labor in Africa alone, Janet got to accompany Bill on nearly all of his crusades. Making eleven extended trips in twelve years, they won thousands of souls, first in Kenya, Tanzania, and South Africa; then, in their primary field of Zimbabwe.

Given his aforementioned childlike persona, Bill was particularly effective in the schools. Janet told me the children absolutely adored him! Because he would later come to believe that he had actually gotten saved at that summer camp (receiving his assurance at thirty-eight), he strongly felt that little ones could definitely be saved. Though he and Janet never had any children of their own, the Lord blessed them with a harvest of spiritual offspring. School administrators often gave Janet glowing reports of how these young people showed a remarkable transformation in their school work and overall character (John 15:16; II Corinthians 5:17).

True to Japheth's spiritual destiny, hundreds of "bad" ole white men had preceded Bill Eubanks to Africa throughout the Philadelphia Church Age. Alfred Saker was a British missionary of the London Baptist Missionary Society who labored for thirty years in Fernando Po Island and Cameroon. After winning scores of Shemites to Christ during his two previous tours to China and India, the veteran missionary, C. T. Studd, spent the last eighteen years of his life serving in and around the Sudan and the Belgian Congo, dying at seventy due to untreated gallstones. Robert Moffat evangelized thousands of cannibals and witch doctors in South Africa, his most notable trophy being the demonic headhunter known as Africana, chief of the Namaquas. His famous son-in-law, David Livingston (of "Dr. Livingston, I presume?" fame), advanced the Gospel 1,400 miles into the heart of Africa, eventually succumbing to the debilitating effects of a dozen jungle ailments.

One of Livingston's protégés, George Grenfell (aka "The Congo Captain"), led a team of one thousand volunteers to haul 800 sixty-five-pound crates, one hundred miles up the crocodile-infested Congo River where their contents were assembled into a seventy-eight-foot screw-steamer. The one-eyed Baptist missionary/explorer then spent the next twenty-five years spreading the Kingdom of God along the Congo's vast system of waterways and tributaries—burying a wife and four children along the way. The Lord even threw in a bad ole single white woman. Known as "The Queen of Okoyong" (a region in Nigeria), Mary Slessor would make *The African Queen's* "Rose Sayer" look like an African pygmy by comparison. Mary spread the Gospel throughout Calabar for over forty years, struggling with intermittent fevers and malaria throughout. When her "beautiful feet" began to fail, she insisted on being pushed along in a handcart. (There is even a lovely missionary family to South Africa out of my own church, Joshua and Meagan Sullivan.) These "racist" Japhethites all shared the same ministry philosophy, as captured in the verse by "C. T." Studd.

> Some wish to live within the sound
> of church, or chapel bell;
> I want to run a rescue shop,
> within a yard of Hell!

"The Wall"

The last time I saw Bill was in 2019. I was preaching for a pastor in Missouri and was staying in their mission house on the church property. Bill also happened to be there at the time and had his spartan motor home parked next to me. I recall how we took a long walk together and reminisced about the goodness of the Lord, etc. One of my final recollections of Eubie was when I peeked through the curtains and watched him bawling out a bunch of stray cats. (He was quite a sight to behold, scooping out cans of cat food in his pajama bottoms and old-fashioned white "muscle" undershirt.)

Jack Chick was so impressed with Bro. Bill's life-long commitment to distributing his tracts that he actually let him write one himself, titled, "The Wall." Similar to Michelangelo's technique of incorporating a self-portrait or two into his paintings, Jack even included a likeness of Bill in the tract (page seven). The storyline is about an unsaved race car driver who dies after "hitting the wall." In March 2021, the so-called Legacy Standard Bible (LSB New Testament) was published (Commode Version Revisited). Two months later, on May 14, 2021, he and Janet departed the States for what would be their last trip to Zimbabwe. In the perfect Romans 8:28 will of God, *this* is where Bro. Bill would finally hit *his* wall (Hebrews 9:27).

As with Mary Slessor, the beginning of the end for Bill began with Ecclesiastes 12:3, *"when **the keepers of the house** shall tremble."* Losing strength in *his* "beautiful feet," as well, Bill spent his *eightieth* birthday on June 16 checking into the local hospital, confirming the veracity of yet another text: *"The days of our years are threescore years and ten; **and if by reason of strength they be fourscore years, yet is their strength labour and sorrow**; for it is soon cut off, and we fly away."* After two days, Bill was diagnosed with Covid-19! He was immediately transferred to the Covid wing of another hospital in Zimbabwe's capital—*with no visitation permitted.* And so, having remained "United to fight for Jesus" for over thirty-eight years, this would constitute their final goodbye. (Janet later told me she thought he was going to recover.) To the surprise of all, the "days of *Bill's* years" were *"cut off"* sooner than later. As the lyrics to the beautiful hymn, "Peace in the Midst of the Storm," say, "When years of living are brought to moments," Bill would *"fly away"* only three days later, on June 21, 2021. What happened during those last seventy-two hours is about as holy as it gets!

"THEY DIED WITH THEIR BOOTS ON"

To "die with your boots on" is a nineteenth-century idiom from the American West that relates to one dying while fighting, or to die while actively engaged in any important action. The expression immortalized George Armstrong Custer and the men of the 7th Cavalry after their defeat at the Little Big Horn. Bill Eubanks epitomized the Pauline charge in II Timothy 2:3 to *"endure hardness, as a **good soldier** of Jesus Christ."* Like Colonel Jim Bowie, who spent *his* final moments at the Alamo fighting the enemy from his sick bed—Bro. Bill would do the same.

My good friend, Brian Green (faithful co-pastor with Danny Farley at Shady Acres Baptist Church in Houston, Texas), was Bill's handpicked successor to continue "Seed for the Cities." He sent me the following text relating some of what he had heard regarding Bill's last moments:

> All I know is that he was in a hospital for about two or three days, but it cost around $800 a day. They moved him to a Covid hospital that didn't have any ventilators, but it was free. He wanted to go there. He was all alone. Miss Janet sent him in there with a box of Chick tracts. He only lasted about three days before he made The Crossing into Glory...*They said* when he died he had been giving tracts to the nurses and doctors. *He died with a Chick tract in each hand.* He finished like he wanted, on the mission field and with Chick tracts in his hands.

Initially, my reaction to this report was one of euphoria. I mean, how could you get a wilder finale than that? But then, my writer's instinct kicked in. As the liberal ABC news commentator, Peter Jennings, used to say, "If you hear a rumor that your mother loves you, check it out." The more I reflected on that final picture of Bill dying "with a Chick tract in each hand," the more apocryphal it sounded. I became even more skeptical when I asked Janet about it and she said that it was news to her. So, I called Bro. Green to "track" down the source of the "tract" story.

Well, as is usually the case, when push came to shove, after Brian had checked with another missionary to Zimbabwe, who claimed he had also heard the same account, the bottom line was that *no* one could pin down the exact origin; everything was second hand. Thus, it quickly dawned on me that our beloved Eubie—though gone less than six months—*already* had a powerful myth circulating about his Homegoing! That, in itself, was significant! Still needing to compose the "closing illustration" for my own book, I was naturally tempted by the classic line from *Who Shot Liberty Valance*, "When the legend becomes fact, print the legend!"

Thankfully, however, the blessed Holy Spirit stepped in and began to direct our thoughts. First of all, Janet did confirm that she had given

Bill a bag of Chick tracts when he entered the second facility. Second, when Bill passed away (on his third evening there), Janet was *not* made aware of her renewed widowhood status from the hospital (which should have been the case, she being the next of kin). Instead, the attending nurse called the Baptist pastor—whose name and church telephone number were stamped on a Chick tract laying in Bill's room—and *he* then notified Janet!

As the saying goes, "Where there's smoke, there's fire," we definitely had some smoke now; we just needed to clarify the extent of the fire. Brian's missionary friend was able to give me the pastor's name, Rozert Zijena, and telephone number in Zimbabwe. When I called him an hour later, not only did the Lord let me discover exactly *what* had transpired during Bill's final moments, but something far greater. As Paul wrote in Ephesians 3:20, *"Now unto him that is able to do **exceeding abundantly** above all that we ask or think,"* at the end of the day—the "fact" exceeded the "legend!"

DEATHBED TRACT RACK

According to the man of God in "Zim," the nurse gave him the following account. When Bill was admitted to the Covid facility, he immediately started doing what he always did—passing out Chick tracts, etc. However, having just tested positive for Covid, he was abruptly informed that he could no longer "hand" *anything* to *anyone*. What Bill asked the nurse in return would make a Chick tract of its own!

And so—as Bill would have said in his former pool hall days—let me "rack 'em up for ya." If you want to see "white privilege" in all of its glory; if you want to see the true purpose of "white supremacy"; if you want to see "Enlarged Japheth" at his best; if you want to experience your *ultimate* "Woke" reality check—just consider the following. What we have here is: an *eighty*-year-old, former Las Vegas pit boss; isolated from his loving wife; dying from the China virus; in an African "hospital" (so primitive they can't even finish him off with a ventilator); some 10,000 miles from his Portland, Oregon, birthplace. And what is "Whitey's" last request? According to what the nurse told the pastor (who personally relayed it to me): He asked her that, since *he* could no longer distribute the tracts, would *she* be so kind as to arrange them across his bed, so that any passing by could simply take one if interested (without the threat of infection from *him*). This, the nurse agreed to do.

Hence, when Bill "finished *his* course" (II Timothy 4:7), he did *not* have a Chick tract in each hand; *he literally died in his own tract rack!* When I shared this revelation with Bro. Green, he responded, "I bet you a dollar to a donut that Bro. Bill grabbed two of those Chick tracts on his "deathbed tract rack" just so he *could* die with them in his hands. I know him...that's *exactly* what he would have done." While I agree, it actually gets even better than that. For the "closing illustration" orchestrated by God Himself, you *could* say that Eubie died—*as a Gospel tract of his own!*

> *Ye are our epistle written in our hearts, known and read of all men: forasmuch as ye are manifestly declared to be the epistle of Christ ministered by us, written not with ink, but with the Spirit of the living God; not in tables of stone but in fleshy tables of the heart.* (II Corinthians 3:2-3)

"I'm Gonna Die on the Battlefield"
(Author Unknown)

One day while I was thinking
On unseen things above,
The Saviour spoke unto me
And filled my heart with love.

Chorus:
Oh, I'm gonna die on the battlefield,
I'm gonna die in this war.
I'm gonna die on the battlefield
With glory in my soul.

I used to have some people
Who walked and talked with me,
But since I've been converted
They've turned their backs on me.

Some say, "Give me silver,"
Some say, "Give me gold."
But I say, "Give me Jesus,"
Who saved my dying soul.

I'll take this gospel trumpet
And I'll begin to blow.
Oh, Lord, if You will help me,
I'll blow it wherever I go.

Photo taken last week of Bill's life

About the Author

William P. (Bill) Grady was born on Manhattan's Upper East Side and reared as a strict Roman Catholic. His grade school diploma was signed by Cardinal Francis Spellman. In 1970, he graduated from Salesianum School in Wilmington, Delaware, the largest parochial high school in the state. While working for the Brandywine Cash Register Company in Wilmington, Bill sold a cutting-edge electronic bar control system to Bill and Jill Stevenson, co-owners of the "First State's" newest nightclub, the Stone Balloon Tavern and Concert Hall in Newark. (Five years later, Jill would marry Senator Joe Biden.)

Bill then accepted a marketing position with British Airways in New York City. Following a promotion to Philadelphia in 1974, he was saved, baptized, and called to preach at the historic Marcus Hook Baptist Church (home church to Clarence Larkin), then grounded in dispensational premillennialism at the equally historic Philadelphia College of Bible (co-founded by C. I. Scofield). Apart from his ministerial degrees (which include a Ph.D. in History from the former Baptist International Seminary, Oxon Hill, Maryland), he also studied business and history at the University of Delaware, Goldey-Beacom College, and the University of Tennessee. As a minister, he founded and pastored two churches, taught Bible and history for ten years on the college level, and preached in over 1,000 churches as a full-time evangelist.

Dr. Grady's best-selling books have been featured in numerous venues, including *USA Today*, *Bill Martinez Live*, and the legendary *Barry Farber Show*. (His 1993 classic, *Final Authority*, is currently in its fifteenth printing.) Bill's lifetime of travel, preaching, and research has spanned forty countries on four continents (including three trips to Asia, five to the Middle East, and eleven to Europe and Russia).

The Lord has also enhanced his writing by affording him unusual favor with several eyewitnesses to history, e.g., Mrs. Nathalie Basilevsky, daughter of Baron Lieutenant-General Pyotr Wrangel, Commander-in-Chief of the anti-Bolshevik White Army; Samuel T. Cohen, Manhattan Project physicist, "Father of the Neutron Bomb"; UNESCO Goodwill

Ambassador, Kim Phuc (aka "the girl in the picture"); World War II fighter aces, Brigadier General Robert Lee Scott, Jr. (author of *God is My Co-pilot*) and Brigadier General David Lee "Tex" Hill (portrayed by John Wayne in *The Flying Tigers*); and Mei-ling Soong (aka Madame Chiang Kai-shek), former First Lady of the Republic of China. (Having produced a documentary on Madame Chiang's life, emphasizing her exemplary Christian testimony, Dr. Grady was honored to attend her 2003 Manhattan funeral at the invitation of Ambassador Andrew Kao, former Director-General of the New York Taipei Economic & Cultural Office.)

Among the many highlights of Dr. Grady's forty-two year ministry, in October 2007, Colonel Eyal Rozen, then-Commander of the IDF Givati Brigade (Special Forces) training camp in the Golan Heights, had the base flag struck and presented to him for his devotion to Israel.

Bill and his wife Linda have been blessed with forty-seven years of marriage, producing three children, sixteen grandchildren, and one great-grandchild. He currently serves as an evangelist out of Fellowship Baptist Church in Maryville, Tennessee, Pastor Tom Hatley.

The New York Times

John Grady, from the pitcher's mound: "They are improving." Son Billy, crouched behind plate: "They are lousy."